Dictionary
of
Information
Technology

Second Edition

DICTIONARY
OF
INFORMATION
TECHNOLOGY

Second Edition

Dennis Longley

and

Michael Shain

MACMILLAN PRESS
LONDON
Macmillan Reference Books

First edition published 1982
Hardcover edition reprinted 1983
Paperback edition reprinted 1984

Second edition first published 1985 by
THE MACMILLAN PRESS LTD
London and Basingstoke

Associated companies in Auckland, Delhi, Dublin, Gaborone,
Hamburg, Harare, Hong Kong, Johannesburg, Kuala Lumpur,
Lagos, Manzini, Melbourne, Mexico City, Nairobi, New York,
Singapore, Tokyo.

British Library Cataloguing in Publication Data

Longley, Dennis
    Dictionary of information technology.——2nd ed.
    1.   Information storage and retrieval systems
    ——Dictionaries
    I.   Title   II.   Shain, Michael
    001.5   Z699

ISBN 0-333-37260-3
ISBN 0-333-37261-1 Pbk

Printed in Great Britain by
St Edmundsbury Press, Bury St Edmunds, Suffolk.

To Annette and Helen

Introduction to Second Edition

The 1970s was the decade in which the industrialized nations lost cheap energy and discovered microelectronics. This technological revolution promised fundamentally new methods for the manufacturing and information industries: the challenge of the 1980s is to exploit these advances and revitalize economic activity.

If the opportunities offered by the new devices for collection, processing and dissemination of information are to be grasped, however, society's attitudes to the nature, processes and impact of information need to be examined and revised. The benefits of Information Technology lie not in the sophisticated hardware but in the exploitation of these devices to harness the power of human intelligence and endeavour within society. The ultimate success thus lies within society's ability and will to communicate and cooperate.

The authors first became involved in this field when they cooperated on a videotex project in early 1980. At that time they remarked upon the wide range of backgrounds amongst workers in that field and the plethora of terms, both derived from the constituent backgrounds and spawned by the videotex industry, that hindered communication. It later became clear that the videotex field exemplified many of the problems arising in the world of Information Technology. It is the nature of this discipline that it not only generates its own advances, but also makes quantum leaps by exploiting the convergence of existing technologies – cable television, word processing, local area networks, fiber optics, video recording, satellite communications, typesetting, microcomputers.

In December 1980 the authors initially considered what was then the first edition of this dictionary and duly checked on the existence of related reference books. A computer search of one and a half million periodicals and two million books failed to reveal a source book or article on this topic. The case for a reference book to assist newcomers into the field, with the relevant technical terms, was thus established.

In October 1984, prior to the publication of this second edition, a subsequent computer search of the INSPEC database revealed over 1000 major journal articles on IT, and the BLAISE database of book titles indicated over 200 books on the subject. IT has now emerged as a discipline in its own right.

At the outset of the compilation the authors were conscious of the continuing role of the traditional technologies in this field, and the fact that the jargon of the old technologies tends to fuse, and confuse, in the new. The constituent fields were thus selected:

Printing and Publishing
Computers and Databases
Computer Newtworks and Communications
Photography and Cinematography
Television and Recording

Microelectronics and Software
Word Processing and Business Systems

Where the focus in the first edition had been to distinguish between the same terms from different disciplines, the emphasis had now shifted to the newer technologies. For this reason there is now more emphasis on technologies such as cable television, computer networks and data communications, cryptography, expert systems, fifth generation computers, machine translation, microcomputers, on line information retrieval, Open System Interconnection, programming and speech synthesis.

The success of Information Technology will depend, ultimately, upon the readiness of society to communicate and cooperate. It is our hope that this dictionary will assist by lowering a few of the barriers to communication.

How to Use This Dictionary

The design of the dictionary is based upon the principle that most readers never consult this section and so, to avoid confusion, sophisticated listing and cross reference techniques have not been employed.

The terms are retained in the normal order, ie **automatic window adjust** is listed under automatic. They are sorted in alphabetical order of the complete term, ie **light pen** comes between **lightemitting diode** and **light stability.** This order contrasts with some dictionaries in which the alphabetical order is based on a heavier weighting of the first word in a term, ie all terms commencing with **light** precede all terms commencing with **lighting.** In the alphabetical ordering digits are ranked after the letter 'Z', ie **S100 bus** appears after **System X** and not at the beginning of the 'S' terms.

The area from which the head word is derived, is usually indicated in the definition, eg In computing, In printing . . . If more than one definition is related to a head word, then the entry is itemized to reflect this and the relevant field indicated in each sub-entry.

The terms normally appear in lower case characters, and proper nouns headed by an upper case, eg **Bildschirmtext.** Acronyms are presented in full upper case and the appropriate letters are amplified in the text, eg:

  PERT – Program Evaluation and Review Technique

The cross references are given under the three headings: 'Compare', 'See' and 'Synonymous with'.

A significant feature of this dictionary is the use of extended entries dealing with important topics of the subject, i.e. cable television, cellular radio, computer networks, cryptography, data communications, data protection, expert systems, fiber optics, fifth generation computer, global satellite communication system, information technology, interactive video disk, local area networks, machine translation, microcomputers, programming, speech synthesis, typesetting, video disk, videotex and word processing.

A

AA See audio active.

AA'S See author's alterations.

A, B and C series of paper sizes In printing, a triple range of paper sizes adopted by International Standards Organization (ISO), of which the A Series is intended for all kinds of stationery and printed matter, the B Series as intermediate alternatives and the C Series for envelopes. The dimensions for the A series are given in millimeters:

A0	1189×841	A6	148×105
A1	841×594	A7	105×74
A2	594×420	A8	74×52
A3	420×297	A9	52×37
A4	297×210	A10	37×26
A5	210×148		

all sizes are proportionate reductions of the basic A0 sheet, sides being in the ratio 1 : sqrt 2, with A0 being equal to one square meter. See International Standards Organization.

abbreviated addressing In computing, a process that enables a user to employ an address having fewer characters than the full address. It provides a faster means of processing data because the shorter address requires less time to decode. See addressing.

ABC (1) American Broadcasting Corporation. (2) Australian Broadcasting Corporation.

ABCA American Business Communications Association.

aberration (1) In optics, any systematic distortion of an image introduced by an optical element, such as a lens, prism, or mirror. Aberrations common in early lenses were astigmatism, chromatic aberration, curvature of field, distortion, and spherical aberration. (2) In television, image distortion caused by signal interference or electron beam misalignment. See astigmatism, chromatic aberration, curvature of field, distortion, spherical aberration.

ABES US Association for Broadcasting Engineering Standards.

abi/inform A database supplied by Data Courier Inc. and dealing with business & industry, business management. See on line information retrieval.

abort In computing, to terminate, in a controlled manner, a processing activity in a computer system because it is impossible or undesirable for the activity to proceed.

above 890 decision In communications, a 1959 FCC decision allowing individual firms to build microwave systems for their own use utilizing frequencies above 890 MHz. This decision established a precedent in the US for the provision of communication channels by entities other than the then established carriers, Western Union Telegraph Company and AT & T. See FCC, microwave.

absolute address In computing, (1) an address in a computer language that identifies a storage location or a device without the use of any intermediate reference, (2) an address that is permanently assigned by the machine designer to a storage location, (3) a pattern of characters that identifies a unique storage location or device without further modification. See address. Synonymous with machine address.

absolute assembler In computer programming, a specific type of assembly language program designed to produce binary programs containing only absolute addresses and address references. See assembly language, absolute address.

absolute code In computing, a code that uses computer instructions with absolute addresses. See absolute address. Synonymous with specific coding.

absolute loader   In computing, a routine that reads a computer program into main storage, beginning at the assembled origin. See main storage, routine.

absolute value   The value of a number regardless of a prefixed plus or minus sign, i.e. the absolute value of -5 is 5.

absorptance   That portion of the quantity of light incident on an object which is absorbed within the object, the energy ultimately being converted into heat. Compare transmittance, reflectance.

absorption   In communications, a loss of power of an electromagnetic wave during propagation through a medium. See electromagnetic radiation.

absorption filter   In photography, any light filter which blocks certain wavelengths of light and transmits others.

ABSTI   Advisory Board on Scientific and Technical Information, Canada.

abstract   In library science, (1) a summary of a book, periodical, feature, report or learned paper, (2) a form of current bibliography in which contributions to periodicals and, sometimes, books are summarized; they are accompanied by sufficient information to enable the publications or articles to be traced. See auto abstract, evaluative abstract, general abstract, indicative abstract, informative abstract, selective abstract, slanted abstract.

AC   See alternating current, accumulator.

ACARD   UK Advisory Council for Applied Research and Development.

ACC   See accumulator.

ACCC   US Ad Hoc Committee for Competitive Communications.

acceleration potential   In electronics, the voltage between the cathode in a cathode ray tube, CRT, and the face of the tube which attracts the beam of focused electrons causing them to impinge on the phosphor dots. See CRT, phosphor dots.

accent   In typesetting, a mark used to indicate a specific sound value, stress or pitch, or to indicate that an ordinarily mute vowel should be pronounced.

acceptance angle   In photography, the angle in two dimensions covered by a lens or light meter.

acceptance testing   In computing, a series of tests designed to demonstrate the functional capabilities of a new computer system. It is usually conducted by the manufacturer to show the customer that the system is in working order.

ACCESS   (1) US Army Automated Catalog of Computer Equipment and Software Systems. (2) In computing, the manner in which files or data sets are referred to by the computer. (3) In communications, the public availability of cable broadcasting time in the US. See direct access, random access, sequential access.

access arm   In computing, a mechanical device in a disk drive that positions the reading and writing mechanisms. See disk drive, head.

access barred   In data communications, a data facility which permits a terminal installation to make outgoing, or receive incoming, calls but not both.

access charge   In communications, a charge made by a common carrier for the use of its local exchange facilities. See common carrier, local exchange.

access control   In computer networks, the control of system usage, imposed by hardware, software and administrative controls. Such controls include system monitoring, user identification, ensuring data integrity, recording system access and changes and methods for granting user access. See hardware, software.

accession number   In library science, an arbitrary serial number given to each item as it enters a collection. See aspect card.

access line   In data communications, a telecommunication line that continuously connects a remote station to a DSE. A telephone number is associated with such lines. See DSE.

access mechanism   In computing, a mechanism for moving read and write heads to the requisite position on the storage device, or moving the storage medium to the heads, so that data may be accessed.

access time   (1) In computing, the time interval from the instant that data is requested from a storage device to the instant it is delivered to the CPU, and vice versa. (2) In recording, the time interval between the moment that information is requested in playback to the moment that it is delivered. See CPU.

accidental destruction   In data security, the unintentional overwriting or deletion of data, e.g. by faulty hardware or software. Backup is needed for recovery. See backup copy.

accordion fold   In computing, a method of folding paper in which each fold is in the opposite direction to the previous one. A printer or paper tape reader can be fed with accordion folded paper without continuous operator intervention. Synonymous with concertina fold, fanfold.

accumulator   In computing, a device that functions as a holding register for arithmetic, logical and input output operations. Normally data words fetched from memory are loaded into the accumulator and words to be stored into memory are first loaded into this register. See input output, register.

accuracy   The degree of exactness of an approximation or measurement. It denotes the absolute quality of the result with respect to its true value, as compared with precision which is concerned with the amount of detail used in specifying a result. Thus a two digit result may be more accurate than an incorrect three digit result, but it will be less precise. See precision.

ac/dc ringing   In telephony, a method of telephone ringing that uses alternating current to operate a ringer and direct current to activate a relay that stops the ringing when the called party answers. See relay.

ACE   Association of Cinema Editors.

achromatic   In optics, pertaining to an optical device, e.g. a lens, which has been corrected in manufacture for chromatic aberration. See chromatic aberration.

ACK   See acknowledge character.

acknowledge character   In data communications, a transmission character transmitted by a station as an affirmative response to the station with which the connection has been set up. Compare negative acknowledgement. See acknowledgement, station.

acknowledgement   In data communications, the transmission by a receiver of acknowledge characters as a response to a sender. See affirmative acknowledgement, negative acknowledgement.

ACK0   See affirmative acknowledgement.

ACK1   See affirmative acknowledgement.

ACLS   American Council of Learned Societies.

ACM   Association for Computing Machinery. A US based organisation which aims to advance computer technology and its applications.

acoustical feedback   In recording, the positive feedback between the microphone and loudspeaker, in a sound system, which usually results in an undesirable howling sound. See feedback, microphone.

acoustic coupler   In data communications, a type of data communication equipment that permits use of a telephone handset as a connection to a telephone network for data transmission by means of sound transducers. See MODEM, transducer.

acoustics   (1) The science concerned with the attributes of sound. (2) The characteristics of an enclosure, e.g. a room, as these affect the sound.

ACR   See audio cassette recorder.

ACRL   Association of College and Research Libraries.

actinic light   In photography, light which is capable of causing photochemical changes in a photosensitive material.

action field   In photography, the portion of the area in front of the camera which is recorded.

action message   In computing, a message issued because of a condition that requires an operator response.

action paper   Synonymous with carbonless paper.

activating   In document copiers, the action of an activator on the exposed sensitized material in some photochemical process to cause development of the latent image. See activator, latent image.

activation   In a computer network, the process by which a component of a node is made ready to perform the functions for which it was designed. See node.

activator   In document copiers, a liquid used for developing certain types of sensitized material. See activating.

active device   In electronics, a circuit which contains an amplifier providing gain. Compare passive. See amplifier, gain.

active file   In computing, a permanent file or a temporary file, having an expiration date that is later than the job date. See job.

active state   In microelectronics, the digital state which causes a given action to occur. It may be either the high state or low state, depending on the circuit and pin in question.

activity   In data processing, the percentage of records in a file that are processed in a run. See volatility.

activity loading   In data processing, a method of storing records on a file in which the most frequently processed records can be located most readily. See record.

activity ratio   In data processing, the ratio of the number of records in a file that are in use to the total number of records in that file. See record.

AC transfer   In recording, a videotape duplication by contact between high coercivity master and low coercivity slave in a high frequency AC field. See coercivity.

ACTSU   US Association of Computer Time Sharing Users.

actual data transfer rate   In data communications, the average number of bits, characters or blocks per unit of time transferred from a data source and received by a data sink. See source, sink.

actuator   A device which is capable of mechanical action under the control of a signal. See robot.

ACU   See automatic calling unit.

acuity   In physiology, (1) the ability of the eye to perceive fine detail, (2) the ability of the ear to detect very low sound levels or small changes in frequency.

acutance   In photography, pertaining to the ability of a lens or film to reproduce edges sharply.

ada   In computer programming, a general purpose, high level language, adopted by the US Department of Defense, and available for scientific and industrial applications on a variety of computers. See high level language.

ADAPSO   US and Canada Association of Data Processing Service Organisations.

adaptation   In physiology, (1) the ability to hear a particular sound in a high level of background noise, (2) the ability of the eye to establish a range of luminance levels about a mean level, after a change in mean level. See luminance.

adaptive channel allocation In communications, a method of multiplexing where channels are allocated according to demand rather than on a fixed predetermined plan. See multiplexing, frequency division multiple access, time division multiple access.

adaptive routing In data communications, a routing scheme for packets or messages in which the behaviour adapts to network changes such as line failures or variation of the traffic pattern. See packet switching, message switching.

adaptive systems Systems which display the ability to learn to change, alter their state or otherwise react to a stimulus.

ADC See analog to digital converter.

ADCCP See advanced data communications control procedure.

added entry In library science, a secondary entry in a catalogue, i.e. any other than the main entry. Compare main entry.

addend In computing, the operand of the addition operation, the number added to the augend to form a sum. See augend, operand.

adder In computing, a device that forms an output resulting from the sum of two or more numbers presented as inputs. See full adder, half adder.

add-in In computing, an expansion board which slots into a microcomputer to provide additional facilities. This is a very simple method of enhancing a microcomputer. The boards available allow for additional RAM, additional operating facilities, particularly CP/M, enhanced graphics, modems, instrumentation etc. See CP/M, MODEM, RAM.

additive colour mixing A means of reproducing colours by mixing lights. Compare subtractive colour mixing.

additive primary colours In television, the red-orange, green and blue-violet colours. In varying combinations, they produce all other

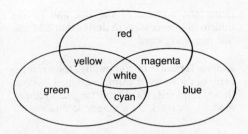

additive colour mixing

colours and white. See primary colours, RGB, triad.

address In computing, (1) a character or group of characters that identifies a register, a particular part of storage, or some other data source or destination, (2) to refer to a device or an item of data by its address. (3) In communications, the part of the selection signals that indicates the destination of a call. (4) In word processing, the location, identified by an address code, of a specific section of the recording medium or storage.

addressability In computer graphics, the number of addressable points within a specified display space or image space. See display space.

addressable horizontal positions (1) In micrographics, the number of positions within a specified film frame at which a full length vertical line can be placed. (2) In computer graphics, a display line. See display line.

addressable vertical positions (1) In micrographics, the number of positions within a specified film frame at which a full length horizontal line can be placed. (2) In computer graphics, a display column. See display column.

address bus In computing, a unidirectional bus over which digital information is transmitted to identify either a particular memory location or a particular input output device. Compare control bus, data bus. See bus, input output devices.

address field In computing, the specific portion of a computer word that contains either the address of the operand or the information necessary to derive that address. See operand, word.

address format In computing, the arrangement of the parts of a simple address, such as those required for identifying a channel, module, or track on a magnetic disk.

addressing (1) In computing, the assignment of addresses to the instructions of a program. (2) In communications, the means whereby the originator or control station selects the unit to which it is going to send a message. See station.

address modification In computing, an operation that causes an address to be altered in a prescribed way by a stored program computer.

address register In computing, a special register used by the CPU to store the address of data to be fetched from, or stored in, the computer memory. See CPU, register.

address track In computing, a track on a magnetic disk containing the addresses of files, records etc. stored on other tracks of the same device. See magnetic disk, track.

add time In computing, the time required by a particular CPU to add two multidigit numbers not including the time taken to read the numbers or store the result. Microcomputers are often rated by comparing add times as a criterion of their relative speed. See microcomputer.

Adherography In printing, the trade name for a duplicating process in which the image is formed by adherence of a powder to a sticky, latent image. See latent image.

ADI American Documentation Institute.

ADIS Automatic Data Interchange System.

adjacency In character recognition, a condition in which the character spacing reference lines, of two consecutively printed characters on the same line, are separated by less than a specified distance.

adjacent channel In communications, the next channel, or the one in close proximity, either physically or electrically to the one in current use. See channel.

adjust In word processing, an editing feature in which the system automatically adjusts the right hand margin for insertion or deletion of copy during playback. Word and sometimes page wraparound is automatically performed as needed. See wraparound.

ADLC See advanced data link control.

ADP See automatic data processing.

ADRES US Army Data REtrieval System.

advanced data communications control procedure In data communications, pertaining to the operation of a data link using an advanced (SDLC, HDLC) protocol. See HDLC, protocol, SDLC.

advanced data link control In data communications, a link protocol used in HDLC and SDLC systems. See HDLC, SDLC.

advanced sprocket feed In computing, pertaining to paper tape sprocket holes that line up with the leading edge of the code holes. Compare center sprocket feed. See paper tape.

AECT US Association for Educational Communication and Technology.

AEDS US Association for Educational Data Systems.

aerial Synonymous with antenna.

aerial cable In telecommunications, a cable connected to poles or similar overhead structures.

aerial image In optics, a real image formed at a plane in space in an optical system.

AEWIS US Army Electronic Warfare Information System.

affective domain In educational theory, the category of instructional objectives relating to attitudes, values and appreciations within human behaviour.

affiliate In communications, a US broadcast station contracted to a network for more than 10 hours of programming a week.

affirmative acknowledgement In data communications, the replies ACK 0 and ACK 1 in binary synchronous transmission indicate that the previous transmission block was accepted by the receiver and that it is ready to accept the next block. ACK 0 and ACK 1 sent alternately provide sequential checking for a series of replies. ACK 0 is also used as an affirmative reply to station selection signal in a multidrop circuit, or to an initialization sequence in a point to point operation. See binary synchronous communications, multidrop circuit, point to point connection.

AFIPS American Federation of Information Processing Societies.

AFNOR Association Française de NORmalisation – the French Standards Organisation.

afterglow Synonymous with persistence.

agate In typesetting, a type smaller than 6 point. Fourteen lines of agate make one inch of matter for newspaper advertising. See matter, point.

agate line See agate.

AGC See automatic gain control.

agenda item In communications, an FCC proceeding which has been placed on the Commission's formal agenda, and a public notice given. See FCC, sunshine notice.

Agricola A database supplied by U.S. Department of Agriculture and dealing with agriculture, food and nutrition. See on line information retrieval.

Agris A database supplied by Food and Agriculture Organization of the United Nations (FAO), AGRIS Coordinating Center and dealing with agriculture. See on line information retrieval.

AI See artificial intelligence.

A & I Abstracting and Indexing.

air gap In recording, the very narrow gap between the two elements of a magnetic recording or playback head. See head.

ALA American Library Association.

alarm A visual or audio signal to signify that an error has arisen or an abnormal situation exists.

albumen plate In printing, a lithographic plate made from a photographic negative using a light sensitive coating, so named because it formerly contained the white of egg. See lithography.

ALC See automatic level control.

ALGOL In computer programming, ALGOrithmic Language, an early block structured language providing many elegant features that were lacking in other early high level languages. See programming, high level language, Pascal.

algorithm A finite set of well defined rules for the solution of a problem in a finite number of steps, for example, a precise description of the steps involved in determining the record with the highest value of a specified numerical attribute. See programming, attribute, record.

algorithmic language A computer language designed for expressing algorithms. See ALGOL.

aliasing An effect that occurs when a signal is sampled at a rate less than twice the highest frequency present in the signal. When a subsequent signal is recovered from the samples it will not contain the high frequency component of the original signal and it will display a false low frequency signal.

aligner On a typewriter, a device that enables the paper to be correctly lined up in the machine for typing.

aligning edge   In optical character recognition, the edge of a form which, in conjunction with the leading edge, serves to correctly position the document that is to be scanned. See scan.

alignment   (1) In printing, pertaining to the position of letters within a line which has an even appearance when looked at horizontally. (2) In radiocommunications, the simultaneous tuning of two or more circuits. (3) In recording, the positioning of microphones or loudspeakers for stereophonic effects.

alignment pin   In electronics, any pin or device that will ensure the correct mating of two components designed to be connected.

all call   In an electronic learning laboratory, a single control which enables the instructor to talk to all stations simultaneously while overriding all educational programming.

all in   In printing, all copy and proofs are available.

all in hand   In typesetting, the state of a job after all copy has been passed out to the typographers. See typography.

allocate   In computing, (1) to assign a resource, such as a disk or a diskette file, to a specific task, (2) to assign main routines and subroutines to storage. See task.

allocation   See assigned frequency.

allophone   In acoustics, a manifestation of a phoneme in a speech signal. A phoneme may be acoustically different depending upon word position and an allophone is a positional variant of the same phoneme. See phoneme, speech synthesis.

all up   In printing, pertaining to the state of a print job after all copy has been set.

Aloha   In computer networks, a packet switched system at the University of Hawaii which uses radio broadcast techniques. See Slotted Aloha.

ALPAC   US National Academy of Sciences Automated Language Processing Advisory Committee.

alphabet   (1) An ordered set of all the letters and associated marks used in a language or work. (2) An ordered set of letters used in a code language, e.g. the morse code alphabet, the 128 characters of the ASCII alphabet. See morse code, ASCII.

alpha beta technique   In artificial intelligence, a technique used in game playing routines to determine the best set of moves for a given player. The player will pick the set of moves to maximise his score whilst the adversary will always attempt to select moves that will minimise his losses. The successive set of moves can be represented by a tree structure, one player having the choice of branches from one level and the adversary the choice at the next level. The alpha beta technique eliminates subtrees to be searched from the tree, thus reducing the effort of searching for optimum moves. See tree structure.

alphabetic character set   A character set that contains letters but not digits. The set may contain control characters, special characters, and the space character. Compare alphanumeric. See control character.

alphabetic shift   A control for selecting the alphabetic character set in an alphanumeric keyboard printer.

alphabetic string   A character string consisting of letters from the same alphabet. See string.

alphabet length   In typesetting, the measurement, in points, of the lower case alphabet of a particular style and size. See point.

alphageometric   In videotex, a standard in which the codes can instruct the terminal to produce line drawings, fill areas with colour, etc. in addition to normal character display modes. Compare alphamosaic. See videotex.

alphamosaic   In videotex, a standard in which the codes determine the alphanumeric character or mosaic pattern to be displayed in a character space. Compare alphageometric. See alphanumeric, videotex, character space.

alphanumeric Pertaining to a character set that contains letters, digits and usually other characters, e.g. punctuation marks.

alphanumeric character set A character set that contains both letters and digits and may contain control characters, special characters, and the space character. See alphanumeric.

alphanumeric data Data represented by letters and digits and perhaps special characters and the space character. See alphanumeric, special character.

alphanumeric display device See character display device.

alphanumeric keyboard In videotex, a keyboard used for entering letters, numbers, and special characters. It is required by IPs for creating frames. Users with this keyboard can send messages via electronic mail or fill response frames with alphanumeric information. Users who are only equipped with numeric keypads enter such information in a format determined by a predefined menu selection. See alphanumeric, electronic mailbox, frame, IP, keypad, response frame.

alphanumerics mode In videotex, the display mode in which the display characters are those of the alphanumerics set. Compare graphics mode. See display mode.

alphanumerics set In videotex, the set of 96 display characters comprising all the alphanumerics characters. See display character.

alphaphotographic In videotex, a method of displaying alphanumeric characters and picture quality graphics from individually transmitted and stored picture elements. See Picture Prestel.

alpha wrap In recording, a method of winding videotape around the drum of a helical scan device. The tape circumnavigates the drum producing a shape like the Greek letter alpha, leaving the drum at a higher level than that which it entered. The video scans are diagonal on the tape and cover the width of it. The edge of the tape is also required for audio recording and thus there is a compromise between good sound recording and drop out. Compare omega wrap. See sound track, drop out.

alternate mode In computing, a method of using a virtual terminal by which each of two interacting systems or users has access to its data structure in turn. The associated protocols include facilities to allow the orderly transfer of control from one user to the other. Compare free running mode. See virtual terminal, data structure.

alternate route In communications, a secondary or backup route that is used if normal routing is not possible.

alternate track In computing, a track on a magnetic disk or other storage device, which is automatically substituted for a damaged track. See track.

alternating current Electric power supply in the form of a sine wave, normally a frequency of 60 Hz in the US, and 50 Hz in the UK. Compare direct current. See Hz.

ALU See arithmetic logic unit.

Alvey A research program, named after Mr John Alvey, of pre-competitive research in advanced information technology costing some £300 million over five years. See ESPRIT.

AM See amplitude modulation.

A-MAC In television, a variant of C-MAC which requires a lower bandwidth per channel. Compare C-MAC. See MAC.

ambient noise level In electronics and recording, random, uncontrollable and irreducible noise level at a location or circuit. See noise.

ambisonics In recording, the use of two or more sound channels to give the effect of more than one spatial dimension. Compare stereo. Synonymous with surround sound.

America; History & Life (AHL) A database supplied by ABC-Clio Information Services and dealing with history, politics & political science. See on line information retrieval.

American National Standards Institute   A body which organizes committees formed of computer users, manufacturers, etc., to develop and publish industry standards, e.g. ANSI FORTRAN, ANSI Standard Code for Periodical Identification.

ammonia duplication process   In printing, a form of diazo process in which a latent image is made visible by exposure to evaporating ammonia. See diazo process, latent image.

ampere   In electronics, the basic unit of electrical current. Compare volt. See current.

amplification   In electronics, (1) the strengthening of a weak signal, (2) the ratio between some measure of the output signal and the input signal of a device. Compare attenuation.

amplified telephone   In teleconferencing, the general term for a hands free telephone, using a loudspeaker and microphone unit rather than a telephone handset.

amplifier   In electronics, a normally unidirectional device which increases the power or amplitude of an electrical signal. See amplitude.

amplitude   The magnitude of the greatest deviation from the midpoint value of a periodic signal or phenomenon. See frequency, wavelength.

amplitude distortion   In electronics, a distortion caused by an undesired amplitude characteristic, e.g. in an amplifier the output signal would not be a faithful reproduction of the input signal.

amplitude frequency characteristic   In electronics, a graphical representation of the variation in output amplitude of a device with changes in input frequency at constant input amplitude.

amplitude modulation   In communications, a form of modulation in which the amplitude of the carrier signal is varied in accordance with the amplitude of the modulating signal. Compare frequency modulation, phase modulation. See carrier, modulation.

analog   In computing and communications, pertaining to the form of continuously variable physical quantities. For example, a telephone conversation can be represented fully in analog form by a voltage derived from the telephone transmitters. Compare digital. See transducer.

analog channel   In communications, a data channel on which the information transmitted can take any value between the limits defined for the channel. Voice grade channels are analog channels. See analog.

analog computer   In computing, a device that performs mathematical functions on variables, usually voltages, and produces a solution in the form of an analog signal. They were used extensively in the study of dynamic systems and as simulators. The basic building block of the analog computer was the operational amplifier, used to produce the mathematical functions of addition, subtraction, integration and multiplication. Non linear effects, e.g. saturation were also effected with special diode units. Unlike digital computers they were parallel in operation, easy to program for their class of problems and relatively fast. They did not benefit, however, from the rapid advances in digital technology and they are now obsolete except for special purpose applications. See digital computer, hybrid computer, simulator, operational amplifier.

analog data   In computing, data represented in a continuous form.

analog recording   A method of recording control information by a continuous but varying signal. Compare digital recording. See analog signal.

analog signal   A signal that varies continuously according to the information in transmission, e.g. sound waves. Compare digital signal.

analog to digital converter   In computing and communications, a device which periodically samples analog signals and produces

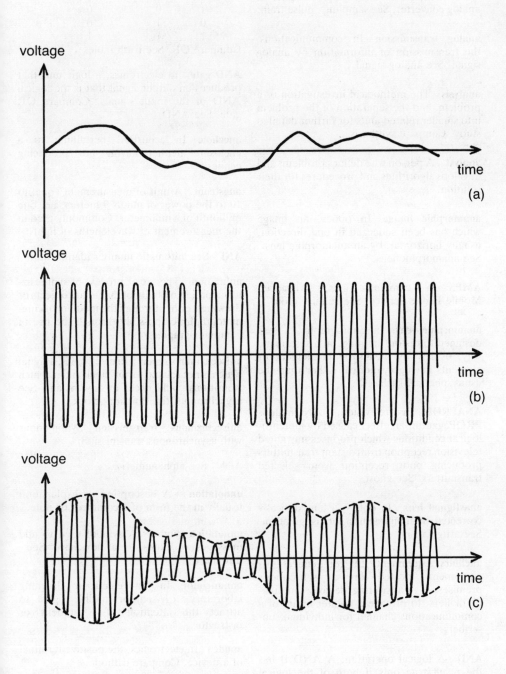

amplitude modulation
(*a*) message signal; (*b*) carrier; (*c*) resulting amplitude modulation

corresponding digital signals, usually in the form of a pulse train. Compare digital to analog converter. See sampling , pulse train.

analog transmission In communications, the transmission of information by analog signal. See analog signal.

analysis The methodical investigation of a problem, and the separation of the problem into smaller related units for further detailed study. Compare synthesis.

analyst A person who defines problems and develops algorithms and procedures for their solution.

anamorphic image In optics, an image which has been squeezed in one direction, usually horizontal, by an anamorphic lens. See anamorphic lens.

AMPS In communications, Advanced Mobile Phone Service. See cellular radio.

anamorphic lens In photography, a lens designed to distort an image in a systematic way, usually by means of an element or elements having cylindrical rather than the usual spherical surfaces.

ANAPROP In television, ANOmalous PROPagation, an effect caused by meteorological conditions which produces unwanted television reception from distant transmitters producing poor reception from selected transmitters. See ghost.

anastigmat lens In optics, a lens optically corrected in manufacture for astigmatism. See astigmatism.

ancillary equipment In communications, equipment located on a subscriber's premises, e.g. answering devices, automatic diallers, to provide a greater utility of a communications channel for individual subscribers.

AND A logical operation, A AND B has the result true only if both of the logical variables A and B are true. The corresponding truth table is

A	B	A AND B
0	0	0
1	0	0
0	1	0
1	1	1

Compare OR. See truth table.

AND gate In electronics, a logic unit that produces an output signal that is the logical AND of the input signals. Compare OR gate. See AND.

anechoic In acoustics, pertaining to a enclosure neither having nor producing echoes.

angstrom A unit of measurement equal to 10 to the power of minus 9 meters, i.e. one millionth of a millimeter. Commonly used in the measurement of wavelengths of light.

ANI See automatic number identification.

animation The art or process of synthesizing apparent mobility of inanimate objects or drawings, either through the medium of cinematography or possibly through the use of computer graphics.

anisochronous signal In electronics, a signal which is not related to any clock and in which transitions could occur at any instant. See asynchronous transmission, clock.

anisochronous transmission Synonymous with asynchronous transmission.

A/N See alphanumeric.

annotation A description or explanation usually in the form of a comment or note.

annotation symbol A symbol used to add messages or notes to a flowchart. See flowchart.

annunciator In an electronic learning laboratory, a visual or audible signal to attract the attention of a student or instructor.

anode In electronics, the positive terminal of a device. Compare cathode.

anomalistic period In satellite communications, the time interval between two con-

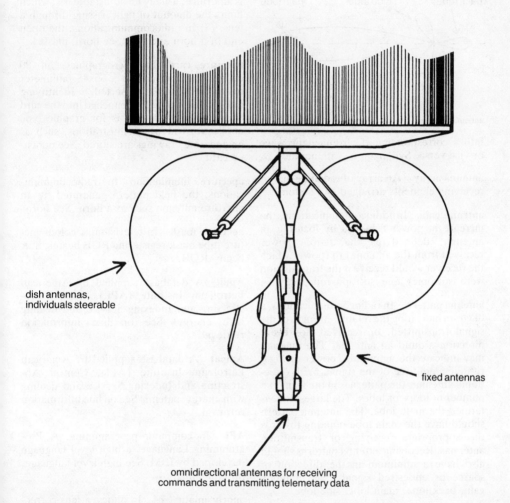

dish antennas,
individuals steerable

fixed antennas

omnidirectional antennas for receiving
commands and transmitting telemetary data

antenna
The three types of antenna on an INTELSAT IV Satellite.

secutive passages of a satellite through its apogee. See apogee.

ANSI See American National Standards Institute.

answer back In communications, signal sent by a receiving unit to the sending station for identification or to indicate it is ready for transmission. See voice answer back.

answering In data communications, the process of responding to a calling station to complete the establishment of a connection between data stations. See station.

answering time The elapse time between the appearance of a signal and the response made to it.

antenna In radiocommunications, a device that converts a high radio frequency signal

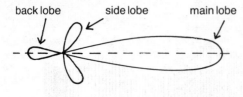

back lobe   side lobe   main lobe

antenna pattern

into a corresponding electromagnetic wave or vice versa. Synonymous with aerial.

antenna array   An array of radiating and/or receiving elements arranged in a system.

antenna gain   In radiocommunications, the increase in power achieved by focusing an antenna, defined as the ratio: (power received from the antenna) to (power which the receiver would receive if the transmission were isotropic). See isotropic radiator.

antenna pattern   In radiocommunications, a diagram indicating the relative strength of the signal transmitted, or received, for every direction around an antenna. The diagram may indicate the amplitude, power or logarithmic amplitude of the signal. With directional antennas the pattern is in the form of a number or loops or lobes. The largest lobe is termed the main lobe. The antenna pattern should have the main lobe pointing towards the appropriate receiving or transmitting antennas. Receiving antenna patterns should also have a minimum in the direction of source of undesired signals. See antenna gain, back lobe, main lobe, side lobe.

anticipatory staging   In computing, a technique in which blocks of data are moved from one storage device to another, with a shorter access time, in anticipation that they will be required by the program and before the program actually requests them. See demand staging.

Antiope   The French standard for character coding and display for videotex terminals.

AP   See Associated Press.

APD   See avalanche photodiode.

aperture   (1) In computing, a part of a mask that permits retention of the corresponding portions of data. (2) In optics, a lens aperture is an orifice, usually an adjustable iris, which limits the amount of light passing through a lens. (3) In radiocommunications, the open end of a horn antenna. See horn, mask.

aperture card   In micrographics, an 80 column card which has a 35x48 millimeter microfilm frame inserted. Identifying information can be key punched into the card and their primary use is for graphic type applications in which illustrations, such as engineering drawings are stored. See punched card.

aperture illumination   In radiocommunications, the field pattern generated by an aperture antenna such as a horn. See horn.

aperture mask   In television, a colour picture tube mask registering RGB beams. See beam, RGB.

Apilit   A database supplied by American Petroleum Institute (APL), Central Abstracting and Indexing Service and dealing with energy. See on line information retrieval.

Apipat   A database supplied by American Petroleum Institute (API), Central Abstracting and Indexing Service and dealing with energy, patents. See on line information retrieval.

APL   In computer programming, A Programming Language, a high level language developed by IBM. See high level language, programming.

apochromatic lens   In optics, a lens corrected for spherical and chromatic aberration.

apogee   In satellite communications, the point at which the satellite is at its maximum distance from earth in its orbit. Compare perigee.

Apple   In computing, a range of popular microcomputers manufactured by Apple Computers. See personal computer.

application layer   In data communications, the topmost layer in the ISO Open Systems Interconnections model. The content of this layer is left to the users and it is expected that standard protocols for specific industries will be developed. Compare data link layer, network layer, physical layer, presentation layer, session layer, transport layer. See Open Systems Interconnection.

application oriented language In computer programming, a language that has facilities or notations useful for solving problems in one or more specific classes of applications, e.g. numerical analysis, business data processing, simulation.

application program In computer programming, a program written for a specific user application.

Applications Technology Satellite-6 In satellite communications, a powerful, all purpose, NASA communications satellite launched in 1974 with 30 foot antenna to utilize higher transmission frequencies.

approach of end of medium indicator On dictation equipment, a device giving an audible or visual signal at a precise distance from the end of the recording medium.

aqualine A database supplied by Water Research Centre and dealing with aquatic sciences, environment. See on line information retrieval.

ARABSAT In communications, ARAB SATellite, a COMSAT project to provide regional satellite communications for countries of the Arab League. See COMSAT, satellite.

archetype A work of communication, e.g. a book, which has the typical pattern, symbolism and forms for works of its kind, especially original, classical works.

architecture In computing, the specification of the relationships between the parts of a computer system, e.g. in a microprocessor, it will involve the organization and capacity of buses, temporary storage registers and control elements. See bus, microcomputer, microprocessor, register.

archival quality In a document copying machine, the quality of the copy image expressed in terms of the specified number of years for which legibility is guaranteed when stored under stated conditions.

archiving In computing, the storage of

backup files and associated journals, usually for a given period of time. See file, journal.

ARDIS US Army Research and Development Information System.

area In databases, the CODASYL definition of an area is a named subdivision of the addressable storage space in the database which may contain occurrences of records and sets, or parts of sets of various types. See CODASYL, record, set.

area code In telephony, a three digit number identifying one of 152 geographic areas in the USA and Canada to permit direct distance dialing on the telephone system. Compare number plan area. See direct distance dialing.

area composition In photocomposition, the operation of setting made up pages in varying formats for advertisements, tables, pages of periodicals etc. following arrangement of these by use of the video layout system. See video layout system.

area exchange In telephony, an area organization established for administrative reasons for a telephone service covered on a single rate basis, usually a city or large division, town, or village. See rate center.

areal density In computing, the number of bits per unit area that can be stored on a recording device. In magnetic and optical disk systems it is equal to the product of bits per inch and tracks per inch. See BPI, magnetic disk, optical digital disks, TPI.

area search In library science, the examination of a large group of documents to select those that belong to one group.

argument (1) Any value of an independent variable. (2) In computer programming, a parameter passed between a calling program and a subprogram or statement function. See subroutine.

arithmetic (1) The branch of mathematics concerned with the study of the positive real numbers and zero. (2) In computing, the operations of addition, subtraction, multiplication and division.

arithmetic capability In word processing,

the ability of a system to be used as a calculator or adding machine.

arithmetic instruction In computer programming, an instruction in which the operation part specifies an operation that follows the rules of arithmetic. See instruction.

arithmetic logic unit In computing, the unit in which arithmetic, logic and related operations are performed. See CPU.

arithmetic mean The average value of a number of values of a variable. It is calculated by summing all the component values and dividing the result by the number of values. Synonymous with average.

arithmetic overflow See overflow.

arithmetic shift In computing, (1) a shift that does not affect the sign position, (2) a shift that is equivalent to the multiplication of a number by a positive or negative integral power of the radix. See radix, shift.

arithmetic unit See arithmetic logic unit.

ARPA In communications, the ARPA project, funded by the US Defense Advanced Research Project Agency, produced one of the first large scale packet switched networks, known as ARPANET. Telenet, a public packet switching service, was derived from this work. See packet switching.

arq See automatic retransmission request.

array (1) In computing, an ordered arrangement or pattern of items or numbers, e.g. a table of numbers. (2) In communications, an assembly of spaced antenna elements designed to give an overall directional characteristic. See vector.

art In printing and filming, an abbreviation for artwork. See artwork.

ARTbibliographies Modern A database supplied by ABC-Clio Information Services and dealing with art. See on line information retrieval.

artificial intelligence In computing, that branch of computer science that studies how make computers smarter. The term has been employed to cover a wide variety of computer developments e.g. efficient rep-

to resentation of knowledge, reasoning, deduction, problem solving and heuristic search. These capabilities have been applied in game playing, automatic theorem proving, automatic computer programming, robots, machine vision, natural language systems and information processing. See expert systems, machine translation.

ARTS In communications, Advanced Radio Telephone Service. See cellular radio.

artwork (1) In printing, matter prepared for photomechanical reproduction. (2) In cinematography, any kind of graphic work for a film, e.g. titles, diagrams, charts, scenery or animation drawings.

ARU In computing, Audio Response Unit. See audio response terminal.

ASA American Standards Association, a body with groups responsible for the establishment of data processing standards.

ASA exposure index In photography, letters used to refer to the numerical exposure index of a film under the system adopted by the American National Standards Institute.

ASC American Society of Cinematographers.

ascender In printing, the portion of a lower case character above the x or z height. Compare descender. See x height.

ascertainment In communications, the FCC licensing procedure requiring broadcast stations to investigate local programming needs. See FCC.

ASCII American Standard Code for Information Interchange, pronounced ASKEE. A standard data transmission code that was introduced to achieve compatibility between data devices. It consists of 7 information bits and 1 parity bit for error checking purposes, thus allowing 128 code combinations. Of these 32 are used for upper case characters and a few punctuation marks, another group of 32 characters are used for numbers, spacing and additional punctuation symbols, the third group of 32 characters are assigned to lower case characters and some rarely used punctuation symbols. The last set of 32 characters are allocated to machine and

CONTROL CHARACTERS

CHAR	OCTAL	BINARY
NUL	000	0000000
SOH	001	0000001
STX	002	0000010
ETX	003	0000011
EOT	004	0000100
ENQ	005	0000101
ACK	006	0000110
BEL	007	0000111
BS	010	0001000
HT	011	0001001
LF	012	0001010
VT	013	0001011
FF	014	0001100
CR	015	0001101
SO	016	0001110
SI	017	0001111
DLE	020	0010000
DC1	021	0010001
DC2	022	0010010
DC3	023	0010011
DC4	024	0010100
NAK	025	0010101
SYN	026	0010110
ETB	027	0010111
CAN	030	0011000
EM	031	0011001
SUB	032	0011010
ESC	033	0011011
FS	034	0011100
GS	035	0011101
RS	036	0011110
US	037	0011111
DEL	177	1111111

PRINTABLE CHARACTERS

CHAR	OCTAL	BINARY
SP	040	0100000
!	041	0100001
"	042	0100010
#	043	0100011
$	044	0100100
%	045	0100101
&	046	0100110
'	047	0100111
(	050	0101000
)	051	0101001
*	052	0101010
+	053	0101011
,	054	0101100
-	055	0101101
.	056	0101110
/	057	0101111
0	060	0110000
1	061	0110001
2	062	0110010
3	063	0110011
4	064	0110100
5	065	0110101
6	066	0110110
7	067	0110111
8	070	0111000
9	071	0111001
:	072	0111010
;	073	0111011
<	074	0111100
=	075	0111101
>	076	0111110
?	077	0111111
@	100	1000000

PRINTABLE CHARACTERS

CHAR	OCTAL	BINARY
A	101	1000001
B	102	1000010
C	103	1000011
D	104	1000100
E	105	1000101
F	106	1000110
G	107	1000111
H	110	1001000
I	111	1001001
J	112	1001010
K	113	1001011
L	114	1001100
M	115	1001101
N	116	1001110
O	117	1001111
P	120	1010000
Q	121	1010001
R	122	1010010
S	123	1010011
T	124	1010100
U	125	1010101
V	126	1010110
W	127	1010111
X	130	1011000
Y	131	1011001
Z	132	1011010

PRINTABLE CHARACTERS

CHAR	OCTAL	BINARY
a	141	1100001
b	142	1100010
c	143	1100011
d	144	1100100
e	145	1100101
f	146	1100110
g	147	1100111
h	150	1101000
i	151	1101001
j	152	1101010
k	153	1101011
l	154	1101100
m	155	1101101
n	156	1101110
o	157	1101111
p	160	1110000
q	161	1110001
r	162	1110010
s	163	1110011
t	164	1110100
u	165	1110101
v	166	1110110
w	167	1110111
x	170	1111000
y	171	1111001
z	172	1111010

CONTROL CHARACTER KEY

NUL	=	All zeros
SOH	=	Start of heading
STX	=	Start of text
ETX	=	End of text
EOT	=	End of transmission
ENQ	=	Enquiry
ACK	=	Acknowledgement
BEL	=	Bell or attention signal
BS	=	Back space
HT	=	Horizontal tabulation
LF	=	Line feed
VT	=	Vertical tabulation
FF	=	Form Feed
CR	=	Carriage return
SO	=	Shift out
SI	=	Shift in
DLE	=	Data link escape
DC1	=	Device control 1
DC2	=	Device control 2
DC3	=	Device control 3
DC4	=	Device control 4
NAK	=	Negative acknowledgement
SYN	=	Synchronous/idle
ETB	=	End of transmitted block
CAN	=	Cancel (error in data)
EM	=	End of medium
SUB	=	Start of special sequence
ESC	=	Escape
FS	=	Information file separator
GS	=	Information group separator
RS	=	Information record separator
US	=	Information unit separator
DEL	=	Delete

ASCII codes.

control commands, e.g. line feed, carriage return. See bit, parity checking, lower case, upper case, carriage control, line feed, carriage return. See bit, parity checking, lower case, upper case, carriage control, line feed.

ASIS American Society for Information Science.

ASLIB In library science, Association of Special Libraries and Information Bureaux, founded in 1926 and merged with British Society for International Bibliography in 1949. Its aims are to facilitate the coordination and systematic use of sources of knowledge and information in all public offices, in industry and commerce and in all the arts and sciences.

aspect card In library science, a card containing the accession numbers of documents in an information retrieval system. See accession number.

aspect ratio (1) In cinematography, the width to height ratio of a motion picture frame, normally 4 to 3 or 1·33 : 1. (2) In television, the ratio of the dimensions of a TV screen, normally 4 to 3.

aspect system In library science, a method of indexing which assumes that a record represents a single subject and contains the necessary information on which documents have this subject in common. See aspect card.

ASR See automatic send receive.

assemble In computer programming, (1) to translate a source program using an assembler, (2) to integrate subroutines into the main program. See assembler, source program, subroutine, translator.

assembler In computing, a program that translates a source program written in a low language to machine code. Compare compiler, interpreter. See low level language, machine code, source program, translator.

assembly language In computer programming, a language that allows a programmer to develop a machine code program using symbols and mnemonics for storage locations and operations. This facility greatly improves the comprehension of the program and enables modifications to be more readily incorpo-

rated. Compare high level language. See low level language, machine code, translator.

assembly listing In computer programming, the printed list produced by the assembler giving details of any syntax errors, a listing of the source program and, normally, an associated listing of the corresponding machine code program. See assembler, machine code.

assembly time In computer programming, the time at which an assembler translates the source program into the corresponding object code. See assembler, object code, source program.

assertion In expert systems, a hypothesis about the problem to be solved. The likelihood of an assertion is established by asking the user questions or, alternatively, rules may be used to deduce the likelihood from other assertions or stored data. Compare object. See rule.

assigned frequency In communications, the FCC license of specific frequency and power to a broadcast station. The available radio frequencies for nongovernment use are reserved by the FCC for specific applications such as FM broadcasting, television, aeronautical radio, amateur radio, etc. In the UK, the Home Office is responsible for such licensing. See FCC.

assigned indexing In library science, a method of indexing in which the indexer assigns the appropriate words to describe the document rather than relying on the author's choice. Compare derived indexing. See indexing.

Associated Press A subscriber news service for broadcasting stations and newspapers. See broadcasting station, Reuters.

associational editing In filming, the juxtaposition of film or video shots in order to present contrast, comparisons, similarities, or ideas.

Association for Computing Machinery A professional computer science organization. Its objective is to advance all aspects of information processing and to promote the interchange of such techniques between computer specialists and users.

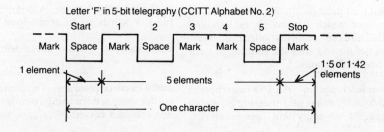

Letter 'F' in 5-bit telegraphy (CCITT Alphabet No. 2)

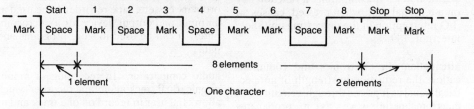

Figure '5' for 8-bit telegraph machines (ASCII codes)

asynchronous transmission

associative processor In computing, a device using associative storage methods, i.e. data is accessed by reading keys and comparing their values with those that identify the item sought. See associative storage.

associative storage In computing, a storage device in which the user identifies data by a part of its content rather than by its physical location. It provides a fast method of searching for data with certain keys. The computer system may also rearrange its storage of data without affecting the user's application programs. See application program, key. Synonymous with content addressable memory.

astigmatism In optics, a defect in the design of a lens which causes light rays passing through the lens to converge improperly.

astonisher In printing, a term for an exclamation mark !

asynchronous Pertaining to actions and events that are not correlated with some reference time.

asynchronous computer A computer in which each operation is initiated as a result of a signal generated by the completion of the previous operation or by the availability of the equipment required for the next operation. Compare synchronous computer.

asynchronous transmission In computing and communications, transmission in which each information character is individually synchronized by the use of start and stop elements because the interval of time between characters can vary. Compare synchronous transmission.

ATM See automated teller mechanism.

atmospheric absorption In radiocommunications, the loss of energy suffered by an electromagnetic wave due to dissipation in the atmosphere. See electromagnetic radiation.

ATR See audio tape recorder.

ATS-6 See Applications Technology Satellite-6.

AT & T American Telephone & Telegraph Co.

attended operation In communications, the transmission and reception of messages with an operator in attendance.

attended trail printer In word processing, a trail printer which has no paper handling facilities and so requires operator intervention before and after the printing of each page. See trail printer.

attention interruption An I/O interruption caused by a terminal user pressing an attention key, or its equivalent. See interrupt, I/O.

attention key In computing, a function key on a terminal that, when pressed, causes an I/O interruption in the processing unit. See interrupt, I/O.

attenuation In electronics and communication, the reduction in strength of an electrical signal as it passes through a circuit or an electromagnetic wave as it propagates through a transmission medium. Compare amplification. See electromagnetic radiation.

attribute In databases, a field that contains information about an entity, e.g. in a personnel database home address would be an attribute of entity employee. See field, entity, display attribute.

audience rating In filming and broadcasting, a statement or scale of judgements made or used by an audience to evaluate a film or TV program.

audio The range of sound wave frequencies that can normally be detected by the human ear (usually between 20 and 20,000 Hz). See Hz.

audio active In an electronic learning laboratory, a facility in which a student can hear a master tape, respond into a microphone and hear his or her response through headphones. Compare audio passive.

audio active compare In an electronic learning laboratory, a facility in which a student can hear a master tape, respond into a microphone, and have both sounds recorded on separate tape tracks for comparison.

audiocard In audiovisual aids, a thin card with a strip of audiotape (usually 12 inches or less) across the bottom. Accompanying pictures or words are located above the tape.

audio cassette Synonymous with compact cassette.

audio cassette recorder In recording, a recorder designed for using compact cassettes. See compact cassette.

audio cassette recorder interface In computing, an interface unit that enables an ordinary cassette tape recorder to be used as an input and output device for a microcomputer. It can be used to store programs and data.

audio comparator In recording, a monophonic, dual track audiotape recorder which allows the user to record on one track and to play back on both. See monophonic.

audio compressor In audio visual aids, an electronic device capable of the compression and expansion of an audio signal with respect to its speed without a corresponding increase or decrease in pitch.

audio frequency The frequency of an audible sound wave, for normal hearing the range of frequencies lies between 20 and 20,000 Hz. See Hz.

audio inquiry See voice answer back.

audio mix In filming, the electronic combination of two or more sound elements into a single track, usually synchronized with a picture projection.

audio monitor In recording, a studio quality speaker for listening to the playback of a tape or record, also used for editing and quality checking.

audio page Synonymous with audiocard.

audio passive In an electronic learning laboratory, a facility in which a student can listen to a master tape, usually through headphones. Compare audio active, audio active compare.

audio response terminal In computing, a terminal which receives spoken information from a computer. Digitized speech in the form of words/phrases or phonemes are accessed by the program, and converted from digital to analog form for transmission. If the receiving unit is a push button telephone, the user can send enquiries via the push button. See phoneme, speech synthesis, pushbutton dialing, voice answer back.

audio response unit See voice answer back.

audioslide In audio visual aids, a 2 by 2 inch slide with a brief audio recording on a magnetic coating on the slide mount. It requires a special projector for operation.

audio tape In recording, a tape having a coating on which sound can be recorded magnetically. See audio tape recorder.

audio tape recorder In recording, a device for making a permanent or temporary record of a signal or program. It usually can play back as well as record. The tape may be on open reels or in a container called a cartridge or cassette. See audio tape.

audio teleconferencing In teleconferencing, group voice communication relying on exchanges among more than two participants via voice.

audiotutorial instruction In audio visual aids, a teaching process in which audiotapes and audio equipment are the main educational tools.

audiovisual A general term for nonbook materials which can be viewed and/or listened to, such as films, filmstrips, tapes and overhead transparencies. See educational technology.

audiovisual aids Any nonbook material which can be used in educational technology. See educational technology.

audit trail In computing, a clerical or automated method for tracing the transactions affecting the contents of a record. See record.

augend The number to which an addend is added to produce the sum in an arithmetic operation. See addend.

aural transmitter In broadcasting, equipment used to transmit the sound signal from a television broadcasting station.

authentication In data security, processes that ensure everything about a teleprocessing transaction is genuine. The parties to the transaction must identify each other reliably, know that each message they receive comes from the other party and has not been stored earlier and replayed. They must verify that the contents of the messages have not been changed by a third party. See replay, wire tapping.

authentication of messages In data communications, the process in which a check field is added to a block of data so that any change to the data will be detected. A secret key enters into the calculation and is known to the intended receiver of the data. In a different form of authentication, the whole block is transformed and this can be a public key cryptosystem. See public key cryptosystem.

authentication of users In data communications, the verification that the user at the terminal corresponds to his claimed identity.

authenticity In data security, controls that either prevent or detect the tampering and/or accidental destruction of data. If the data to be protected is already encrypted, then authenticity requires that a cryptoanalyst would not be able to substitute a false ciphertext without detection. See ciphertext, accidental destruction, digital signature, masquerading.

author The writer of books or articles on computer software.

authoring In interactive video disk, a structured approach to developing all elements of an interactive video disk program with emphasis on preproduction. See preproduction.

authoring system In computing, a computer system capable of executing an author language. See author language.

authority file In library science, a file of records relating to the decisions taken in the use of an indexing language. It identifies established forms of headings, index terms, preferred synonyms, etc. which may be used for information retrieval. See indexing language.

authorization   In computing, the right given to a user to communicate with or make use of a computer system.

authorization code   In computing, a code used to protect against unauthorized access to data and system facilities. The code normally consists of a user id (identification) and password. See user id, password.

authorized power   In communications, the maximum power which may be used by a licensed radio station in the US, or a station which broadcasts any form of radio signal. The power limit is authorized and assigned by the FCC, and is necessary to prevent interference with the many other users of the radio spectrum. It is set in accordance with the specific usage involved: television, FM, broadcast, CB, police radio, etc. See FM, CB.

authorized user   In communications, a person or firm which, under the Communications Satellite Act of 1962, is permitted in the US to deal directly with the Communications Satellite Corporation (COMSAT) to secure space segment and associated ground facilities. See COMSAT.

author language   A programming language used for designing instructional programs for computer assisted instruction and computer based training systems. See computer assisted learning, computer based training.

author's alterations   In printing, an indication in a proof that the cost of a correction is to be borne by the author or publisher and not the printer.

auto abstract   In library science, an abstract produced by computer analyses. Sentences containing a high frequency of particular words are printed out in sequence. Compare evaluative abstract, general abstract, indicative abstract, informative abstract.

auto answer   See automatic answering.

autodialer   In computing and videotex, a device that automatically dials a prerecorded telephone number for connection to a host computer.

autoidentifier   In computing and videotex, a device by which a terminal automatically identifies itself to a computer.

auto indexing   In computing, a system of indexing that superimposes additional information at any of several given addresses. Compare automatic indexing.

auto kerning   In typesetting, the automatic reduction of unwanted white spaces between characters to produce a more aesthetic image. See kerning.

automata theory   A mathematical study of the systems that receive discrete inputs, change their internal states according to the input and their current states and deliver outputs according to their internal states and inputs. See Turing machine.

automated teller mechanism   A device which provides for cash withdrawals, deposits into accounts, payment of bills, account balance enquiries and transfers of funds between accounts. See self banking.

automatic   Pertaining to a process or device that, under specified conditions, functions without intervention by a human operator.

automatic abstracting   In library science, pertaining to the production of an abstract by a computer. The abstract comprises complete sentences, derived from the original document, which are normally selected on the basis of the frequency of relevant terms within them. More refined methods introduce other criteria of significance, e.g. comparison with the expected frequency of occurrences; cue words in sentences - significantly, important - which indicate the author's emphasis; title and heading words and position of the sentence in the overall structure. Compare automatic indexing. See abstract.

automatic answering   In communications, a system in which the called station automatically responds to the calling signal, the call may be established whether or not the called station is attended. Synonymous with auto answer.

automatic answering device In telephony, a machine feature that enables incoming phone calls to be answered and gives a prerecorded message. At the end of the message the unit usually switches from playback to record thus permitting callers to leave recorded messages.

automatic calling In communications, a machine feature that allows a station to initiate a call automatically over a switched line. See station.

automatic calling unit In telephony, a device that enables a business machine to automatically dial calls over a network. See automatic dialer.

automatic carriage In typewriters, a control mechanism that can automatically control the feeding, spacing, skipping, and ejecting of paper or preprinted forms.

automatic carriage return In word processing, the automatic performance of a carriage return when the last word, which will fit onto a line of print, is typed. A system which has this facility will usually employ a buffer to hold the word currently being typed until it can decide whether to place the word on the current line, or to wrap it onto the next line. See carriage control, wraparound.

automatic centering In word processing, the automatic ability to center a word or portion of text.

automatic data processing Data processing performed by computer systems as compared with manual systems. See electronic data processing, manual data processing.

automatic decimal alignment In word processing, the feature of a machine that enables numbers to be aligned automatically on either side of a decimal marker.

automatic decimal tab Synonymous with automatic decimal alignment.

automatic dialer See autodialer.

automatic dictionary (1) In machine translation, a database which provides a word for word substitution from one language to another. (2) In information retrieval, a system which substitutes codes for words or phrases in the encoding operation. See term bank.

automatic document feeder On a document copying machine, a device in which a quantity of original documents may be placed for automatic feeding.

automatic document handler On a document copying machine, an automatic document feeder that incorporates additional facilities in order to recycle originals.

automatic exposure In photography, the use in a camera of a device which opens up or closes down the lens iris depending on subject brightness.

automatic file select In word processing, a facility for making a selection from a data file based on the characters which appear in a specified data field. For example, using a zip code field, the system can select all the addresses with a 1248 zip code for one letter, and type a different letter for all other codes, etc.

automatic file sort In word processing, a facility for performing sorts on files in alphabetical, or other order. This feature is useful for manipulating address lists so that changes need not be performed in alphabetical order.

automatic footnote tie in In word processing, a system which ties a footnote to the appropriate text segment. If the text segment is moved to another page or document, the footnote will travel with it.

automatic frequency control In radiocommunications, a method of negative feedback in which a tuning error generates a control voltage, which is used to change the local oscillator frequency so as to minimize the error. See negative feedback.

automatic gain control In electronics, circuitry which provides a consistent average output signal level for a wide range of input levels. For example, in a radio receiver this facility will automatically adjust the output volume to compensate for variations in signal strength. See gain.

automatic headers/footers   In word processing, the ability to place header/footer text at the top or bottom of each page of a multipage document. The operator specifies the text once, and the header/footer (usually document title, company name or confidentiality requirements) is automatically added during printout.

automatic indexing   In library science, pertaining to the selection of keywords from a document by a computer in order to develop index entries. Simple word counts techniques proved to be defective on several counts and a more effective method is to count the number of occurrences of a word and compare it with an expected number derived from a predetermined frequency norm. Compare automatic abstracting. See index.

automatic letter writing   In word processing, the ability to produce a standard document as though it were typed specially for the recipient.

automatic level control   Synonymous with automatic gain control.

automatic line/paragraph numbering   In word processing, a facility whereby the system automatically supplies an identifying number for each line or paragraph during input for use in defining locations during subsequent editing. The line/paragraph numbers are automatically deleted during final printout.

automatic line spacing   In word processing, the ability of a printer to perform different line spacings without the need for operator intervention.

automatic loader   In computing, a loader program implemented in a special ROM that allows loading of binary paper tapes or the first record or sector of a mass storage device. See loader, mass storage, ROM.

automatic lock   See pix lock.

automatic logging   In word processing, a facility in which a system automatically records titles and log numbers with all documents. Thus data can be played back separately when required. See log.

automatic margin adjust   In word processing, a facility to change margins with a single command. Line endings are adjusted without further intervention.

automatic message accounting   In telephony, a process for automatically recording all data of customer dialed long distance calls for billing purposes.

automatic message switching center   In communications, a location at which messages are automatically routed according to the information they contain. See message switching.

automatic noise suppression   In electronics, a means of suppressing unwanted signals. For example, on a dictation machine, automatic noise suppression automatically reduces electrical noise during input to the recording medium or during playback or both.

automatic number identification   In communications, the automatic line identification of outward dialed calls.

automatic page numbering   In word processing, a facility to generate automatically page numbers within documents. When text is rearranged and page numbers change, the system can generate a new set of correct page numbers.

automatic pagination   In word processing, a facility to take a multipage document and divide it into pages of a specified length in terms of line numbers. Often, this feature is joined with the capability to automatically generate page numbers. See automatic page numbering.

automatic polling   In computing and data communications, a feature of a transmission control unit that enables it to handle negative responses to polling without interrupting the CPU. See CPU, polling.

automatic programming   In computer programming, the use of a computer to convert a program written in a convenient language for the programmer into a set of machine code instructions that can be executed by the computer. See high level language, translator.

automatic program transfer In an electronic learning laboratory, a facility which enables the transfer of program material to all students by the instructor.

automatic repeat key A typewriter key, such as the underscore, which will continue to operate as long as the key is depressed. See typamatic key.

automatic request for repetition In communications, a feature that automatically initiates a request for retransmission when an error in transmission is detected.

automatic restart In computing, a facility to perform automatically the initialization functions necessary to resume operation following an equipment or power failure. See initialization.

automatic retransmission request In data communications, a technique to ensure accurate transmission of data. Data to be transmitted is held in a buffer until the communication link is ready to deal with it. The data is then despatched and a copy made at the same time. The copy is deposited in the buffer and erased when the sending device receives acknowledgment of correct receipt, as verified by CRC checking. If the receiving device detects an error in the data it informs the sending device which then retransmits the buffered copy. See CRC.

automatic reverse In recording, a facility in some recorders to reverse at the end of a tape without having to change reels.

automatic send receive In communications, a teletypewriter unit with keyboard, printer, paper tape, reader/transmitter and paper tape punch. This combination may be used for unattended on line operations. See unattended operation.

automatic stop In recording, a facility of a cassette recorder or dictation machine that enables it to automatically stop the tape when it reaches the end of its travel and which may also switch off the machine.

automatic tab memory In word processing, a facility of a system which enables it to store a format of tab settings to be automatically restored to the typewriter at the time of printing. See tabulation.

automatic threading In filming and recording, the insertion and automatic direction of a film or tape through a film projector or recorder mechanism.

automatic toning control In a document copying machine, a built in monitoring facility that regulates the supply of toner to the developing system of an electrostatic machine. See xerography.

automatic typewriter The simplest form of word processor, used for repetitive output with little or no text editing. See text editing.

automatic volume control In recording, a method of automatically maintaining a constant audio output volume over a range of variation of input signals.

automatic volume switching In computing, access to a sequential data set that extends across two or more volumes, and to concatenated data sets stored on different volumes. See sequential data set, concatenate, volume.

automatic widow adjust In word processing, a facility which prevents the first line of a paragraph, title or heading from being the last line on a page. It may also prevent the last line from being the first line on a new page. See widow.

automatic word recall In office systems, an adjustable feature of an audio transcriber unit, whereby each time a foot pedal or hand control is depressed, a measured portion of the previous dictation is replayed.

automatic word wraparound In word processing, the automatic placing of a word onto the next line if it does not fit onto the line being typed. Frequently combined with the automatic carriage return feature. Also used to denote systems which can wrap words during margin adjust procedures. See automatic carriage return.

automation The technology concerned with the design and development of processes and systems that minimize the necessity of human intervention in their operation. See feedback.

autopositive In photography, a material or process which provides a positive image of an original without the intervening negative stage.

auto stop Synonymous with automatic stop.

auxiliary equipment In computing, equipment not under the direct control of the central processing unit. See central processing unit.

auxiliary storage In computing, data storage other than the main storage, usually with slower access, e.g. magnetic tape or direct access devices. See direct access storage.

availability (1) In computing, the degree to which a system or resource is ready when needed to process data. (2) In communications, broadcast time open for purchase in the US. See available time.

available light In photography, light which is existing and not supplemented by additional photographic light.

available point In computer graphics, an addressable point at which characteristics such as colour, intensity, or on/off condition, may be specified. See picture element.

available time The time during which a system can be used. Synonymous with uptime.

avalanche photodiode In electronics, a photodiode operated with a high reverse voltage. Hole electron pairs are produced by incident infrared or light energy and these carriers are swept to the appropriate electrode. The electron carriers collide with other atoms releasing more electrons, hence increasing the sensitivity of the device. Compare pin photodiode. See photodiode, semiconductor.

AVC See automatic volume control.

average See arithmetic mean.

average access time In computing, the average time between the instant of a request for data and the delivery from a storage device.

average delay In communications, the average time that a caller must wait for access to a communication facility.

AVIP See BAVIP.

azerty keyboard A keyboard arranged as on the standard typewriters of continental Europe, with the keys a, z, e, r, t, y on the upper left-hand side. Compare qwerty keyboard.

azimuth alignment In recording, the precise alignment of recording/playback heads with the edge of tape or film. A very slight irregularity in alignment can cause a very considerable degradation in either or both recording and playback. See azimuth loss.

azimuth loss In recording, the signal loss due to misalignment between the playback head and the signal recorded on tape.

azo dye In a document copying machine, dye formed by the reaction between diazo compound and a coupler. See diazo process, coupler.

B

babble In communications, the aggregate cross talk from a number of interfering sources. See cross talk.

background In computing, the processing of low priority jobs. See job.

background colour In videotex, the colour filling the parts of the character rectangle not occupied by the colour itself. The background colour may be black or one of the seven display colours. It may be changed within a row by control characters. See character rectangle, display colour, control character.

background ink In optical character recognition, a type of ink which is not detected by the scan head because of its high reflective characteristics. It is used for print location guides, logotypes, instructions and any other desired preprinting that would otherwise interfere with the scan head reading.

background job In computing, a low priority job, usually a batched or a noninteractive job. Compare foreground. See batch processing, job.

background noise In communications, a noise signal received and demodulated with the required signal. See signal to noise ratio.

background noises In filming, small sounds which are either synchronous or nonsynchronous and often used to add realism to the sound track.

background plate In photography, an image on a glass slide used in a rear projection unit.

background printing See off line printing.

background processing (1) In computing, the execution of lower priority computer programs when higher priority programs do not require any system resource. (2) In word processing, the execution of an operator's request such as printing a document whilst the operator is performing other tasks. See priority, background.

background program In computing, the program with the lowest priority in a multi-programming environment. See background, batch processing, multiprogramming.

background projection In filming, projection from the rear of still or moving images on a translucent screen in front of which titles or action are photographed.

background region In computing, a region in main storage to which a background job is assigned. See background job, main storage.

backing In filming, a coating on the back of a film stock, e.g. an anti-abrasion coating or an antihalation coating. See halation.

backing copy In recording, the first video tape duplicate of a master, taken for protection purposes. See master.

backing sheet In a duplicator, a sheet of material attached to the back of a stencil master to strengthen and support it during the preparation of the image. The backing sheet is discarded before the duplicating begins.

backing store In computing, an intermediate storage medium, e.g. magnetic tape, magnetic disk etc., on to which data is entered from an off line terminal for later processing by the central computer. Also any auxiliary storage medium. See magnetic disk, magnetic tape, paper tape.

backlash Unwanted play in mechanical systems due to looseness.

back lobe In radiocommunications, a lobe opposite the main lobe in an antenna pattern. See antenna pattern, main lobe, side lobe.

backlog Work scheduled to be processed, but not yet completed.

back number In library science, any issue of a periodical which precedes the current issue.

back office box In point of sale equipment, a device, in the back office of a store, which is connected to a customer operated information device. The customer may press a button requesting help from a sales assistant. The back office box gives an audible warning plus information on the customer's interaction with the device so that the assistant is prepared for the nature of the enquiry.

backpack In recording, a lightweight, portable television recording or camera signal transmitting equipment. See porta pak.

backplane Synonymous with motherboard.

back porch In television, a picture signal that lies between the trailing edge of the line sync pulse and the trailing edge of the corresponding blanking pulse. Compare front porch. See blanking, line sync pulse.

backscatter In radiocommunications, a radio wave produced as a result of scattering of an incident wave but travelling in the reverse direction. See forward scatter.

backspace (1) In computing, to move the printing head on a printer back one character position, or the cursor on a VDU back by the same amount. (2) On a typewriter, escapement that occurs in a direction contrary to that of the writing direction without a character being typed on the paper. See escapement, VDU.

backspace character In computing, a control character that causes the print or display position to move one position backward along the line without producing the printing or display of any graphic character. See control character, display.

backspace control On dictation equipment, a device that causes the return of the recording medium to a predetermined position.

backspace mechanism On a typewriter, a device that performs an incremental movement between the paper carrier and the typing position contrary to the writing direction.

backup copy In computing and word processing, a copy of a file or data set that is kept for reference in case the original file or data set is destroyed. See file, data set.

backup diskette In microcomputing and word processing, a diskette that contains information copied from another diskette. It is used in case the original information is unintentionally altered or destroyed.

Backus Naur form In computer programming, a metalanguage used to specify or describe the syntax of a language in which each symbol represents a set of strings of symbols. See metalanguage, syntax.

backward channel In data transmission, a channel used for supervisory or error control signals, but with a direction of transmission opposite to that in which user information is being transferred. Compare forward channel.

backward lobe Synonymous with back lobe.

backward read In computing, a technique used in a magnetic tape drive whereby data can be read when the tape is running backwards. See tape drive.

backwards learning In data communications, a method of routing in which the switching nodes are able to deduce the network by observing the packets passing through, noting their source and the number of links through which they have travelled. See node, packet switching.

backward supervision In data communications, the use of supervisory sequences sent from the slave to a master station. See station, supervisory signal.

bad break In typesetting, pertaining to an incorrect end of line hyphenation or a page beginning with a widow or the end of a hyphenated word. It may be produced by a manual operator or computer software. See hyphenation, software, widow.

bad copy In printing, a manuscript that is indistinct, illegible, improperly edited or otherwise unsatisfactory.

badge reader In computing, a card, usually of plastic, containing a notched or magnetic stripe code for identifying an operator at a computer terminal. See magnetic stripe.

bad letter In printing, a letter that does not print or reproduce fully or clearly.

baffle In recording, a nonresonant surface mounted on a loudspeaker to prevent air pressure cancellation effects between the front and rear of the speaker.

balance (1) In printing, the appropriate placement of the various units of composition, illustration and ornamentation so that the appearance of the whole does not look disproportionate. (2) In recording, the arrangement of instruments and microphones to the best advantage.

balanced circuit In communications, a line that is terminated with a matched load. See matched load.

balanced merge In computing, a sort carried out on auxiliary storage equipment that places strings created by an internal sort phase on half of the available storage devices and then merges strings by moving them back and forth between an equal number of devices until the merging process is complete. See merge, sort, string.

balance stripe In filming, the narrow band of magnetic coating on a magnetic film applied to the edge opposite the magnetic sound track to make the film lie flat when it passes over magnetic heads. The balance stripe is sometimes used to carry additional audio or magnetic cueing information. See magnetic film, magnetic head.

ballistic technique In printers, a method used in the printing head of a matrix printer. The needle is driven forward by a clapper which stops its own motion before the pin head meets the ribbon. The pin is thus in free flight at the point of contact. Compare non-ballistic technique. See matrix printer, clapper.

balun In radiocommunications, a passive device used to match an antenna to a cable having a different impedance. See impedance matching.

band (1) In computing, a group of tracks on a magnetic drum or on one side of a magnetic disk. (2) In communications, a range of frequencies between two defined limits, e.g. the voice band in telephony is about 300 to 3,000 Hz. See Hz.

banding In recording, an uneven variation in the rotational speed on a video tape playback head which causes variations in the picture hue. See hue.

bandpass In electronics, pertaining to an amplifier or circuit having a frequency response characteristic that is uniform, within defined limits, across a given frequency range.

bandwidth (1) In communications, the difference between the limiting frequencies in a band. (2) In electronics, the range of frequencies within which a device can operate and meet a specified performance characteristic.

bandwidth compression In television, a method of reducing the bandwidth normally required for transmission by suppressing redundant information. See bandwidth, redundancy, video compressor.

banking In optical character recognition, a misalignment of the first character of a line with respect to the left margin.

bank paper In office systems, uncoated paper produced for typewriting, similar to bond but lighter, used for carbon copies. See bond paper.

bar chart A coordinate graph in which values are represented by vertical or horizontal bars, as distinct from a straight line graph. See coordinate graph.

bar code In computing, a code of parallel lines of discrete thickness printed on paper and used for fast error free data entry into a computer. There is a wide variety of codes which may be numeric, limited alphabetic,

alphanumeric and even encompass the full
ASCII set. Often 2 bar widths are used but
some codes use 4 bar widths although such
codes have less tolerance in printing and
present the scanning device with problems
of resolving multiple bar widths. The code is
read by moving a bar code pen across the
code, or the code itself is moved past a fixed
reader. Header and tailer codes are used
before and behind the data bars so that the
scanning device can synchronise to the speed
of pen movement, the coding may also allow
for correct reading even when the code is
scanned in the reverse direction. Check codes
may be employed either by appending a
block check character or using parity check
on bar combinations. The bar code is commonly used on product labels for retail outlets, on library books for check in and check
outs and can be printed in computing books
for entry of sample programs into microcomputers. See alphanumeric, ASCII, EAN,
optical bar reader, parity checking, UPC.

bar code

bar code scanner   Synonymous with optical
bar reader.

bar printer   In computing, an impact printer
in which type characters are carried on a print
bar. See impact printer.

barrel distortion   (1) In optics, a type of lens
image distortion in which the sides of square
objects are bent outwards. (2) In television, a
form of distortion in the display, produced by
the scanning system, which is identical in

effect to the optical version. See pincushion
distortion.

barrel printer   In data processing, a printer
in which the print characters are located on
the surface of a rotating barrel. At any
moment, all print positions have the same
character on the barrel and those required
are printed.

barrier box   In telephony, an isolation unit
that electrically separates a customer's equipment from a telephone line.

baryta paper   In printing, special matt
coated paper suitable for repro proofs. See
repro proof.

base   In mathematics (1) a reference value,
(2) a number used in the floating point representation of numbers, (3) the value in
which a number system is established. For
example, binary arithmetic uses a base of 2.
(4) In printing, and filming, a supporting
material for an emulsion or other sensitizing
agent, usually cellulose triacetate. (5) In
semiconductors, a region in a transistor into
which minority carriers are injected.
Compare collector, emitter. See floating
point, transistor, radix.

base address   In computing, an address
which is used as a reference value. It is
combined with a relative address to form an
absolute address. See relocatable program,
absolute address, relative address.

baseband   In communications, the frequency range of the information bearing
signals prior to combination with carrier
wave by modulation. See carrier wave, modulation.

baseband modem   Synonymous with limited
distance modem.

baseband signalling   In communications,
transmission of a signal at its original frequencies, i.e. unmodulated. See baseband,
modulation.

baseline   In typesetting, a horizontal reference line from which the location of characters and signs is derived. Normally char-

acters without descenders are positioned on the base line. See descender.

baseplate In word processing, an interface device which connects to a typewriter converting it into a low level word processor.

BASIC In computer programming, Beginners All Purpose Symbolic Instruction Code. A high level language with a simple syntax and small repertoire of commands widely used in microcomputers. Normally used in the interpretive mode, it is usually regarded as too slow and too unstructured for complex applications. See high level language, interpreter.

basic line space On a typewriter, the basic distance provided on the machine between two consecutive typing lines.

basic mode link control In data communications, control of data links by use of the control characters of the ISO/CCITT 7 bit character set for information processing interchange. See data link, CCITT.

basic service In communications, a common carrier service limited to the provision of transmission capacity for the movement of information. Basic services are regulated by the FCC. See enhanced services, computer inquiry 1980, FCC.

basic telecommunication access method In computer networks, an access method that permits communication between terminals and computers. See terminal.

basic weight In printing, the weight in pounds of a ream (500 sheets) of paper to a given standard size. The basic weight of continuous forms for computer output is based on the size for bond paper (17 x 22 inches). See bond paper.

bass In recording, a standard audio frequency range of 0 - 60 Hz.

bass boost In audio, the intensification of low frequencies in a sound by electronic means.

bastard size In printing, any matter used in

printing which is of nonstandard size. See matter.

batch In computing, (1) an accumulation of data to be processed, (2) a group of records or data processing jobs brought together for processing or transmission. See job.

batch control In data processing, a control system where fixed quantities of work are given to an employee at regular intervals.

batched communication In data communications, the transmission of a large body of data from one station to another in a network without intervening responses from the receiving unit. Compare inquiry/response.

batch processing In computing, (1) the processing of data where a number of similar input items are grouped for processing during the same machine run, (2) the technique of executing a set of computer programs such that each is completed before the next program is started. Compare on line system.

batch region In computing, one of several regions in main storage controlled by the operating system, where batch processing can be performed in a multiprogramming environment. See multiprogramming.

batch total In data processing, a sum of a set of items in a batch of records used to check the validity of operations involving the batch.

baud In communications, a measure of signalling speed in a digital communication circuit. The speed in bauds is equal to the number of discrete conditions or signal events per second. For example, one baud equals one half dot cycle per second in Morse code, and one bit per second in a train of binary signals. Since the baud is a measure of all the signalling elements transmitted, including those used to coordinate transmission as well as the actual message transmitted, it is not necessarily equivalent to the data signalling rate. See data signalling rate, morse code.

baudot code In communications, a code for the transmission of data in which five equal length bits represent one character. This code is used in some teletypewriters where one start element and one stop element are added.

BAVIP British Association of Viewdata Information Providers.

BBC British Broadcasting Corporation.

BCC See block character check.

BCD See binary coded decimal.

BCPA British Copyright Protection Association.

BCS British Computer Society.

BDN See Bell Data Network.

beam (1) In electronics, the unidirectional, pinhead electron stream generated by the cathode gun in a CRT. (2) In radiocommunications, the radiation in a lobe of a directional antenna. See CRT, directional antenna.

beam deflection In electronics, the process of changing the orientation of the electron beam in a CRT. See CRT.

beam diversity In satellite communications, a method of transmitting a band of frequencies twice, e.g. when a satellite is orbiting over the Atlantic Ocean one frequency can be used for different transmissions to both the United States and Europe simultaneously. See frequency reuse.

BEAMOS In microelectronics, BEAM addressed MOS, a memory device in which bits are written by directing a beam of electronics to the surface of a MOS semiconductor chip. The reading action involves the detection of voltage changes on the chip when the electron beam is directed to the appropriate point on the surface, which contains a surplus or deficit of electrons. Packing densities of up to 30 megabits per square inch with access times of 30 nanoseconds have been obtained. See bit, electron beam accessed memory, MOS, nano.

beam splitter In optics, any prism or partial mirror which reflects part of a light beam and lets the rest pass through, used to separate colours or to produce two images in two different places.

beam width In radiocommunications, the angular width of a beam within which the radiation exceeds some specified fraction of the maximum value. See beam.

beard In typesetting, the space extending from the baseline of the typeface to a lower limit of body as it appears on the page. See baseline, bevel.

bearer In data communications, a high bandwidth channel.

beating the shift In a typewriter, an action whereby a very fast or erratic typist may cause a malprinting of a character following or preceding a shift.

beginning of tape mark In recording, an indicator on a magnetic tape used to indicate the beginning of the permissible recording area, e.g. a photo reflective string, a transparent section of tape etc. See magnetic tape.

beginning of volume label See label.

bel In electronics and communications, the basic unit of a logarithmic scale (to base 10) used for expressing ratios of powers. Two powers, A and B are related by N bels when $\log (A/B) = N$. See decibel.

BEL See bell character.

bell character In computing, a control character which causes an audible tone, often a ringing bell such as in a teletype terminal. See teletype.

Bell Data Network In data communications, an AT&T system intended to provide subscribers with an extensive range of communication and database access facilities.

benchmark test In computing, a procedure designed to evaluate the performance of a computer system under typical conditions of use. A program or group of programs can run in several computers for purposes of comparing speed, etc.

bessel functions In radiocommunications, a mathematical series which gives the relative amplitudes of the spectral components of a frequency modulated carrier wave. See frequency modulation.

Beta In recording, a video cassette format for half inch tapes developed by Sony. Compare U-matic, VHS.

between-lines entry In data security, the use of active wire tapping by an unauthorized user to gain access to a computer system when the legitimate user's terminal is momentarily inactive. See wire tapping, piggyback entry.

bevel In typography, the sloping surface of a typeface extending from the top of the face to the shoulder. See shoulder.

bias (1) In electronics, a reference electrical level. (2) In recording, a high frequency AC carrier current (50 - 100 KHz) combined with an audio signal in a magnetic recording circuit to minimize nonlinear distortion. (3) In statistics, a systematic deviation of a value from a reference value. (4) In communications, the uniform shifting of the beginning of all marking pulses on a teletypewriter from their proper positions in relation to the beginning of the start pulse. (5) In telegraphy, a type of distortion in which the significant intervals of the modulation do not all have their exact theoretical duration.

biased data In data processing, a distribution of records which is nonrandom with respect to the sequencing or sorting criteria.

bibliographic coupling In library science, a method of detecting documents dealing with the same subject by examining the articles cited in the bibliographies of the documents. If two documents contain many common references to other articles, then both documents are likely to deal with the same subject. See citation indexing.

bibliography (1) An annotated catalogue of documents. (2) A list of documents relating to a specific subject or author. (3) An enumerative list of books. (4) The process of compiling catalogues or lists.

bicycling In cable television, pertaining to showing of a program on several cable networks.

bid In data communications, an attempt by a computer or station to gain control of a circuit so that it can transmit data.

bidirectional bus In microcomputers, a bus structure in which a single conductor is used to transmit data or signals in either direction, usually used for data transmission between a peripheral unit and a CPU or memory. See bus, CPU, memory, peripheral.

bidirectional microphone In recording, a microphone that picks up sound primarily in two directions along a single axis. Compare unidirectional microphone. See microphone.

bidirectional printing In data processing, a method of printing in which a line is printed from left to right and the next from right to left, saving time by avoiding unnecessary carriage movement.

bifurcation A condition where two, and only two, outcomes are possible, e.g. on or off, 0 or 1.

Big Blue In computing, a nickname for IBM. See IBM.

Bildschirmtext The Federal Republic of Germany public interactive videotex system.

binary In mathematics and computing, a numbering system in which there are only two states, or conditions. The binary system is represented by the numbers 0 and 1. It is used in computing, because bistable storage devices are reliable and cheap. See bistable.

binary arithmetic In mathematics and computing, arithmetic performed with binary numbers. The arithmetic rules are extremely simple (e.g. $1 + 0 = 1$, $1 + 1 = 10$) and they can be implemented with simple logic circuits. See full adder, half adder, logic circuit.

binary code A coding system employing the binary digits 0 and 1 to represent a letter, digit or other character in a computer, e.g. the decimal number 6 is represented by binary 110, (i.e. 1X4 + 1X2 + 0X1). See binary.

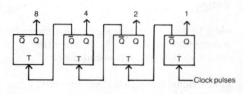

binary counter

binary coded decimal   In computing, a 4 bit binary representation of the ten decimal digits 0 to 9.

binary counter   In electronics, a digital circuit, usually a series of cascaded flip flops, each storing one bit of a binary number. See flip flop.

binary digit   In binary notation, either of the characters 0 or 1, often abbreviated to 'bit'. See bit.

binary number   In computing, a number expressed in binary notation. See binary code.

binary search   In computing, a method of searching an ordered file or table. The value of the key at the midpoint of the file, or table, is compared with the search key. If the search key value is less than that of the midpoint value, then the half of the file with low key numbers is selected and vice versa. The procedure is repeated with the appropriate half of the search area until the required item is found. See key.

binary synchronous communications   In data communications, pertaining to data communications in which synchronization is established between the sending and receiving station before the message is sent. The synchronization is checked and adjusted during transmission. The continuous stream of transmitted bit patterns are separated by the receiving hardware using the synchronization information. Commonly used for medium and high speed communication. Compare asynchronous transmission. See handshaking.

binary to decimal conversion   In mathematics, the conversion of a binary number to the equivalent decimal number. For example, the binary to decimal conversion of the binary number 111 is the decimal number 7. See binary.

binaural   In recording, the use of two separate sound channels on headphones so that the left hand sound channel is heard only in the left ear, and the right hand channel is confined to the right ear. The spatial dimension in binaural sound is not confined to the location of the sound source. See monaural.

binding time   In computer programming, the stage at which the compiler replaces a symbolic name or address with its machine language form. See compiler.

Biocodes   A database, supplied by the BioSciences Information Services of Biological Abstracts and dealing with biology and life sciences. See on line information retrieval.

bionics   In technology, pertaining to the branch that relates the functions, characteristics and phenomena of living systems to the development and exploitation of machine systems.

biosensor   A mechanism for detecting and transmitting biological data from an organism so that the results may be displayed or stored.

BIOSIS Previews   A database supplied by BioSciences Information Service (BIOSIS) and dealing with life sciences. See on line information retrieval.

bipolar coding   In communications, a method of transmitting a binary stream in which a binary zero is sent as no pulse and a binary one is sent as a pulse which alternates in sign for each one that is sent. See binary.

bipolar transistor   See transistor.

birdies   In recording, extraneous whistles and chirps generated when two high frequency tones intermodulate. It can occur in a tape recorder if the bias intermodulates with a high frequency tone or its harmonics. See bias, intermodulation distortion.

bistable Pertaining to a system or device that can only occupy one of two states. See flip flop.

BISYNC See binary synchronous communications.

bit See binary digit.

bit density See packing density.

bit interleaving In data communications, a method of time division multiplexing in which the channel receives one bit in turn from each active terminal and delivers one bit in turn to each receiving terminal. Compare character interleaving. See time division multiplexing.

bit map (1) In computing, a map where each item is represented by a single bit of information. For example, a file directory may contain a bit map, the presence of a 1 bit denoting that the block is being used, an 0 that it is unused. (2) In computer graphics, the information displayed on a screen, corresponding to the contents of the memory mapped part of main storage. See memory mapping.

bit packing See packing.

bit pattern In computer programming, the pattern of bits in a string, often a computer word. See string, word.

bit rate In data communications, the speed at which bits are transmitted over a communications link, usually expressed in bits per second. See baud.

bit sequence independence In communications, the property of a network which enables the transfer of digital data, as a sequence of binary digits, without placing any restriction upon the sequence of binary digits. See binary digit, transparent data communication code.

bit slice In computing, an arithmetic logic unit realized as an LSI circuit which handles 2 or 4 bits at a time. See bit slice microprocessor.

bit slice microprocessor In computing, a

microprocessor with an LSI arithmetic logic unit, made from bit slices, and associated control unit. See bit slice, LSI, arithmetic logic unit.

bits per inch In recording, the number of bits recorded per inch of track on a magnetizable recording surface.

bits per second See bit rate.

bit stream In computing and communications, a binary signal without regard to grouping by character. See bit.

bit string In computing and communications, a string of binary digits in which each bit position is considered as an independent unit. See bit, string.

bit stuffing In data communications, a technique in which frames are delimited by the bit pattern 01111110. When 5 consecutive 1 bits appear in the message or control data an 0 bit is added to avoid confusion with the delimiter. Compare character stuffing. See synchronous data link control.

black and white In photography, the rending of colour images into monochromatic values which are visually equivalent to, and acceptable as, substitutes for the colours of the images producing them.

black body See colour temperature.

black box In electronics, a device or system which has accessible inputs and outputs but where the internal functions are unknown. All knowledge obtainable from a black box is derived solely from the output and input signals.

black crush In television, an electronic effect which converts a live action image into a total black/white contrast without half tones. See halftone.

black level In television, a signal corresponding to zero luminance on the screen. Compare white level. See luminance.

black signal In facsimile, the signal produced by scanning the darkest areas of a source document.

Blaise-Line   In databases, an information retrieval service operated by the British Library and covering books published in the UK and USA, education and audio-visual materials. See on line information retrieval.

Blaise-Link   In databases, an information retrieval service operated by the British Library and covering medicine. See on line information retrieval.

blank   (1) In computing, a part of a data storage medium in which there are no characters. (2) In computer graphics, to suppress the display of all or part of a display image.

blank character   In computer graphics, the visual representation of the space character.

blanket cylinder   In printing, a cylinder in an offset lithographic machine which takes the ink image from the plate cylinder and transfers it to paper or other printing material via a rubber sheet. See offset printing, plate cylinder.

blanketing   In radiocommunications, the action of a powerful radio signal, or interference signal, in rendering a receiving set unable to detect the desired signals. See jamming.

blanking   In television, the suppression of the picture signal information during the return trace of the scanning line on the picture or camera tube. See scanning line.

blanking interval   In television, the time interval occupied by the blanking pulse.

blanking level   In television, the level of a composite picture signal which separates the signals containing picture information from those containing synchronizing information. It usually corresponds to the black level. See black level.

blanking pulse   In television, a pulse used in a television signal to effect blanking. See blanking.

blast through alphanumerics   In videotex, the set of letters and digits which may be displayed on a videotex terminal whilst it is being used in the graphics mode. See graphics mode.

bleed   In printing, to run a line or halftone image off the edge of a trimmed page or sheet. See halftone.

blind dialing   In data communications, a facility of some modems which allows the modem to dial when a dial tone is supposed to be present but none is detected. This facility is important in some PBX systems which use non standard lines that certain modems will interpret as a dead line. See MODEM, PBX.

blind keyboard   In typesetting, a keyboard which outputs data to paper tape, magnetic tape or magnetic disk for photocomposition but provides neither a visual display nor hard copy. See hard copy, magnetic disk, magnetic tape, photocomposition.

blinking   In computer graphics, a flashing effect caused by an intentional change in the intensity of a character or group of characters on a VDU. See VDU.

BLLD   British Library Lending Division.

block   In computing (1) a group of words, documents or files treated as a unit, (2) a collection of contiguous records stored as a unit. (3) In data communications, a group of bits transmitted as a unit and encoded for error control purposes. (4) In word processing, the ability to define information so as to move it from one position to another within a text element or into another text element. See contiguous, text move.

block cancel character   In computing, a specific operational character designed to cause the portion of a block preceding it to be cancelled. See block.

block character check   In data communications, an error control procedure used to detect errors on a block of data transmitted over a network. See block.

block diagram   A diagram of a system in which the principal parts are represented by suitably annotated geometrical figures to show both the function of components and their interrelations. See flowchart.

block error rate In communications, the ratio of the number of blocks incorrectly received to the total number of blocks sent. See block.

block gap See interblock gap.

blocking See denial.

blocking factor In data processing, the number of logical records in each block. See logical record, block.

block length In computing, the number of bytes or words which form a block. See block.

block move Synonymous with text move.

block multiplexer channel In communications, a multiplexer channel that interleaves blocks of data. See multiplexer, channel.

block parity In data communications, a method of parity checking in which an error in a block of data can be detected and corrected without the block being retransmitted. See parity checking.

block structure In computer programming, a technique by which a program is segmented into blocks of information or subroutines. See subroutine.

block sum check See longitudinal redundancy check.

bloom In television, excessive luminosity of the spot due to excessive beam current. See beam, spot.

bloop In recording, the removal of unwanted sound from a magnetic sound track by erasing it by hand with a small magnet.

blooping tape In recording, a tape used to cover unwanted portions of sound tracks. See bloop.

BNF See Backus Naur form.

board In television, the control panel in a studio control room for the switching and mixing of video or audio program elements. See mixing.

BOB See back office box.

body In word processing, the main text of a letter or other document.

body size In typesetting, measurement from the top to bottom of a piece of type measured in points. See point.

boilerplate In word processing, sections of standard text held as a library in memory for retrieval and use in documents. Synonymous with standard paragraphs.

bold face In printing, a heavier version of a particular typeface.

bomb In computing, a term used to denote a spectacular failure in a program which results in the disruption of the entire computer system.

bond paper In printing, a grade of paper made for hand writing and used in typewriters. It can also be used for printing.

boolean algebra In mathematics, an algebra for expressing logical relationships between truth values. It is associated with such logical operations as AND, OR , NOT etc. See AND, NOT, OR, truth table.

boom In antennas, a metal backbone to which the array elements are attached.

boomy In recording, a description of a sound which, when reproduced, lacks definition or contains an accentuation of low frequencies.

bootleg In recording, pertaining to illegally produced material. Compare copyright.

bootstrap In computing and electronics, a technique or device designed to bring itself into a desired state by means of its own action, e.g. a machine routine where the first few instructions are sufficient to initiate loading action into the computer from a peripheral device. See routine.

borrow An arithmetically negative carry. It occurs in direct subtraction by raising the low order digit of the minuend by one unit of the next higher order digit. See minuend.

bottom up method   In computer programming, a technique in which the lowest levels
of instructions are combined to form a higher
level operation which in turn may be used in
the formulation of even higher level routines.
In this manner the programmer effectively
forms a new instruction set which contains
useful forms for a particular application area.
Compare top down method. See instruction.

bounce   (1) In photography, diffused light
having no direction. (2) In television, a short
duration variation in the luminance following
a step change in the video signal. (3) A fault
on a keyboard in which a single key depression causes two or more characters to be
transmitted. See luminance, debounce.

boxed mode   In teletext, a facility whereby
an item of information from the teletext
database is superimposed on the broadcast
picture displayed on the television set. It is
usually displayed as white characters on a
rectangular black background, giving a
boxed effect, often used for news flashes or
subtitles.

box in   In printing, to enclose or encompass
typed matter with a border of rules. See rule.

BPCC   British Printing and Publishing
Communication Corporation.

BPI   See bits per inch.

BPMM   In recording, bits per millimeter.
Compare bits per inch.

BPS   See bits per second.

bracketed   In printing, a typeface having
serifs which are joined to the stem of the type
character by a continuous curve or bracket.
See serif.

bracketing   In photography, the practise of
taking several camera shots with exposures
around a mean value indicated by the light
meter.

braille marks   In audiovisual aids, special
raised markings on equipment function controls which permit identification and operation by touch.

branch   In computer programming, a jump
instruction. See jump.

breadboard   In electronics, a portable
board on which experimental circuits can be
laid out.

break   (1) In communications, to interrupt
the transmitting end and seize control of the
circuit at the receiving end. (2) In printing, a
separation of continuous paper forms,
usually at the perforation.

break line   In printing, a short line, particularly when at the end of a paragraph.

breakpoint   In computer programming, (1)
an instruction whose execution may be interrupted by an external intervention or by a
monitor program, (2) a point in a program
where control returns from the program to
the user. The current state of the program can
be examined for debugging purposes. See
debug, monitor.

breakup   In television, a momentary distortion in a picture.

breezeway   In television, a synchronizing
waveform used in colour transmission and
representing the time interval between the
trailing edge of the horizontal synchronizing
pulse and the start of the colour burst. See
waveform, horizontal sync pulse, colour
burst.

bridge   In communications, equipment and
techniques used to match circuits to each
other ensuring minimum transmission
impairment.

bridging   In optical character recognition, a
combination of peaks and smudges that may
close or partially close a loop of a character
thus making it unreadable.

brightness   In optics, the visual and psychological sensation due to the perception of a
luminous source. Compare luminance.

brightness range   In photography, the variations in intensity of light reflected from
various objects or persons in the action field
of a camera as measured by a light meter. See
action field.

brilliance In photography, pertaining to the perceived brightness or darkness of a subject.

Bristol board In printing, fine pasteboard with a smooth surface, ideal for drawing up artwork. See artwork.

British Education Index A database supplied by The British Library and dealing with education & educational institutions. See on line information retrieval.

British Standards Institution The UK national body having a similar standards role to the American National Standards Institute.

British Telecom The telecommunications part of the United Kingdom PTT. See PTT.

broadband In communications, pertaining to transmission facilities whose bandwidth is greater than that available on voice grade circuits, and therefore capable of higher speed data transmission. Synonymous with wideband.

broadband exchange service In communications, a public switched system of Western Union in the United States and CNCP Telecommunications in Canada.

broadcast (1) In communications, the simultaneous transmission of data to a number of stations. (2) In radiocommunications, the transmission, by means of radiowaves, of programs of sound and vision for general reception. Compare narrowcasting.

broadcast homes In communications, a household owning one or more radio or television broadcast receivers.

broadcasting station In radiocommunications, a center consisting of one or more transmitters and associated antennas.

broadcast satellite technique In satellite communications, a method of maximizing channel bandwidth on a geostationary satellite. See geostationary satellite.

broadcast videotex See videotex. Synonymous with teletext.

broadsheet In printing, a sheet of paper in its basic, uncut size. Also one which is printed on one side only.

bromide print (1) In photography, a normal photographic print made from a negative. (2) In printing, a preproduction plate in photolithography for proofing. See photolithography.

browsing In data security, the unauthorized searching of data held on a computer for information (e.g. confidential data or proprietary software). It is similar to passive wire tapping on communication channels, but is potentially more serious since data stored in a computer has a longer lifetime. Access controls are designed to prevent browsing. See access control, wire tapping.

BRS In databases, an information retrieval service operated by Bibliographic Retrieval Services Inc. (USA). See on line information retrieval.

brute force technique Any technique that depends mainly on computer power and time to arrive at a nonelegant solution to a problem.

BSC See binary synchronous communications.

BSI See British Standards Institution.

BT See British Telecom.

BTX See Bildschirmtext.

bubble memory In microelectronics, a nonvolatile solid state storage device utilizing microscopic magnetic domains in an aluminium garnet substrate. The domains, or bubbles, are circulated within the substrate and directed to the output by magnetic fields. This technology has the advantage over RAM that it is nonvolatile and the advantage over magnetic disk in that it has no mechanical moving parts. However it is expensive compared with floppy disk and there are no facilities to remove one set of data to a physical store, e.g. a cupboard, and replace it with another. See magnetic disk, nonvolatile memory, RAM.

bubble sort In data processing, a computer sort achieved by exchanging, if necessary, pairs of keys, beginning with the first pair and exchanging successive appropriate pairs until the file is ordered. See sort, key.

bucket In computing, an area of storage which is referred to as a whole by some addressing system.

buckling In audiovisual aids, the bending of film in a projector caused by a combination of tight winding and dryness.

buffer (1) In computing, an area of storage that is temporarily reserved for use in performing an input output operation, into which data is read or from which data is written. (2) In data communications, a storage area used to compensate for differences in the rate of flow of data, or time of occurrence of events, when transferring data from one device to another. (3) In electronics, a device to allow one circuit to drive another when a direct interconnection would produce an excessive load on the driving circuit. See input output, load.

buffered device In computing, a device that has I/O elements queued to a direct access device before being written. See direct access, I/O.

buffered input In computing, the ability to enter new data or control instructions into the machine before current operations are completed. See buffer.

buffered network In data communications, a system which employs buffers associated with each terminal to maximize the efficiency of the operation. See buffer.

buffer size In word processing, the number of characters of text and command codes a system can manipulate at one time.

bug In computing, an error in a program or system. The term is reputed to have originated in the days of an electromechanical computer using relays. An inexplicable error was traced to the wing of an insect lodged between the contacts of a relay. See debug, relay.

bulk eraser In recording, a device which magnetically aligns all of the iron oxide molecules on a magnetic tape or film, thus eliminating any sound recording.

bulk storage Synonymous with mass storage.

bulk update terminal In videotex, a terminal used by an IP for off line preparation, storage and fast transmission of pages to a videotex computer. See IP, off line, page.

bulletin boards In computing, a term to denote information in a computer based message system that is available to all authorized users. See computer based message system.

bullets In typesetting, (1) solid patches exposed onto phototypesetting film, or paper, to enable densitometer evaluation of the image density, (2) large dots used to draw attention to, or to set paragraphs apart from the rest of the text. See densitometer, phototypesetting.

Bundespost The West German PTT. See PTT.

bundle In optical fibers, a number of fibers grouped together in a single enclosure.

Bureau of Standards US Government agency which is concerned with standards for measurement and performance.

burn in (1) In photography, a prolonged exposure of image or part of an image to light. (2) In television, the after-image in a video tube when the camera has remained focused for too long on a bright or contrasting light source.

burning In computing, the process of programming a read only memory. See PROM programmer.

burn resistance In electronics, the ability of the CRT phosphor dots to withstand local overheating due to the conversion into heat of the residual energy of the electron beam, i.e. that part of the electron beam energy that is not converted into visible light. See phosphor dots.

burnt out   In electronics, a device in which the essential working parts are inoperable due to abnormal use or excessive heat.

burst   (1) In data communictions, a sequence of signals counted as a single entity in accordance with some defined criteria. (2) In printing, to separate continuous form paper into discrete sheets using a burster. See burster.

burster   In printing and office systems, a form handling device for detaching continuous forms at the cross perforation, usually using two sets of pressure rollers rotating at different speeds.

burst mode   In data communications, a mode in which data is transmitted at a specific data signalling rate during controlled, intermittent intervals.

bus   In data communications (1) a network topology in which workstations are connected by T junctions to one main cable. (2) In computing, an electrical connection between the components of a computer system along which the data is transmitted. Compare ring, star. See address bus, control bus, data bus, local area network, microcomputer, S100 bus, T junction.

business data processing   Data processing for business purposes, for example, maintaining the financial transactions of a business.

bussback   In communications, the connection, by a common carrier or PTT, of the output portion of a circuit back to the input portion of a circuit. See loopback test.

bustrophedon printing   Synonymous with bidirectional printing.

busy   (1) In filming, pertaining to a background or setting which is distractingly over elaborate or detailed. (2) In telephony, a line or plant which is unavailable for more traffic. See busy hour.

busy hour   In telephony, the 60 minute period of business day in which the traffic volume is at its maximum. See traffic.

butted slugs   In printing, a term used to describe type matter too wide to set in one line.

buzz   In television, an undesirable audible noise resulting from the interaction between sound and vision signals in a receiver.

B-Y   In television, the blue primary colour difference signal.

bypass   In electronics, a parallel path, or shunt, around one or more elements of a circuit.

byte   (1) In computing, a binary character operated upon as a unit and usually shorter than a computer word. A byte is the smallest addressable unit of storage and is usually eight bits long. (2) The representation of a character. See bit, word.

byte mode   Synonymous with multiplex mode.

byte multiplexer channel   In communications, a multiplexer channel that interleaves bytes of data from different sources. See multiplexer.

byte serial transmission   In communications, the transmission of data in which successive bytes follow one another in sequence. The individual bits of each byte may be transmitted serially or simultaneously. See serial transmission.

C

C In computer programming, high level language for use on microcomputers. See high level language.

cable In electronics, a flexible electric wire sheathed in insulation.

cable television A subject of considerable interest in the UK following the publication of the Hunt Report in October 1982. Cable television was originally developed as a relay, or classic cable, service to provide high quality reception to homes which found it difficult to obtain a good picture from domestic antennae. This system involved the siting of a main antenna at a strategic, normally elevated, site and transmission of the received signal into homes via cable. Since about 1970 growth has been confined to MATV systems which distribute locally receivable UHF TV and VHF radio signals on coaxial cables, usually at the received frequency, in blocks of apartments or small housing schemes. The two types of cable TV networks in common use, in the UK, are coaxial cable and multipair systems. The coaxial cable systems usually operate in the VHF spectrum using frequency division multiplexing to carry a number of channels. The multipair, or HF, system carries signals which were originally in the UHF, or VHF, band and were then translated down to HF for transmission; a separate cable pair is allocated to each television signal using a space division multiplex system. UK systems currently have limited channel capacity with HF systems offering some 4-6 TV channels whilst coaxial cable systems might be capable of carrying up to nine or ten channels.

The UHF terrestrial broadcast transmitter network has been improved in recent years to the point where most parts of the UK can enjoy a perfectly satisfactory reception from domestic antennae. Thus the Government regulations which forbade alternative and additional programs caused a stagnation in the UK cable TV business. In 1980 the situation began to change when the Home Secretary licensed a small number of pilot subscription services over existing cable systems. This was followed by a Home Office report in 1981 on DBS and the general acceptance of the complementary nature of cable networks and DBS. The ITAP report of Wideband Cable Systems, December 1981, produced the view that broadband cable systems, capable of supporting new information technology based services, could be financed by the private sector. It was postulated that an initial entertainment led business would both provide an early return on investment and provide the infrastructure for new interactive domestic services. This report led to the formation of the Hunt Committee and the subsequent Hunt Report, published in October 1982, proposed a liberal regulatory framework aimed at the encouragement of private sector investment in, and the establishment of, new wideband cable systems. The Government White Paper in April 1983 declared the following broad strategy.

(i) Cable investment should be privately financed and marketed.

(ii) Regulations should be as light as possible so that investors are free to develop a wide range of services and facilities.

(iii) The regulatory framework should be flexible so that it can adapt as technology constantly changes to what is practicable and economic.

(iv) A small number of key safeguards are needed both to ensure that existing broadcasting and telecommunication services are not impoverished and to take account of the fact that cable services will be directly available at home.

There has been considerable debate both on the topology of proposed cable networks, i.e. tree and branch or switched star, and the transmission medium choice between coaxial cable and fiber optics. Such debate arises from the possibility of providing consumers with many more TV channels than those of existing networks. Many consumer receivers, however, can only be tuned to a limited number of frequencies and will therefore require a frequency changer, or set-top convertor, to interface the TV set to the cable system. Such a convertor can also contain decoding circuits which allow the viewer to receive premium services. Such services are subject to subscription charges and the signals are encoded to prevent unauthorized, i.e. unpaid, viewing. The decoder itself may be addressable so that it can be programmed from a central point to receive different tier of programs and information. The set-top convertor may also be enhanced to enable user originated information to transmit information upstream and thus provide the interactive information services envisaged in the ITAP report.

The tree and branch topology, as the name suggests, takes the form of a main trunk cable with periodic branches serving a cluster of subscribers; each individual subscriber is served by a further branch from this cable. Such a system provides a fixed amount of downstream bandwidth available throughout the system, all channels are simultaneously piped to a subscriber even though at any one time only one is used. A return, i.e. upstream path can be provided for two way communications but suitable protocols must be employed to avoid the collision of such signals converging at the head end. In the alternative configuration, switched star, downstream video and data information is carried over trunk and subtrunk cables to local switching centers and thence are selected so that only the required signal is transmitted from the switching center to the subscriber. Each subscriber is equipped with a keypad so that signals can be sent to the switching center indicating the channel or service required. Alternatively subscriber's data can be routed upstream, from the switching center to the head end, usually via a data concentrator which serves a number of switching centers. The switching center can also receive signals from the head end to predetermine the range of services made available to each subscriber. Thus this type of system is inherently interactive and two way communication forms an integral part of the design. The switched star system requires no set top encoding for premium services, since a subscriber can be allowed, or denied, access to particular services by programming the switching center appropriately.

The transmission media may be coaxial cable or fiber optics. Whilst fiber optic cables are well suited to digital signals there are technical problems in putting several analog TV channel signals on a fiber system at a price low enough for the mass market. Fiber optic transmission is ideal for point-to-point connections but does not lend itself readily to successive tapping or subdividing since there is an unacceptable loss of energy at each tap. Thus fiber optics are fully compatible with the switched star system with its series of connections from set to switching centers etc., and it is unlikely that fiber optics will be applicable in the final distribution network of tree and branch systems which require successive taps onto the final distribution lines. See coaxial cable, DBS, fiber optics, head end, frequency division multiplexing, HF, Hi-Ovis, Hunt Report, ITAP Report, MATV, Qube, set-top converter, space division multiplexing, switched star, tree and branch, UHF, VHF.

cable television relay pickup station In cable television, a mobile broadcast station used to pick up programs from a location other than the studio, and to transmit them to the head end by microwave transmission. See head end, microwave transmission.

cable television relay station In cable television, formerly community antenna relay service, a fixed or mobile station that picks up signals and transmits them by a microwave link to a terminal point from which they are distributed to users by cable. See microwave transmission.

cable text In cable television, a teletext system transmitted over a cable network. Unlike conventional broadcast teletext the system can employ the whole frame for codes instead of just a few lines not carrying video information. This enables a much larger database to be transmitted with acceptable user waiting times. See frame, teletext.

cache memory In computing, a very high speed buffer memory into which instructions from main storage are loaded and executed at a faster rate than if executed directly from main storage. See main storage.

CAD See computer aided design.

cadmium sulphide meter In photography, a light meter which uses cadmium sulphide as its light sensitive component.

CAF See content addressable filestore.

CAI See computer assisted instruction.

caliper In printing, thickness of a sheet of paper.

call (1) In computer programming, the action of bringing a program, routine or subroutine into effect, usually by specifying the entry conditions and jumping to an entry point. (2) In data communications, a transmission for the purpose of identifying the transmitting station for which the transmission is intended. (3) In telephony, an attempt to reach a user, whether or not successful. See entry point, station.

call accepted signal In data communications, a call control signal that is transmitted by the called DTE to indicate that it accepts the incoming call. See call control signal, DTE.

call control character In data communications, a character which is used for call control. It may be used in association with defined signal conditions on other interchange circuits.

call control procedure In data communications, the implementation of a set of protocols required to establish and release a call.

call control signal In data communications, one of the set of signals necessary to establish, maintain and release a call.

call duration In telephony, the time interval between the moment when a connection is established between the calling and called stations, and the moment that the connection is broken by the operator or the calling station giving the clearing signal. See station.

called party In communications, the location to which a connection is established on a switched line.

call forwarding In telephony, a diverter

feature of certain central offices and PABXs, using a call device which causes an incoming telephone call to one station to be transferred automatically to another station. See central office, station.

callier effect In optics, the scattering of light as it passes through successive lenses.

calligraphy The art of beautiful handwriting.

calling In data communications, the process of transmitting selection signals to establish a connection between data stations. See data station.

call letters In radiocommunications, broadcast station identification, usually assigned by a licensing authority. In the U.S. the rule is generally 'W' - prefix, east of the Mississippi River; 'K' - prefix, west. See allocation.

call not accepted signal In data communications, a call control signal sent by the called DTE to indicate that the incoming call has not been accepted. See call control signal, DTE.

call progress signal In data communications, a call control signal transmitted from the DCE to the calling DTE to indicate the status of the call being established, the reason why connection could not be made, or any other network condition. See call control signal, DCE, DTE.

call redirection In data communications, a facility that allows calls to be automatically passed on to a nominated address when the recipient's user terminal is not operational.

call request In data communications, a call control signal sent by a DTE to the DCE (or network) that it wishes to make a call. See call control signal.

call restriction In telephony, a facility on a PABX system that prevents users from making toll calls without operator intervention. See PABX, toll call.

call transfer In telephony, a facility that enables a called subscriber to transfer incoming calls to another user.

CAM See computer aided manufacture, content addressable memory.

CAMA See centralized automatic message accounting.

CAMAC Computer Automated Measurement and Control Association.

Cambridge Ring In data communications, a local area network standard using a coaxial cable or twisted pair ring topology and a transmission rate of 10 megabits. It uses a message slot protocol. Compare Ethernet. See coaxial cable, local area network, message slot, megabit, ring, twisted pair.

cameo (1) In printing, typefaces in which characters are reversed white out of solid or shaded ground. (2) In filming, the lighting of foreground objects, with a solid, dark tone background. See background.

camera In photography, a device consisting basically of a lens attached to a light tight box holding film for exposure.

camera chain A television camera and its associated equipment, including power supply, cables and video controls.

camera light In television, a small spotlight mounted on a television camera and used for additional fill light on a performer, object or graphic card.

camera ready copy In printing, matter prepared for reproduction that is ready to go before a process camera. See process camera.

camp on In telephony, a method of holding a call for a line that is in use and of signaling when it becomes free.

CAN See cancel character.

cancel character In computing, an accuracy control character used to indicate that the data with which it is associated is in error and is to be ignored.

Cancerlit A database supplied by US National Institutes of Health, National Cancer Institute, International Cancer Research Data Bank Program and dealing with biomedicine. See on line information retrieval.

candela In optics, the intensity of light given off by one sixtieth of a square centimeter of platinum at a temperature of 2045 degrees Kelvin. See intensity.

candidate key In relational databases, a key that has the properties of a primary key. See primary key.

canonical schema In databases, a model of a data system which represents the inherent structure of that system. It is independent of the software and hardware mechanisms used to store and manipulate the data. See schema.

capacitance In electronics, the property of a system of conductors and dielectrics that permits the storage of electrically separated charges when a potential difference exists between the conductors. Compare resistance, inductance. See capacitor.

capacitance disk In video disk, a video disk system that uses capacitance signals embedded on the disk and a stylus that touches the surface of the disk to read encoded information. Compare optical disk.

capacitor In electronics, a device which is designed to introduce capacitance into an electric circuit. See capacitance.

capacitor microphone In recording, a microphone which uses a two plate capacitor with one plate, the diaphragm, flexing under sound pressure. See microphone.

capacity activated transducer In electronics, a device operated by a change in capacitance, e.g. a switch operated when a finger is placed close to it. See capacitance, transducer.

capstan In recording, a rotating device in a tape recorder used to drive the recording medium at a constant speed. See pinch roller.

CAPTAIN In videotex, Character And Pattern Telephone Access Information Network, the Japanese videotex system.

caption (1) In printing, the explanatory comment accompanying an illustration or diagram separated from the text. (2) In filming, a line of explanatory comment inserted into, or superimposed over, the action of a shot. See matte.

carbonless paper In typing, paper especially treated to achieve write through without the use of carbon interleaves or carbon coating.

carbon microphone In recording, a microphone where the transducer is a container filled with carbon granules, the resistance of which varies as sound waves impinge on a diaphragm connected to the granules. See transducer.

carbon ribbon In typing, a Mylar ribbon backed with a carbon film producing a cleaner print impression than that usually achieved with fabric ribbon. See Mylar.

carbon ribbon supply indicator In typing, a device that indicates the amount of carbon ribbon still available for use.

carbon sets In office systems, forms and paper manufactured with attached carbon paper.

carbon tissue In printing, light sensitive gelatine coated pigment used for the preparation of the cylinder or plate in the photogravure process. See photogravure.

card (1) In computing, a machine processable information storage medium of special quality paper stock, generally 7 x 3 inches. (2) In computing and electronics, a unit bearing circuit components which can be plugged into a piece of equipment. See card cage, expansion card, punched card, module.

card cage In computing, a structure containing standard sockets for plug in printed circuit boards and a motherboard for the interconnection of units used for microcomputers. It provides a basic system that can be configured with I/O boards etc. to meet users'

requirements. See printed circuit, motherboard, I/O.

card code In computing, the combinations of punched holes that represent characters (for example, letters, digits) in a punched card. See punched card.

card column In computing, a simple line of punch positions parallel to the short edge of a punched card. A column normally corresponds to an alphanumeric character. See punched card, alphanumeric.

card holder In typing, a device for holding a card in close contact with the platen on a typewriter so that it follows the curvature of the platen. See platen.

card image In computing, a set of contiguous locations in main or auxiliary storage which contain an exact representation of the data on a punched card. See auxiliary storage, main storage, memory mapping.

cardioid response In radiocommunications and recording, a heart shaped curve depicting the performance in a specified plane of a device such as microphone or antenna. See antenna pattern, microphone.

card punch In computing, a device that punches holes in a card to represent data. See punched card.

card reader In computing, an input device that senses hole patterns in a punched card and produces corresponding signals.

card row In computing, a line of punch positions parallel to the longer edges of a punched card. Compare card column. See punched card.

caret mark In printing, a proof reading symbol in the form of an inverted V to indicate that something is to be inserted. See proofreading.

carriage (1) In printing, the bed of a cylinder machine on which the forme is laid and which carries it under the impression cylinder. (2) In office systems, a control mechanism for a typewriter or other listing device that can automatically control the feeding, spacing, skipping and ejecting of paper or preprinted forms. See form.

carriage control In computing, a means of controlling the movement of a printer carriage via a control character.

carriage control tape In data processing, a continuous strip of tape which has punched holes so positioned as to control movement of the carriage on some printers. See carriage.

carriage return In typewriters and printers, the operation that prepares for the next character to be printed at the given first position on the same line, or the next line if it is accompanied by a line feed. See line feed.

carrier (1) In printing, the substance in a xerography developer which conveys the toner, but does not itself become part of the viewable record. (2) In micrographics, a device for holding a frame, or frames, of microfilm e.g. an aperture card. (3) In communications, a continuous frequency voltage or electromagnetic wave capable of being modulated or impressed with a second signal which carries the information to be transmitted. (4) In IBM Selectric typewriters that part which carries the type element. See aperture card, modulation, toner, xerography.

carrier sense multiple access - collision detection In data communications, a protocol in which a node with data to transmit listens to the network until it becomes quiet. Still listening it then transmits data, if it hears what has been transmitted then it knows that transmission is successful. Otherwise it is clear that two or more nodes have transmitted simultaneously and the collision has caused a corruption in the data. The nodes then await a random interval before attempting to retransmit. Compare control token, message slot. See local area network, Aloha.

carrier signalling In communications, pertaining to signalling techniques used in multichannel carrier transmission. See in band signalling, out of band signalling, separate channel signalling, signalling.

carrier system In communications, a method of using a single path to obtain a number of channels. Signals are modulated with a different carrier frequency for each channel and the received signals are demodulated at the receiving end. See frequency division multiplexing.

carrier telegraphy In communications, a transmission technique in which the telegraph transmitter signals modulate on alternating currents. See modulation, AC.

carrier wave See carrier.

carry In computing, a value, to be added to a digit in an addition process, which arises when the sum obtained, by adding the digits in the preceding position, exceeds the number base.

carry forward In typesetting and word processing, an instruction to transfer text to the next column or page.

CARS In cable television, Community Antenna Relay Service, now known as cable television relay station. See cable television relay station.

Carterfone In radiocommunications, a device for connecting a two way mobile radio system with the telephone network. See Carterfone Decision.

Carterfone Decision In the U.S. the landmark interconnect decision of the FCC. In 1968, the FCC ruled that AT & T tariffs, which had forbidden the connection to the Bell network of any non Bell company equipment, were unlawful. AT & T had banned the use of the Carterfone device on the grounds that its interconnection would cause harm to the network. The FCC decision resulted in tariff revisions which permitted the interconnection of customer provided equipment to the telephone network with appropriate terminating facilities to protect the network from harm. It subsequently evolved into the FCC's Registration Program for terminal equipment.

cartridge In filming, recording and computing, a container holding film or magnetic tape, or disks, which permits quick insertion without threading.

cartridge disk In computing, a hard disk storage medium contained in a cartridge. See hard disk.

cartridge paper In printing, closely woven paper for drawing and offset printing. See offset printing.

CA Search A database supplied by Chemical Abstracts Service (CAS) and dealing with chemistry. See on line information retrieval.

cassette (1) In recording, a case or container for audio and videotape, motion picture film in reel to reel format. (2) In computing, a popular, low cost microcomputer bulk storage medium. See cartridge, magnetic tape cassette.

cassette recorder In recording, a magnetic tape recorder using compact cassettes. See compact cassette.

casting off In printing, the process of calculating the amount of space required to print a defined amount of text in a specified font. See font.

CAT See capacity activated transducer.

catalog In computing, a directory of all the files available to the computer.

catchline In printing, a temporary descriptive headline on galley proofs etc.

catch word In printing, a word placed at the end of a block of text to indicate the first word of the next block or text following.

cathode In electronics, the negative terminal of a device. Compare cathode.

cathode ray tube In electronics, a device that converts electrical signals to a visual display. It comprises an evacuated glass envelope shaped as a television tube, an electron gun, focussing deflection systems and a screen coated with phosphors. The gun provides a stream of electrons that are focussed into a thin beam and accelerated towards the tube face. When the beam strikes the phosphor screen a spot of light is produced. Voltages applied to the deflection system move the beam horizontally and vertically and trace a display. Alternatively the beam traces out a regular raster pattern on the screen and signal voltages applied to the gun vary the intensity of the beam and hence the brightness of the spot. See oscilloscope, gun.

CATLINE CATalog on LINE. A database supplied by National Library of Medicine (NLM) and dealing with biomedicine, books & periodicals - library holdings. See on line information retrieval.

CATV See cable television, community antenna television.

CAV See constant angular velocity.

CB See citizen band.

C band In communications, the frequency range 3·9 - 6·2 GHz. See GHz.

CBEMA Canadian Business Equipment Manufacturers Association.

CBMS See computer based message system.

CBX See computerized branch exchange.

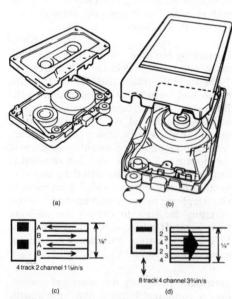

(a)   (b)

4 track 2 channel 1⅞in/s

8 track 4 channel 3¾in/s

(c)   (d)

cassette
(a) compact cassette; (b) cartridge; (c) cassette tracks (stereo); (d) cartridge tracks (stereo).

CCC See Copyright Clearance Center.

CCD See charge coupled device.

CCETT Centre Commune d'Etudes de Television et de Telecommunications.

CCIR Comité Consultatif International Radio.

CCITT Comité Consultatif International Telegraphique et Telephonique.

CCLN US Council for Computerized Library Networks.

CCTA UK Central Computer and Telecommunications Agency.

CCTV See closed circuit television.

CCU See communications control unit.

CD See compact disk.

CE See customer engineering.

CED In video disk, a Capacitance Electronic Disk developed by RCA. See capacitance disk.

cedilla In typesetting, an accent positioned under the 'c' to indicate that it should be pronounced as an 's'. See accent.

Ceefax In videotex, See Facts, the British Broadcasting Corporation's teletext system. See teletext.

cell In computing, the storage for one unit of information, usually one character or one word. Compare data cell.

cellular radio In communications, a method of providing a mobile radio telephone service in which a computer automatically searches for open channels to establish a user's call. Stored program computer controlled switching equipment is essential. The other special aspect of cellular technology, frequency reuse in each service area, is possible because low power transmitters and receivers are used to divide the area into cells. The low power radio signals have limited range and can be configured to cover cells as small as one mile in diameter. Each cell is assigned a set of channel frequencies and arranged so that its neighbouring cells use different sets of frequencies. This arrangement enables different conversations to use the same frequencies in areas only several miles apart. As a mobile phone user moves from one cell to another, the switching center compares signal strength as received at nearby cells. It searches the frequency spectrum, of the cell receiving the strongest signal, for an open channel set, and commands the mobile unit to tune to that frequency. The system can now accept another call originating in the first cell on the previously occupied channel. To ensure that a minimum of calls are dropped cells typically overlap. When a call in progress moves into a busy cell, where there are no open channels, it can remain on its original cell until a channel opens or the user moves closer to a third cell with an open channel.

Cellular radio systems facilitate calling from a normal telephone to a mobile telephone even if the location of the called subscriber is not known and his equipment is not in use. The base station in each cell transmits regular identification signals that are constantly monitored by all mobile telephones in the area. If a mobile set detects a change of signal, indicating that it has travelled from one cell to another, it automatically transmits a brief identification to a new base station to inform the system that it has moved and to indicate the latest location. The specification for UK networks call for operation on a wide band of frequencies around 900 MHz. The specification allows for 600-1000 channels which should be adequate for the projected demand of 100,000 subscribers by the year 2000. See MHz.

center holes In telegraphy, holes punched in the middle of a telegraph tape which enable it to be moved backwards or forwards. Synonymous with feed holes.

centering In word processing, the positioning of a text string, so that its midpoint is aligned with a given reference location.

center of perspective The eye position from which the image in a photograph would coincide dimensionally with the real subject.

center operator   In videotex, an organization responsible for operating a service.

center sprocket feed   In computing, pertaining to paper tape sprocket holes that line up with the middle of the code holes. Compare advanced sprocket feed. See paper tape.

centi   A prefix indicating a hundred or one hundredth.

centimeter   One hundredth of a meter.

CENTO system   In communications, Central European Treaty Organization, an international microwave system. See microwave.

central computer   Synonymous with host computer.

centralized adaptive routing   In data communications, a method of routing in which the network routing center controls routing based on data supplied to it by each node. See node.

centralized automatic message accounting   In telephony, an automatic message accounting system located in a central office and serving various adjacent central offices. Any calls not processed by automatic number identification are routed through an operator who dials the calling number into the equipment. See central office.

centralized computer network   A computer network configuration in which a central node provides computing power, control or other services. See node.

central office   In telephony, the place where common carriers locate their switching equipment and terminate customer lines etc. Synonymous with exchange, end office, local central office.

central processing unit   In computing, the unit containing the circuits that control and perform the execution of instructions. It generally contains the ALU, a number of special registers and control circuits. The CPU handles the decoding and execution of instructions, performs arithmetic and logic functions, provides timing signals etc. See ALU, microcomputer, register.

centrex   In telephony, a switching system enabling direct dialing without going through a switchboard. The system allows such services as direct inward dialing and direct distance dialing. See direct distance dialing, direct inward dialing.

CEPT   Conference of European PTTs. See PTT.

CEPT videotex standard   In videotex, a European standard for alphamosaic systems harmonising the British, French and West German standards. Compare NAPLPS. See CEPT.

chad   In computing and communications, the material removed when a hole is punched in paper tape or punched cards.

chadless tape   In computing and communications, perforated tape with the chad partially connected like a hinged flap. See chad.

chain   (1) A set of operations that are to be performed sequentially. (2) In data structures, a set of data items linked in sequence by a series of pointers. See chain list.

chain delivery mechanism   In a duplicator, a delivery system in which a number of chain mounted gripping devices extract paper from the machine and pass it along into the delivery tray. See conveyor delivery mechanism.

chaining search   In computing, a search in which each item contains the means for locating the next item to be considered in the search. See chain.

chain list   In data structures, a list in which each item contains a pointer to the next item in the list so that consecutive items do not have to be physically adjacent in storage.

chain printer   In computing, a printer in which the type characters are joined to form a chain which rotates at high speed. Characters are printed when they are at the appropriate position in the print line. Compare barrel printer.

change dump   In computing, a selective

dump of those storage locations whose contents have changed. See dump.

channel In computing and communications, (1) a path along which signals can be sent, e.g. a data channel, output channel, (2) the portion of a computer's storage medium which is also accessible to a given I/O device. See input output devices, I/O.

channel bank In communications, equipment performing the operation of multiplexing. Typically used for multiplexing voice grade channels. See multiplexer.

channel capacity In communications, the maximum rate at which information can be transmitted over a given channel. Channel capacity is normally measured in bauds, but may be stated in bits per second when specific terminating equipment is implied. See channel.

channel group In communications, an assembly of 12 channels in a carrier system which occupy adjacent bands in the spectrum and are frequency division multiplexed. See carrier system, channel, frequency division multiplexing, supergroup, master group.

channel isolation In communications, a measure of the degree of cross talk between two channels, measured in decibels. See cross talk, decibel.

channel overload In computing, a condition in which data transfer to or from a processor and I/O devices reaches a rate that approaches the capacity of the data channel. See I/O.

chapel In printing, a term applied to local branches of printers' and journalists' U.K. trades unions.

chapter In video disk, a consecutive sequence of frames. See frame.

chapter stop In video disk, a code embedded in the vertical blanking interval of the video disk that enables the player to locate the beginning of chapters. See chapter, vertical blanking interval.

character (1) In printing, a letter, number,

punctuation mark or special graphic used for the production of text. (2) A letter, digit or other symbol that is used as part of the organization, control or representation of data. A character is often represented in the form of a spatial arrangement of adjacent or connected strokes or in the form of other physical conditions in data media. (3) In computing, any letter, number, punctuation mark or graphic stored or processed by computing equipment.

character assembly (1) In printing, a generic term covering all methods in which letters, figures, special characters and spaces are generated for reproduction. (2) In data communications, the process by which bits are put together to form characters as the bits arrive on a data link. Compare character disassembly.

character at a time printer Synonymous with character printer.

character byte In videotex, the byte obtained by appending an odd parity bit to a character code. See parity.

character code In computing, a method of representing characters by means of a unique value. The two most common character codes are ASCII and EBCDIC. See ASCII, EBCDIC code.

character disassembly In data communications, the process by which characters are decomposed into bits for transmission over a data link. Compare character assembly. See bit.

character display device In computing, a display device that gives a representation of data only in the form of characters. Synonymous with alphanumeric display device.

character fill In computing, the insertion into a storage medium of a representation of a specified character that does not itself convey data but may delete unwanted data.

character generator (1) In computer graphics, a functional unit that converts the coded representation of a graphic character into the shape of the character for display. (2) In word processing, the means within the equipment for generating visual characters or symbols from coded data.

character interleaving In data communications, a method of time division multiplexing in which the multiplexer stores a complete character before transmitting it down the line. Compare bit interleaving. See time division multiplexing.

characteristic The numeral that represents the exponent of a floating point number. See exponent, floating point.

characteristic curve In photography, a graph displaying the relationship between the density in developed photographic emulsion and exposure.

character key In word processing, a control used to process text one character at a time.

characterplexer In communications, a system in which data from a low speed asynchronous channel is organized on a character basis and each character is gated onto a high speed synchronous trunk. See asynchronous transmission, synchronous transmission.

character printer In data processing, a device that prints individual characters in succession, for example, a typewriter. See line printer. Synonymous with serial printer.

character recognition In computing, the identification of graphic, phonic, or other characters by automatic means including magnetic, optical or mechanical. See optical character recognition, magnetic ink character recognition.

character rectangle In videotex, one of the 960 units in the regular matrix of 24 rows of 40 character positions in which characters are generated in the display of a page. See page.

character rounding In computer graphics, the technique of improving the shape of a displayed character within the constraints of the dot matrix. See dot matrix.

character set (1) In computing and data communications, a finite set of different characters that is considered complete for a particular application, for example, each of the characters in ISO Recommendation R646 6 bit and 7 bit coded character sets for information processing interchange. (2) In computing, the set of characters available on a particular computer.

character size control In word processing, a display option where the operator can choose between a full page of text at normal character size or one half page at double (vertical) size.

character skew In optical character recognition, the angular rotation of a character relative to its intended or ideal placement. See skew.

character space In videotex, the space occupied by a character or graphic symbol on a videotex display. See contiguous graphics, page.

character spacing display In word processing, a facility whereby the operator can view the character spacing for either 10 or 12 pitch or for proportionally spaced characters. The screen display line may be identical to the line to be printed. See pitch, proportional spacing.

character spacing reference line In character recognition, a vertical line used for determining the horizontal spacing of characters.

characters per pica In printing, the average number of characters in a given font that will fit within a given pica measure. See pica.

characters per second In data communications, a measure of transmission rate, usually between a terminal device and a computer. Compare baud.

character string (1) In data structures, a string which consists solely of characters. (2) Connected sequence of characters.

character stuffing In data communications, a method of delimiting frames with a special end of frame character. Compare bit stuffing.

character subset A selection of characters

from a character set comprising all characters which have a specified common feature. For example, in the definition of a character subset, the digits 0-9 constitute a character subset.

character terminal In data communications, a terminal which cannot form its own packets; it is connected to a PAD for connection to a packet switched network. Compare packet terminal. See packet switching, PAD.

charge In electronics, a quantity of unbalanced electricity in a body, i.e. the excess or deficiency of electrons, giving the body negative or positive potential respectively.

charge coupled device In microelectronics, an MOS recirculating memory. Electrons are injected into the device and are moved along it as the result of voltages applied to a series of electrodes thus providing an action similar to that of a shift register. See MOS, memory, shift register.

charging In a document copying machine, the process of creating an electrostatic surface charge on an insulating medium.

chassis In electronics, the metal base upon which the sockets, wiring, and other electronic parts of an assembly are mounted.

chatter In electronics, a rapid closing and opening of contacts on a relay. See relay.

check bit In control and communications, a binary digit used in the process of determining the accuracy of processed or transmitted data. See parity checking.

check digit In computing, one or more redundant digits used to check for the presence of errors in an associated set of digits.

check key In data processing, a group of characters, derived from and appended to a data item, that can be used to detect errors in the data item during processing.

checkpoint In computing, a point at which information about the status of a program execution can be recorded so that the execution can be later restarted.

checkpoint restart In computing, the action of continuing processing from the last checkpoint in the case of an abnormal termination of a run, instead of the beginning. See checkpoint.

checksum In data processing and data communications, the summation of a set of data items associated with the set for checking purposes. The data items are either numerals, bits or other character strings regarded as numerals for the purpose of the calculation. See hash total.

Chemical Engineering Abstracts A database supplied by The Royal Society of Chemistry and dealing with chemistry engineering. See on line information retrieval.

Chemical Industry Notes A database supplied by Chemical Abstracts Service and dealing with chemical industry. See on line information retrieval.

chip In microelectronics, an integrated circuit device including its encapsulating package and circuit terminations. The phenomenal growth in the microelectronics industry is due to the technology that produces circuits of increasing complexity, high reliability, low power dissipation and cost on minute wafers of silicon. Silicon itself is a gray semiconductive material commonly found in the earth's crust.

The processes involved in the production of a chip are purification, ingot growth, wafer generation, imaging process, deposition and growth process, testing, chip separation, wiring and encapsulation. A silicon rod is initially purified by the zone refining process; heating coils move along a cylinder containing the rod and the impurities tend to collect in the localized molten region. As the heating coils move from one end of the rod to the other, the impurities are gradually separated from it. The polycrystalline silicon is then melted and a single crystal seed is placed in contact with it; the seed crystal is slowly rotated and drawn away from the molten silicon forming a monocrystalline silicon cylinder. The ingots are then ground to produce a 'flat' that parallels the growth axis and sliced, into wafers of 500 micron thickness and 5 centimeter diameter, with diamond slicing saws. These wafers are then

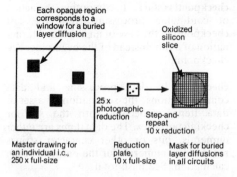

Each opaque region corresponds to a window for a buried layer diffusion

Oxidized silicon slice

25 x photographic reduction

Step-and-repeat 10 x reduction

Master drawing for an individual i.c., 250 x full-size

Reduction plate, 10 x full-size

Mask for buried layer diffusions in all circuits

chip
Fig 1 The production of one of a series of photographic masks required for the manufacture of an array of integrated circuits (not to scale).

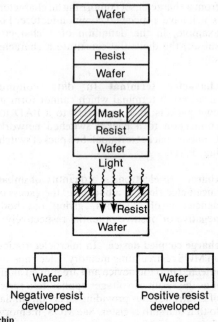

Wafer

Resist
Wafer

Mask
Resist
Wafer

Light

Resist
Wafer

Negative resist developed — Wafer

Positive resist developed — Wafer

chip
Fig 2 Resist imaging.

cleaned and chemically etched to produce a highly polished surface. The wafer forms the basis of a large number of individual chips, each with surface areas of the order of square millimeters. Each chip will comprise a complicated pattern of embedded zones of various semiconductor materials.

The zones are produced by successive imaging and deposition or growth processes; an individual bipolar transistor, for example, is produced by forming minute zones of p- and n- type semiconductor material corresponding to the base, collector and emitter regions. The imaging process exposes certain areas of the chip surface, corresponding to circuit components, or parts thereof, to provide access windows for subsequent processes. In the photographic process a large mask is cut accurately by machine and its image then reduced photographically to wafer size. The wafer surface is coated with a photoresist material, and like all operations in chip manufacture, extreme precautions are taken to protect the surfaces from contamination. The mask is placed over the wafer surface which is then exposed to ultraviolet light; the photoresist is developed with the consequent removal of the exposed (positive resist) or unexposed (negative resist) areas. An etching process then removes the exposed portions of the surface layer material and finally the remainder of the photoresist is removed. The deposition and growth processes add new layers to the wafer or introduce changes into the properties of chip material through windows produced by the

imaging process. Silicon dioxide is a very stable material and is used to inhibit diffusion processes over certain parts of the surface or as an insulating layer, i.e. in Metal Oxide Silicon components. The oxide layer is produced by heating the wafer in an oxygen or steam atmosphere.

Epitaxy is a deposition process wherein a single crystal layer is applied to a silicon wafer of the same crystal orientation. In this case the wafer surface is chemically cleaned and the wafer is heated in a carefully controlled atmosphere of silicon tetrachloride and hydrogen which deposits silicon onto the wafer surface. The new layer is usually required to have a different level of p- or n-type concentration to that of the substrate and the necessary dopant can be introduced into the vapour in the reactor.

Diffusion and ion implementation techniques enable impurity atoms to be introduced into zones of the wafer thus producing the individual circuit components or parts thereof. In the diffusion process windows, cut in the silicon dioxide layer by the imaging process, reveal the areas of surface that are to receive the impurity atoms. Dopants are introduced onto the surface of the heated wafer and are allowed to diffuse into the material. Ion implementation techniques are used to place impurity ions in semiconductor layers at variously controlled depths and with accurate control of the dopant ion concentrations. A beam of ions, produced by the collisions of electrons and neutral atoms, are accelerated and focused, by electric fields, onto the surface of the chip. The surface of the chip is masked by thick layers of silicon diode or photoresist material according to the required patterns of circuit components.

Aluminium metallization is used to provide an interconnection layer on the integrated circuits, making low resistance contacts to the devices formed in the silicon, and connecting these to bonding pads on the chip's edge. Various techniques are employed to deposit a layer of aluminium some 2 microns thick on the chip. When the circuit components have been produced by the successive operations described above the circuit operation is tested so that deficient chips can be eliminated before the subsequent, costly, packaging operation. The wafer is separated into the individual chips by diamond scribing and cleaving. Each circuit chip is fixed to a suitable header and fine wires, of gold or aluminium, are bonded to circuit terminal pads to form connections between the chip components and the outside world. The chip is then encapsulated and circuits tested. See base, collector, dopant, emitter, epitaxial layer, etching, integrated circuit, metal oxide silicon, micron, negative resist, n-type material, photoresist, positive resist, p-type material, resistance, semiconductor, transistor, wafer.

chip architecture In computing, the arrangement of chips forming a microprocessor chip, i.e. the ALU, general purpose registers and the control bus structure. See ALU, control bus.

chip microprocessor In computing, a set of LSI circuits on a single silicon chip capable of performing the essential functions of a CPU. See chip architecture, LSI, chip, CPU.

chip modem In data communications, a modem contained in a single silicon chip. See chip, MODEM.

chip select line In microcomputers, a circuit which, when activated, enables or selects one and only one of several units. See chip.

chipspeech In microelectronics, an integrated circuit which stores the sound of speech in digital form for playback. See speech synthesis.

chord keying In data processing, a keyboard safeguard in which two or more keys must be depressed simultaneously in order to action critical commands from the keyboard.

CHPS See characters per second.

chroma The measure of hue and saturation of a colour, undiluted with white, black or gray. See saturation.

chroma control In television, the control regulating colour saturation in a receiver. See saturation.

chroma detector In television, black and white circuitry eliminating colour burst by sensing absence of chrominance signal in a receiver. See colour burst, chrominance signal.

chromakey In television, a colour effect produced by a special effects generator, used like an optical matte to cut a portion of one picture into another via the blue colour signal. See matte, special effects generator.

chromatic aberration In optics, a lens defect which causes colours to be focused at different points and so producing coloured fringe haloes.

chromatic dispersion In optoelectronics, dispersion or distortion of a pulse in an optical waveguide due to differences in wave velocity caused by variation in the indices of refraction for different portions of the guide. See refractive index.

chromaticity In optics, the colour quality of light definable by its dominant wavelength and its purity.

chrominance signal In television, the transmitted signal providing information on hue and saturation. See hue, saturation, luminance signal.

chromium dioxide In audio recording, a

magnetic tape coating which offers improved signal to noise ratio. See signal to noise ratio.

CIA See communications interface adapter.

CICIREPATO Committee for International Cooperation in Information Retrieval among Examining PATent Offices. See ICIREPAT.

CIM See computer input from microfilm.

cine The prefix meaning motion pictures or film.

cine camera A motion picture film camera.

cinematography (1) Motion picture photography. (2) The creation of the illusion of motion through motion picture techniques.

cine oriented image In micrographics, an image appearing on a roll of microfilm in such a manner that the top edge of the image is at right angles to the long edge of the film.

cine 8 film In cinematography, the older 8mm motion picture film having a width of 8mm and one perforation per frame at the frame line on one side.

cipher In communications, a cryptographic technique where the sequence of characters or bits is changed by means of a secret transformation. See cryptography.

ciphertext In communications, text or data which has been transformed by encipherment.

CIPS Canadian Information Processing Society.

circle of confusion In photography, the circular image of any subject point on a piece of film.

circuit (1) In communications, a link between two or more points. (2) In electronics, the path of an electric current in a conductor or arrangement of conductors.

circuit breaker In electronics, a device that opens electric circuits under abnormal operating conditions, e.g. excessive current, voltage, heat, etc.

circuit diagram In electronics, a schematic diagram using conventional symbols to show the connections between components in an electronic device.

circuit grade In communications, the information carrying capability of a circuit, in speed or type of signal. The grades of circuits are wideband, voice, subvoice and telegraph. See wideband channel, voice grade channel, telegraphy, subvoice grade channel.

circuit noise level In communications, the ratio of the circuit noise to some reference level. The ratio is usually measured in decibels above the reference noise. See decibel, noise.

circuit switched digital circuitry In data communications, a technique for making end to end digital connections. The user places calls normally and then employs the same connection to transmit high speed data. See circuit switching.

circuit switching In data communications, a method in which a connection is established on demand and maintained between data stations in order to allow the exclusive use of a data circuit until the connection is released. Compare message switching. See data station.

circular buffer In computing and communications, a form of a queue with two pointers indicating the head and the tail. When a pointer reaches the end of the buffer it returns to the start. See queue.

circular file In data processing, a file organized for high volatility in which new records added replace the oldest records. See volatility, record, file.

circular orbit In satellite communications, an orbit in which the distance between the satellite and the center of the earth is constant.

circular waveguide In communications, waveguides of circular cross section which can transmit higher frequencies than rectangular waveguides. Circular waveguides can be used for frequencies up to about 100GHz and can be used for long distance communication channels. Compare rectangular waveguide. See waveguide, GHz.

circulating register In electronics, a shift register in which data moved out of one end of the register is re-entered into the other end as in a closed loop. See shift register.

circumflex In typesetting, an accent in the shape of an inverted 'v' positioned over the character. See accent.

citation indexing In library science, a method of indexing in which a list of documents, subsequent to the appearance of the original article, refer to, i.e. cite, that article. Such an index enables a user to find recent articles appertaining to a known document. See indexing.

citizen band In radiocommunications, a 40 channel short wave broadcast band in the 27 MHz range for private communication over a limited range of 8 to 10 miles. See MHz, short wave.

cladding In optoelectronics, an optical conductive material with a lower refractive index, than the core, around the core material of an optical fiber; it serves to reflect or refract light waves so as to confine them to the core. See fiber optics, refractive index.

Claims / Citation A database supplied by IFI/Plenum Data Company and Search Check Inc. and dealing with patents. See on line information retrieval.

Claims / Compound Registry A database supplied by IFI/Plenum Data Company and dealing with chemistry - structure & nomenclature, patents. See on line information retrieval.

Claims / US Patents A database supplied by IFI/Plenum Data Company and dealing with patents. See on line information retrieval.

clamping In electronics, the action of establishing the voltage level of a signal.

clapper In printers, a component of a matrix printer that is moved by the action of an electromagnet and hence drives the print needle. See ballistic technique, matrix printer, non ballistic technique. ·

classification In library science, the arrangement of items in a logical order according to their degree of similarity. See Dewey Decimal Classification.

class of service In communications, (1) the type of communications service to which a customer subscribes, (2) the type of telephone equipment used by a customer, (3) the calling privileges and restrictions of a given line in switching. See PBX.

Clayton Act Legislation that prohibits price discrimination, anticompetitive mergers and certain restrictive agreements. The act empowers the FCC to enforce certain sections applicable to common carriers engaged in wire or radio communication or transmission of energy. See FCC, common carrier.

CLC See communications link controller.

cleaning down In a duplicator, the cleaning of the blanket, inker and damping system so as to make the equipment ready for subsequent use. See blanket cylinder, lithography.

clean proof In printing, a proof containing no errors or corrections. See proof.

clear (1) In computing, the action of erasing data from storage. (2) In telephony, the release of a circuit in a controlled manner so that each of the various links and devices is correctly returned to its idle condition.

clearance Permission to use material which is subject to copyright protection, especially music in a film. See copyright.

clear area In character recognition, an area that is kept free of printing and other markings not related to machine reading.

clear data Data that is not enciphered. Synonymous with plaintext.

clear display In computer graphics, the

action of deleting all information from a display.

clear to send   In data communications, a signal sent from a modem to a DTE, when received the DTE commences sending data. See DTE.

clip   (1) In broadcasting, a short film insert used in live TV transmission. (2) In audio recording, the accidental omission of a note, syllable or word from the beginning or end of an audio track. (3) In electronics, to remove the upper or lower portion of a waveform or to remove the high frequency components of a signal.

clipping   (1) In telephony, the loss of the initial or final parts of words or syllables due to the operation of voice activated devices, e.g. TASI. (2) In computer graphics, to remove parts of a display that lie outside a selected area. See TASI. Synonymous with scissor.

clock   (1) In electronics, a device that generates periodic signals used for synchronization. (2) In computing, a register whose content changes at regular intervals in such a way as to give a measure of time. (3) In data communications, equipment that provides a time base used in a transmission system to control the timing of certain functions such as sampling and to control the duration of signal elements. See register, sampling, time base.

clocking   In data communications, the use of clock pulses to control synchronization of data and control characters in a binary synchronous communication. See binary synchronous communications.

clock oscillator   In electronics, a crystal controlled high frequency oscillator (200 kHz - 30 MHz) used in the basic timing device in a clock. See clock, kHz, MHz.

clock pulse   In electronics, a synchronization signal generated by a clock.

clock rate   In computing and electronics, (1) the rate at which timing pulses are emitted from a clock, (2) the rate at which bits are transferred from one internal computer element to another.

clock run in   In teletext, a sequence of alternating bits at the start of a dataline, enabling a receiver to achieve bit synchronization. See dataline, synchronization.

close   In computer programming, an instruction to close a file disconnects a program from the stored file. The closure may consolidate changes in the file produced by the program or purge it from the storage device depending upon options exercised by the program. The action of closure releases the file for use by other programs. Compare open. See file.

close classification   In library science, the arrangement of documents in a classification system in as minute subdivisions as possible; necessary for the adequate definitions of documents in a specialist collection. See classification.

closed circuit television   A system in which a TV signal is fed to a limited number of viewing monitors by cable.

closed loop   A system in which the output is fed back to the input to effect a control action. Compare open loop. See feedback.

closed subroutine   In computer programming, a subroutine that is stored in one place. A call to that routine causes a jump to the appropriate storage location and a subsequent return to the instruction immediately following the calling instruction. Compare open subroutine. See subroutine.

closed user group   (1) In videotex, a service to which only predefined users have access. (2) In communications, a number of users of a public switched data communication service who have the facility to communicate with one another but access is barred to and from all others.

close spacing   In printing, text with as little space as possible between the words.

close up   (1) In printing, the action of bringing together type matter by taking out spaces. (2) In photography, a shot in which an image of the subject fills most of the negative.

cluster   (1) In communications, a group of

terminal devices grouped in one specific location and interfaced to the communication facility through a cluster controller. (2) In word processing, a group of workstations attached to a central control unit. See work station.

CLV See constant linear velocity.

C-MAC In television, a standard to be used in DBS which will provide enhanced picture quality. The synchronization, luminance, chrominance and sound signals are transmitted in time division multiplex. Compare A-MAC. See chrominance signal, luminance signal, MAC.

CMOS See complementary metal oxide silicon.

CNP See communications network processor.

COAM In communications, Customer Owned And Maintained communication equipment, e.g. terminals.

coaxial cable In electronics, a low loss cable, used for high frequencies, which consists of a conductor within, and insulated from, a tube of braided copper. See shielded cable.

COBOL In computer programming, COmmon Business Oriented Language, a high level language designed for business data applications. See high level language.

co-citation indexing In library science, an indexing method which pairs documents which have been cited in common by other documents. See bibliographic coupling.

CODASYL In databases, COnference for DAta SYstem Languages. A group created by the US Department of Defense, including users and manufacturers, for developing COBOL and hardware independent software for database management. See COBOL, database management system.

CODATA Committee on data for science and technology of the International Council of Scientific Unions.

code (1) In computing, the instructions or statements of a program, or the act of generating them. (2) In communications, a system of symbols used to convert alphanumeric information into a form suitable for communications transmission. (3) A set of rules outlining the way in which data may be represented. See ASCII, baudot code, character code.

code area In micrographics, a part of the film frame reserved for the retrieval code.

CODEC In communications, COder DECoder, a device to convert analog signals, e.g. speech, television, music to digital form, for transmission over a digital medium and to reconvert them back to analog form. See analog signal, analog to digital converter, digital to analog converter.

code conversion In computing and communications, a process for changing the bit

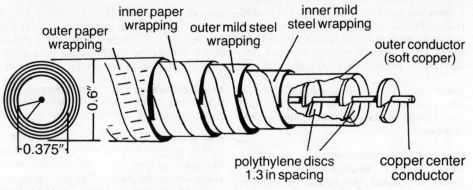

coaxial cable
A long-distance telephone cable for transmission at frequencies up to 60 MHz.

grouping of one character in one code into the corresponding bit grouping for a character in a second code.

coded character set In computing and communications, a set of rules for establishing a character set and the one to one relationships between the characters in the set and their coded representations.

coded image In computer graphics, a representation of a display image in a form suitable for processing.

code extension character In computing, a control character used to indicate that one or more of the succeeding code values are to be interpreted according to a special code. See escape character, shift codes.

code holes In data processing, the information holes in perforated tape, as opposed to the feed or other holes.

code independent system In data communications, a mode of transmission that uses a character oriented link protocol that does not depend on the character set or code used by the source of data. See link protocol.

code key In word processing, a special typewriter key that, when depressed in conjunction with a designated key, initiates special modes of operation.

code level In computing and communications, the number of bits used to represent a character. See byte.

code line In micrographics, a series of horizontal bars placed adjacent to each frame of a microfilm used to assist in the location of required frames. As the film passes rapidly in searching the bar is seen to rise (or fall) and the search is stopped when it attains a predetermined position. See microfilm.

coder In computer programming, a person who produces a program from a detailed specification of that program. Compare programmer.

code set In computing and communications, a finite and complete set of representations defined by a code. Synonymous with code.

code value In computing and communi-

cations, one element of a code set, e.g. the eight bit binary digit code value for the delete character.

coding sheet In computer programming, a sheet of paper used by a programmer for coding a program and subsequently transcribed into machine readable form. See coder, machine readable.

coercivity In ferromagnetic materials, the reverse magnetic field necessary to reduce the magnetic flux to zero after the field has been increased to produce flux saturation and then reduced to zero. See flux, ferromagnetic, remanence, saturation.

cognitive domain The category of instructional objectives relating to knowledge, information, and other intellectual skills within human behaviour.

cogwheel effect In television, a staggered vertical image produced by the relative displacement of alternate scan lines. See scanning line.

coherence In optics, pertaining to electromagnetic radiation, e.g. light, where the individual waves are in phase. See LASER, in phase.

coherent bundle In optoelectroncs, a bundle of optical fibers in which the spatial coordinates are the same, or bear the same spatial relationship to each other, at the two ends of the bundle. See bundle, fiber optics.

CoI Central Office of Information. UK Government agency dealing with information and publicity.

coincidence circuit In electronics, (1) a digital comparator circuit which detects the equality of two binary words, (2) a circuit which detects the simultaneous occurrence of two digital events and produces an output.

coin denomination use In telephony, a tone sent to an operator to indicate the value of a coin inserted in a coinbox.

cold standby In computing, the use of a backup computer in the event of a failure in the main system. Any data in the main computer at the time of failure, and not recorded in backing store will be lost. Compare warm standby, hot standby. See backing store.

cold start In computing, the restart process used when a serious failure has occurred in a realtime system such that the contents of the store become inaccessible and all information on the recent processing is lost. The computer must be reloaded and activity restarted as though at the beginning of the processing. See realtime.

cold type In typesetting, type that is set on any photographic process. Compare strike on, hot type, etch type.

collate (1) In data processing, to combine two or more similar sets of items to produce another similar set. (2) In printing, to check through the pagination or signatures of the sections of a book to ensure that they are complete and in the correct sequence for binding. See signature.

collating marks In printing, marks used to check for any displacement of printed material after gathering. They are black step marks printed on the back folds of sections and in progressively different positions.

collect call In telephony, a call in which the caller requests that the charge be paid by the called party.

collector In electronics, a terminal on a transistor. Compare base, emitter. See transistor.

collimator In optics, a device for measuring the position of an image formed by a lens in relation to the film plane of a camera.

collotype In printing, a photomechanical non screen planographic process in which the printing is performed from a gelatine film. Used in art reproductions. See photomechanical, planographic.

colophon In printing, an inscription, placed usually at the end of a book, with information relating to the production of the book.

colour (1) The psychological sensation arising as a result of ocular perception of and discrimination between various wavelengths of light. (2) In printing, the degree of lightness or heaviness in appearance of a particular typeface.

colour balance (1) In photography, the relative sensitivity of film to light of various wavelengths. (2) In television, adjustment of the colour controls to give a visually satisfying image, usually based on skin tones.

colour bar signals In television, a video test signal for colour television equipment.

colour break up In television, a separation of the primary colour components of an image due to a rapid horizontal movement in the field of view.

colour burst In television, a signal of 8 cycles of 3·58 MHz transmitted on the back-porch of a composite colour signal. The phase of the following video signal is compared with that of the colour burst to determine the hue of the colour signal. See hue, back porch, composite colour video signal.

colour cell In television, the smallest area of the phosphor screen of a display tube that can reproduce complete colour information.

colour compensating filter In photography, a yellow, magenta, or cyan filter which absorbs small amounts of either red, green or blue used on cameras or in printers to make slight corrections in the colour of the light used.

colour contamination In television, an error in the colour reproduction of an object due to defects in the optical, electronic or mechanical paths of the system.

colour decoder In television, the apparatus for deriving the receiver primary signals from the colour picture signal and the colour burst. See colour burst.

colour encoder In television, a device that produces an NTSC encoder colour signal from separate red, green and blue video inputs. It may also generate the colour burst. See video standards, colour burst.

colour saturation See saturation.

colour separation In printing, an electronic or photographic process to separate the various colours of an original, by the use of colour filters, so that separate printing plates can be produced. See filter.

colour shift In television, an unwanted colour change in a transmitted picture.

colour temperature In photography, a concept formulated for the purpose of reference to and standardization of colour of light sources. When a black body, such as a carbon filament, is heated until it glows, the colour of the radiant light is directly related to the temperature of the filament. It is measured in degrees Kelvin. See black body.

colour transparency In photography, a usually positive colour picture on a transparent film.

colour work In printing, the process of printing more than one colour on a sheet.

columnar graph See bar chart.

column move and delete In word processing, a facility permitting text to be manipulated by column as compared with normal row manipulation. Used in tabular work.

COM See computer output microfilm.

coma In optics, a lens aberration resulting in a variation of magnification with aperture. Rays through the outer edges of a lens form a larger image than those through the center.

comb In computing, an assembly of seek arms in a multiple disk, movable head magnetic disk unit. The seek arms hold the read/write heads that are moved to the appropriate track of the disks. See head, magnetic disk, movable head disk, track.

combination A given number of different elements selected from a set without constraint on the order in which the selected elements are arranged. See permutation.

combinational circuit See combinational logic.

combinational logic In electronics, a logic circuit in which the output depends only upon the instantaneous discrete states of the circuit inputs and is not a function of any previous inputs. Compare sequential logic.

combined station In data communications, the station used in HDLC procedures. A combined station generates and interprets both commands and responses. See HDLC.

combiner (1) In cable television, a device enabling two or more input signals to be fed

to a single output without interaction. (2) In antennas, a device enabling two or more transmitters to use a single antenna simultaneously.

comic strip oriented image In micrographics, an image appearing on roll microfilm in such a way that the long edge of the film and the top edge of the image are parallel.

command In computing, (1) an electronic pulse, signal or set of signals to start, stop or continue an operation, (2) the portion of an instruction word specifying the operation to be performed, (3) a character string from a source external to a system that represents a request for system action. See instruction.

command language In computer programming, a source language consisting principally of procedural operations, each capable of invoking a function to be executed. See procedure, source language.

comment In computer programming, a phrase included in a computer program to assist the programmer in debugging operations by highlighting some aspect of the program. Comments are ignored by compilers and have no effect upon the program execution. See compiler, debug.

commentary In filming, the narration for a film spoken by an off screen voice in voice over situations. See voice over.

common carrier In communications, a company whose business is to supply communication facilities to the public. The term is derived from the interstate commerce concept of carrying goods. A communication common carrier comes under the jurisdiction of relevant state organizations and if it operates interstate facilities it will be subject to FCC regulations. Common carriers can carry telemetry, facsimile, television and data messages. See FCC, facsimile, telemetry, PTT.

common channel signalling In communications, a signalling technique in which signalling information relating to a multiplicity of circuits, and information for network management, are conveyed over a single channel by addressed messages. Compare separate channel signalling. See signalling, System X.

communicating word processing In data communications, word processing equipment capable of transmission and reception of text and data.

communication The process of transferring information in the various media from one point, person or device to another. See telecommunications.

communication buffer In communications, a terminal that has a buffer. See buffer.

communication link The physical means of connecting one location to another for the purpose of transmitting and receiving information.

communications act of 1934 Act of Congress that established the FCC. See FCC.

communication satellite act 1962 Act of Congress that established COMSAT. See COMSAT.

communication scanner In data communications, a device that monitors lines for service requests.

communications computer In data communications, a computer which manages the control of lines and the routing of data in a network. See routing.

communications control unit In data communications, a device that controls the transmission of data over lines in the network.

communications interface adapter In computing, an intelligent device, on a bus organized computer system, that provides interface functions between the bus and a modem. See bus, MODEM, peripheral interface adapter, UART.

communications link controller In data communications, an intelligent unit which provides line oriented interface functions, e.g. error detection, synchronization, acknowledgements, between a group of modems and a computer or communications

network processor. See communications network processor.

communications network processor In data communications, an intelligent unit which performs interface functions, e.g. buffering, code conversion, queue management, between a computer and one or more communications link controllers. See communications link controller.

communications satellite system A system of earth orbiting communications satellites and associated earth stations for the purpose of transmitting telephone, television and data signals. See earth station, INTELSAT, satellite.

communication theory The mathematical discipline dealing with the transmission of messages in the presence of noise. See noise.

community antenna television In cable television, a subscriber system in which a single master antenna provides television reception for a whole geographic area. See master antenna television system.

compact cassette In recording, a 3·81mm audio tape attached to two hubs inside a plastic container for self threading, which may be used in fast forward and rewind modes. See cartridge.

compact disk Synonymous with DAD.

COMPANDOR In telephony, COMPressor expANDOR, a device that compresses the range of signal amplitudes during transmission to provide a more uniform response to strong and weak inputs. At the transmitting end, strong signals are attenuated and weak signals amplified, a reverse process occurs at the receiving end to restore signals to their original volume. See VOGAD.

comparator (1) In electronics, a circuit that provides an output indicating if two input signals are, or are not, equal. (2) In computing, a device for determining the similarity, or otherwise, of two words or patterns. See word.

compare instruction In computer programming, a machine code instruction which checks for a zero difference between two specified words and returns a result true or false, which is then normally used by a conditional jump instruction. See conditional jump.

compatibility (1) In computing and communications, pertaining to pairs of devices that have met the requirements for code, speed and signal level conversion to enable direct interconnections. (2) In computing, pertaining to machines on which programs may be interchanged without appreciable modification. See program.

COMPENDEX COMPuterized ENgineering InDEX. A database supplied by Engineering Information Inc. and dealing with engineering. See on line information retrieval.

compile and go In computing, an operating system which loads, compiles and executes a high level language source program without intermediate operator intervention. See compiler, operating system.

compiler In computer programming, a program designed to translate a high level language source program into a corresponding machine code program. The compiler checks for, and reports, any syntax errors in the source program. If the source program is syntax error free then a complete object code program is produced. Compare interpreter. See high level language, source program, machine code, object code, syntax.

complement A number that is derived by subtracting the given number from another specified number. Often used in the representation of negative numbers. See two's complement.

complementary colours In optics, those pairs of colours which give the effect of white when combined, e.g. red-cyan, green-magenta, blue-yellow.

complementary metal oxide silicon In microelectronics, a semiconductor integrated circuit logic system using two complementary p- channel and n-channel transistors. Power consumption is very low because virtually no

current flows except when the input changes from one logic value to the other. See MOS, n-channel MOS, p-channel MOS, transistor.

component An essential functional part of a subsystem or apparatus.

composite circuit In communications, a circuit that can be used simultaneously for telephony and DC signalling.

composite colour video signal In television, the complete transmitted signal for colour television comprises the front porch, horizontal sync pulse, breezeway, colour burst and video signal. The phase of the video signal relative to the colour burst determines the hue, and the amplitude of the signal determines the saturation. See front porch, horizontal sync pulse, breezeway, colour burst, hue, saturation.

composition size In printing, sizes of type up to and sometimes including 14 point. See point, type size.

compositor A typographer. See typography.

compressed audio In video disk, a method of digitally encoding and decoding several seconds of voice quality audio per individual disk frame thus producing a potential for several hours of audio per disk. See frame. Synonymous with still frame audio.

compression In communications, a process in which the effective gain applied to a signal is varied as a function of the signal magnitude, the effective gain being greater for small signals. Compare overmodulation. See gain, bandwidth compression, COMPANDOR.

computation In computing, a process involving many calculations and often requiring high utilization of the CPU. Compare data processing.

computational stereo In computing, pertaining to the recovery of three dimensional characteristics of a scene from information on multiple two dimensional images, taken from different viewpoints.

computer (1) A device which performs prespecified computations on any valid set of input data and delivers results within defined levels of accuracy. (2) A term which is used for electronic digital computer. See analog computer, electromechanical computer, electronic digital computer, hybrid computer.

computer aided design In computing, a system employing keyboard, light pen and VDU to manipulate design data in a computer memory and generate design diagrams on the VDU or X-Y plotter. See light pen, VDU, X-Y plotter.

computer aided manufacture The use of computers to control manufacturing processes.

computer aided translation Synonymous with machine aided translation.

computer animation The use of computer display facilities to provide animation effects. Since the computer can store the coordinates of three dimensional objects, it is possible to provide a display of changing perspective as the observer moves through the scene. Techniques were originally developed for flight simulators but now are used in cinema and television. See simulator.

computer assisted instruction See computer assisted learning.

computer assisted learning The use of a computer to provide information to a student, pose questions and react to the student's response, e.g. by providing remedial information in the case of an incorrect response. The system may provide sophisticated graphic displays or simulations of complex systems. Speech recognizers, speech synthesizers, touchscreen inputs etc. provide opportunities for very sophisticated student machine interaction. See computer based training, simulator, touchscreen, Plato computer system, speech recognizer, speech synthesizer.

computer based message system In communications, a facility to permit users to create and edit messages at a terminal, file them in computer store, deliver them by a communications computer via electronic mailbox

addresses or terminals equipped to answer incoming calls. See electronic mailbox.

computer based training The use of a computer in a training environment. The distinction between computer assisted learning and computer based training is not well defined but computer based training tends to be applied to application areas in which a limited, well defined training objective is specified and often microcomputers are employed. See computer assisted learning.

computer conferencing In teleconferencing, the use of a computer to handle group communication in simultaneous or asynchronous meetings, the latter allows participants to enter the conference at random.

computer graphics In computing, the manipulation and presentation of data in the form of dots on a graphic display terminal to give a picture like image. The terminal stores data as a set of discrete picture elements, or pixels, each of which may be individually addressed. The greater the number of pixels on a given screen, the higher the resolution of the displayed image. See bit map, display attribute, refresh.

computer input from microfilm In micrographics, pertaining to the equipment and techniques employed to interpret microfilm images and convert them into a form suitable for input to a computer. Compare computer output microfilm. See microfilm.

computer inquiry 1980 FCC decision to restrict common carrier regulation only to the carrier's provision of basic services, and to free enhanced services from regulation. This decision encourages competition in the telecommunications market and increases the range of customer services and equipment. See basic service, common carrier, enhanced services.

computerized branch exchange In telephony, an intelligent private switchboard which may provide extra facilities, e.g. facsimile, database interrogation, in addition to routing incoming and outgoing telephone calls. Compare private branch exchange.

computerized composition In typesetting,

the use of a computer to make the mathematical decisions necessary to drive the typesetting machine. An idiot tape is produced on a keyboard and subsequently input to the computer which sums the set widths of individual characters and spaces on a line, makes the necessary end of line decisions, such as hyphenation and justification, and then outputs a justified tape used to drive the phototypesetter or metal linecasting machine. See hyphenation, justify, linecaster, phototypesetting, set width.

computer managed instruction The use of a computer to assist in the management of a student's progress through a course. The system may be fully integrated with computer assisted learning such that the students' responses are recorded and new units are delivered according to a preset curriculum and satisfactory performance in prerequisite units. The system may also be used in conventional teaching environments with details of student course marks and progress input into the computer and printouts produced for course tutors. See computer assisted learning.

computer micrographics In computing, a technique in which a computer is used to convert data to or from film, or any other appropriate medium, in which the images are too small to be read by the naked eye. See micrographics.

computer networks A computer network is a network for interconnecting computer systems to allow the fast and easy flow of data between the systems and users of the systems. Computer networks have evolved from the developments in data communications and computers. The earliest form of telecommunication was telegraphy in which the data took the form of morse code signals, and in recent years the Telex and Datel services in the UK have experienced considerable rates of growth. The pressure on data communications facilities over the last decade has arisen predominantly from computer based data and such traffic has highlighted a mismatch between the requirements of computer systems and the traditional data communication networks. Computer requirements have also evolved rapidly over the last decade with users demanding on line access to both

local and remote computing facilities, together with the demands for automatic transfer of data between computing systems. The data itself may comprise one or two commands or it may span continents and be transmitted over the networks of several common carriers.

See (a) Telephone network, (b) circuit and packet switching, (c) packet switching operation, (d) standards, (e) future developments.

(a) Telephone network. The telephone network has been designed for voice communication and therefore many of its characteristics are inadequate for data communications. The main, interrelated problem areas are: (i) noise; (ii) baud rate; (iii) analog medium; (iv) response time. The nature of voice communication is such that although a telephone conversation is continuous, the information content is low and so contains a certain amount of redundancy. Consequently the common carrier is able to employ low bandwidth circuits on which it is possible to tolerate a lot of noise - clicks, hum etc. This low bandwidth, of the order of 3KHz, gives rise to the relatively low data rates possible, about 4800 baud. Another constraint with the telephone network is the analog nature of the transmission medium. Computer data is digital and therefore an interface is required, usually a modem, between it and the telephone network. Data transmission is frequently performed as short bursts of activity which means the transmission medium is under used. In addition, the response time may also be unsatisfactory as many exchanges are still based on electromechanical technology and allocating a route through a network may take tens of seconds, a relatively long time for a message lasting perhaps only for milliseconds. The telephone network is, therefore, a poor environment for computer communication which ideally requires a high bandwidth, digital, noise-free circuit. However a modern, all digital network as proposed, for example, by the British Telecom based on System X exchanges will solve directly many of the problems currently experienced.

(b) circuit and packet switching. Two main methods of operating data networks have been proposed, circuit switching and packet switching. Circuit switching is the method of allocating calls currently used on the telephone network. A circuit is found between

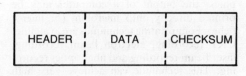

computer networks
Fig 1 A packet of data.

two customers and once allocated it is used exclusively for these customers and the data passes through the network without any further intervention. In packet switching, messages are split into a series of small packets and each packet has a header, a data section and an error checksum (fig. 1). The header contains sufficient control information to allow the packet to be routed independently through the network. The packets are usually of a fixed, short length of the order of 1K bits. This means that they can be transmitted with only a small delay through a network. An important advantage for packet switching is that the packets of various calls may be interleaved on the transmission links thus allowing a high, and therefore efficient, usage of these facilities. This interleaving is a form of time division multiplexing. The checksum on each packet enables error checking to be performed after transmission along a link, and should corruption have occurred, the packet can be retransmitted. A copy of the packet is retained at the sending exchange until successful receipt is signalled by the receiving exchange, see (c) for a more detailed explanation. This error correction scheme, which is sometimes referred to as store and forward, gives rise to an important feature of packet switching which is the ability to connect users operating at dissimilar transmission rates. For example, if a customer receives at a slower rate than the sender is transmitting, the network can temporarily store packets until they can be received. This does imply, however, that there must be packet flow control within the network to prevent log-jams.

(c) packet switching operation. Fig. 2 shows four packet switching exchanges interconnected with duplex links and the description illustrates in a simplified way how packets might be transmitted through the network. A user X, connected to exchange A

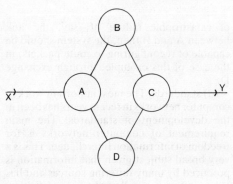

computer networks
Fig 2 Packet switching exchange.

is sending a message to a second user, Y, connected to exchange C. Both users are assumed to be operating in packet mode, implying that the message is split into packets by the sending user's equipment and the receiving apparatus performs message reassembly. Packets are handled one at a time in each exchange and a duplicate is maintained, in a repeat queue, during transmission so that a corrupted packet may be retransmitted.

Suppose X sends a packet X1 from A to exchange B. If X1 is received correctly at B then an acknowledgement control packet is returned to A and will cause the duplicate of X1 to be deleted. At the same time as the acknowledgement is returned, exchange B will be forwarding X1 to C and then to user Y. Now suppose a short burst of noise had corrupted X1 between A and B. Upon receipt at B the checksum would show an error had occurred and the packet would be ignored. Assuming X2 now follows successfully, an acknowledgement will be triggered back to A. At A, when the acknowledgement is received and compared with the repeat queue, it will be shown that no acknowledgement was received for X1 and that therefore this packet must now be retransmitted. This very simple error recovery scheme does not provide protection in all cases. Although X1 and X2 here were consecutive packets of the same message, in reality X2 could have been replaced by an interleaved packet of another message from another user. This description has covered normal operation and short-lived errors; in the event of catastrophic failure of, say, the link between A and B then, the system should be capable of reconfiguring to route packets, in the case of this example, through exchange D.

(d) standards. The most important work in computer networks in recent years has been in the development of standards. The main requirement of computer networks is for freedom of information interchange. This is a very broad subject given that information is produced by many differing sources and has to be used by an equally wide range of entities. The only feasible solution currently is to build communicating systems to an agreed set of standards for common interface working. Much pioneering work has been performed by the CCITT with the X series standards. X25 is one of the most important as it describes the interface between a packet switching network and a terminal capable of communicating in packet streams. However, these standards are still fairly restrictive in scope, they do not define, for example, the protocol for transporting a file between users. The International Standards Organisation (ISO) has proposed a model for interconnecting open systems, the Reference Model of Open Systems Interconnection (OSI model). Open in this context implies 'the mutual recognition and support of the applicable standards'. The model is intended to coordinate the development of standards at all levels of communications and to incorporate and improve existing standards, for example X25.

(e) future developments. From a users' viewpoint, the most important future development will be the widespread acceptance of standards enabling the easy flow of data between any type of system. Developments in transmission techniques, both satellite and cable, will improve technical accessibility to the data and the greater transmission rates, perhaps in the order of 100 million baud, will give a very fast and efficient response. See analog, bandwidth, baud, bit, CCITT, checksum, circuit switching, data communications, Datel, duplex, Hz, ISO, MODEM, morse code, noise, packet switching, Open Systems Interconnection, protocol standards, store and forward, System X, telex, time division multiplexing, X-Series of recommendations of CCITT.

computer output microfilm In micrographics, the output of a computer may be printed directly onto microfilm (or microfiche). Four printing techniques are available: CRT recording, electron beam recording, laser beam recording and fiber optics recording. This technique can achieve very high throughput rates, of the order of 90,000 lines per minute, and microform indexes can be automatically generated by the computer. Compare computer input from microfilm. See CRT recording, electron beam recording, fiber optics recording, laser beam recording.

computer to plate In typesetting, the production of plates from computer stored format without film or other intermediaries.

COMSAT Communications Satellite Corporation.

concatenate In computer programming, the joining of two or more strings into a single string. See string, character string.

conceal In videotex, a display mode during which certain characters are displayed as spaces until the viewer chooses to reveal them. This facility can be used in games, quizzes etc. Compare reveal.

concentrator (1) In telephony, a circuit switching mechanism which connects a number of lines that are not all used simultaneously to a small group of lines for economical transmission. (2) In data communications, a device that buffers incoming data and retransmits it over appropriate output lines.

conceptual schema In databases, the overall logical structure of the database. See schema.

concertina fold See accordion fold.

concurrent programming See multiprogramming.

condenser lens In audiovisual aids, one or more lenses between the projection lamp and slide, or film aperture, to concentrate the light in the aperture area. See aperture.

conditional jump In computer programming, an instruction to jump to another specified instruction if a specific condition exists, e.g. the equality of two computed variables, otherwise to select the next instruction in sequence. Compare unconditional jump.

conditioning In communications, procedures to ensure that transmission impairment on a circuit lie within limits specified in a tariff. It is used on telephone lines leased for data transmission to improve the transmission speed.

cone In recording, a component of certain types of loudspeakers, used as a vibrator. See loudspeaker.

conference call In telephony, a call established among three or more stations so that each of the stations is able to communicate with all others. See dial up teleconferencing. Synonymous with conference connection.

conference connection Synonymous with conference call.

Conference Papers Index (CPI) A database supplied by Cambridge Scientific Abstracts and dealing with science & technology. See on line information retrieval.

congestion In communications, a state arising when the traffic demand exceeds the system capacity.

Congressional Record Abstracts A database supplied by Capitol Services Inc. (CSI) and dealing with government - US Federal. See on line information retrieval.

connect time In computing, the time in which a user of an interactive system is logged on. See log on.

console (1) In audiovisual aids, a control panel for an instructor using an electric learning laboratory, with built in devices for originating, controlling and monitoring student stations. (2) In computing, controlling terminal of a computer system.

constant (1) In mathematics, a value that does not change. (2) In computer programming, a value set in a program at compilation time and not allowed to be altered during the

execution of the program. See compiler, literal.

constant angular velocity In video disk, a disk with one frame reproduced for each revolution giving freeze frame facilities and individual frame addressability, a basic requirement for interactive video disk. Compare constant linear velocity. See freeze frame.

constant linear velocity In video disk, a disk with a constant length for each frame giving longer playing per side, but sacrificing individual frame addressability. Reference to locations on such disks is limited to playing time in minutes and seconds. Compare constant angular velocity. See frame.

constant ratio code Synonymous with M out of N code.

contact In electronics, part of a switch designed to touch a similar contact to permit current to flow.

contact print In photography, a print with direct emulsion to emulsion contact with the film being printed. See emulsion.

content addressable filestore In computing, a disk based associative processor used for storing and accessing large data files. The heads on the multidisk, magnetic disk system read data simultaneously as they scan each cylinder. Various fields of the accessed record can be used as a key, thus providing for very flexible search strategies. See associative processor, cylinder, field, head, key, magnetic disk, record.

content addressable memory See associative storage.

contention (1) In computing and communications, a situation in which two or more devices simultaneously attempt to access a common piece of equipment, e.g. two terminals attempting to access a processing unit. (2) In communications, a method of line control on which terminals request or bid to transmit. If the channel is not available the terminals must wait until it is free.

contention control In data communications,

a control strategy for a local area network in which any node that wishes to transmit does so. If two nodes transmit at the same time a collision occurs and both messages are garbled, the transmitting notes detect the collision and await a random interval before retransmitting the message. See Aloha, carrier sense multiple access-collision detection, Ethernet, local area network.

contention delay   In communications, the time spent waiting for a facility that is occupied by other using devices. See contention.

contiguous   Adjoining.

contiguous graphics   In videotex, the set of graphic characters in which there are no gaps between adjacent cells in the character space. Compare separated graphics.

continuation page   In videotex, a page which cannot be addressed directly by its page number. If a continuation page exists, it is displayed by first retrieving the main page either via menu selection or its page number. The user must then view in sequence the associated continuation pages. See page.

continuity check   In communications, a check made to verify that an information path exists in a channel or channels.

continuous loop   In audiovisual aids, a loop of film or tape made by splicing the ends together for continuous projection or operation.

continuous stationery   In data processing, paper forming one continuous piece, perforated at page intervals and with sprocket holes along the edges. See accordion fold, sprocket feed.

continuous wave   In communications, pertaining to a transmission technique in which a constant carrier wave is turned on and off in patterns to represent the signal, e.g. morse code. See morse code.

contrast   (1) In optics, the ratio between the maximum and minimum intensities of incident light on a subject. (2) In photography, the ratio between the optically most dense and least dense areas of a positive or negative

film. (3) In television, the subjective assessment of the difference in appearance of two parts of a field of view seen simultaneously or successively. (4) In computer graphics, the difference in brightness or colour between a display image and the area in which it is displayed. See crushing.

control block   In computing, an area of storage used by a program to hold control information. See data control block.

control bus   In microcomputers, a bus used to select and enable an area of main storage, and to transmit signals required for regulating the computer operation. Compare address bus, data bus. See bus, main storage.

control character   In computing and communications, a character whose occurrence in a particular context initiates a control action, e.g. carriage return on a printer.

control computer   A special purpose computer that controls a device or process. It receives input signals from device or process transducers, or commands from operators, processes them according to a prestored program and produces signals to device or process activators, e.g. to move a robot arm, provide information for the operator etc. See transducer, robot.

control driven   In computing, pertaining to an architecture, in which instructions are executed as soon as they are selected by the control sequence. Compare data driven, demand driven. See architecture, Von Neumann.

controlled reading device   In audiovisual aids, a device for progressively disclosing or exposing visual information.

controlled vocabulary   In library science, a fixed list of terms used in an indexing language. See indexing language.

controller   In data communications, a device, which may contain a stored program, that directs the transmission of data over a network.

control mode   In data communications, a

necessary state for all terminals on a line to allow time control actions or terminal selection to occur.

control read only memory In computing, a memory in a microprocessor based device that holds one or more programs which are used to schedule or supervise the execution of other programs. See operating system, ROM.

control token In data communications, a bit pattern passed around a local area network for control purposes. Any node, upon receiving the control token, may remove it from the network, send a message and then pass on the control token. Compare daisy chain, message slot. See local area network.

control track In video recording, a track containing timing pulses to facilitate synchronisation of reading head on playback. See tach pulse.

control unit In computing, a part of the central processing unit holding the instruction code of the computer and performing such functions as fetching instructions and operands, decoding instructions, allocating instructions to arithmetic logic units, storing results of ALU operations etc. See arithmetic logic unit, central processing unit, instruction.

conversational mode Synonymous with interactive mode.

conversational remote job entry In computing, pertaining to the input of job control statements and operands from a remote terminal for remote on line control of batch processing. See batch processing, job control language.

converter See code conversion.

conveyor delivery mechanism In a duplicator, a delivery system which transports paper by means of an endless belt.

coordinate graph A visual representation of a relationship between two variable quantities by plotting a series of points according to axes at right angles.

copperplate printing In printing, an intaglio process in which the printing is performed direct from an engraved copper plate. See intaglio.

copy (1) In printing, matter that is to be set in type or reproduced. (2) In computing, the reproduction of source data in an identical form but not necessarily on the same storage medium, e.g. from magnetic disk to magnetic tape. (3) In office equipment, a product of a document copying process.

copyreader In printing, one who assists an editor in preparing copy for printing.

copyright The legal ownership of the duplication rights for a computer program, literacy work, musical composition, photograph, motion film etc. Copyright is usually considered to vest with the author, unless assigned to another party, such as a publisher. With the advent of direct broadcast by satellites, where a TV transmission may be picked up by several countries within the footprint of a satellite, copyright protection will be a major issue. See direct broadcast satellite, footprint.

Copyright Clearance Center A US non profit making organisation offering licensing arrangements for the photocopying of documents.

core In optoelectronics, the central primary light conducting region of an optical fiber. See fiber optics.

coresident In computing, pertaining to the condition in which two or more subroutines are located in main storage at the same time. See subroutine.

coroutine In computer programming, a procedure that can pass control to any other coroutine, suspend itself and continue later. Compare subroutine See procedure.

corporate identity See house style.

corrective maintenance In computing, the activity of detecting, isolating and correcting failures after occurrence. Compare preventive maintenance.

corruption In computing and communications, data that has been changed in an undesired manner either during transmission or in storage, e.g. a corrupt floppy disk. See floppy disk.

COSATI US Committee on Scientific and Technical Information of the Federal Council for Science and Technology. COSATI is composed of federal agency officials with responsibility for operating scientific and technical information systems.

coulomb In electronics, the unit of electric charge, representing the quantity of charge passing in a conductor when a current of one ampere flows for one second. See ampere.

counter In computing, a register for storing a number which is increased or decreased by a fixed amount each time an event occurs. See register.

counting perforator In typesetting, a device that stores character codes, character widths and function codes on paper tape for subsequent processing. By storing character width details the operator is able to receive sufficient information so as to make justification and hyphenation decisions. See hyphenation, justification.

coupler (1) In optoelectronics, a component used to interconnect three or more optical conductors. (2) In printing, a chemical compound that reacts with another compound to form a dye in a document copying machine.

coverage In broadcasting, the population within the service area of a transmitter capable of receiving the programs.

CP/M In computing, Control Program/Microcomputer, a widely used operating system for microcomputers based upon the Z80 microprocessor. Compare MS-DOS, Unix. See MP/M, operating system.

CPM See critical path method.

cps cycles per second. See hertz.

CPU See central processing unit.

CR See carriage return.

crash In computing and communications, a failure in a component or system, during operations, which renders it unavailable for use.

crawl In filming, a device upon which television or film credits are mounted and which makes them appear to crawl up the screen.

CRC See cyclic redundancy check.

critical fusion frequency In computer graphics and filming, the frequency of a flickering stimulus at which the flicker appears to stop and the individual sensations are fused into a continuous, uniform sensation. See flicker, persistence of vision.

critical path method A management technique for control of large scale projects involving analysis and determination of each critical step necessary for project completion. See PERT.

CRJE See conversational remote job entry.

CROM See control read only memory.

cross check A method of validating the results of a calculation by repeating it with an alternative method.

cross compiler In computer programming, a compiler which generates object code for execution on a different computer than that on which it is running. See compiler.

cross fade In recording, a transition in sound or image with the element fading out as a second element fades in.

crossfire Synonymous with cross talk.

cross modulation In communications, an interference between two or more modulated signals, with different carrier frequencies, produced by nonlinearities in the transmission path. See modulation, interference, nonlinear.

cross referenced page In videotex, a page

which can be selected from a page which is not its parent. See parent.

cross section In communications, the signal transmission capacity of a transmission system normally measured in terms of the number of two way voice channels.

cross talk In communications, an unwanted transfer of energy from one circuit to another. Synonymous with crossfire.

CRT See cathode ray tube.

CRTC Canadian Radio Television and Telecommunications Commission.

CRT recording In micrographics, a technique used in the production of computer output microfilm. The image on the face of a cathode ray tube is focussed onto the microfilm. Compare electron beam recording, fiber optics recording. See cathode ray tube.

crushing In television, an unwanted change in the contrast gradient of a picture. See contrast.

cryptoanalysis In data security, the science and study of methods of breaking ciphers. A cipher is breakable if it is possible to determine the plaintext or key from the ciphertext, or to determine the key from plaintext-ciphertext pairs. See cryptographic key, cryptography.

cryptographic algorithm In data security, a set of rules specifying the procedure required to encipher and decipher data. See cipher.

cryptographic control In data security, the use of cryptographic techniques to protect information when transmitted over a link or when stored in a computer. See wire tapping.

cryptographic key In data security, a code used in association with a cryptographic algorithm, for enciphering and deciphering data. See code.

cryptography The science and study of secret writing. A cipher is a secret method of writing, whereby plaintext (or clear text) is transformed into ciphertext. The process of transforming plaintext into ciphertext is called encipherment or encryption; the reverse process of transforming ciphertext into plaintext is called decipherment or decryption. Both encipherment and decipherment are controlled by one or more cryptographic keys (see diagram).

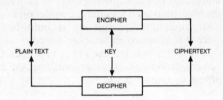

cryptography
Fig 1

Classical cryptography provided secrecy for information sent over channels where eavesdropping and message interception were possible. The sender selected a cipher and encryption key, and either gave it directly to the receiver or else sent it indirectly over a slow but secure channel, typically a trusted courier. Messages and replies were transmitted over the insecure channel in ciphertext (see diagram).

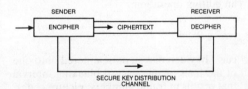

cryptography
Fig 2 Classical information channel.

A cryptographic system is analogous to a resettable combination lock used to secure a safe. The combination is kept secret and can be changed whenever it is suspected of having fallen into the wrong hands. Even though the unauthorized person knows the set of all possible keys or combinations, he may be unable to discover the exact combination in a reasonable expenditure of time and money. The effort to try all possible combinations is a measure of the security of the lock, or cipher.

Modern cryptography protects data transmitted over high-speed links or information stored in computer systems. There are two principal objectives: secrecy (or privacy) to prevent the unauthorized disclosure of data; and authenticity (or integrity), to prevent the unauthorized modification of data. Modern ciphers, such as the Data Encryption Standard, offer a high degree of security and can only be broken by an attacker with knowledge of the key being used. In general, the algorithm used for encryption/decryption with modern cryptosystems is published, since it is assumed an attacker would in any case find this out, but the key is kept secret. See cryptanalysis, cryptographic key, DES, digital signature, RSA.

crystal microphone In recording, a microphone in which the transducer is a piezoelectric crystal. When the crystal is deformed by a sound wave, the small voltage generated is used as an audio signal. See piezoelectric.

CSDC See circuit switched digital circuitry.

CSMA-CD See carrier sense multiple access - collision detection.

CTRL In computing, a key on a computer terminal which, when pressed in conjunction with another key, is used to perform a control or manipulation function, e.g. to terminate an editing operation.

CTS See clear to send.

cue In video disk, a pulse entered onto one of the lines of the vertical blanking interval that results in frame numbers, picture codes, chapter codes, white flags, etc. on the disk. See chapter, frame, vertical blanking interval, white flag.

CUG See closed user group.

CULT In machine translation, Chinese University Language Translator, a human aided machine translation system for English-Chinese and Chinese-English text developed by the Chinese University of Hong Kong. The system is interactive with a specially designed Chinese keyboard. See human aided machine translation.

cumulative index In library science, an index which comprises the combination of a number of separate indexes. See index.

current In electronics, an electric current flows through a conductor when there is an overall movement of electrons or other charge carrying elements through it. See electron.

cursor In computing, a short line or character on a VDU indicating where the next character is to be typed.

cursor control In computing, a facility in some VDUs enabling the cursor to be moved around the screen under keyboard control. See cursor, keyboard.

cursor home In computing, the operation of moving the cursor to the top left hand corner of the screen.

curvature of field In optics, an aberration in which the focal point of a lens image falls on a curved rather than a flat plane. See aberration.

customer engineering Pertaining to the department of a manufacturer which is responsible for field maintenance and repair of installed equipment.

cut and paste In word processing, the facility to delete a section of text and relocate it elsewhere, in one or more places, of the stored document.

cut in notes In printing, notes set into the text at the outer edge of a paragraph with white space forming three sides of a square around them.

cutoff In communications, the point of degradation at which a signal becomes unusable because of attenuation or distortion. See attenuation, distortion.

cutoff frequency In electronics, the upper or lower frequency limits of the useful frequency band of a filter. See filter.

CW See continuous wave.

CWP See communicating word processing.

cyan In optics, the colour that is the complement of red, (i.e. blue-green). See complementary colours.

cyberamics The study of computer controlled robots.

cybernetics The technology concerned with the study of control and information flows in artificial and natural systems.

cycle In computing, the basic time unit of a central processing unit. See central processing unit.

cycle stealing In computing, a technique where a peripheral uses one or more processor cycles to access main storage, locking out the processor from main storage for that period. Compare direct memory access.

cycle time In computing, the time required for one cycle, usually between 500 nanoseconds and one microsecond. See microsecond, nanosecond.

cyclic code See gray code.

cyclic redundancy check In data communications and computing, a method for detecting errors in the transmission or transfer of data using a polynomial code and a cyclic check character. See polynomial code.

Cyclops In audio visual aids, a novel system developed by the Open University in which a stereo audio cassette tape stores both graphical and audio information. One track of the tape holds an audio commentary and the other contains digital information which is fed into a microprocessor system and produces a graphical display on a TV set. The play back units may also be equipped with light pens to provide electronic blackboard facilities. See electronic blackboard, light pen.

cylinder In computing, the set of tracks of magnetic disks, on a unit with multiple read write heads that can be read without mechanical movements of the heads. See magnetic disk.

cylinder machine In printing, a machine bed from which impressions are made by a cylinder. Compare platen press. See cylinder.

cyphertext See encipher.

Cyrillic alphabet The Russian alphabet, derived from Greek and incorporating characters expressing Slavic sounds.

D

DAA See data access arrangement.

DAC See digital to analog converter.

DAD In recording, Digital Audio Disk, a system in which sound signals are converted to a train of binary digits and recorded on an optical disk. The disk is scanned by a laser beam, thus ensuring that it is not subject to mechanical wear. Synonymous with compact disk, DAD.

dagger In printing, a type character used as a second order of reference marks in footnotes, sometimes called an obelisk or long cross. See reference mark.

daisy chain (1) In computing, a method by which signals are propagated along a bus, allowing the CPU interrupt control signal to pass along the chain. The first device in the chain, next to the CPU, has the highest priority. (2) In data communications, a technique in a local area network to pass permission for a node to transmit; dedicated wires are used to pass control information from one node to the next. Compare control token, message slot. See bus, interrupt, local area network.

daisy wheel In computing, a print element used in conjunction with a daisy wheel character printer. This is a removable flat disk with spokes radiating out on stalks from a central hub, the entire print 'wheel' resembling a daisy. The daisy wheel is available in a variety of type styles and may be 10, 12 or 15 pitch or proportionally spaced. See pitch, proportional spacing.

DAMA See demand assigned multiple access.

dark current In optoelectronics, the current that flows in a photodetector when there is no radiant energy or light flux incident upon its sensitive surface. See photocell.

dark trace tube In computer graphics, a CRT in which the electron beam causes the phosphor surface of the tube to darken rather than to brighten. See CRT.

DASD In computing, Direct Access Storage Device. See direct access storage.

data (1) In computing, information which is to be input, processed in some way and output by the computer. There is usually no restriction on the meaning associated with the data when it is processed by a computer but it must be in a format that the computer can interpret. This is usually the responsibility of the programmer who has to define whether the data is numeric or alphanumeric and its method of coding, e.g. binary, octal, etc. (2) A representation of facts, concepts, or instructions in a formalized manner in order that it may be communicated, interpreted, or processed by human or automatic means.

data above voice In data communication, a system for carrying digital data on a portion of the microwave radio spectrum above the frequency used for voice transmission. Compare data in voice, data under voice.

data access arrangement In communications, a unit containing an isolation transformer, for interconnecting user equipment to a telephone network. It is designed to prevent harmful voltages or signals entering the network.

data access management See MODEM.

data acquisition In computing, the process of identifying, isolating and gathering source data to be centrally processed. See data capture.

data aggregate In databases, a CODASYL term for a named collection of data items within a record. See CODASYL.

databank Synonymous with database.

database (1) A collection of interrelated data stored so that it may be accessed by authorized users with simple user friendly dialogs. The database structure is independent of the programs that use the data and a common controlled approach is employed in adding, deleting or modifying the data contained therein. (2) In CODASYL terms a database consists of all record occurrences, set occurrences and areas which are controlled by a specific schema. An installation with multiple databases must have a separate schema for each database. The contents of different databases are assumed to be disjoint. See record, set, area, CODASYL, schema.

database administrator A person who is responsible for a database system, particularly for defining the rules by which data is accessed and stored. See database.

database machine In computing, a special combination of hardware and software specifically designed to speed up database operations. Most current developments are concerned with either enhancing the technology of magnetic disk storage mechanisms or finding suitable roles for other memory technologies, e.g. bubble memory. See bubble memory, magnetic disk.

database management system In computing, a set of programs which facilitates the creation and maintenance of a database and the execution of programs using the database. See database, data independence.

Data Base Task Group In databases, the CODASYL committee responsible for producing their database facilities and associated languages, DDL and DML. See CODASYL, DDL, DML.

data bus (1) In computing, a bus system which interconnects the CPU, memory and all the peripheral input output devices of a computer system for the purpose of exchanging data. (2) In optoelectronics, an optical waveguide used as a common trunk line to which a number of terminals can be interconnected using optical couplers. Compare address bus, control bus. See bus, coupler, microcomputer.

data bus coupler In optoelectronics, a component that interconnects a number of optical waveguides and provides an inherently bidirectional system by mixing and splitting all signals in it. See data bus.

data capture In computing, the act of obtaining data by means of peripheral devices, e.g. a point of sale terminal. See point of sale terminal.

data carrier In computing, any medium such as magnetic tape or disk used for carrying data.

data carrier detect In data communications, an interface signal from a modem to a DTE indicating that a carrier of adequate quality is being received. See carrier, DTE.

data cell In computing, the smallest unit of data which cannot be further subdivided, e.g. a bit. See bit.

data circuit In data transmission, a circuit which enables two way communication to be carried out between any two data terminating devices such as teleprinters, computers, visual display units, etc.

data circuit terminating equipment In data communications, a piece of equipment located at either end of a data circuit which provides all the functions needed to establish, maintain and terminate a connection. It also carries out the signal conversion and coding between the data terminal equipment and the telephone line. Compare data terminal equipment. See MODEM.

data collection In computing, an activity in which data from several locations is accumulated at one place prior to processing.

data collection platform In satellite communications, a small, unattended earth station used to automatically transmit data to a central point via a satellite. See earth station.

data communications The transmission of data between person and program, or program to program, between geographically separated locations. Data communications may take place between workstations and computers within a limited geographic region such as an office building, or college campus, in which case the network is classified as a local area network. If the various install-ations are located at different cities con-nected by public telephone networks, high speed data communication lines or satellites, then the network is classified as long haul. Local area networks are normally owned and operated by a single organization whereas long haul networks will comprise hosts, belonging to one or more organizations and a communication system operated by a common carrier. A typical long haul network is illustrated in the diagram.

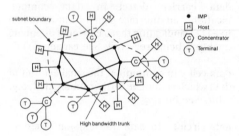

data communications
Fig 1 A typical point to point long haul network.

The IMP's (interface network processors) are normally minicomputers and they provide an interface between the host computers and the network. The IMP's allow for store and for-ward facilities so that messages may be routed from one IMP to another, temporarily stored and then rerouted towards their desti-nations.

At the lowest level of operation the net-work may be considered as simply passing pulses, representing bits, from one location to another. In long haul networks the communication can be organized on a circuit or packet switching basis. In circuit switching a connection is established between sender and receiver which is only released when one party terminates the call, i.e. telephone con-nections. In packet switching, on the other hand, the user establishes a connection between his terminal or host, and the nearest IMP. Whenever data is to be transmitted it is sent as a series of packets, typically 10-1000 bytes long. Packets are routed from IMP to IMP, within the communication network,

until they reach the IMP that services the destination host.

In local networks the minicomputer IMP's are replaced by interface cards in the consti-tuent workstations or microcomputers. The networks are organized either on a bus or ring basis as shown in the diagram.

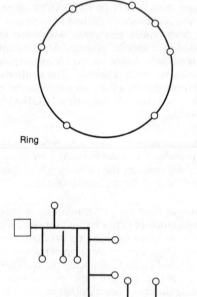

data communications
Fig 2 Ring and bus networks.

The Ethernet network, properly a trademark of the Xerox Corporation, is now commonly used as a generic term for a linear or tree shaped network using CSMA-CD (Carrier Sense Multiple Access-Collision Detection) mode. When a host wishes to send it first listens to check if the bus is free, if it is not then it awaits the termination of the current transmission before putting its packet onto the cable. Of course it is possible for two hosts to initiate a packet transmission at the same time causing a collision to occur. This condition is detected by the host monitoring to the cable and checking the results with the data transmitted. If a collision is detected then the current transmission is aborted and a noise burst is broadcast to inform all units of the situation. The host then awaits a random interval before retransmission. Ring networks operate on a different principle and the whole ring is regarded as a massive circular shift register. After each shift the host interface can read or write the bit just shifted into it.

The consideration of the physical transfer of bits around the network does not allow for the problems which can arise from transmission errors or the possibility that a receiver is unable to accept data as fast as the sender can transmit. This aspect of data communications is handled by agreed protocols governing the exchange of signals, between transmitters and receivers, concerning the states of data transmission. A typical protocol is HDLC (High Level Data Link Control). The raw data must first be organised into groups, or frames, so that each individual frame can be checked and acknowledged. The frames must, of course, be delimited and three common techniques are character count, character stuffing and bit stuffing. With character count a fixed format frame header indicates the number of characters in a frame. In theory the receiver simply counts the incoming characters and hence detects the end of the frame. However, this technique is extremely sensitive to transmission errors in the count field and lost characters can wreck frame synchronization. Character stuffing uses a special 'end of frame' character to terminate frames but this forces a specific character code into the protocol. Bit stuffing is used by modern protocols for long haul networks; in this case frames are delimited by the bit pattern 0 111 111 0, if 5 consecutive ones appear in the data stream a zero is stuffed into the bit stream and subsequently removed by the receiver. Local area networks can use any of the above methods but can also simply detect the end of a frame by the absence of a signal on the cable. Frame headers will also contain some form of checksum to provide for the detection, but not correction, of transmission errors. With the increased use of satellite communication with their long propagation times the use of error correction codes (e.g. Hamming codes) becomes increasingly economic but conventional local and long haul networks simply call for the retransmission of corrupted frames.

When two people communicate over a telephone they automatically employ a number of informal conventions to ensure that meaningful conversation takes place; the speaker will listen for comments of affirmation and if the listener is silent for an extended period then the speaker will enquire 'if he is still there'. Similar protocols are required between the sender and receiver in a communication network and the design of standardized effective protocols is an essential element of a successful system. At the simplest level there is the stop-and-wait protocol. In this case host A sends a frame to B and awaits specific permission from B to send the next one. If host A puts a sequence number on the frame header, together with some error detection code, then on receipt of a positive acknowledgment from B it forwards the next frame; on receipt of a negative acknowledgment, indicating errors detected by B, the frame is retransmitted by A. Unfortunately such simple protocols can easily fail and as additional features are built into the protocol to overcome problems closer investigation reveals additional sources of difficulty so that the design of effective protocols is a task of some complexity. In the case that host A awaits receipt of positive, or negative, acknowledgment from B, before forwarding another frame, a complete deadlock arises if either the message, or acknowledgment, frame is lost in transmission. To overcome this problem host A can be required to retransmit a frame if no acknowledgment is received after a specified period. However, if a satellite transmission is employed, then the minimum propagation delay for message and acknowledgment frame is 540 milliseconds. In this case host A must await at least this period of time before it can assume that a frame is lost. Thus a 1000 bit frame sent over a 1 megabit per second channel takes only 1 millisecond but frames can only be sent every 540 milliseconds if the simple stop and wait protocol is employed. The transmission rate can be improved by the use of sliding window protocols in which the sender is allowed to have multiple unacknowledged frames outstanding simultaneously. If each frame is given a unique sequence number then host A could send out frames at high speed and retransmit individual frames if either negative acknowledgments are received or if no acknowledgment for a particular sequence number arrives in a given time interval. However, this technique produces a problem because the sequence numbers will become very large, thus necessitating an excessive overhead in the size of the frame header. The frame sequence numbers can simply be limited to a fixed size and thereafter repeat themselves. The protocols then need to be designed with care to ensure that losses in message, or acknowledgment frames, do not lead to confusion between frames with identical sequence numbers.

The HDLC (High Level Data Link Control) protocol uses bit stuffing to delimit frames and a checksum field for error detection. There are three types of frame – information, supervisory and unnumbered. The information frames from A to B contain data but also indicate the sequence number of the current frame and an indication of the frames correctly received from B to A. Attaching an acknowledgment field to an outgoing data frame is known as piggybacking. Supervisory frames are used to send acknowledgments when no information frames are transmitted and for other control purposes, e.g. negative acknowledgment, receiver temporarily not ready. Unnumbered frames are employed for a variety of control purposes.

The protocols described so far relate to point to point transmissions. Radio or satellite data communication networks, and some local area networks, operate in a broadcast mode, i.e. every host receives every message transmitted. The broadcast mode can lead to collisions when two hosts are transmitting simultaneously and protocols are required to enable recovery and successful retransmission following such collisions.

In the Cambridge Ring network the 10 megabit per second ring contains several small slots around it, each slot consisting of 16 bits of data, an 8 bit source address, an 8 bit destination address, a bit indicating whether the slot is empty or full and a number of control bits. A host transmits by awaiting a free slot and filling it up, the corresponding destination accepts the data and inserts acknowledgment information in the control bits which are subsequently read by the transmitting host.

A long haul network provides for a variety of paths from a transmitting to a receiving host and inevitably some of these paths will be subject to congestion whilst others may be relatively idle. Routing decisions must be taken to pass a packet onto the appropriate output lines of an IMP and such routing decisions should also aim to minimise link congestion. The network can either provide a datagram or a virtual circuit service. In the first case each packet carries a full destination address and is treated in a manner unrelated to any other packet, thus there is no guarantee that packets will be delivered in the same sequence that they were transmitted. In the case of a virtual circuit service a setup packet chooses a route for subsequent traffic and initializes all IMP's along the route accordingly. The simplest routing technique is static or directory routing in which each IMP has a table, indexed by destination, stating which outgoing line is to be used. This static technique makes no attempt to respond to network conditions and can therefore lead to unnecessary congestion. Attempts to provide a more flexible approach, with monitoring of traffic and centralized routing decisions, are, however, fraught with problems. Unlike congestion problems of rail or road traffic the information about traffic conditions flows at the same speed as the packets themselves and difficulties arise because the information about congestion is often out of date when it is received. Hot potato routing simply assigns a packet to the output line with the shortest transmission queue until it, hopefully, reaches the IMP immediately serving the destination host.

The X25 protocol is a CCITT recommendation which relates to the interface between a host computer and a packet switching network. The interface is defined in three layers; the first deals with the circuit interface between DTE and DCE, the second with the frames in which packets are sent whilst layer 3 is concerned with the packet level interface. To set up a virtual circuit a CALL REQUEST packet is sent into the network. This packet contains the addresses of the source and destination host, a number selected by the host to designate the virtual circuit details of facilities requested by the host and optional user data. The called host accepts or rejects the set up request by sending back a control packet with appropriate bits in one of the specified fields. When the virtual circuit has been established full duplex operation between the hosts is permitted and data packets are transmitted with facilities, similar to HDLC, for the acknowledgement of error free packages. The call is terminated by a CLEAR REQUEST packet sent by either host and the return of corresponding CLEAR CONFIRMATION packet. See bit, bit stuffing, Cambridge Ring, checksum, circuit switching, common carrier, computer networks, CSMA-CD, datagram, DCE, DTE, Ethernet, frame, full duplex, hamming code, HDLC, host computer, hot potato routing, IMP, local area network, long haul network, Open Systems Interconnection, packet switching, piggybacking, point to point, protocol, ring, satellite, sliding window protocol, stop and wait protocol, store and forward, virtual circuit, X-Series of recommendations of CCITT.

data compaction In computing, any method for encoding data to reduce the amount of storage space required in a computer system. See data compression.

data compression In computing, a technique that saves storage space by eliminating gaps, empty fields, redundancies, or unnecessary data to shorten the length of records or blocks. See null suppression.

data connection In data communications, the interconnection of a number of circuits designed to carry data signals. Special switching equipment is required so that data may be transmitted between data terminal equipment. See data terminal equipment, switching.

data control block In computing, a control block used for input output operations. See control block, input output.

data corruption In computing, a deliberate or accidental violation of data integrity. See data integrity.

data coupler In data communications, a device which enables the connection of customer provided modems to the telephone network. It limits the power applied to the line and provides network control and signalling functions. See MODEM.

data description language In databases, the language for describing the data. Such lan-

guages will provide very detailed definitions of the structures and relationship of the data. In some cases the language is only concerned with the logical structure of the database, in others it is also concerned with descriptions relating to the manner that the data is organized on physical storage devices.

data dictionary In databases, a catalog giving details of the names and structures of data types.

data diddling In data security, the changing of stored data values for illegal purposes.

data division In computer programming, a section of a COBOL program that contains full information on the nature and characteristics of the data to be processed. See COBOL.

data driven In computing, pertaining to a new computer architecture in which instructions wait until the necessary data becomes available, whereupon they are obeyed. Compare control driven, demand driven, Von Neumann. See architecture, instruction.

data element Synonymous with data item.

data encryption standard In data security, a method of data encryption formulated by the US Bureau of Standards in which the encrypting algorithm is standard but the key is restricted. Semiconductor chips, which work to this standard, are available. See encryption.

data entry In computing, the method of entering data into a computer system for processing. The equipment used can include a card reader, badge reader or keyboard. See card reader, badge reader, visual display unit.

dataflow See data driven.

datagram In packet switching, a self contained packet that contains sufficient routing information to enable it to reach its required destination. See packet.

datagram service In packet switching, a service in which packets from a source, each of which contain the destination address, are entered into the network and are delivered to the destination in an order which may be independent of their order of entry. Compare virtual call service. See datagram.

data independence   In databases, pertaining to the structure of data that removes the close coupling with user programs, so that the logical or physical structure of the database may be changed without affecting the application programmer's view of the data. See logical data independence, physical data independence.

data input voice answerback   In data communications, a system in which a user sends input to a computer using a terminal, e.g. a touchtone telephone, and receives a voice answerback from the computer which may be either actual recorded or synthesized human voice. See speech synthesis, touchtone.

data integrity   In computing, the preservation, against loss or corruption, of computer programs or data for their intended purpose.

data in voice   In data communications, the type of transmission in which digital data displaces voice circuits in a microwave channel. Compare data under voice, data above voice.

data item   In databases, the smallest unit of data that has meaning, e.g. an employee's name in a personnel record. Synonymous with data element, field.

dataline   In teletext, one of the lines of the television field blanking interval used to carry information for the teletext character row. A dataline is identified by the clock-run in sequence followed by a framing code at the appropriate time on a line in the field interval. See clock run in, field blanking, framing code.

data link control   See protocol.

data link   In data communications, (1) a physical means of connecting two locations, e.g. a telephone wire, (2) the physical medium of transmission, the protocol and the associated devices and programs that together enables data to be transferred from a data source to a data sink. See data source, data sink.

data link control standard   In data communications, a set of conventions for sending and receiving data to and from a data network.

data link layer   In data communications, a layer in the ISO Open Systems Interconnections model. The function of this layer is to convert an unreliable transmission channel into a reliable one for use by the layer above it, i.e. the network layer. The raw data bit stream is organized into frames each containing a checksum for detecting errors. Compare application layer, network layer, physical layer, presentation layer, session layer, transport layer. See bit stream, checksum, frame, Open Systems Interconnection.

data management   In databases, pertaining to the organization and performance of functions that provide for the creation of stored data, access to it, regulation of input output devices and the enforcement of data storage conventions.

data manipulation language   In databases, a language used by a programmer to manipulate the transfer of data between the database and the application program. It is normally hosted by another language to provide a framework for it and the necessary routines to handle the data.

data name   In computing, a character or group of characters used to identify an item of data. For example, the constant PI can be used to refer to the number 3·14159.

data origination   In computing, the translation of information from its original form into machine readable form or directly into electrical signals.

Datapac network   The packet switched data network provided by the Computer Communications Group of the Trans Canada Telephone System. See packet switching.

dataplex   In data communications, a generic term used in the UK for services which involve multiplexing. See multiplexing.

data pointer In computing, a special purpose register which stores the address of the next byte or word of data to be fetched from memory. See register.

data preparation In data processing, the operation of transferring information in written form into a machine readable form.

data processing The systematic performance of operations on data to achieve a desired objective. These operations can include the handling, merging, sorting and computing of data. Compare word processing.

Data Processing Management Association A professional data processing organization whose main objective is the development and promotion of business methods and education in data processing and data processing management.

data protection In computing, the problems arising from the use of computers to store and correlate personal information on private citizens has been the subject of a number of UK and European Committees. This matter was considered by the Younger Committee (1972), two White Papers (1975), Lindop Committee (1976), Council of Europe Convention, OECD guidelines and a 1982 White Paper. The Data Protection bill issued in June 1983 is based on eight Data Protection principles broadly in line with the recommendations of the Council of Europe Convention for the Protection of Individuals with regard to the automatic processing of personal data. The eight principles are:

(a) The information to be contained in personal data shall be obtained, and personal data shall be processed, fairly and lawfully.

(b) Personal data shall be held only for one or more specified and lawful purposes.

(c) Personal data held for any purpose or purposes shall not be used or disclosed in any manner incompatible with that purpose or those purposes.

(d) Personal data held for any purpose or purposes shall be adequate, relevant and not excessive in relation to that purpose or those purposes.

(e) Personal data shall be accurate and, where necessary, kept up to date.

(f) Personal data held for any purpose or purposes shall not be kept for longer than is necessary for that purpose or those purposes.

(g) A data subject shall be entitled:

(i) to access at reasonable intervals and without undue delay or expense to personal data of which he is the subject; and (ii) where appropriate, to have such data corrected or erased.

(h) Appropriate security measures shall be taken against unauthorised access to, or alteration, disclosure or destruction of personal data and against accidental loss or destruction of personal data.

In addition, the Act establishes a new office of Data Registrar, a national position, and a Data Protection Tribunal. It will be the responsibility of the Registrar to set up and maintain a register of data users and persons carrying on computer bureaux. The Tribunal will hear appeals on behalf of users against decisions of or actions by the Registrar. The Act requires that all users of automated personal data must register their systems with the Registrar and comply with the principles except in specified exempted categories, which will include, for example, national security. It will be an offence to process or exchange automated personal data:

(a) while not being registered as a user (b) while being prevented by order of the Registrar from so doing (c) for purposes or exchanges which have not been registered.

The person who is the subject of information contained in a computer file is given the right to check that information, to receive a copy of the record and to take actions against loss where data is inaccurate or has been misused. See Lindop Committee, privacy, Younger Committee.

data reduction In computing, the process of transforming raw data into a useful simplified form. This often involves such operations as adjusting, scaling, smoothing, compacting, and editing of data.

data retrieval See information retrieval.

data security The science and study of methods of protecting data in computer and communications systems against unauthorized disclosure, transfer, modifications or destruction whether accidental or intentional. See access control, cryptographic control, cryptography, inference control.

data set   (1) In databases, a named collection of data items, bearing a logical relation to each other and ordered in a prescribed manner, it may also contain data for accessing the data, e.g. indices. (2) In data communications, a modem. Synonymous with MODEM.

data set ready   In data communications, a signal from a modem to a DTE which indicates that the modem is ready to operate. See DTE, MODEM.

data signalling rate   In data communications, the aggregate rate at which binary digits are transmitted over a circuit, expressed in bits per second. See bit.

data sink   In data communications, that part of a data terminal device that receives data. Compare source. See sink.

data source   In data communications, that part of a data terminal device that inputs data into a link. Compare data sink. See source.

Data-Star   In databases, an information retrieval service operated by Information Industries Ltd (UK). See on line information retrieval.

data station   In data communications, the assembly of equipment which includes the data terminal equipment and data circuit terminating equipment. See data circuit terminating equipment, data terminal equipment.

Datastream   A database supplied by Datastream International Ltd and dealing with corporate accounts (UK and US), international exchange rates, fiinancial futures, commodities, fiancial news, fixed interest stocks and portfolio investments. See on line information retrieval.

data stream   In data communications, a continuous stream of serial data being transmitted in character or binary digit form through a channel.

data structure   In computing, a system of relationships between items of data. Well designed high level languages permit the programmer to define and manipulate appropriate data structures which greatly reduce the complexity of programs. See stack, list, array, queue.

data switching exchange   In data communications, equipment installed at a single location used to switch data traffic. Compare packet switching. See line switching, message switching.

data terminal equipment   In data communications, any piece of equipment at which a communication path begins or ends, e.g. a VDU or teletype. Compare data circuit terminating equipment.

data transactions   Synonymous with data processing.

data transmission   The transmission of data from one place for reception elsewhere.

data transparency   In data communications, a technique whereby any pattern of bits, including those normally reserved for control purposes, may be transmitted as a block.

data transport system   See wide area network.

data under voice   In data communications, a transmission system which carries digital data on a portion of the microwave radio spectrum below the frequency used for voice transmission. Compare data above voice, data in voice.

data validation   In data processing, the act of checking that data fits certain defined criteria.

data word   In computer programming, an item of data stored as a single word. See word.

data word size   In computing, the length of a data word, in bits, that a particular CPU is designed to handle. See CPU, data word.

Datel   In data communications, a generic name for British Telecom data transmission services other than dedicated data networks. See PSS.

DAV   See data above voice.

db See decibel.

DBA See database administrator.

DBMS See database management system.

D & B-Principal International Businesses Formerly Principal International Businesses Directory File, a database supplied by Dun & Bradstreet International Ltd and dealing with corporations; corporations - finance; directories. See on line information retrieval.

DBS See direct broadcast satellite.

DBTG See Data Base Task Group.

DC See direct current.

DCD See data carrier detect.

DCE See data circuit terminating equipment.

DC signalling In communications, the use of direct current pulses at signalling speeds below 150 baud over a wired circuit, e.g. telegraphic communication. See baud, telegraphy.

DDC See Dewey Decimal Classification.

DDD See direct distance dialing.

DDL See data description language.

dead In acoustics, an enclosed space in which reverberation is reduced to a very low level.

dead keys In an electric typewriter, keys which do not normally advance to the next character position when struck, e.g. the shift key.

deadlock In computing, an error condition in which processing cannot continue because each of two elements of the process is waiting for an action from the other. Synonymous with deadly embrace.

deadly embrace Synonymous with deadlock.

dead matter In printing, set type no longer intended for use.

dead spot In audio recording, a point in space where sound waves originating from a common source cancel one another because of a 180 degree phase difference. See out of phase.

de-archive In word processing, the process of retrieving stored text held on a disk or diskette and placing the text on the system disk or diskette.

debounce In electronic circuits, the prevention of spurious signals arising from mechanical bounce of electrical contacts.

debug In computing, the detection, isolation and correction of a mistake in a computer program or the computer system itself. See bug. Synonymous with trouble shoot.

debugging aids In computing, special purpose routines that are useful in debugging programs. These routines include the ability to trace the steps executed by a program as well as listing the contents of the computer store once the program has finished running. See debug.

DEC Digital Electronic Corporation.

decade A group, set or series of ten objects or events.

decade counter In electronics, a four bit binary counter which has been modified to count from 0 to 9 and then reset to 0. Normally, a four bit binary counter would increment up to 1111 (decimal 15) before returning to 0. See bit.

decentralized computer network In data communications, a computer network where some of the functions that control the network are distributed over several network nodes. See node.

decibel In electronics and communications, one tenth of a bel, a measure of signal strength relative to a given reference level. A decibel is ten times the common logarithm (base 10) of that ratio. See bel, logarithm.

decibel meter   An instrument for measuring electric power level in decibels above or below an arbitrary reference level. One application is for the measurement of sound intensity. See decibel.

decimal tab   See automatic decimal tab.

decimonic ringing   In communications, a method of party line selective ringing using frequencies 20, 30, 40, 50 and 60 Hz. See party line, selective ringing, Hz.

decision table   A table listing all the contingencies to be considered in the analysis of a system, together with the corresponding actions that have to be taken. Decision tables represent a very concise method of describing a system and are often used in computing applications.

decision tree   In computing, a set of rules in the form of a tree, at each node the rule is examined and a decision is correspondingly made to take a particular branch which leads either to the next rule to be examined or a leaf denoting the end result. See expert systems, leaf, tree structure.

deckle edge   In printing, the ragged edge of handmade paper, sometimes simulated on machine made paper.

declaration   In computer programming, a statement in a language which defines the attributes of data used in the program.

decode   To translate or determine the meaning of coded information. Compare encode.

decoder   (1) In television, the receiver circuitry, between the signal detector and the screen, which decodes the broadcast signals. (2) In computing, a logic device designed to convert data from one number system to another, e.g. from binary to decimal. (3) In videotex, a device used to decode videotex signals and to display them on a TV screen.

decollator   In data processing, a forms handling device for separating out the folds of a continuous form into singles.

decrement   The numerical quantity by which a variable is decreased, e.g. the numerical contents of a counter or store in a computer program.

dedicated   A term indicating equipment reserved for one user or type of application. For example, a dedicated word processor may be reserved for the use of specific individuals or types of word processing.

dedicated access   In data communications, a permanent connection between a terminal and a service network or computer.

dedicated channel   In data communications, a circuit or channel that has been reserved or committed for a specific use or application, e.g. for emergency purposes.

deep etched plate   In printing, a lithographic plate made from a photographic positive in which the image is slightly recessed below the surface of the plate, allowing a thicker film of ink to be carried and permitting longer print runs. See lithography, print run.

default   In computing, pertaining to the choice selected by the computer in the absence of specific instructions by the user, e.g. in a write operation the user may specify one of several devices that is to receive the data, if no device is indicated then the computer sends the information to its default device, usually the VDU screen.

default format statement   In word processing, a facility which is automatically invoked whenever the operator fails to specify some or all of the details relating to the layout and design of the printed work. See format, default.

defect skipping   In magnetic disk recording, a technique in which magnetic material defects are identified during the manufacturing stage and their size and location are written on a defect map track on the disk. See track.

definition   In visual reproduction, a measure of perceivable detail.

deflection yoke   In television, an assembly of one or more coils, whose magnetic field deflects an electron beam and hence moves the spot to another point on the screen. See cathode ray tube.

defocus In filming, to cause the action to become out of focus during a shot by focusing the lens to a close point and reducing the depth of field. See depth of field.

degausser In magnetic tape recording, a device used to erase information on magnetic tapes and films or to demagnetize magnetic recording heads.

degaussing pencil In audio recording, an electromagnetic device for delicate sound track editing.

degradation (1) In data communications, a deterioration in the characteristics of a signal for whatever reason. (2) In photography, any loss of image quality caused by duplication.

DEL See delete character.

delay distortion In data communications, a distortion caused by different propagation speeds of electric signals in a transmission medium due to their difference in frequency. This type of distortion does not affect voice but can have a serious effect on some data transmission.

delay equalizer In communications, a corrective network used to render the phase delay, or the rate of change of phase shift with frequency, of a system, substantially constant over the desired frequency range. See phase delay.

delay flip flop See flip flop.

delay line In electronics, a device which causes a time delay in the transmission of a pulse.

delay vector In packet switching, a list of the estimated transit times for a packet from one node to every other node in the network. Used in adaptive routing systems. See adaptive routing.

delete In word processing, a function that enables portions of text held in storage to be deleted.

delete character In computing, a control character used to delete an erroneous or unwanted character, for example a character wrongly punched on a paper tape, or transmitted down a communications circuit.

delimiter In computing, a specified character used to denote the end of a field. See field.

delta modulation In data communications, a form of differential PCM in which only 1 bit for each sample is used. See differential PCM.

delta routing In packet switching, a method of routing in which a central routing controller receives information from nodes and issues routing instructions, but leaves a degree of discretion to individual nodes. See node.

demagnetize The elimination of unwanted magnetic fields, especially in audio or video tape recording heads. See degausser.

demand assigned multiple access In satellite communications, the capability of a satellite to allocate circuits to users only at those times when they are actually required for traffic.

demand driven In computing, pertaining to a computer architecture in which instructions are only selected when the value they produce is required by another, already selected, instruction. Compare control driven, data driven, Von Neumann. See architecture.

demand multiplexing In data communications, a form of TDM in which time slots are allocated according to demand. See TDM.

demand staging In databases, a technique in which blocks of data are moved from a storage device to one with a shorter access time when they are requested by a program. Compare anticipatory staging.

demarcation strip In data communications, a terminal board which acts as a physical interface between a business machine and the common carrier. See common carrier. Synonymous with barrier box.

democratic network In data communications, a synchronized network in which no one clock has priority over any other. Compare hierarchical network.

demodulation In communications, the process by which an original modulating signal is recovered from a modulated wave. Demodulation techniques are used in both radio and television receivers and in data communications equipment. Compare modulation.

demodulator In communications, (1) a device which performs the function of demodulation in a radio or television receiver, (2) a device which performs the function of demodulation on a data transmission circuit. It is usually found in conjunction with the device performing the modulation, together forming a modem. See modulation, MODEM.

demon In computer programming, a suspended process that waits for a certain kind of event to occur, it is then automatically actuated, performs its job and either terminates or suspends itself in wait for the next event. Used in artificial intelligence applications. See artificial intelligence, coroutine.

demultiplexing In data communications, the dividing of one or more information streams into a larger number of streams. Compare multiplexing.

denial In communications, a condition that occurs in a network when no circuits are available and a busy tone is returned to the calling party. Synonymous with blocking.

denial of service In data security, the loss or delay of messages through active wire tapping, e.g. overloading the system with false messages having acceptable protocols. See wire tapping.

dense index In databases, an index that contains an entry for every record to be searched. Compare nondense index. See index, record.

densitometer In photography, a device used for measuring the density of photographic images.

density (1) In photography, a quantitative measure of the light-stopping characteristics of developed film. The density of a transparent surface is the logarithm of the ratio between the amount of incident light and the amount of light transmitted. (2) In printing, the blackness or darkness of a typed, printed or carbon image. Density control is determined by the nature of the hammer or type impact; on a typewriter it is often called 'impression control'. See opacity.

depth indexing In library science, indexing as fully as possible by making specific entries for all relevant concepts mentioned in the text. See exhaustivity.

depth of field In photography, the distance range before a camera in which objects are considered to be in sharp focus. The depth of field increases with smaller lens apertures. Compare depth of focus.

depth of focus In photography, the range of positions of a film in relation to the camera lens in which an acceptably sharp focus can be obtained. Compare depth of field.

derived indexing In library science, a method of indexing in which the indexing information is derived solely from the document. A method well suited to the derivation of indexes by computer processing. Compare assigned indexing. See indexing.

derived sound In audio recording, sound taken from the left and right and stereo tracks and played on a third, middle speaker.

DES See data encryption standard.

descender In typesetting, the lower portion of the letters g,j,p,q, y with the addition of f in italic. Compare ascender. See italic.

descriptor In library science, a word or symbol which is given to a document to describe it and by means of which the document can be discovered when required. Synonymous with keyword.

despotic network In data communications, a synchronized network in which a single master clock controls all other clocks in the network. See democratic network, hierarchical network.

despun antenna In satellite communications, an antenna whose main beam points to a fixed area on the surface of the earth even though the satellite rotates.

destructive cursor In computing, a cursor on a VDU that erases any character through which it passes as it moves. See VDU.

destructive readout In computing, pertaining to a reading action of stored data that necessarily erases the data held. Compare nondestructive readout.

detail paper Thin, hard, semi-transparent paper used for sketches and layouts.

developing In photography, the chemical process of bringing forth permanent image in film. Developing represents the first stage of this process, the later stages being fixation and drying. See fixation.

device control In data communications, a character in a data transmission code available for controlling a device, e.g. turning it on or off.

device independence In computer programming, the technique of writing application programs so that they are independent of the physical characteristics of peripheral devices. See peripheral.

Dewey Decimal Classification In library classification, a system devised by Melvil Dewey to classify areas of knowledge, and still in use in a modified form. In this system, there are ten main numbered classes (e.g. philosophy=100) and each area is subdivided progressively into ten subclasses and so on.

D/F See depth of field.

DGT Direction Generale des Telecommunications.

DG XIII Directorate General Section XIII of the Commission of European Communities which deals with the information market and innovation.

diacritic In typesetting, an accent placed above or below certain letters. See accent.

diagnostics In computing, programs and techniques used to detect and isolate faults in a system, component or program. A diagnostic program will usually produce a printout containing an analysis of the operation being checked in order to assist with fault finding and correction.

diagonal cut In photography and recording, a joint at an oblique angle to the edges of the film or tape. The diagonal cut is commonly used with magnetic tape to minimize the noise of the splice.

dial access In data communications, the connection through the public switched telephone network from a terminal to a service, network or computer.

Dialcom In communications, a US electronic mail service. See electronic mailbox, Telecom Gold.

dial conference In telephony, a PABX facility enabling an extension user to call several parties, all of whom are able to communicate with one another.

Dialog In databases, an information retrieval service operated by Dialog Information Systems Inc. (USA). (Previously Lockheed Information Systems Inc). See on line information retrieval.

dial pulse In telephone switching, a DC signal produced by, or simulated to look like, the opening and closing of contacts in a rotary telephone dial.

dial tone In telephone switching, a single frequency signal indicating to the caller that the receiving unit is ready to receive dial pulses. See dial pulse.

dial up In telephony, the initiation of a station to station telephone call through the use of a rotary, dial or touchtone telephone. See touchtone.

dial up teleconferencing In telephony, a teleconferencing network which is established over dial up circuits with or without operator assistance.

DIANE Direct Information Access Network for Europe. Refers to information services offered over the Euronet system. See Euronet.

diaphragm (1) In photography, an iris in a lens used to control the amount of light passing through the lens; the diaphragm setting will affect the depth of field. (2) In audio recording, a sound wave sensing element in a microphone. See depth of field.

diapositive In photography, a positive transparency.

diascope See slide projector.

diazo process In a document copying machine, a process in which a transparent or translucent original is exposed to an ultraviolet light source. The copy is produced on diazonium sensitized material and is developed using ammonia vapor.

dibit In communications, a group of two bits. The four possible states of a dibit are 00, 01, 10, 11. See tribit, bit.

dichroic In optics, a thin, layered coating used on filters and mirrors to control the spectral qualities of light. Dichroic filters are used to alter the colour temperature of lights, and in colour printers to absorb certain wavelengths and pass others. See wavelength.

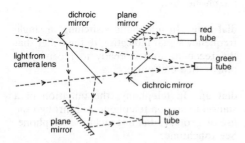

dichroic
A simplified diagram showing the use of dichroic mirrors for colour separation in a television camera.

dictionary In computer programming, a list of names generated by a compiler. See compiler, data dictionary.

DID See direct inward dialing.

Didot point In typography, a measurement system established by François Didot, now used in most European countries as an alternative to the Anglo-American point system. The Didot point is now accepted as 0·375mm (0·0148in).

dielectric In electronics, a material which resists the passage of electricity, i.e. an insulating material.

differential PCM In data communications, a version of pulse code modulation in which the difference in value between a sample and the previous sample is encoded. Because fewer bits are required for transmission than under PCM, this technique is used in satellite communications. See pulse code modulation, sampling.

diffusion In microelectronics, a process in which controlled amounts of an impurity dopant material are inserted into a silicon crystal. See chip.

digipad See digitizing pad.

digipulse telephone In telephony, a pushbutton telephone containing equipment that converts calling signals from the keypad into pulses similar to those generated by a rotary dial. See touchtone.

digit A graphic character that represents a whole number, e.g. one of the characters 0 to 9.

digital Pertaining to digits or the representation of data or physical quantities by digits. Compare analog.

digital computer In computing, one that operates on discrete data by performing arithmetic and logic processes. See electronic digital computer.

digital multiplex switching system In data communications, the use of PCM and TDM systems over circuit switched lines. See circuit switching, PCM, TDM.

digital plotter In computing, a plotter in

which an automatically controlled pen is moved in incremental steps.

digital recording In recording, the use of digital techniques to store sound or pictorial information on tape or disk. Digital recording offers an increased frequency range and lower tape noise compared to analog methods. See DAD, optical digital disks.

digital signal A discrete or discontinuous electric signal, one whose various states are at discrete intervals apart. Compare analog signal.

digital signalling In data communications, the use of a digital transmission channel for the setting up, control and release of calls. See System X.

digital signature In cryptography, a property private to a user or process that is used for signing messages over a communications link. For example, if customer A's bank receives an electronic message requesting a large withdrawal, the bank must be certain the request came from A; if A later disavows the message, the bank must be able to prove to a third party that the message originated with A, i.e. that A's electronic signature is fully authenticated. See authentication.

digital speech interpolation In communications, a technique used to enhance the effective capacity of telephone networks in which speech is conveyed by PCM. The channel does not transmit bits during pauses in speech. Compare TASI. See PCM.

digital switching In data communications, a process in which connections are established by operations on digital signals without their first being converted to analog signals. See digital signal.

digital to analog converter In computing, a device that accepts a series of values in the form of binary numbers and produces a corresponding analog signal, e.g. for converting stored digital speech signals into analog voltages to drive a loudspeaker. Compare analog to digital converter.

digital transmission system In data commu-

nications, a network in which analog information is digitized via a modulation technique and transmitted in a discrete form as a series of pulses. At the receiving station, the analog data is reconstituted from the digitized signals. Digital transmission systems support high data rates, error detection and minimize effects due to noise. See digitize

digital typography In typesetting, the production of type from data stored in digital form. Individual letter forms are represented by digital code stored in a computer. Algorithms convert this code into the appropriate graphic form which is then displayed on a CRT, and projected onto film, or written directly onto film by a laser. The number of bits required to represent a particular letter form may be reduced by the use of splines to represent its constituent curves. The algorithms can provide a high degree of flexibility in the production of the individual letterforms thus enabling the designer to produce visually pleasing images for a wide range of type sizes. See algorithm, CRT, LASER, spline.

digitize The process of converting analog signals to digital form. Once the signal is in a digital form, it can be processed using digital techniques and then reconverted to analog form. Compare analog to digital converter. See quantize.

digitizing pad In computing, an input device on which free hand drawing is translated into digitized form. The resulting image is displayed on a VDU screen and may be permanently stored. See VDU.

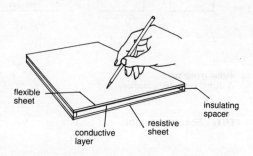

digitizing pad
A graphics encoding device using a flexible writing surface.

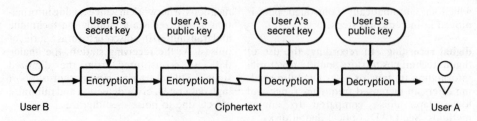

digital signature
A can prove that the message was enciphered by B. B can prove that the clear text was deciphered by A. In each case secret keys available only to B and A were used.

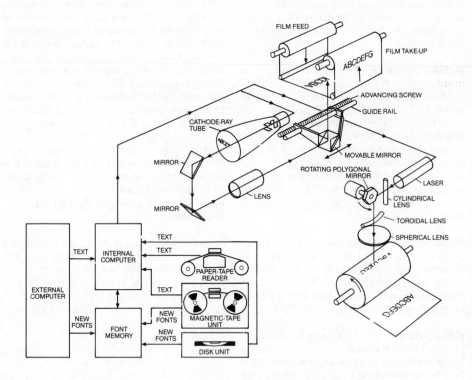

digital typography
A digital typesetting machine.

DIL See dual in line.

DIMDI Deutsches Institute für Medizinische Dokumentation und Information.

din (1) In photography, a European unit of measurement used to indicate film exposure indexes. (2) In electronics, a multipin connector based on West German standards. See DIN.

nector based on West German standards. See DIN.

DIN Deutsche Industrie Norm, West German Standards organization.

diode In electronics, a device that has a low electrical resistance in one direction and a very high resistance in the other, thus enabling current signals to pass in only one direction. See rectifier, semiconductor devices.

diode transistor logic In microelectronics, a logic circuit with diodes performing the logic function and the transistor providing amplification and inversion action. They may have a large number of inputs in a relatively small chip area. See chip, diode, inversion, logic circuit, transistor.

diopter In optics, a unit expressing the power of a lens.

diopter lens In photography, a lens attachment for close up work.

DIP In computing, Dual Inline Package. See dual in line.

diplex In communications, a facility that permits two signals to be transmitted simultaneously, and in the same direction, over a channel. Compare duplex.

diplex operation In communications, the use of a single circuit, carrier or antenna for the simultaneous transmission or reception of two signals. Compare duplex. See antenna, carrier.

dipole In radiocommunications, a symmetrical antenna which is center fed. In its simplest form it consists of a single straight wire a half wavelength long which radiates uniformly in all directions. See wavelength.

direct access In computing, pertaining to the ability to obtain data from a storage device, or to enter data into a storage device in such a way that the process depends only on the location of that data. Compare sequential access.

direct access storage In computing, a storage device that provides direct access to data in such a way that the access time is independent of the location of the data. Comapre magneric tape, See magnetic disk.

direct address Synonymous with absolute address.

direct broadcast satellite In television, a geostationary satellite used for broadcasting television and radio services. The satelite receives signals from an earth station which it then retransmits over a wide geographical area. Consumers may receive such services via a domestic disk antenna or a cable network employing a master antenna. DBS services are due to commence in the UK in 1986 and the BBC will program two of the five channels allocated to the UK. It is intended that the standard for these broadcasts will be C-MAC. See antenna, cable television, C-MAC.

direct colour print In photography, a colour print made in one step from the original colour film.

direct current In electronics, current produced by a constant voltage source, e.g. a rectifier or a battery. Compare alternating current. See rectifier.

direct data access arrangement In communications, a unit containing an isolation transformer, for interconnecting user equipment to a telephone network. It is designed to prevent harmful voltages or signals entering the network.

direct distance dialing In telephony, a service that enables the subscriber to call other subscribers outside the local area without operator assistance. Synonymous with subscriber trunk dialing.

direct image film In photography, a film that will retain the same polarity as the previous generation or the original material, i.e. black for black.

direct impression In printing, a method of type composition using a typewriter.

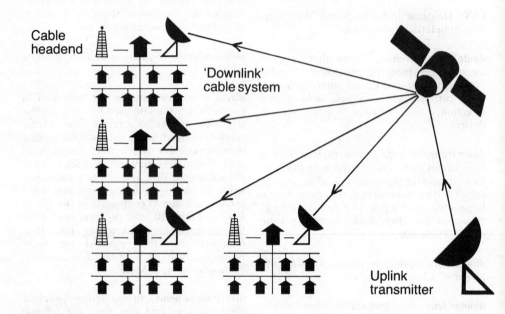

Cable headend

'Downlink' cable system

Uplink transmitter

direct broadcast satellite
One application of satellite transmission in which a direct broadcast satellite relays a television signal to CATV networks.

direct inward dialing In telephony, a feature of some private branch exchanges where incoming calls are routed to extensions without the need of an operator. Compare direct outward dialing. See private branch exchange.

directional antenna In radiocommunications, an antenna that radiates, or receives, radio waves more effectively in some directions than others. Compare isotropic radiator.

directional microphone A microphone which has greater sound sensitivity in one direction than in others. Directional microphones are often used in film and television production in order to avoid recording unwanted sounds. Compare omnidirectional microphone. See unidirectional microphone.

directional pattern In audio recording, the directional sensitivity of a microphone. The basic patterns are omnidirectional (nondirectional), bidirectional and unidirectional. See unidirectional microphone, omnidirectional microphone, bidirectional microphone.

directivity In antennas, the ratio in decibels of the radiation intensity produced in a given direction to the average value of the radiation intensities in all directions in space. See decibel.

direct memory access In computing, a means of accessing or writing stored data without requiring the attention of the CPU. It enables block transfer of data between the main memory and peripherals whilst the CPU is performing other processing tasks. Compare cycle stealing. See CPU, peripheral.

directory In databases, a file that stores relationships between records in other files. The directory contains an overview of the data held, and since it occupies less storage space than the data files, searches and operations performed on the directory are more efficient than those performed on the data files themselves. Compare data dictionary.

directory routing In message and packet switching systems, a routing method that uses a directory at each node. The directory contains details of the preferred, and possibly second preference, outgoing link for each destination.

direct outward dialing In telephony, a feature of private branch exchanges that allows a user to gain access to the exchange network without the assistance of the operator. Compare direct inward dialing.

direct ray In radiocommunications, the shortest possible path for a wave between the transmitting and receiving antennas.

direct read after write In video disk, a record once optical disk technique used for the mass storage of digital data. See optical disk.

DIRS DIMDI Information Retrieval Service. See DIMDI.

disable In computing, the prevention of a function from being recognized or acted upon.

disassembler (1) In computer programming, a routine that accepts machine code and produces a mnemonic code listing corresponding to the assembly language. An essential facility for debugging stored machine code programs. (2) In packet switching, a device that extracts the message content from packets. See assembly language, packet switching, packet assembler/-disassembler.

disclosure In data security, the unauthorized acquisition of information. See masquerading.

disconnect signal In telephony, a signal transmitted over the line to indicate that the established connection should be broken.

discrete In computing, data which is in the form of distinct elements such as characters. Compare analog signal.

discretionary hyphen In word processing, a hyphen inserted by an operator to divide a word when there is insufficient space on the line to produce the whole of that word. See hyphenation.

dish In communications, an antenna having a concave reflecting surface. See antenna.

disjoint Having no common areas.

disk See floppy disk, magnetic disk, video disk.

disk drive In computing, a mechanism for rotating a disk pack or a magnetic disk and controlling its movements. See disk pack, magnetic disk unit.

diskette Synonymous with floppy disk.

disk operating system In computer programming, an operating system for systems with disk drives in which the relevant routines are loaded from disk as required. See operating system.

disk pack In computing, a set of disks on a common spindle, handled as a single unit. See disk.

displacement Synonymous with relative address.

display In word processing, a device for visual presentation of information on any temporary character imaging device.

display attribute In computer graphics, a particular property that is assigned to all or part of a display, e.g. character colour, size, blinking status, intensity etc. See pixel.

display character In videotex, one of many different shapes which can be generated in a character rectangle as part of a page. The display characters consist of alphanumeric, separated graphics and contiguous graphic sets. See contiguous graphics, separated graphics.

display character generator In computing, a device on a VDU that converts the digital code for a character into signals that cause the electron beam to create the character on the screen. See character generator, VDU.

display colour   In videotex, one of the seven colours (white, yellow, cyan, green, magenta, red and blue) used to depict a display character. See display character.

display column   In computer graphics, the display positions that form a vertical line on the display screen.

display highlights   In word processing, the ability of the system to emphasize certain portions of the display screen. This may be achieved by intensifying or blinking a selected portion of the text, or the screen area behind the text. Display highlighting is often used to isolate a text segment that is to be deleted or moved.

display line   In computing, the series of positions that may be occupied by a character, or other element of display, that constitute a horizontal line on the display surface.

display mode   In videotex, pertaining to the three character sets used in creating and displaying a videotex page, i.e. alphanumerics set, separated graphics set and contiguous graphics set. See alphanumerics set, contiguous graphics, separated graphics.

display size   In printing, any size of type above 14 point, as distinct from text size or composition size. See composition size, text size, point.

display space   In computer graphics, the portion of a display surface that is available for the display of the image.

display tube   See cathode ray tube.

display unit   In computing, a terminal device capable of producing a visible record or display of information. Normally used in reference to CRT displays. See CRT, visual display unit.

Dissertation Abstracts Online   A database supplied by University Microfilms International Inc. and dealing with dissertations. See on line information retrieval.

distortion   (1) In optics, any systematic malformation of an image caused by the optical system involved. Common optical distortions include positive (barrel) distortion, and negative (pin cushion) distortion. (2) In audio, any discrepancy in signal waveform or phase between the input and output signal of an amplifier or transmitting system. (3) In data transmission, an undesired change in waveform. The principal sources of distortion of waveforms are: (a) nonlinear relationship between input and output, (b) nonuniform transmission at different frequencies and (c) a phase shift not proportional to frequency. See harmonic distortion, intermodulation distortion.

distortion optics   In photography, optical devices used on a camera to achieve special image effects.

distribute   In printing, to break up composed type and melt it down for subsequent reuse.

distributed adaptive routing   In packet switching, a method of routing in which the decisions are made on the basis of exchange of information between the nodes of a network. See adaptive routing.

distributed data processing   In computing, the processing of jobs at a number of geographically separated locations. See job.

distribution point   (1) In cable television, a point from which signals are taken from the trunk network, or head end, to feed branch or spur cables serving subscribers. (2) In telephony, the final point on a local line network from which twisted pairs of wires are run to a subscriber's premises. See head end.

dittogram   In printing, a repeated letter caused by a typesetting error, e.g. a worrd.

DIV   See data in voice.

DIVA   See data input voice answerback.

divergence   In television, the failure of the

beams in a colour display tube to land at the same colour cell on the screen.

DMA See direct memory access.

DML See data manipulation language.

DMS See digital multiplex switching system.

DOC Canadian Department of Communications.

docket In communications, the record of an FCC or US State regulatory proceeding. See sunshine notice.

document In word processing, a portion of text treated as a single unit, whether it be a few short lines or a multipage report. See standard document.

document assembly See document merge.

documentation In computing, the preparation and production of documents for systems analysis, programming and system operation. Good documentation is an essential element in maintaining a computer system, particularly when changes or modifications have to be made subsequently to the computer software or hardware. See hardware, software.

document delivery service In databases, a service in which the user searches a database for information on relevant publications and then orders a copy of a selected publication via the terminal. The appropriate print copy is then delivered by post. See on line information retrieval.

document mark In micrographics, an optical mark, usually rectangular, within the recording area, and usually below the image on a roll of microfilm used for counting images or frames automatically.

document merge In word processing, the ability of the system to create a new document from previously recorded text. This facility is very useful in applications such as contracts preparation, where a company's standard clauses can be selected, assembled

and then merged on a word processor. See boilerplate.

document retrieval system In information retrieval, a system that provides a complete copy of the document instead of just a citation or reference. See citation indexing.

document stop In micrographics, a device incorporated in most rotary cameras which prevents the entry of more than one document at a time. See rotary camera.

Dolby In recording, a proprietary noise reduction system used on audio tape and cassettes.

domain (1) In computing, the resources under the control of one or more associated host processors on a network. (2) In computer programming, the set of values assigned to the independent variables of a function.

Domestic Digital Bus A proposed standard, published by Philips, for the interconnection of television receivers, VCR's, video disk and stereo audio equipment. See VCR, video disk.

domestic satellite carrier In satellite communications, an interstate common carrier which provides communication services within the US via DOMSAT. See DOMSAT decision.

DOMSAT decision In satellite communications, an FCC decision allowing open entry into the provision of domestic satellite communication services. Synonymous with open skies policy.

dongle In computing, a chip that must be present in a microcomputer to enable it to operate proprietary software. It is used to prevent illegal copying. See chip, hardware.

don't care In logic circuits, pertaining to outputs corresponding to a subset of input signals that will not arise, e.g. in a device that is designed to accept a 4 bit binary number and produce a corresponding decimal digit there are 5 inputs corresponding to numbers, 10 - 15, that should not arise. The circuit designer is not constrained to produce particular outputs for such inputs and this provides for flexibility and optimization in the circuit design.

dopant   In microelectronics, an element that is diffused into semiconductor material to give it n- or p- type properties. See diffusion, n-type material, p-type material, semiconductor.

DOR   In video disk, Digital Optical Recording. See optical digital disks.

DOS   See disk operating system.

dot matrix   (1) In computer graphics, a two dimensional pattern of dots used for constructing a display image. This type of matrix is used to represent characters by dots. (2) In data processing, a pattern of dots used as the basis for character formation in a matrix printer. See matrix printer.

dot printer   Synonymous with matrix printer.

dot signal   In telegraphy, a signal composed of a continuous sequence of alternate marks and spaces of equal duration. See mark, space.

double dagger   In typesetting, a character used as a third order of reference marks; also known as double obelisk. See reference mark.

double density   In computing, a method of recording data on floppy disks using a modified frequency modulation process. See modified frequency modulation.

double document   In micrographics, a defect in a microfilm in which two documents have been photographed simultaneously on a rotary camera. See rotary camera.

double exposure   In photography, the recording of two or more images on a single strip of film. Synonymous with multi-exposure.

double precision arithmetic   In computing, pertaining to arithmetic performed on a number comprising two words. Used when the limited number of bits in one word does not provide sufficient precision. See precision.

double sideband   In radiocommunications, the frequency bands occupied by a modulated carrier wave, above and below the carrier frequency. See modulation, carrier.

down line load   In computing, the process of loading programs into a computer from a remote location using a communications channel such as a telephone line. See telesoftware.

download   See down line load.

downstroke   In printing, the heavy stroke in type character derived from the broad line created by the downward movement of a pen in calligraphy. See calligraphy.

downtime   In data processing, the time during which a device is inoperable due to a fault. See MTBF.

dp   See data processing.

DPM   In computing, Data Processing Manager.

DPMA   Data Processing Management Association.

drain   In electronics, (1) the current supplied by a battery or power supply to a circuit, (2) a terminal on an FET. See FET, source, gate, terminal.

DRAM   See dynamic RAM.

DRAW   See optical digital disks. Synonymous with direct read after write.

DRCS   See dynamically redefinable character set.

D region   In radiocommunications, that part of the ionosphere, between 50 and 90 kilometers, responsible for most of the attenuation of radio waves in the frequency range of 1 to 100 MHz. See attenuation, MHz.

drift   In electronics, the natural tendency of a circuit to alter its characteristics with time and temperature changes. In sound recording circuits, drift may cause a frequency modulation of the signal in the range below 0·5 Hz, resulting in a distorted waveform which may be perceived as a slow changing of the average pitch.

driver In computer programming, a routine which performs low level input output functions for an input output device. See input output devices.

drop In communications, that portion of outside telephone plant which extends from the telephone distribution cable to the subscriber's premises.

drop cap In typesetting, the initial at the beginning of a line of text set in a larger size type and extending into lines of type below.

drop line In cable television, a cable which branches off from a feeder cable to provide signals to the subscriber's home. See feeder cable.

drop out (1) In data transmission, the loss of discrete data signals due to noise or attenuation. (2) In video recording, loss of video information caused by irregularities in the oxide surface of the tape. Drop out results in a horizontal streak in the television picture during playback.

drum (1) In cinematography, a flywheel which is used in a film projector to ensure smooth film movement over the sound head. (2) In a video recorder, slotted helical scan record/playback head assembly. (3) In photocomposition, an image carrier in drum form. (4) In computing, an early form of magnetic storage device.

drum plotter In computing, an output device in which the writing tool moves laterally across the width of a roll of paper which is at the same time being rotated on a drum. The drawings so produced are reasonably accurate, though not as good as a flatbed plotter. See flatbed plotter.

drum printer In computing, a line printer in which the type are mounted on a rotating drum that contains a full character set for each printing position.

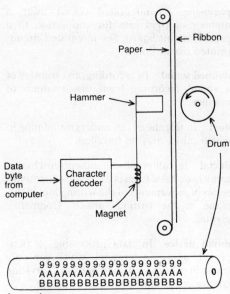

drum printer

dry circuit In communications, a circuit for the transmission of voice signals that carry no direct current. See DC.

DS See data set.

DSE See data switching exchange.

DSI See digital speech interpolation.

DSR See data set ready.

DTE See data terminal equipment.

DTL See diode transistor logic.

DTMF In communications, Dual Tone MultiFrequency signalling, a signalling method in which two frequencies, each selected from a group of four, are used to transmit numerical address information. See multifrequency signal.

dual channel In recording, a device with two separate paths that do not interact unless deliberately mixed, e.g. stereo equipment.

dual column In word processing, a facility for printing in two columns on a page when the text was entered in a single column format.

dual in line In microelectronics, a method of

packaging an integrated circuit using a number of rigid pins for connection to a printed circuit board. See integrated circuit, printed circuit board.

dubbed sound In recording, the transfer of a sound recording from one medium to another.

duct In telephony, an underground pipe in which cables may be installed.

ductal In calligraphy, handwritten characters whose basic form is the result of a smooth series of movements of the writing tool in the plane of the writing surface. Compare glyptal.

dumb device In data processing, a peripheral, usually a terminal, which can only transmit or receive data to or from a servicing computer. Compare intelligent device.

dump In computer programming, a bulk transfer of data from one medium to another, e.g. the transfer of the contents of a part of main memory to a line printer. See line printer, main memory.

duplex (1) In photography, photographic paper having emulsion coating on both sides. (2) In micrographics, an image positioning technique in a rotary camera, the front side of the document is photographed on one half of the film whilst the image on the reverse side of the document is simultaneously photographed on the other half of the film. (3) In data communications, pertaining to the simultaneous two way independent transmission over a circuit. Compare half duplex. See rotary camera. Synonymous with full duplex.

duplex circuit In communications, a circuit used for transmission of signals in both directions at the same time. See full duplex, half duplex.

duplicator In printing, a device that uses lithographic or other methods to produce multiple copies from a master. See lithography, spirit duplicator.

duplicator paper In printing, a soft, absorbent paper used in a duplicating machine.

DUV See data under voice.

dyeline See diazo process.

dynamic allocation In computing, the assignment of system resources to a program at the time of execution rather than when it is loaded into main storage. See main storage.

dynamically redefinable character set In videotex, the ability to load a new character set in a videotex terminal by transmitting the set over the telephone network from a videotex computer. See character generator.

dynamic microphone In acoustics, a microphone which generates a voltage in proportion to the sound pressure changes on a diaphragm. This is achieved by attaching a voice coil to the diaphragm. See microphone.

dynamic multiplexing Synonymous with demand multiplexing.

dynamic RAM In computing, an inexpensive MOS random access memory where the contents need refreshing every 2 milliseconds. Compare static memory. See MOS, RAM.

dynamic range In audio recording, the difference in amplitude between the softest and loudest sounds. See distortion.

dynamic storage allocation In computing, a technique in which storage is allocated to a program according to its actual demand as compared with an allocation based upon a fixed or anticipated demand.

dynamic track following In video recording, a technique adopted by Philips in which the read head is dynamically aligned with the correct track position through the use of guidance signals.

E

EAN In computing, European Article Number, a four bar width bar code said to be the European counterpart of UPC. See bar code, UPC.

EAPROM In computing, Electrically Alterable Programmable Read Only Memory. Synonymous with EPROM.

Early Bird In communications, the world's first communications satellite operated by COMSAT, in orbit over the Atlantic. It had 240 telephone circuits, equivalent to 1 TV channel, and generated 40 watts of power. It is no longer in commercial use. See satellite.

EAROM See electrically alterable ROM.

ear print In computing, a warmbody device

technique which uses a small microphone and sound emitter. The emitter and microphone are held close to the ear and a series of clicking noises from the emitter causes an audible response, from the middle ear, which is unique to each individual. Compare voice print. See warmbody device.

earth See ground.

earth coverage In satellite communications, pertaining to antenna systems with a beam for maximum cover of the earth's surface. Compare spot beam.

earth station In satellite communications, a dish shaped antenna, and associated electronic equipment, for transmitting and receiving

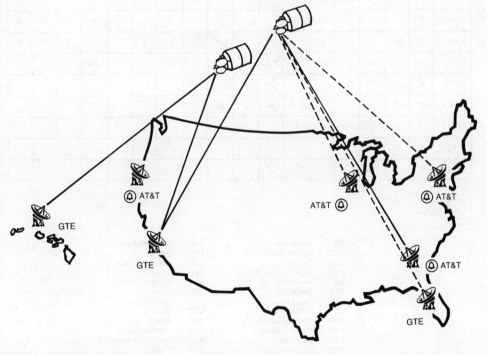

earth station
Antennas of 105 feet in diameter are used in the long-distance telephone networks of AT & T and GTE.

satellite telecommunication signals. The size of the antenna has been reduced in recent years, from several hundred feet to a few feet, as the power generated from satellites has increased. See satellite.

EAX   See electronic automatic exchange.

EBAM   See electron beam accessed memory.

EBCDIC code   In data transmission and computing, Extended Binary Coded Decimal Interchange Code, one of two international data codes used in IBM equipment.

Bit Positions 4, 5, 6, 7	Hex	Bit Positions 0, 1, 2, 3															
		0000	0001	0010	0011	0100	0101	0110	0111	1000	1001	1010	1011	1100	1101	1110	1111
		0	1	2	3	4	5	6	7	8	9	A	B	C	D	E	F
0000	0	NUL	DLE			SP	&	$\overline{RHY}$						2	3	½	0
0001	1	SOH	DCI			RSP		/		a	j	°		A	J	NSP	1
0010	2	STX	DC2	SYN						b	k	s		B	K	S	2
0011	3	ETX	DC3	WUS	IRT					c	l	t		C	L	T	3
0100	4									d	m	u		D	M	U	4
0101	5	HT	NL	LF						e	n	v		E	N	V	5
0110	6	RCR	BS	ETB	NBS					f	o	w		F	O	W	6
0111	7	DEL		ESC	EOT					g	p	x		G	P	X	7
1000	8				SBS					h	q	y		H	Q	Y	8
1001	9	SPS			IT	!	±			i	r	z		I	R	Z	9
1010	A	RPT	UBS	SW	EOP	¼/$	¾/	#/¾	:					$\overline{SHY}$			
1011	B			CU2		.	$/£	,	£/#								
1100	C	FF				<	*	%	@								
1101	D		IGS	ENQ	NAK	(	)	—	'								
1110	E		IRS			+	;	>									
1111	F		ITB	BEL	¢/¼	μ	?	"									

Options

BS	Backspace	RHY	Required hyphen
CRE	Carrier return	RPT	Repeat
DEL	Delete	RSP	Required space
CU2	MCII Format control	SBS	Subscript
HT	Horizontal tab	SHY	Syllable hyphen
INX	Index	SP	Space
IRT	Index return	SPS	Superscript
IT	Indent tab	STP	Stop
NBS	Numeric backspace	SW	Switch
NSP	Numeric space	UBS	Unit backspace
PE	Page end	WUS	Word underscore
RCR	Required carrier return	PRE	Prefix

EBCDIC code

This 8 bit code gives 256 combinations. Compare ASCII, ISO 7 bit code.

EBR   See electron beam recording.

EBU   European Broadcasting Union.

ECDIN   Environmental Chemicals Data and Information Network, a database supplied by the Commission of the European Communities and dealing with chemistry-structure and nomenclature, environment, toxicology. See on line information retrieval.

echo   (1) In broadcasting, a sound generated in an echo chamber to simulate reverberation. (2) In audio recording, an electronic technique for creating a time delayed signal to be added to the original source. (3) In high frequency radio communications, a signal received after travelling around the world. (4) In television, the second image on a display due to a signal received via a reflecting path. This image is displaced to the right of the original. (5) In telephony, an interference due to reflection of the transmitted signal from the receiving end. See high frequency, echo suppressor.

echo chamber   An acoustic or electronic device that can prolong the decay of a reverberating sound wave by up to 2 seconds. See echo.

echocheck   See echoplex.

echoplex   In data communications, a visual method of error detection in which the signal from the originating device is looped back to that device so that it can be displayed. See CRT.

echo suppressor   In telephony, a voice operated device used on long distance lines to prevent the propagation of echos. Echo suppressors must be disabled if a speech circuit is to be used for full duplex data transmissions. See echo, full duplex.

ECL   See emitter coupled logic.

ECMA   European Computer Manufacturers Association.

ECOM   See electronic computer originated mail.

ECOMA   European Computer Measurement Association.

Economics Abstracts International   A database supplied by Dutch Ministry of Economics Affairs and dealing with business management, economics. See on line information retrieval.

ECSA   European Computer Services Association.

EDAC   In data communications, Error Detection And Correction. See forward error correction.

edge card   In microcomputers, a circuit board with contact strips along one edge, designed to mate with an edge connector. See edge connector.

edge connector   In microcomputers, an electrical slot shaped socket enabling an edge card to be connected to the motherboard. See motherboard.

edge emitting LED   In optoelectronics, an LED with a spectral output that emanates from an edge, having a higher output intensity and greater coupling efficiency to an optical fiber, or integrated optical circuit, than a surface emitting LED. See fiber optics, LED.

edge notched card   In manual data processing, a card in which notches representing data are punched or clipped around the edges.

edge notched card index   In manual data processing, a coordinating indexing system in which edge notched cards are removed by one or more needles passing through the

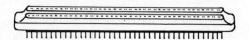

edge connector

pack. Those cards remaining in the box will contain information relevant to the search. See edge notched card.

edit (1) In filming, the creative alteration of a recorded original, whether by assembling, shortening, transposing or synchronizing the original film or tape material. (2) In computing, a procedure used to change or modify the form of data input to the system. This may involve testing input for correct format and adding or deleting characters. See editor.

editing run In computer batch processing, a program which will check new data for validity against a series of predefined rules and identify any errors for correction and resubmission. Typical tests include checking that dates and numbers fall within expected ranges, verification of check digits etc.

editing symbols In micrographics, alphanumerical and geometric symbols on microfilm readable with the unaided eye and used to provide cutting, loading and other preparation instructions.

editing terminal (1) In typesetting, a VDU on which the result of keyboarding held on tape or disk, is displayed for editing purposes, using an attached keyboard, prior to processing the copy on a typesetting machine. (2) In videotex, a terminal used for building up a page display consisting of alphamosaic characters. Compare page view terminal. See alphamosaic.

edition In publishing, the complete output of a publication from one set of printing forms. An edition may be of one or more impressions, but a new edition implies some change in content and/or style of production. See form.

editor (1) In filming, one who edits film. (2) In computing, a software tool which is used as an aid in modifying and debugging programs under development. See debug, line editor, screen editor, text editor.

editorial processing center In publishing, a center enabling a number of small publishing operations to be combined into one which is sufficiently large to render the application of computer techniques economically sound.

The center permits functions such as writing, refereeing, editing and proofing to be performed on line. It also facilitates computer typesetting and the automation of certain business management functions. See on line.

EDP (1) Educational Data Processing, (2) Electronic Data Processing.

EDP capability In word processing, the ability of a machine to either perform some associated data processing, or else for it to be used independently for data processing tasks. See electronic data processing.

EDS See exchangeable disk storage.

educational technology A systematic approach to the design and evaluation of teaching and learning methods and methodologies and to the application and exploitation of media and of the current knowledge of communication techniques in education, both formal and informal.

educational television A generic term applied to any television program, or equipment, related to some form of education or instruction.

EEMAC Electrical and Electronic Manufacturers' Association of Canada.

EEROM See electrically erasable ROM.

effective address In computing, the address that is derived by performing an address modification. See address.

effective aperture (1) In optics, the ratio between the focal length and the diameter of the iris diaphragm. Thus although the geometry of the lens may indicate an f-number of 2·8, due to shortcomings of the camera system the lens may only have an effective value of 4·0 (2) In communications, the effective aperture of an antenna is a measure of the power available at the terminals of the receiving antenna. See f-number, antenna.

effective bandwidth In telecommunications, the frequency range over which the performance of the system is within the specified operational limits. See bandwidth.

effective isotropic radiated power In microwave transmission, the product of the power supplied to an antenna and its gain. It is used as a measure of satellite transmission. See antenna gain, isotropic radiator.

effective search speed In computing, the rate at which a storage medium, e.g. a floppy disk, can be searched to reach the beginning of a particular text passage.

EFT See electronic funds transfer.

EHF See extremely high frequency.

EIA Electronic Industries Association.

EIAJ standards In video recording, the tape standards promoted by the Electronic Industry Association of Japan which allows for the compatibility of the equipment of several manufacturers.

EIN See European Informatics Network.

EIRP See effective isotropic radiated power.

electret In electronics, a dielectric solid which retains a charge at its opposite sides after a voltage application in the assembly process.

electret microphone See electret, microphone.

electrically alterable ROM In microelectronics, a read only memory that can be programmed by applying a voltage to selected pins and erased either by exposure to ultraviolet light (FAMOS) or by reversing the polarity used in writing (MNOS). Compare EPROM. See FAMOS, NMOS, ROM. Synonymous with electrically erasable ROM, EROM.

electrically erasable ROM Synonymous with electrically alterable ROM.

electrically programmable read only memory In microelectronics, a read only memory that can be programmed by applying a voltage to selected pins. The term is applied both to devices that may, and may not, be reprogrammed. See electrically alterable ROM, PROM.

electric typewriter A typewriter in which all the output functions, such as a keystroke, tabulation etc. are controlled by an electric motor. Compare electronic typewriter.

electrode In electronics, that part of a circuit that acts as source of electrical charges or controls or collects them.

electroluminescence In computer graphics, the emission of light from a phosphor dot excited by an electromagnetic field. See phosphor dots.

electromagnet A device consisting of a ferromagnetic core and an electric coil that produces an appreciable magnetic effect whilst a current flows in the coil.

electromagnetic interference In communications, induced magnetic fields originating from high energy electrical disturbances which can cause data corruption in signals passing through cables.

electromagnetic radiation In communications and optics, a radio or light energy wave associated with electric and magnetic fields. Electromagnetic radiation requires no supporting medium and is propagated through space at a velocity of approximately $3 \times (10$ to the power $8)$ metres per second. The nature of electromagnetic radiations depends upon their frequency and includes light waves and microwaves. In radiocommunications, the carrier signal is an electromagnetic wave which is transmitted and received by an antenna. See antenna, carrier wave, light, microwave.

electromagnetic spectrum The range of frequencies over which electromagnetic radiations are propagated. The lowest frequencies are radio waves; increases of frequency produce infrared radiation, light, ultraviolet radiation, X-rays, gamma rays and finally cosmic rays. See electromagnetic radiation, infrared, light, ultraviolet.

electromechanical computer A device using relays or electrically driven mechanical counting devices for computation. The first

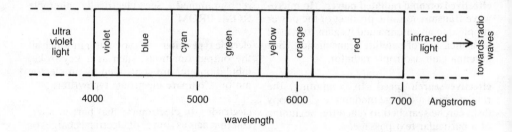

electromagnetic spectrum
Visible light is part of the electromagnetic spectrum.

generation of electronic computers were preceded by such devices. See first generation computer, relay.

electromechanical switching   In telephony, the connection of an input point to an output point using an electrically operated mechanical device such as a relay. See relay.

electron   In electronics, an elementary particle containing the smallest electrical charge. The mass of the electron is approximately 1/1837 of the mass of the hydrogen atom. Compare proton.

electron beam accessed memory   In computing, a memory that is written and read by an electron beam. In the writing action the beam either does, or does not, deposit electrons according to a one or zero input. In the reading action the effect of the beam on the charged or uncharged area is detected. See BEAMOS, memory.

electron beam recording   In micrographics, a technique used in the production of a computer generated microfilm, a beam of electrons is directed onto an energy sensitive microfilm. Compare CRT recording, fiber optics recording. See microfilm.

electron gun   See gun.

electronic automatic exchange   In telephony, an automatic exchange in which electronic circuits are used to route calls. See exchange, System X.

electronic blackboard   In teleconferencing,

a system for sending handwriting, and hand drawn graphics, over a telephone line. The sender may use either a light pen or digitizing tablet, and the appropriate image will appear on a television monitor at the remote location. See Cyclops.

electronic composition   In printing, the use of a computer for text manipulation prior to typesetting.

electronic computer originated mail   In computing and communications, a proposed mail service for large organizations. Mail originated in a computer is transmitted by data communication networks to regional centers where it is printed, placed in envelopes and addressed for posting to local recipients. Compare electronic mailbox.

electronic data processing   Data processing performed largely by electronic, as compared with manual and mechanical equipment. Compare manual data processing.

electronic digital computer   In its simplest form a device, with an electronic CPU, that accepts a set of instructions and data, performs computations or manipulations upon that data according to the instructions and delivers the results. The basic computer comprises an input device, a memory, a control and arithmetic unit and an output device. The input device translates sets of signals from some external form, e.g. a keyboard on a computer terminal, into a set of voltages that represent binary codes of the input data. These voltages are directed to the memory where they cause an electronic device to assume one of two states, i.e. they store the bits of the input data. The control unit of CPU takes each instruction from the program, held in memory, in a sequence determined by the program and previous results of program computations. The instruction is decoded and the corresponding actions are performed in the arithmetic unit. For example, a sequence of three instructions might require that a number be extracted from a memory location and stored in an arithmetic unit register, the second instruction extracts another number from a second memory location and adds it to the first number in the register, the third instruction moves the sum held in the register to a third memory location. At another part of the program an instruction will require that the certain memory locations be sent to an output device such as a lineprinter. This operation involves the reverse of the input operation, i.e. the states of the memory location are converted to a pulse train and sent to an output device. See arithmetic unit, byte, binary code, CPU, information processor, memory, microcomputer.

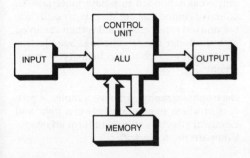

electronic digital computer
The five functional elements.

electronic editing In video recording, the insertion or assembling of program elements on video tape without physically cutting the tape. See editor.

electronic funds transfer An automated system for transferring funds from one bank account to another using electronic equipment and data communications rather than paper media, e.g. cheques, and the postal system.

Electronic Industries Association A stand-

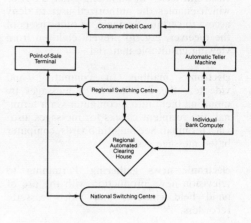

electronic funds transfer

ards organization specializing in the electrical and functional characteristics of interface equipment.

electronic journal In publishing, an electronic publishing system which can bypass traditional scientific journal publishing. All the stages in the preparation of the electronic journal, i.e. writing, refereeing, editing, proofing and publishing, are performed within a distributed computing system. See electronic publishing.

electronic keyboard A keyboard in which characters are generated or encoded by electronic means as opposed to mechanical methods. Electronic keyboards have a different feel and in order to simulate their mechanical equivalent some have an artificial bottoming feel and/or audible click to assure the operator a key has actually been depressed.

electronic learning laboratory In educational technology, a system consisting of instructors, control equipment and a number of student positions or stations. The control equipment is capable of producing, copying, monitoring and distributing educational material to one or more students for study or response. The communications network may be either wired, or broadcast, and student positions are usually equipped with headphones, microphones, signalling devices, recording and viewing facilities.

electronic lock   In cable television, a device which enables the authorized user to deny access to certain channels, to other users of the receiver, e.g. to prevent children from viewing unsuitable material.

electronic mailbox   In computing and videotex, the distribution of messages by inputting them into a computer via a terminal; the recipient checks for messages also via a terminal. See bulletin boards, computer based message system.

electronic news gathering   Pertaining to television news production with the use of hand held cameras and video cassette recorders.

electronic office   Synonymous with office of the future.

electronic pen   Synonymous with digitizing pad.

electronic publishing   A generic term for the distribution of information on computer databases linked by communication networks. Videotex is an example of this method of publishing. See information provider, videotex, database.

electronic pulse   See pulse.

electronics   A branch of technology dealing with the motion and behaviour of electrons, especially those in semiconductor circuits. Although the term derives from vacuum tube technology, it now encompasses the solid state circuits and devices used in computing and communications. See chip, microelectronics, solid state device.

electronic stylus   Synonymous with light pen.

electronic switching system   In telephony, a switching system using a special purpose computer to direct and control the switching of telephone circuits.

electronic telephone   A telephone set which contains extra circuitry to provide additional features and improved performance.

electronic typewriter   In word processing, a typewriter with limited word processing facilities, it normally has a marching display which allows text to be corrected before it is printed. Compare electric typewriter. See marching display.

electronic viewfinder   In television, a small CRT built into a camera to enable the operator to view the camera image.

Electronic Yellow Pages Files   A collection of databases, supplied by Market Data Retrieval Inc. and dealing with company information. See on line information retrieval.

electrooptic effect   In optoelectronics, the change in refractive index of a material when subjected to an electric field. The effect can be used to modulate a light beam in a material. See modulation, refractive index.

electrophotoadhesive process   In printing, an electrophotographic imaging process in which a toner image is formed xerographically on a photoconductive layer which is only weakly bonded to a base material. An adhesive coated transfer sheet is pressed onto the unfixed toner image and is then removed with the toner image adhering. See electrophotography, photoconductivity, xerography.

electrophotography   In photography, a process in which interaction between light and electrical effects is utilised to form an image. Compare photoelectric.

electroplating   In printing, the creation of a duplicate plate by electrolysis.

electrosensitive paper   Printer paper with a thin coating of aluminium, or other conductive material. The print becomes visible after a matrix print head causes an electric current to flow onto the conductive surface, producing a darkening effect.

electrostatic loudspeaker   A speaker consisting of two large conducting electrodes, one or both of which are flexible. The electrodes are maintained at a high voltage and separated by an insulating material. Voltages at audio frequency are applied to the electrodes, the resulting movement creates a sound wave. See electrode.

electrostatic printer In printing, a device for printing an optical image on paper, in which dark and light areas of the original are represented by electrostatically charged and uncharged areas on the paper. The paper is dusted with particles of finely powdered dry ink, and the particles adhere only to the electrically charged areas. The paper with ink particles is heated, causing the ink to melt and become permanently fixed to the paper. See xerography.

electrostatic storage The storage of data on a dielectric in the form of charges that can persist for a short time after the electrostatic charging mechanism is removed, e.g. the screen of a CRT can be used for this purpose. See dielectric.

electrotype In printing, a duplicate letterpress plate made from an original by electroplating. See electroplating, letterpress.

electrowriter See digitizing pad.

ELF See extremely low frequency.

element (1) In a printer, the removable type element. (2) In a set, an object, entity or concept having the properties that define the set. See daisy wheel, set.

elementary cable section In communications, the physical means of transmission between the output terminals of one device, e.g. a repeater, and the input terminals of the next device in the system. See repeater.

elite Typewriter spaces of 12 characters to the inch. See typewriter faces. Synonymous with twelve pitch.

ellipsis In printing, a sign used to indicate that something has been left out of a phrase or sentence, thus.....

elliptical orbit In communications, an orbit in which the trajectory of a communications satellite around the earth maps out an ellipse.

em (1) In printing, the surface area taken up by type of a given size. Thus an 8 point type occupies a print area of 8 point em. (2) In computing, an ASCII control character, end of medium. See en, pica, type size.

embedded code In computer programming, sections of assembler, or machine language, embedded into a high level language program. It is used to reduce storage requirements, increase execution speed or to provide some function not available in the high level language. See high level language, assembler, machine language.

embedded computer A computer serving as an intelligent active component in an electronic or electromechanical system, e.g. a camera or a washing machine.

embedded pointers In databases, pointers that are embedded within the data records rather than stored in the directory. See directory, pointer.

EMF ElectroMotive Force. Synonymous with voltage.

EMI See electromagnetic interference.

emitter In electronics, a terminal of a bipolar transistor. Compare base, collector. See transistor.

emitter coupled logic In microelectronics, a transistor logic circuit characterized by fast action and high power dissipation used in high speed mainframe computers. See emitter, logic circuit, mainframe, transistor.

empty set A set that has no elements. See element, set.

empty slot In computer networks, a packet which continually circulates around a ring network. Whenever a node on the circuit wants to send information it waits for an empty packet and then fills it with data and address information. See Cambridge Ring, packet switching.

em quad In printing, a type having no face and used for creating white space in letterpress printing. The width of the space is equal to an em. See em.

em rule   In typesetting, a sign used to indicate the omission of a word.

ems per hour   In typesetting, a unit of measurement used to evaluate the speed of text production by an operator or machine. An average of two characters is assumed to equal one em. See em.

emulator   In computing, special purpose hardware or software which enables one machine to act as if it were another. It is used to minimize reprogramming effort when a new computer replaces an existing one.

emulsion   (1) In photography, the essential light sensitive coating on photographic film comprising gelatine and silver salts. (2) In recording, iron oxide on magnetic tape.

emulsion laser storage   In computing, a digital storage medium in which a controlled laser beam is used to expose very small areas on a photosensitive surface.

en   In typesetting, a measure equal to half the width of an em. See em.

enable   In electronics, a pulse signal used for control purposes, e.g. to open a gate thus permitting other operations. See gate.

encipher   In data security, (1) to scramble data or convert it, prior to transmission, to a secret code, (2) to convert plain text to ciphertext. See cryptography.

encode   In data communications, (1) to convert data, by means of a code, in such a way that it may be subsequently reconverted to its original form, (2) to convert from one system of communication to another. Compare decode. Synonymous with code.

encoder   In computing, a device capable of translating from one method of expression to another.

encryption   In data security, the conversion of a clear text signal to a coded form for security reasons. See cryptography, data encryption standard. Synonymous with encipher.

end   In computer programming, a statement in a high level language program to inform the translator that the end of the source program has been attained. See translator.

end around carry   In electronics, a carry generated in the most significant bit of a number in a register, and carried around to be added to the least significant bit of the same register. See least significant bit, register, most significant bit.

endless loop   (1) In recording, a sealed continuous loop of magnetic cassette tape. (2) In computer programming, an error state in which there is no exit from a loop of instructions.

end of address   In data communications, a control character which indicates to the receiver that the last character of the address has been transmitted and successive characters relate to the message.

end of block   In data communications, a control character which indicates to the receiver that the last character of a block has been transmitted. See block.

end of copy signal   In document transmission, a signal indicating the end of transmission.

end of document   In character recognition, a mark on a document, recognizable by a detector, to indicate that the last position where data can be entered has been passed.

end office   Synonymous with central office.

end of file   In computing, a character indicating that the last record of a file has been read. See file, record.

end of message   In data communications, a control character which indicates an end of message; used to separate messages in a multimessage stream. See end of text.

end of page indicator   On a typewriter, a device giving a warning of the approach of the end of page during the typing operation.

end of text   In data communications, a control character which indicates to the receiver that the previous character was the last in a message text. Compare start of text.

end pages In videotex, the pages, at the leaves of a tree structured database, containing the information. See leaf, routing page, tree structure.

end to end control In data communications, a technique for ensuring that information transferred between two data terminals is not lost or corrupted. See data terminal equipment.

end to end signalling In communications, a method of signalling in which signals are sent from one end of a multilink connection to the other without intermediate storage.

end user In communications, a person who is the ultimate recipient of information flowing through the system.

end user device In computing and communications, a device, e.g. a VDU, that provides the final output of an operation without need for further processing. See VDU.

energy The capacity for doing work. Energy exists in many different forms and in any system the sum of the mass and energy remains constant. See photon.

Energyline A database supplied by EIC/-Intelligence and dealing with energy. See on line information retrieval.

ENG See electronic news gathering.

enhanced services In communications, a service that uses the basic facilities supplied by a common carrier to provide additional, different or restructured benefits. Enhanced services are not regulated by the FCC. See basic service, computer inquiry 1980.

ENQ See enquiry character.

en quad In printing, a spacing bar of half the width of an em quad. See em quad.

enquiry character In data communications, a control character used to request a response from a remote station. The response may include station identification and the type of equipment in service.

enter In computing, to input a message for transmission from a terminal to the computer.

entity In databases, an object or event about which information is stored in a database. Compare attribute.

entity identifier In databases, a key that uniquely identifies an entity or data relevant to that entity. See entity, key.

entropy In information theory, the mean value of the measure of information conveyed by the occurrence of any one of a finite number of mutually exclusive events. The entropy $H(x)$ for event x with a probability of occurrence of $p(x)$ is given by $H(x) = -p(x) \log p(x)$. See information theory.

entry (1) In library science, the record of a book publication, or other item in a catalogue or other library record. (2) In word processing, the typing and entry of text into the system. (3) In databases, information stored about an object or event.

entry point In computer programming, the starting address of a subroutine to which control is passed from the main program. See subroutine.

enumerative classification In library science, a classification which attempts to list specific subjects. Most classifications are necessarily selective due to the difficulty of enumerating all possible specific subjects. Compare hierarchical classification. See classification.

envelope (1) In electronics, the gas tight enclosure of a CRT or vacuum tube. (2) In communications, the amplitude variations of an amplitude modulated carrier wave. (3) In data communications, a byte to which a number of additional bits have been added for control and checking purposes. See amplitude modulation.

envelope delay See delay distortion.

envelope detection In communications, a

method of recovering the signal from an amplitude modulated waveform. The received signal is rectified and smoothed so that the envelope of the modulated waveform is recovered. Compare synchronous detection. See amplitude modulation, rectification.

Enviroline A database supplied by EIC/Intelligence and dealing with environment. See on line information retrieval.

environment In computing, the state of all registers, memory locations and other operative conditions.

EOA See end of address.

EOB See end of block.

EOD See end of document.

EOF See end of file.

EOM See end of message.

EOT In data communications, a control character which indicates to the receiver that transmission has been completed.

EPA Electronic Publishing Abstracts, a database supplied by The Research Association for the Paper and Board, Printing and Packaging Industries and dealing with computers and computer industry, information systems and services, publishing and publishing industry. See on line information retrieval.

EPC See editorial processing center.

EPIC In computing, Exchange Price Information Computer. The UK Stock Exchange information system providing data to information services including TOPIC. See TOPIC.

episcope In audiovisual aids, a projector for displaying opaque subject matter on a screen, e.g. the pages of a book.

epitaxial layer In microelectronics, a thin layer of the order of 10 microns, of doped semiconductor material that is grown onto a substrate. See chip, micron.

EPO European Patent Office.

EPOS Electronic Point of Sale. See point of sale.

EPROM In microelectronics (1) Erasable Programmed Read Only Memory, (2) Electrically Programmable Read Only Memory. See electrically programmable read only memory, erasable programmed read only memory.

equalization In electronics and communications, a general term for a system designed to compensate for some form of deficiency in frequency response. See loading.

equatorial orbit In satellite communications, the path of a satellite when its orbital plane includes the earth's equator. Compare inclined orbit.

EQUIVALENCE A logical operation, A EQUIVALENCE B has the result true if A EXCLUSIVE OR B is false. The corresponding truth table is

A	B	A EQUIVALENCE B
0	0	1
1	0	0
0	1	0
1	1	1

compare EXCLUSIVE OR. See truth table.

equivalent service In telephony, a multiline telephone service in which calls are automatically routed to the next available line of a group when the dialed number is busy.

erasable programmed read only memory See PROM.

erasable storage In computing, (1) a storage device whose data may be altered during the course of computation, (2) an area of storage used for temporary purposes, (3) a storage medium which can be erased and reused repeatedly, e.g. magnetic disk storage.

erase In computing, (1) to replace all the binary digits in a storage device by binary zeros, (2) to replace all hole patterns on a punched paper tape by holes in every position. (3) In computing and recording, to remove the information and signals on magnetic media. See binary digit, paper tape.

erase head In recording, a small degaussing device in the path of the tape which removes previously recorded signals. See degausser.

erecting system In optics, a system which produces a top side up image, e.g. a camera viewfinder.

E region In radiocommunications, a layer in the ionosphere occupying a region between 90 and 150 kilometers above the earth. Compare D region, F region. See ionosphere.

ergonomics The study of people in relation to their working environment. It is concerned with the design of man machine interfaces to improve factors affecting health, efficiency, comfort and safety.

ERIC Educational Resources Information Center, a database supplied by US Department of Education, National Institute of Education and dealing with education & educational institutions. See on line information retrieval.

erlang In communications, a unit of telecommunication traffic intensity determined by the product of the number of calls, carried by the circuit in one hour, and the average duration of the call in hours. See erlang hour, traffic.

erlang hour A unit of traffic volume, equal to the mean traffic intensity of one erlang maintained for one hour. See erlang, traffic.

EROM In microelectronics, Erasable Read Only Memory. Synonymous with electrically alterable ROM.

erratum In publishing, an item omitted from a book and acknowledged by subsequent inclusion of an erratum slip.

error A discrepancy between a computed, or measured, value and some objective standard. See error condition.

error burst In communications, a series of

consecutive errors. It is not unusual for errors to occur in groups or clusters.

error condition In computing, a state that results from an attempt to execute invalid instructions or operate on invalid data. See instruction.

error correction code In computing and communications, a code designed to detect an error, in a word or character, identify the incorrect bit and replace it with the correct one. Compare error detection code. See hamming code.

error detection code In computing and communications, a code designed to detect, but not correct, an error in a word or character. Compare error correction code. See parity checking.

error message In computing, a statement indicating that the computer has detected an error in the translation or execution phase of a program.

error rate In data communications, the frequency of occurrence of errors, defined as the ratio of the number of bits incorrectly received to the total number of bits received.

ESA European Space Agency.

ESA-IRS In databases, an information retrieval service operated by the European Space Agency (Italy). See on line information retrieval.

ESC See escape codes.

escape character See escape codes.

escape codes In data terminal equipment, a code combination which causes a device to recognize all subsequent code combinations as having an alternate meaning to their normal representation. Escape codes are used for indicating a sequence of control messages in ASCII. See ASCII.

escapement On a typewriter, movement of the paper perpendicular to the typing line over a predetermined distance.

ESPRIT European Strategic Program for

Research in Information Technology, launched in 1984, which aims at concentrating on long term research for IT product leadership. Compare Alvey.

ESS See electronic switching system.

etching (1) In graphical processes, the use of acid to bite an image into a metal plate. (2) In microelectronics, the process of removing material, on a chip, left exposed by the exposure and development of the photoresist. See chip.

etch type In typesetting, type that is produced by direct etching of a printing surface, e.g. by a laser, electron beam etc. Compare strike on, cold type, hot type.

Ethernet In data communications, a local area network standard using baseband mode of transmission at 10 megabits per second, coaxial cable, bus topology and CSMA-CD access protocol. Originally developed by Xerox. Compare Cambridge Ring. See baseband signalling, bus, coaxial cable, CSMA-CD, local area network, megabit.

ETS Japanese satellite program.

ETV See educational television.

ETX See end of text.

Euler circle See Venn diagram.

EURODICAUTOM In machine aided translation, EUROpean DICtionaire AUTOMatique, a term bank operated by the EEC to provide assistance in translation of scientific and technical documents. It can give corresponding phrases or sentences in several languages, terms or expressions accompanied by illustrative contexts and/or definitions as well as term by term definitions. See term bank.

Eurolex A database supplied by European Law Centre Limited and dealing with law - international; law - UK. See on line information retrieval.

Euronet The data transmission network provided for the European Economic Community by the telecommunication authorities of member countries. Users on Euronet are able to access specialized scientific, technical and economic information via a packet switched network, which in turn is connected to the public telephone system of member countries. See packet switching.

European Informatics Network In communications, a European project established to coordinate research into networks and to promote agreement on standards. Its first task was to construct a packet switched subnet which became operational in 1976. See packet switching.

Eurotra In machine translation, proposed state of the art system. The proposal was initiated by the EEC in 1977 and is mainly intended for the translation of committee minutes, technical memoranda etc. See machine translation.

Eurovision The European television program distribution service.

evaluative abstract In library science an abstract which comments on the value of the original. Compare auto abstract, general abstract, indicative abstract, informative abstract, selective abstract, slanted abstract. See abstract.

even parity See parity.

even word spacing Synonymous with fixed word spacing.

even working In printing, a piece of print which is contained in sections of 16, 32, 48 or 64 pages.

EX See exchange.

exception dictionary In word processing and computer aided photocomposition, a store of word breaks which do not conform to the usual rules. See hyphenation.

Excerpta Medica A database supplied by Excerpta Medica and dealing with biomedicine. See on line information retrieval.

exchange In telephony, the generic term for an assembly of telephone equipment providing for the interconnection of incoming and outgoing lines, with the necessary signalling and supervision facilities, housed in one building. See central office, toll center.

exchangeable disk See disk pack.

exchangeable disk storage In computing, one or more disk units with disk packs that can be replaced by an operator. See disk pack.

exchange line Synonymous with local loop.

exchange text string In word processing, a function that enables a text string to be changed for another text string at one, or a number, of points throughout the text. See search and replace, string.

exclusion (1) In some telephone systems, a feature permitting a user to exclude or prevent other users from access to a line or channel. (2) In logic A EXCLUSION B is true if A is true and B is false. The corresponding truth table is:

A	B	A EXCLUSION B
0	0	0
1	0	1
0	1	0
1	1	0

See truth table.

exclusion word dictionary In computing, a dictionary of syntactical words, articles and propositions which are ignored when a computer scans titles in the making of a KWIC index. See KWIC.

exclusiveness In library science, a classification principle that it should not be possible to class a specific subject in more than one term of an array. See array.

EXCLUSIVE OR A logical operation. A EXCLUSIVE OR B is true if either, but not both, A or B is true. The corresponding truth table is:

A	B	A EXCLUSIVE OR B
0	0	0
1	0	1
0	1	1
1	1	0

See truth table, OR.

execute In computing, to run a program or

to carry out an instruction. Synonymous with run.

execution time In computing, the time taken for a CPU to carry out a sequence of instructions. See run time, CPU.

executive In computing, a master program that controls the execution of other programs. See operating system.

executive control program See operating system.

exerciser In computing, a test system or program designed to detect faults in a program or circuit under development.

exhaustivity In library science, the extent to which a document is analysed to establish the subject content that has to be specified for search and indexing purposes. The greater the proportion of concepts covered the greater the exhaustivity. Compare specificity. See depth indexing.

exit In computing, an instruction which upon execution relinquishes all further control by that program.

expander board Synonymous with expansion card.

expansion card In a microcomputer, a card added to the system in order to mount additional chips or circuits so as to extend the system capability, e.g. modem, additional RAM. See MODEM, RAM. Synonymous with add-in.

expert systems In computing, a computer system which reflects the decision-making processes of a human specialist. It embodies organized knowledge concerning a defined area of expertise and is intended to operate as a skilful, cost effective consultant. An expert system comprises a knowledge base, inference machine, explanation program, knowledge refining program and natural language processor.

The knowledge base contains the distilled and codified knowledge of the human expert, or experts. It is much more than a simple database of facts; the expert must formulate

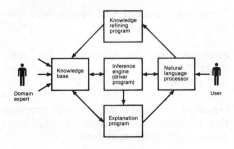

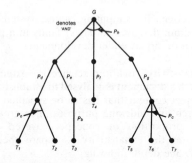

expert systems
Fig 2 AND/OR tree representing rules.

rules, often based upon years of experience rather than deterministic laws, and in many cases such rules will be probabilistic. Much research is being conducted into the methods of structuring knowledge bases, one of the most common is the production system in which rules are formulated on an IF... THEN... basis. The knowledge base may be constructed directly by the expert or by a knowledge engineer who assists the expert to express his knowledge in the required format.

The inference machine is a program which drives the system; attempting to match known facts, elicited from the user, with the rules in the knowledge base. The ultimate goal, e.g. decision on the presence of minerals in a given region or identification of a disease, will not be attained in one step and the inference machine must set up subgoals, those successful subgoals are then used in higher level rules. The facts elicited from the user, and inferred from application of the productions, may often be expressed only in terms of probabilities. Sometimes the requirement for more information from the user is recognised by the inference machine

and the user may be asked to input that information or even to perform (say) laboratory tests to obtain it. If the user does not supply the requested information, then the system will attempt to infer it. The inference machine may establish subgoals from an AND/OR tree.

The initial facts (T) are entered at the bottom of the tree causing rules to be fired and thus establishing goals or subgoals. An essential part of the design of the inference machine lies in the strategy for exploring the trees to determine the most efficient method of goal achievement. The explanation program is essential to establish user confidence in the system. It is human nature to query the conclusions of an expert and the explanation program will enable the system to state the rule and input information leading to a particular conclusion. This facility can also expand upon the requirement for further information giving explanations of the terms used or a statement on why the additional information is required. A 'what if' facility in the explanation program can also enable the user to explore certain paths in the knowledge base.

The knowledge refining program enables the expert to update the knowledge base in the light of experience of the system or the acquisition of new knowledge in this field. The natural language processor facilitates the man-machine dialog and enables the user to communicate with the system in a natural manner.

Expert systems software is available on current computer systems and can even be implemented on microcomputers. Expert systems have been employed by chemists to determine chemical structures (CONGEN), in geology to provide a consultant system for mineral exploration (PROSPECTOR), in medicine to provide advice on diagnosis and therapy for infectious diseases (MYCIN). The range and versatility of current systems is, however, limited both by the substantial effort involved in the development of the knowledge base and by the power of the inference machine necessary for determining goals in a massive knowledge base. The current research on artificial intelligence and the power of the future generation of computers opens up the possibility of extensive, powerful systems of the future. In the meantime, however, one can speculate that the expert system may prove to be an entirely new medium for reference material publishing. Compare database. See inference machine, intelligent knowledge based system, knowledge engineering.

expiration date   (1) In photography, the date past which a film may not be expected to yield good results. (2) In computing, the date set at which a file is no longer protected from deletion by the system.

exponent   A number indicating how many times another number, the base, is to be repeated as a factor. Positive exponents denote multiplication, negative exponents denote division and fractional exponents denote a root. See base.

exposing   In photography, the action of submitting any sensitized material to radiation, light or heat, which will act upon it to form an image or latent image. See photography.

exposure end point   In photography, the energy required to expose light sensitive material to a stated density value. See density.

expression   (1) A mathematical identity or relationship. (2) In computer programming, a source language combination of one or more operations, (3) a notation, within a program, that represents a value.

extended area service   In telephony, a telephone service in which exchange subscribers pay flat monthly, or measured, rates instead of long distance call charges for calls to adjoining exchange areas. See exchange.

extender   In photography, a device used to hold a lens away from the camera for close up work. See diopter lens.

extensible language   In computer programming, a language that permits a user to define new elements, e.g. data structures, operators, types of statements, control structures, in terms of existing elements in the language.

extension group hunting   In telephony, a PABX facility whereby a number of extensions can be associated in a group so that an incoming call automatically hunts for, and is connected to, the first free extension.

extension tube   See extender.

extent   In computing, a contiguous space on a computer direct access storage medium occupied by, or reserved for, a particular file.

external data file   In computing, a file containing data that is stored separately from the program that processes it.

external label   In computing, an identification label attached to the outside of a file medium holder, e.g. a sticky label attached to the case of a magnetic disk.

external schema   In databases, the structure of the data from a user's or programmer's viewpoint. Synonymous with subschema.

external sort   In a computer program sort, the second phase of a multipass sort in which strings of data are continually merged until one string of sequential data is formed. See multipass sort.

external storage   See auxiliary storage.

external timing   In data communications, an option on some modems in which the clock or synchronizing bits are externally generated, normally by the data terminal to which the modem is connected. See MODEM.

extra   In radio telegraphy, a spurious mark condition, recorded at the end, usually due to atmospheric noise. See mark.

extract   In computing, the process of removing specific information from a computer word by the logical action of a mask. See mask.

extra terrestrial noise   In communications, random noise originating in outer space and detected on the earth. The sun produces extra terrestrial noise. See noise.

extremely high frequency   In radiocommunications, the range of frequencies from 30-300 GHz. See GHz.

extremely low frequency In communications, frequencies less than 100 Hz. See Hz.

eye legible copy Pertaining to a microform record which contains title, or other lettering, legible to the naked eye. See microform.

eyepiece In photography, the lens of a camera viewfinder at which the operator's eye is placed.

E13B In character recognition, a magnetic ink character recognition font consisting of ten numerals and symbols widely used in automatic cheque sorting and banking. See font, magnetic ink character recognition.

F

face In printing, (1) the printing surface of type, (2) the design of a particular type, hence typeface. See typeface.

facilities management In commercial data processing, the use of an independent service organization to manage and operate a computing installation.

facility In data communications, a transmission path between two or more locations without terminating or signalling equipment.

facsimile (1) A system of still picture transmission and reception, using synchronized scanning at the transmitter and receiver, and telegraphy types of modulation such as frequency shift keying. The reconstructed image at the receiving station is either duplicated on paper or film. (2) A precise reproduction of an original document. (3) A hard copy reproduction. See frequency shift keying.

facsimile character generation In computer graphics, the technique of writing characters on a display screen by copying those already

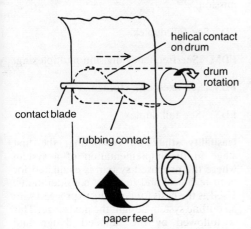

facsimile
A facsimile receiver using a rotating helix to produce the line scan.

written and stored in a master set. See character generator.

factor In a multiplication operation, any of the numbers or quantities that are the operands. See operand.

factoring In cryptography, the security of the RSA system depends on the computational infeasibility of factoring a large number of, say, 200 digits, made up of two prime numbers each of about 100 digits. Unless the prime numbers are known, the fastest computer would take several billion years to factor it using current technology. See RSA.

fading In radiocommunications, pertaining to variations in the received signal strength due to varying ionization conditions over the propagation path. Fading can affect television reception of a broadcast signal.

fail safe system In engineering and computing, a system designed to avoid catastrophe by reverting to a predetermined state in the event of a failure, e.g. the fail safe position of a computer controlled rail traffic light system might be to leave all lights at red. See fail soft system.

fail soft system In engineering and computing, a system that continues to operate in a degraded manner even when a part of the system has failed.

fall back In a real time computer system, backup procedures to be used in the event of a services machine failure. These procedures may be manual or involve the use of other computers and databases.

false drop In information retrieval, irrelevant items, retrieved during an on line search, which arise from the use of inappropriate search terms. See on line information retrieval. Synonymous with noise.

FAM See fast access memory.

family   (1) In printing, a complete range of design variants of a particular typeface. (2) In computing, a manufacturer's range of central processing units marketed to enable a customer to upgrade an installation with a more powerful unit without having to change the rest of his installation or programs.

FAMOS   See floating gate avalanche injection MOS.

FAMT   Fully Automatic Machine Translation. See machine translation.

fan antenna   In communications, an antenna in which the elements are spread in relative positions similar to the ribs of a fan.

fanfold   Synonymous with accordion fold.

fan in   In computing, the maximum number of inputs that can be connected to the processing unit, without affecting operation of the unit. Compare fan out.

fanning strip   In communications and electronics, a strip of insulating material with holes through which individual pairs of a cable may be passed for support and identification.

fan out   In computing, the maximum number of outputs that can be serviced by the processing unit, without affecting operation of the unit. Compare fan in.

farad   In electronics, the unit of capacitance. A capacitor has a capacitance of one farad when a charge of one coulomb produces one volt of potential difference between its terminals. See coulomb, volt.

far end cross talk   In telecommunications, cross talk that travels along the disturbed circuit in the same direction as signals in that circuit. See cross talk.

fast   In photography, pertaining to lenses which have an f-value near one, and to films having a relatively high sensitivity to light. See f-number.

fast access memory   In computing, a memory with a speed intermediate between that of main memory and fixed head disk. See fixed head disk, main memory.

fast lens   In photography, a lens which has a large light collecting capacity, i.e. an f-number of 2·8 or less. See f-number.

father file   In computing, a method of updating disk or magnetic tape files so that in the event of a serious corruption or loss of data, the master file can be reconstituted. When a new file is created as a result of updates to a current file, the old master file is termed the "father file". The new, updated file is called the "son file", whilst the file used to create the father file becomes the "grandfather file".

fault   In systems, a condition that causes a device, component or element to fail to perform in a required manner. The fault may be either physical or logical. Compare error. See bug.

fault trace   In computing, a record of faults and the circumstances of their occurrence as determined by a specially designed monitor system.

fax   See facsimile.

FC   See font change.

FCC   See Federal Communications Commission.

FD   See full duplex.

FDM   See frequency division multiplexing.

FDS   See fixed disk storage.

FDX   See full duplex.

feasibility study   In computing, the first stage in the implementation of a system where the proposed system is evaluated for both technical and financial considerations. Used as the basis for deciding to proceed with an outline system design, the next stage. This is followed by the detailed design and implementation, with each stage representing a more substantial financial commitment.

FEC See forward error correction.

Federal Communications Commission The independent regulatory agency, established by Congress in the Communications Act of 1934 and empowered by that Act to regulate interstate and foreign radio and wire communications services originating in the United States.

Federal Register Abstracts A database supplied by Capitol Services Inc. (CSI) and dealing with government - US federal. See on line information retrieval.

Federal State Joint Board In communications, a board established by the FCC and composed of commissioners representing state and federal jurisdictions. See Federal Communications Commission.

FEDS See fixed and exchangeable disk storage.

feed The mechanical process of transporting a continuous medium, such as line printer paper, printer ribbon, magnetic tape, etc. along to the required operating position.

feedback A process in which part of the output of a system is returned to it as input. Feedback may be positive, tending to increase the overall output, or negative, which will have the opposite effect. See negative feedback, positive feedback.

feed control In a duplicator, a control for starting and stopping the feed mechanism of the machine.

feeder cable (1) In telecommunications, the principal cable from a central office. (2) In cable systems, a transmission line that supports one or more signals over a number of receiving points. See central office.

feed holes In computing, holes punched in a paper tape to enable it to be driven by a sprocket wheel.

feed horn In microwave transmission, a horn which directs power to the reflector of a microwave antenna. The arrangement of feed horns on a satellite is important in shaping the beam to fit the area it serves. See horn, footprint.

feed reel A reel from which film or tape is passed through a mechanism and onto a take up reel.

femtosecond A thousandth of a picosecond, i.e. 10 to power minus 15 seconds. Approximately the time required for light to traverse one third of the width of a human hair. See picosecond.

FEP See front end processor.

ferric oxide In magnetic recording media, the magnetizable constituent deposited on tape or disk in the form of a dispersion of fine particles within the coating.

ferrite In electronics, a nonmetallic solid used in radio frequency operations. Ferrite materials have high permeability, high resistance and low eddy current loss. See permeability, resistance.

ferromagnetic In electronics, pertaining to a material such as iron or nickel that has a very high magnetic permeability. See permeability.

FET See field effect transistor.

fetch In computing, the process of getting the next instruction from memory. See memory.

FF See form feed character.

FHDS In computing, Fixed Head Disk Storage.

fiber crosstalk In optoelectronics, exchange of light wave energy between a core and the cladding, the cladding and the ambient surrounding or between differently indexed layers. The crosstalk is deliberately reduced by making the cladding glossy. See cladding, core, fiber optics.

fiber optics In communications, a technique which deals with the communication of signals by the transmission of light through extremely pure fibers of glass or plastic. A fiber optic cable comprises a plastic or glass

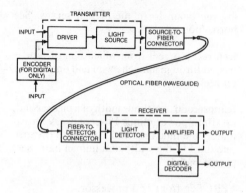

fiber optics
Fig 1 Basic elements of a fiber optic transmission system

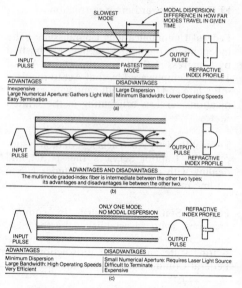

fiber optics
Fig 2 (a) multimode step index fiber; (b) multimode graded index fiber; (c) single mode step index fiber.

core surrounded by a layer of plastic or glass cladding which in turn is surrounded by a plastic jacket to protect the core from moisture and abrasion. The diameter of the core varies, with the type of fiber, from 2 to 200 microns. Light signals are inserted from LED's or injection lasers, propagated by refraction or internal reflection and are collected by light detectors at the receiving end.

The propagation along the cable is either reflective or refractive depending upon the type of cable - stepped index monomode, stepped index multimode or graded index multimode. Here the term index refers to refractive index and as the names suggest the refractive index of stepped index fibers is constant throughout the core and changes sharply at the core-cladding interface, whereas in the case of multimode graded index fibers, the index falls off gradually from the center of the core to its outer edges. In monomode cables the core diameter is very low (2-10 microns) and there is only one path - along the center of the core - for the light signals. With multimode graded index fibers the light rays travel at varying angles to the axis and are internally reflected at the core-cladding interface. In this case rays will travel along paths of different lengths and thus signal pulses are spread out and distorted. In the graded index fiber light rays will travel faster near the outer edge of the core, than along the axis, because the refractive index is lower. This effect tends to reduce the dispersion because rays travelling along the longer paths tend to travel faster.

The light signals are produced either by LED's or injection lasers. The comparative advantage of the injection laser over the LED are higher power output and a narrow beam but they tend to be more expensive and have shorter working lives. The transmitted light is normally in the infrared bandwidth, the signal attenuation is very sensitive to wavelength, tending to decrease with increased wavelength. The British Telecom system used wavelengths of 1·5 microns and transmit signals over 100 kilometers without intermediate amplification. The advantages of fiber optic cables, over conventional coaxial, are immunity from electromagnetic interference, high data carrying capacity, low signal attenuation, security, raw material cost, chemical stability and freedom from co-channel interference. A British Telecom 204 kilometer fiber optic telephone link has been established and the high bandwidth has encouraged the user of fiber optics for both video and data communication. See infrared, injection laser, LED, micron, refractive index, total internal reflection.

fiber optics recording In micrographics, a technique used in the production of computer output microfilm. A matrix of luminous fibers is selectively illuminated to form a single line of characters. The film is exposed to this line of characters and then incremented to permit the next line of characters to be generated. Compare CRT recording, electron beam recording. See fiber optics.

fibonacci sequence (1) In mathematics, a series of numbers in which each number is equal to the sum of the two preceding numbers in series : 0, 1, 1, 2, 3, 5, 8, 13, 21, etc. (2) In computing, a search in which at each step a division is made in accordance with the fibonacci sequence.

fiche See microfiche.

FID International Federation for Documents.

fidelity In audio frequency systems, the ability of a reproducing unit to recreate at its output a faithful reproduction of the input signal. See hi fi.

field (1) In physics, the energy associated with magnetic and electric sources. Electromagnetic fields are types of composite fields radiated from a source into the surrounding space, e.g. light waves. (2) In television, a scan of a picture by a series of evenly spaced lines from top to bottom. (3) In data processing, a physical space on a data\ recording medium which is reserved for one or more related data elements, e.g. a specified number of columns on a punched card might be reserved for employee numbers and would be designated as a field. (4) In photography, the portion of the object in front of the camera represented within the limits of the camera aperture at the focal plane. Area of field thus varies with the focal length of lens and camera to subject distance. (5) In data structures, an element of a record. See record.

field blanking In television, the time interval between two successive fields within which picture information is suppressed, and field sync pulses are transmitted. See field sync pulse, teletext.

field correlator In video disk, a device used to overcome field dominance problems during recording. The correlator accepts two successive fields and compares them line by line. If any difference is detected then one field is selected to be dominant and the device replaces the second field with a copy of the dominant field. See field, field dominance.

field data code In data communications, a standardized military data transmission code consisting of 7 data bits plus one parity bit. See bit, parity.

field dominance In videodisk, pertaining to a phenomenon in freeze frame recording on a CAV disk. The two fields selected for recording on one rotation should relate to the same instantaneous scene. If video material is mixed then the field dominance may change so that the fields selected for freeze frame viewing relate to successive video scenes giving a flicker effect. See CAV, field, freeze frame.

field effect transistor In electronics, a semiconductor device that combines the small size and low power consumption of a bipolar transistor with a high input impedance. Named field effect because the control action is effected by a field produced by an input voltage as compared with the control effect of the base current in a bipolar transistor. See transistor, impedance.

field frequency In television, the number of fields scanned per second. Field frequency is usually the same as that of the power supply, e.g. for a power supply of 60Hz the field frequency will be 60 fields/second, interlaced to produce 30 pictures/second. See field, interlace, Hz.

field separator In computing, a character that may be used to delimit fields or other items of data in the storage, transfer or transmission of data. See field.

field strength In radio wave propagation, the value of either the electric or magnetic field for a specified direction of the field.

field sweep In television, a general term for the movement of the electron beam spot in the vertical direction on the screen. See field sync pulse.

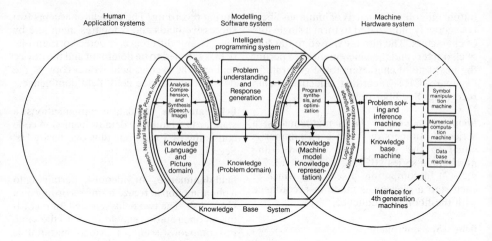

fifth generation computer
A conceptual diagram of a fifth generation computer system

field sync pulse In television, a pulse used for initiating the field sweep and generated during the field blanking interval. See field blanking, field sweep.

FIFO See first in first out.

fifth generation computer In computing, a knowledge-information processing system based on innovative theories and technologies, that can offer the advanced functions expected to be required in the 1990's, overcoming the technical limitations inherent in conventional computers. The previous four generations of computers have exploited successive developments of new hardware techniques but all were based upon the same Von Neumann architecture. The fifth generation machine breaks with this tradition and represents a unification of four current separate areas of research: knowledge based expert systems, very high level programming languages, decentralized computing and VLSI technology.

Knowledge based systems embody modules of organized knowledge which support sophisticated problem solving and inference functions to provide users with intelligent advice on specialized topics. This development will involve the production of large database machines employing relational database organization and linked to storage systems with 10 gigabytes capacity. The processing involved will be performed initially by powerful serial inference machines. These knowledge based systems will communicate in an extremely user friendly manner using voice images and graphics; the dialog will be conducted in genuine natural languages.

The very high level programming languages allow the programmer to specify 'what is to be performed' rather than the traditional 'how to perform it' approach of current languages such as Cobol or Pascal. Prolog is an example of such a language and is regarded as a stepping stone for the new machine. The demands on computer processors produced by the above mentioned developments force a radical rethink of the conventional Von Neumann architecture. The fifth generation computer systems will involve multiple processors comprising in some cases geographically separated computers, linked by communications networks, and in other cases miniature microcomputers residing on the same board or even on a single chip. The control mechanisms must ensure highly efficient non-sequential operations and employ dataflow or reduction architectures. Dataflow devices operate with individual actions performed when the input data becomes available. In reduction program organization the requirement for a result triggers the execution of the instruction that generates the value and the control mechanism is recursive rather than sequential or parallel. VLSI technology can yield high performance general and special purpose computers at a modest cost.

The fifth generation computer systems may be viewed as forming a new computer family in which members provide powerful facilities for problem solving and inference, database management and intelligent input output. Interfaces will be developed allowing both software modules and hardware units to be configured for applications or sets of applications. The resultant configuration can then be considered as building blocks for even larger systems. High speed local area networks will interconnect hardware units of a single system whilst global networks will link together computer systems for social organizations. Compare fourth generation computer, supercomputer. See byte, COBOL, database machine, dataflow, expert systems, general purpose computer, giga, hardware, inference machine, local area network, parallel computer, Pascal, PROLOG, recursive routine, relational database, software, VLSI, Von Neumann.

FIGS   See figures shift.

figure   In printing, a traditional term for a line illustration incorporated within the body of type in the pages of a book, as distinct from a photographic plate. See plate.

figures case   In telegraphy, a group of characters consisting mainly of figures and signs.

figures shift   (1) In communications, a code combination in the five level baudot code which causes all subsequent code combinations to be recognized as upper case characters, i.e. numerics, special symbols or control codes. (2) In a teletypewriter, a physical shift that enables the printing of images such as numbers, symbols and upper case characters. See escape codes, teletypewriter, shift codes.

figures shift signal   In telegraphy, a signal that causes the receiving apparatus to translate subsequent signals as secondary characters included in the figures case. See figures case.

file   In computing, a collection of records which are logically related to each other and handled as a unit, for example, by giving them a single name. A file may exist on

magnetic tape, disk etc. See magnetic disk, magnetic tape, record.

file cleanup   In data processing, the removal of superfluous data from a file. Synonymous with file tidying.

file conversion   In data processing, the process of changing the file medium or structure, often because of the requirements of a new program or change of hardware. See hardware.

file gap   In data processing, an area on a tape or disk used to signify the end of a file, and possibly the start of the next file. See file.

file layout   In data processing, the arrangement and structure of data in a file, including the order and field size of each element. See field, file.

file maintenance   In computing, the activity of keeping a file up to date by adding, changing, or deleting data, e.g. the addition of new programs to a program library on magnetic disks. See file management, file organization.

file management   In computing, a procedure or set of processes for creating and maintaining files. See file maintenance, file organization.

file organization   Synonymous with file layout.

file processing   In computing, the periodic updating of master files to reflect the effects of current data, e.g. a monthly stock run updating the master stock file. See run.

file protection   In data processing, a technique or device used to prevent accidental erasure of data from a file. See file protect ring.

file protect ring   In data processing, a ring which when removed from a magnetic tape reel will prevent data from being written to the tape. See file protection.

file security   In a computer system, the arrangements for ensuring the privacy or inaccessibility of files from unauthorized users. See data security, file protection.

file storage   In a computer system, peripherals which can store a mass of data. These include magnetic disk units, magnetic tape units, and magnetic card units.

file tidying   Synonymous with file cleanup.

fill character   (1) In office systems, a character used on form to fill out a field so that nothing can be added to the field once the form has been issued. (2) In computing, a character, usually a space, added to a set of characters to make the set a given length.

filled cable   In communications, a cable in which the gaps between the pairs are filled with a jelly like compound to prevent the ingress of moisture.

film advance   In typesetting, distance in points by which the film in the photounit of a phototypesetting machine is advanced between lines. See phototypesetting, point.

film assembly   In printing, the arrangement of film negatives or positives in position for making photolithographic printing plates. See photolithography.

film base   In filming and recording, the flexible, usually transparent, support on which photographic emulsions and magnetic coatings are deposited.

film chain   In television, equipment necessary to present film or slide images via television. It ordinarily includes a pickup TV camera, motion picture projector adapted for TV frame rate, slide projector and a multiplexer all mounted on a rigid frame. Compare multiplexer. See film pickup.

film makeup   See photomechanical.

film mechanical   See photomechanical.

film pickup   In television, the electronic scanning of motion picture film and transmission of the images by television. See film chain.

filmsetter   Synonymous with photocomposition.

film strip   In audiovisual aids, a series of still pictures on a strip of film, usually single frame 35 mm, but sometimes 110, Super 8 or 16 mm formats. The film strip may be silent or provided with an accompanying sound program (tape or record). Film strips may be advanced manually as desired or in response to an audible beep in the audio source. Some film strip equipment can be automatically advanced through inaudible pulses on the tape or record.

filter   (1) In electronics, a circuit which is frequency selective and so capable of attenuating some components of a signal whilst allowing other components to pass through uniformly. For example, a low pass filter attenuates all frequencies in a signal which are above a specified frequency. (2) In optics, an element commonly used in conjunction with a lens system and designed to absorb selectively specific components of the visible spectra. See electromagnetic radiation.

filter factor   In an optical system, a number designating the extent to which light is absorbed through the introduction of a filter. This attenuation can be remedied either by increasing exposure time (shutter speed) by an amount indicated by the filter factor, or by opening the diaphragm an amount sufficient to compensate for this absorption.

final route chain   In telephony, the final part of a network over which telephone calls are routed when all other direct, or high usage, paths are busy.

Financial Times Company Information   A database supplied by Financial Times Business Enterprises Limited and Predicasts Inc. and dealing with business & industry, corporations, news - economics and finance. See on line information retrieval.

find text string   In word processing, a command that enables a word or series of words to be found within the text.

firmware   In microcomputers, a program or data which has been permanently stored in a computer memory ie. a ROM, PROM,

EROM, or EPROM. This method of implementing software contrasts with programs held on magnetic media and which must first be loaded into the RAM memory of the computer before they can be used. See EPROM, EROM, PROM, RAM, ROM.

first computer inquiry   See computer inquiry 1980.

first generation computer   In computing, vacuum tube based electronic computers, of which the Univac 1 in 1951 was one of the earliest. Compare second generation computer, third generation computer, fourth generation computer, fifth generation computer. See vacuum tube, second generation computer.

first generation image   In duplication, the copy of a document, generally used as a master, produced directly by a camera.

first in first out   In computing, a method of storing and retrieving items from a list, table, or queue, such that the first element stored is the first one retrieved. Compare LIFO. See list, table, queue.

first line form advance   In a word processor, a forms feeding device that automatically advances the stationery to the first line on a new page once the current page is completed. This avoids the need to record keystrokes for multiple line advances.

first normal form   In relational databases, pertaining to data that can be expressed in flat file form. See flat file, normal forms.

first party release   In telephony, a method of operation in which the release of a connection begins as soon as either party restores his telephone, modem, etc. to its quiescent state.

fisheye lens   In photography, an extreme wide angle lens, about 150 degrees to 180 degrees, producing a very distorted circular image.

FIU   US Federation of Information Users.

five unit code   In telegraphy, a binary code in which the character signals are composed of five unit elements.

fix   See fixation.

fixation   In photography, that part in the chemical development of films and prints where the images are made permanent.

fixed and exchangeable disk storage   In computing, pertaining to a magnetic disk unit in which some disks are fixed and others may be exchanged by an operator. See exchangeable disk storage, fixed disk storage.

fixed data   (1) In word processing, data, text, or format instructions entered initially and available for subsequent reuse in documents. (2) In computing, data that is written on the display screen of a VDU but which cannot be altered by the operator. See format, VDU, protected field.

fixed disk storage   In computing, storage on non exchangeable magnetic disks . Compare exchangeable disk storage.

fixed head disk   In computer peripherals, a disk system with a dedicated magnetic head fixed over each track. In the more common type of disk unit, the head is located on an arm and so there is a delay whilst the head is positioned to seek the data. By eliminating the head positioning delay, this method provides very high speed access. See head, magnetic disk.

fixed length record   In computing, a record that always has the same length as all other records with which it is logically or physically associated. Compare variable length record. See record.

fixed point   In mathematics, a number system in which each number is represented by a set of digits and the position of the radix point is implied by the manner in which the numbers are used. Compare floating point. See radix.

fixed point arithmetic   Arithmetic using fixed points. See fixed point.

fixed routing   In data communications, a method of routing messages in which the behaviour of the network is predetermined, taking no account of changes in traffic or network components. Compare adaptive routing.

fixed word spacing In typesetting, printing in which word spaces are all standard, any extra space being left at the end of the line. Synonymous with even word spacing.

FL See focal length.

flag (1) In a packet switching network, a character (typically consisting of eight digits) used to mark the start of a frame. (2) In a computer, a signal set up to indicate that a specific condition has occurred. For example, when a buffer is full. See frame, packet switching.

flag bit See flag.

flag code Synonymous with escape character.

flagging In video recording, television picture distortion caused by incorrect video tape playback head timing coordination. See time base corrector.

flag sequence In a packet switching network, a sequence of bits used to identify the beginning and end of a frame. See frame, packet switching.

flare (1) In television, an unwanted component in the picture signal output from a camera, caused by the scattering of light in the optical system. Flare is often described in terms of its position in the picture, e.g. edge flare, bottom flare. (2) In film emulsion, an area exposed in some way other than directly through the lens, such as internal reflections between the various surfaces of the lens component. See halation.

flash In computer graphics and videotex, a display mode in which the characters are blanked out at regular intervals under the control of a timing device in the receiver. In videotex it is used to highlight a part of the page. See character.

flash card In micrographics, a document introduced during the recording of a microfilm to facilitate its indexing. See index.

flashing (1) In telephony, a signal used by a telephone operator to gain the attention of another, or a signal sent by a subscriber held by an operator to gain the latter's attention. (2) In cinematography, the process of exposing film to a weak light before or after camera exposure, but before processing, to reduce contrast.

flat In printing, (1) an assemblage of various film negatives or positives attached, in register, to a piece of film or suitable masking material ready to be exposed to a plate. (2) A lack of contrast and definition of material in printed matter.

flat bed camera See planetary camera.

flatbed cylinder press In printing, a mechanical press which uses a rotating cylinder to force the paper into contact with the flat inked typeface, as distinct from a platen press. Compare rotary press. See platen press.

flatbed editing machine In filming, a rigid table on which various pieces of equipment are mounted for editing films.

flatbed plotter In computing, a peripheral that provides point or continuous line plotting of subject matter on a flat surface. See plotter.

flatbed transmitter In facsimile, apparatus which hold the source document flat for scanning line by line.

flat file In data processing, a file comprising a collection of records of the same type which do not contain repeating groups. A flat file can be represented by a two dimensional array of data items. A relational database comprises a set of well structured flat files. See record, relational database, repeating group.

flat pack In integrated circuits, a package that has leads extending from the package and in the same plane, so that they can be spot welded to terminals on a substrate or soldered to a printed circuit board. See substrate.

flat rate A method of pricing for a service. For example, a telephone subscriber may pay a fixed monthly charge and be allowed to make an unlimited number of local calls.

flexography In printing, a relief or surface process which uses curved rubber plates. It is particularly convenient for printing on paper bags and packaging material.

flexowriter In office equipment, a form of typewriter accepting paper tape input.

flicker (1) In video disk, a phenomenon that occurs in a freeze frame display when the two fields are not identically matched, creating two different alternating pictures. (2) In television, a visual awareness that the luminance is being interrupted at a constant rate. (3) In computer graphics, an effect caused by a low refresh rate. See freeze frame, field, field dominance.

flip flop In electronics, a circuit which can be used as a one bit storage device for digital data. It can assume either one of two stable states at a given time.

floating accent In printing, an accent produced on a separate piece of metal and placed over the type character to which it belongs.

floating gate avalanche injection MOS In microelectronics, a type of programmable read only memory using storage cells similar to field effect transistors. An applied voltage produces a static charge, which allows the storage cell to conduct during the read action, for a 1 bit. Exposure to ultraviolet light enables the charge to leak away thus permitting reprogramming. See bit, field effect transistor, MOS, programmable read only memory.

floating point In computing, a form of number representation in a given base where a number is expressed as a mantissa multiplied by an exponent of the number base. Numbers with a very large range of magnitude, but limited precision, can be expressed with a fixed number of digits, one set of digits is allocated to the mantissa and another to the exponent. Compare fixed point. See mantissa, exponent.

floating voltage In electronics, a network or component having no terminal at ground potential. See ground.

flooding In packet switching, a routing method in which each node replicates incoming packets and send copies to its neighbours, thus ensuring that the actual destination is reached quickly and with certainty, though with considerable use of transmission capacity. See node, routing.

floppy In computing, an abbreviation for floppy disk or a floppy disk drive.

floppy disk In computing, a thin, flexible magnetic disk and a semi rigid protective jacket, in which the disk is permanently enclosed. There are three sizes of floppy disk: 8, 5·25 and 3·5 inches; the 3·5 inch disks have a rigid protective jacket. They may have data stored on one or both sides, at either single or double density. Depending on the size and type a floppy disk may store between 100 kilobytes to 1 megabyte. See double density, byte.

floppy disk controller In microcomputers, an interfacing device, which may be a combination of both hardware and software, that enables the CPU in a microcomputer to read or write to a floppy disk resident in a floppy disk unit. See CPU, floppy disk.

floppy disk unit In microcomputers, a peripheral storage device into which a floppy disk is inserted and from which data may be read or written to. The unit is linked or interfaced to a microcomputer via a floppy disk controller. See floppy disk controller.

flowchart In computer programming, a pictorial representation of an algorithm. With languages such as COBOL, BASIC and FORTRAN, the construction of a flowchart is one of the first steps in writing a program. The programmer initially lays out a broad brush general flowchart, replacing it with more detailed charts on the second and successive iterations. Plastic templates with standard symbols are available to facilitate construction. This method of program devel-

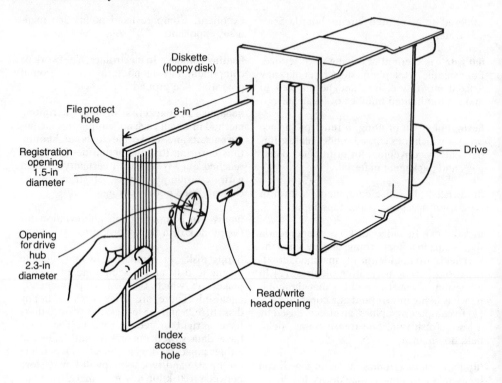

Diskette
(floppy disk)

File protect
hole

8-in

Registration
opening
1.5-in
diameter

Drive

Opening
for drive
hub
2.3-in
diameter

Read/write
head opening

Index
access
hole

floppy disk
An 8 inch floppy disk and floppy disk drive.

opment is being largely replaced by structured programming methods. See algorithm, BASIC, COBOL, flowchart symbol, flowchart template, FORTRAN, structured programming.

flowchart symbol   A symbol used to represent operations, data, flow or equipment on a flowchart. See flowchart.

flowchart template   A plastic template containing cutouts of the flowchart symbols used in the preparation of a flowchart. See flowchart.

flow control   In data communications, the control of data flow to prevent overspill of queues or buffers or loss of data because the intended receiver is unable to accept it. See buffer.

flush left   In typesetting, type that lines up vertically on the left, with a ragged right margin. Compare flush right. See ragged right.

flush right   In typesetting, type that lines up vertically on the right, with a ragged left margin. Compare flush left. See ragged left.

flutter   In recording, a form of audio frequency distortion arising in reproduction from disk, film or tape, caused by variations of speed in the transport system. See wow.

flux   (1) In recording, a measure of the magnetic effect produced by a magnetic recording head, or a tape as it passes a head. (2) In optics, the amount of light energy incident or reflected from a body, measured in lumens. See lumen, magnetic head.

fly back   In a television, the rapid return of a scanning beam from the end of a line or field scan, to the start of the next.

fly fold   A method of folding paper.

flying spot scanning In television, a method of scanning used for film transmission in which a moving, horizontal spot of light from a CRT is passed through the film and detected on a photocell. See photocell, scan.

FM See frequency modulation.

FNP See front end network processor.

f-number In optics, a measure of the amount of light passed by a lens, the smaller the f-number the 'faster' the lens. It is the ratio of the focal length to the maximum diameter of the lens opening and is usually inscribed on the lens. See focal length, f-stop.

focal length In optics, the distance from the optical center of a lens to the film plane when the lens is focused at infinity. Generally, a shorter focal length lens when used in a projector will give a larger image size on a screen for a given projection distance.

Focus Committee A UK Department of Industry committee formed to coordinate British national and international information technology standards activities.

focusing (1) In a cathode ray tube, a process for ensuring that the electron beam is contained in a small spot area on the phosphor screen. (2) In photography, the maximum definition of image attainable with a lens on a screen or film.

fog In a photographic emulsion, a region which has developed as a result of exposure to unwanted light, such as that arising from leaks in the camera.

follow me diversion In telephony, a PABX facility which enables a user to have incoming calls automatically diverted to another extension. See PABX.

font In printing, a character set of given size, style and face. The set will contain lower case, capitals, small capitals, numerals, ligatures, punctuation marks, reference marks, signs and spaces. See face, ligatures.

font change A control character to change the font of a printing or display device. See font.

font disk In typesetting, (1) a plastic or glass disk containing the master character images which are used to form typeset characters. (2) the master characters stored in digital form on a magnetic disk. See magnetic disk, photo-typesetting.

foot candle A measure of light illumination, defined as that illumination falling on a surface of one square foot when the uniform flux is one lumen. See lumen.

footcandle meter A lightmeter calibrated in foot candles.

footprint (1) In satellite communications, the geographical area throughout which signals may be transmitted to, or received from, a particular satellite. Within this area, the field strength of the beam from the satellite must exceed a specific value. (2) In computing, the area of a desk occupied by a microcomputer. See field strength.

forbidden combination In data processing, a combination of bits that is not valid according to the criteria set by the programmer or system designer.

foreground In computer programming, the environment in which high priority programs are executed. A large computer is capable of running a number of programs at any one time, those programs with high priority will reside in the foreground, e.g. online terminal users, whilst low priority processing, such as a batch program, will be kept in the background. Compare background. See multiprogramming.

foreground colour In videotex, the colours in which characters are presented on an alphamosaic display. Compare background colour. See alphamosaic, videotex.

foreground program In computing, a program that has a high priority and so takes precedence over other programs that are running concurrently in a multiprogramming environment. See foreground, multiprogramming.

foreign exchange In telecommunications, a form of private line service which enables a

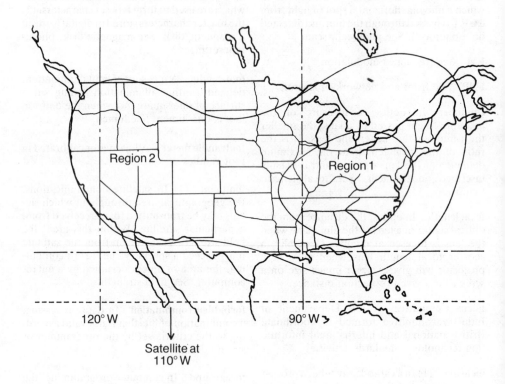

footprint
Contours of signal strength from 12/14 GHz SBS (Satellite Business Systems).

customer to maintain a local call service in another service area.

foreign exchange line   In telephony, a subscriber's telephone line connected to an exchange or local office, other than the one that would normally be used.

forest   In data structures, a collection of trees. See tree.

fork-join   In computer programming, a control instruction in parallel computation systems. Fork indicates the next instructions that may be performed in parallel. Join indicates the instructions that must be executed before the designated instruction can be obeyed. See parallel computer.

form   (1) In office systems, a document in

which certain items have been precoded and against which variable information is entered. (2) In printing, type matter, blocks and spacing material encompassed in a chase as a complete letterpress printing unit. Also, a complete lithographic plate for printing on one side of a sheet. See lithography.

formant   In acoustics, pertaining to a resonent frequency of the vocal tract. See speech synthesis.

format   (1) In filming, the dimensions of a film stock and its perforations, and size and shape of the image frame. (2) In computing, the predetermined mandatory order, organization or position of symbols in a computer instruction, data or word, data transmission message etc. The order is mandatory so that the computer can understand and interpret the information. (3) In a book, the dimensions of the printed page. See instruction, word, data transmission.

formatted dump In computing, a dump in which certain data areas are isolated and identified. See dump.

formatting In typesetting, translating the designer's type specifications into format, or command, codes for phototypesetting equipment. Compare type markup. See phototypesetting.

form feed In computing, a command from the CPU to a line printer to move the paper onto the next sheet for printing. See continuous stationery, line printer.

form feed character In data processing, a control character that causes a printer to move a form to the next predetermined position.

form letter In word processing, a repetitive letter sent to more than one person in which the name and address are either individually or automatically typed. See mail merge.

form mode In data communications, pertaining to sophisticated microprocessor based terminals intended for data entry. Typically the computer displays a form for the operator to fill out using cursor control and local editing facilities. Compare page mode, scroll mode.

forms flash In micrographics, the method by which document formats are superimposed on a frame of computer output microfilm containing other data. See microfilm.

forms mode In word processing, the storing of a format for a particular form. The format will provide automatic carriage position and other operator aids. See format.

formula In mathematics, a rule expressed as an equation, e.g. $F = MA$ is a formula derived from Newton's laws of motion.

fortnightly decision In CATV, the 1968 Supreme Court decision which allows CATV operators to record and retransmit broadcast television programs without regard to any copyright restrictions. See CATV.

FORTRAN In computing programming, FORmula TRANslator, a high level problem oriented programming language used principally by engineers and scientists. See high level language, problem oriented language.

forward busying In an automatic switching telephone system, the process of successively changing the states of devices and links from idle to busy as a telephone call is set up. Compare forward clearing.

forward channel In data communications, a transmission channel in which the direction of transmission coincides with that in which the user information is being transferred. Compare backward channel.

forward clearing In an automatic switching telephone system, the process of returning devices and links from busy to idle successively in the direction in which the call was established. Compare forward busying.

forward echo In a transmission line, an echo travelling in the same direction as the original wave, and formed by energy reflected back from one irregularity and then onwards again by a second. If forward echoes add in a systematic way, they can impair the overall performance of the transmission line. See echo.

forward error correction In data communications, a method using redundant code which enables both error detection and some error correction without retransmission. See error correction code, hamming code.

forward scatter In radiowave propagation, a wave produced as a result of scattering and propagating in the same general direction as the incident wave.

forward supervision In data communications, use of supervisory sequences sent from the primary to a secondary station or node. See node, supervisory sequence, primary station, secondary station.

FOSDIC In micrographics, Film Optical Scanning Device for Input into Computers.

A storage and retrieval system using direct input into a computer from 16mm microfilm. See computer input from microfilm.

FOTS Fiber Optics Transmission System. See fiber optics.

fount See font.

four colour process In printing, a method of producing full colour pictures by superimposing impressions from plates with cyan, magenta, yellow and black inks. See subtractive colour mixing.

fourier series In communications, a mathematical series which can be applied to the analysis of periodic waveforms. Any periodic waveform may be expressed as the weighted sum of the fundamental frequency and its harmonics. See fundamental frequency, periodic, harmonic.

fourth generation computer In computing, pertaining to the generation of computers developed in the mid 1970's using LSI technology. Compare first generation computer, second generation computer, third generation computer, fifth generation computer.

fourth generation languages In computer programming, a family of programming languages designed for use by end users rather than professional programmers. They are designed to speed up the process of application building, reduce the maintenance costs, minimize debugging problems and make languages user friendly so that end users can solve their own problems. See debug, spreadsheet.

four track recorder In audio recording, the ability to store four different sound or data channels on an audio tape. Conventionally, tracks 1 and 3 are recorded in the 'forward' direction, with tracks 2 and 4 recorded in the 'reverse' direction.

four wire circuit In communications, a two way circuit where the signals simultaneously follow separate and distinct paths in opposite directions in the transmission medium. A telephone circuit carries voice signals both ways and in the local loop this is achieved over two wires because the waveforms travel-

ling each way can be distinguished. In the trunk network where amplifiers and multiplexers are used, the two directions of transmission have to be physically separated. It is called a four wire circuit because, in its primitive form, it uses a pair of wires for each direction. See local loop, trunk.

fpm frames per minute.

fps See frames per second.

FRA Federal Radio Act.

frame (1) In computing the array of bits across the width of magnetic or paper tape. (2) In an automatic switching telephone system, a complete cycle during which all the devices in a group are inspected by a common control system. (3) In a packet switching network, a complete sequence of bits identified by an opening synchronization character, and usually including a field containing the user's data. (4) in filming, an individual picture on a film, filmstrip or videotape. The size of the frame is determined by the limits of the camera aperture. (5) In television, a single television tube picture scan combining interleaved information. (6) In videotex, a page of data displayed on a terminal. (7) In artificial intelligence, a data structure for representing a stereotype situation; this concept may be useful in dealing with linguistic ambiguities which arise in machine translation. See bit, data structure, page.

frame frequency In television, the number of frames transmitted per second; it is 30 in the U.S., 25 in Britain. See frame.

frame grabber In recording, an electronic technique for storing and regenerating a video frame from a helical video tape signal. This method avoids the need for the continuous head to tape contact that would otherwise be required in freeze frame operation. See freeze frame.

framesnatch In cable television, a home control unit for receiving and storing a particular frame, transmitted as one of many.

frames per second (1) In cinematography, film speed through a camera or projector gate. (2) In television, a transmission standard related to the power supply frequency. See frame, gate.

frame store In television, special apparatus for storing analog signals in digital form on magnetic disk. A frame store is capable of storing many thousands of TV frames in an efficient way. See analog signal.

framing (1) In filming, the positioning and movement of a camera by a cameraman so as to eliminate unwanted action and to achieve good composition. (2) In data communications, the process of selecting the bit groupings represented by one or more characters from a continuous stream of bits. (3) In time division multiplexing, the method by which individual frames are recognized so that the time slots can be correctly identified. See framing bit, time division multiplexing.

framing bit In data communications, bits used to make possible the separation of characters in a bit stream, but otherwise carrying no information. See bit stream. Synonymous with sync bit.

framing code In teletext, a technique for enabling a receiver to achieve byte synchronization with the broadcast teletext signal. See synchronization.

framing pattern A unique pattern of framing bits. See framing bit.

FRC Federal Radio Commission.

free indexing In library science, a method of coordinate indexing in which words or phrases assigned as index terms for a given document are considered by the indexer to be appropriate even though they may not appear in the document. See index.

freeline In telephony, the state of a line when it is available for traffic.

free running mode In computing, a method of allowing two or more users of a database to have access simultaneously. The possibility that conflict between them may cause difficulties must be taken into account in the system design. This problem is avoided in the alternate mode. Compare alternate mode.

free space loss In satellite communications, a measure of the radiation dilution with distance of an antenna transmitting uniformly in all directions. Defined as the ratio of the power received by an isotropic antenna to the power transmitted by an isotropic antenna, in decibels. See antenna gain, isotropic radiator.

free wheeling In data communications, a technique in which the simplest protocol is used by teletype compatible terminals. The computer transmitting the data does not know whether it is received or not, or whether it is received correctly. Compare stop and wait protocol. See protocol, teletype compatible terminal.

freeze frame (1) In cinematography, a frame of motion picture film that has been repeatedly printed to give the appearance of frozen motion. (2) In recording, a disk player or video tape recorder in which an identical effect is created by continually re-reading the frame. Compare frame grabber. Synonymous with still frame.

F region In radiocommunications, that part of the ionosphere lying more than 150km from the surface of the earth. Compare D region, E region. See ionosphere.

frequency In communications, the frequency of a periodic wave is the number of times the cycle of the waveform is repeated in a second, measured in hertz. Compare period. See hertz.

frequency changer In radiocommunications, a device used in a receiver which changes the frequency of an input signal to a lower value for amplification purposes. See intermediate frequency, receiver.

frequency coordination In radiocommunications, an internationally agreed consultative procedure designed to prevent interference between terrestrial and satellite services sharing the same frequency bands. See band.

frequency divider In electronics, one or more flip flops used to divide down a square wave input frequency. Each flip flop output changes at half its input frequency. See flip flop.

frequency division multiple access In communications, a technique in which a pool of frequency bands, in a frequency division multiplexing system, are allocated to users according to demand. This enables the capacity of the channel to be dynamically switched according to demand, as compared with a fixed allocation system. Compare time division multiple access. See frequency division multiplexing.

frequency division multiplexing A process whereby two or more signals may be transmitted over a common wideband path, by using different parts of the frequency band for each signal. At the other end of the line the signals are separated and identified by selective filters which demultiplex them. Compare time division multiplexing. See filter, signal.

frequency domain In electronics, pertaining to the computation of the effect of a linear circuit on a periodic waveform by an analysis of the effects upon individual sinusoidal components of the waveform. Compare time domain.

frequency modulation (1) In computing, a form of modulation in which the instantaneous frequency of a carrier wave is caused to depart from the normal carrier frequency by an amount proportional to the instantaneous amplitude of the modulating wave. (2) In computing, a method of recordng data on a magnetizable surface. The direction of current in the recording coil is reversed at intervals determined by a clock sequence. If a 1 bit is to be recorded then the current is also reversed at the midpoint between clock pulses. These current changes produce corresponding changes in the orientation of the particles on the disk surface. Compare amplitude modulation, modified frequency modulation, phase modulation. See magnetic disk, modulation.

frequency multiplexing See frequency division multiplexing.

frequency response See amplitude frequency characteristic.

frequency reuse In satellite communications, a method of increasing traffic through-put by using allocated frequency bands more than once. The same frequencies are used to link different geographical areas, provided that the antennas have sharply defined beams and suppressed side lobes. See side lobe.

frequency shift keying In data communications, a method of signalling in which a carrier is frequency modulated by a signal which has a fixed number of discrete values. See frequency modulation.

friction feeder In a document copying machine or duplicator, a device that feeds single sheets of paper into the machine from the paper stack.

frilling In photography, the puckering and peeling of a photographic emulsion from its support during processing.

front end network processor In computing, a front end processor that handles the interface functions between a computer and a data network. See front end processor.

front end processor In computing, a small computer used to handle communication interfacing, e.g. polling, multiplexing, error detection for another computer. See multiplexing, polling.

front porch In television, that part of the video signal waveform between the start of the line blanking pulse and the leading edge of the line sync pulse. See line sync pulse, video signal.

front projection In filming, TV and still photography, a method of projecting a background image along the axis of a camera lens on a particular subject and a screen behind the subject. Usually, a two way mirror is interposed between the camera and main subject. Compare rear projection.

frying In a carbon microphone, noise produced by small irregularities in the current in the absence of any input.

FS See field separator.

FSK See frequency shift keying.

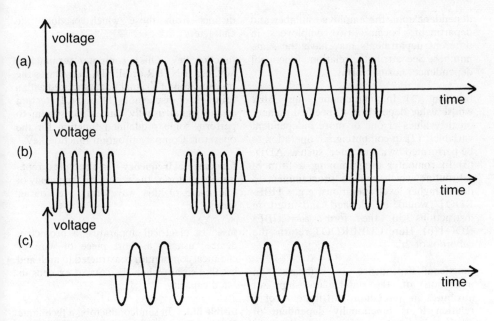

frequency shift keying
The frequency of the carrier wave (a) is shifted by discrete steps due to the combination of (b) and (c).

f-stop In optics, a lens calibration equal to the ratio : focal length divided by aperture opening. The lowest f-stop of a given lens is the setting which passes the most light and is equal to the f-number of the lens. See f-number.

full adder In computing, a binary arithmetic circuit which can add two numbers, producing a sum and an output carry, taking into account and adding in a carry from a less significant bit stage, should this be necessary. See binary arithmetic, half adder.

full coat magnetic film In recording, magnetic film, as distinguished from magnetic audio tape, which is completely covered on one side with an iron oxide coating. Magnetic film is used in conjunction with a magnetic film recorder. See magnetic film, magnetic film recorder.

full duplex In data communications, a mode of information transmission in which data is transferred in both directions simultaneously. Compare half duplex, simplex.

full frame time code In video recording, a standardized SMPTE method of address coding a video tape. It gives an accurate frame count rather than an accurate check time. See SMPTE.

fully connected network A network in which each node is directly connected with every other node. See node.

fully distributed costs In communications, a system for determining the costs of different services provided by a common carrier. The total allowable operating expenses and rate base are apportioned among the various services in accordance with fixed procedures established by the FCC. See FCC.

fully formed character In computing, pertaining to printers in which the character is produced by a single action, as in a typewriter. Compare dot matrix.

fully functional dependent In databases, a collection of attributes A of a relation R is fully functionally dependent on another collection of attributes, B, of relation R if A is functionally dependent on the whole of B but not on any subset of B. Suppose a relation contains employee name, employee number and department, and every employee in a particular department has a unique number. Then the employee name is fully functionally dependent upon the employee number and department, because two employees in different departments may have the same number. See attribute, relation, functional dependence, normal forms.

function (1) In mathematics, an entity whose value depends in a specified manner on the values of one or more independent variables. (2) In computing, an operation to be performed by a computer, such as ADD. (3) In computer programming, a form of subroutine which enables programmers to define higher level operations, e.g. CUBE-ROOT would be defined and used in instructions in the form a:=CUBE-ROOT(b). Here CUBEROOT returns the cuberoot of 'b'.

functional dependence In databases, an indication of the interrelationships of attributes in a relation. Attribute A of a relation R is functionally dependent of attribute B of relation R if, at every instant of time, each value of B has no more than one value of A associated with it. Suppose a relation contains employee name, employee number and department, if every employee has a unique number then the employee name is functionally dependent upon the employee number. Note that the employee number is not functionally dependent upon the employee name since two employees may have identical names. See attribute, fully functional dependent, normal forms, relation.

functional diagram A diagram that represents the working relationships among the parts of a system.

functional unit In a computer system, a piece of hardware, software, or both, capable of accomplishing a specified objective. See hardware, software.

function codes In typesetting, codes which control the operation of the typesetter as

distinct from those which produce the characters.

function key On a computer terminal, a key, e.g. ENTER or SEND, that causes the transmission of a signal not associated with a printable or displayable character. Detection of the signal usually causes the system to perform some predefined function for the operator. Compare program function key.

fundamental frequency In a complex, repetitive waveform, the repetition frequency of one cycle of this waveform. See fourier series.

fuse In electrical apparatus, a protective device, usually a short piece of wire or chemical compound, constructed to melt and break a circuit when the current exceeds its rated capacity.

fusible link In semiconductors, a technique for entering and storing data or a program in a PROM. A large current is used to destroy a metallized connection in a storage device, creating a '0', for instance, if a conducting element is interpreted as a '1'. See PROM.

fuzzy logic In mathematics, a form of logic in which the variables may assume a continuum of values between 1 and 0. It is used in expert systems when logical rules relate the input data and assertions to goals and subgoals but the data is often expressed in terms of likelihood rather than certainty. See assertion, expert systems, fuzzy set, rule.

fuzzy set In mathematics, a set in which membership can be expressed as a continuum of values between 0 and 1. A value of 1 corresponds to definite membership, a value of 0 corresponds to definite non membership. The concept of fuzzy sets have applications in information retrieval where it may not be possible to give a definite yes/no answer on the relevance of a document to a given area of search. See fuzzy logic, sets.

G

G See giga.

gain In electronics, (1) the degree to which the amplitude of a signal is increased when it passes through an amplifier, repeater or antenna, (2) the ratio of output power from an amplifier system, to the input power. Gain is normally measured in decibels. See decibel.

gain control In electronics, a control for varying the gain in a signal path. Gain control can be manual (such as a sound volume control) or automatic. See gain, automatic volume control.

galactic In databases, pertaining to data that is extensive and accessible from many places and by many applications.

galactic noise Noise originating in outer space. See noise.

galley proof In printing, a rough proof of composed text, normally in a column produced before the text is made up into a page. See proof.

galley slip See galley proof.

gamma (1) In photography, a measure of the extent of development, and hence the contrast characteristics of a film. (2) In television, the relationship between the logarithm of the reproduced signal luminance on the screen to the logarithm of the original scene luminance. For the reproduction of a visual scene, it is important that variations in light and shade are reproduced with similar variations in luminance. See contrast, luminance.

ganged controls In electronics, two or more manual switches which can either work in unison or independently.

gap (1) In communications, a process of communicating in which a normally continuous signal, such as a radio frequency carrier, is interrupted so as to form a telegraph type message. (2) In computing, the space between two records or blocks on a tape or disk. A gap is usually set to a predetermined value, such as all zeroes. It allows blocks to be rewritten in a slightly expanded or reduced format due to speed variations of the driving mechanism. See air gap, disk drive.

gap loss In magnetic disk recording, the loss of signal when the reading head is not directly in line with the information that has been recorded.

garbage (1) In radio reception, radio frequency spillover interference onto adjacent frequency bands. (2) In computing, data and programs in store that are no longer required.

garbage collection (1) In computing, an expression for cleaning dead records from a file, (2) the removal of items marked deleted from main memory to provide space for new programs or data. See file, main memory.

garbage in garbage out A computing adage, reflecting the fact that the quality of the output of a computer is dependent on the quality of the input.

gas plasma displays See plasma panel.

GAT See graphics art terminal.

gate (1) In a camera or projector, a hinged opening in which each picture frame is held momentarily for exposure or projection. In electronics, (2) the input terminal of an FET, (3) a generic term for a circuit element that can be turned on or off in response to one or more control signals. See NAND gate, FET.

gateway In telecommunications, equipment used to interface networks so that a terminal on one network can communicate with a terminal or computer on another. For example, in Prestel gateway in the UK, a subscriber to the Prestel viewdata service can access a third party database via the gateway facility. See interface, network, third party database, viewdata.

gaussian distribution A probability distribution derived by Gauss for the distribution of errors in experimental measurement. In communications, it is used to determine the probability that a signal carrying information will exceed a random noise voltage on the channel.

general abstract In library science, an abstract which covers all the essential points of the article and is provided when the interests of the reader are varied. Compare auto abstract, evaluative abstract, indicative abstract, informative abstract, selective abstract, slanted abstract. See abstract.

general purpose In computing, a system that can be applied to a wide variety of tasks without essential modification. Compare special purpose.

general purpose computer A digital computer designed to operate upon a wide variety of applications. It may be contrasted with a dedicated computer which would have special hardware and/or software for a specific purpose, such as the control of an industrial process. Compare special purpose. See hardware, software.

general purpose interface bus In micro-

processors, the name used for the IEEE (Institute of Electrical and Electronics Engineers) interface bus standard. See bus.

general purpose terminal In computing, a terminal that may be employed for a variety of functions, e.g. database interrogation, on line program development, data entry. See terminal.

general register In computing, a register used for such operations as binary addition, subtraction, multiplication and division. General purpose registers are used primarily to compute and modify addresses in a program. See address, binary arithmetic, register.

generation In computing, (1) a measure of the remoteness of a file from the original file, (2) pertaining to the technology used for fabricating the components of a computer. (3) In typesetting and micrographics, a measure of the remoteness of the copy from the original matter, the first copy being the first generation. See father file, first generation computer, second generation computer, third generation computer, fourth generation computer, fifth generation computer.

generator In computing, a program that creates other programs that carry out specific tasks, e.g. a report program generator. See report program generator.

genlock In television transmission, a device for synchronizing video signals generated from different sources.

Geoarchive A database supplied by Geosystems and dealing with earth sciences. See on line information retrieval.

geometric distortion (1) In television, a defect in the displayed picture in which the two dimensional linearity is distorted. (2) In recording, video tape velocity and time base changes which produce a distorted image on playback. See barrel distortion, pincushion distortion, time base corrector.

Georef A database supplied by American Geological Institute and dealing with earth sciences. See on line information retrieval.

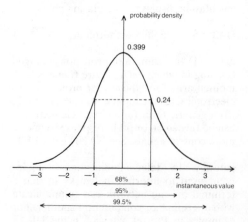

gaussian distribution

geostationary orbit   See geostationary satellite.

geostationary satellite   A satellite that appears stationary to observers on the earth's surface. These satellites have to be located at a height of about 35,800 km above the equator where the combined effect of the satellite's momentum and the earth's gravitational pull keep the craft in the desired circular orbit with respect to the earth's center. A satellite in such an orbit offers the following advantages:
   (a)   it remains almost stationary to the earth antennas, so the cost of computer controlled tracking of the satellite is avoided. A fixed antenna is sufficient;
   (b)   there is no necessity to switch from one satellite to another as one disappears over the horizon;
   (c)   there are no breaks in transmission;
   (d)   because of its considerable distance from the earth, the satellite is in line of sight from 42·4% of the earth's surface. A large number of earth stations may thus intercommunicate;
   (e)   there is almost no Doppler Shift, i.e. an apparent change in frequency of the signal from the satellite were it to move relative to the earth station. This is the case of satellites in ordinary elliptical orbits and more complicated receiving equipment is required, especially when a large number of earth stations intercommunicate.
   The disadvantages of geostationary satellites;
   (f)   the polar regions are not covered;
   (g)   because of the distance of the satellite from the earth, the received signal power is weak and the signal propagation delay is 270 milliseconds from earth station to satellite. See antenna, earth station.

get   (1) In computing, to obtain a record from an input file. (2) In word processing, the retrieval of a block of text from one document and its incorporation into another. See block, input, file, record.

ghost   (1) In filming, an unanticipated disturbance of an image arising from the original illumination of the subject, image transfer in duplication or in projection. (2) In television, a secondary picture tube image, displaced to the right of the main image and generally caused by a reflected signal arriving at the antenna. Sometimes ghosting can be caused in cable systems where there is a long mismatched feeder cable between the antenna and the television receiver. See ANAPROP, impedance matching.

GHz   See gigahertz.

Gibson Mix   In commercial data processing, a statistically balanced mix of instructions representative of the type of workload associated with commercial computing. It is one of several variations used for evaluating computer performance. See benchmark test.

GIDEP   US Government Industry Data Exchange Program.

giga   A thousand million, i.e. 10 to the power 9.

gigahertz   In communications, a frequency of one thousand megahertz. See megahertz.

GIGO   See garbage in garbage out.

glare   A visual condition caused by excessive luminance variations within the field of vision, e.g. when bright sources of light such as windows or lamps or their reflected images fall in the line of sight. See luminance.

glitch   (1) In television, random picture noise appearing as an ascending horizontal bar. (2) In digital systems, a short duration disturbance which can affect a timing or pulse waveform.

global   In computer programming, a variable whose value is accessible throughout the program. Compare local.

global satellite communication system   The commercial system set up by INTELSAT to provide world wide communications facilities. Geostationary satellites are positioned above the Atlantic, the Pacific and the Indian ocean to provide global common carrier telephone and data circuits. The INTELSAT system is characterized by large, expensive, highly reliable earth stations designed for interconnection to the circuits of national telephone administrations. INTELSAT represents an evolutionary system of satellite communications, the first step being taken in 1965 with the launch of the satellite Early Bird (later renamed INTELSAT 1). This had 240 telephone circuits, equivalent to one television channel and was operational through to 1968. In July 1980 there were 12 INTELSAT satellites providing over 17,000 international voice circuits, in addition to facilities for television and other services. The INTELSAT VI series of satellites to be launched in the mid 1980's will each provide up to 30,000 voice circuits plus 2 TV channels. As the cost of earth stations drop more antennas will be constructed and more traffic will be generated, making it economical to use more powerful satellites. This in turn will reduce the cost of earth facilities. By the end of this decade one can confidently expect that satellite communication technology will provide:

(a) a means to reach isolated places on earth. This is especially relevant to third world countries where the availability of very low cost satellite communications will reduce the need for expensive terrestrial telephone plant;

(b) an alternative to suboceanic cables. For example, multinational corporations will enjoy instantaneous global communications;

(c) the ability of a cheap receive only antenna to pick up hundreds of different TV broadcast channels;

(d) a data facility capable of interlinking computer terminals and computer databases everywhere;

(e) a multiple access facility capable of carrying all types of signals on a demand basis.

These facilities are in direct consequence of the falling costs of satellite communications and the opportunities for new services that are opened up. What is harder to predict are the social, economic and political implications of a technology that can make information available either to an all powerful minority or to mankind everywhere. See earth station, geostationary satellite.

global search and replace See search and replace.

glyptal In printing, pertaining to characters

engraved onto a steel punch. Compare ductal.

GND See ground.

go ahead tone In data processing, an audible signal indicating that the system is free to carry out an instruction.

goal In computing, an outcome of the application of rules in an expert system. The ultimate goal, or goals, of the system will provide the user with the desired results of the consultation, e.g. the probability that the site contains specified minerals. In general the goal will only be attained after investigation of a hierarchy of subgoals. See expert systems, rule.

golf ball Colloquial name for the spherical typing head of an IBM 72 typewriter and its derivatives.

GPIB See general purpose interface bus.

GPT See general purpose terminal.

grabber In electronics, a fixture on the end of a lead wire, with a spring activated hook and claw designed to make electrical contact with a circuit or component. See frame grabber.

grade of service In telecommunications, a measure of the quality of the service in terms of the availability of circuits when calls are to be made. Grade of service is measured during the busiest hour of the day and is usually expressed as the fraction of calls likely to fail at the first attempt owing to equipment limitations. See busy hour, circuit.

grain (1) In cathode ray tubes, the particle size of the phosphor coating in the interior surface of the tube face. (2) In printing, direction of the fibers in a sheet of paper. See phosphor dots.

graininess In film emulsion, the characteristic of a photographic image which under normal viewing conditions appears to be made up of small particles or grains. This effect is due to the grouping together, or clumping, of the individual silver grains.

grammatical mistake In computer programming, a violation of the rules of a particular language. See syntax.

graph A diagram representing some form of relationship between two or more variables. See coordinate graph.

graphic A symbol produced by a process such as handwriting, drawing or printing.

graphic arts quality In photocomposition, a machine that can offer the facilities of traditional composition methods of change of type face and font, variable spacing, right hand justification, proportional spacing for characters and variable leading between lines. See face, font.

graphic display terminal (1) In computing, a VDU which is capable of displaying graphical information. The screen is divided into discrete addressable elements which form the display picture, (2) In typesetting, a VDU which enables the phototypeset matter to be viewed as it appears on the font disk. See computer graphics, font disk, phototypesetting, pixel. Synonymous with page view terminal.

graphic language In computer graphics, any language used to program a display device.

graphics (1) In filming, printed or hand painted titles, charts, graphs etc. (2) In computing, the ability to present data in the form of drawings, pictures, diagrams etc.

graphics art terminal In typesetting, a terminal with an output that is used for typesetting. The output is, typically, encoded alphanumeric characters and control characters on magnetic disk or paper tape. The terminal is used in conjunction with a photographic typesetter. See alphanumeric, control character, phototypesetting.

graphics character In videotex, one of 127 different shapes which can be generated in a character rectangle as part of a page. There are alphanumerics characters to provide text, and graphics characters to provide an elementary, mosaic type of pictorial representation. There are three sets, alpha-numerics, contiguous graphics and separated graphics, each of 96 display characters, some of which are common. See alphanumerics set, character rectangle, contiguous graphics, separated graphics.

graphics mode In videotex, the display mode in which the display characters are those of one or other of the graphics sets, depending on whether contiguous or separated graphics are used. See display character, display mode, contiguous graphics, separated graphics.

graphics set See contiguous graphics, separated graphics.

graphic terminal See graphic display terminal.

graph plotter See plotter.

graticule In a CRT, a transparent sheet with a ruled reference scale used to cover the tube screen for waveform calibration.

grave In typesetting, an accent above the letter in the form of a diagonal stroke downwards left to right. See accent.

gravure See photogravure.

gray code In computer programming, a binary code in which sequential numbers are represented by binary expressions, each of which differs from the preceding expression in only one place. Synonymous with cyclic code.

gray scale In filming and television, a range of ten discrete luminance values (1 = pure white, 10 = pure black) for evaluating the shading in a black and white television or for exposure tests. A television picture tube cannot adequately reproduce the extremes of the scale.In colour television, the gray scale test is important since at no place on the scale should colour be visible. See luminance.

Green Thumb In videotex, the US Department of Agriculture's service for farmers. See videotex.

grid In optical character recognition, two sets of parallel lines crossing at right angles

Decimal	Natural Binary	Gray Code
0	0000	0000
1	0001	0001
2	0010	0011
3	0011	0010
4	0100	0110
5	0101	0111
6	0110	0101
7	0111	0100
8	1000	1100
9	1001	1101
10	1010	1111
11	1011	1110
12	1100	1010
13	1101	1011
14	1110	1001
15	1111	1000

gray code

used for specifying or measuring character images.

grid gauge   In micrographics an inspection tool which is used to check the position of images on microfiche. See microfiche.

grotesque   Synonymous with sans serif.

ground   In electronics, a conducting connection, whether by design or accident, by which an electric circuit or piece of equipment is connected to the earth.

ground absorption   In radiocommunications, absorption of energy from a wave at or near the surface of the ground.

ground station antenna   In communications, an antenna used to receive and transmit signals to and from a communications satellite. See satellite.

group   (1) In telecommunications, an assembly of 12 telephone channels forming a 48kHz frequency band of a carrier transmission system. (2) In telegraphy, a word consisting six characters in length. (3) In computing, a set of related records that have the same value for a particular field in all of the records. See field. channel, record, kHz.

group delay   In communications, a modulated radio frequency signal consists of a group of waves, within an overall wave envelope which may travel at slightly different speeds. The group delay is the time of propagation of the modulated wave envelope transmitted between two points. See modulation.

GSIS   US Group for the Standardization of Information Services.

guard band   (1) In recording, the blank portion of a magnetic tape which separates two tracks of information, thus preventing signal interference. (2) In communications, a narrow band of unused frequencies between allocated channels, intended to minimize the possibility of mutual interference. For example, most television channels have a guard band of 0·5MHz on each side of the channel. See interference, MHz, frequency division multiplexing.

guarding   (1) The function of preventing the false operation of device. (2) In book production, a method of attaching a single leaf to a section of a book or periodical.

guide bars   In computing, lines on a bar code that indicate the beginning and end of the bar code pattern and also separate items in the coding pattern. In UPC the guide bars comprise two thin black lines that are slightly longer than the code lines. See bar code, UPC.

guided wave   In radiocommunications, an electromagnetic wave travelling along a waveguide. See electromagnetic radiation, waveguide.

gun   In television, that part of the cathode ray tube which provides a continuous source of electrons for the beam. In a colour tube, there are three guns, one for each of the additive primaries: red-orange, green and blue-violet. See additive primary colours, cathode ray tube.

gutter In printing, the space between pages of type when laid on a form, including an allowance for trimming. See form.

H

hacker In computing, a computing enthusiast. The term is normally applied to people who take a delight in experimenting with system hardware, software and communication systems.

halation (1) In photography, a flare or halo effect caused by excessive light bouncing back through the emulsion of a film base. (2) In television, a dark area on a picture tube surrounding an overloaded bright area. See emulsion, overload.

half adder In computing, a combinational logic circuit which is capable of adding two binary digits, A and B, to produce a sum, S, and a carry, C. It is so named because it is not designed to add an input carry from a less significant digit. Consequently, the half adder has little use except as a component of a full adder. See full adder.

Input A	Input B	Output sum S	Output carry C
0	0	0	0
1	0	1	0
0	1	1	0
1	1	0	1

See binary digit, EXCLUSIVE OR, full adder, truth table.

half duplex In data communications, transmission which takes place one way at a time on a two way circuit. See duplex.

half space In word processing, the vertical distance advanced by a sheet of paper when moved through a distance of half a character space parallel to the typing line.

half title In a book, a right hand page containing only the title, preceding the title page of the book.

	Direction	No. of Channels	Typical Application
Half-Duplex (HDX)	Both directions, alternately	One	Communications between a low speed terminal and a computer.
Full Duplex (FDX)	Both directions, simultaneously	Two	High speed data transfers, e.g. between two computers.
Simplex (SPX)	One	One	Outputting commands from a computer to servo-mechanisms in a factory.

half duplex
A comparison of half duplex, full duplex and simplex transmission.

halftone (1) In facsimile, a picture having a range of tones lying between picture black and picture white. (2) In printing, an image having a continuous shading, in contrast to a line subject.

halftone process In printing, a photo-mechanical reproduction of a continuous tone original. The subject is photographed through a finely ruled glass screen, which splits the image into white or black dots according to tonal variations in the original.

half wave rectifier In electronics, a device that passes current in only one half of an applied AC voltage cycle. See AC, rectification.

halfword In computing, a contiguous sequence of bits, bytes or characters that occupy the space of half of a computer word and is capable of being addressed as a unit. See word.

halide In photography, a chemical compound of halogen and silver which renders the silver light-sensitive.

halo See halation.

halt In computer programming, an instruction to stop the CPU which may be restarted by a switch on the console. See console.

hamming code In data transmission, a code that is capable of being corrected automatically by the receiving terminal. For example, in the teletext system the hamming code used is a byte containing four message bits and four protection bits. A single bit error in such a byte can be corrected, without the need for retransmission. See error correction code.

HAMT See human aided machine translation.

hand held In filming, (1) a shot made with a hand camera, (2) the somewhat wobbly image on the screen which can result from such a shot.

handler In computing, a program under the control of the operating system which controls a specific peripheral such as a disk or printer and also handles interrupts. See interrupt, operating system.

hand receiver In telephony, a rigid combination of a microphone and earphone designed to be held in the hand.

handshaking In data communications, the exchange of predetermined signals when a connection is first made across an interface, in order to confirm it is working satisfactorily and to prevent data loss. See interface.

hand viewer In micrographics, a small portable magnetizing device used for viewing microfilm with magnification ranges from 5X to 15X. See microfilm.

hangover (1) In television, an effect due to the camera tube in which a field image will persist after a scan to contaminate the following field scan. (2) In facsimile, a defect whereby an abrupt tonal change on the original copy is reproduced as a gradual transition at the receiving terminal. See scan.

hang up In computing, an unwanted or unforeseen halt in a program run, due to faulty coding, hardware errors or operator mistakes. See run.

hard (1) In photography, any paper which produces a high contrast image. (2) In electronics, pertaining to materials which retain their magnetism where the magnetic field is removed. Compare soft.

hard copy In data processing, output in a permanent form, usually by printing on paper, but can include COM. Compare soft copy. See COM.

hard disk In computer peripherals, a rigid storage disk which is capable of storing more information and being accessed more quickly than a floppy disk. At one time because of cost and size considerations, they were only used in conjunction with large central processing units, but increasingly they are being used in microcomputers. See central processing unit, floppy disk, Winchester.

hard sector In computing, a floppy disk which is physically divided into sectors by holes punched through the disk. Largely superseded by soft sectored disks. See soft sectored disk.

hardware In computing, a term used to describe physical equipment such as a disk drive, central processing unit or printer, as opposed to programs, procedures, rules and associated documentation. Compare software.

hardware breakpoint In computing, the ability to halt a program at a predetermined point in its execution via manual switches on a central processing unit. A program can then analyse the contents of registers associated with the program for diagnostic purposes. See central processing unit, diagnostics.

hardware interrupt In computing, an interrupt request made by a peripheral, or some other external, device. Compare software interrupt. See interrupt.

hardwired (1) In teleconferencing, telephone equipment which is permanently connected into a wall rather than attached to a telephone jack. (2) In microelectronics, the implementation of a facility using logic circuits (hardware) rather than by using software. See hardware, logic circuit.

harmonic In waves, an oscillation with a frequency that is a multiple of a fundamental frequency. See fundamental frequency, fourier series.

harmonic distortion In electronics, a distortion caused by the nonlinear processing of an input signal. For example, in an overloaded amplifier, additional sinusoidal components in the output signal are produced, these being integral multiples of the sinusoidal components of the input. See distortion, overload.

harmonic telephone ringer In telephony, a ringer in a telephone that only responds to a very narrow frequency band of alternating currents. A number of such ringers, each responding to a characteristic frequency, are used for selective ringing when there are several parties on a subscriber's line. See selective ringing.

hartley In information theory, a unit of information based on a scale of ten, i.e. the amount of information that can be derived from the knowledge of the occurrence of one random event out of ten equiprobable events. See information content.

Hart's Rules In printing, rules contained in a book first published in 1903 by Horace Hart for compositors and print readers in connection with abbreviation, hyphenation, punctuation and spelling.

hashing In computing, a method of allocating storage locations to records of a file. An algorithm is applied to the record key to produce the location address; with suitably designed algorithms this method provides for a more uniform distribution of locations than if a simple linear relationship were employed, particulary if the keys have a very large range and the records are clustered in certain bands. See file, key, record.

hash total In data processing, a figure obtained by some operations upon all the items in a collection of data and used for control purposes. A recalculation of the hash total, and comparison with a previous computed value, provides a check on the loss or corruption of the data.

HASP See houston automatic spooling program.

hazard In electronics, an undesirable transient output that may occur when a circuit changes its state. For example, a flip flop condition in which both outputs are at zero for an instant during a change in state. Compare race. See flip flop.

HD See half duplex.

HDLC See High Level Data Link Control.

HDVS In television, High Definition Video System, a proposed new television standard with 1125 lines and a wide TV screen. It requires a higher bandwidth signal, equivalent to about 4 current channels and it may, therefore, be limited to satellite or cable systems. See bandwidth.

HDX See half duplex.

head (1) In filming, the beginning of a reel of tape or film. (2) In recording and computer peripherals, a specially designed electromagnetic transducer which can read, record or erase data on a magnetic disk, tape, cartridge or cassette. (3) In printing, the top edge of a book. (4) In computing, a special data item that points to the beginning of a list. See cassette, list, magnetic cartridge, magnetic disk, magnetic tape, transducer, magnetic head.

head alignment In recording, the electrical adjustment of a magnetic tape head for optimum performance characteristics. See magnetic head.

head crash In computer peripherals, a failure in a disk drive in which the head touches the rapidly rotating surface of a hard disk resulting in physical damage and data corruption. See hard disk, head.

head demagnetizer In video recording, a device which provides an alternating magnetic field used during routine maintenance to remove any residual magnetism from recording or playback heads. See residual magnetism.

head end In cable television, equipment which interfaces the antenna output with the cable network. It performs the function of pre-amplification, a combination of channels and change of frequency levels. See CATV.

header In data communications, the first part of a message or packet which contains all necessary information for directing that message to its destination. See packet switching.

header card In computing, a punched card that contains information related to the data in the rest of the cards in a batch. See punched card.

header label In data processing, a label that precedes data records of a file and contains descriptive information about the file, e.g. file name, reel number, retention period etc. See file.

heading In library science, the word, name or phrase at the beginning of an entry to indicate some special aspect of the document,

e.g. authorship, subject content, title. See entry.

headlife In recording, the nominal maintenance period for servicing a video recording head.

head of form In computing, the first line that data can be entered on a form. In continuous stationery it is the first printing line, typically the fourth line below the fold. See form.

headset In telephony, a lightweight microphone and telephone assembled on a headband and worn by switchboard operators, so freeing their hands.

head wheel In video recording, the rotating wheel holding the read/write heads of a tape record/playback assembly.

heat fixing In document copying, the use of heat to retain an image on the copy material.

heat sink In electronics, a material used to conduct heat rapidly away from an active component.

heaviside layer In radio wave propagation, the original name for the E region in the ionosphere, after the British physicist who discovered it in 1902. See E region ionosphere.

helical scan In video tape recording, a format in which the video heads and tape meet at an angle to produce a long, diagonal series of tracks, each diagonal stripe containing the full information for one field of video picture. It is so called because of the helical path the tape describes between supply and take up reels. It offers a still picture, but is more susceptible than quadruplex to tape stretch and slippage. Compare quadruplex. See field, freeze frame.

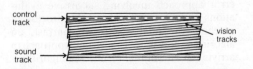

helical scan
Track layout in video tape recording.

helios noise In satellite communications, interference caused by the sun when an orbiting satellite passes between it and a tracking earth station. See earth station, sun outage.

help In computer programming, a facility provided by some software packages which enables a user to obtain information on certain aspects of the package during operation. See software package.

Hermes In communications, a proposed teletex based electronic document delivery service sponsored by the UK Department of Industry. It provides an electronic mail and document delivery service suitable for general use and for the specific needs of the publishing industry, libraries and information departments. See document delivery service, Teletex.

hertz The unit of frequency, one cycle per second. Abbreviated Hz.

heterodyne In electronics, a device which operates on two input sinusoidal signals to produce an output of two signals having frequencies equal to the sum and the difference of the frequencies of the inputs. See intermediate frequency, superheterodyne.

heterogeneous computer network In computing and data communications, a network of dissimilar host computers, such as those produced by different manufacturers. Compare homogeneous computer network. See host.

heterogeneous multiplex In data communications, a multiplex structure in which the information bearing channels are not transmitting at the same data signalling rate. Compare homogeneous multiplex. See data signalling rate.

heuristic In problem solving, a trial and error approach involving successive evaluations at each step made in the process of reaching the final result. In contrast, an algorithm represents a consistent approach in arriving at an optimal result. See algorithm.

heuristic searching In library science, a search for information, or a document, by the user in which the search may be modified as each bit of information, or document retrieved, influences the user's view on it.

hex See hexadecimal.

hexadecimal In computer arithmetic, a numbering system with a radix of 16. This system is used because a byte, comprising 8 bits, can be conveniently expressed as 2 hexadecimal digits. Digits between decimal 10 and 15 are represented by the letters A to F respectively, e.g. the decimal number 26 can be represented as hexadecimal 1A. See radix.

HF See high frequency.

hidden line In computer graphics, a line which is obscured from view in a two dimensional projection of a three dimensional object. Hidden lines may be used to show the shape of an object and are usually displayed in a different format to lines representing the visible edges of the object.

hierarchical classification In library science, a classification which splits items into initial sets and then successively splits those sets into even finer ones. Compare enumerative classification. See classification, Dewey Decimal Classification.

hierarchical computer network In computing, a network in which operations relating to control and processing are performed at several levels by computers specially suited for the tasks they have to execute.

hierarchical database A database that allows records to be related to one another on a 1 to n mapping, e.g., an employee's record may point to a number of dependents' records. The records are thus interrelated by a tree structure. Compare network database, relational database. See tree structure.

hierarchical network In data communications, a network which is synchronized through the use of clocks, where some clocks exert more control than others. Thus the operating rate of the network is a weighted average of the rates of all the clocks. Compare democratic network.

hierarchy In databases, a method of organizing data into ranks, each rank having a higher precedence than those below it. See hierarchical database.

hieroglyph A picture standing for a word or concept or sound. Derived from the Greek for sacred writing, used to describe the mode of writing used by the ancient Egyptians. Compare alphabet. See Hiragana.

hi fi In recording, pertaining to high quality audio reproduction from radio, disk, tape or microphone.

high frequency In radiocommunications, the range of frequencies from 3 - 30 MHz. See MHz.

High Level Data Link Control In data communications, a standard data communications interface defined by the ISO. It has a data format that is virtually identical with SDLC. See ISO, protocol, synchronous data link control.

high level data link control station In data communications, a process located at one end of a communications link which sends and receives HDLC frames in accordance with the HDLC procedures. See frame, HDLC.

high level language In computer programming, a language that enables programmers to specify a set of instructions in a form geared to the nature of the problem rather than the detailed operation of the computer. As a comparison, consider the instruction 'take the next flight to New York' with the mass of detailed instructions implied by this action : 'stand up, turn left, walk three paces, open door ....'. High level languages can be designed for specific application areas and provide facilities geared to the requirements of that area. The programs must adhere to well defined rules of syntax. There are three programs involved when a high level language is used: the source program, the translator and the object program. The programmer writes a source program. A specially designed computer programs the translator, converts and checks the syntax of the source program and either reports errors or, if error free, produces the corresponding set of machine code instructions, or instructions in some lower level language, i.e the

object program. See programming, source program, syntax, translator, FORTRAN, COBOL.

high level protocol In data communications, a protocol that enables users to carry out functions at a higher level than merely transporting streams or blocks of data. See protocol.

highlight In word processing, a facility which intensifies the characters on the display screen. Usually used in such text operations as deleting, copying and moving words or characters, to make the operator fully aware of which portions of the text will be affected when the command is executed. See command, display.

high pass filter In electronics, a filter passing signals having frequencies above a predetermined cut off frequency. See cutoff frequency.

high reduction In micrographics, a reduction in the range 31X to 60X. Compare low reduction, medium reduction, very high reduction, ultra high reduction. See reduction.

high speed In data communications, transmission speeds in excess of those normally attainable over voice grade channels, i.e. in excess of 9600 bits per second. See medium speed, narrow band.

high speed carry In computer logic circuits, any method which can be used to speed up the processing of carries when numbers are added in parallel. See carry, full adder.

high speed duplication In video recording, the production of one or more tape copies from a master tape at a speed many times faster than the original recording.

high speed multiplex link In data communications, a high speed link over which many signals are combined, but which can be uniquely separated at the far end of the circuit. See multiplexing.

high speed skip In word processing, a rapid vertical advance of a form on a printer to the areas where information is to be printed.

Synonymous with form feed, slew, vertical tab.

high usage trunk In telephony, a voice circuit directly connecting switching centers generating high volumes of traffic to each other. Since these trunks are specially designed for such traffic, they will always be selected first in routing calls between the locations they connect. See switching center.

hill climbing In artificial intelligence, a search technique for finding an optimum value. Starting from an arbitrary point the value of the appropriate function is measured at a number of test points in the vicinity, a move is then made in the 'best' direction as indicated by the test values. The process is repeated until all the neighbouring test points indicate 'lower' function values than that of the search point.

Hi-Ovis In cable television, Higashi Ikoma Optical Visual Information System. An experimental Japanese system employing switched star fiber optics and a computer system. Subscribers are provided with a keyboard, video camera and microphone, thus allowing them to participate in programs dealing with community affairs, education etc. Teleshopping comprises direct haggling with shopkeepers over a video link. Users can request programs stored on video cassette and loaded by robot arms. A form of computer information retrieval is also provided. See Qube.

Hiragana A character set of symbols used in one of the two common Japanese phonetic alphabets. See Katakana.

hiss In recording, audio frequency noise having a continuous spectrum, often audible during tape playback.

histogram In graphs, a representation of some type of distribution in which the frequency percentage is plotted on the ordinate and the varying quantity on the abscissa.

Historical Abstracts A database supplied by ABC;Clio Information Services and dealing with history, social sciences and humanities. See on line information retrieval.

hit (1) In computer databases, a comparison of two items of data in which specified conditions are satisfied. (2) In data communications, a momentary line disturbance which could result in the corruption of characters being transmitted. (3) In personal computing, an abbreviation of Hobbyist's Interchange Tape Standard, a tape cassette recording format designed to facilitate a broad exchange of cassettes and programs among hobbyists. See Kansas City Standard, format.

hit on the line In communications, a general term used to describe short term disturbances caused by external interferences such as impulse noise caused by lightning or man made interference. See noise.

HLL See high level language.

HOF See head of form.

hold In television, the synchronization of a sweep time base with a pulse signal. In some receivers, preset controls are marked vertical hold and horizontal hold. See time base.

hold current In electronics, the minimum current needed to keep an electrically operated switch, such as a relay, in the operating position. See relay.

hold graphics In videotex, a display mode which removes a gap in a graphic display when the colour is changed. The new colour code occupies a character space but in this mode the screen space is occupied by a repeat of the previous graphic character. See alphamosaic.

holding line In artwork, an outline for indicating the boundary of a solid or halftone image. See halftone.

holding time In communications, the total time that a circuit or device is occupied in connection with a particular call.

hole In semiconductors, a vacancy for an electron in an atomic structure. An electron in a neighbouring atom may move into this vacancy thus creating a similar vacancy in its own atom. This movement of electrons produces the effect of a positive carrier moving in the opposite direction of electron flow. p type impurities have such holes in their atomic structure and therefore introduce carriers when they are added to pure semiconductors. See electron, semiconductor, p-type material.

hollerith code In computing, a code used to represent data on punched cards. Data is represented by holes punched in one or more of twelve positions in each column, divided into two sections.

hologram A three dimensional image produced through a combination of photography and laser beams. Diffracted laser light from a subject is used to capture a two dimensional interference pattern in photographic film. These interference patterns, when illuminated by light from a similar laser, produce a three dimensional image of the original subject. See LASER, interference pattern.

holograph In publishing, a manuscript written entirely in the author's own hand.

holographic memory In computing, a system in which an image of a page of binary data is stored as a two dimensional interference pattern. This memory is illuminated by a laser beam and the image is formed on the surface of an array of photocells. The system is experimental but it is claimed that extremely high bit packing densities can be achieved. See bit, hologram, interference pattern, LASER, packing density, photocell.

holography See hologram.

home address In computing peripherals, an address written on a disk or drum indicating a track's address relative to the beginning of the storage medium. See track.

home banking The use of a domestic communication terminal, usually viewdata, to conduct transactions on the user's bank account. Compare self banking.

home computer In computing, a microcomputer intended for use in the home. Home computers range from small video game and educational computers to business microcomputers. Compare personal computer. See microcomputer.

Homelink In videotex, a home banking service operated by the Nottingham Building Society and the Bank of Scotland, using the Prestel system. See home banking, Prestel.

Homenet In communications, a cable like an electrical ring main that will connect together domestic appliances, heating, lighting and alarm systems providing timing and user control, energy management and connection to fire, police and medical services.

homing (1) In automatic switching, the automatic return of a wiper switch to a predetermined position following its release. (2) In audiovisual aids, the act of the projector automatically returning to its starting position. See wiper switch.

homodyne detection See superheterodyne.

homogeneous computer network In computing and data communications, a network of similar host computers, such as those of one model of one manufacturer. Compare heterogeneous computer network.

homogeneous multiplex In data communications, a multiplex structure in which the information bearing channels are transmitting at the same data signalling rate. See data signalling rate.

homograph One of several words having the same spelling but different meaning. Compare synonym.

hooking In recording, television picture distortion caused by errors in the head timing coordination of a video tape recorder. See video tape recorder.

hop In radiocommunications, a transmission path from one point on the earth to another via the ionosphere without any intermediate reflections from the earth's surface. See ionosphere.

horizontal In television, a signal which produces a scanning line 0·4 nanosecond duration across a television tube. See nanosecond, scanning line.

horizontal blanking In television, the blanking out of the retrace path area on the screen during the horizontal retrace. See horizontal.

horizontal parity See longitudinal redundancy check.

horizontal sync pulse In television, the pulse that follows the front porch in the composite colour video signal. It is used to synchronize the sweep circuits of the receiver with those of the camera. See composite colour video signal, front porch.

horizontal wraparound In visual display units, the continuation of cursor movement from the last character position in a row to the first character in the next row, or vice versa. Compare vertical wraparound.

horn In radiocommunications, a form of directional radiator or antenna, in which a feed waveguide is flared at its end in one or more dimensions to provide a radiating aperture. See antenna, waveguide.

host See host computer.

host computer (1) In a network, a computer that primarily provides services such as computation, database access or special programming languages. (2) In distributed processing, the primary or controlling computer in a multiple computer installation. (3) A computer used to prepare programs to be run on other systems; for example, a computer used to test programs to be run on a microcomputer. See cross compiler.

hot frame In filming, an overexposed frame and so one which is consequently producing a very bright image.

hot metal composition In printing, any typeset matter originating in hot metal casting. This traditional typesetting technique is now being largely replaced by photocomposition methods. See typesetting, photocomposition.

hot potato routing In data communications, a method of routing in which a packet of data is transmitted from a node as soon as possible, even though this may not be the best choice of outgoing line. See packet switching.

hot spot An area of too much brightness.

hot standby In computing, a method of hardware backup which is automatically switched into operation when a system failure is detected. Compare cold standby, warm standby.

hot type See hot metal composition.

hot zone In word processing, an area of adjustable width immediately to the left of the right hand margin. The system detects any word starting in the hot zone that will exceed its width. It may then pause to allow an operator to decide whether to hyphenate and start a new line, or to overrun the margin. Some word processing systems are programmed to make such decisions automatically. See hyphenation.

house corrections In printing, errors made during composition and corrected at printer's cost.

housekeeping In computing and word processing, supporting operations that are secondary to the main processing objectives. For example, initialization, file creation and maintenance activities. See file, initialization.

housekeeping information In data communications, signals which are added to

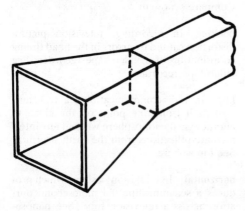

horn

information signals but intended only for the receiving equipment so that it may function properly.

house style   A set of design rules by which an organization establishes and maintains a public identity in its publicity, promotion, stationery and packaging. Synonymous with corporate identity.

houston automatic spooling program   In IBM computer systems, a program that provides a number of system management functions in a batch processing environment, including line printer spooling and internal scheduling activities. See spooling.

howler   In telephony, a device used to indicate that a telephone handset is off the receiver. It is connected at the exchange end of the subscriber's line.

HR   See high reduction.

Hseline   A database supplied by Health and Safety Executive, Library and Information Services (England) and dealing with safety. See on line information retrieval.

ht   See halftone.

hue   The name of a colour e.g. red, yellow, or the quality of a colour as determined by its frequency in the spectrum. Compare saturation. See colour.

hue control   In television, an essential control with NTSC receivers used for adjusting the hue of the picture. See hue, video standards.

huffman code   A code in which frequently occurring characters are assigned fewer symbols than less frequently occurring characters.

hum   In electronics, undesirable low frequency currents interfering with a desired signal, and usually caused by a poorly screened alternating mains supply.

human aided machine translation   In machine translation, a system in which the computer retains the initiative but which works with a human consultant, who need

not be a translator. The computer recognizes reliably when a certain difficulty has arisen and communicates the nature of the difficulty to the consultant. Compare machine aided translation.

humanist   In printing, an example of typeface.

hum bars   In television receivers, broad moving or stationary horizontal picture bars due to a variation in the DC power supply at the AC power supply frequency. See picture, field frequency.

hunting   (1) In control systems, an undesired oscillation generally of low frequency that persists after external stimuli disappear. (2) In telephone switching, searching for an available, idle circuit from a group. See group, feedback.

Hunt Report   In cable television, report of the Hunt Committee submitted in October 1982 in response to ITAP Report on Wideband Cable Systems. It proposed a liberal regulatory framework intended to encompass the private sector investment in the establishment of wideband cable systems. See ITAP Report, wideband.

hybrid circuit   In electronics, a complex circuit which is made by connecting a number of dissimilar elements such as semiconductor devices, integrated circuits, resistors etc. on a thick film. See thick film.

hybrid computer   In computing, a system which combines the elements of both digital and analog techniques. See analog computer.

hyphenation   In typesetting and word processing, the practice of dividing a word into two parts if it cannot fit on the current line. Word processing sytems are designed to handle hyphenation in various ways, one of which may call for the use of an exception dictionary. See exception dictionary.

hyphen drop   In word processing, a software facility which ensures that a hyphenated word at the end of a line loses its hyphen if it subsequently appears elsewhere in the text and no longer requires hyphenation. See hyphenation.

hypo In photography, a common abbreviation for sodium hyposulfate, incorrectly referred to as the fixing solution for film and paper. It is, in fact, sodium thiosulfate. See fixation.

Hz See hertz.

I

IACBDT UNESCO International Advisory Committee on Bibliography, Documentation and Terminology.

IACDT UNESCO International Advisory Committee for Documentation and Technology.

IADIS Irish Association for Documentation and Information Services.

IAM See intermediate access memory.

IARD Information Analysis and Retrieval Division of the American Institute of Physics.

IBA UK Independent Broadcasting Authority.

IBI Intergovernmental Bureau for Informatics, an organization developed by UNESCO with the remit 'to permanently assist people in the field of informatics to help them live in the context created by this discipline, to understand better its impact on society and to derive the maximum benefit from its possibilities'. See informatics.

IBM International Business Machines.

IBM PC In computing, a 16 bit personal computer produced by IBM. See microcomputer, personal computer.

IC See integrated circuit.

ICAI See intelligent computer assisted instruction.

ICIC UNESCO International Copyright Information Center.

ICIREPAT International Cooperation in Information Retrieval among Examining Patent offices.

ICL International Computers Limited.

ICOGRADA The International COuncil of GRAphic Design Associations, a body set up to provide a central focus for all aspects of graphic design.

icon In computing, a pictorial representation of an object in a computer graphic display. Used in display systems for an executive workstation to represent the functional component of an executive desk, e.g. documents, folders, in trays. See Lisa, mouse.

ICOT In computing, Institute for New Generation Computer Technology. The Japanese fifth generation computer research laboratory. See fifth generation computer.

ICR International Council for Reprography.

ICSSD International Committee for Social Sciences Documentation and Information.

ID See identification character.

IDD International Direct Distance Dialing.

ideal format In photography, a popular negative format (60 x 70mm), an alternative to 35mm format (24 x 36mm), which is smaller and more elongated.

identification In data communications, the procedure carried out by a host computer in determining the identity of an individual line, device, subscriber, etc. requiring access. See host computer.

identification character In data communications, a character that identifies a remote data station to the central station. See identification.

identifier In computing and communications, a character or group of characters used to identify, indicate or name a body of data. See terminal identity.

identity operation In boolean operations, a process which results in a boolean value of 1 only if all the operands have the same boolean value. See boolean algebra, operand.

ideogram In Chinese, a character which symbolizes the idea of a thing, without expressing the name of it. See Kanji.

idiot tape In typesetting, an unhyphenated, unjustified tape which cannot be used to set type until format codes are added and processed by a computer that makes end of line decisions. See hyphenation, justify.

idle In communications, the state of a line, or switching equipment on the line, when it is not in use.

idle character In data communications, a control character transmitted on a telecommunication line when there is no information to be transmitted. The character will not be displayed, printed or punched by the accepting terminal.

idle time In computing, operable time during which some or all of a computer system is not being used. Compare operating time.

IDMS See Integrated Data Management System.

IDP UK Institute of Data Processing.

IEC The International Electrotechnical Commission, a body responsible for electrical standardization, including standards for materials, components and methods of measurement. Some of the IEC's work relates to telecommunications applications in the fields of wires, cables, waveguides and CATV systems. See CATV.

IEE UK Institution of Electrical Engineers.

IEEE US Institute of Electrical and Electronics Engineering.

IEEE 802 In data communications, a proposed standard for local area networks dealing with the physical and data link layers. See data link layer, IEEE, physical layer.

IERE UK Institution of Electronic and Radio Engineers.

IF See intermediate frequency.

IFD International Federation for Documentation.

IFIP The International Federation for Information Processing, a federation of professional and technical societies concerned with information processing. One society is admitted from each participating country.

IFRB The International Frequency Registration Board, a body responsible for maintaining a master list of radio frequencies used throughout the world. It tries to prevent a country from introducing a new frequency if it would interfere with existing radio services. See International Telecommunications Union.

IF statement In computer programming, a conditional statement that specifies a condition to be tested and the action to be taken if the condition is satisfied. See conditional jump.

IIC International Institute of Communications.

IIL See integrated injection logic.

I Inf Sc US Institute of Information Scientists.

IIS See I Inf Sc.

Ikarus In digital typography, a widely used computer program which produces letterforms from splines. See Metafont, spline.

IKBS See intelligent knowledge based system.

ILD In optoelectronics, Injection Laser Diode, a semiconductor laser. See LASER, semiconductor laser.

ILL See inter library loan.

illegal character In computing, a character or combination of bits not valid according to some predetermined criteria, e.g. with respect to a specified alphabet for which that character is not a member. Compare forbidden combination.

illegal operation In computing, a process that a computer is unable to perform.

illuminance In optics, that part of the luminous flux that is incident on a unit area of a surface, i.e. a measure of the quantity of light with which a surface is illuminated. Measured in units of lux. See lux.

image (1) In computing, an exact logical duplicate stored in a different medium. (2) In reproduction, a faithful likeness of the subject matter of the original.

image area (1) In micrographics, that portion of the film frame reserved for an image. (2) In word processing, the area of a display device where characters can be displayed.

image carrier In phototypesetting, a disk, grid, filmstrip, or magnetic tape which holds details of typefaces used by a phototypesetter. It has the same function as a set of type matrices in machine composition. See machine composition, matrix.

image converter In television, a camera tube which produces a visible image of an object illuminated by infrared or ultraviolet light.

image degradation In photography, a loss of picture detail and good contrast as a result of successive duplication.

image distortion In optics, a fault in a lens which produces an unwanted modification in the appearance of an object. See aberration.

image master In typesetting, the matrix holding the type fonts in a phototypesetter, i.e. disk, filmstrip etc. See matrix, phototypesetting.

image plane In photography, the plane, perpendicular to the optical axis of a lens, at which an image is formed by the lens. This plane is normally coincident with the plane occupied by the emulsion surface of the film.

image retention See lag.

image sensors In television, devices that produce an electrical signal corresponding to the intensity of incident light. An optical image is focused on a matrix of sensors which are then scanned to produce a television picture signal. See pickup tube.

image spread In photography, the slight extension of the developed silver grains beyond the edges of images formed by the action of light striking the film emulsion.

image stability In visual display units, the perceived degree of freedom from flicker and movement of character images on the display screen. The main causes of image instability are fluctuations of the voltage supply. See flicker, jitter.

image storage space In computer graphics, the storage locations occupied by a digitized or coded image. See coded image.

imaging In phototypesetting, pertaining to the techniques used for creating and displaying an image, e.g. on a CRT. See CRT.

immediate access store In computing, main storage having a very fast access time. See main storage.

immediate address In computing, an instruction which contains the value of a required operand, rather than the address of the operand. See immediate data.

immediate data In computing, data contained in an instruction rather than in a separate storage location. Used for data that is predefined by the program and does not change in the course of the program execution. See immediate address.

IMP See interface message processor.

impact paper In printing, a coated paper used for multipart forms in which pressure on the top sheet causes the character to appear on the front of all sheets, thus eliminating the need for ribbon and carbon paper.

impact printer In word processing, a printer in which printing is the result of mechanical impacts. A key or ball with the desired symbol strikes a carbon or nylon ribbon and then the paper. Compare ink jet printer.

impairment scale   In television, a subjective scale used in the classification of degradations caused to the screen image by imperfections in transmission links or equipment. Usually the scale will have five levels ranging from imperceptible to very annoying.

impedance   In electronics, the property of a circuit that determines the magnitude and phase of the current flowing for a given applied voltage. The three basic elements of impedance are resistance, capacitance and inductance. See capacitance, inductance, phase, resistance.

impedance matching   In electronics and communications, the process of matching the impedance of a load or terminating device to that of the driving unit or network. Impedance matching is performed to maximize power transfer or to avoid reflection of signals back into the network. See impedance.

impedance matching transformer   In audio recording, a small transformer used to match a low impedance microphone output with the high impedance input of an amplifier. See impedance matching.

impedance mismatch   In networks, a terminating device whose impedance does not match that of the network. Compare impedance matching.

implementation   In data processing, the process of installing a computer system or an enhancement to an existing system. It represents the last stage of a series of steps prior to daily operation, including some or all of the following: feasibility study, outline system definition, detailed system specification, programming, integration tests and acceptance tests. In parallel with these activities, the user may be involved in equipment selection, staff training and establishing computer control policies. In very large computer projects, the industrial relations aspects of commissioning a new system may have to be thoroughly explored and agreed. See acceptance testing, feasibility study, systems analysis.

imported signal   In cable television, a program that is taken off the air outside the system's normal reception area and forwarded for local distribution over the cable.

impression   In printing (1) all copies of a book or other work printed at one time, (2) the degree of pressure on a sheet of paper in a press.

impression cylinder   In printing, the pressure drum in a cylinder press which receives paper and takes it into contact with the inked typed matter or plate and makes the impression. See impression.

imprint   (1) In publishing, the publisher's name printed on the title page of a book. (2) In printing, the printer's name, usually placed at the back of the title page.

imprint position   The position on a sheet of paper where a character is to be typed.

impulse   Synonymous with pulse.

impulsive noise   In communications, interference characterized by short duration disturbances separated by quiescent intervals. For example, the interference with radio reception caused by the ignition system on a car.

in band signalling   In communications, a system in which control signals are transmitted inside the band normally used for voice transmission. Compare out of band signalling. See band.

in camera process   In photography, a camera in which the development of the image takes place within the device itself, as in Polaroid and Kodak Instant Picture cameras.

incandescent   A light produced by a current passing through a filament at high temperature in a gas filled tube or bulb.

in circuit emulator   In electronics, a development tool used for debugging a microprocessor system ahead of hardware design. The emulator plugs into the circuit into which the microprocessor will be connected. See debug, emulator.

inclined orbit   In communication satellites, an orbit that is neither equatorial nor polar. Compare equatorial orbit, polar orbit.

inclusive OR   Synonymous with OR.

incoming message   In data communications, a message transmitted from a station to the computer. See station.

incoming traffic   In communications, traffic passing through a network and having its origin in another network. See traffic.

incoming trunk   In communications, a trunk coming into a central office. See trunk, central office.

increment   In computer programming, (1) a value used to alter a counter or register, (2) to alter the value of a counter or register by a specified value. (3) In computer peripherals, to move a card from one column to the next in the punch station so that each column presents itself for punching. (4) In a document reader, to move a document forward from one timing mark to the next so that a new line of characters is visible to the scan head.

incremental plotter   In computing, a plotter which is able to draw straight lines, and curves produced as a sequence of straight lines.

indefeasible right of use   In cable networks, a guarantee given to a subscriber for access to facilities on the network either until ownership of the network changes or else they are conveyed to another subscriber.

indent   In printing and word processing, to begin a line or lines with a blank space. In word processing systems a margin indent is usually handled automatically.

independent telephone company   Any telephone company in the United States which is not part of the Bell System.

index   (1) In library science, an organized or systematic list which specifies, indicates or designates the information, contents or topics in a document or groups of documents. Indexes can be organized under a variety of ways, e.g. authors, titles, dates, countries, institutions. (2) In publishing, an alphabetical list of subjects contained within a book together with page numbers. (3) In computer programming, a subscript of integer value that identifies the location of an item of data with respect to some other data item. (4) In word processing, to move the paper or display pointer in the direction used for normal printout. (5) In data structures, a list of the contents of a file or of a document with keys or references for locating the contents. (6) In micrographics, a guide for locating information on microform. See code line, file, indexing language, index register, key.

index build   In databases, the automatic process of creating an alternate index based on results from using the current access methods.

indexed address   In computing, an address that is modified by the contents of an index register prior to the execution of a computer instruction. See index register.

Indexed Sequential Access Method   In databases, a method of file access in which a stored index contains the address of a group of records and the highest key value of that group. See key, record.

indexed sequential storage   In databases, a method in which records are stored in ascending order of primary keys and one index points to the highest key on a physical sector, e.g. track, cylinder, bucket, etc. See bucket, cylinder, nondense index, primary key, track.

indexing   In computing, a technique of address modification by means of index registers. See index register.

indexing language   In library science, a language used for naming subjects in an index. Its vocabulary introduces a measure of control of the terms used in indexing and its syntax is formalized to permit only certain constructions, e.g. aluminium, heat treatment instead of heat treatment of aluminium. See syntax.

index page   In videotex, a page which classifies a particular subject into divisions along with routing numbers to branch the user to the appropriate pages. See end pages. Synonymous with routing page.

index register In computing, a register whose contents may be used to modify an operand address during the execution of computer instructions. An index register may be used as a counter, or to control the execution of a loop.

indicative abstract In library science, an abstract which indicates the content of the document rather than its methods and findings. Compare auto abstract, evaluative abstract, general abstract, informative abstract, selective abstract, slanted abstract. See abstract.

indicator In computing, a device, usually a light, that registers a particular condition in the system.

indirect address In computing, a memory location which contains the address of an instruction or data word, rather than the information itself. Compare direct address. See address.

indirect electrostatic process In document reproduction, an electrostatic process in which the image is formed within the machine and subsequently transferred to the unsensitized copying material. See xerography.

indirect letterpress Synonymous with letterset.

indirect ray In radiocommunications, a wave travelling along a path between transmitter and receiver which is not the shortest, e.g. at VHF or UHF frequencies reflection from an aircraft. See ghost, UHF, VHF.

induced interference In communications, noise induced in a circuit as a result of electromagnetic coupling with an external source. See noise.

inductance In electronics, an electromagnetic phenomena in which a change in current will induce a change in voltage in the same or adjoining circuit. Due to the very rapid current changes in digital computing circuits, even a straight connecting wire has significant inductance, and computer circuits must be

designed to avoid undesired inductive coupling.

induction coil (1) In telephony, a transformer used in a hand set for interconnecting the transmitter, receiver and line terminals. (2) In electronics, a transformer for converting interrupted direct current into a high voltage alternating current.

inductive coordination In communications, consultation agreements between the electricity supply authorities and the communications authorities designed to prevent induced interference. See induced interference.

INFAIS US National Federation of Abstracting and Indexing Services.

inference In data security, the deduction of confidential data about a particular person by correlating released statistics about groups of individuals.

inference control In data security, database controls for determining which statistics can be released without disclosing sensitive data. Compare inference.

inference engine See inference machine.

inference machine In expert systems, the part of an expert system that drives the system. It attempts to match the known facts about a particular problem with one, or perhaps more, of the rules. When a successful match is found the rule fires and the action part of the rule is used to update the known facts database.

inferior figures In printing, small characters, either figures or lower case, set at the bottom of larger characters, e.g. in chemical formulae, and projecting slightly below the line.

infinity (1) In optics, the position of a subject with respect to a camera lens which produces parallel light beams, in practice, a distance exceeding thirty feet. (2) In mathematics, a quantity greater than any assignable number.

infix notation In computing, a notation

where operators are embedded within operands. Compare prefix notation, postfix notation.

InfoLine In databases, an information retrieval service operated by Pergamon Info-Line Ltd. (UK). See on line information retrieval.

informatics (1) The science concerned with the collection, transmission, storage, processing and display of information. (2) Translation of the French term informatique which is normally considered to be equivalent to data processing.

information (1) Knowledge that was unknown to the receiver prior to its receipt. Information can only be derived from data that is accurate, timely, relevant and unexpected. (2) The meanings assigned to data by the agreed conventions used in its representation. If the content of a message is known prior to its receipt then no new information is conveyed. The information $I(x)$ for event x of probability $p(x)$ is given by $I(x) = -\log p(x)$, i.e. the information is highest for the least probable event. See information theory, information content.

information bearer channel In data communications, a channel capable of carrying both control and message information. It may therefore operate at a greater signalling rate than that required solely for user's data. See bearer.

information content In information theory, a measure of the information conveyed by the occurrence of a symbol emitted by a source, measured in hartleys or shannons. Defined as the negative of the logarithm of the probability that this particular symbol will be emitted. If logarithms to the base 2 are used, the unit is the shannon, if base 10 is chosen, the unit is the hartley. In practice, the probability of a particular symbol being emitted may be conditional on the symbols that preceded it. For example, a string of T's or H's representing the successive results of a toss of a coin would have an information content of 1 shannon.

information flow control In data security, controls concerned with the right of dissemination of information, irrespective of what object holds the information. Whilst access controls regulate the accessing of objects, information flow control addresses what subjects might do with the information contained in them. See access control, leakage.

information management system In computing, a system designed to organize, catalog, locate, store, retrieve and maintain information. Such systems are usually operated in realtime and are accessed via visual display units. See catalog, realtime.

information networks In databases, the interconnection of a physically dispersed group of databases linked via telecommunications so that the total information resource may be shared by larger population of users.

information processor A device that has stored information and instructions, receives input data or signals, processes its input and stores information according to its stored program and delivers output information or signals. The term computer is really a misnomer because the vast majority of the world's computers are not concerned with arithmetic or mathematical operations but with the processing of textual information or communication and control signals. See communications computer, control computer, word processing.

information provider In videotex, a name given to an organization providing information. Unlike other forms of publishing, an information provider is required to create an integrated system of cross references to aid user access. See cross referenced page.

information rate In data communications, the number of symbols emitted by a source per second multiplied by the average information content per symbol. See information content.

information retrieval In computing, pertaining to the techniques for storing and searching large quantities of data and making selected data available. These techniques can include on line storage, KWIC indexes and database methods. See KWIC, on line information retrieval, database.

information retrieval center In computing, a system designed to recover specific information for a user from a mass of data. See on line information retrieval.

Information Science Abstracts A database supplied by IFI/Plenum Data Company and dealing with library and information science. See on line information retrieval.

Information Technology The acquisition, processing, storage and dissemination of vocal, pictorial, textual and numerical information by a microelectronics-based combination of computing and telecommunications.

Information Technology (IT) has arisen as a separate technology by the convergence of data processing techniques and telecommunications, the former providing the capability for processing and storing information, the latter the vehicle for communicating it. This convergence has been catalyzed by the availability of complex, reliable and cost-effective microelectronic components and equipment. Global developments in electronics have also stimulated the search for common international standards in data processing and telecommunications and are beginning to pave the way for wide scale applications of IT.

The introduction of digital techniques into telecommunications which are compatible with modern data processing technology has done much to hasten the arrival of IT. The prospects now offered by satellite transmission, coaxial cables and optical fibers will eventually reduce costs of data transmission to the point where bandwidth is almost free. Many consumer services which are currently impracticable will become entirely possible in the foreseeable future.

See (a) Information as a resource, (b) digitization of information, (c) factors affecting progress, (d) cable systems.

(a) Information as a resource. Current developments in the technologies associated with the processing, storage and transmission of information by electronic means are creating an information based society within the industrial nations of the world. Information has become to these nations what coal and steel were to the pioneers of the industrial revolution.

Today, information is considered as a resource, essential to the operation of a country's economy. Unlike most resources, however, information is not exhausted by use, rather its value can be increased by its circulation.

Accurate and adequate information is a major component of industrial and commercial operations, and an increasing proportion of the labour force in an industrialized country is employed in information handling. Statistics from the US labour bureau show that almost half of the civilian workforce in the US are information workers (fig. 1). Within Western Europe a similar situation exists in that a large part of the workforce in the private sector is concerned with generating, recording, processing, reproducing and transmitting information in numbers or in words.

So far, computers have affected only a small part of this activity, mainly that part concerned with the storage and processing of numerical data. The availability of computerized systems which allow the processing of textual information has precipitated a complete re-appraisal of the working methods employed in offices, in the printing and publishing industries and in the postal and telecommunications services of Western Nations.

As a result of developments in IT, there will be a marked increase in the quantity of rapidly accessible information and in the ability to manipulate it. Access to constantly updated information is already possible in offices and homes through videotex systems. As printing and distribution costs rise and communications and computing costs fall, such systems may come to replace some paper publications. Business videotex systems enable information to be disseminated rapidly within a company. Further developments will provide individual users with the ability to interact in a simple way with financial, mail order, and other transaction based computer systems.

(b) digitization of information. Before information can be handled by a computer or transmitted on a data communications link, it must first be converted into a digital form. Information may be regarded as being discrete, such as the individual characters of a printed word, or continuous, as in a speech waveform.

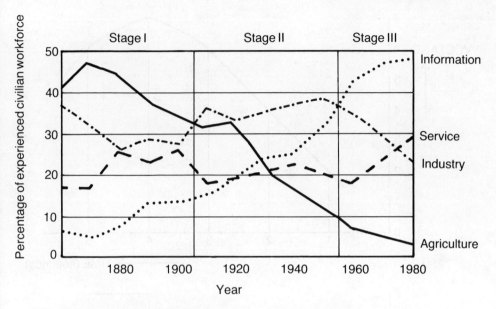

Stage 1 has been described as the agricultural economy
Stage 2 the industry economy
Stage 3 the information economy
Source: Bureau of Labor Statistics USA

Information Technology
Fig 1 Changing pattern of employment in US 1860–1960.

When data is entered into a computer via a keyboard, the equipment will automatically generate the appropriate binary signals uniquely corresponding to the character being typed. Here, digitization is automatically carried out by the data entry equipment.

The process of handling continuous information is different since the data must be first segregated into discrete elements in such a way that it can be eventually reconstituted from these elements. This requires that the information is sampled at a high enough rate to permit reconstruction and that the sampled data is quantified into defined signal levels.

In fig. 2a, a continuously varying waveform has a maximum amplitude excursion of 7 volts. Fig. 2b shows the waveform sampled at 1 second intervals, with the voltage measured to the nearest volt. Thus a sampled measurement can have a value from 0 to 7 volts, or 8 levels of quantization. For speech

purposes between 8 to 16 levels of quantization are just about sufficient for reasonable intelligibility, but for practical purposes, speech supply is carried out at a rate of 8000 samples per second.

In theory, it would be possible to transmit directly the signals sampled in fig. 2b as pulses of varying (although quantized) heights. But with discrete or numbered voltage levels, each level can be coded before transmission. This simplifies signal handling and has the advantage that the information capacity of a coded system is greater than that of an uncoded one.

The coding scheme of Pulse Code Modulation (PCM) is an example of this process. Fig. 2d represents the quantized equivalent of the sampled waveform, and in fig. 2e under PCM, the signal is converted into a group of binary (on-off or plus-minus) pulses of fixed amplitude. Since more than one pulse must be transmitted in the sampling

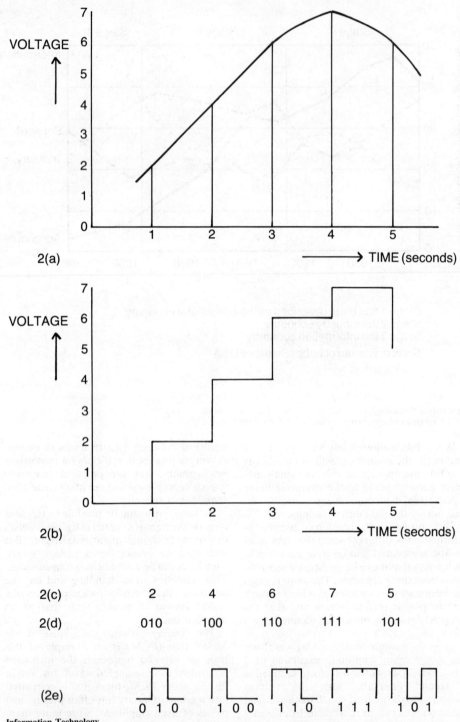

Information Technology
Fig 2 Pulse modulation. A continuous waveform is quantized into a pulse train: (a) continuous waveform; (b) sampled waveform; (c) quantized sample heights; (d) binary coded sample values; (e) pulse train.

period of 1 second, the pulse widths are decreased and the bandwidth goes up.

Using the reverse process it is possible to reconstruct the original signal from the coded pulses. The important point is that once information is in digitized form it can be handled using computing and data communications techniques, and the microelectronic circuits to do this are fast, reliable and inexpensive.

(c) factors affecting IT innovation. The success or failure of an innovation or a new medium, such as videotex, can depend critically on whether it succeeds in developing an aura of social need. In many instances, this may well depend on how effectively new devices and services are marketed.

A major difficulty in trying to anticipate the role of IT lies in trying to predict how particular elements within society will react. For example, in the mid 1930's it was suggested that the new medium of television would have little effect on newspaper circulation because no one would wish to strain his eyes to read print on a television screen. It was not realized that news could be presented in an entirely different way, and that technical developments would accelerate to fulfil the demands of the new medium.

In the fields of communications and computing, the problem of predicting how our lives will be affected is complicated by an ever increasing rate of change, so that technical developments always seem to be several steps ahead of professional prophecy.

The rate of innovation in IT represents a dynamic balance between technical developments within IT, possible areas of application, the interests of pressure groups involved and social, economic and other constraints. These inter-relationships are shown in fig. 3.

The new technology may make possible technical options which will blur the current distinction between telecommunications, broadcasting, press and publishing. Technical developments are causing these fields to converge with each capable of offering similar new information services. A two-way cable television network, for example, will support a variety of convenience services, such as mail order, whilst providing channels for the equivalent of a local newspaper, education and film request services (see next section).

Increasing attention is being paid in developed countries to privacy invasion made possible by developments in information processing. There is little doubt that the scope for information pollution, as it has been called, will increase. It is important that legislative process is fast enough to deal with practices which are irritating or offensive, such as surveillance, but not actually illegal.

A further constraint on the application of IT must to some extent be governed by the need to protect the copyright of information. Once information is in machine readable format it can very easily and quickly be duplicated. This applies equally to audio and video cassette recordings on magnetic tape as well as computer programs for microcomputers. The relative ease in being able to copy a program represents a disincentive in the development of the microcomputer software market.

The take up of new IT services or the expansion of existing ones is much influenced by their being offered at an economic tariff rate. Some new services in the US, such as satellite communications, are economically justifiable because of their geography, with three time zones and the pattern of their business traffic. Others, such as Prestel in the UK, are easier to introduce because of the central position that British Telecom currently enjoys. Once a data communications infrastructure has been developed there is considerable scope for organizations to exploit it through applications, products and services at much lower levels of investment.

In recent years there has been a considerable growth of digital traffic between computers and computers, and between computers and terminals used by operators. The advantages of digital transmission have led to the establishment of all digital networks which will gradually take over a substantial portion of the present network capacity. The result of this change towards digital working is to make feasible and economic equipments, systems and services which previously have been in the realm of pipe dreams, e.g. digital facsimile, intercommunicating word processing, teleconferencing, electronic mail and optical character recognition. Fig. 4 depicts the process by which new electronic media will emerge as a result of the convergence of information and entertainment services (software), the means of distribution, and the consumer electronic devices capable of displaying these services (terminal hardware).

Such developments could either result in or be accelerated by changes in organization structure, particularly in the business area. The 'small is beautiful' approach to business enterprises is thought to result in greater job satisfaction. This view is entirely compatible with what IT can now support: smaller, semi-autonomous units connected by sophisticated communications systems. This trend

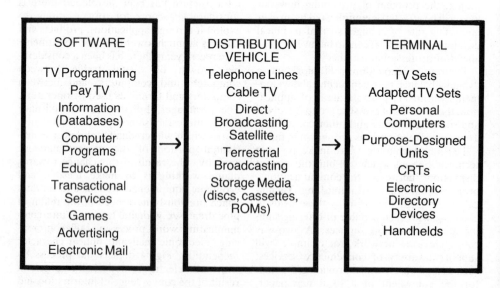

Information Technology
Fig 3 Factors affecting IT innovation.

could, however, lead to a reassessment of responsibilities and practices within industry.

If a large proportion of office staff have access to a terminal connected to integrated computer-communications facilities, the current distinctions between responsibilities of the Data Processing Manager, the Communications Manager, the Office Manager and the Line Manager will become blurred. Thus the rate of take up of IT in business will depend largely on the attitudes to organizational change of both management and staff. A flexible outlook and an extensive education and training programme will be essential.

(d) cable systems - an example of IT. Modern cable systems, based on coaxial or optical fibers, are capable of providing many new telecommunications based services to homes and businesses. The main role of cable systems will be the delivery of information, financial and convenience services to the home and the joining of businesses and homes by high capacity datalinks.

The key to the capacity of a cable system in supplying these services lies in the concept of bandwidth. The greater the bandwidth of a communications system, the more information can be transmitted at any one time. Band-

SOFTWARE	DISTRIBUTION VEHICLE	TERMINAL
TV Programming	Telephone Lines	TV Sets
Pay TV	Cable TV	Adapted TV Sets
Information (Databases)	Direct Broadcasting Satellite	Personal Computers
Computer Programs	Terrestrial Broadcasting	Purpose-Designed Units
Education	Storage Media (discs, cassettes, ROMs)	CRTs
Transactional Services		Electronic Directory Devices
Games		Handhelds
Advertising		
Electronic Mail		

Information Technology
Fig 4 New electronic media–common elements.

width is a measure of the frequency range over which a system can operate and of its information carrying capacity. In the US, for example, cable systems now being installed will support up to 50 TV channels, together with high quality sound transmission.

Individual channels on a cable may be subdivided into different services, all apparently as far as the user is concerned on different channels. This is because a moving video transmission will occupy the full bandwidth allocated for a channel (350 MHz in the US), but a service where no movement is required, such as teletext, would not need as much bandwidth. Thus some systems now being planned in the US will carry 80 to 100 different services.

Two-way communications capability is now being provided on American cable networks, and is mandatory under FCC regulations for all new systems. In this context, two-way means a video capability from transmitter to the home subscriber, and a relatively slow channel for the reverse path. This is used for sending instructions to a computer on the network which supervises and monitors requests for services. Virtually all extra services being promoted on US cable systems are based on videotex principles pioneered in the UK.

The possible applications of a cable system for which a high bandwidth is essential include:

(i) a wide choice of conventional TV programmes. Both terrestrial transmissions, and those via satellite (DBS) can be relayed down one cable;

(ii) channels for specialist interest, i.e. narrowcasting;

(iii) local programmes, such as a local news service. In the US, some cities have required the cable company to provide one or two channels for city council business as a condition of cable franchise;

(iv) education and training at a distance;

(v) film request services;

(vi) rapid transmission of digitized data, thus supporting local area networking requirements of business workstations linked to one or more computers, as on Ethernet;

(vii) support for new ways of selling such as mail order, home banking, holiday bookings, etc.

The natural convergence of cable and local area network technologies mentioned in (vi) above will encourage the development of new relationships between home and work activities, and a reduction in the need to travel. A large international market for advanced cable technology is likely to develop since the concept of interactive entertainment and information services which cable can support is universally attractive.

information theory In communications, the mathematical theory concerned with the information rate, channel capacity, noise and other factors affecting information transmission. Initially developed for electrical communications, it is now applied to business systems and other areas concerned with information units and the flow of information in networks. See information content, Shannon's Law.

information transfer channel In data communications, the functional connection between the source and sink data terminal equipments, including the circuit and associated line plant. See data terminal equipment, source, sink.

informative abstract In library science an abstract giving detailed information about the original, i.e. summarizing the principal arguments, giving conclusions and, if appropriate, methods. Compare auto abstract, evaluative abstract, general abstract, indicative abstract, selective abstract, slanted abstract. See abstract.

infotainment A combination of information and entertainment services to consumers. Videotex, employing the domestic TV set as a display device, created the first consumer link between information and entertainment services and its database may contain both information pages and interactive games or quizzes. Cable television provides the major example of this form of service, particularly with its potential for educational programs, cable text, telebanking, teleshopping etc. See cable television, cable text, telebanking, teleshopping.

infrared In electromagnetic radiation, wavelengths extending from visible red light to the shortest microwaves (780 - 100,000 nanometers).

infrared cinematography In cinematography, using film which is sensitive to infrared light and may either be black and white or colour.

infrasonic frequency In audio recording, a frequency below that of sound waves audible to the human ear, usually taken as a frequency below 15Hz. Synonymous with sub-audio frequency.

inhibit In electronics and computing, to prevent a process from taking place. Thus an inhibit input will prevent a logic element from carrying out its defined function.

in house (1) In film production, a unit which is a part of the company for which it makes films. (2) In computing, a system whose parts, including terminals, are situated at one location. (3) In printing, work carried out by an organization whose main business is not printing but which has its own printing plant.

initialization In computer programming, the process of setting the values of a variable to a specified value at the start of program execution.

initial program loader In computing, a machine program that loads into main memory the initial part of the operating system so that the system can then proceed under its own control. See bootstrap, operating system.

injection laser In optoelectronics, a semiconductor laser used as a light source for optical fiber communication systems. See fiber optics, semiconductor laser.

inking (1) In computer graphics, creating a line by moving the pointer as in a line drawing on paper. (2) In film animation, drawing lines for artwork. (3) In duplication, the process by which ink is transferred from the master to copy paper.

ink jet printer In computing, a nonimpact printer that forms characters by the projection of high speed ink droplets onto paper. The ink droplets are deflected by electric fields and thus these printer heads have no mechanical moving parts, hence they are capable of high speed and reliability.

inlay In television, a method of combining video signals from two sources into the one picture.

in line In computing, a method of processing data without their previously having been edited or sorted.

in line recovery In computing, a recovery in which the affected process is resumed from a safe point preceding the occurrence of the error. See recoverable error.

INMARSAT In communications, INternational MARitime SATellite organization, an international organization using satellite communications and providing maritime telephone, telex, facsimile, telegram, data communication, distress and safety services.

INPADOC A database supplied by INternational PAtent DOCumentation Center and dealing with patents. See on line information retrieval.

in phase (1) In cinematography, the precise coordination of the film movement through a gate with the rotation of the camera shutter. (2) In electronics and communications, pertaining to signals that have a zero phase shift relative to each other, e.g. two sinusoidal waves of the same frequency whose maximum and minimum values coincide. Compare out of phase. See gate, phase.

in pro In printing, an abbreviation of 'in proportion', used when giving instructions for reducing or enlarging originals.

input (1) In computing, a signal transmitted from a peripheral device to the central processing unit. (2) In electronics, a signal transmitted into a circuit or unit, usually to achieve some desired output or else to induce a change in the state of the circuit. Compare output. See central processing unit.

input area   In computing, an area of storage reserved for holding input data on a temporary basis prior to further processing.

input data validation   In computing, a control technique used to detect inaccurate or incomplete input data. This may include format checks, completeness checks, reasonableness checks and limit checks. See format, limit check, reasonableness check.

input device   Synonymous with input unit.

input field   In computer graphics, an unprotected field on the display surface of a VDU in which data can be entered, modified or erased. Compare protected field. See VDU.

input output   In computing, a general term for the equipment used to communicate with a computer and the data involved in the communication. Synonymous with I/O.

input output channel   In data processing, a device which is controlled by the central processing unit and handles the transfer of data between main storage and the peripheral equipment connected to the channel. See channel, main storage, peripheral, central processing unit.

input output devices   In computing and communications, any external equipment used to enter data into the computer or transmission system, or accept data from the computer or network for display, storage, further processing or transmission.

input output interface   In computing, an interface which will transmit an interrupt signal from a peripheral device to the CPU. See interface, interrupt, CPU.

input output statement   In computing, any instruction which results in a transfer of data between main storage and input output devices. See statement, input output devices.

input output symbol   In programming, a flowcharting symbol used to indicate an input

to or an output from a process. See flow-chart.

input output unit   In data processing, any device used to enter data into the computer or accept data from the computer or both. See input output devices, peripheral.

input primitive   In computer graphics, a basic data item from an input device, e.g. a keyboard or keypad. See data item, keypad.

input stream   In commercial data processing, a sequence of job control statements and input data entered via a device activated by the computer operator to the central computing system. See job control language.

input unit   In data processing, a device by which data can be entered into a computer system.

inquiry   In computing, a request for information from storage which may be initiated at a local or remote point by use of a keyboard terminal or similar device.

inquiry/response   In computing, a method of transaction handling in which a user interrogates the computer via a conversational type terminal keyboard and obtains a response almost immediately. See conversational mode.

insert   (1) In word processing, adding characters, words, sentences or paragraphs into copy. (2) In publishing, adding a separately printed piece into a book or periodical after binding.

insertion loss   In communications, the power which is absorbed by the insertion of a passive element into a channel or electronic device. This usually occurs when a filter or equalizer is added to a communications channel. See channel, equalization, filter.

INSPEC   A series of abstracts comprising: Computer and Control Abstracts. An abstracting publication covering computer and control engineering. Electrical and Electronics Abstracts. An abstracting publication covering electrical and electronics engineering. IT Focus. An abstracting publication covering information technology. Physics Abstracts. An abstracting publication covering physics. See abstract.

installation In data processing, a general term for a particular computing system in the context of the work it does and the staff who manage, operate and service the system.

instant replay In video recording, the ability to playback immediately a shot often in slow motion or freeze frame. See freeze frame, slow motion.

instruction In computing, (1) a basic directive made by a programmer in a form which the computer can accept and execute, (2) a statement which specifies what operation is to be performed and the value or location of the operands. A computer operates by executing sequentially a series of instructions. See location, operand.

instruction counter In computing, a counter that indicates the location in main memory of the next instruction to be interpreted. Synonymous with program counter.

instruction cycle In computing, the sequence of fetching an instruction stored in computer memory and then executing it.

instruction cycle time In computing, the time taken to complete one instruction cycle. It represents a measure of computer speed. See instruction cycle.

instruction execution time See execution time.

instruction processor Synonymous with order code processor.

instruction register In computing, a register that is used to hold an instruction during its decoding and execution. See instruction counter.

instruction repertoire Synonymous with instruction set.

instruction set In computing, the complete list of instructions which a processor can decode and execute. These instructions are supplied by the manufacturer of the processor. See central processing unit.

instruction time See execution time.

instrumentation In electronics, devices utilized to test, monitor record and/or control physical properties and movements.

in sync In recording, the exact alignment of sound and picture. See synchronization.

intaglio In printing, a general term for graphic printing carried out under pressure, usually in a cylinder or rolling press. In intaglio printing, the printing plate holds ink in etched lines and paper is forced into these recesses under the action of the cylinder. Compare letterpress, lithography.

integer In mathematics, a whole number that may be positive, zero or negative.

integer BASIC In computer programming, a version of the BASIC language that can perform arithmetical operations on only integers. See BASIC, integer.

integral boundary In computer programming, a location in main storage at which a fixed length field, e.g. a halfword or doubleword, must be positioned. The address of an integral boundary is a multiple of the length of the field, in bytes. See byte, field, word.

integrated circuit In electronics, a combination of interconnected circuit elements inseparably associated on or within a continuous substrate. An integrated circuit may contain anywhere from a few to many thousands of transistors, resistors, diodes, capacitors. See large scale integration, very large scale integration.

integrated database A database which has been consolidated to eliminate redundant data. See database.

Integrated Data Management System In databases, a proprietary system, specified by CODASYL, which provides facilities for

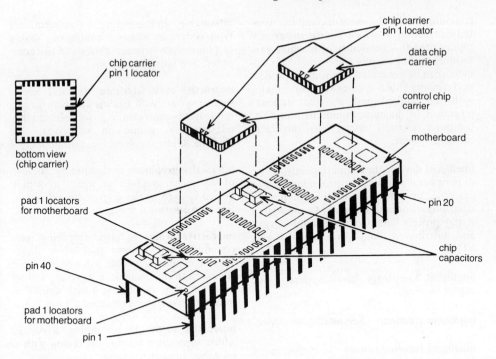

integrated circuit
The LS1-22/23 data and control chip manufactured by Digital Equipment Corporation (courtesy Digital Equipment Corporation).

structuring and using large databases. See CODASYL.

integrated data processing In computing, a systematic approach to all aspects of data capture and data processing in order to maximize overall efficiency. See data processing.

integrated digital network In data communications, a network in which digital transmission and digital switching are used. See digital switching, digital transmission system.

integrated injection logic In microelectronics, a logic circuit of very low power consumption in which the switching speed is proportional to the amount of current injected. Widely used in electronic wrist watches. See logic circuit.

integrated modem In data communications, a modem that is an integral part of the device with which it operates. See MODEM.

integrated optical circuit In optoelectro-

nics, the optical equivalent of a microelectronic circuit. It acts on the light in a lightwave system to carry out communications functions; generating, detecting, switching and transmitting light.

integrated service digital network In digital communications, an integrated digital network used for more than one service, e.g. telephony and data. See integrated digital network.

integrated word processing equipment In word processing, equipment that has its associated control unit contained within the body of the machine, as opposed to a general purpose microcomputer system which runs a word processing software package.

integrity In computing, the preservation of files for their intended purpose. See data integrity.

intelligent computer assisted instruction In

computing, a development of computer assisted instruction in which course material is represented independently of teaching procedures so that exercises and remedial comments can be generated according to student performance. Such systems carry on a dialog with the student and use the student's responses to diagnose comprehension. See computer assisted instruction, intelligent tutoring system.

intelligent device In computing, any device or peripheral which can be programmed. For example, an intelligent VDU will have a microprocessor and some RAM store so that it may process data. Compare dumb device. See distributed data processing, RAM, VDU.

intelligent knowledge based system See expert systems.

intelligent terminal See intelligent device.

intelligent tutoring system In computing, a computer assisted instruction system employing the principles of artificial intelligence and expert systems to provide a reactive learning environment. See artificial intelligence, expert systems, intelligent computer assisted instruction.

INTELSAT INternational TELecommunications SATellite organization, a body responsible for the design, development, construction, operations and maintenance of the space segment of the global satellite communication system. It is an organization of governments and their designated telecommunications authorities with each participating member holding a quota of investment shares based on its use of the system. See COMSAT, global satellite communication system.

intensity (1) In wave propagation, the intensity of a beam is proportional to the square of the amplitude of oscillation. It is a measure of the strength of the radiation. With light waves, intensity is an indication of brightness and in sound it is a measure of loudness. (2) In computer graphics, the amount of light emitted at a display point. See decibel.

interactive In computing, a conversational type system in which a continuous dialog can take place between a user and the computer. See inquiry/response.

interactive cable television In cable television, a system with facilities for the user to send signals upstream, e.g. for telebanking, teleshopping, voting on referenda. See Hi-Ovis, Qube, telebanking, teleshopping.

interactive graphics In computing, the use of computer graphics in which a display device is used in the conversational mode. See conversational mode.

interactive media In teleconferencing, telecommunication systems that allow direct exchanges among people via one or more communication channels, e.g. voice, writing or vision, thus supporting a high degree of interpersonal communication.

interactive mode In computing, a system which supports a continuous dialog with a user. See inquiry/response.

interactive routine In real time computer systems, a program which accepts data from a keyboard operator and reacts in an automatic fashion to these inputs. See conversational mode.

interactive video disk systems In video recording, some video disk systems provide facilities for freeze frame, fast/slow motion and random access to individual frames. These facilities can be exploited for a variety of applications, e.g. education, training, sales promotions, information storage/retrieval. Four forms of interactive systems are classified as level one, level two, level three and level four.

Level one systems include consumer video disk players and are characterized by individual frame addressability, worst frame access (1 - 54,000) less than 20 seconds, limited memory and no processing power. At the simplest level the user controls the playback with a keypad; e.g. search for a particular frame, playing from that point in normal mode, stopping at a point of interest, moving forward or reversing frame by frame, fast or slow motion and so on. The disk can also contain coded control information so that, for example, the player automatically switches from normal play to freeze frame when a control code is read from the disk. Some disks also contain teletext coded information so that the user may view teletext menus which display details of starting frame numbers for various sequences or select teletext style subtitles providing additional information relating to sequences.

Level two systems, sometimes called industrial players, have the capabilities of level one systems plus improved worst case access times, two way computer/communications capabilities and a built in microprocessor. Such systems provide capabilities for automatic programming of control sequences. These systems relieve the viewer of the requirement for manual control during playback but require control sequences to be manually keyed in prior to playback. A possible development is to encode the control program onto the beginning of the disk and to download it from the disk to the inbuilt microprocessor.

Level three systems comprise a level one or level two player interfaced to a microcomputer. This provides the most versatile form of interaction since the control program can employ the processing and memory power of the microcomputer and is independent of the information contained on the disk. The facilities depend upon the player, some systems provide for two way communication so that the computer awaits acknowledgement signals, or even frame numbers, from the player. Level four systems are sophisticated players with extensive memory, control and processing facilities.

Some players have teletext encoders so that computer generated text or alphamosaic graphics can be superimposed upon the video disk pictures. More advanced user friendly facilities - touchscreen, voice recognition etc. can also be incorporated into most microcomputer configurations. See frame, freeze frame, teletext, touchscreen, voice recognition, video disk.

interactive videotex See videotex. Synonymous with viewdata.

interblock gap In computer peripherals, the space on a magnetic tape between the end of one block of data and the beginning of the next. Such spacing facilitates tape stop-start

operations. Synonymous with file gap, interrecord gap.

intercarrier buzz In television receivers, an occasional noise heard on the reproduced sound which may have several causes, including intermodulation between the sound and vision carrier signals. See carrier, intermodulation distortion.

intercharacter spacing In word processing, the creation of variable spaces between the characters of individual words in order to create a justified column of text. Some sophisticated systems offer spacing assigned according to character width, giving a print like quality. See justification.

intercom In communications, a service which supports voice intercommunications between two or more stations located in the same building or localized area.

interconnection In communications, the connection of a piece of telephone equipment to the telephone network, also applies to the interconnection of common carrier networks. See Carterfone Decision, interface.

interexchange In communications, services and channels supported by one or more exchanges or rate centers. See exchange, rate center.

interface In electronics, a shared boundary between two related devices or components defined for the purpose of specifying the type and form of signals passing between them. For example, the EIA RS 232 interface represents a standard set of signal characteristics (time, duration, voltage and current) specified by the Electronic Industries Association for use in communications terminals. It also includes a standard plug/socket connector arrangement. See RS 232.

interface message processor In packet switching, a term originating in the ARPA network to describe a packet switching computer. See ARPA, TIP, interface processor.

interface processor In computing and data communications, a processor that acts as the interface between another processor or terminal, and a network or a processor controlling data flow in a network. See interface.

interference In communications, any unwanted signals appearing in a channel at a level sufficient to impair the performance of the channel to a significant extent. Interference may be a result of natural or man made noises and signals. (2) In wave propagation, the addition or combination of waves. If a crest of one wave meets the trough of another of equal amplitude and frequency, the wave is destroyed at that point, and conversely the superimposition of one crest upon another leads to an increased effect.

interference fading In radio reception, fading caused by the interaction of two or more radio waves of similar amplitude but differing in phase. See fading.

interference immunity In radio reception, (1) the degree to which a receiving system will reject interfering signals, (2) the effectiveness of a directional antenna system designed to reject interfering signals. See antenna.

interference pattern (1) In optics, the resulting distribution of energy when waves of the same frequency and kind are superimposed. (2) In television, a visual pattern of lines impressed on the display picture. See hologram.

interlace In television and computer graphics, a system of scanning a picture using two fields. The first line-by-line scan sweeps alternate line positions on the picture, the second sweeps the gaps between the first, completing the total structure of the picture. Interlace scanning reveals a higher level of character detail in a VDU or videotex terminal, and helps to reduce flicker. See flicker, scanning line, VDU.

interleaving (1) In printing, extra sheets, usually blank, placed between printed sheets as they come off a press to avoid ink being transferred from one printed sheet to another. (2) In computing, the act of accessing two or more bytes or streams of data from separate storage units simultaneously. Also, the alternating of two or more operations or

functions at the same time from the one computer. See set off.

inter library loan In library science, a book or microform lent between libraries for a particular reader. See microform.

interlinear spacing In phototypesetting, the electronic equivalent of the mechanical insertion of spaces between print lines.

interlock (1) To prevent a machine or device from commencing further operations until the current one is completed. (2) In recording, an arrangement which will synchronize separate sound and picture tracks. The simplest method is through the use of a synchronous drive motor connecting both picture viewer and sound reproducer. See interlock projector.

interlock projector In audiovisual aids, a projector used to produce the picture while synchronized sound is played back on an accompanying machine. See interlock.

intermediate access memory Synonymous with fast access memory.

intermediate frequency In radio communications, the frequency to which the received signal is changed by the frequency changer in a superheterodyne receiver. See frequency changer, superheterodyne.

intermediate materials In video disk, all the media selected for assembly onto the video disk premaster (i.e. 16 mm film, video tape, 35 mm slides etc).

intermediate reversal negative In film processing, a negative made directly from another negative without the creation of a positive, used to eliminate one generation of printing. See generation.

intermediate text block In data communications, a control character used to end an intermediate block of characters. See end of text.

intermittent error In computing and data communications, an error that occurs intermittently in a random way, is extremely difficult to reproduce and therefore to correct.

intermodulation distortion In electronic systems, a distortion resulting from the interaction of two or more frequencies when there is a nonlinear relationship between input and output signals, e.g. an overloaded audio amplifier may cause such distortion. In wideband FDM transmission systems, the result of intermodulation is usually called intermodulation noise. See FDM, noise.

internal label In computing, a machine readable label recorded on a data medium such as magnetic tape or disk, that provides information about a set of data recorded on the medium. Compare external label.

internally stored program In microcomputers, a program stored in read only memory, as compared to one loaded into the machine from disk or cassette tape. See read only memory.

internal sort In computing, a sort program that uses main storage only. Compare external sort.

internal storage In microcomputers, internal solid state memory in the form of RAM and ROM chips. See RAM, ROM.

International Network Working Group A forum for discussing network standards and protocols. It is a working group within IFIP with the title 'International Packet Switching for Computer Sharing'. See IFIP.

International Nuclear Information System INIS, a database supplied by International Atomic Energy Agency (IAEA), INIS Section, in cooperation with participating member states and dealing with nuclear science. See on line information retrieval.

international number In telephony, all the digits that have to be dialed after the international prefix to obtain access to a subscriber in another country. See international prefix.

International Packet Switched Service In packet switching, a system operated between Europe and the US.

international paper sizes See A, B and C Series of paper sizes.

international phonetic alphabet In communications, an internationally agreed code for spelling out letters of words over a voice circuit. A Alpha, B Bravo, C Charlie, D Delta, E Echo, F Foxtrot, G Golf, H Hotel, I India, J Julia, K Kilo, L Lima, M Mike, N November, O Oscar, P Papa, Q Quebec, R Romeo, S Sierra, T Tango, U Uniform, V Victor, W Whisky, X Xray, Y Yankee, Z Zulu.

international prefix In telephony, the dialing code for access to an exchange controlling international calls.

International Record Carrier In telecommunications, a common carrier engaged in providing a service between the United States and foreign destinations, and between the continental United States and other areas such as Puerto Rico, Hawaii and Guam. These services include telex, private line service and alternate voice data service. See common carrier.

International Software Database A database supplied by Imprint Software and dealing with computers and computer industry. See on line information retrieval.

International Standard Book Number In book publishing, a unique, ten digit number allocated to each published book, with a separate number for each edition. The first part of the number consists of a group identifier (country or group of countries), second part is the publisher identifier, third part is the title identifier, and the last part is a single check digit.

International Standard Serial Number In library science, a unique number for the identification of serial publications. It consists of 8 digits, 7 of which uniquely identify the serial and the eighth is a check digit. Compare International Standard Book Number.

International Standards Organization An agency of the United Nations concerned with international standardization across a broad field of industrial products.

International Telecommunications Union   A body that promotes international collaboration in telecommunications with a view to improving the efficiency of world services. It is a specialized agency of the United Nations and has three permanent committees, the IFRB, the CCIR and the CCITT. Its regulations have the status of formal treaties between the participating countries and are binding on signatories who have acceded to them. See CCIR, CCITT, IFRB.

internegative   In film processing, a colour negative duplicate made from a colour positive. Internegatives are used for release printing in order to protect the source film from damage. See print.

interpolation   The process of filling in intermediate values, or terms, of a series between known values of the terms.

interpositive   In film processing, any positive duplicate of a film, used for further printing.

interpreter   In computer programming, a translator that accepts one line of a source program at a time, produces the corresponding machine code instructions and executes them. Interpreters differ from compilers in two important respects. Firstly, they do not check the syntax of the whole program before execution. Secondly, they repeat the process of translation every time a particular source program is executed. Debugging is easier and less frustrating than with compilers, but interpreted programs are much slower than compiled programs in execution. Moreover, a syntax error can lurk undetected, for many program test runs in a program instruction that is only accessed in exceptional circumstances. Compare compiler. See BASIC, execute, machine language, source program, translator.

interrecord gap   Synonymous with interblock gap.

interrupt   (1) In computing, a facility that enables a CPU to handle concurrently a number of input output devices on a priority basis. An interrupt is sent from an I/O device to the CPU requesting action, e.g. to receive data. The CPU will suspend execution of the current task, transfer control to a specified location in memory which then calls a routine to deal with the interrupt. On completion, control is returned to the interrupted task. (2) In data transmission, to take an action at a receiving station that causes the transmitting station to terminate a transmission. Compare DMA. See CPU, input output devices.

interrupt mask   In computing, a mechanism that enables certain interrupt lines to be inhibited by setting appropriate bits in a special register. See interrupt.

interrupt request   In computing, an interrupt from a peripheral unit indicating that it requires the CPU to perform a predetermined task. See interrupt.

interstate communicator   In telecommunications, any service which crosses the boundary of two or more states of the United States, and which may therefore be subject to FCC regulation. See FCC.

interstation muting   In radio receivers, the suppression of the audio output during a tuning change from one broadcast station to another. With FM receivers this is particularly useful since in the absence of an input signal the receiver is a noise generator. See FM, noise.

intertoll trunk   In communications, a trunk between toll switching offices in different exchanges used for routing long distance calls. See toll switching office, trunk.

intervention signal   In data communications, a control signal designed for the equipment at either end of a channel rather than for the channel itself.

interword spacing   In word processing, creating spaces between words to create justified columns of text. See intercharacter spacing, justification.

intrusion   In telephony, the intervention by a telephone operator wishing to speak to both parties in an established call, e.g. announcing an incoming international call.

intrusion tone   In telephony, an audible

signal superimposed on a conversation when a third party takes part in a call.

inverse square law In electromagnetic radiation, the intensity of the radiation falling on a given surface varies inversely as the square of its distance from the source. In light, the intensity of illumination on an object will thus vary as the square of the distance from the object to the light source. See intensity.

inverse video   Synonymous with reverse video.

inversion In binary arithmetic, a complementation process where all the 1's in a binary number are changed to 0's and vice versa. See complement.

inverted file In databases, a file structure that facilitates searches for attributes by the provision of special lists or indices, e.g. a personnel file uses an employee number as the primary key but an inverted file might provide a list in departmental order, with associated employee numbers. Thus all the employees in a given department could be accessed without an exhaustive search of the total personnel file.

inverter In electronics, a logic circuit to perform a NOT operation. See NOT.

invitation In data communications, the process in which a processor contacts a station in order to allow the station to transmit an available message. See polling.

invitation to send In data communications, a transmission control character used in an ASR system causing the tape transmitter of a remote device to send its data on the line. See ASR.

INWG See International Network Working Group.

IOB A UN Inter-Organization Board for Information Systems and Related Activities.

I/O See input output.

I/O bound In data processing, pertaining to computer applications in which there is rela-

tively little processing compared to the amount of reading or writing to external devices. This is often the case in commercial processing, e.g. for payroll, stock control processing. See batch processing, multiprogramming.

ion A charged particle. An atom is normally electrically neutral, the total charge of the electrons being equal and opposite to the positive nucleus. If an atom gains an extra electron, it becomes a negative ion, if it loses an electron it is then a positive ion.

ionic In printing, a range of typefaces commonly used in newspaper work.

ionosphere In radiocommunications, a layer in the earth's atmosphere consisting of charged particles which cause a radio wave to be reflected back to earth. For reference purposes the ionosphere is divided into three regions: the D region occupying the spherical shell from 50km to 90km above the earth, the E region from 90km to 150km and the F region. See D region, E region, F region.

I/O port In a microcomputer, a special chip which sits on the CPU data bus, enabling an external device to be connected to the computer for input output operation. See bus, input output.

IP See information provider.

IPA International Pharmaceutical Abstracts, a database supplied by American Society of Hospital Pharmacists and dealing

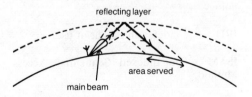

ionosphere
Radiowaves in the band 3-30 MHz are reflected back to earth. Since the upgoing beam covers a range of elevation angles, the signal is received over a relatively large area.

with pharmaceuticals and pharmaceutical industry. See on line information retrieval.

IPG Information Policy Group of the Organization for Economic Cooperation and Development.

ips inches per second

IPSS See International Packet Switched Service.

IP terminal In videotex, an editing terminal used for creating or updating videotex pages. The terminal is designed to facilitate the use of colour, alphanumeric and graphics characters. Page creation can be carried out either on line, or else in an off line mode where pages are held on disk for subsequent on line connection to the videotex database. See bulk update terminal, page.

IR See information retrieval.

IRC See information retrieval center, interrecord gap.

IRE US Institute of Radio Engineers.

IRIS International Reporting Information System, an ambitious information system designed to provide governments and large corporations with sophisticated analyses of political and economic events. It was formed in 1981 but collapsed fifteen months later.

irradiation In film processing, the scattering of light by the silver grains in the emulsion, producing a noticeable reduction of image definition in thick emulsions. See emulsion.

IRT UK Institute of Reprographic Technology.

IRU See indefeasible right of use.

ISAM See Indexed Sequential Access Method.

isarithmic control In packet switched networks, the control of flow so as to maintain the total number of packets in transit below a certain limit. See flow control.

ISBN See International Standard Book Number.

ISDN See integrated service digital network.

ISO See International Standards Organization.

isochronous transmission Synonymous with synchronous transmission.

isolated adaptive routing In packet switching, a method of signal switching in which the routing decisions are made solely on the basis of information available in each node. See adaptive routing.

isolation The separation of the section of a system from undesired influences of other sections.

ISO OSI See Open Systems Interconnection.

isotropic Pertaining to systems or substances, that demonstrate the same properties in all directions. See isotropic radiator.

isotropic radiator In microwave communications, a theoretical antenna radiating uniformly in all directions. See antenna gain, free space loss.

ISO 7 bit code In data transmission, one of two international data codes. The US version of this code is ASCII. Compare EBCDIC code. See ASCII.

ISSN See International Standard Serial Number.

IT See Information Technology.

italic In printing, a 15th century typeface with characters which have a noticeable inclination to the right.

ITAP Report In cable television, a report on Wideband Cable Systems produced by the Information Technology Advisory Panel in December 1981. It suggested that broadband cable systems capable of supporting new information technology based services could be financed by the private sector on the basis of an entertainment led business. See Hunt Report.

ITB   See intermediate text block.

item   In computing, a group of related characters treated as a unit. For example, a record may consist of a number of items, which in turn may consist of other items. See record.

iteration   In computer programming, a process that repeats the same series of processing steps until a predetermined state or branch condition is reached. Compare recursive routine. See loop.

ITS   See intelligent tutoring system, invitation to send.

ITU   See International Telecommunications Union.

IVIPA   International Videotex Information Providers Association.

IWP   International Word Processing Organizations.

IX   See interchange.

J

jam (1) In photography, a fault in a camera due either to mechanical failure or a pile up of film. (2) In computer peripherals, a pile up of cards in a card reader.

jamming In communications, deliberate interference with a signal on a common channel by the transmission of a powerful disturbing signal.

JCL See job control language.

jitter (1) In television and digital systems, a signal instability resulting in sudden, small, irregular variations, due mainly to synchronizing defects in the associated equipment. (2) In facsimile, raggedness in the received copy caused by erroneous displacement of recorded spots in the direction of scanning. See synchronization.

JK flip flop In electronics, a logic storage element having two inputs (J and K), and two outputs whose states are always complementary. See flip flop.

job In data processing, a full description of a unit of work for a computer. A job will normally include all the necessary application programs, files and instructions to the operating system. See background job, foreground.

job control language In data processing, a problem oriented language used for specifying the environment for running a particular batch of work.

job oriented terminal In computer peripherals, a terminal designed for a particular application.

job priority In data processing, a value assigned to a job that determines the priority used in scheduling the job and allocating resources to it in a multiprogramming environment. See batch processing, multiprogramming.

job queue In data processing, the set of programs and data being processed by a computer, the order of processing being determined by the job priorities. See job priority.

job step In data processing, a unit of work associated with an application program. See application program.

job stream See input stream.

jog In recording, a frame by frame movement of a video tape during editing. This is possible on helical scan systems because of their freeze frame capability. See freeze frame, helical scan.

joggle (1) In punch cards, to align a deck, usually before placing in a card hopper. (2) In stationery, to align the edges of a stack of sheets by using vibration.

johnson counter In electronics, a shift register ring counter commonly used in the timing and control of digital circuits. See ring counter, shift register.

join In relational databases, an operator in relational algebra. A join operation on two relations which share a common data item type produces a combined relation with attributes specified in the join operation. See relational algebra.

journal (1) In communications, a list of all messages sent and received by a terminal. (2) In computing, a chronological record of changes made to a set of data, often used for reconstructing a previous version of the set in the event of corruption. See corruption.

joystick (1) In visual display units, a rotary lever which enables an operator to alter or move images on the display. (2) In filming, a device connected to a cable for remote lens control.

j-type defects In micrographics, defects in microfilm appearing as tiny spots 10-150 microns in diameter. See micron.

judder In facsimile, an irregular movement of the moving parts in a transmitter or receiver causing straight lines in the source document to be reproduced in a wavy manner.

jumbo chip See wafer silicon integration.

jump (1) In printing, to carry over a portion of a newspaper or periodical feature from one page to another. (2) In computer programming, a departure from the consecutive sequence in which instructions are executed. Synonymous with branch, transfer.

jumper In electronics, a short wire used for the temporary connection of two points in an electric circuit.

jumper selectable In electronics, the selection of a particular facility in a piece of equipment by connecting jumper wires across appropriate terminals. See jumper.

junction In electronics, the boundary region between two semiconductors having different electrical properties, or between a metal and a semiconductor. This boundary region is used to control the current flow through a semiconductor. See semiconductor.

junk In satellite communications, satellites which are still in orbit but are no longer operating.

justification (1) In word processing, the vertical alignment of right or left margins. (2) In computing, the act of adjusting, arranging or shifting digits to the left or to the right to fit a given pattern.

justify (1) In printing, to set lines of type to their full measure. (2) In word processing, to print a document with even right and left hand margins. (3) In computing, to shift the contents of a register to a specified position. See justification, register.

justify inhibit In word processing, to inhibit the justification routine so that text is processed without being justified. See justification.

K

K See kilo.

Kanji A set of ideograms used in Chinese and Japanese writing. Compare Hiragana, Katakana, See ideogram.

Kansas City Standard In microcomputers, a format standard for writing and reading data from a cassette. See cassette.

Karnaugh map In logic design, a method of representing a logical expression that facilitates the simplification of that expression. Consider the expression A AND (B OR NOT B) = A, the Karnaugh map facilitates the recognition of such combinations in a complex expression. See AND, NOT, OR.

Katakana A character set of symbols used in one of the two common Japanese phonetic alphabets. See Hiragana, Kanji.

Kb See kilobyte.

keep in In typesetting, instruction to a compositor to use narrow wordspaces.

keep out In typesetting, instruction to a

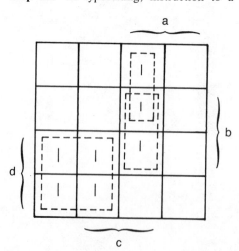

Karnaugh map

compositor to set type matter widely spaced so that it makes as many lines as possible. See type matter.

kern In printing, that part of a piece of type that overhangs the body and so overlaps onto an adjacent piece. See kerning.

kernel In computer programming, (1) that part of an operating system that must always be in main memory when any part of it is loaded. It comprises the routines that perform basic loading and supervisory functions, (2) that part of a segmented program that must always be in main storage when any other segment is loaded. See main memory, operating system, segment.

kerning In photocomposition, a backspacing technique whereby one character is tucked into another in order to avoid the optical impression of excessive spacing that can arise from the varying shapes of characters and combinations of characters.

key (1) In computing, one or more characters used for identifying a set of data. (2) In communications, a switching device having one or more sets of contacts that can be operated manually by means of a small handle or pushbutton. (3) In keyboard equipment, a lever on a manually operated machine, such as a typewriter, teletypewriter or keypunch. (4) A cryptographic key. See cryptographic key, keypunch, teletypewriter, primary key, secondary key.

keyboard (1) In data processing, a device for the encoding of data by key depression, which causes the generation of the correct coding sequence. (2) A systematic arrangement of keys by which a machine is operated, or by which data is entered. (3) In typewriters, an arrangement of typing and function keys laid out in a standard manner. (4) In videotex, a cluster of numeric keys, alphabetic keys and special keys for colour and graphics creation used for displaying information on a screen and entering data in a videotex computer. See data entry, key, videotex.

keyboarding In printing, the operation of entering text via keyboards for subsequent photocomposition. See photocomposition.

keyboard scan In microcomputers, the periodic sampling of the switches activated by the keys of a keyboard by the central processing unit, to determine if a key has been depressed and its identity. See central processing unit.

keyboard send receive In communications, a teletypewriter having a keyboard and page printer. See teletypewriter. Synonymous with page send receive.

keyboard to disk system In data processing, a system by which data can be entered directly onto magnetic disk from a keyboard. See magnetic disk.

keyboard to tape system In data processing, a system by which data is captured directly onto a magnetic tape from a keyboard. See magnetic tape.

keyboard transmitter In telegraphy, a transmitter controlled by a keyboard so that selection of a character results in the corresponding coding symbol being sent down the line.

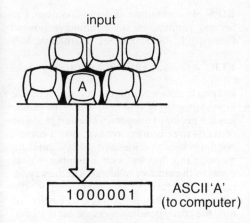

keyboard
Pressing a key generates an 8-bit code.

keyboard typing reperforator In communications, a teletypewriter device with a keyboard, paper tape punch and printer which prints the characters of incoming and outgoing messages on the paper tape, adjacent to the corresponding punched holes.

key click In radio communications, impulsive noise produced by the opening and closing of circuit contacts. See impulsive noise.

keyforce On a keyboard, the force required to depress a key to ensure positive contact and the actioning of the keystroke.

keying In telegraphy, the forming of signals by the interruption of a direct current.

key letter in context In library science, a method similar to KWIC but based on letters instead of terms. Permuted term lists are sorted on each letter in every term with the balance of term displayed. See keyword in context.

key management In cryptography, secret keys are required for encipherment and authentication. These procedures provide no security when the keys have been handled incorrectly. Key management implies the effective creation, storage, transmission, installation and eventual destruction of keys. See authentication, cryptography.

keypad A simplified keyboard consisting of a small set of pushbuttons, as on certain telephones or on the control unit of a videotex terminal. See keyboard, touch-tone, videotex.

keyplate In printing, the first plate used in the production of a coloured print. Subsequent plates overprint the first image, which provides the key for registering other colours. See register.

keypunch In computing, a keyboard operated device for punching holes in punch cards to represent data. It consists of a keyboard, punching and reading mechanisms and a mechanism to transport and stack cards during the keypunching operation. See punched card.

keystone waveform   In television, a correction waveform sometimes used in scanning to correct for certain types of geometric distortion. See geometric distortion, keystoning.

keystoning   (1) In optics, a geometrical image distortion arising when a plane surface is photographed at an angle other than perpendicular to the lens axis. (2) In audiovisual aids, distortion of a projected image, usually of a wide top, narrow bottom effect. To avoid keystoning, the screen must be placed at right angles to the projection axis.

keystroke   The act of depressing one of the keys on a keyboard or a typewriter.

keystrokes per hour   In printing, the total number of text and command code keystrokes that are made by a compositor in one hour.

keystroke verification   In data processing, the re-entry of data by a keyboard operator to check the accuracy of the prior entry of the same data by a different operator. See verify.

key telephone set   In communications, a telephone set with special buttons to provide such capabilities as switching between lines, call holding or alerting of other telephone users.

key travel   On a keyboard, the displacement of a key from its rest to fully depressed position.

keyword   In information retrieval, one of the significant and informative words in a title or document that describes the content of that document. See key, KWAC, KWIC, KWOC.

keyword and context   In library science, an index of titles of documents permuted to bring each significant word to the beginning, in alphabetical order, followed by the remaining words which follow it in the title, and then followed by that part of the original title which came before the significant word. See KWIC.

keyword in context   In library science, a form of automatic indexing. Keywords are extracted from the title, abstract, or some portion of the text and stored with the associated title or surrounding portion of text. A search for the keyword can produce the context of that keyword in the document plus a document number. Compare KWOC. See indexing, keyword.

keyword out of context   In library science, a method of indexing in which the titles are printed in full under as many keywords as the indexer considers useful. Compare KWIC. See indexing, keyword.

kHz   See kilohertz.

kilo   A prefix denoting 1000 but in some computer applications it refers to 1024 because it corresponds to the binary number 10 000 000 000.

kilobit   1024 bits. See bit, kilo.

kilobyte   1024 bytes; See byte, kilo.

kilohertz   One thousand hertz. See hertz.

Kilostream   In data communications, a fully digital service provided by British Telecom which operates over a specially provided digital network that links main telephone exchanges. See X-Stream.

kinesthetic feedback   In physiology, an indication that an action has been effected, e.g. the actioning of a keystroke, by the sensation of touch, position or movement.

KIPS   In computing, Kilo Instructions Per Second, a measure of computing power. Compare LIPS, MIPS. See instruction.

KLIC   See key letter in context.

knapsack cipher   In data security, a public key cryptography system in which the public key is a vector of integers. The encryptor first converts the plaintext message into a corresponding binary code and breaks up the message into blocks, with a number of bits equal to the number of integers in the key. A sum is produced by including, or not, the integer of the key according to whether, or not, the corresponding message bit is 1 or 0. The term knapsack is used because the breaking of the the code is equivalent to the 'knapsack problem', i.e. given a knapsack of cylindrical shape and a set of rods, of the same diameter as the knapsack, but of varying lengths (corresponding to the integers of the key) find a subset of rods that will be of total length equal to that of the knapsack. The knapsack cipher has proved vulnerable to cryptanalytic attack. See public key cryptosystem, RSA.

knowledge base In computing, a database containing the codified knowledge of a human expert or experts. See expert systems.

knowledge engineering In computing, the process of building expert systems. See expert systems.

KTR See keyboard typing reperforator.

KWAC See keyword and context.

KWIC See keyword in context.

KWOC See keyword out of context.

L

label (1) In computer programming, one or more characters or a symbol used to identify a program statement, or the entry point of a subroutine. The use of labels in place of statement numbers saves time and avoids the possibility of error when the program is amended or enhanced. (2) In data processing, an identification record for a tape or disk file. (3) In cinematography, words superimposed on a film to indicate names, or functions, of objects shown in the film. See program statement, subroutine.

laboratory effects In recording, special audio and optical effects which can be produced in the processing of film or video tape, e.g. a night effect or the sound of an explosion.

lag (1) In electronics, the delay in change of an output with respect to changes in the input voltage, current or power. (2) In telegraphy, the time elapsing between the operation of the transmitting device and the response of the receiving device. (3) In television, a persistence of the electrical charge image on the phosphor screen for a small number of frames. (4) In visual perception, the retention of an image by the eye after removal of the stimulus. When a succession of still pictures is presented to the eye, as in films or television, the visual sensation retained by the retina decays relatively slowly, thus providing an illusion of continuous movement. See persistence of vision.

LAN See local area network.

landing pad In video disk, (1) a range of frames within which a player can locate a frame or frame sequence (2) a command that modifies the number of times a player attempts to locate a frame following an unsuccessful search. See frame.

language In computing and communications, a set of characters, conventions and rules used to convey information. A language may be formally considered to consist of pragmatics, semantics and syntax. See pragmatics, program language, semantics, syntax.

language support environment In computing, hardware and software facilities supplied by a manufacturer to assist in the development of programs written in a particular language.

language translator See translator.

lap In printing, a small overlap where two colours meet to safeguard against a gap which might otherwise occur due to a lack of register. See register.

lapel microphone In recording and audiovisual aids, a microphone clipped to a performer's clothing. Compare lavalier microphone.

large face In typesetting, the larger of two sizes available on the same body of typeface. See type size.

large scale integration In microelectronics, pertaining to a fabrication technology which produces between 100 and 1000 gates per chip. Compare MSI, SLSI, SSI, VLSI. See chip, gate.

LASER In optoelectronics, Light Amplification by Stimulated Emission of Radiation. A device that emits light rays which are in phase, travelling in the same direction and essentially of the same wavelength, i.e. colour. A laser beam does not diverge by a significant amount and maintains a high energy density. Conventional light sources accept energy, in some form, and use it to raise the energy level of electrons, bound to nuclei; when these electrons return to their original state photons are produced. The light wavelength corresponding to these emitted photons depends upon the energy level changes of the electrons. In lasers a large number of electrons are raised to a specific energy level. An incident photon of the correct frequency causes an excited electron to fall to its lower energy level and to emit a photon, these two photons can now stimulate two more excited electrons to undergo similar energy jumps. This multiplier effect produces the virtual simultaneous emission of photons of identical frequencies, thus providing a high energy pulse of coherent, monochromatic light. Lasers are used in optical signalling devices, high speed printers, fiber optics and holography. See coherence, electron, fiber optics, hologram, laser printer, photon.

laser beam recording   In micrographics, a technique employed in a microfilm recorder whereby the output characters from a computer are written directly into a microfilm by a laser. Typically the beam is divided into a number of separate beams that produce a dot matrix pattern by on-off actions of the beam. Compare electron beam recording. See dot matrix, LASER.

laser COM   In micrographics, the use of a laser to write directly on a microfilm to produce instantaneous storage without any need for chemical processing. See COM.

laser printer   In printing, an electrostatic printing device in which a laser beam is scanned across the surface of an electrically charged selenium coated drum by a rotating polygonal mirror. The beam is modulated corresponding dot matrix character patterns and produces corresponding changes in the charge on the drum surface. The image is then transferred to paper as in conventional xerographic printers. Speeds of 18,000 lines per minute can be produced. See LASER, xerography.

laser xerography   See laser printer.

last in first out   A system in which the next item to be selected is the one most recently added to the list. Compare first in first out. See stack.

latch   In electronics, a circuit that maintains an assumed position or condition until it is reset to its former state by external means. See flip flop.

latency   In computing, a delay between the instant a request is made for a record and the instant the transfer starts.

latent image   In photography and document copiers, the invisible image formed in the sensitized material after exposure but before development.

lateral reversal   To reverse an image from right to left so that it will appear as a mirror image.

LAU   See line adaptor unit.

launch amplifier   In cable television, the final amplifier at the head end of a system. See head end.

launch vehicle   In satellite communications, a rocket or space shuttle used to lift a satellite into orbit.

lavalier   microphone   In   recording   and audiovisual aids, a small microphone suspended from a cord around a performer's neck. Compare lapel microphone.

layer   In radiocommunications, one of the three regions which form the ionosphere. See D region, E region, F region.

lay in   In recording, the synchronization of sound tracks to a picture.

layout   (1) In printing, a plan designed to show how the printed result is to be produced and to give an indication of how it would look. (2) In computing, the specification of the format for input output data. See format.

LBR   See laser beam recording.

LC   US Library of Congress.

LCA   Lower case alphabet. See lower case.

LCD   See liquid crystal display.

Lcmarc   A database supplied by Library of Congress (LC) and dealing with books and periodicals - catalogs. See on line information retrieval.

LCP   See link control procedure.

LDDS   Limited distance data set. See limited distance modem.

LDS   See local distribution service.

LDX   See Long Distance Xerography.

LD4   In data communications, a high speed, coaxial cable, digital transmission system operating at 274 megabits per second. See bit.

lead   In printing, a thin metal strip inserted between lines of type in order to give a wider separation between the lines of print.

leader   (1) In photography and cinematography, any kind of nonimage film used for editing, threading or identification purposes. (2) In printing, a line of dots ...., used to direct the eye along a printed line. (3) In computing, the blank section of magnetic or paper tape preceding the start of the recorded information, used for threading purposes.

leading   In typesetting, the insertion of interline spaces. See lead.

leading edge   In computing, the edge of a punched card which is the first to be put into a card reader. See card reader, punched card.

leading zero   In computer programming, a zero, used as a fill character, which precedes the most significant digit of a number.

lead in pages   In videotex, routing pages which direct a user to required areas of the database. See end pages.

leaf   (1) In printing, the two backing pages of a book. (2) In data structures, the node at the end of a path in a tree structure. See tree structure.

leakage   In data security, the transmission of data to unauthorized users by processes with legitimate access to data. A compiler, for example, could leak a proprietary program whilst it is being compiled. See information flow control.

leased circuit   In communications, a circuit hired by a subscriber for his or her exclusive and permanent use. It may be a point to point or multidrop connection. See multidrop circuit, point to point connection.

leased line   See leased circuit.

least cost network design   In communications, a network of optimum design which meets the design specification at the least possible cost.

least significant bit   In computing, the bit which occupies the rightmost position in a binary number. See bit.

least significant digit   In computing, the digit which occupies the rightmost position in a number and therefore has least weight.

LED   See light emitting diode.

left hand margin indent   In word processing, a feature that enables blocks of recorded text to be identified with different left hand margins, irrespective of any amendments made to the text and while still retaining the original, fixed, left hand margin settings.

left justified   (1) In computing, the shifting of a number to the left hand end of a register. (2) In printing, the control of the printing positions of characters on a page so that the left hand margin of the printing is regular. See ragged setting, register, justification.

lens speed   In photography the f-number of a lens. See f-number, lens stop.

lens stop   Synonymous with f-stop.

letterpress   In printing, a process in which an impression is taken from the inked surfaces of type or blocks. Compare intaglio, lithography. Synonymous with relief printing.

letter quality printing   In word processing, a print quality equal to that provided by standard office typewriters.

letters case   In telegraphy, a group of characters consisting mainly of letters.

letterset   In printing, a contraction of letterpress offset, a process in which a rotary letterpress transfers an inked image from an offset cylinder, as with offset lithography. See letterpress, offset printing, lithography.

letterspacing In printing, the insertion of spaces between the letters of a word or words to lengthen the measure, improve the appearance of the line, or for emphasis. See measure.

letters shift signal In telegraphy, a signal that causes the receiving apparatus to decode following signals as characters in the letters case. See escape codes, letters case, shift codes.

level (1) In electronics and communications, a general term for the magnitude of a signal, used for voltage, current and power. (2) In data communications, the number of bits in each character of an information coding system. (3) In data communications, the number of discrete signal elements that can be transmitted in a given modulation scheme. See modulation.

level four In video disk, pertaining to a sophisticated player with extensive memory, control and processing facilities. Compare level one, level two, level three. See interactive video disk systems.

level one In video disk, pertaining to a player with freeze frame, picture stop, chapter stop, frame addressability and dual channel audio but with limited memory and virtually no processing power. Compare level two, level three, level four. See freeze frame, interactive video disk systems, picture stop, chapter stop.

level three In video disk, pertaining to a level one or level two player interfaced with an external computer. Compare level one, level two, level four. See interactive video disk systems.

level two In video disk, pertaining to a player with level one facilities plus on board programmable memory and improved access times. Compare level one, level three, level four. See interactive video disk systems.

lexicon A vocabulary, not necessarily in alphabetical order, with definitions or explanations for all terms.

Lexis A database supplied by Mead Data Central and others and dealing with communications, energy, industry, government - US Federal, labour and employment, law - finance, law - international, law - UK, law - US Federal, Law - US State, patents, securities - US, taxes, trade - US. See on line information retrieval.

LF See low frequency.

library In computing, (1) a collection of subroutines and programs written for a particular computer and available to a programmer for insertion into his own coding, (2) a repository for demountable recorded media, such as magnetic disk packs and magnetic tapes, (3) any collection of related files.

library directory In computing, the directory component in a library which contains such information as the number, name and location of each member in the library. See library.

library science The knowledge and skill concerned with the administration of libraries and their contents.

LIFO See last in first out.

lifter In audio recording, a device which removes the magnetic tape from contact with the head on fast wind or rewind.

ligatures In printing, two or more letters joined together, forming one type character, or a stroke connecting two letters.

light In physiology, that part of the electromagnetic spectrum, from 400 to 750 nanometers, of which the human observer is aware through the stimulation of the retina. It is not synonymous with radiant energy, nor is it merely a sensation. See electromagnetic radiation.

light conduit In fiber optics, an assembly of fibers used for the transmission of light sources rather than encoded optical signals. See fiber optics.

light emitting diode In semiconductors, a diode which glows when supplied with a specified voltage. LEDs are commonly used as alphanumeric display devices, but can be used as light sources in optical fiber transmission systems, although their low power output and relatively wide bandwidth make them less attractive than lasers. See LASER, fiber optics.

lightface In printing, a design of type style in which the image area is less in proportion to the width than in normal typestyles.

light guide See fiber optics.

light pen In computer graphics, a light sensitive device that is shaped like a pen and connected to a VDU. The tip of the light pen contains a light sensitive element which, when placed against the screen, will register a pulse from the scanning spot. A coincidence pulse is generated from which a computer can identify the location of the pen on the screen. See scanning spot, VDU.

light stability In optical character recognition, the resistance to change of colour of the image when exposed to radiant energy.

limit check In computing, a test on a number to see if it is within a stipulated range. See validation.

limited distance modem In data communications, a modem which does not apply a complex modulation scheme to the data before transmission but which applies the digital input (or a simple transformation of it) to the transmission channel. Used only for short distances of transmission. Synonymous with baseband modem.

limiter In electronics, a device that restricts the amplitude of a signal to a predetermined threshold level. Limiters may act on positive or negative values of a signal, or both.

limiting resolution In television, a measure of overall system resolution usually expressed in terms of the maximum number of lines per picture height discriminated on a test chart. For a number of lines N (alternate black and white lines) the width of each line is 1/N times the picture height. See resolution.

Lindop Committee In computing, a committee which considered the problems of data

protection and privacy, and reported in 1976. See data protection, privacy.

line (1) In communications, a metallic conductor used for transmission purposes. (2) In television and facsimile, the path traced by a scanning spot. (3) In computing, one or more characters entered on a terminal before a return to the first printing or display position. (4) In data communications, a string of characters accepted by a central computer as a single block of input, e.g. all the characters entered prior to a carriage return command. (5) In printing, a unit of measurement used to describe the body size of large faces, e.g. wood letters for posters. See block, scanning spot.

line adaptor unit See MODEM.

linear In electronics, a circuit which produces an output that varies in direct proportion to the input. No actual device is ever linear because there will always be an upper limit on the output, however the term is usually applied to devices that provide a linear response over the normal range of input signals.

linear array In radiocommunications, an antenna array in which the centers of the radiating elements lie in a straight line. See radiating element.

linear function A function which comprises the sum of terms, each of which is a constant multiplied by one, and only one, of the variables which are of first order only, e.g. $P = 5X + 10Y$.

linear integrated circuit In electronics, a type of integrated circuit suitable for analog signals. See analog signal.

linear predictive coding In computing, a technique of encoding sampled speech sounds in which redundant information is ignored. See speech synthesis.

linear programming A technique for finding the maximum or minimum value of a linear function when certain constraints are placed upon linear functions of the variables. A widely used optimizing technique in business and industry. See linear function.

line blanking interval In television, the time interval represented by the line blanking pulse width. See blanking interval.

line busy tone In telephony, an audible signal sent to a calling party to indicate that the called party is busy. See busy.

linecaster In typesetting, a machine which can cast an entire line of type as compared with one casting a character at a time.

line communications In communications, the transmission and reception of electric signals over a cable. See cable.

line concentrator In telephony, a switching stage in a local office which concentrates the traffic from a number of incoming lines to a smaller number of outlets to subsequent switching stages. Compare multiplexing.

line control In data communications, the sequence of signals used to control a channel.

line counter In word processing, a facility for counting and possibly controlling the number of lines printed on each page.

line drive signal In television, the signal applied to the camera control unit to initiate scanning. See scanning line.

line editor In computing, a text editor where the user must select individual lines to modify the text. Compare screen editor. See text editor.

line engraving (1) In printing, a letterpress printing block consisting of solid areas and lines, reproduced direct from a black and white original without any intermediate tones. (2) In graphics, an intaglio print taken from a hand engraved copper plate. See intaglio, letterpress.

line extender In cable television, an amplifier which compensates for signal loss in a spur feeder, enabling the network to cover a greater area. See attenuation, spur.

line feed In computing and data processing, advancement of paper or a form on a printer one line at a time so that the printing mechanism is positioned for printing the next line.

line folding In communications, when a teletypewriter or similar equipment receives a text message longer than the maximum allowed by the printer, the excess characters will be printed on the next line through the generation of a local new line signal. Although the appearance of the message may be marred, the meaning is preserved. See teletypewriter.

line frequency In television, the number of scanning lines swept in one second. In a 525 line, 30 pictures per second system, the line frequency is 525 x 30 = 15,750 Hz. See Hz, scanning line.

line group In communications, one or more lines of the same type that can be activated and de-activated as a unit.

line impedance In communications, the impedance of a telecommunication line. See impedance.

line increment In typesetting, the smallest separation possible between two lines of type for a particular machine. In hot metal type setting, it is a half point (0.0069 inch), but in photocomposition it may be as low as one eighteenth of a point (0.00077 inch). See point, photocomposition, hot metal composition.

line level In data communications, (1) the signal strength on a communications channel, (2) a set of protocols concerned with the transmission and control of a transparent stream of bits along a communications channel. See decibel, protocol, transparent.

line load In communications, the amount of traffic on a line, expressed as a percentage of its utilization to its total capacity. See traffic.

line number In computer programming, a number associated with a line in a program. In some languages such as BASIC they are mandatory and act as labels for reference purposes. See label.

line of sight In radiocommunications, pertaining to a situation in which there is an unobstructed straight line path from the transmitting to the receiving antenna. A necessary condition for microwave relay systems. See microwave relay, antenna.

line printer In computer peripherals, a device that prints an entire line of characters as one unit, at speeds of 500 - 2000 lines per minute. Compare character printer.

line spacing See automatic line spacing.

line speed In data communications, the rate at which signals may be transmitted over a given channel, measured in bauds. Effective speed varies with the capabilities of the equipment used and the amount of noise on the line. See baud, Shannon's Law.

lines per minute In computing, a measure of the speed of a line printer. See line printer.

line sweep In television, the horizontal movement of the scanning spot at line frequency. See line frequency, scanning spot.

line switching See circuit switching.

line sync pulse In television, a synchronizing pulse transmitted during the line blanking interval. See line blanking interval, video signal.

line termination equipment In data communications, data circuit terminating equipment, usually for a non telephone circuit. See data circuit terminating equipment.

line transient In electronics, an unwanted voltage pulse of very short duration, which can often produce errors in digital circuits not designed to minimize the effects of such interference. See pulse.

lining figures In printing, numerals that align horizontally at the top and bottom, e.g. 1234567890, as opposed to old style numerals. See old style figures.

link (1) In communications, a transmission path of specified characteristics between two points, e.g. a telephone wire or a microwave beam. As well as the physical aspect of transmission, a link includes the protocol, and associated devices and associated software, i.e. it can also be logical. (2) In computer programming, a routine that interfaces two separate programs, and through which control information is passed. See protocol, logical channel.

link control procedure In data communications, a procedure or set of rules for the transfer of data in an orderly and accurate way over a channel. Synonymous with link protocol.

linking In computer programming, a process of integrating two or more separately written, assembled or compiled, programs into a single entity. This function is normally carried out by the linking loader. See linking loader.

linking loader In computer programming, an executive routine which links different program segments, renumbers and relocates them in main memory, so that the program can be run as one unit. See linking,

link loss In satellite communications, the mcrowave transmission loss, in decibels, of signals between the transmitting and receiving earth stations. See decibel, footprint, microwave transmission.

link protocol Synonymous with link control procedure.

LIPS In computing, Logical Inferences Per Second, a measure of the power of an inference machine and denoting the number of syllogistic inferences per second that can be performed. One syllogistic inference is equivalent to 100-1000 conventional computer instructions. Compare KIPS, MIPS. See inference machine, syllogism.

liquid crystal display In computing, a visual

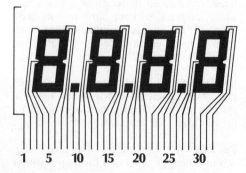

liquid crystal display
The numbers represent pin connections.

display used in pocket calculators, made of two glass plates sandwiched together with a special fluid. The liquid darkens when a voltage is applied. Compare light emitting diode. See optoelectronics.

Lisa (1) A database supplied by The Library Association and dealing with Library and Information Science.(2) In computing, a microcomputer hardware and software system produced by Apple and designed to facilitate its use by executives. The cursor is moved across the screen by use of a mouse and documents can be selected, modified and filed by reference to icons representing filing cabinets, in trays, waste paper baskets etc. Text can be cut from one document and pasted to another again by mouse controlled cursor movements See cursor, cut and paste, icon, mouse, on line information retrieval.

LISP In computer programming, LISt Processing, a language designed for the manipulation of lists and symbolic strings. It was one of the first high level languages and is now of considerable importance in the artificial intelligence field. See artificial intelligence, list, list processing.

list (1) In computing, an ordered set of items of data. (2) In programming, to print or display items of data that meet specific criteria. See chain list.

listening center In audiovisual aids, an audio distribution device which allows several individuals to listen to audio materials at the same time.

list processing (1) In computing, the manipulation of lists. Items may be added to, or deleted from, lists by modification of pointers on the affected and adjacent items. It is not necessary to physically move the adjacent records in storage. (2) In word processing, a facility to maintain and manipulate files in the form of lists, e.g. customer/address list. See list, LISP.

literal (1) In printing, an error by the compositor in substituting one character for another. (2) In computer programming, an item in a source program that contains a value rather than the address of that value.

literature search In library science, a syste-

matic and exhaustive search for published material on a specific subject, together with the preparation of annotated bibliographies or abstracts. Such searches are now commonly performed using on line databases. See database, information retrieval, on line.

lith film In printing, a photographic film having a high definition and contrast, used for lithographic printing. See photolithography.

lithography In printing, a method in which a very thin metal plate, usually made of zinc or aluminium, is bent to fit around a printing cylinder. A greasy substance is applied to the area to be printed, and the non printing areas, which have a fine, grained surface are dampened with water. A very fine film of water is retained by the fine surface. A greasy printing ink is used which adheres to the greasy image but is rejected by the water on the non image area. See offset printing.

LLL See low level language.

load (1) In computer programming, to enter data or a program into a computer memory. (2) In electronics, a device that receives power. (3) In computing, to prepare a peripheral device so that data can be accessed.

load and go In computing, an operating technique in which there are no stops for operator intervention between the loading and execution phases of a computer program.

loader In computing, a program designed to load other programs into main memory from external bulk storage devices. See main memory.

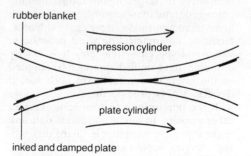

rubber blanket

impression cylinder

plate cylinder

inked and damped plate

lithography
The printing surface lies in the same plane as the non-printing areas on the plate cylinder.

loading (1) In paper making, the addition of a substance such as china clay to paper pulp during the manufacturing process for improved opacity and high finish. (2) In communications, a method of improving the transmission characteristics of a telephone line by inserting a series of inductances along the line at regular intervals. Such a line behaves in a similar way to a low pass filter. See inductance, low pass filter.

load life In electronics, the number of hours a device may dissipate power under specified operating conditions whilst remaining within its specified operational performance.

load point In computing, the beginning of the recording area on a reel of magnetic tape.

load sharing In computing, a technique whereby computers on a network share work loads to achieve a reasonably uniform distribution. This is achieved by the off loading of jobs from a heavily loaded computer to one more lightly loaded. See job.

lobe See antenna pattern.

local In computer programming, a variable which is defined and used only in one part of a program. Compare global. See variable.

local area network In data communications, a high bandwidth bidirectional communications network which operates over a limited geographic area, typically on office building or a college campus. The incentive for the development of LANs arose from the proliferation of micro- and mini-computers in large organizations and the perceived trend to supply office workers with more communication devices - videotex, facsimile, communicating word processors, video and speech system etc. It is clearly desirable that a unified approach be adopted to the intercommunication of such varied devices. LANs provide the computer user with the opportunity to communicate with other workers, to supply and access data and share expensive peripherals - hard disk storage devices, sophisticated printers etc. The LAN comprises a cable network linking the constituent nodes. Each node corresponds to a user workstation equipped with a physical

net work interface device. The topology of the network may be ring, star or bus.

The star network is the logical successor to the traditional mainframe computer-multi-terminal configuration but although it provides for a simple access protocol it has three disadvantages - network failure with central controller breakdown, low speed with controller bottlenecks and extensive wiring. The current trends tend to favour bus and ring topologies.

The mode of transmission may be either baseband or broadband; the transmission medium may be twisted pair copper wire, coaxial cable or fiber optics although the latter is unlikely to be extensively employed for some years due to the problems of implementing T junctions at each node.

The access protocols available for bus and ring networks are CSMA-CD, control token or message slot. The success of LANs will depend upon the confidence of users in the establishment of standards which will guarantee trouble free interconnection and operation of a wide range of user devices. Two of the most widely discussed standards

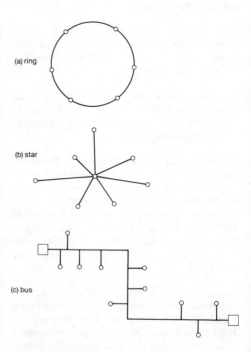

local area network
(a) ring; (b) star; (c) bus.

are Ethernet and Cambridge Ring. Other systems using CSMA-CD protocols often describe themselves as Ethernet-type. Both these systems transmit data in the baseband mode at 10 megabits per second. IBM have also developed a LAN standard using a baseband ring and token passing protocol. The ECMA approved a LAN standard in 1982 which is compatible with Ethernet.

An important consideration to the LAN user is the interface card which connects the workstation to the network. The internal high speed bus structures of computers, e.g. S100, facilitate the interconnection to the LAN and the interface card can be simply plugged into the backplane. The interface must also contain the software to handle data transfers. The ISO-OSI seven layer structure is significant in the design of LAN standards particularly where the LANs will require gateways to other LANs and wide area networks. See backplane, bandwidth, baseband, signalling, Cambridge Ring, coaxial cable, control token, CSMA-CD, ECMA. Ethernet, facsimile, fiber optics, gateway, ISO OSI, LAN, message slot, node, protocol, S100 bus, T junction, topology, twisted pair, videotex, wide area network.

local automatic message accounting   In telephony, a system which automatically captures and processes long distance call information for accounting purposes.

local central office   Synonymous with central office.

local distribution service   In cable television, a CAR station located within a system and used for the transmission of signals, by microwave link, to one or more locations from which they are distributed to users by cable. See CARS, microwave transmission.

local exchange   See local office.

local loop   In telephony, a link connecting a subscriber to the local central office. See central office.

local mode   In data communications, an internal operating state of a data terminal. In this condition a terminal is not able to accept incoming calls.

local office   In communications, a telephone exchange in which subscriber's lines are terminated. Synonymous with local exchange.

local service area   In telephony, the geographical area containing the telephone stations that a flat rate customer may call without incurring toll charges.

local switching office   See toll office.

local variable   See local.

location   In computing, any place where an instruction or data is stored.

locator device   In computer graphics, an input device that provides coordinate data, e.g. tablet. See tablet.

loc cit   In printing, an abbreviation for 'loco citato', Latin for 'in the place cited', used particularly in footnotes.

lock   In electronics and computing, a mechanism for controlling multiple accesses to a common device such as a bus or memory. See bus, memory.

locking   In electronics, a term used for the process of synchronizing a repetitive signal source with timing signals. See clock.

lockout   (1) In communications, the inability of a subscriber on a circuit controlled by an echo suppressor to get through to a called party because of either excessive local noise or continuous speech from one party. (2) In computer programming, a technique used to prevent access to critical data by two separate programs in a multiprogramming environment. Compare lock up. See echo suppressor.

lock up   In computing, an unwanted state of a system from which it cannot escape, e.g. a deadly embrace in the claiming of common resources. See deadly embrace.

log   In computing, a record or journal of a sequence of events of the jobs run through a computer.

logarithm   In mathematics, the logarithm of

a number is the power to which the base must be raised to give that number. Thus in decimal arithmetic the logarithm of 100 (to base 10) is 2, since 10 x 10 = 100. See base.

logarithmic graph   In mathematics, a coordinate graph in which the scale of the vertical axis is in logarithmic proportions, whilst the horizontal axis remains linear. See logarithm.

logic   (1) In philosophy, the discipline concerned with reasoning and thought. (2) In electronics, the physical circuits which implement logical operations and functions. (3) In computing, the electronic components of the system. See logical operator.

logical channel   In data communications, a circuit that is used for packet switching operations between a terminal and a network node. The circuit may be a permanent virtual connection or one set up for the duration of the call. See packet switching, virtual circuit.

logical comparison   In programming, a logic operation to determine whether two character strings are equal. See logical operator, string.

logical database   A database as viewed by its users. This structure of the data need not be the same as that of the physical database. Compare physical database.

logical data independence   In databases, pertaining to the structure of the data that permits the schema to be changed without affecting the application programmer's view of the data. Compare physical data independence. See data independence, schema.

logical expression   In Boolean algebra, a statement that contains logical operators and operands and that can be reduced to a value that may only be either true or false. For example, the Boolean formulae for an EXCLUSIVE OR function Z = (A AND NOT B) OR (NOT A AND B) is a logical expression. See EXCLUSIVE OR, logical operator.

logical operator   In computer programming, an operator that can be used in a logical expression to indicate the action to be per-

formed on the terms in the expression. The logical operators are AND, OR, and NOT. All logic expressions can be written in terms of these three basic operations. See AND, OR, NOT.

logical record   In computer programming, a record which is defined in terms of its functions rather than the physical manner in which it is stored. Compare physical record. See record.

logical unit   In data communications, a port through which a user gains access to the sevices of a network. See port.

logical variable   In Boolean algebra, a variable in a logical expression. It may only assume one of two values, true or false.

logic bomb   In data security, a part of a program which is triggered by a combination of events in the system. The illegal section of the program activates a fraud when triggered by the events.

logic card   In computing, a circuit board that contains components and wiring which performs one or more complex logic functions or operations. The board is designed for easy removal from the motherboard of a computer. See motherboard.

logic circuit   In computing, a circuit comprising one or more gates or flip flops that performs a particular logic function. See gate, flip flop.

logic device   See logic circuit.

logic level   In electronics, the value of a physical quantity, e.g. a current or voltage, used to represent the logic state of a signal in a circuit. In binary logic there are two logic levels corresponding with the two logic states of 1 and 0. For example, in a circuit, a signal of +5 volts may correspond to a logical 1 (the high or true state) and -2 volts may correspond to a logical 0 (the low or false state). See logic state.

logic map   See Karnaugh map.

logic state   In digital circuits, one of the two

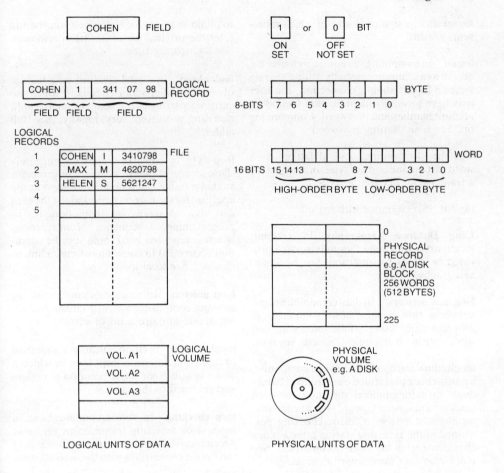

logical record
A comparison of logical and physical data storage.

possible states of a binary variable, usually designated the 1 state and the 0 state.

logic state analyzer In electronics, a digital test and diagnostic system equipped with an oscilloscope, and capable of displaying bus and other digital states as O's and 1's. See oscilloscope, logic timing analyzer.

logic symbol In electronics, a symbol used to represent a logic element graphically.

logic timing analyzer In electronics, a digital test equipment incorporating a special oscilloscope capable of handling and display-

ing 8 or more separate inputs in the time domain. See time domain.

log in See log on.

Logo In computer programming, a high level, interactive language developed for educational applications. See high level language, turtlegraphics.

logo See logotype.

log off In computing, an instruction to a computer system by a user that a session is to be terminated.

logogram A sign or character which represents a word.

log on In computing, a request by a user for access to a computer, usually a time sharing system. In initiating a connection, the user may have to supply identification such as an account number and password. Compare log off. See time sharing, password.

logotype In printing, several letters, or a word cast on one body of type, often used for a trade name. See house style.

log out Synonymous with log off.

Long Distance Xerography In communications, a wideband facsimile service provided by Xerox Corporation. See facsimile, xerography.

long haul network In data communications, networks that connect host computers in different cities using public telephone network, satellite communications etc. See host.

longitudinal parity check (1) In computing, a parity check performed on a group of binary digits in a longitudinal direction for each track on a magnetic tape. (2) In data communications, a system of error checking performed at the receiving station after a block check character has been accumulated. See block character check, parity checking.

longitudinal redundancy check In data communications, a redundancy code technique using one 8 bit check byte per transmitted block of data. The most significant bit of the check byte provides a parity check bit for the most significant bits of the characters in the block and so on for all other bit positions. See bit, byte, parity checking, redundant code.

long letters In printing, letter designs that occupy the maximum area of the typeface and include an ascender or descender. See ascender, descender.

long persistence phosphors See long persistence screen.

long persistence screen In display devices, a screen with a coating of phosphors designed to retain an image for a relatively long period after the original signal has been removed. See lag, storage tube.

look ahead In digital electronics, a feature of some parallel adder circuits in which the carries occurring as the result of binary addition are processed very rapidly. See full adder.

loop (1) In cinematography, a purposely slack section of film in a camera or projector so that a frame can remain motionless at the aperture for the correct period whilst the feed and take up spools are in motion. (2) In programming, a sequence of instructions which is repeated until some specific condition occurs. (3) In communications, a link or channel. See local loop.

loop antenna In radiocommunications, an antenna comprising a closed circuit consisting of one or more turns of wire.

loopback test In communications, a method of fault isolation on a local loop in which a signal is sent from a test point on a modem and returned to the modem.

loop checking In data communications, a method of detecting transmission errors in which received data is returned to the sending station for comparison with the original data.

looped outlet In cable television, a junction box in a subscriber's premises through which a spur cable passes. The box usually contains isolation and attenuation circuits. See attenuation, isolation, spur.

loop film In recording, a length of film or tape spliced head to tail for continuous playing.

loop network In computing and communications, a network configuration in which there is a single path between all nodes and the path is a closed circuit. Compare star. See node, ring.

loop plant In communications, all the cables, ducts, joint boxes, cabinets, poles and ancillary equipment used to connect subscribers to their local office. See local office.

loose gate In audiovisual aids, a projector which has a loosened gate in order to reduce the possibility of film damage. See gate.

loss In communications, a general term for the loss of signal energy during transmission along a circuit, expressed as the ratio of the signal power at the start of the circuit to the signal power at the receiver, usually expressed in decibels. See attenuation, decibel, signal.

lost call In telephony, a request for connection that is abandoned owing to congestion.

lost time In facsimile transmission, that fraction of the scanning line period which is not available for the transmission of picture information. See scanning line.

LOTUS 123 In computer programming, a combined database management, spreadsheet and graphics package. See spreadsheet.

loudness In audio, a subjective experience of the intensity of a sound wave. The loudness of a noise is determined by the amplitude of the wave, its frequency, and the sensitivity of the listener to sound waves at a particular frequency. See frequency, intensity.

loudspeaker In acoustics, a transducer which converts electrical energy into sound energy. Most loudspeakers are of the moving coil variety where signals are supplied to a coil, attached to a large diaphragm, which is relatively free to move in a strong, transverse magnetic field. See electrostatic loudspeaker.

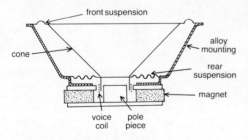

loudspeaker
Cross-section of a moving coil loudspeaker.

lower case In printing, the small letters in typefaces, e.g. a, b, c etc. Compare upper case.

lowest useful frequency In radiocommunications, the lowest frequency in the high frequency band that can be used for transmission over a given path at a specified time.

low frequency In radiocommunications, the frequency range from 30-300 kHz. See kHz.

low level language In computer programming, a language that is closely related to the machine code language of a computer, i.e. one that is translated by an assembler. Low level languages may be more efficient in operation, i.e. faster, require less memory etc. However, such languages are difficult to write and their application is restricted to specific hardware configurations. Compare high level language. See assembler, machine language, portability, translator.

low pass filter In electronics, a frequency selective network that attenuates signals with frequencies above a predefined value, but passes signals with lower frequencies. Compare high pass filter. See attenuation, cutoff frequency.

low reduction In micrographics, a reduction of less than 15X. Compare medium reduction, high reduction, very high reduction, ultra high reduction. See reduction.

low speed (1) In data communications, systems which operate at less than 2400 bits per second.

LPC See linear predictive coding.

LPM See lines per minute.

LR See low reduction.

LRC See longitudinal redundancy check.

LSB See least significant bit.

LSD See least significant digit.

LSI See large scale integration.

LTE See line termination equipment.

lumen In optics, a unit of illumination, defined as the luminous flux emitted by a standard candela into a solid angle of 1 steradion. See flux, candela, steradion.

luminance In optics, the measured radiance of a light source using a photometer as distinguished from brightness, the subjective visual sensation of luminance. See brightness.

luminance signal In television, that part of the composite colour video signal responsible for the luminance information. Because the eye is less sensitive to colour changes than changes in contrast, more bandwidth is required for the luminance signal than the chrominance signal. See chrominance signal, composite colour video signal.

lux In optics, one lumen per square millimeter. See lumen.

M

MAC (1) In television, Multiplexed Analog Components, the technique adopted as a standard for DBS in which the transmission format is a multiplex of time compressed video components and a digital burst which carries synchronization, sound and data services. (2) In data communications, Message Authentication Code, a code which is transmitted along with a message to confirm both the validity of the data and the data source. See A-MAC, authentication, C-MAC, DBS.

machine A system of interrelated parts with separate functions designed to carry out some particular tasks. Synonymous with computer.

machine address Synonymous with absolute address.

machine aided translation A system in which the computer relieves the human translator from routine tasks, e.g. dictionary look up, text processing. See machine translation, term bank, text processing.

machine check In computing, an error condition caused by equipment failure.

machine code See machine language.

machine composition In printing, any process which results in the production of type matter by means of composing machines and keyboards.

machine cycle In computing, the minimum length of time taken by a computer to perform a given series of tasks. See memory cycle.

machine independent In computer programming, pertaining to a program or procedure created without regard to the actual computer on which it will run. A machine independent program is therefore portable across computers. See portability.

machine instruction In computer programming, an instruction written in machine language. See instruction, machine language.

machine language In computing, a language providing programs that can be expressed directly in a binary format acceptable to the central processing unit. All other programming languages, e.g. assembler or high level, have to be translated into binary machine code before being executed in the central processing unit. See translator.

machine learning In computing, a process where a device improves its performance based on the results of past actions. See artificial intelligence.

machine proof In printing, the first copies taken off a printing machine for checking purposes before full production starts.

machine readable In computing, data which is in a form that can be input directly into the machine, e.g. on magnetic tape. See magnetic ink character recognition, magnetic tape, optical character recognition.

machine ringing In telephony, automatic ringing that persists until a call is either answered or abandoned.

machine sheet In printing, a printed sheet off the press during a run.

machine translation In computing, pertaining to the use of a computer to translate natural language text into the corresponding text of another language. A significant proportion of conventional computing activity is spent in compilation, or interpretation; processes used when a program expressed in a high level language is translated into another lower level language. The processes involved in accepting several pages of a Pascal program with paragraphs written in English-like phrases such as
WHILE ONGOING DO

BEGIN CALC-TAX into a stream of binary numbers representing machine instructions, have considerable similarity with that of translating from English to French. The program text is subjected to parsing and the syntactical rules of the words and phrases are identified, then the subcomponents are looked up in a dictionary and substitutions of the target language terms are made. Computer scientists have devoted considerable effort to the design of highly efficient compilers and it was natural that the parallels with the tasks of foreign language translation were spotted in the 1950's and 1960's when attempts were made to produce natural language translation. These early attempts did not, however, produce the expected rates of success in spite of the money and expertise expended on research projects.

The human translator has three important functions not required of the compiler. He must resolve ambiguities which arise from the very free syntax of natural language, often without the opportunity to refer back to the original author, he must deal with a very large and dynamic vocabulary and finally he must produce a final text which has a 'style' acceptable to the ultimate user. The resolution of ambiguities demands a knowledge of the conceptual framework surrounding the text. Consider the sentences - The boy went into a supermarket. He put a bag of flour into the basket and some chocolate into his pocket. At the checkout counter his face reddened and he said 'I didn't mean to take it.' In the translation into German it is necessary to give a gender to 'it' contained in the phrase - 'mean to take it.' To do so requires that 'it' is assigned to 'chocolate' and not 'bag of flour' but how does the human translator know this? He must use the concepts of supermarket shopping, shoplifting, sense of guilt and blushing to perform this task. The vocabulary can present problems particularly with homographs that again require a knowledge of context for correct translation. Finally the process of learning to produce prose, which is acceptable to a well educated reader, is not amenable to codification in a computer program.

The resolution of ambiguities will be a formidable task for the artificial intelligence field and it is unlikely that computer systems will be able to emulate the skill and versatility of human translators in the foreseeable future. The demand for translations is so massive, however, that the search for methods to reduce the cost of human translators is imperative for organizations such as the EEC, which currently spends an estimated £300 million on the translation activities.

The use of a computer in the translation task becomes feasible when one or more of the demands on the fully automated process are dropped. If the subject area of the source text is well defined then the syntax and vocabulary can become a manageable subset of natural language. Thus the Canadian Meteo system successfully translates weather forecasts from English to French. If the requirement for a style of target text similar to that of a good human translator is relaxed then a crude form of translation with mechanical translation of words and phrases can be achieved by computers. In military intelligence work it is necessary to scan vast quantities of foreign documents but the reader is often only interested, initially, in the appearance of a combination of key phrases or words. This very crude translation process is often adequate for the task of selecting those documents that prove to be of sufficient interest to warrant full human translation. The most important relaxation, however, is that the process be fully automated. There is a continuum of translator/computer arrangements that promise to reduce the cost and improve the turnaround, of the translation task, i.e. from the fully automated machine translation, through the human assisted machine translation to the machine assisted translation down to the provision of comprehensive text processing facilities for translators. The fully automated machine translation can be successfully employed if the user is prepared to accept an incredibly crude translation for scanning purposes or if the subject area is rigidly defined, e.g. Meteo and Titus.

The human assisted machine translation systems interact with a consultant and the computer reports detected errors in the text which prevents it from continuing with the analysis, or finding a term in the internal dictionary. The English-Chinese CULT system developed in the Chinese University of Hong Kong employs this interactive process. Machine Aided Translations can range from translation systems which demand pre- and postediting by human translators through automatic dictionaries to merely word processing systems of greater or lesser complexity. Pre-editing enables the translator to remove ambiguities and simplify the syntax of the source text whilst post editing involves the redrafting of output text to produce a style more acceptable to the user. Translators argue that the effort of post editing can exceed that of a complete translation from scratch so that pre-editing is often the more productive task. Systems like SYSTRAN which are said to be fully automated machine translation either require a rigid adherence to input syntax, e.g. pre-editing by the author or a degree of post-editing to convert phrases such as 'on a street large motion' into 'there is a lot of traffic in the street'.

The provision of an electronic dictionary, or term bank, can substantially reduce the manual effort of translation particularly in areas where new definitions arise from technological developments. EURODIC-AUTOM provides an interactive service in the EEC in which users can input phrases from terminals and conduct a dialog with the system to obtain equivalents in several languages. The TEAM system, developed by the Languages Services Department of Siemens AG, combines the advantages of a term bank with a sophisticated text processing facility.

The EEC Commissioners intend to move forward in the machine translation area with the development of the Eurotra system with the hope that it will overcome many of the problems experienced with SYSTRAN and reduce the cost and effort of routine translations of Commission papers, e.g. committee agenda, minutes, technical reports etc. SYSTRAN is essentially a bilingual system only and past attempts to tune its performance have proved to be expensive and of limited success. The EEC administration produces massive demands for multilingual translation and Eurotra will separate out the analysis and synthesis stages so that the analysis is independent of the target language and the synthesis is independent of the source language. This degree of modularity will reduce the total effort of translating from one to many languages and, it is hoped, simplify the problems of improving the total system per-

formance. See compiler, CULT, EURODI-CAUTOM, Eurotra, Meteo, syntax, TEAM, Titus, text processing.

mackle   In printing, a spot or blemish on a printed sheet caused by a double impression, wrinkling etc.

macroassembler   In computer programming, an assembler equipped with a facility for defining and expanding macroinstructions. See macroinstruction, assembler.

macrobend loss   In fiber optics, the leakage of light when the optical cable is bent. Compare microbend loss.

macro chip   See wafer silicon integration.

macrocode   See macroinstruction.

macroinstruction   In computing, an instruction which stands for a predefined sequence of other instructions. When a macroinstruction is encountered within a program, it is called by the controlling system and expanded into a series of machine language instructions. Compare closed subroutine. Synonymous with open subroutine.

macrolanguage   In computer programming, the representations and rules for writing macroinstructions. See macroinstruction.

macroprogramming   In computer programming, the use of macroinstructions. See macroinstruction.

magazine   (1) In teletext, a group of up to a hundred pages, each carrying a common magazine number in the range of 1-8. Up to eight magazines may be transmitted in sequence, or independently, on a television program channel. (2) In filming, a container for film which is used for supply, shooting or storage purposes. (3) In typesetting, a slotted metal container used to store matrices in linecasting machines. See linecaster, matrix, page.

MAGB   Microfilm Association of Great Britain.

mag film   Synonymous with magnetic film.

Magicall In telephony, a telephone access-ory which can hold up to 400 telephone numbers and dial any of them automatically at the push of a button.

magnetic bubble memory See bubble memory.

magnetic card (1) In audiovisual aids, a card with a magnetizable stripe on which sound can be stored by magnetic recording. (2) In word processing, a recording medium in the form of a paper or plastic card on which recordings can be made on one side only.

magnetic card reader In audiovisual aids, a device for recording and reproducing sound on a card having a magnetic stripe along one edge. The card usually contains pictorial and/or typed information and separate tracks on the magnetic stripe may provide for a protected master and erasable student responses. See magnetic card, magnetic stripe, audioslide.

magnetic cartridge Synonymous with mag-netic tape cassette.

magnetic disk In computing, a flat disk with a magnetizable surface layer on which data can be stored by magnetic recording. There are two main types of disk : hard and floppy, the former being rigid using a metal or glass base, the latter having a flexible, plastic base. The hard disk rotates at high speed (2400rpm) so that data may be accessed with-out undue delay. A disk is logically for-matted into tracks, with each track having a number of sectors. See floppy disk, magnetic disk unit, sector, track, Winchester.

magnetic disk unit In computing, a device containing a disk drive, magnetic heads and associated controls. See magnetic disk.

magnetic drum In computing, a cylinder with a magnetizable surface layer on which data can be stored by magnetic recording. A magnetic drum offers very fast retrieval of information but it is very expensive and to some extent has been superseded by fixed head disks. See fixed head disk.

magnetic film In recording, standard width film which is coated with an iron oxide compound. Used for recording and repro-ducing sound. Synonymous with mag film.

magnetic film recorder In recording, a sound recorder which uses perforated mag-netic film, as distinguished from a magnetic tape recorder. See magnetic film.

magnetic focusing In electronics, the focus-ing of an electron beam in a CRT by a magnetic field. See CRT.

magnetic hand scanner In computing, a hand held device that reads information from a magnetic stripe. See magnetic stripe.

magnetic head In computing and recording, a transducer for converting electric vari-ations into magnetic variations for storage on magnetic media, or for reconverting informa-tion stored in this way into corresponding electric signals. See transducer.

magnetic ink In computing, an ink contain-ing magnetic particles which can be detected by a suitable magnetic sensor. See magnetic ink character recognition.

magnetic ink character recognition In char-acter recognition, the identification of char-acters printed with ink that contain particles of a magnetic material. MICR is used in the banking industry to record transmitted codes and account numbers on checks for data processing. Compare optical character recognition. See magnetic ink.

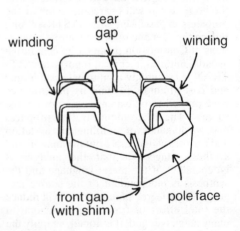

magnetic head

magnetic keyboard   A term used to describe a word processor. See word processing.

magnetic master   In recording, the soundtrack from which the release print soundtrack is made.

magnetic original   In recording, a magnetic tape or film soundtrack containing the original, live sound.

magnetic printing   In printing, a process in which a magnetic image is formed on a ferromagnetic layer, the image is developed by applying fine ferromagnetic particles, then transferring and fixing the image to paper. Compare xerography. See ferromagnetic.

magnetic recording   In recording, a method of impressing signals onto a moving magnetic material by means of a magnetic field produced by a magnetic head. See magnetic head.

magnetic screen   In electronics, a sheet of metal used to confine a magnetic field within a prescribed volume.

magnetic sheet   See magnetic card.

magnetic sound   In recording, sound recorded on a magnetic medium. Compare optical soundtrack.

magnetic sound recording   See magnetic recording.

magnetic storm   In communications, a disturbance in the earth's magnetic field, associated with abnormal solar activity, and capable of seriously affecting both radio and wire transmission.

magnetic stripe   (1) In cinematography, a stripe of iron oxide placed on a clear film for recording and reproduction. (2) In computing, a stripe of magnetic material, e.g. on a credit card, on which data, usually identification information, can be recorded and from which the data can be read.

magnetic tape   In recording and computing, a tough plastic base material coated with a thin film of finely divided magnetic particles of iron, iron oxide, chromium dioxide or similar materials. See magnetic tape transport. Synonymous with audio tape.

magnetic tape cartridge   Synonymous with magnetic tape cassette.

magnetic tape cassette   In microcomputers and recording, a container holding a magnetic tape that can be used without separating it from its container. Synonymous with magnetic tape cartridge.

magnetic tape drive   Synonymous with magnetic tape transport.

magnetic tape label   In computing, one or more records at the beginning of a magnetic tape that identify and describe the data recorded on the tape and contains other information, such as the serial number of the reel holding the tape. See record.

magnetic tape recorder   See tape recorder.

magnetic tape transport   (1) In computing, a tape drive mechanism under the control of a computer that moves tape past a read/write head. (2) In recording, a tape transport. See magnetic head, tape transport.

magnetic thin film storage   See thin film memory.

magnetic transfer   In recording, a transfer from one magnetic medium to another, e.g. magnetic tape to perforated magnetic film for editing.

magnetic workprint   In recording, a rerecorded sound track used for editing purposes, usually on a perforated magnetic film with coded edge numbers.

magnitude   In mathematics, the absolute value of a number, irrespective of sign.

magoptical   In recording, a sound track which has both an optical and a magnetic stripe track. See optical soundtrack, magnetic sound.

MAHT   Machine Aided Human Translation. See machine aided translation.

mail box   See electronic mailbox.

mail merge In word processing, a program for producing form letters in which a name and address file is merged with the text file containing the letter. See form letter, merge.

main beam In communications, the electromagnetic waves contained within the main lobe of an antenna array. See antenna, electromagnetic radiation, main lobe.

main cable In communications, a cable linking to a cross connection point in a local line network to which other main cables are connected.

main distributing frame In telephony, the cable racking on which all distribution and trunk cables into a central office are terminated. The bulky processing units of the early computers resembled the MDF, hence the origin of the term mainframe for a large computer. See mainframe.

main entry In library science, the basic catalog entry with the fullest particulars for the complete identification of the work. Compare added entry.

mainframe In computing, a term normally applied to a large general purpose computer installation serving a major section of an organization or institution. Compare microcomputer, minicomputer.

main index In videotex, the topmost index in the database that directs a user to other indexes or services. See routing page, tree structure.

main lobe In radiocommunications, the predominant lobe in an antenna pattern. Compare side lobe, back lobe. See antenna pattern.

main memory Synonymous with main storage.

main station In communications, a telephone, telex or teletypewriter exchange terminal connected to the local central office via a local loop and having a unique dial number. See local loop, teletypewriter exchange service.

main storage In computing, that part of a computer which holds data and programs for random access by the central processing unit in the form of binary digits. Storage and memory are synonymous. Main storage usually has a fast access time (between 100 nanoseconds and 1 microsecond) but because it is relatively costly its size is usually restricted. However, memory size is also restricted by the addressing capability of the computer, for example on an 8 bit microcomputer it is 64K bytes. On a large computer which has a 24 bit address field, it is 16 Megabytes. See access time, address, RAM, random access, word size.

maintained In audiovisual aids, a switch which when operated remains in an operating state and only changes either to another operating state or an off state when activated again. Compare momentary.

maintenance Any activity intended to keep a machine in a specified, operational condition, including preventive maintenance and corrective maintenance. See preventive maintenance, corrective maintenance.

majuscule In printing, a capital letter. Compare minuscule.

make up In printing, the arrangement of type matter into pages.

Management Contents A database supplied by Management Contents and dealing with business & industry, business management. See on line information retrieval.

management information system (1) A system designed to provide management and supervisory staff with required data that is accurate, relevant and timely, possibly on a realtime basis. (2) A system in which data is recorded and processed for operational purposes. The problems are detected for higher management decision making and information is fed back to higher levels on the progress, or lack of it, in achieving management objectives. See realtime.

man machine interface In computing, pertaining to technologies designed to improve the communication between the user and the computer. In hardware terms this includes voice analysis and synthesis, touchscreen, mouse, light pen etc. In software terms it relates to methods which render packages more user friendly, e.g. natural language dialogs. See light pen, mouse, speech recognizer, touchscreen, voice synthesis.

man made noise In communications, interference caused by electrical machines, car ignition systems etc. See interference.

mantissa In mathematics, the positive fractional part of the representation of a logarithm. In the expression $\log 643 = 2·808$, the mantissa $= 0·808$ and the characteristic $= 2$. See logarithm.

manual central office In telephony, a central office, or exchange, in which all call connections are established and released by operators.

manual data processing The processing of data without the use of a computer.

manual input In data processing, the entry of data by hand into a computer, usually involving a keyboard. Compare machine readable.

manuscript In printing, any handwritten matter intended for typesetting. Synonymous with copy.

MAP See Microprocessor Application Project.

mapping (1) In mathematics, a relationship between two or more quantities. (2) In databases, the relationship between a given logical structure and its physical representation. See logical database, physical database.

MAR See memory address register.

MARC In library science, MAchine Readable Catalog, a system initially developed in the US Library of Congress with the purpose of organizing and disseminating bibliographic data, in machine readable form, for incorporation into national and local records for the purpose of documentation. See machine readable.

marching display In photocomposition, a

display device which shows the last 30 to 40 characters keyed.

margin (1) In telegraphy, a measure of the ability of the receiving apparatus to cope with timing errors in the received signal. (2) In printing, the space surrounding the type area, comprising head, tail, back and foredge. See head, tail.

Maritime Satellite Service In satellite communications, a service that enables calls to be made to ships in the Atlantic and Pacific oceans. It has a geostationary satellite over each ocean, with an earth station in California serving the Pacific and another in Connecticut serving the Atlantic. See earth station, geostationary satellite.

mark In communications, an impulse on a data circuit which corresponds to the active condition of the receiving apparatus, i.e. a one binary condition that causes a morse printer to mark the paper. Compare space. See bit, morse printer.

mark hold In telegraphy, the normal no traffic line condition whereby a steady mark is transmitted. See mark.

marking interval In telegraphy, a period of time corresponding with a mark condition. See mark.

markov process A random process in which the probability of a transition to a new state depends only upon the current state. See random process, probability theory.

mark scanning In optical character recognition, the automatic optical sensing of marks usually recorded manually on paper or other data carrier.

mark sense In character recognition, to mark a position on a form with an electrically conductive pencil for machine reading. See machine readable.

mark sensing In character recognition, the automatic sensing of conductive marks usually recorded manually on a form. See mark sense.

mark sensing card In computing, a card on

which mark sensible fields have been printed. See mark sense.

mark space   In telegraphy, the states of a two condition telegraph code. The mark corresponds to the active condition of the receiving apparatus.

markup   Synonymous with type markup.

MASER   In electronics and communications, Microwave Amplification by Stimulated Emission of Radiation, a stable, low noise amplifying device. Masers were frequently used for amplifying microwave signals received from the first generation of communication satellites, but their low bandwidth and special low temperature operating requirements have made them unsuitable for use with later generations of satellites. Compare LASER. See travelling wave tube.

mask   (1) In photography, a device used to restrict the light from one area, while admitting whole or reduced illumination to another area. (2) In electronics, a photographically produced stencil used in semiconductor manufacture to control areas of metal deposited on a silicon substrate, or to limit the regions of doping during the diffusion process. (3) In computing, a pattern of characters used to control the retention and elimination of portions of another pattern of characters. For example, the selective enabling or prevention of an interrupt from one of several I/O units connected to the bus system of a central processing unit. See bus, dopant, input output devices, interrupt, masked ROM.

masked ROM   In computing, a ROM whose contents are produced during its manufacture by a masking technique in contrast to a PROM whose contents are programmed after manufacture by means of a PROM programming device. ROM masking is a high volume method of production used when 1000 or more of the same identical ROM are to be made. See PROM, ROM.

masking   (1) In audio, an effect in which a sound may apparently be suppressed by another which might be louder or at a different frequency, or both. (2) In television, the minimizing of colour errors that may appear in the process of synthesizing colour information to three primary signals. See RGB.

mask register   In computing, a storage location used to store mask bits for the selective control of interrupts. See interrupt, main storage, mask.

masquerading   In data security, the unauthorized access to a database by using the password of a legitimate user. Similarly, a program might be able to obtain confidential information from database users (e.g. their login passwords). Protection against masquerading requires the system and user to be able to mutually authenticate each other. See authenticity, digital signature, Trojan Horse.

massaging   In typesetting, the manipulation of input copy, particularly on a VDU, in order to produce a desired layout. See VDU.

mass media   In communications, newspapers, television and radio. See media.

mass storage   In computing, the storage of a large amount of data which is also readily accessible to the processing unit of a computer. Synonymous with bulk storage.

mass storage device   In computing, a device having a large storage capacity, e.g. magnetic disk, magnetic drum. See magnetic disk, magnetic drum.

mass storage system   In computing, a storage system with more than a terabit capacity. Such systems normally hold the data cells in a rack, or honeycomb, of storage units. A mechanical system moves the appropriate cell to and from the read/write head. The data cells may be magnetic tape cartridge or cassette, magnetic card or photodigital systems. Access times range from three to about twenty seconds. See bit, magnetic card, magnetic tape, photodigital memory, tera.

master   (1) In recording, a sound track on which other tracks have been combined. (2) In printing, a sheet of material that carries an image of the text or other material to be copied. See master proof.

master antenna television system   In cable

television, an antenna arrangement which serves a localized cluster of television receivers. Compare community antenna television.

master clock In computing, the primary source of timing signals used to control the sequencing of pulses. See clock.

master file In data processing, a file containing relatively permanent information that is used as a source of reference and is updated periodically. See file.

master group In communications, an assembly of ten supergroups in a 2520 kHz band, the basic master group extending from 564 to 3084 kHz. In the UK, a master group contains only 5 supergroups separated by 8 kHz in a 1232 kHz band. See supergroup.

mastering In video disk, a real time process in which a premaster video tape is used to modulate a laser beam onto a photosensitive glass master disk.

master proof In printing, the final version of a galley proof or page proof used for a print run. See galley proof.

master station In data communications, a station that has accepted an invitation to pass data to one or more slave stations. At any one time, there can only be one master station on a link. See station, slave.

MAT See machine aided translation.

match dissolve In audiovisual aids, a dissolve which links images having similar form or content.

matched load In electronics and communications, a load connected to the output of a device or at a node on a transmission system which absorbs all the transmitted signal without reflection. See impedance matching.

matching In data processing, the process of comparing two files to determine whether there is a corresponding item, or group of items, in each file. See file, item.

matching transformer In electronics, a transformer used for coupling two systems having different impedances, e.g. a low impedance microphone and a high impedance amplifier. Compare mismatch. See impedance matching.

mathematical model A formal statement of the mathematical relationship between the elements of a system which are of particular interest. Mathematical models usually represent a simplified form of reality and are often used for prediction.

mathematics The study of the relationships between quantities or objects, organized so that certain facts can be proved or derived from others by the use of logic. See logic.

Mathfile A database supplied by the American Mathematical Society and dealing with mathematics. See on line information retrieval.

matrix (1) In mathematics, a multidimensional array of quantities, manipulated in accordance with the rules of matrix algebra. (2) In computing, a logic network whose configuration is an array of intersections of its input output leads, with logic circuits connected at some of these intersections. The network usually functions as an encoder or decoder. (3) In television, the means by which colour data is transformed from one reference system to another. (4) In printing, a copper mould which has been struck by a punch and from which type is cast. (5) In photocomposition, the set of type faces used by a machine. (6) In photography, a dyed emulsion image strip which together with two other strips are combined on a film base to produce colour film. See decoder, encoder, logic circuit.

matrix printer In computing, a printer in which each character is represented by a pattern of dots. It is commonly used as a microcomputer peripheral; it has the advantage of relatively low cost and high flexibility. The font is determined by an internal ROM holding the matrix patterns for each code. The quality of the printed output, with various machines, can range from the functional, e.g. for program listings, to that approaching letter quality. Compare daisy wheel. See font, letter quality printing. Synonymous with dot printer, needle printer.

matte (1) In cinematography, a mask used to blank off one part of a negative during exposure to allow superimposition of another shot. (2) In television, the electronic insertion of an image into a selected background. See chromakey.

matter In printing (1) the body of a printed work as distinct from headings, (2) type set up. See type matter.

MATV See master antenna television system.

Mavica In photography, a new camera system developed by Sony, the images of which are stored on a magnetic disk and can be replayed on a television set. Up to 50 individual pictures can be stored on one disk.

maximum usable frequency In radiocommunications, the highest frequency that can be used for transmission purposes via the ionosphere. See ionosphere.

Mb See megabyte.

MCC See miscellaneous common carrier.

MDF See main distributing frame.

mean busy hour In telephony, an uninterrupted period of one hour, starting at the same time on each of a number of weekdays, during which the highest average traffic is measured. See traffic, busy hour.

mean grade In audio and television, the average of a subjective assessment by a number of observers of the quality of a reproduction. See impairment scale.

mean time between failure In computing and communications, for a given period in the life of a piece of equipment, the average of the periods of time between consecutive failures under stated conditions.

mean time to repair In computing and communications, the average time needed to repair, or to correctively maintain, a piece of equipment.

measure In printing, the width to which type is set, i.e. the maximum length of the lines.

measured service In communications, service which is provided on the basis of the number of message units accrued during the charging period, rather than on a flat rate basis. Compare flat rate. See message unit.

media (1) In computing, the material on which data and instructions are recorded, e.g. magnetic disk, paper tape, floppy disk, magnetic tape, punch cards, etc. (2) In communications, the means whereby information is conveyed within the communications industry; book, cinema, newspaper, radio, TV.

media center In audiovisual aids, a place where a full range of media related information sources and associated equipment are available.

media drive In word processing, the device used for recording on or reading from a recording medium, such as floppy disk. See floppy disk.

media technology The range of activities and techniques which lie on the intersection of computing, publishing and film making.

mediated instruction In audiovisual aids, a package which is designed for use without the need for a teacher or instructor.

medium frequency In radiocommunications, the range of frequencies from 300 - 3000 kHz.

medium lens In photography, a lens whose focal length is near the normal focal length for the film dimensions being used. See focal length.

medium reduction In micrographics, a reduction in the range 16X to 30X. Compare low reduction, high reduction, very high reduction, ultra high reduction. See reduction.

medium scale integration In microelectronics, pertaining to a fabrication technology which produces between 10 and 100 gates per chip. Compare LSI, SSI, SLSI, VLSI. See chip, gate.

medium speed In data communications, transmission rates between 2400 baud and the limit of a voice grade circuit, 9600 baud. See baud, voice grade channel.

Medline A database supplied by National Library of Medicine and dealing with biomedicine. See on line information retrieval.

meet me conference In teleconferencing, a switchboard facility enabling a conference call to be established by each participating extension user dialing a designated conference code. See conference call.

megabit One million bits. See bit.

megabyte In computing, a unit of storage equal to 1,048,576 bytes. See kilobyte.

Megadoc In computing, an optical digital disk produced by Philips. See optical digital disks.

megahertz One million hertz. See hertz.

Megastream In data communications, a very high speed digital communications service on a point to point basis offered by British Telecom. Initially it will be used for connecting directly to users' digital telephone exhanges. See X-Stream.

memomotion In filming, a time lapse photographic technique, used mostly in connection with time and motion study analysis. See time lapse cinematography.

memory Synonymous with main storage.

memory access time See access time.

memory address register In computing, an internal register of a CPU which contains the address of a data item, or instruction, to be accessed in the memory. See address, CPU, register.

memory allocation In computing, the setting aside of contiguous memory locations for programming or device handling purposes. See memory map.

memory bank In computing, a block of memory locations corresponding to contiguous addresses. See address.

memory cycle In computing, the time required to send an address to memory and the reading or writing into that memory location. Compare machine cycle. See address.

memory dump In computer programming, a listing of the contents of a storage device, or selected parts of it. See dump. Synonymous with storage dump.

memory management In computing, a combination of hardware and software elements which allocate main memory to programs and data in a multiprogramming system. See main memory, multiprogramming.

memory map In computing, a drawing or table showing the allocation of main memory to input output devices and programs. See input output devices, main memory, memory mapping.

memory mapping In computing, an addressing technique in which I/O devices are addressed as memory locations. For example, a memory mapped VDU is one in which each character or pixel location on the screen corresponds to a unique main memory location which the central processing unit may access. See address, central processing unit, pixel.

memory protect In computing, a facility whereby specified locations in main memory can be protected from accidental overwriting or unauthorized access.

memory workspace In computer programming, the amount of memory required by a program in addition to that required for its own storage. Workspace is generally used for input output device buffer areas and for holding temporary results. See input output devices. Synonymous with work area.

menu (1) In computing, a display of a list of available functions for selection by an operator. (2) In videotex, a list of up to 9 choices on a page for selection by a user for routing to various parts of the database. See page, menu selection, main index.

menu selection In computing, a technique in which a user is provided with a list of options and details of the keys to be depressed for the selection of each option. Thus the user needs no specific training or reference manuals to use the system. See menu.

MEP In computing, Microelectronics Education Program, a UK government scheme designed to enhance the teaching of computing in schools.

Mercury In communications, a private consortium of Cable and Wireless, British Petroleum and Barclays Bank, acting as a carrier for voice and data traffic. They offer all digital services in the UK based upon a combination of high speed fiber optics and microwave techniques. See fiber optics, microwave transmission.

merge In computer programming, the combining of two ordered files of information items in such a way as to maintain the ordering of the original files in the resulting file. See file.

merge sort In computer programming, a sort program in which the sorted subsets of a set are merged. See merge, sort.

meridional ray In fiber optics, a ray of light that passes through the axis of the fiber as a result of an internal reflection, and is confined to a single plane. See total internal reflection.

mesh In computer networks, a configuration in which there are two or more paths between any two nodes. Compare ring, star. See node.

meshbeat See moire.

message (1) In communications, an arbitrary amount of information whose beginning and end are defined or implied. (2) In telephony, an answered call or the information content thereof. (3) In telegraphy and data communications, an assembly of characters and sometimes control digits, which is transferred as an entity from transmitter to receiver, the format being determined by the transmitter. See message format.

message analysis In communications and computing, the study of the structure, length and on line time of a typical message. This information may be used to plan enhancement to an existing network.

message format In data communications, rules for the placement of such portions of a message as the heading, address, text and end of the message. See address, message heading, message text.

message heading In data communications, the leading part of a message that contains such information as the source or destination code of the message, the message priority, and the type of message. See message text.

message numbering In data communications, a unique number given to each message in a system for identification purposes.

message routing In data communications, the process of selecting a route in a message switching system. See message switching.

message slot In data communications, sequences of bits, sufficient to hold a full message, which are continually circulated around a ring local area network. A slot may be empty or full, and any node, on detecting an empty slot, may mark the slot as full and place a message in it. Compare daisy chain, control token. See Cambridge Ring, local area network.

message switching In data communications, a technique for increasing the throughput of a network by the sequential switching of prestored messages. Unlike packet switching, messages are transmitted in their entirety and once in a network the system takes over responsibility for their delivery. Compare packet switching. See store and forward.

message switching center In data communications, a center in which messages are routed according to information contained within the messages themselves.

message telephone service In telephony, a long distance toll telephone service with charging subject to the calling distance, call duration and time of day.

message text In data communications, the part of a message that is relevant to the party receiving the message. The message text excludes the header and control information. See message heading.

message unit In telephony, a method of charging for a local telephone service, based on the number, distance, and sometimes the duration of calls. A single local call may be equal to one message unit. A more distant call or lengthy call would be counted as several message units. See measured service.

messenger cable In telephony, a steel strand used to support an aerial cable. See aerial cable.

Metadex A database supplied by American Society for Metals and The Metals Society and dealing with metallurgy. See on line information retrieval.

Metafont In digital typography, a computer program which produces letterforms from stored splines. See Ikarus, spline.

metalanguage In computer programming, a language that is used to describe a class of languages. See Backus Naur form.

metal oxide semiconductor Synonymous with metal oxide silicon.

metal oxide silicon In semiconductors, a technology for fabricating high density integrated circuits, named after the three successive layers of the materials used. Most LSI devices, such as microprocessors, are based on MOS technology. See LSI.

Meteo In machine translation, a Canadian system used for translating weather reports from English to French. See machine translation.

MF See medium frequency, microfiche, microfilm, multifrequency signal.

MF keypad In communications, a keypad producing multifrequency signals that can be used with suitable types of telephone exchanges both for call set up purposes and subsequently to transmit slow speed data, i.e.

less than 600 baud. See keypad, multifrequency signal, touchtone.

MFM See modified frequency modulation.

MHD See movable head disk.

MHz See megahertz.

MICR See magnetic ink character recognition.

micro (1) A Greek word meaning small. (2) A prefix representing one millionth.

microbend loss In fiber optics, the leakage of light caused by minute sharp curves in the optical cable that may result from imperfections when the glass fiber meets the sheathing that covers it. Compare macrobend loss.

microcassette In recording, an audio cassette much smaller than the compact cassette, used mainly for office work. See compact cassette.

microcode In computing, microinstructions used in a product as an alternative to hardwired circuitry to implement given functions of system components or the processor. In large systems this code will not be available to the programmer. See hardwired, microinstruction, software.

microcomputer In computing, a term applied to desktop computers designed for hobbyists, small businesses or educational applications. The power of some current business microcomputers rivals that of early minicomputers and exceeds that of small mainframe computers produced in the 1960's. The term microcomputer is used to describe a stored program desktop digital computer built from microelectronic components (chips). These components consist of integrated circuits manufactured by using one or other variant of the Metal Oxide Silicon (MOS) process. During processing (sometimes called fabrication), a number of layers of aluminium, silicon oxide, or silicon containing a large number of separate microscopic regions, are deposited on a slice (wafer) of very pure silicon. The complexity of the circuit, which can be produced, is dependent on the number of transistors (gates) which can be contained on a single chip. The term Very Large Scale Integration (VLSI) is used to describe processes by which the most complex chips can be produced.

Processed chips are sealed into carriers of ceramic or plastic material and are attached to external pads or pins with fine gold wires. Packages come in a range of standard sizes. The Dual in Line (DIL) package is frequently used. This has two rows of pins (leads) on the longest pair of sides of a rectangular carrier. There are also leadless packages which have pads rather than pins on the edges of a square carrier. Packages are described physically by the number of pins and type, e.g. 40 pin DIL. The use of standard components, produced in high volumes, keeps prices low and permits cheap but powerful microcomputers to be marketed.

The components making up the computer are assembled on printed circuit boards, which are then mounted in cases with power supplies and peripherals to produce the complete system. Many microcomputers are now supplied as three separate units. The main unit contains circuit boards, power supplies and disk drives whilst the keyboard unit and monitor (display) unit are connected to it by cables.

See (a) overall view of a microcomputer (b) the bus structure (c) memory (d) peripheral controllers (e) future developments.

(a) Overall view of a microcomputer. The main components in a microcomputer are: (i) Processor (ii) Memory (iii) Peripheral Controller. The processor is the Central Processing Unit (CPU) and communicates with the other components by means of logic signals carried on a group of electrical conductors (copper tracks on the circuit board), known as the bus. The memory holds lists of binary numbers which represent numerically coded program instructions or other numerical information (data). Memory capacity is usually quoted in units of bytes or kilobytes. A byte is a group of eight binary digits (bits) and a kilobyte, by convention is 1024 bytes. A peripheral controller provides the means for connecting peripheral equipment such as keyboards, printers, disks and displays.

The actions of the microcomputer are controlled by the processor which in turn is controlled by program instructions in the memory. When the system is switched on the processor starts fetching and executing instructions from the memory. A fetch-execute cycle, which is performed for each instruction, consists of the following steps: (i) obtain the next instruction from the memory (ii) interpret the code (iii) execute the actions specified. This cycle is repeated indefinitely until the processor is switched off, or instructed to stop. It is of course necessary for a suitable program to be present in the memory when the computer is switched on. This program is sometimes called the firmware and may provide the means for a user to operate the system (e.g. Basic systems for home computers) or may read a copy of an operating system program from a disk unit and put it in the memory (e.g. PC-DOS for the IBM PC).

The power of a computer system is partly dependent on the amount of information, measured in bits, which the processor can handle in a single operation. Here it is necessary to consider both the operations inside the processor chip, using the internal bus, and outside using the external bus. The first microprocessors to become widely used (MOS6502, Intel 8080, Zilog Z-80) were designed to handle 8 bits internally and externally. Currently available products offer a variety of alternative combinations from families of compatible processors. For example, one may have 16 bit systems with a 32 bit processor using the Motorola 68000, or 16 bit systems with a 16 bit processor using the Intel 8086 or Zilog Z-8000. The number of bits handled externally by the processor not only influences the power of a system but also the cost. The IBM PC design adopts a compromise approach by using the Intel 8088 processor (internally 16 bit and externally 8 bit). In this way the advantages of having 8086 instructions are obtained, while avoiding the extra cost of a full 16 bit system.

(b) The bus structure. The collection of conductors connecting the processor to the other components in the computer is referred to as the processor bus. The detailed structure of each bus is dependent on the particular processor design being studied. There is, however, a general similarity in structure for all processors. Communication on the bus uses electronic signals which assume either a low voltage or high voltage state in order to represent: (i) binary zero or one digit (ii) true or false logic states (iii) active or inactive control signal states.

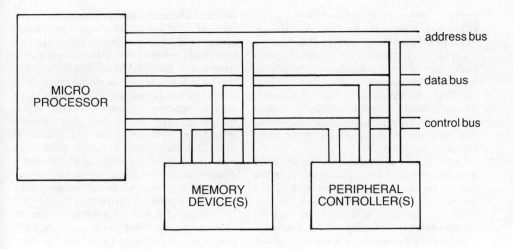

address bus

data bus

control bus

MICRO PROCESSOR

MEMORY DEVICE(S)

PERIPHERAL CONTROLLER(S)

microcomputer
bus structure of a microcomputer

The processor bus consists of the following three parts (Fig. 1): (i) the address bus (ii) the data bus (iii) the control bus.

The address bus: This bus is used by the processor to present a binary number which identifies a place in memory, or a particular peripheral controller, for a data transfer operation. Typically 8 bit processors have 16 bit address buses, other microprocessors use up to 24 bits. The number of bits in the address bus determine the maximum limit for directly addressable memory which can be connected. 16 bit addresses allow a maximum of 64K bytes of memory to be directly addressed.

The data bus: This is the external bus referred to in the overall view above. It carries binary numbers between the processor and memory or peripheral controllers selected by the address on the address bus. Most microcomputer systems currently have 8 or 16 bit buses, but there are also very powerful systems using 32 bit buses.

The control bus: This bus conveys control signals to the various parts of the system. The details here are most heavily dependent on the processor being considered. Examples of necessary control functions are: synchronisation of use of the data bus, or specification of the direction of data transfer.

Bus operation: The processor uses the bus in order to transfer binary data between itself and other components in the system. The term read transaction refers to a transfer into the processor, and write transaction to a transfer out of the processor. Transactions are synchronised by a master clock signal (typically from 1 to 8MHz), and take one or more clock cycles depending on processor design. A bus transaction starts with the address being provided by the processor. Logic circuits connected to the address bus use this address to select the appropriate place in memory, or particular peripheral controller (referred to as address decoding). Finally data is transferred using the data bus. A fetch-execute cycle in the processor will in general require one or more read transactions to obtain the instruction from memory followed by other read or write transactions during instruction execution.

Other miscellaneous circuits: The foregoing description explained the nature and operation of the main components in the microcomputer. The need for logic circuits for address decoding has been mentioned. There is also a need for transmitter, receiver and buffer circuits for the bus signals and for other control logic. Reducing the numbers of the separate components used in a design reduces costs and increases reliability. One method of achieving this goal, which has been favoured recently, is the production of custom designed integrated logic components for a given product based on the use of Uncommitted Logic Arrays (ULA).

(c) Memory. The memory of the computer holds lists of binary numbers representing program instructions and data. These numbers are stored in a line of separate memory locations 'identified by a unique integer address ranging from zero upwards. The memory locations are all of the same capacity, usually 8 bits.

Individual semiconductor memory components are offered in a variety of capacities and arrangements. For example, 64K x 1 components, which have 65,636 1-bit locations, can be used in a bank of eight to provide 64K bytes of memory. Alternatively, a single 8K x 8 component alone can provide 8K bytes of memory. Two main types of memory component are used, Read Only Memory (ROM) and Random Access Memory (RAM). ROM is used for holding fixed program (firmware) or data and, as its name implies, can only be read by the processor, not written to. The contents of ROM are nonvolatile, which is to say that the contents are not lost when power is switched off. Some ROM components are manufactured containing the required program and data values and these cannot be altered, this is economic where a large number (say more than 1,000) of components are required all with the same contents.

For lower volume requirements, where perhaps program and data will be subject to change during development and testing, so-called programmable memories are available (PROMs). Program or data values can be written to these after manufacture by a special process called, confusingly, 'programming'. Most PROM's can also be erased and reprogrammed. The most popular of these, the EPROM, requires exposure to high intensity ultra violet light, through a quartz glass window in the package, for around 20 minutes, for data erasure. Capacities commonly found are from 2K x 8 bits to 8K x 8 bits with the newest products offering capacities up to 32K x 8. A newer type is electrically erasable, the EPROM, and erasure is achieved electronically in about 10 milliseconds. Typical capacity is lower for this type, though, commonly being 2K x 8 bits.

The term RAM is applied to components which can be read from, or written to, by the processor. (A better name would be random access read write memory). There are two types of circuit used: static and dynamic. The circuits in a static RAM are flip-flops (bistables) which will retain the stored bit value as long as power is maintained. The other type uses a capacitor to store a charge representing the bit value and this requires refreshing, by being read and rewritten, every 2 milliseconds. Although more complex circuitry is required to implement a memory using dynamic components they are favoured for large memories because they have a 4:1 advantage in cost over static types. Both types of RAM are volatile in that the contents are lost when power is switched off. In some equipment this limitation is overcome by the use of battery backup techniques.

(d) Peripheral Controllers. A microcomputer requires peripheral equipment in order to perform a useful function. Input peripherals provide data for the processor to read (e.g. a keyboard), output peripherals accept data written by the processor (e.g. a printer). There are also peripherals used for file storage which the processor can both read from and write to (e.g. magnetic disks). In order to connect peripherals to a microcomputer an interface is necessary. Externally this takes the form of a socket which brings the electronic signals, at the appropriate voltage levels, to the specified pin positions. Internally a peripheral controller is necessary to provide the means for the processor to operate the signals via the processor bus. Peripheral controller circuitry may be dedicated to a specific peripheral type (e.g. a display or a disk) or may be a general purpose type, which can handle a number of different applications by program control. Two main types of general purpose interface are used, parallel and serial.

With the parallel interface, a number of ports are provided to permit the transfer of a collection of bits, (e.g. 8), simultaneously. Each bit requires its own wire to carry the signal. Generally there will also be control and status signals on separate wires for control of the data flow in a similar manner to that of control signals on the processor bus. This type of parallel interface is commonly used for keyboard and printer interfaces. Provided that a suitable program can be produced the interface can also be adapted for many other purposes (e.g. control of a robot arm, motors, valves or lamp displays).

The serial interface uses a single wire for transmitting data one bit at a time to a receiver. This technique originated for tele-communications purposes and is widely used for remote communication over the tele-phone network. There is an internationally agreed standard (RS 232), which, among other things, specifies connector size, allocat-ion of pins, voltage levels, rates of trans-mitting bits. The standard was originally specified for connections to modems but has found much wider usage for interconnection of assorted microcomputers and (suitable) peripherals. RS 232 interfaces in microcom-puters provide both a transmitter circuit and a receiver circuit which are capable of independent and simultaneous operation. Over short distances it is possible to intercon-nect two systems with only three wires, trans-mitter data out, receiver data in and a ground return. (e) Future developments. Fierce international competition in microelectronic technology will spur continuing refinement of existing processes and the development of new processes. The CMOS (Complementary MOS) process is being widely introduced because of its lower electrical power con-sumption. Reduction in the size of circuit elements is increasing the scale of integration which is possible. Also new semiconductor materials capable of higher speeds of opera-tion (e.g. Gallium Arsenide) are opening up new areas of application for microelectro-nics. The results will be further increases in raw computing power, lower costs and wider penetration of microcomputers in the marketplace.

The trend towards higher levels of inte-gration will also be evident in the design of new microcomputer systems with fewer sepa-rate components being used. Services to support both the design and manufacture of custom components (silicon foundries) are being introduced by the major semicon-ductor companies. Customers will be able to design their own components for new systems using sophisticated Computer Aided Design (CAD) facilities, which will have available libraries of standard logic circuits ready for integration. Batches of these components will then be fabricated in the silicon foundry.

Progress in peripheral design is set to conti-nue at a more modest pace but here a move away from keyboards, cathode ray tube dis-plays and disks is predictable. The increased work potential of individual microcomputer systems will heighten the pressures on the development of data communications links at local, national and international levels with the emergence of hierarchies of systems on a worldwide basis.

The provision of cheap and reliable soft-ware will continue to be of major importance in the marketing of microcomputer systems. This will lead to the dominance of one stand-ard software system which supports an exten-sive catalogue of program packages. Com-pare mainframe, microprocessor, minicom-puter. See BASIC, binary number, bistable, bit, bus, byte, CAD, cathode ray tube, chip, CMOS, CPU, data communications, DIL, EPROM, firmware, flip flop, IBM PC, instruction, magnetic disk, memory, MHz, microprocessor, MOS, parallel transmis-sion, peripheral, program, PROM, RAM, ROM, RS 232, semiconductor, serial trans-mission, software, silicon foundry, ULA, VLSI, wafer. Synonymous with home com-puter, personal computer.

Microcomputer Index A database supplied by Microcomputer Information Services and dealing with computers and computer indus-try. See on line information retrieval.

microcontroller In computing, a microcom-puter used for industrial control purposes, as opposed to data processing. See control computer.

microelectronics The branch of electronics concerned with the design and manufacture of chips and integrated circuits. Advances in this field over the past decade fundamentally changed the economics and power of com-puting, communication and information technology devices. See chip, micro-computer.

microfiche In micrographics, a microform storage medium in which many microimages are arranged in a grid pattern on a sheet of film, usually containing a title that can be read without magnification. The most common microfiche has dimensions 148·75 x 105mm and reductions range from 20X to

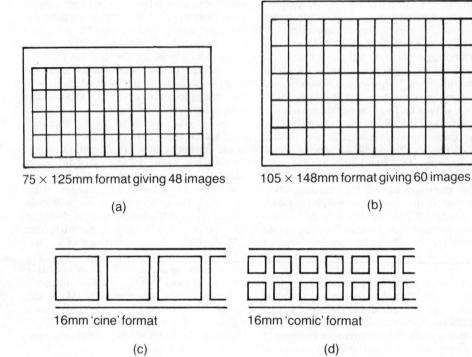

75 × 125mm format giving 48 images   105 × 148mm format giving 60 images

(a)   (b)

16mm 'cine' format   16mm 'comic' format

(c)   (d)

microform
(a) microfiche in a 75 × 125mm format; (b) microfiche in a 105 × 148mm format; (c) microfilm in a 16 mm 'cine' format; (d) microfilm in a 16 mm 'comic' format.

48X. Compare ultrafiche. See microform, microimage, reduction.

microfilm In micrographics, a film in the form of a roll that contains microimages arranged sequentially. Used in data processing and for documentation and record compilation. See microimage.

microfont In micrographics, an upper case font designed by the NMA specifically for microfilm applications. See font, microfilm, NMA.

microform In micrographics, a medium that contains microimages, such as microfiche and microfilm. See microimage, microfiche, microfilm.

microformat In micrographics, any audiovisual format containing images too small to be seen without magnification.

microform reader In micrographics, a display device with a built in screen and magnification arranged so that a microform may be read comfortably at normal reading distances. See microform.

microform reader/printer In micrographics, a microform reader with a printer attachment for producing hard copy printout at the original size. See microform reader.

micrographics In photography and data processing, the condensing, storing and retrieving of graphic information. Micrographics involves the use of all types of microforms and microimages. See microform, microimage.

microimage In photography, an image too small to be read without some form of magnification.

microinstruction In computing, (1) a small, single, short, add, shift or delete type of instruction, (2) a bit pattern which is stored in a microprogram memory word and specifies the action on individual computing elements and associated subunits, e.g. main memory, input output interfaces. See microprogramming.

micron One millionth of a meter.

Micronet In videotex, a service for microcomputer users supplied via Prestel. The users gain access to the Prestel database with special adaptors. The database contains telesoftware programs and information pages relevant to microcomputer users. See Prestel, telesoftware.

micro-opaque In micrographics, a sheet of opaque material bearing one or more microimages. See microimage.

microphone In recording, a transducer which generates electrical voltages from air pressure waves. Microphones vary in their pick up patterns, i.e. directionality, and the method used to generate the electric signal. The pickup pattern may be omnidirectional, cardioid, bidirectional and unidirectional. There are several methods of generating signals from soundwaves, and they vary in sound quality, impedance and cost. Generating methods include ceramic where a piezoelectric transducer is used, condenser where a change in capacitance of a diaphragm is detected, dynamic where a diaphragm induces vibrations in a moving coil, and electret which is similar to the condenser microphone except that the diaphragm is permanently charged. See bidirectional microphone, cardioid response, impedance, omnidirectional microphone, transducer, electret, unidirectional microphone.

microphone pickup pattern In recording, the locus of maximum sensitivity of a microphone.

microphonics In electronics, a noise caused by mechanical vibration of one or more components of a system.

microphotography In micrographics, the application of photography to produce copy in sizes too small to be read without magnification. Compare photomicrography.

microprint In micrographics, microimages on opaque stock produced by printing as distinct from microimages produced on photosensitive materials. See microimage.

microprocessor In computing, an LSI implementation on a single chip of a complete central processing unit consisting of an arithmetic logic unit, and a control unit. Various microprocessors are capable of accepting coded instructions for execution in 8, 16 or 32 bit word format and acts as the central processor unit in a microcomputer. See arithmetic logic unit, central processing unit, control unit, microcomputer, word.

Microprocessor Application Project A project launched by the UK Department of Industry to encourage UK manufacturing industries to exploit microelectronics and information technology in its products and processes.

microprocessor development system In computing, a system based on a particular microprocessor used for developing associated hardware and software for that microprocessor. The system usually includes an assembler, text editor, monitor, system console, PROM programmer, and disk/tape units. See assembler, PROM programmer, text editor.

microprogram In computing, a sequence of microinstructions maintained in a special storage. These instructions are initiated by the introduction of a computer instruction into an instruction register of the computer. Compare microcode. See hardwired, microinstruction.

microprogrammable computer In computing, a computer where the instruction set is not fixed but can be tailored to individual needs by the programming of ROMs or other memory devices. See microprogram, ROM.

microprogramming In computer programming, programming using microinstruction. See microcode, microprogram.

microprojector In audiovisual aids, a device for enlarging and projecting microscope slides.

micropublishing In micrographics, the issue of new or reformatted information in multiple copy microform for sale or distribution to the public. See microfilm.

microsecond One millionth of a second. See micro.

microwave In radio communications, a range of frequencies from about 1 GHz to the lower end of the infrared spectrum (3000 GHz), i.e. a wavelength range from 30cm to 0·1mm. See GHz, infrared.

microwave interference In satellite communications, the interference between satellite earth station communications and terrestrial receivers. See earth station, main beam, microwave transmission.

microwave relay In radiocommunications, a station used for the reception and retransmission of microwave signals. See microwave.

microwave transmission In radiocommunications, the transmission of microwaves which due to their high frequency may be modulated for very high information throughput. Many individual telephone and telex circuits may be multiplexed for transmission over trunk routes by microwaves. They are transmitted via highly directional dish shaped antennas in line of sight in both terrestrial and satellite communication. See geostationary satellite, line of sight, microwave, dish.

Microwriter In word processing, trade name for a battery powered hand held keyboarding device for use by executives. The device has six keys and a marching display. The user inputs individual characters by depressing combinations of keys. After text has been entered it can be modified to correct errors etc. The stored text can be downloaded to a television set for document readout or to a word processor for hard copy output. See hard copy, marching display.

mid user In databases, an operator, with detailed knowledge of the search methods and techniques, who conducts a search on behalf of an end user.

migration In databases, a technique in which the use of fast access store is optimized by moving the less frequently accessed items to a slower, low cost storage device.

migration imaging In printing, an electrophotographic imaging process in which the charge receptivity of photoconductive particles in a softenable resin layer, on a film base, is increased by exposure to light. When the resin is softened the particles migrate to the film base to form an image. See electrophotography, photoconductivity.

mill Synonymous with arithmetic logic unit.

milli A prefix representing one thousandth.

milliampere In electronics, a current flow of one thousandth of an ampere. See ampere.

millisecond A unit of time equal to one thousandth of a second.

MIMD See multiple instruction stream multiple data stream.

mimeography In printing, a popular name for a stencil ink duplicating process, derived from the trade name, Mimeograph.

minicomputer In computing, a term first used to distinguish smaller computers from mainframes. There is no universally accepted definition of a minicomputer, but they are usually faster and more expensive than a microcomputer, the cost being largely a function of memory size. See bit, mainframe, microcomputer, word.

minimax In artificial intelligence, a state which is a minimum when considered from one viewpoint and a maximum when viewed from another. In game playing it represents a local optimum move from the viewpoint of both players. See alpha beta technique.

minimum weight routing. In data communications, a method of optimizing the transmission of a message by associating a weighting factor with each link in the network. The chosen route is the one which minimizes the sum of the weights of the lines it uses. If the weights chosen are the transit delays associated with lines, a minimum delay routing is obtained. See adaptive routing, directory routing.

minuend In mathematics, the number from which another number, the subtrahend, is subtracted.

minuscule In printing, a lower case character. Compare majuscule. See lower case.

MIPS In computing, Million Instructions Per Second, a measure of computing power. Compare KIPS, LIPS. See instruction.

MIRIAM In computing, Major Incident Room Index and Action Management, a police computer system intended for use in the investigation of a major crime or incident.

mirroring In computer graphics, the rotation of all or part of a display image through 180 degrees about an axis in the plane of the display.

MIS See management information system.

miscellaneous common carrier In communications, common carriers not engaged in providing telephone or telegraph services. Usually these carriers are responsible for radio and TV transmission services using terrestrial microwave links. See common carrier, microwave.

MISD See multiple instruction stream single data stream.

mismatch In electronics and communications, the conditions in which the impedance of a load does not match the impedance of the source to which it is connected. In recording, mismatch will cause a loss of signal level and distortion. See impedance matching, level. Synonymous with impedance mismatch.

mixed highs In television, the high frequency components of the picture signal that are intended to be reproduced in monochrome in a colour picture. Systems such as NTSC and PAL use this principle, which is based on the fact that the eye cannot observe colour in fine detail, but is aware of variations in luminance. See composite colour video signal, luminance signal.

mixer (1) In electronics, a circuit that accepts two signal inputs at different frequencies, and generates an output consisting of combinations of sum and difference frequencies. (2) In broadcasting, equipment for combining signal inputs prior to being modulated for transmission. See modulation.

mixing (1) In printing, the use of more than one typeface in a word or line of text. (2) In recording, the process of combining sound tracks to produce a master.

mixing studio In recording, a facility equipped with electronic mixers capable of combining two or more audio signals into a single final sound track, usually synchronized with a picture. See mixer.

MKS system A system of units based on the meter kilogram second.

MLA Bibliography A database supplied by Modern Language Association of America and dealing with language and linguistics. See on line information retrieval.

MMI See man machine interface.

mnemonic An abbreviation or set of symbols chosen to help the reader to remember by association.

mnemonic code See symbolic language.

mobile earth terminal In communications, a mobile radio station used for space communication. See satellite.

mobile unit In filming and television, a production equipment system for use away from a studio.

modal position In telephony, the position a telephone handset assumes when the receiver of the handset is held in close contact with the ear of a person with head dimensions that are modal for a population. See mode.

mode (1) A state of a vibrating system which corresponds to one of the possible

TERMINALS   COMPUTER

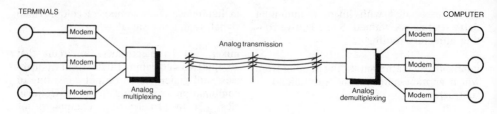

modem
Digital signals may be transmitted over an analog circuit using a MOdulator-DEModulator.

resonant frequencies. (2) In computing, an option in a method of operation, e.g. binary mode, alphanumeric mode etc. (3) In mathematics, the most frequently occurring value in a statistical sample. (4) In fiber optics, pertaining to the manner in which light rays travel along the fiber. See mode dispersion, monomode fiber, multimode fiber, total internal reflection.

mode dispersion   In fiber optics, the dispersion which arises from the different paths traversed by the light rays in an optical fiber. This dispersion causes a distortion of the received pulse. See mode. monomode fiber, multimode fiber,

MODEM   In data communications, MOdulator-DEModulator, a device that modulates the transmitted signal and demodulates the received signal at a data station. For example, a modem is used to convert a digital signal from a computer into an analog signal for transmission over a network and is commonly employed for the intercommunication of microcomputers over the telephone network. See modulation, limited distance modem. Synonymous with data set.

modern face   In printing, a class of typeface having considerable differences between thick and thin strokes, serifs at right angles to their strokes, and central thickening of curves. See serif.

modified frequency modulation   In computing, a method of recording data on a magnetic disk similar to frequency modulation but requiring fewer flux reversals to encode a given amount of data; thus giving a greater

number of bits per unit length of track. See bit, frequency modulation, magnetic disk, track.

modular   In computing, a building block approach to hardware and software design in which a system is first analyzed in terms of functional subassemblies (modules) and then synthesized using these modules. Electronic fabrication consists largely in assembling circuits out of standard hardware components. See hardware, software.

modulating signal   In communications, a signal which is impressed upon a carrier wave to vary it in some specified manner. See carrier.

modulation   In communications, a process by which information is impressed upon a carrier wave for transmission purposes. The term covers processes where some characteristic of a continuous wave, such as its frequency or amplitude, is varied in accordance with a modulating signal such as speech, television or facsimile waveform. See amplitude modulation, frequency modulation, modulating signal, pulse modulation, phase modulation.

modulation rate   In communications, the reciprocal of the shortest time interval between successive significant instances of the modulated signal. If this measure is expressed in seconds, the modulation rate is in bauds. See baud, modulation.

modulator   In communications, the equipment or apparatus which modifies some characteristic of a signal. See modulation.

module   In computing, a hardware or software subassembly used in a modular system. See modular.

modulo N check   In computer programming, a means of checking the values of data whereby an operand is divided by a number N and the remainder used as a check digit. Often N is taken to be 11, thus 81 modulo 11 is 4. See operand.

modulo 2 addition   In computing, binary addition without carries, i.e. $1+0 = 1, 1+1 = 0$. See EXCLUSIVE OR.

modulus of a counter   In electronics, the number of input pulses required to recycle a counter to its starting position. See counter.

moiré   (1) In optics, an undesirable effect caused by one set of closely spaced lines moving in relation to another. (2) In television, the spurious pattern in the reproduced picture caused by interference beats between two sets of periodic structures in the image. The most common cause of moiré is the interference between scanning lines and some other periodic structure such as a line pattern or dot pattern in the original scene, a mesh or dot pattern in the camera sensor, or the phosphor dots or other structure in a shadowmask picture tube. See interference, scanning line, shadowmask.

momentary   In audiovisual aids, a switch which reverts to its normal state when it is not activated. Compare maintained.

monaural   In recording, the use of a single sound channel applied to one ear. Compare binaural.

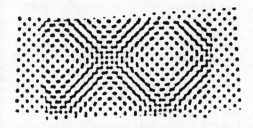

moiré
Moiré fringes.

monitor   (1) In television, a high quality viewing unit, often used in closed circuit systems. (2) In filming, a rear projection unit used in editing. (3) In computing, a program, or collection of programs, implementing the fundamental set of commands required to operate a computer system. (4) In electronics, a supervisory system which can detect a circuit failure, e.g. a voltage monitor which signals a failure condition when a power supply goes outside given limits. See closed circuit television, operating system.

monitor speaker   In recording, a loudspeaker used for listening during recording and mixing.

monochrome   (1) In photography, pictures which have no colour, only black, white or gray tones. (2) In television, the signal used for controlling the luminance values in the picture. See luminance.

monograph   A publication dealing with a single subject or person.

monoline   In printing, a typeface in which all the letter strokes are of equal thickness.

monolithic   In electronics, an integrated circuit fabricated on a single monocrystalline silicon chip. See integrated circuit.

monomode fiber   In fiber optics, a fiber with a very narrow core (2-10 microns); the only path for transmission is along the axis giving low dispersion. Compare multimode fiber. See mode, mode dispersion.

monophonic   In recording, sound reproduction using a single output signal or made with a single channel audio tape recorder. Compare stereophonic.

monostable   In electronics, a circuit used for delaying or lengthening a pulse. It remains in its stable state until it receives an input pulse when it then moves into a second state for a specified period.

monte carlo method   In mathematics, a technique of numerical analysis whereby statistical sampling techniques are used to obtain approximations to the correct solution. Often used when a purely analytical approach is unsuitable. See numerical analysis.

morse code In telegraphy, an early code in which the characters are formed from signal elements called dots and dashes. Ideally, the dash has a duration of three dots, and the elements making up a character are separated by spaces with a duration of one dot. The spacing between characters is equivalent to the length of a dash, that between words to the length of two dashes:

```
A . -
B - ...
C - . - .
D - ..
E .
F .. - .
G -- .
H ....
I ..
J . ---
K - . -
L . - ..
M --
N - .
O ---
P . -- .
Q -- . -
R . - .
S ...
T -
U .. -
V ... -
W . --
X - .. -
Y - . --
Z -- ..
1 . ----
2 .. ---
3 ... --
4 .... -
5 .....
6 - ....
7 -- ...
8 --- ..
9 ---- .
0 -----
```

morse key In telegraphy, a contact unit operated by hand to form signals according to the morse code. See morse code.

morse printer In telegraphy, a printer

which converts a morse code signal to an alphanumeric character and then prints it. See morse code.

mortising Synonymous with kerning.

MOS See metal oxide silicon.

mosaic In videotex, a display character which can have one of 128 different shapes. See alphamosaic, display character.

MOSFET In semiconductors, Metal Oxide Silicon Effect Transistor. A device which has an extremely high input impedance, low switching speed and low power consumption. See field effect transistor.

most significant bit In mathematics, the left-most bit in a binary number, having the greatest impact on the value of the number. Compare least significant bit. See binary number.

most significant digit In mathematics, the leftmost digit in a number. Compare least significant digit.

motherboard In computing and electronics, an interconnecting assembly with female connectors into which other printed circuit boards are inserted. It carries the system buses. See bus, printed circuit. Synonymous with backplane.

motion picture In filming, a succession of still images which gives the subjective impression of motion when used in a device which maintains persistence of vision. See persistence of vision.

motor boating In audio, a very low frequency oscillation often resulting from a positive feedback path in an amplifier system. See positive feedback.

mouse In computing, a palm sized unit equipped with a number of control buttons, used to manipulate a screen display and invoke utility functions. The mouse is rolled over a tablet surface and the movement of the ball is measured and fed to the computer. Control functions are invoked by moving the mouse to designated tablet areas or pressing the button. It may be employed to input graphics or to manipulate text on displayed documents, e.g. scrolling, cut and paste. See cut and paste, icon, Lisa, scrolling.

mouth In communications, the open end of a microwave antenna such as a horn. See horn, microwave.

M out of N code In data communications, a transmission code with inbuilt error detection facilities. A specified number of bits (M), in a character of N bits, must be 1 bits. Any received character not containing a total of M one bits initiates an error procedure. See error detection code. Synonymous with constant ratio code.

movable head disk In computing, a magnetic disk unit in which the heads are mounted on a seek arm which moves radially to position the heads over the appropriate track. Compare fixed head disk. See head, magnetic disk, track.

move instruction In computer programming, a microprogram which transfers data from one part of the main memory to another. See main memory, microprogram.

moving coil microphone In audio, a microphone with a transducer consisting of a coil in a magnetic field attached to a flexible diaphragm. Incident air pressure waves on the diaphragm will generate voltages in the coil. See microphone, transducer.

moving coil pickup In audio, a transducer for sound reproduction from a disk recording. A stylus is connected to a coil in a magnetic field, thus developing voltages resulting from stylus movement. See transducer.

MP/M In computing, Multiprogramming control Program for Microprocessors, a multiprogramming and multiterminal version of the CP/M operating system from Digital Research. See CP/M.

MPU Microprocessor Unit. See microprocessor.

MR See medium reduction.

MRDF In computing, Machine Readable Data Files. See machine readable.

ms See millisecond.

MSB See most significant bit.

MSD See most significant digit.

MS-DOS In computing, an operating system employed on the IBM-PC and similar microcomputers. Compare CP/M, Unix. See operating system.

MSI See medium scale integration.

M signal In audio, the signal represented by the sum of the right and left signal sources in a stereo sound broadcast. See stereophonic.

MSS See mass storage system.

MTBF See mean time between failure.

MTC See magnetic tape cassette.

MTTR See mean time to repair.

multi A prefix meaning many.

multi-access computing In computing, a mode of computer usage in which the user controls the operation interactively from a terminal. The user inputs commands, modifies program statements etc. and awaits the results before proceeding to the next stage. A common method of computer operation for program development, computer aided design, graphics applications etc. Compare batch processing, transaction processing. See computer aided design, on line.

multiburst signal In television, a video test signal comprising a series of short duration bursts of continuous waves, with different frequencies but constant amplitude.

multidimensional language In computing, a language which can be represented in more than one way, for example, flow charts, logic diagrams, block diagrams and decision tables. See block diagram, flowchart decision table.

multidrop circuit In communications, a circuit rented to a customer for the transmission of data between a central site, usually a computer, and a number of outstation terminals. Both way transmission is possible between any terminal and the central site, but not directly between terminals. Compare point to point. See circuit. Synonymous with multipoint circuit.

multi-exposure   Synonymous with multiple exposure.

multifrequency pushbutton set   See MF keypad.

multifrequency signal   In telephony, a signal made up of several superimposed audio frequency tones.

multi-image   In audiovisual aids, the simultaneous projection of two or more images on adjacent screens using 35mm slide projectors and sometimes 16mm and 8mm motion picture images and multisourced sound. Synchronization and control is carried out using special programmer units. See programmer.

multilayer   In electronics, a type of compact, printed circuit board that has several layers of circuit etch or pattern, one over the other, interconnected by electroplated holes. These holes can also receive component leads. See printed circuit.

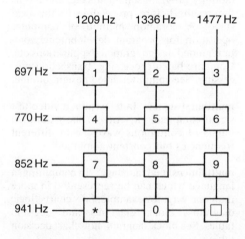

multifrequency signal
Allocation of pairs of tones to a keypad for local signalling to CCITT standards.

multilayer colour film   In photography, colour film with two or more layers each sensitive to a different range of colours.

multilink   In data communications, a branch between two nodes consisting of two or more data links. See data link.

multilist organization   In data structures, a method of segmenting long chains with an index for the start address of each chain segment. In large databases pointers may be used to link records with common fields, e.g. in a personnel database, chains of all employees in given departments may be formed. Searches along long chains may be excessively time consuming and a multilist organization enables the search to commence at an intermediate point in the chain. See chain, list.

multimedia   In audiovisual aids, any combination of motion pictures, slides, video, sound and live action.

multimode fiber   In fiber optics, a fiber having a core large enough to permit optical energy to propagate in a number of different modes. Compare monomode fiber. See mode, mode dispersion.

multipass overlapping   In printers, a technique used in dot matrix printers in which the printing head makes several passes, with slight offsets, so as to improve the quality of the printed character. See matrix printer.

multipass sort   In computer programming, a sort program that is designed to sort more items than can be held in main storage at one time. See sort, main storage.

multipath   (1) In fiber optics, a pulse dispersal resulting from the fact that the light rays through a fiber have different velocities and paths. (2) In radiocommunications, the reception of a direct VHF or UHF wave and another reflected from a surface. The reflected wave travels a longer path, and the two waves can interfere at the receiver. See interference, mode dispersion.

multiple access   Synonymous with multi-access computing.

multiple exposure In filming, an optical effect caused by re-exposing camera film more than once.

multiple instruction stream multiple data stream In computing, pertaining to a form of parallel computer with multiple control units, arithmetic logic units and memories which virtually operate as individual computers with facilities for work sharing and interaction. Compare MISD, SIMD, SISD. See arithmetic logic unit, control unit, memory.

multiple instruction stream single data stream In computing, pertaining to a form of parallel computer with multiple control units which control a single arithmetic logic unit operating on a single stream of data. Compare MIMD, SIMD, SISD. See arithmetic logic unit, control unit, parallel computer.

multiple key retrieval In databases, the technique of retrieving records based upon the value of several keys, some or all of which are secondary keys. See key, record, secondary key.

multiple precision In computing, the use of two or more computer words to represent a number so that its precision may be enhanced. See double precision arithmetic, precision.

multiple routing In data communications, a method of sending a message where more than one destination is specified in the header of the message. See message heading, routing.

multiplexer (1) In data communications, equipment which takes a number of channels and combines the signals into one common channel for transmission. At the remote end, a demultiplexer extracts each of the original signals. (2) In filming, a unit designed for the selective projection of 16mm film, 2 inch x 2 inch slides or filmstrips into a stationary television camera. See film chain, film strip, multiplexing.

multiplexing In communications, the process of combining a number of signals so that they can share a common transmission facil-

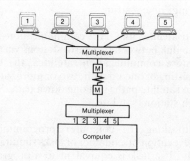

multiplexer

ity, thereby making more efficient use of the shared resource. See frequency division multiplexing, time division multiplexing.

multiplex mode In data communications, a means of transferring data to or from low speed I/O devices, such as printers, on a multiplexer channel by interleaving bytes of data. See byte, input output devices, multiplexer.

multipoint circuit Synonymous with multidrop circuit.

multipoint connection In data communications, a communication link that joins three or more data stations, with the link going from one station to the next in sequence rather than a star arrangement. See star.

multiprocessing In computing, the technique of executing programs using multiple processors. See multiprocessor.

multiprocessor In computing, a system which has a number of separate central processing units. They may be either linked or autonomous, but all having access to a part of the main memory. Processing units are now relatively inexpensive, but backing store remain expensive, and a multiprocessor environment represents an economic way of achieving a high throughput. See central processing unit, throughput.

multiprogramming In computing, a method of achieving apparent simultaneous execution of multiple programs in a single processor machine, by interleaving their execution. See central processing unit, interleaving, time sharing.

multisatellite link In communications, a radio link between two earth stations via two or more communication satellites, the link consisting of one up path, two or more satellite to satellite paths and one down path. See earth station, satellite.

multitasking In computer programming, the execution of a number of tasks simultaneously. If a task is equivalent to a program, multitasking is synonymous with multiprogramming, but a task may often be a part of a program. See multiprogramming, task.

multi-unit call In telephony, a call for which more than one basic charge unit is levied for an initial minimum interval.

multivibrator In electronics, a circuit that oscillates between two states producing output pulses of desired specifications.

multiwire element In communications, an antenna consisting of a number of wires connected in parallel. See antenna.

Munsell colour system In photography and television, a method of colour assessment in which a colour is defined according to its hue, chroma and value. See hue, chroma, value.

MUPID In videotex, Multipurpose Universally Programmable Intelligent Decoder, a personal computer integrated into an intelligent videotex terminal. The device virtually treats the viewdata base as a backing store, both downloading programs and data and also recording them back onto the database. A version of BASIC is employed which provides SAVE and FETCH commands to facilitate the interaction. A range of enhanced videotex facilities, including alphageometric display, is available for this device. See alphageometric, BASIC, telesoftware.

mush area In broadcasting, a region where signals from two or more synchronized transmitters are comparable in strength, producing fading and distortion of received signals.

mutual isolation In cable television, the attenuation between two system outlets on the network. A minimum figure is normally specified to prevent a spurious signal from one receiver on the network from interfering with another. See attenuation, interface.

MUX See multiplexer.

Mylar A polyester film manufactured by DuPont, often used as a base for magnetically coated or perforated information media.

myopia A visual disorder caused by excessive refractive power of the eyes with the result that only objects close to the eyes appear to be in focus.

N

NAK See negative acknowledgement.

NAND A logical operation, A NAND B has the result true if the result of the logical operation A AND B is false. The corresponding truth table is

A	B	A NAND B
0	0	1
1	0	1
0	1	1
1	1	0

Compare AND. See truth table.

NAND gate In electronics, a unit which produces an output signal that is the logical NAND of the input signals. Compare AND gate. See NAND.

nano A prefix indicating 10 to the power -9.

nanosecond one thousandth of a microsecond. See microsecond, nano.

NAPLPS In videotex, North American Presentation Level Protocol Syntax, (pronounced naplips) the American viewdata standard. See PLP, viewdata.

narrow band In communications, pertaining to a channel with a bandwidth less than that of a voice grade channel. Normally used for communication speeds of less than 300 bits per second. See bandwidth, voice grade channel.

narrowcasting In cable television, pertaining to a program designed to meet the interests of a minority group.

NASA A database supplied by National Aeronautics and Space Administration (NASA) and American Institute of Aeronautics and Astronautics (AIAA) and dealing with aeronautics and astronautics, science and technology. See on line information retrieval.

National Newspaper Index A database supplied by Information Access Co. and dealing with news. See on line information retrieval.

natural language A language in which the rules reflect current usage without being specifically prescribed. The language employed by users in normal communication as compared with restricted language used for communication with computers, indexing documents etc. Compare indexing language, program language.

NBM See non book materials.

NBS US National Bureau of Standards.

NCC National Computing Centre.

n-channel MOS In microelectronics, a MOS device in which all conduction is through n-type silicon. Compare PMOS. See field effect transistor, MOS, n-type material.

NDR See nondestructive readout.

necessary bandwidth In communications, the width of bandwidth which is just sufficient to ensure that the transmission of information is of the speed and quality required. See bandwidth.

needle printer Synonymous with matrix printer.

need to know In security of information systems, a policy that restricts access to classified information to personnel whose duties necessitate such access.

negate To reverse the sign of a numerical quantity.

negative acknowledgement In data communications, a signal sent from receiver to transmitter to indicate that a message with detectable errors has been received. The transmitter then repeats the message. Compare affirmative acknowledgement.

negative feedback In electronics, a feedback arrangement in which the output signal is effectively subtracted from the input signal and the resulting signal is fed into the system. Amplifiers with negative feedback have lower gains, but greater stability, than the corresponding amplifier with the feedback path removed. Compare positive feedback. See feedback.

negative resist In microelectronics, pertaining to an imaging process in which the unexposed region of the photoresist is removed in the development process. Compare positive resist. See chip.

nest In computer programming, to embed a subroutine in a larger routine or to embed a loop instruction inside another loop instruction. See subroutine, loop.

network (1) A series of interconnected points. (2) In communications, a system of interconnected communication facilities. (3) In data structures, a structure in which any node may be connected to any other node. Compare tree. See node.

network architecture In data communications, the layers, interfaces and protocols of a network. See Open Systems Interconnection, protocol.

network controlling signal unit In telephony, a device that controls the operation of a telephone network by initiating, dialing, completing and performing supervisory functions on a call. All telephones and switchboards contain such components.

network control program In computer networks, a part of the operating system of a host computer that establishes and breaks logical connections. It communicates with the user processes in the host computer on one hand, and the network on the other. See host computer, operating system.

network control station In communications, a station that coordinates the use of a communications network.

network database A database structure that permits a linkage from any item to any other item. Compare hierarchical database, relational database, tree database. See database. Synonymous with plex database.

network diagram A diagram indicating the nodes, and their interconnections. See node.

network interface machine In communications, a device that enables a nonintelligent terminal to access the Datapac network. It formats the data from the terminals into packets to be transmitted over the network. See Datapac network.

network layer In data communications, a layer in the ISO Open Systems Interconnection model. This layer is primarily concerned with routing techniques in a point to point system and the effects of poor routing, i.e. congestion. Compare application layer, data link layer, physical layer, presentation layer, session layer, transport layer. See congestion, Open Systems Interconnection, routing.

network management system In data communications, a system which enables the network supervisor to monitor the status of every communication line, modem and terminal in the network and to locate failures. Usually a controlling unit monitors the network via a low speed secondary channel independent of the main data channel. See MODEM.

network management In communications, the systematic procedures necessary to plan, organize and control an evolving commu-

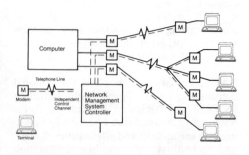

network management system

nication network with optimum costs and performance.

network operating center In computer networks, an installation that facilitates reliable network operation by the monitoring of network status, supervision and coordination of network maintenance, collecting usage and accounting data etc.

network redundancy In communications, a property of networks that have more links than are strictly necessary to connect the nodes, thus enabling the network to continue to function if certain links fail.

network structure In data structures, a structure in which any node can be connected to any other node. Compare tree structure.

network television station In communications, an earth station that can receive and transmit signals of television network quality. See earth station.

network termination unit In communications, the part of the network equipment that connects directly with the data terminal equipment, it operates between the local transmission lines and the subscribers' interface.

network timing In data communications, timing signals transferred from DCE to DTE to control the transmission of digits across the transmitted and received data circuits. See DCE, DTE.

network topology In communications, the geometric arrangement of nodes and links in a network.

network user identifier In packet switching networks, the identification code used by a customer on a public dial port to identify himself for accounting purposes. See public dial port.

Network User Identity In data communications, a code required for dial up access to a data network.

neutral density filter In photography, a gray filter used to reduce exposure and contrast without affecting the colours.

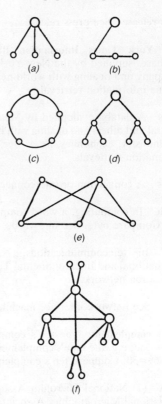

network topology
(a) star; (b) multidrop; (c) loop; (d)tree; (e) mesh; (f) mesh of trees.

neutral transmission Synonymous with unipolar transmission.

new line character A control character that instructs a printer or typesetter to commence a new line.

Newsearch A database supplied by Information Access Co. and dealing with business and industry, general interest, law, news. See on line information retrieval.

newsflash page In teletext, a page in which the information for display is boxed and may be automatically inset or added to a television picture.

newspaper lines per minute In typesetting, a setting speed used for newspaper typesetters; the newspaper line is usually one of 8 point type to an 11 pica line. See pica, point.

news release   See press release.

New York Times Information Bank   A database, supplied by the New York Times Company and dealing with world news. See on line information retrieval.

Nexis   A database supplied by Mead Data Central and others and dealing with business and industry, economics, news. See on line information retrieval.

nexus   A connection or interconnection.

nibble   In computing, a word comprising 4 bits. Compare byte. See bit, word.

NIIT   In telecommunications, National, International and Intercontinental Telecommunication network.

NIM   See network interface machine.

nine's complement   The ten's complement minus one, e.g. the nine's complement of 69 is 99-69=30. Compare ten's complement.

NMA   (1) National Microfilm Association, (2) National Micrographics Association.

NMOS   See n-channel MOS.

no circuit signal   In telephony, a low tone, periodically interrupted, indicating that no circuit is available.

node   (1) In data communications, a place that has significance for data routing, a point of interconnection to a network. (2) In data structures, an entity on two or more access paths.

node computer   In computer networks, a computer used to interconnect the host computers. The host computers are connected to the communications network via a node computer. See host computer.

no flash   In typesetting, a command code in phototypesetters that positions the matrix and film but does not expose the character. The film is thus moved on by a required amount without the formation of an image. See matrix, phototypesetting.

noise   In electronics and communications, (1) any signal disturbance that tends to interfere with the normal operation of a device or system, (2) a random undesired signal. (3) In information retrieval, a false drop. See false drop, thermal noise.

noise bar   In video recording, a momentary distortion of the picture during playback of a helical scan device, it occurs most commonly during still framing. See still frame, helical scan.

noise cancelling   In microphones, pertaining to devices designed to reduce the effect of ambient noise. The housing is arranged so that ambient noise strikes both sides of the diaphragm, thus cancelling itself out, sound from a close speaking voice strikes only one side of the diaphragm. See diaphragm.

noise factor   In library science, the proportion of nonrelevant items produced by a search. See noise.

noise temperature   In electronics, the temperature of a thermal noise source producing the same output noise power, in the same bandwidth, as the device under consideration. See thermal noise.

nomenclature   A consistent method for assigning names to elements of a system.

nomogram   A graphical method of determining the value of a variable from the values of two other related quantities. Three horizontal lines are marked with scales, a straight line through the known values of two of the quantities passes through the corresponding value of the third quantity. Synonymous with nomograph.

nomograph   Synonymous with nomogram.

nonaligned   In printing, pertaining to a line of characters in which the baseline varies. Most phototypesetting systems employ automatic procedures to correct this condition. See baseline, phototypesetting.

non ballistic technique   In printers, a method used in the printing head of a matrix printer. The needle is forced forward by a clapper and does not lose contact with it during its flight. Compare ballistic technique. See clapper, matrix printer.

non book materials In library science, pertaining to library materials which do not come within the definition of a book, periodical or pamphlet and which require special handling, e.g. vertical file materials, audio visual materials.

noncompatibility In computing, pertaining to a situation in which one system is unable to retrieve information stored in another or to run programs developed on another. Compare compatibility, programming.

noncounting keyboard In typesetting, an input device that provides no information to the operator for decisions on line justification etc. See idiot tape, noncounting perforator, justification.

noncounting perforator In typesetting, a device that punches character and function codes onto paper tape, for subsequent processing, but does not store character widths. Compare counting perforator. See idiot tape.

nondense index In databases, an index that provides information on the location of a group of records. Once the location is accessed the records must be scanned sequentially until the one corresponding to the appropriate key is found. Compare dense index. See index, record, key.

nondestructive cursor In computer displays, a cursor that can be moved about the screen without destroying or changing the information displayed.

nondestructive readout In computing, pertaining to reading action that does not change the data held. Compare destructive readout.

nondirectional microphone Synonymous with omnidirectional microphone.

nonerasable storage In data processing, storage media that cannot be erased and reused, e.g. paper tape. See paper tape.

nonlinear In electronics, pertaining to devices in which a change in the input signal does not necessarily produce a proportional change in the output signal. Amplifiers may only be considered to be linear devices over a limited range of signal amplitudes. Nonlinear effects in amplifiers can produce output signals of different frequencies to those of the input and hence produce interference between signals. Compare linear. See cross modulation, amplifier.

non linear optics Pertaining to devices in which light flows are controlled by light signals. Compare optoelectronics.

nonlining figures Synonymous with old style figures.

nonmaskable interrupt In computing, an interrupt that cannot be disabled by a masking operation, used for operations that must be serviced as soon as the interrupt is activated, e.g. reading data on an incoming line. See mask, interrupt.

nonpolarized return to zero recording In computing, a storage technique in which binary zeros are represented by the absence of magnetization. Compare polarized return to zero recording.

nonprime attribute In relational databases, an attribute that is not a prime attribute, i.e. it is not a member of a candidate key. Compare prime attribute. See candidate key.

non procedural language In computer programming, a language in which the user specifies the desired end result rather than the processes required to attain it. For example, having specified a family tree and defined grandson as the son of a son or daughter then the user may input a request for the grandsons of a specified person. Compare procedural language. See PROLOG.

nonreflective ink In optical character recognition, ink that absorbs light and hence used to write machine readable characters.

non return to zero (1) In data communications, a method of data transmission in which a voltage of one polarity represents a 1 bit and the other polarity represents a 0 bit.

The circuit carries data whenever it is enabled. It is a common method of data transfer between a computer and its peripherals. (2) In computing, a method of recording data on a magnetizable surface so that magnetization in one direction represents a 1 bit and vice-versa . Compare non return to zero inverted. See bit, polar signalling.

non return to zero inverted   In computing, a method of recording data on a magnetizable surface in which the current in the read/write head is reversed to write a 1 bit and left unchanged for a 0 bit. Compare non return to zero. See bit.

nonswitched line   Synonymous with leased line.

nontransparent mode   In communications, transmission of characters in a defined format, e.g. ASCII, in which all defined control sequences and characters are recognized and treated. Compare transparent data communication code. See ASCII.

nonvolatile memory   Synonymous with non-volatile storage.

nonvolatile storage   In computing, storage media that retain information when the power supply is removed, e.g. bubble memory, magnetic disks. Compare volatile storage. See bubble memory, magnetic disk.

no op   In computer programming, an instruction that causes no action. It may be used as a convenient point to which a program branches. See branch.

NOR   A logical operation, A NOR B has the result true if the result of the logical operation A OR B is false. The corresponding truth table is

A	B	A NOR B
0	0	1
1	0	0
0	1	0
1	1	0

Compare OR. See truth table.

NOR gate   In electronics, a unit that produces an output signal that is the logical NOR of the input signals. Compare OR gate. See NOR.

normal forms   In relational databases, a class of relations with defined properties of interrelationship between the attributes. The use of normal forms in a database reduces problems in the manipulation and storage of data which can arise from inherent interrelationships between attributes. See relation, attribute, first normal form, second normal form, third normal form.

NOT   A logical operation, NOT A has the result true if the logical variable A is false. The corresponding truth table is

A	NOT A
0	1
1	0

See truth table.

not hole   In logic diagrams, a small circle on the input or output of a symbol for a gate indicating the action of negation, e.g. a circle attached to an AND gate would convert it to a NAND gate. See AND, NAND, gate.

notice of enquiry   In communications, a public notice issued by the FCC and inviting information, and opinions, to be used in formulating policies, modifying rules or making new rules. See FCC.

notice of proposed rulemaking   In communications, a public notice issued by the FCC and inviting comment on a new rule or the modification of an existing rule. See FCC.

n-p-n transistor   In electronics, a bipolar transistor with the emitter and collector connected to n-type semiconductor material and the base connected to p type material. Compare p-n-p transistor. See transistor.

NRCd   UK National Reprographic Center for documentation.

NRZ   See non return to zero.

NRZI   See non return to zero inverted.

NTIS   National Technical Information Service, a database supplied by National Techni-

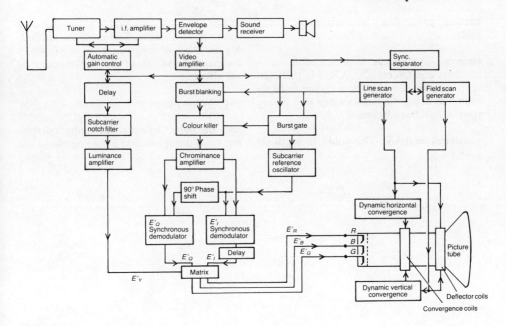

NTSC
An NTSC decoder.

cal Information Service and dealing with science and technology. See on line information retrieval.

NTSC See video standards.

NTSC decoder In television, the receiver circuitry between the signal detector and the screen which decodes the broadcast signals. See video standards.

NTT In communications, the Japanese PTT. See PTT.

n-tuple A collection of n elements, normally ordered. See tuple.

n-type material In electronics, a semiconductor material doped with an impurity that provides nuclei with loosely bound electrons. These electrons provide negative charge carriers. Compare p-type material. See semiconductor devices.

NUI See Network User Identity.

null modem In computer networks, an imit-

ation modem which interfaces a local peripheral, normally requiring a modem, and a nearby computer, which expects to drive a modem to interface with that device. See MODEM.

null string In data structures, a string which contains no characters. See string.

null suppression In computing and communications, the bypassing of null characters to be stored or transmitted to save transmission time or storage space. See data compression.

number A mathematical entity indicating a quantity or amount of units.

number crunching In computing, pertaining to processing activities that involve a high proportion of mathematical operations on the data, usually arising in scientific applications. Such applications make heavy use of the CPU and involve comparatively few input output operations. Compare data processing. See CPU.

number plan area Synonymous with area code.

number processing See arithmetic capability.

numeral A discrete representation of a number, e.g. twenty, 20, XX, 14, 10100 all represent the number 20, with the last two examples using the hexadecimal and binary system. See hexadecimal.

numerical analysis The study of methods relating to the development of quantitative solutions to mathematical problems, including the study of errors and the efficiency of the methods in terms of the total computational effort.

nut Synonymous with en-quad.

nuts and bolts In cinematography, pertaining to an unsophisticated training film.

O

obey In computing, the process whereby the computer performs the set of instructions specified in a program.

object In expert systems, a quantity which may be assigned a numerical value and allows the system to reason about real physical quantities. Compare assertion. See rule.

object code In computer programming, the code of a user's program after it has been translated. Compare source code. See translator.

objective In optics, the image forming component of the system.

object language In computer programming, the output language of a translation process. Compare source program. See translator. Synonymous with target language.

object program In computer programming, a program in object code form. See object code.

Oceanic Abstracts A database supplied by Cambridge Scientific Abstracts and dealing with aquatic sciences. See on line information retrieval.

OCI US office of Computer Information. An office of the Department of Commerce.

OCP See order code processor.

OCR See optical character recognition.

OCR-A In optical character recognition, a special typeface intended for optical character recognition. Compare OCR-B.

OCR-B In optical character recognition, a special typeface for optical character recognition considered to be more pleasing to the eye than OCR-A. Compare OCR-A.

OCR font In computing, a set of characters designed to be read by optical character recognition. See OCR-A, OCR-B, optical character recognition.

octal In computing, pertaining to the number 8. Octal notation uses a base of 8 and is a convenient form of representing binary numbers, e.g. decimal 66 = octal 102 = binary 1 000 010. Compare hexadecimal. See binary.

octet In computing and communications, a group of eight binary digits treated as an entity. See octal.

odd even check Synonymous with parity checking.

odd parity See parity.

OEM See original equipment manufacturer.

off air In broadcasting, a programme received either on radio or television.

offcut In printing, paper left over when the sheet is trimmed to size.

off hook In telephony, a condition in which a unit indicates a busy condition to incoming calls. Compare on hook.

office of the future An office in which all recorded information is held in computer readable form and there exists a highly integrated database, communication, word and transaction processing system. See database, transaction processing, word processing. Synonymous with electronic office, paperless office.

off line In computing and communications, pertaining to processing equipment that is not connected to a computer or network, or the operations performed on such equipment. Compare on line.

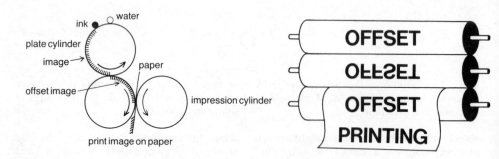

off line printing In computing, printing that takes place without the continual supervision of a computer. See background.

off microphone In filming, pertaining to the area outside a microphone's pickup pattern.

off mike Synonymous with off microphone.

offprint In printing, a feature or other portion of publication made available separately from the whole work.

off screen In filming, pertaining to unseen action that is presumably not far from the perceived action.

offset In filming, sound overlapping from a previous or succeeding scene.

offset lithography Synonymous with photolithography.

offset printing A lithographic method of printing in which the ink is first transferred from the printing surface to a rubber offset blanket and then to the paper or other printing material. See lithography.

ohm In electronics, a unit of electrical resistance. One ampere flowing through a one ohm resistance produces a voltage drop of one volt. See resistance.

Ohm's Law In electronics, the voltage drop across a resistance is directly proportional to the current flowing through it. See voltage, current, resistance.

O.K. In printing, a mark to indicate that a proof is error free. See proof.

old style figures In typesetting, a set of type numerals that vary in size, some having ascenders and other descenders. Compare lining figures. See ascender, descender.

omega wrap In video recording, a method of winding videotape around the drum of a helical scan device. The tape is wrapped almost 360 degrees around the drum to form a Greek letter omega. The tracks are diagonal on the tape, there are no video tracks at the top and bottom edges of the tape and the signal is not recorded on tape as the recording head crosses the gap between tracks. Compare alpha wrap. See helical scan.

omission factor In library science, the number of documents that are relevant to a query but are not retrieved in a search.

omnidirectional microphone A microphone that is equally sensitive in all directions. Compare unidirectional microphone.

OMR See optical mark recognition.

on chip In microelectronics, pertaining to a circuit that is on the same chip as other elements. See chip.

one address computer A computer with a machine language set that only uses one address, e.g. an add instruction will add the contents of the specified address to the contents of the accumulator. See accumulator, machine language.

one and one half spacing In word processing, an instruction to place one and one half spaces between lines of text during playback printing.

one for one In computer programming, an assembler in which one assembler instruction produces just one machine code instruction. See assembly language.

one line initial In printing, an initial letter larger than the text and lined up with the bottom of the text.

one's complement In computing, a method of representing a negative binary number. In this convention, a binary number is negated by interchanging the ones and zeros. The most significant digit is a sign bit, i.e. one indicates a negative number. Unlike the two's complement, a zero is represented both by all ones or all zeros. Compare two's complement.

one time pad In cryptography, a cipher which uses a nonrepeating random key stream. One time pads are the only ciphers that achieve perfect secrecy. See cryptoanalysis.

on hook In telephony, a condition in which the telephone is not in use. Compare off hook.

onion skin architecture In computing and communications, a layered structure that facilitates communication between processes at the same level, employing lower level processes in a manner that is largely transparent to the user process. In communication systems this approach facilitates the design and use of complex networks and systems. Processes receive messages from the layer above and pass them to corresponding processes at the same layer by initially transmitting them to the layer below. These processes need only be concerned with the passage of messages through two layer interfaces although the total system may have many layers. See transparent, onion skin language, Open Systems Interconnection.

onion skin language In databases, a computer language to manipulate a hierarchy of systems. A database system may be constructed as a set of systems of increasing complexity such that one system is a subset of the next. An onion system language will manipulate the most complex system and subsets of the language will manipulate the successive system subsets. See onion skin architecture.

on line In computing and communications, pertaining to data processing and communication equipment that is connected to a computer or communication channel. Compare off line.

on line information retrieval A system that enables a searcher at a remote terminal to interactively interrogate databases, containing bibliographical information or source data, held on a host computer.

Since the end of the Second World War there has been a dramatic growth in the amount of scientific and technical information published, particularly in the form of journals and conference proceedings, and this has resulted in a significant increase in the number of abstracting and indexing journals. On line information retrieval originated in the 1960's when computers were introduced for phototypesetting these abstracting and indexing journals. Information Centres obtained the machine-readable tapes and developed software to enable them to be interrogated, although initially only in batch mode. During the late 1960's the Lockheed Missiles and Space Company and the System Development Corporation (SDC), were instrumental in developing interactive on line systems, and, by the mid 1970's, such systems were being offered by a number of organisations on a world-wide basis.

The producers of the databases are normally professional institutions, government bodies, commercial companies etc. and the databases are leased or sold to the suppliers offering the on line services. There are now databases covering all subjects and disciplines and although originally they were bibliographical in nature, many now contain factual information and even the full texts of original articles and papers.

To interrogate a database the searcher uses a terminal, with printer attached, connected by a modem or acoustic coupler, to a telephone. The searcher can access the supplier's computer - the 'host' computer - either by dialling directly, if nearby, or by dialling the local node of a data telecommunications network. Having entered his password he specifies which database he requires for his search.

On accessing a relevant database the searcher specifies search terms of keywords which best describe his topic. These are matched with the index to the records on the database and the system responds with the number of matches, or 'postings' found. By combining the search terms using Boolean Operators, (AND, OR, NOT), the search can be narrowed or widened. In bibliographical databases it is usually possible to narrow a search by specifying the language of the original articles, by searching for matches in titles only, or matches with the terms used by the abstractor to index the publications, by retrieving references to works by a particular author, by specifying the formats of original articles (e.g. journal articles, conference papers) etc. The retrieved references or abstracts can be output on the searcher's printer, or, if large numbers are involved, may more economically be printed off line by the supplier and posted to the searcher. Various formats may be specified, e.g. bibliographical citation, full record including abstract and indexing terms, etc. On some systems it is possible to order reprints of original articles and papers directly at the terminal. Also useful are the Selective Dissemination of Information (SDI) services available on many systems. A search profile (i.e. a combination of search terms), is entered and details of new relevant references are regularly sent to the searcher as the database is updated.

The initial cost of using an on line information retrieval system is incurred in purchasing or leasing the necessary equipment or hardware; the terminal, printer, modem, telephone etc. It is sometimes necessary to pay a subscription to access a particular information system, and manuals, and thesauri of indexing terms will have to be purchased. The direct costs of a search are the telecommunications charges, (i.e. telephone call and use of a data communications network); the database connect-time charges, (charges vary from database to database and from one supplier to another); and the charges made for off line printed references. Frequently a charge is also made for any references printed on line during a search. On many systems an estimated cost of the search, (excluding any telephone charges), is printed when a searcher logs off from the system. Before undertaking on line searches it is necessary to have some training in searching techniques and be familiar with some of the retrieval languages used on the various systems. Searches are therefore usually undertaken for enquirers by trained intermediaries such as information scientists or librarians. See abstract, acoustic coupler, AND, boolean algebra, keyword, MODEM, OR, SDI.

on line storage   In computing, storage devices, and the media they contain, under the direct control of the computer system. See on line.

on line system   In computing, an information processing system in which the data or instructions are inserted directly from the point of origin and the output data is transmitted directly to the appropriate recipient. See on line.

on the fly   (1) In microcomputers, examining data obtained during program execution without affecting the execution. (2) In printing, pertaining to a printing method using a moving font, e.g. as on a barrel printer. See barrel printer.

on the nose   In photography, pertaining to the use of exposure as indicated by the light meter.

opacity   In optics, the reciprocal of transmittance. Compare transmittance. See density.

op amp   See operational amplifier.

opaque projector   In audiovisual aids, a device using the principle of reflection to project an image held on a nontransparent medium, e.g. coins, photographs, diagrams, in black and white or colour. Compare overhead projector.

op code   See operation code.

open   In computing, an instruction to open a file associates it with the calling program. Compare close. See file.

open loop Pertaining to any system in which the input information or signal is not influenced by the output of the system. Compare closed loop, feedback.

open reel In filming and recording, film, video or audio tape on a reel and not enclosed in a cassette or cartridge. See cassette, cartridge.

open skies policy See DOMSAT decision.

open subroutine In computing, a subroutine whose code is inserted at every call instruction in the program. Compare closed subroutine. See call, subroutine. Synonymous with macroinstruction.

Open Systems Interconnection In data communications, pertaining to an ISO reference model intended to coordinate the development of standards at all levels of communication. The model has seven layers - physical, data link, network, transport, session, presentation and application. These layers are illustrated in the figure.

The concept of the layers provide for a considerable degree of independence between the multifarious and complicated operations involved in data communications. At each level the process believes that it is communicating with its corresponding layer in the receiving host and it does this by accepting messages from the layer vertically above it, adding control information to it and passing it on to the layer immediately below

it. At the receiving end the process is reversed, messages are received from the layer below it, control information is stripped off and the message passed up to the next level. The concept can be illustrated by the business communicating in different countries. Businessman A in Turin is only concerned to pass a business analysis to Businessman B in Tokyo. He passes on the analysis to a translator who only speaks Italian and English. The translator produces an English version of the business analysis and hands the result to a post office for transmission. The post office forwards the message by letter to Tokyo where it is handed to a local translator who converts the text from English to Japanese and hands it up to Businessman B. The degree of independence is obvious, the translator could agree on a different common language and the post office could select a whole variety of message transmissions and the other layers are unaware and unaffected by the changes.

The physical layer is concerned with the transmission of a raw bit stream. The data link layer uses error detection codes and host to host control messages to convert an unreliable transmission channel into a reliable one. The network layer in a point to point network is primarily concerned with routing and congestion. The transport layer provides reliable host to host communication and hides the details of the communication network from the session layer. The session layer is responsible for setting up, managing and tearing down process to process connections, whilst the presentation layer performs useful transformations in the text, e.g. text compression, and allows for dialogs with incompatible intelligent terminals. The content of the application layer is left to the users and standard protocols for specific industries, e.g. banks, are expected to develop. Compare SNA. See application layer, bit, data link layer, error detection code, host, physical layer, point to point, presentation layer, routing, session layer, text compression, transport layer.

operand The quantity that is to be the subject of a mathematical operation. Compare operator.

operand field In computer programming, the section of an assembler or machine code

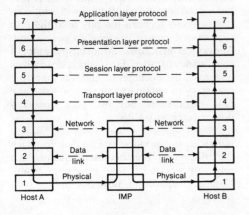

open systems interconnection

instruction designated for the operand. See operand, assembler, machine code.

operating system In computing, a software programming package that controls the operation of user programs. Operating systems may typically perform the supervision of input output operations, allocation of storage, sequencing of user programs, etc. Operating systems are of particular importance to microcomputer users; application programs written for one system cannot be run under another. The three most common systems for microcomputers are CP/M, MS-DOS and Unix. See CP/M, MS-DOS, Unix.

operating time In communications, the total time required for dialing the call, waiting for connection to be established and coordinating the subsequent transaction with the personnel or equipment at the receiving end.

operational amplifier In electronics, an amplifier that produces outputs in specific mathematical relationships to the analog input signals. Operational amplifiers can perform the functions of addition, subtraction, integration and are the essential components of analog computers. See analog computer.

operation code In computer programming, the part of a machine code instruction that specifies the action to be performed. Compare operand field. See machine code.

operator (1) A person charged to enable a piece of equipment to fulfill its function. (2) A character that designates a mathematical or logical operation, e.g. +.

operator number identification In telephony, the intervention of the operator on DDD calls to request the calling subscriber's number, for billing purposes, where no automatic number identification equipment is available. See DDD.

optical axis An imaginary line drawn through an image forming system such that the image forming properties of the system are symmetrical in any plane perpendicular to the line.

optical bar reader In computing, a reader which focuses a beam of light on a bar code label and receives the pulses of reflected light of varying strength and duration. See bar code.

optical character recognition In computing, pertaining to techniques and equipment for reading printed, and possibly handwritten, characters on a document and converting them to digital code for input to a computer. In its simplest form light is beamed onto the character and the reflected light is projected onto a matrix of photocells. The output of the matrix is scanned and the received signal is read into a storage cell matrix where a match is sought with a set of stored character patterns. Compare magnetic ink character recognition, optical mark recognition. See OCR font, photocell.

optical digital disks In computing, optical video disks in which the information is encoded as bits representing the characters of text or data. Such disks cannot be used to view documents on a consumer disk player plus TV receiver but they can input information into a computer or word processor. They provide a very efficient storage mechanism with capacities in the region of 4 gigabytes on a 30 centimeter disk; this represents a capability to store one million pages of typed text or 2500 average sized text books. The mass production methods for consumer video disks is not appropriate for business document storage and thus the players for optical digital disks also require record facilities. DRAW (direct read after write) systems have been produced using 10 milliwatt semiconductor lasers to burn the bits onto the disk surface at a rate of 10 megabits per second. The optical digital disks do not have the inbuilt redundancy of video disks, which store visual images of the documents, and it is therefore necessary to obtain extremely low write and read error rates. See bit, giga, semiconductor laser, video disk.

optical disk In video disk, a disk in which the information is etched on the surface as a series of pits and is read by a laser beam. Compare capacitance disk. See optical digital disks.

optical mark recognition In computing, a

technique for recording marks on documents. The marks are usually short lines or filled-in squares on formatted documents, e.g. answers to multiple choice questions on examination papers, customer order documents. The document is positioned and scanned by a light beam, and transmitted, or reflected light, is collected by photocells. The significance of the data depends upon its coordinate position on the document and the signals from the photocells are input to a computer. Compare optical character recognition. See photocell.

optical memory See optical digital disks.

optical scanner A device that optically scans an image and generates a corresponding analog or digital signal. See optical character recognition, scanner.

optical soundtrack In filming, a photographic soundtrack. Light passes through the variable density striations of the track and is then incident upon a photocell. The electric current variations from the cell are amplified and fed to a loudspeaker system. See photocell, amplifier.

optoelectronics In microelectronics, pertaining to a device that is responsive to, or that emits, coherent or noncoherent electromagnetic radiation in the visible, infrared or ultraviolet regions. See coherence, fiber optics.

OR A logical operation, A OR B has the result true if either, or both, of the logical variables A, B are true. The corresponding truth table is

A	B	A OR B
0	0	0
1	0	1
0	1	1
1	1	1

Compare AND. See truth table.

ORACLE In videotex, Optional Reception of Announcements by Coded Line Electronics, the teletext service operated by the UK Independent Broadcasting Authority. See teletext.

Orbit In databases, an information retrieval service operated by the System Development Corporation (SDC), (USA). See on line information retrieval.

order code processor In computing, the processor, in a multiprocessor system, which decodes the user program instructions and performs the corresponding arithmetic logic unit operations. It is the central processor of a system which has separate processors for storage management, communications interfacing, etc. Synonymous with instruction processor.

ordering bias In library science, the degree to which the distribution, or sequence, of items renders the effort of producing a specified order greater, or less, than that required for producing the same order from a random distribution.

OR gate In electronics, a unit that produces an output signal that is the logical OR of the input signals. Compare AND gate. See OR.

original An initial photographic image or sound recording as compared with one produced by a duplication or reproduction process.

original equipment manufacturer A manufacturer who purchases equipment, adds value to it, e.g. by enhancing its capabilites, making it suitable for an application area, and resells it.

original typing In office systems, typing from dictation, handwritten copy or other originating sources.

origin directive In computer programming, a statement in an assembly program that specifies the memory address for the start of the program. See assembler.

orthochromatic film In photography, a black and white film insensitive to the colour red.

ortho film Synonymous with orthochromatic film.

oscillator In electronics, a device to produce a sinusoidal signal of a specified frequency. See sinusoidal.

oscilloscope In electronics, a test instrument comprising a cathode ray tube, time base and amplifiers. Used for displaying voltage waveforms. See time base, amplifier, cathode ray tube, waveform.

OSI See Open Systems Interconnection.

osmosis method In library science, the implementation of a new classification scheme by the classification of all literature received after a given date and the reclassification of older active material as, and when, it is returned after use.

OTP In communications, Office of Telecommunications Policy, in the Executive office of the U.S. President. An agency that develops and recommends U.S. public policy in the area of telecommunications.

outage (1) In communications, a period when a system cannot function. (2) A period of system nonfunction due to a power supply failure. See sun outage.

outline letter In printing, a letter in which each stroke is represented by two lines, i.e. one in which the inner part has been removed.

outlining capability In word processing, a function that permits the system to deal with a multi-indented format and automatically generates the number scheme of the outline.

out of band signalling In communications, a system in which control signals are transmitted at a frequency within the passband of the circuit but outside the band normally used for voice transmission. Compare in band signalling. See passband, signalling.

out of phase In electronics and communications, a condition between two waveforms of the same frequency in which the waveform peaks do not coincide in time. If the maximum value of one sinusoidal waveform coincides with the minimum value of the other, the waveforms are 180 degrees out of phase. Compare in phase. See sinusoidal.

output (1) In computing, pertaining to the action, or the result, of transferring data from the internal storage of a computer to an external device or user. (2) Signals delivered from an audio or video device.

overflow (1) In computing, pertaining to a state in which the result of an arithmetic operation is greater than the value that can be stored in the associated storage location. (2) In communications, traffic in excess of the capacity of channels on a particular route which is offered an alternative route. (3) In word processing, pertaining to a condition in which the information exceeds the available storage capacity. (4) In databases, a situation in which a record is allocated a storage area, by an addressing algorithm, and that location is already occupied. The system places the record in an appropriate free area and sets pointers to that area. Compare underflow. See hashing.

overhead bit In computing and communications, a bit that transmits no information but is included for control or error checking purposes. See parity checking.

overhead projector In audiovisual aids, a device that projects an image held on a flat, transparent acetate sheet up to about 10 x 10 inches square. The lecturer can write on the sheet during projection or successively build up a total projected image. See progressive disclosure.

overlay In computing, a method of running a large program with a limited allocation of internal storage. Specified sections of the program are held in backing store until they are required for execution, when they are read into the internal storage, overwriting some other routine not currently required. See backing store, overwrite, virtual storage.

overlay network In communications, a network of transmission links and switching centers superimposed upon another network and interconnected with it at specific points.

overload (1) In electronics, to draw an excessive current from a device. (2) In filming, to record sound at an excessive level.

overmodulation In communications, an amplitude modulated signal in which the amplitude of the carrier is reduced to zero for some part of the cycle of the modulating waveform. See amplitude modulation.

overpunching In computing, a method of changing the character represented on punch tape or a punched card by punching additional holes. See paper tape, punched card.

overscan In television, the part of the TV raster outside the visible area of the screen. See raster.

overstrike In word processing, a method of producing a character not in the typeface by the appropriate superimposition of two other characters, e.g. a dollar sign produced by the superimposition of an S and a l.

overtones Frequencies that are multiples of the fundamental frequency. Any periodic waveform can be decomposed into a series of sinusoidal waveforms at the fundamental frequency and overtones. See fourier series. Synonymous with harmonic.

overwrite In computing, to write data to a storage location that already holds other data. The original data is lost.

ownership In data security, the right of users to dispense and revoke privileges for objects they own, e.g. access on programs and data sets. See access control, data set.

P

PABX See private automatic branch exchange.

pacing In data communications, a method by which a receiving station controls the rate of transmission in order to avoid a loss of data.

pacing device In audiovisual aids, a device to improve reading skills by indicating a word or phrase for a controlled period. See tachistoscope, controlled reading device.

package In electronics, an integrated circuit chip and its housing. See integrated circuit. software package.

package count In electronics, the number of integrated circuits necessary to perform a specified function. See integrated circuit.

packed BCD In computing, a coding in which two 4 bit binary coded decimal digits are packed into one 8 bit computer word. See BCD, packing, word.

packed decimal In computing, a data representation in which two or more BCD digits are present in each word. See BCD, word.

packet In data communications, a self-contained component of a message, comprising address, control and data signals, that can be transferred as an entity within a data network. See packet switching.

packet assembler/disassembler In packet switching networks, a device that converts the character stream, suitable for a simple terminal, to packets and vice versa. See packet.

packet interleaving In packet switching networks, a form of multiplexing in which packets from various subchannels are interleaved onto a main channel. See packet, multiplexing.

packet radio In packet switching, a network with radio links so that a packet may be received by more than one station. See Aloha.

packet sequencing In packet switching, a method of ensuring that packets arrive at the receiving station in the same sequential order that they were transmitted.

packet switching In data communications, a method of message transmission in which each complete message is assembled into one or more packets that can be sent through the network, collected and then re-assembled into the original message at the destination. The individual packets need not even be sent by the same route. The communication channels are only occupied during the transmission of a packet as compared with a convential circuit switching in which a connection is made and maintained for the duration of the complete message transmission. Compare circuit switching. See computer networks, packet.

packet switching exchange In packet switching, the computer system that provides the interface between users and the node to node network. The functions of the exchange include network protocol, packet sequencing and routing. See routing.

packet switching network In data commu-

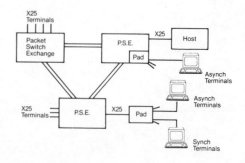

packet switching network

nications, a network of devices that communicate between each other by transmitting packets addressed to particular destinations. See packet switching.

packet terminal   In packet switching, a terminal capable of forming its own packets and interacting with a network character terminal. Compare character terminal.

packing   In computing, the process of making the most effective use of storage by placing data elements into contiguous bit positions of words. See packed BCD, packed decimal.

packing density   (1) In computing, the number of bits that may be stored per unit length of recording medium. (2) In microelectronics, the number of individual logic circuits per unit area on a chip. See chip. PAD.

PACX   In computing and communications, Private Automatic Computer Exchange, a switching and contention system which allows a range of terminals, with different speeds, to communicate through a number of output ports with several other devices such as computers. See contention, port.

PAD   See packet assembler/disassembler.

paddle   In computing, a hand held controller used with microcomputers and video games to control the movement of the cursor, or graphic display, on the screen. See video game.

page   (1) In word processing, the amount of text designated by the operator to fit onto a sheet of paper. The usually accepted maximum for an A4 sheet is 52 single spaced lines of 80 characters, i.e. 4160. (2) In computing, an area of storage space. (3) In videotex, a screenful of information (24 lines x 40 characters) that can be accessed directly. Compare frame.

page frame   In computing, an area of storage than can store a page. See page.

page header   In teletext, the top row containing general information, e.g. magazine and page number, day and date, program source and clock time. See page.

page make up   Synonymous with make up.

page mode   In data communications, pertaining to terminals that usually have cursor addressing or some local editing capability. Compare form mode, scroll mode.

page number   In videotex, a number which uniquely identifies a page. See page.

page numbering   See automatic page numbering.

page printer   In computing and printing, a device that composes a whole page of text before printing. Compare line printer.

page reader   In optical character recognition, an optical scanning device that examines many lines of text with a scanning pattern determined by program control and/or control symbols intermixed with input data.

page scrolling   In computing, scrolling through a whole page of a document, displayed on a VDU, instead of just a line at a time. See vertical scrolling, VDU.

page send receive   Synonymous with keyboard send receive.

page store   In videotex, a memory unit, or audio cassette device, capable of storing videotex pages for later playback. See memory, page.

page view terminal   Synonymous with graphic display terminal.

pagination   See automatic pagination.

paging   (1) In computing, the transfer of pages of instructions or data between the main and backing store. (2) In printing, making up in pages or numbering pages. (3) In communications, the use of a pocket sized device to alert the user that he or she is required on the telephone. See page, virtual storage, paging receiver.

paging rate   In computing, the average number of pages read in and out of the main store, per unit time, when a virtual storage system is used. See virtual storage, page, thrashing.

paging receiver In communications, a pocket sized electronic device that emits an audible signal when a telephone call is made to the user. See radio paging.

paint In computer graphics, to fill an area of display, e.g. with a colour, a cross hatched pattern, etc.

pairing In television, a display fault in interlacing in which alternate scan lines are very close or superimposed. See interlace.

PAIS International A database supplied by Public Affairs Information Service and dealing with social sciences and humanities. See on line information retrieval.

PAL See video standards.

PALAPA An Indonesian common carrier domestic communication satellite. See satellite.

PAM See pulse amplitude modulation.

pamphlet In printing, an unbound treatise on a subject or current topic of interest.

panchromatic film In photography, black/-white film which is sensitive to all colours thus giving good gray tones.

pan film Synonymous with panchromatic film.

pan scrolling In computing, a form of vertical scrolling with a smoother movement of the text up the screen, similar to the movement of credits following a TV program. See vertical scrolling.

paper bail A device on a printer to hold the paper against the platen. See platen.

PAPERCHEM PAPer CHEMistry, a database supplied by The Institute of Paper Chemistry (IPC) and dealing with pulp, paper and packaging. See on line information retrieval.

paper jam In printing devices, a condition in which the paper flow is inhibited causing overprinting of lines, etc.

paperless office Synonymous with office of the future.

paper tape In computing and communications a medium for recording data in binary coded format. Characters are recorded by punching a pattern of holes across the width of the tape in some specified code. The paper width is typically $\frac{7}{16}$ or 1 inch. It normally has 5 or 8 holes per character.

paper tape code In computing and communications, the relationship between the set of holes across the width of the paper and the data that it is intended to convey. See paper tape.

paper tape reader In computing and communications, a device that senses the holes in paper tape and converts them into electrical signals. See paper tape.

paper throw In printing devices, paper movement at a rate in excess of the speed for normal line spacing.

parabolic antenna In communications, an antenna of parabolic shape. It is used to focus the transmitted waves to a narrow beam, or to receive a narrow beam.

paragraph In computer programming, a section of a COBOL program that represents a logical processing entity. See COBOL.

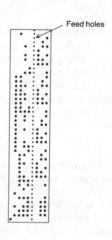

paper tape

paragraph assembly In word processing, a term used for the process of producing completed documents from portions of text held in computer store.

paragraph mark See reference mark.

parallax In optics, the apparent change of position of an object produced by an actual change of point of observation, e.g. two telegraph poles in a line of sight appear to move relative to one another if the eye is moved to one side.

parallel (1) In optics, pertaining to rays or lines that neither converge or diverge. (2) In computing and communications, pertaining to processes operating concurrently or systems performing simultaneous actions or in simultaneous active states.

parallel circuit In electronics and communications, two or more circuits that share common input and output nodes or connections. Compare series circuit.

parallel computer A computer with multiple logic or arithmetic units enabling it to perform parallel operations or parallel processing. Compare serial computer. See parallel processing.

parallel conversion In computing, the simultaneous operation of an old and new data processing system for a transition period following the installation of the new system.

parallel fold In printing, a folding method in which a sheet is folded and then folded again along a line parallel to the first fold.

parallel interface In electronics, a device that supports the parallel transmission of data when a number of bits, usually a byte, are transmitted at the same time. Compare serial interface.

parallel mark See reference mark.

parallel operation The performance of simultaneous, and usually similar actions, on a related set of inputs. Compare serial operation. See parallel processing, parallel transmission.

parallel processing In computing, pertaining to the concurrent operation of two or more devices to perform simultaneous tasks within an overall job, e.g. outputting to several peripheral devices simultaneously.

parallel storage In computing, a storage device in which the words or bytes are accessed simultaneously or concurrently. See word, byte.

parallel to series converter In electronics, a device that converts a word, or byte, represented in the form of parallel data into an appropriate series of pulses for serial transfer. Compare series to parallel converter. See serial transmission.

parallel transmission In communications and computing, the simultaneous transmission of elements constituting the same code, e.g. each bit of a word is sent simultaneously on an individual wire. It has a higher bit rate than corresponding serial transmission but requires 8 wires to convey individual bytes and is therefore mainly used for transmission over comparatively short distances, e.g. to convey data from a computer to its peripherals. Compare serial transmission. See bit rate, peripheral.

parameter (1) A quantity that, individually, or as part of a set, specifies a system or process. (2) A specified variable of a system or process that temporarily assumes the properties of a constant.

parent In any hierarchical system the element that is immediately superior to the element in question, e.g. in a tree structure the node that points to the particular node in question. See tree structure.

parenthesis free notation Any notation for mathematical expressions that does not require the use of parentheses to indicate the order in which individual parts of it are to be evaluated. See prefix notation, postfix notation.

parity In computing and communications, pertaining to a condition in which the number of items in a group is odd or even. See parity checking.

parity bit In computing and communications, the bit added to a bit grouping, if necessary, in order to produce parity. See parity checking, parity.

parity checking In computing and communications, a form of redundancy checking. The convention odd or even parity is selected, the number of bits in a grouping is counted and a parity bit is added, if necessary, to produce parity with the selected convention. Upon receipt of the grouping the number of bits is checked and an error reported if the selected parity is not found. Parity checking detects the loss, or incorrect addition, of an odd number of bits. See parity, parity bit, redundancy checking.

parse In computer programming, to resolve a string of characters, representing for example a program statement, into its elemental parts as defined by (say) the programming language. See compiler.

part A piece of equipment or a component.

partial dial tone In telephony, a high tone indicating to the caller that dialing has not been completed within a specified time or that not enough digits have been dialed.

party line In telephony, a line shared by several subscribers, possibly with selective calling. See selective calling. Synonymous with shared line.

Pascal (1) A database supplied by Centre National de la Recherche Scientique, Centre de Documentation Scientifique et Technique (France) and dealing with science and technology. (2) In computer programming, a block structured language favoured by computer scientists for its compatibility with structured programming, and becoming increasingly popular in the microcomputer field. See block structure, structured programming, ALGOL. on line information retrieval.

pasigraphy A proposed universal system of writing in which the characters represent ideas rather than words.

pass In computing, (1) a complete cycle, i.e. input, processing, output, of a program

execution, (2) a complete scan of the source code by the compiler or assembler. See compiler, assembler.

passband In communications, the range of signal frequencies that can be satisfactorily transmitted on a given channel, e.g. the passband on voice grade channels is 300-3000 Hz. See Hz.

passim In printing, a term used in footnotes meaning, 'here and there'.

passive In electronics, equipment incapable of amplification or power generation. Compare active device. See amplifier.

passive mode In computer graphics, a mode of operation in which the user is unable to modify or interact with the displayed image.

password In computing, a unique string of characters input by an authorized user in order to gain access to a system or to protected information in the system. Passwords are usually not displayed on terminal screens upon input, in order to preserve their secrecy.

PA system Synonymous with public address system.

patch In computer programming, (1) to replace a small set of instructions with a corrected or modified set, (2) to modify a program by changing its object code rather than its source code. (3) In electronics, to make an electrical connection. See object code, source code.

patch cord In electronics, a small length of cable with suitable end connectors for use in a patch panel. See patch panel.

patch panel In electronics, a unit to facilitate the interconnection of systems. It normally takes the form of a board with a matrix of electrical sockets that can be interconnected by specially prepared leads, e.g. a telephone switchboard.

pattern recognition In computing, the automatic recognition of shapes, patterns and curves. The human optical and brain system is much superior to the most advanced computer system in matching images to those stored in memory. This area is subject to intensive research effort because of its importance in the fields of robotics and artificial intelligence, and its potential areas of application, e.g. reading handwritten script. See artificial intelligence, robotics.

pattern sensitive fault   In computing, a fault that occurs in response to a particular pattern of data.

pause control   In recording, a feature of some tape recorders that permits the tape movement to be stopped without switching from the play or record settings.

pause instruction   Synonymous with halt.

pause retry   In communications, a network control program option enabling a user to specify the number of times that a message should be transmitted in the event of transmission errors, and the time interval between each attempt.

PAX   See private automatic exchange.

pay cable   In television, a wired subscription service with a surcharge for special optional programs. See cable television.

pay per view   In cable television, a charging system in which a user pays for viewing a particular program. See premium television.

pay television   A form of broadcast television in which the signals are scrambled and can only be normally viewed by coin operated sets with a decoder. See scrambler.

PBX   See private branch exchange.

PC board   See printed circuit board.

p-channel MOS   In microelectronics, a MOS device in which all conduction is through p-type silicon. Compare NMOS. See field effect transistor, MOS, p-type material.

PCK   See processor controlled keying.

PCM   See plug compatible manufacturer.

PCU   See peripheral control unit.

PDC   See permanent data call.

PDM   See pulse duration modulation.

PDN   See public data network.

PE   See printers' errors.

peak   In electronics and communications, the maximum positive or negative signal excursion.

peak envelope power   In radio communications, the average power supplied to the antenna transmission line by the transmitter during one radio frequency cycle, at the crest of the modulation envelope, under normal operating conditions. See modulation.

peculiar   Synonymous with special sort.

peek   In computer programming, a high level language instruction that retrieves a value from a program specified memory address location. Compare poke. See high level language.

peek a boo system   In manual data processing, a card index system in which individual attributes are represented by holes in certain areas of the card. The presence or absence of a particular attribute can be checked by placing one card on top of another.

pegging   In recording, a sharp swing in the needle of VUmeter caused by a sudden noise. See VUmeter.

pel   In computing, picture element. Synonymous with pixel.

percent denial   In communications, the average percentage of attempted calls, in the busy hour, that are blocked due to network loading. A measure of the grade of service in a dial access circuit group. See busy hour, dial access.

perfector   In printing, a rotary press that prints first one side, then the other, of a sheet, in one pass through the machine.

perforated tape Synonymous with paper tape.

perforations A series of small linearly spaced holes or cuts on a form to facilitate tearing along a desired line.

perforator In paper tape equipment, a tape punch operated by a keyboard, by received signals or by another unit.

perigee In satellite communications, the point at which the satellite is at a minimum distance from earth in its orbit. Compare apogee.

period In periodic systems, the time interval between two corresponding points on successive cycles. Compare frequency.

periodic Pertaining to any phenomenon that consistently repeats the same cycle of events.

peripheral In computing, a device to perform an auxiliary action in the system, e.g. input output, backing store. See input output, backing store.

peripheral control unit In computing, a unit which provides the necessary interfacing between a peripheral device and the computer input output system. It provides the decoding of the computer commands relating specifically to a particular device, it also develops the necessary control voltage levels and the timing for the operation of the peripheral device. See peripheral.

peripheral equipment operators In large computer systems, staff involved in loading disks on disk drives, removing printouts from line printers etc.

peripheral interface adapter In computing, a device that provides interface functions between the computer bus and its peripherals. Typical functions include bit serial/-bit parallel conversion, buffering, addressing, monitoring status and generating interrupts. See bus, interrupt, microcomputer, peripheral.

peripheral software drivers In computing, small programs that enable a user to control

and communicate with a peripheral. See peripheral.

permanent data call Synonymous with permanent virtual circuit.

permanent file In word processing, a file that is usually held in backing store. Compare working data file.

permanent memory In computing, a memory storage device that retains its contents when the power is removed. Compare volatile storage. Synonymous with nonvolatile storage.

permanent virtual circuit In data communications, a special type of virtual call service in which the logical links between specific terminals are permanently set up so that call set up and release procedures are eliminated. See virtual circuit.

permeability In electronics, the ratio of magnetic flux density, in a material, to the magnetic field acting on it.

permutation Any one of the total possible number of positional arrangements in a group.

permutation index In library science, a technique used in machine indexing, each entry in the index is a cyclic permutation of all the words in the original document title. See KWIC.

persistence In cathode ray tube displays, the continuation of light emission from phosphor after excitation by the electron beam. See phosphorescence, flicker. Synonymous with afterglow.

persistence of vision A physiological effect in which the eye's response to a visual stimulation remains for a short period after the removal of the stimulus. At the average cinematic screen illumination, the average eye detects no flicker for frequencies of intermission above approximately 16 per second.

persistent conductivity imaging In printing, an electrophotographic imaging process using photoconductive materials, which, after exposure to light, retain their increased conductivity for relatively long periods after the light source has been removed. See electrophotography, photoconductivity.

personal computer In computing, a term generally applied to more powerful microcomputers intended for business applications. Compare home computer. See microcomputer.

personal identification number See PIN.

PERT Program Evaluation and Review Technique, a method used to facilitate the supervision and control of complex projects. See critical path method.

pertinent A quality implying a close logical relationship with, and importance to, the matter under consideration.

PESTDOC PEST control literature DOCumentation, a database supplied by Derwent Publications Ltd and dealing with agriculture. See on line information retrieval.

PET In computing, a popular microcomputer developed by Commodore Business Machines. See home computer.

petal printer See daisy wheel.

pf See picofarad.

phantom ROM See shadow memory.

phantom telegraphy circuit In communications, a telegraph circuit superimposed on two circuits reserved for telephony.

phase An aspect when brought into relation with another aspect. See in phase, out of phase, phase delay.

phase angle A measure of the phase relationship between two sinusoidal waveforms. 'In phase' corresponds to a phase angle of 0, 360, 720.... degrees. See phase, in phase, out of phase.

phase delay In communications, the time delay represented by a change in the phase of a sinusoidal wave in passing through two points on a transmission path.

phase equalizer Synonymous with delay equalizer.

phase modulation In communications, a method of modulation in which the phase of the sinusoidal carrier is varied in accordance with the modulating signal. See phase, modulation, sinusoidal, carrier.

phasing In facsimile transmission and reception, an adjustment, achieved by a phasing signal, to ensure that the reproduced picture corresponds with the original.

phon In acoustics, a measure of sound intensity equivalent to one decibel at 1000 Hz. See decibel, Hz.

phoneme In acoustics, the smallest element of spoken language which distinguishes one utterance from another, e.g. the word bit comprises three phonemes 'b', 'i' and 't'. See allophone, speech synthesis.

phonetic transcription A means of suggesting the pronunciation to the reader using a transformation of the text into another alphabet.

phosphor dots In electronics, the matrix of dots on a CRT screen, or TV set, that emit light when bombarded by an electron beam. In colour displays three different types of dots, emitting the colours red, green or blue, are tightly clustered.

phosphor efficiency The ratio of the quantity of light energy emitted by a phosphor dot to the quantity of energy received from the excitation beam. See phosphorescence.

Phosphor dot triad

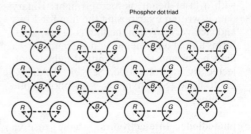

phosphor dots
Arrangement of phosphor dot triads in a shadow mask tube (R=red; G=green; B=blue).

phosphorescence The phenomenon in which certain materials emit light following irradiation by an appropriate form of energy. See phosphor dots.

photo (1) A prefix meaning light. (2) An abbreviation for photograph.

photocell In optoelectronics, a device employing a photoelectric effect. See photoelectric.

photochromism In optics, a reversible change of colour produced by exposure to light.

photocomposition Synonymous with phototypesetting.

photoconductivity A phenomenon in which the resistance of a piece of semiconductor material decreases if it receives light energy. See semiconductor.

photoconductor A photocell which employs the phenomenon of photoconductivity. See photocell, photoconductivity.

photocopy A photographic copy from an original. See photostat.

photodielectric process In printing, an electrophotographic imaging process in which a photoconductive layer is charged and exposed to a light pattern and an image is produced on a nonphotosensitive dielectric surface. See dielectric, electrophotography, photoconductivity.

photodigital memory In computing, a storage cell produced by writing data onto a film with a laser beam or focused light. Binary data is written by exposing the film for 1 bits and vice-versa. When the film is developed it forms a read only memory; it is scanned by a light beam and the transmitted light is collected by a photodiode. See bit, LASER, photodiode. Synonymous with photo-optic memory.

photodiode In electronics, a light sensitive semiconductor diode; the conductivity varies with the intensity of received light. See photoconductivity.

photodirect lithography In printing, a process in which lithographic plates are made direct from the original without an intermediate negative stage. See photolithography.

photoelectric In optoelectronics, pertaining to phenomena in which incident light energy produces an electrical effect. Compare electrophotography. See photoconductivity, photocell, photoemission, photovoltaic.

photoelectric cell Synonymous with photocell.

photoemission In optoelectronics, a phenomenon in which incident light onto a material causes the emission of electrons from the surface. Compare photoconductivity, photoresistive, photovoltaic.

photoengraving In printing, the process of making metal relief plates by acid etching on a photographically produced image on metal. See relief printing.

photography The formation of a permanent record of an optical image by exposing a sensitized surface to light or other form of radiant energy.

photogravure In printing, a photomechanical process in which the printing is performed from a recessed surface and the paper comes into direct contact with the plate. Compare offset printing. See photomechanical.

photoheadliner In photocomposition, a machine that produces display type by photographic methods. In some versions the machines have special lenses for producing condensed, expanded, slanted or other distorted letter forms.

photolettering See photoheadliner.

photolithography A method of selectively etching a surface according to a pattern on a mask. The surface is coated with a photoresist material and the mask is placed in contact with it. The masked surface is exposed to light, the mask removed and the photoresist developed chemically. The photoresist is then selectively wasted away according to whether it has or has not been exposed to light. The surface, unprotected by developed photoresist, is then etched away and finally the remaining photoresist is removed. See chip, etching, photoresist, lithography.

photomechanical In printing, a complete assembly of type, line art and halftone art, in the form of film positives onto a transparent base from which autopositive diazo proofs can be obtained for checking, and from which a control film negative can be made for the production of printing plates. See diazo process, halftone.

photomechanical plates In printing, plates produced by exposing positive or negative film on a photosentive coated plate and then applying chemicals to produce a distinction between printing and non printing parts. See photoengraving, photolithography, photomechanical.

photometry The science of light measurement.

photomicrography In photography, a photograph of a magnified image, usually made through a microscope, of a small object. Compare microphotography.

photomontage In photography, the production of a composite image by the superimposition and juxtaposition of images from various sources.

photon A packet of electromagnetic energy. According to Planck's quantum theory, energy is not transmitted in continuous amounts but in discrete quanta, or photons, and the quantity of energy in a photon is directly proportional to the frequency of radiation.

photonics Technology employing optical-electronic effects.

photo-optic memory Synonymous with photodigital memory.

photoplastic An image recording technique that employs heat or light to deform the surface of a special plastic film.

photopolymer In printing, a plastic printing plate material which is rendered insoluble in certain solutions by the action of light.

photoprint In typesetting, the final proof with all typographic elements in position ready to be pasted into a mechanical. See proof.

photoresist Pertaining to photosensitive materials that react to light by hardening. See chip, negative resist, photolithography, positive resist.

photoresistive In optoelectronics, pertaining to a phenomenon in which incident light onto a semiconductor releases electrons from parent atoms causing a reduction in resistance, i.e. increase in conductivity. Compare photoemission, photoresist, photovoltaic. See photoconductivity.

photostat In printing, a thin photocopy used as part of a paste up layout.

phototelegraphy Synonymous with picture transmission.

phototext In typesetting, text matter set by means of photocomposition. See photocomposition.

phototransistor In electronics, a device which combines the ability to detect light and to provide gain in a single unit. Compare photodiode.

phototypesetting In printing, the production of textual typsetting, by photographic means. See typesetting.

phototypography In typesetting the process of producing matter from graphic reproductions via the use of all photomechanical means; cameras, photoenlargers, photocomposing machines and photosensitive substrates. See photomechanical.

photounit In typesetting, the unit of a phototypesetter housing the optics, light and energy source and photographic material, on which the typographic image is produced. See phototypesetting.

photovoltaic In optoelectronics, pertaining to a phenomenon in which incident light onto the device produces a voltage across it. Compare photoconductivity, photoemission, photoresistive.

physical database   A database in the form that it is held on the storage media including any pointers that it may contain. A number of different logical databases may be based upon the same physical database. Compare logical database.

physical data independence   In databases, pertaining to the structure of databases that enable the physical storage structure to be changed without affecting the logical structure. Compare logical data independence. See data independence.

physical layer   In data communications, the bottom layer in the ISO Open Systems Interconnection model. This layer is concerned with the transmission of the raw bit stream. Compare application layer, data link layer, network layer, presentation layer, session layer, transport layer. See bit stream.

physical record   In computing, (1) a record associated with a specific area of physical storage, (2) the largest unit of data that can be transmitted in a single read or write operation. Compare logical record.

PIA   See peripheral interface adapter.

pica   (1) In typesetting, a point system of measurement equivalent to twelve points or 4·217 mm. (2) In typewriters, spacing of 10 characters to the inch. Compare elite. See point, typewriter faces.

pi character   In printing, a type character not included in the font. See font. Synonymous with special sort.

pick up   In recording, the stylus, cartridge and supporting arm of a disk player.

pickup tube   In television, the tube in a television camera that accepts a visual image and provides an electrical signal corresponding to that image. The image is focused upon a surface coated with a photoconductive material. This surface is scanned by an electron beam which produces an electrical signal corresponding to the conductivity, and hence illumination, at the corresponding point on the surface. See photoconductivity.

pico   A prefix for one million-millionth, i.e. 10 to the power of minus 12.

picofarad   In electronics, a capacitance of one million-millionth of a farad. See farad, capacitance.

picosecond   One millionth of a microsecond. See pico, microsecond.

pictograph   A pictorial sign resembling the thing that the sign represents.

picture   In computer programming, a description of a character string used to describe the length and type of data that may be stored in a field of a record etc., e.g. in COBOL 999 is used as a picture of a 3 digit word. See field, record.

picture element   (1) In computer graphics, the smallest element of a display space that can be addressed. A picture element will have one or more attributes of colour, intensity and flashing. (2) In optical character recognition, an area on a document which coincides with the scanning spot at a given moment. (3) In micrographics, the area of the finest detail that can be effectively reproduced. Synonymous with pixel.

picturephone   In communications, a telephone device that also provides a simultaneous picture of the caller. See picturephone meeting service.

picturephone meeting service   In teleconferencing, a broadband video conferencing facility provided by A T & T in which microwave, satellite and cable may be employed to transmit full motion images.

Picture Prestel   In videotex, an experimental system for displaying a small TV quality picture on a viewdata page. The transmission of a complete TV frame, by viewdata codes over telephone lines, would require about an hour to transmit. In Picture Prestel only a small area of the screen is used to display a picture, e.g. a signature in a bank retrieval system, and data compression techniques are employed to minimize the transmission time and terminal storage requirements.

picture stop   In video disk, an instruction

encoded in the vertical blanking interval on the video disk to stop the player on a predetermined frame. See frame.

picture transmission In communications, a facsimile system with special regard to tone reproduction in which the photographic process is used at the receiving end. See facsimile. Synonymous with phototelegraphy.

picture writing The use of pictures to literally or figuratively represent things or actions, in the recording of events.

piece accent Synonymous with floating accent.

piece fractions In printing, a fraction that is contained within one symbol and to which one character width is allocated.

pie graph A diagram representing proportions as various sized slices of a circular pie, e.g. to represent the manner in which a corporation's budget is spent under the various expenditure headings.

piezoelectric In electronics, pertaining to the property of certain crystals which change their electrical characteristics, i.e. resistance or voltage, when physical pressure is applied, or change their physical dimensions when an electric current is applied. See resistance.

piggyback entry In data security, the illegitimate access to a computer system via another's legitimate connection, e.g. via an unattended terminal logged onto a remote system. See log on.

piggyback form In word processing, a continuous form carrying stationery, which is usually pasted on. Often used for printing continuous letters and envelopes.

piggybacking In data communications, a method of sending acknowledgements with outgoing messages, e.g. in HDLC messages from A to B contain information on the frames received by A from B. See HDLC, acknowledgement, frame.

PILOT In computer programming, a textually based computer language developed

for computer assisted learning applications. See computer assisted learning.

PIN In computing, Personal Identification Number, a number that must be entered by a user before a remote terminal, or point of sale terminal, can be used to transfer information or complete a transaction. See password.

pin board A device containing a perforated board to control the action of a piece of equipment. The desired control action is achieved by placing pins in designated holes. Compare patch panel.

pinch roller In recording, a roller on a tape recorder that holds the tape against the capstan during play and record. See capstan.

pincushion distortion In optics, an image distortion in which square objects appear with the corners stretched out. It is caused by lens aberration. Compare barrel distortion.

pin feed platen In printing devices, a cylindrical platen that moves the paper by sprocket feed. See platen, sprocket feed.

pin photodiode In electronics, a P-Intrinsic N-photodiode. A comparatively large segment of intrinsic silicon is sandwiched between p- and n- type silicon layers. The diode is biased so that no current flows in the absence of light radiation. When visible light or infrared radiation strikes the diode, hole-electron pairs are formed and the carriers are swept to the appropriate electrode causing a current flow in the external circuit. Compare avalanche photodiode. See semiconductor, photodiode, hole, electron.

pipelining In computing, a method of speeding up computer operations by simultaneous operations on instructions. In a strictly sequential processor all operations on one instruction are completed before processing of the next begins. In a pipelining system the third (say) instruction may be fetched from store at the same time as the second one is being decoded and the operations required by the first one are in execution. Only used in comparatively powerful computers. See parallel operation.

Pira A database supplied by The Research Association for the Paper and Board, Printing and Packaging Industries and dealing with pulp, paper and packaging. See on line information retrieval.

pitch (1) In typing, the horizontal spacing of characters. (2) In cinematography, distance between leading edges of film sprocket holes. (3) In acoustics, the frequency of a sound wave. (4) In satellites, a rotation about a horizontal axis perpendicular to the direction of flight. See typewriter faces, roll, yaw.

pixel Synonymous with picture element.

pix lock In video recording, a state in which the playback system is in synchronism with the external synchronizing pulses. Synonymous with automatic lock.

PLA See programmable logic array.

plaintext In data security, messages which are in readable forms, i.e. not encrypted.

PLAK In videotex, Public service Look AliKe system.

plan A scale drawing with a view vertically above the object or area.

planetary camera In micrographics, a type of microfilm camera in which the document being photographed and the film remain in a stationary position during exposure and the document is on a plane surface at the time of filming. Compare rotary camera, step and repeat camera. See microfilm.

planographic In printing, pertaining to processes in which the printing surface is neither raised nor incised. Compare relief printing, intaglio. See lithography.

plasma display See thin window display.

plasma panel In computing, a display device which can replace the cathode ray tube in VDUs. The device consists essentially of two optically flat glass plates separated by a few hundredths of a millimeter, sealed and filled with neon argon gas. Vertical parallel conductors are etched on the inside of the front plate and horizontal parallel conductors

are similarly etched on the inside of the rear plate. Each junction, individually addressable, forms a pixel and when activated with a voltage produces a light point of ionized gas. The device has the advantage of simplicity, ruggedness and shape over a conventional CRT. It requires no refresh circuitry, has no flicker and is much flatter than a CRT. It can, however, only be used for monochrome displays. See cathode ray tube, pixel, VDU.

plate In printing, (1) a relief, intaglio or planographic printing surface, (2) an illustration of a book printed separately from the text and usually on different paper. (3) In photography, a photographic image on a sheet glass support. See intaglio, relief printing, planographic.

plate cylinder In printing, the cylinder carrying the inked plate in an offset lithography process. See offset lithography, blanket cylinder.

platen (1) A rubber covered cylinder in a typewriter, or printer, around which the paper is guided. (2) In photography, a mechanical device which holds the film in the focal plane during exposure.

platen press In printing, a letterpress machine that has a flat impression surface as compared with a cylindrical plate. See letterpress, cylinder machine.

Plato computer system In computer assisted learning, a highly sophisticated system manufactured by Control Data Corporation using touchscreen terminals and associated audio visual facilities. See touchscreen.

playback The retrieval of recorded signals, data or information in a form suitable for a human operator.

playback print rate In computing and word processing, the automatic printing speed of a printer.

PLC In computer programming, Programming Language Committee, a body responsible for the development of the COBOL language. See COBOL.

plex database Synonymous with network database.

plex structure Synonymous with network structure.

PL/M In microcomputers, Programming Language for Microprocessors, a high level language for microprocessors derived from PL/1. See PL/1.

plotter In computing, an output unit used to produce graphs or diagrams. See drum plotter, flatbed plotter, digital plotter, incremental plotter, X-Y plotter.

plotting mode In word processing, a form of printer operation in which dots, or some other suitable characters, are printed at appropriate points to produce a graph or diagram.

PLP In videotex, AT&T Presentation Level Protocol, an alphageometric standard. See alphageometric, NAPLPS.

PLTTY Private line teletypewriter service.

plugboard In computing and communications, a device for making a set of complex interconnections using removable wires terminated in plugs or pins. See patch panel.

plug compatible manufacturer A manufacturer who produces equipment that can be operated in conjunction with another manufacturer's equipment when connected by plug and cable. A term commonly employed in connection with IBM equipment.

plug in To make an electrical connection.

plug in unit In electronics, an assembly of permanently interconnected components that can be easily plugged into an item of equipment.

PL/1 In computer programming, a high level language designed to encompass both commercial and scientific applications. It contains many of the features of ALGOL, COBOL and FORTRAN plus some facilities not available in previous languages. See high level language, ALGOL, COBOL, FORTRAN.

PMBX In telephony, Private Manual Branch Exhange. See private branch exchange.

PMOS See p-channel MOS.

pn-junction In electronics, an interface between p- and n-type semiconductor material; such an interface produces a diode effect. See semiconductor, diode, transistor.

p-n-p transistor In electronics, a bipolar transistor with the emitter and collector connected to p-type semiconductor material and the base connected to n-type semiconductor material. Compare n-p-n transistor. See transistor.

point In typesetting, the Anglo-American unit of type measurement, one point is equal to 0·351 mm. Compare Didot point. See pica.

pointer In data structures, a variable that holds the address of an item of data. In a simple chained list a pointer will hold the address of the next item in the list. See chain list.

point of sale A position where a customer pays for goods or services. See point of sale terminal.

point of sale terminal In computing, a terminal used at a location where real life transactions are performed, and designed for particular input functions. In many cases they will be operated by unskilled staff and have facilities for direct reading of data, e.g. automatic reading of coded tags or bar codes. See bar code.

point to point connection In communications, a circuit connection between two, and only two, terminal installations. The connection may include switching facilities.

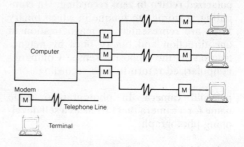

point to point

point to point In communications, pertaining to connection between two, and only two, terminal installations. The connection may include switching facilities. Compare multidrop circuit.

poisson distribution A probability distribution pertinent to traffic flows in computing and communication systems. It is used to estimate the size, and waiting times, of queues for service systems in which the arrival and service rates have certain specified statistical properties. See probability distribution.

poke In computer programming, a high level language instruction that places a value in a program specified memory address location. Compare peek. See high level language.

polar diagram In recording, a diagram of the pick up pattern of a microphone.

polarity reversal In television, an effect in which the polarity of an electronic signal is reversed. The gray scale and colours of the corresponding picture are also reversed. See gray scale.

polarized Pertaining to electromagnetic radiation in which the electromagnetic vectors are not uniformly distributed in the transverse plane.

polarized return to zero In communications, a method of signalling with three states, positive and negative signals represent one each of the binary states and the line condition returns to zero voltage between the signals. Compare polar signalling. See bit.

polarized return to zero recording In computing, a storage technique in which binary zeros are represented by magnetization in one direction and binary ones by magnetization in the opposite sense. Compare nonpolarized return to zero recording.

polaroid camera In photography, trade name for a camera that produces a self developing photograph.

polaroid filter In photography, a filter that attenuates the intensity of transmitted light according to the plane of polarization. See polarized.

polar orbit In satellite communications, the trajectory of a satellite whose orbital plane includes the axis of the earth. Compare equatorial orbit.

polar signal See return to zero signal.

polar signalling In communications, signalling as used in telegraphy where a direct current of one polarity represents a 1 bit and the opposite polarity represents a 0 bit. Compare polarized return to zero. See NRZ.

polar transmission In communications, a telegraphy type signalling system with three states, one representing no signal, the second a binary one signal and the third a binary zero signal.

pole tips In video recording, the part of the magnetic head that protrudes radially beyond the head wheel. See head wheel.

POLIS Parliamentary On-Line Information System, a database supplied by Scicon Limited for the House of Commons Library (England) and dealing with government - UK. See on line information retrieval.

Polish notation See prefix notation.

polling In data communications, a method of controlling terminals on a multidrop or clustered data network where each terminal is interrogated in turn by the computer to determine whether it is ready to receive or transmit data. Data transmission is only initiated by the computer. See cluster, multidrop circuit.

polling list In computing and communications, a list specifying the sequence in which terminals are to be polled. See polling.

polling overhead In computing and communications, the time spent by the computer in the polling interrogation of terminals. See polling.

Pollution Abstracts A database supplied by Cambridge Scientific Abstracts and dealing

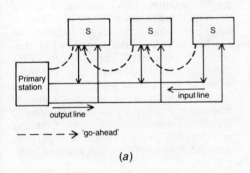

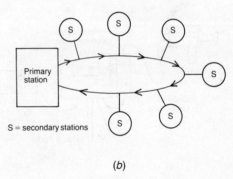

S = secondary stations

(a) (b)

polling
(a) hub polling; (b) loop polling.

with environment. See on line information retrieval.

polynomial code In data communications and computing, an error detection code in which a mathematical operation is performed on the data to be sent and is repeated at the receiving end; a check is then performed to detect any data corruption in transmission or transfer. Typically the total obtained from the summation of the binary numbers, corresponding to the bit patterns of the transmitted characters, is divided by an arbitrarily selected constant. The remainder is transmitted as the cyclic check character at the end of the message. At the receiving location the total is then performed as above with the cyclic check character added. If division by the same arbitrarily selected constant is performed and the remainder is zero the message is accepted as uncorrupted. See error detection code.

POP Post Office Preferred, pertaining to a range of envelope and post card sizes recommended by the UK Post Office.

pop filter In recording, an acoustic filter for use on microphones to reduce overload effects arising from the sound of hard p's and breath blasts etc.

pop instruction In computer programming, an instruction to retrieve an item from the stack. Compare push instruction. See stack.

pop off In animation, pertaining to the instantaneous removal of a pictorial information, e.g. a title from a frame. Compare pop on.

pop on In animation, pertaining to the instantaneous appearance of a new image on an existing scene. Compare pop off.

port In computing and communications, a functional unit of a node through which data can leave or enter a data network or a computer. See node.

portability In computer programming, pertaining to programs in a form that enables them to be run on more than one computer system. High level language source programs will be more portable than their corresponding object programs. See high level language, source program, object program.

portapak In television, a self-contained, portable, battery operated video recorder, often with a monitor that can be employed as a viewfinder or for playback. See video recorder, monitor.

POS See point of sale terminal.

position independent code In computer programming, code that can be loaded into, and executed from, any area of store without modification or relinking. See linking, relocate.

positioning time In computing, the total

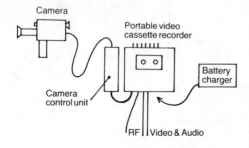

time required to access an item of data on an auxiliary storage unit.

positive feedback In electronics, a feedback arrangement in which the output signal is effectively added to the input signal and the resulting signal is fed into the system. In some cases this can result in a self sustained oscillation. Compare negative feedback. See feedback.

positive interlace In television, a camera system producing exactly spaced sequential scanning of picture tube field lines. Compare random interlace. See field, interlace.

positive resist In microelectronics, pertaining to an imaging process in which the exposed region of the photoresist is removed in the development process. Compare negative resist. See chip.

positive response In communications, a response indicating that the message was received successfully.

post In data processing, to enter data into a record. See record.

postcoordinate indexing In library science, a method of indexing in which the indexing terms are assigned individually and the searcher uses his own combination of terms. Compare precoordinate indexing.

postediting In machine translation, the editing of material produced by the machine translator to improve the style and make it more acceptable to the end user. Compare pre-editing.

postfix notation In computing, a logical notation for the representation of arithmetic operations which removes the necessity for brackets to indicate the order in which they are to be performed. The operators follow their associated operands, e.g. (a+b)—c would be represented as ab+c—. This form considerably facilitates the production of machine code instructions corresponding to high level language statements. Compare infix notation, prefix notation. See operator, operand, high level language, machine code.

post mortem In computing, pertaining to the analysis of an operation after its execution.

post mortem dump In computing, a dump undertaken after execution to facilitate post mortem analysis. See post mortem, dump.

postprocessor In computing, (1) a program that converts the output data from an emulator into the form of the emulated system, (2) a program that performs some final computation or organization. Compare preprocessor. See emulator.

post production premastering In video disk, the process of editing, assembly, evaluation, revision and coding of intermediate materials. See intermediate materials.

Post Telephone and Telegraph In communications, a government operated common carrier outside the USA, e.g. British Telecom. See common carrier.

pot See potentiometer.

potentiometer In electronics, a resistor with a movable contact that may be used as an adjustable resistor or voltage attenuator. See resistor, attenuation.

POTS In telephony, Plain Old Telephone Service, i.e. one used for a conventional telephone service as compared with data communications.

power (1) In mathematics, the number of times that a quantity is multiplied by itself. (2) In electronics, the product of the instantaneous voltage and the corresponding instantaneous current. In AC circuits, the power consumed in a circuit will be zero if the voltages and currents are exactly 90 degrees out of phase with each other. See out of phase, exponent.

powerhouse In communications, an FCC licensed radio station permitted to operate at 50 kilowatts power on a frequency assigned to no other full time licensee. See FCC, watt.

power keyboard See magnetic keyboard.

power pack In electronics, a unit to supply power voltages for equipment.

power restart In computing, a facility that detects a fall off in the supply voltage and initiates an interrupt routine enabling the computer to prepare itself for the power loss. The program can be resumed without error when power is restored.

power supply In electronics, a circuit for converting AC voltage to low voltage DC in such a way that the output is regulated to minimize noise and voltage fluctuations. See power pack.

power typing In word processing, low level repetitive processing applications, e.g. typing standard letters.

POWU In computing, Post Office Work Unit, a measure of computer performance devised by the UK Post Office.

PPM See pulse position modulation.

pragmatics The relationship between signs and those who use them. See semiotics.

pre-amplifier In electronics, a unit to boost very weak input signals, e.g. the unit that accepts the antenna signals in a TV set. See amplifier.

precedence In computing, rules that govern the order in which operators are applied to operands, e.g. consider a + b x c, the expression is ambiguous unless it is understood that multiplication has precedence over addition. See postfix notation.

precedence prosign In communications, a group of characters indicating the the the manner in which the message is to be handled.

PRECIS In library science (1) PREserved Context Index System. A subject indexing system developed for the British National Bibliography. (2) PRE Coordinate Indexing System. See precoordinate indexing.

precision The degree of discrimination with which a quantity is quoted, e.g. a two digit number can be selected from a 100 possibilities. Compare accuracy.

precision ratio Synonymous with relevance ratio.

precoordinate indexing In library science, an indexing method in which the terms are combined at the time of indexing a document, the combination of terms being shown in the entries. Thus the document can be found listed under the combination of terms. Compare postcoordinate indexing. See entry, index, term.

predicate In relational databases, a term of a relational calculus expression that specifies the condition to be satisfied by the terms in the retrieved set. See relational calculus.

pre-editing In machine translation, the editing of source material to make it compatible with the syntax expected by the translator, to remove ambiguities etc. Compare postediting.

pre-emphasis In video recording, pertaining to the amplification of the high frequency components of the video signal prior to the frequency modulation process. See frequency modulation.

preferred term In definitions, a term recommended as a standard.

prefix In communications, a code at the beginning of a message.

prefix notation In computing, a method for the representation of one dimensional expressions, without the need for brackets, by preceding an operand string with a string of operators, the operand string may itself contain operators. Compare postfix notation, infix notation.

premium television Any television system that exacts a charge for program viewing. See pay cable, pay television.

premix In recording, to combine sound tracks onto one track which will later be combined with other tracks. See sound track.

prepotent In library science, pertaining to a symbol that has the major effect in determining the position of a heading in an indexing sequence.

preprint In printing, an advanced issue of an article to be published in book or journal form.

preprinted data In word processing, data printed on forms to reduce typing effort, e.g. the year in a date field. Compare variable text.

preprocessor In computer programming, (1) a program that converts data from an emulated system into a format suitable for the emulator, (2) a program that undertakes some preliminary computation or organization, (3) a program that examines preprocessor statements in a source program, which are then executed resulting in some alteration of the source program. Compare postprocessor. See emulator, source program.

preproduction In video disk, the set of design tasks - flowcharting, story boarding, scriptwriting, software design etc., prior to video disk production. See story board.

prerecording (1) In cinematography, the action of recording sound which will later be played back and used in shooting. (2) In word processing, the action of storing text on magnetic media for subsequent playout as part of a repetitive letter or a letter created from boilerplate. See boilerplate.

presentation layer In data communications, a layer in the ISO Open Systems Interconnection model. This layer performs generally useful transformations on the data to be sent, e.g. text compression, and performs the con-

versions required to allow an interactive program to converse with any one of a set of incompatible intelligent terminals. Compare application layer, data link layer, physical layer, presentation layer, session layer, transport layer. See intelligent terminal, Open Systems Interconnection, text compression.

press proof In printing, the last proof to be checked before approval for printing. See proof.

press release A statement circulated to newspaper and periodical editors for publication on the specified release date.

pressure pad In recording, a pad that holds the magnetic tape against the record/playback heads.

Prestel The British public viewdata service. See viewdata.

prestore In computing, to store data before it is operated on by a computer program or subroutine. See subroutine.

preventive maintenance A regular routine of checking equipment and replacing substandard parts to minimize the possibility of equipment failure.

primary colours That minimum set of colours from which all other colours may be obtained. See additive primary colours, subtractive primary colours.

primary distribution In publishing, the initial distribution of a document from its publisher to more than one destination.

primary group In communications, an initial grouping of channels in a multiplexed system. The multiplexing of a large number of channels is often performed in stages, the basic signals are first multiplexed into a primary groups, these primary groups are then multiplexed and so on. See multiplexing.

primary key In databases, a key that uniquely identifies an entity. Compare secondary key. See entity, candidate key.

primary letters In printing, lower case characters that have neither ascenders or descenders, i.e. a, c, e, etc. See ascender, descender.

primary station In communications, a station on a data link with the right to select a secondary station and transmit a message. There should only be one primary station on a data link at any one time. Primary status is temporary, allocated to a station so that it may transmit a message. Compare secondary station.

prime attribute In relational databases, an attribute that is a member of at least one candidate key. See attribute, candidate key.

primitive A basic or fundamental unit.

print (1) In graphics, an inked impression of an engraved or lithographic plate. (2) In printing, an impression from type of the actual printed matter. (3) In photography, a positive image produced from a negative.

print contrast ratio In optical character recognition, the quantity obtained from the formula $(M-I)/M$ where I = reflectance at an inspection area and M = maximum reflectance found within a specified distance from the inspection area. See reflectance.

print contrast signal In optical character recognition, the signal generated by the contrast of the zone under examination and its background. See print contrast ratio.

print control character A control character used in print operations to perform a non-printing action, e.g. carriage return. See carriage control.

print drum In printing devices, a rotating drum holding print characters.

printed circuit In electronics, a method of fabricating printed circuit boards in which a copper clad card is treated with light sensitive emulsion and exposed. Areas to be retained are fixed and an acid is used to etch away the remaining portions. See fixation, printed circuit board.

printed circuit board In electronics and computing, a plastic board upon which elec-

tronic components such as resistors, capacitors and integrated circuits are mounted and interconnected by plated or etched foil conducting paths. Printed circuit boards are used as plug-in modules in microcomputers. See expansion card, integrated circuit, resistor, capacitor, printed circuit.

printers' errors In typesetting, a mistake made by the typesetter. Compare author's alterations.

printing (1) The production of an image by applying an ink bearing surface to paper. (2) In photography, to produce a picture by the transmission of light through a negative to light sensitive paper. (3) In cinematography, the duplication of a film, it can include the addition of colour and exposure corrections, optical and other effects, and a sound track.

printout microfilm In computer output microfilm, each frame of the microfilm contains data that would otherwise occupy one page of continuous stationery.

print out See hard copy.

print run In printing, (1) the action of producing a prescribed quantity of copies, (2) the number of copies produced.

print to paper An instruction to a printer to use all the available supply of paper rather than produce a prescribed number of copies.

printwheel Synonymous with daisy wheel.

priority In computing and communications, a rank assigned to a task that determines its precedence in receiving system resources.

priority interrupt In computing, an interrupt that is given precedence over other system interrupts, e.g. an alarm interrupt in a real time control system. See interrupt.

priority processing In computing, a method of operating a computer system so that the sequence in which programs are processed is fully determined by a system of priorities.

priority scheduler In computing, a system

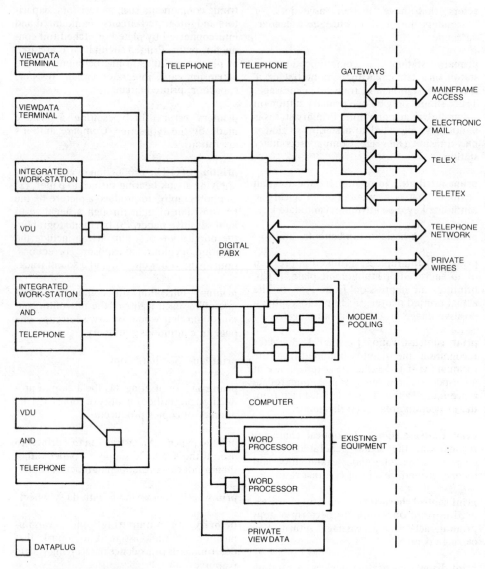

```
[ ] DATAPLUG
```

private automatic branch exchange
Local Area Network (LAN) based on a digital telephone exchange (courtesy Plessey Ltd).

that uses input and output queues in its job scheduling to improve overall performance.

privacy The right of an individual to exercise some form of control both over the information that is stored about him or her, and the personnel that are allowed to access such information. A cause of severe concern among many communities particularly when the developments of information technology facilitate the collection, correlation and distribution of sensitive personal information. The legislation governing such activities varies considerably from country to country. See data protection.

private address space In computing, a range of computer addresses assigned to a particular user. See address.

private automatic branch exchange In telephony, a small automatic branch exchange. In recent years the function of PABX's have moved beyond the interconnection of internal and external telephone users to a role of the central controller of a star based local area network. In a conventional PABX system each separate telephone handset is directly connected by a twisted pair cable to a central switch. A connection is made by numerical signalling at relatively low speed and, if the connection cannot be completed, an engaged signal advises the sender to try again. In the great majority of systems this is a limiting factor because it places responsibility for pursuing the connection on the human user. In more advanced PABX systems the problem is eliminated because the switch takes over responsibility for persisting until the connection is made. The same advanced switch can store and forward messages, and carry data as well as voice at speeds of up to 64 Kb/sec.

The important advantage of this type of switching technology is that it is fully proven in decades of use. Its numerical message coding principle is understood by all users. Its operational speed is common to every terminal and is not divided by the number of terminals wishing to communicate. The limit is only reached when all circuits of the switch are simultaneously operated. The ability of the computer program controlled integrated circuitry to seek out open lines, and to store and forward data as lines become available, overcomes the previous disadvantage of individual relay switches dedicated to a single traffic line.

Thus a star network based on a PABX switch using digital technology can have terminals to perform the functions of LAN terminals. A PABX's ability to handle data traffic, like a LAN, is determined by software. In a PABX star network the data terminal is connected through a data port or data plug which translates the data into a form of traffic intelligible to the PABX. Modification to the PABX itself can provide gateways to mainframe computers, in public and private data networks such as Prestel in the UK, to telex and facsimile.

The star network thus develops from an existing cable installation using familiar technology and satisfies all the requirements of a LAN with the added benefit of voice communication integrated into data traffic. See local area network, signalling, star, store and forward.

private automatic exchange In telephony, a dial telephone system, provided to an organization, which does not permit calls to be made over the external telephone network. See private automatic branch exchange.

private branch exchange In telephony, a service provided to an organization comprising switching office trunks, a local switchboard and extension telephones. The extension telephone sets may be connected to each other or to the external trunks. PBX's may be manual, or dial, depending upon the methods used by extensions to place local and outgoing calls.

private dial port In a packet network, a dial-in port providing an access port for one customer, with an unlisted telephone number. Compare public dial port. See packet switching.

private line See leased circuit.

privilege In computing, pertaining to a program or user and characterizing the type of operation that can be performed. Privileged users or programs can perform operations normally considered to be the domain of the operating system and which can affect the system performance. See operating system.

probabilistic model See stochastic model.

probability distribution A function giving the probability that a random quantity will lie within a given interval. The shape of the probability distribution curve will depend upon the mechanisms governing the random event, the two most common in science and technology are the gaussian and the poisson distributions. See gaussian distribution, poisson distribution.

probability theory A branch of mathematics dealing with the study of chance events, used to predict quantities that characterize the behaviour of a population of such events.

problem oriented language In computer

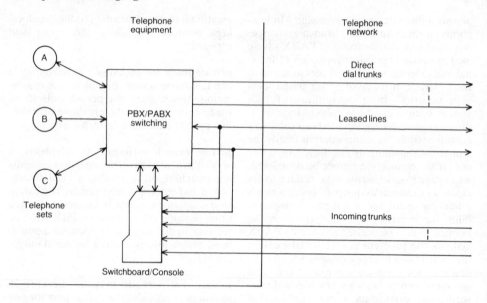

Telephone
equipment

Telephone
network

A

B

C

Telephone
sets

PBX/PABX
switching

Direct
dial trunks

Leased lines

Incoming trunks

Switchboard/Console

private branch exchange

programming, a high level language developed for the convenient expression of a
specified set of problems. See report program generator, procedure oriented
language.

procedural language   In computer programming, a conventional high level language,
e.g. Pascal, in which the programmer specifies the actions necessary to attain the desired
result. Compare non procedural language.
See Pascal.

procedure   In computer programming, (1)
the course taken for the solution of a problem, (2) a subroutine. See subroutine.

procedure oriented language   In computer
programming, a high level language oriented
towards a given class of procedures. See
FORTRAN, COBOL, PL/1.

process   A course of events occurring in
accordance with an intended purpose or
effect.

process camera   (1) In printing, a camera
specially designed for process work, e.g. halftone making, colour separation. (2) In cine-
matorgraphy, a camera designed for special
effects. See halftone.

process control   The use of feedback control
systems in the context of a manufacturing or
industrial process. See feedback.

process engraving   In printing, the production of a letterpress printing plate by printing
down a photographic image onto a plate and
etching it to form a relief printing surface.
See letterpress, relief printing.

processing   In computing, the manipulation
of data in solving a problem.

process inks   In printing, inks used in three
colour and four colour printing processes.
See four colour process, three colour
process.

processor   In computing, a device or system
capable of performing operations upon data.
A central processing unit is a hardware processor, a compiler is a language processor.
See central processing unit, compiler,
hardware.

processor controlled keying   In computing, a
technique in which a data entry operator is
assisted by a computer which provides
prompts, performs formatting and validation
checks.

processor utilization In computing, the proportion of processor time spent in performing useful and necessary tasks in relation to the total available time.

product The result of multiplying two quantities.

production cycle In printing, the cycle towards final production includes mark up, original keyboarding, correction keyboarding, typesetting, proof reading, corrections, page make up and author's corrections. See markup, proofreading, typesetting.

production run In computing, a routine execution of a commonly used program, e.g. calculation of pay checks.

program In computing, a complete series of definitions and instructions, conforming to the syntax of a given computer language, that when executed on a computer will perform a required task. See source program, object program, programming, syntax.

program call In an electronic learning laboratory, a system that enables an instructor to make announcements to those students listening to specific program channels. Compare all call.

program check In computing, a condition arising when programming errors are detected by an I/O channel. See I/O.

program counter In computing, a register that holds the address of the next program instruction to be executed. Program counters are incremented for most instructions but branch instructions cause new address values to be inserted. See branch, register.

program development In computer programming, the process of writing, inputting, translating and debugging a source program. See source program, translator, debug.

program execution time In computing, the interval during which the instructions of an object program are executed. See object program.

program function key In computing, a key on a computer terminal that (1) invokes a

utility, e.g. to perform scrolling, (2) can be programmed by the user, e.g. to insert a repetitive line of data. Compare function key.

program language In computer programming, a set of rules to define the manner in which data structures are formulated and the processing instructions are written and organized. See high level language, low level language, programming.

program library In computing, a collection of available general purpose computer programs held off line or on backing store. See backing store, off line.

program listing In computer programming, a printout produced by a translation process displaying the source program, error messages and relevant information on the object program. See source program, object program.

programmable In computing, (1) pertaining to a device that can store a sequence of user defined instructions and perform them, (2) pertaining to a microcomputer device that can be adjusted by the user as compared with fabrication. See programmable read only memory.

programmable logic array In computing, a read only memory programmed to perform logic operations. Compare uncommitted logic array. See logical operator, read only memory.

programmable read only memory In computing, a form of ROM that can be programmed by a user. Blank memory chips are purchased and the required data is input to the chip in a special device (PROM programmer). See ROM, EPROM, PROM programmer.

programmer (1) In computing, a person who writes programs. (2) In audiovisual aids, a multifunction, multichannel controller. A programmer operates in conjunction with a tape recorder or computer with stored instructions, or it may contain its own internal storage. Upon receipt of a signal from an external, or possibly internal synchronizer, the programmer selects the next control function from storage and performs the corresponding action, e.g. turning on lights, selecting a new slide for projection etc. See synchronizer, program.

programming The process by which a computer is made to perform a specialised task. It involves the creation of a formalised sequence of instructions which can be recognised and implemented by the machine. These instructions (the program) are a static entity, but when executed they result in a useful information handling process. All programs are concerned, either directly or indirectly, with the flow of information. Data, whether stated explicitly or made an intrinsic component of the program, is used as an input which is then processed, or computed, to generate an output. All of the functions performed by a computer depend, at some stage, upon a program.

The instructions are encoded into a specific programming language, different languages vary both structurally and syntactically, thus programs are specific to one language, the choice of which depends on both the application and computer for which it is intended. Common examples include BASIC, Pascal PL/1, COBOL, APL, LISP and various low level languages, each having its characteristic uses and limitations.

See (a) The components of a program, (b) Data representation and structure, (c) Languages, (d) Future trends.

(a) The components of a program. Very broadly speaking, all program commands may be split into two categories. Firstly, those responsible for the manipulation of data within a system: these perform what we recognise as the actual computation. They can be divided into three fundamental classes:

(i) Reading in values from the external environment.

BASIC: INPUT A, B, C

(ii) Assigning values to the variables.

BASIC: A = A + 2

T$= 'The quick brown fox'

(iii) Sending data to output.

BASIC: PRINT Q.

The range and power of such commands varies enormously between languages. This is particularly noticeable when comparing high and low level languages.

The second category comprises commands

governing the flow of control through a program. Whilst their syntactic construction may vary, virtually all programming languages embody four basic structures:

(i) Sequential commands or statements. The instructions are expressed as a simple list, and are executed consecutively in the order given. Each command is thus only performed once.

PASCAL: A: = B; B:= C; WRITELN(B);

(ii) Conditions. These are used to select between different sets of commands, depending upon the parameters specified within them. They can thus alter the sequence of execution through a program and options will be taken or omitted depending on whether the boolean expressions attached to them evaluate as true or false.

PASCAL: IF (K = 0) AND NOT FLAGSET THEN K: = 10;

(iii) Repetition. Almost inevitably, groups of commands will need to be performed many times during the execution of a non-trivial program. This is achieved by creating a loop, within the program, which retains control of the machine until a certain condition has been fulfilled. Often this is arranged so that the loop will be executed a predetermined number of times.

PASCAL: WHILE K>6 DO K: = (K + DELTA) / 2;

or FOR COUNT: 1 TO 10 DO WRITELN (COUNT);

(iv) Abstraction or encapsulation. This involves labelling a subset of commands in some manner and then later accessing them via that label. Hence the programmer can attain increasing levels of abstraction from the original instruction set by attaching an intricate computation to a single label. This can give rise to two entities: a procedure (or subroutine) which produces an effect, or a function which yields a value. PASCAL; PROCEDURE MESSAGE;

BEGIN

WRITE ('Hello')

END;

.

.

.

BEGIN (—Main program body—)

MESSAGE (—Causes 'Hello' to be printed—)

These structures can be combined by nesting one within another, for example, conditions can be embodied within a sequence of statements, i.e. one after another, or else the branches from one condition can lead to further conditions, and so on, thus creating a decision tree. Loops may also be enclosed within other loops and subroutines may call other subroutines, or even themselves (recursion). As a result, very complex structures can be developed.

The universality of these structures is of great importance to the design of algorithms (which detail the abstract method by which a task is to be performed), for it allows them considerable independence from the programming language ultimately to be used. For an application of any complexity top down programming is generally preferred, whereby the task is split into a few large modules, whose interaction is described using similar structures to those above. Each of these modules is in turn reduced to a few submodules etc. and thus a hierarchical descent to ever lower levels of abstraction is obtained. Eventually the finest subdivisions will approach the same degree of abstraction as the data manipulation instructions available in the chosen programming language, and program coding may now begin.

(b) Data representation and structure. All of the information used by a computer has to be stored as a series of binary bits. Usually only the machine code programmer need be concerned with this, because high level languages seek to provide their users with more natural data structures.

Typically, decimal numbers are handled directly in either real or integer form. Real values are not represented exactly and their precision will depend on the number of bits allocated to store them. For exact work, care must be taken to ensure that cumulative rounding errors don't erode accuracy too far. The programmer will also have to be aware of the largest and smallest values the language can handle, and in some cases a choice of precisions will be available. High precision, however, will be less economical in storage and processing time.

Text can normally be employed direct, i.e. literals or manipulated via text variables or strings. Typical string operations allow access to substrings and concatenation ('AB' + 'CDE' = 'ABCDE'). Note that spaces will also count as characters, and that non-printing control characters can usually be included in strings. Boolean variables and expressions are often implemented, being restricted to the values true or false they are invaluable for condition processing.

In addition to these fundamental data types, most languages provide data structures within which many variables can be ordered and contained. The most common of these is the array, analogous to the mathematical matrix, which holds a value in each of its elements and may be multidimensional. Elements are accessed via their subscript(s), one for each dimension, e.g. a rectangular array would require the row and column to be given. Using these structures, many variables can be accessed in turn through the application of program loops.

PASCAL: FOR K: = 1 TO 10 DO VECTOR (K):= K — K;

The above example would place the first ten perfect squares in VECTOR (1) TO VECTOR (10) respectively, so that e.g. VECTOR (7) = 49.

More advanced structures such as records allow the user to collate different data types into a framework of their own design. Thus many facets of an item can be stored and processed conveniently, e.g. a personnel record may contain fields for NAME, EMPLOYEE, NUMBER, DEPARTMENT, ADDRESS.

The distinction between literals and variables should be clearly understood. A literal is an explicitly declared value (e.g. 4·5 whilst a variable comprises an identifier which can adopt a particular value (e.g. x = 2).

Fundamental data types are not generally interchangeable except where one is a subset of another (integer values may be assigned to real variables but not vice versa) and the programmer must exercise caution when mixing them. There are usually some facilities for converting between types, e.g. functions to truncate real values to integers, or to yield numbers in character string format.

(c) Languages. Perhaps surprisingly, programming languages do not generally vary in their ultimate power of computation. Once they have passed a certain 'critical mass', as all but the most trivial must do, each becomes capable of implementing any intuitively computable function. The huge variety of languages now available have arisen to satisfy other considerations.

Current programming languages divide most significantly into the low level, which closely relate to the machine code instruction set of the computer and consists mainly of symbolic assemblers, and the high level which offer radical abstraction from the internal workings of the machine towards more convenient notations. Variations within the first category primarily reflect different machine architectures (number/size of registers, addressing facilities, ALU capabilities).

Low level languages have two great advantages: speed and compactness. As a result, they may be used for writing operating systems, I/O handling etc. where time and storage space are at a premium. Unfortunately, they are not so well suited to everyday applications for the following reasons:

(i) In order to use such a language, the programmer must have substantial familiarity with the internal organization and functioning of the machine. The constraints imposed by the instruction set and data representation make apparently trivial tasks (like the addition of two decimal numbers) very complex tasks.

(ii) The actual program code is very difficult to read, thus making correction and debugging time-consuming.

(iii) There exists no clear distinction between instructions and data, and these can easily be interposed due to a program error. It can also prove difficult for the operating system to protect against loss of user control or valuable information under such circumstances.

(iv) Low level languages are specific to one microprocessor.

For these reasons, high level languages have gained widespread popularity. Their command sets are far more versatile and operate upon handy data types, programs are easier to understand (most noticeably in the structured languages, e.g. PASCAL) and there is no danger of confusion between instructions and data. A good degree of protection can be provided against accidental interference with prohibited areas of memory and advanced debugging facilities are normally available. In theory they also provide for program portability between machines, but the emergence of dialectic variations within most has greatly impaired this, particularly amongst microcomputers.

Speed and memory consumption are not such prominent concerns when choosing a high level language, and the main differences between them fall under the headings:

(i) Ease of use. Certain languages encourage structured, readable programming far more than others. This is crucial to large computing installations where software maintenance is frequently more expensive than its initial development and any factors that simplify modifications are at a premium.

(ii) Applications. The facilities offered by a language determine its suitability to a given task. Certain environments may require advanced file handling, precision maths, automatic graph plotting etc. and the user will naturally give preference to a language that supports their demands. Several languages are strongly biased towards a quite specialised field, e.g. LISP (list processing, AI), PILOT (computer assisted learning). Programs do not have to be written entirely in one language. For instance, most high level languages allow calls to be made to machine code subroutines and the resultant hybrid may combine the advantages of both categories.

(d) Future trends. Computing folklore holds that small programs are rarely correct: large programs, never. The truth behind this seemingly cynical outlook has dogged users and support programmers alike as ever more large software installations become unwieldy, unreliable and often downright impenetrable. As a result much attention has focused upon software engineering, whose aims are far broader than just tidying up slipshod techniques for serious theoretical questions centre around both program proving and task specification. Experience has also shown ease of modification to be critical, as few big systems, no matter how carefully conceived, can avoid the need for small functional alterations. Good program structure alone is insufficient here, since the best laid out code may conceal a minefield of assumptions and logical niceties from the unwary.

The most significant development, then, in the next few years, will probably be a radical alteration in the way that we program, in the form of fourth generation, very high level languages. These exemplify the 'non-procedural' approach of telling the computer

WHAT you require as opposed to the 'procedural' languages of today which have to be told HOW to do it. These languages will have to employ artificial intelligence techniques, especially knowledge-based, in order to achieve this and a strong element of heuristics may emerge. Nevertheless, the attainment of 100% program reliability seems a long way off.

The popularity of standard business packages may also be at stake. Most are too inflexible to serve the wide range of individual needs found in the real world and customization, where available, is expensive for the reasons discussed above. Conversely, few end users are willing to write programs from scratch. The resultant demand gap is widening so that spreadsheet programs like VISICALC and its derivatives, which provide an environment easily tailored by even the inexperienced to a variety of applications, are likely to corner a large section of the market. See algorithm, APL, BASIC, boolean algebra, COBOL, data structure, decision tree, field, fourth generation languages, high level language, instruction, I/O, LISP, low level language, machine code, non procedural language, Pascal, PILOT, PL/1, procedural language, real number, record, software, string, variable.

programming aids In computer programming, computer programs provided to aid the user, e.g. compilers, debugging packages, linkage editors, mathematical subroutines, etc. See compiler, linking, debug.

program monitor In an electronic learning laboratory, a system that enables the instructor to monitor the content and volume level of an audio stimulus, before, or during transmission to students.

program specification In computer programming, a document providing complete details of a program, giving its function, files accessed, input output requirements, etc.

program stack In computing, an area of storage reserved for a system stack, e.g. to store computer states during an interrupt. See stack, interrupt.

program statement In computer programming, an expression or a generalized instruction in a source language. See source language.

program stop In computer programming, an instruction that will cause the execution to stop, e.g. upon completion of the process. See halt.

program switch In computer programming, a branch point in a program such that the subsequent path depends upon a condition elsewhere in the program or by some physical state in the system. See branch.

progressive disclosure In audiovisual aids, the process of building up a composite image, e.g. by removing masks on an overhead transparency or adding a new element, or a new slide, whilst retaining images already exposed. See overhead projector.

progressives In printing, pertaining to a set of proofs showing each plate of a colour set printed in its appropriate colour and in registered combination. See register.

projection In relational databases, an operation in relational algebra. A projection on a given relation, specifying attributes of that relation, produces a second relation containing only those attributes with all duplicates removed. See relational algebra.

projection/sound programmer In audiovisual aids, a device that controls a combined system of sound recorders and projection equipment.

projector (1) In cinematography, a device to throw motion picture images onto a screen and, with some devices, to reproduce sound from the film soundtrack. (2) In audiovisual aids, a device to throw slide images onto a screen.

projector dissolve control In audiovisual aids, a device that controls two or more images so that one can dissolve into or over another.

PROLOG In computer programming, PROgramming in LOGic, a non procedural language used in development of expert systems. See non procedural language.

PROM See programmable read only memory.

PROM burner See PROM programmer.

PROM programmer In computing, a device to input data into a PROM chip. See microcomputer, programmable read only memory.

prompting In computing, a method of requesting specific types of data input from a terminal user by visual messages and, sometimes, audible signals.

proof In typesetting, a sample of a printed output taken for proofreading. See proof-reading.

proofing press In printing, a press used for producing proofs rather than an extensive number of copies. See proof.

proofreading In printing, a detailed examination of a proof for punctuation, spelling and typographical errors. See proof.

propagated error In computing, an error in one operation that affects data used in subsequent operations so that the error spreads through much of the processed data.

propagation delay In communications, the transit time for a signal from one point in the circuit to another.

proportional spacing In printing, pertaining to printed or displayed text in which each alphanumeric character is given a weighted amount of space according to its width, i.e. an 'i' occupies less space than an 'm'.

Prospector In computing, an expert system designed to emulate the reasoning process of an experimental geologist in assessing a given prospective site or region for its likelihood of containing ore deposits of the type represented by the model. See expert systems.

protected field In computing, data on a visual display screen that may not be modified by an operator. Compare unprotected field.

protected location In computing, an area of storage whose contents are protected against accidental or improper alteration, or unauthorized access.

protected space In word processing, an empty space and associated words treated as an entity. If a text is reformatted the space and the words will be contained in a single line and not split. Synonymous with required space.

protected storage See protected location.

protection key In computing, an indicator used to check if a specified program may access a given block of storage.

protection master In filming and recording, (1) an intermediate duplicate of a film from which prints are made, to protect the original, (2) a spare, reserve copy of a sound recording.

protection ratio In communications, the minimum value of the required to unrequired signal ratio, at the receiver input, under specified conditions, such that the specified reception quality of the required signal is achieved at the receiver output.

protocol In data communications, a formally specified set of conventions governing the format and control of inputs and outputs between two communicating systems.

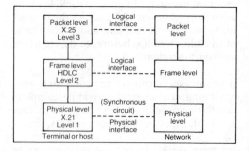

protocol
Levels of communication protocols.

protocol standards In data communications, defined protocols which facilitate communication amongst a wide body of users. Early protocols merely provided for the interconnection of similar devices and the Arpanet was an exception which permitted the interconnection of any two devices. Some early protocols, e.g. BISYNC, became ad hoc standards since they were adopted by many other manufacturers. There are two international bodies concerned with standards - CCITT and ISO. CCITT is responsible for standards in the field of public telecommunication services. It is a permanent committee of the ITU and its best known recommendations are the V and X-series for analog and digital data transmission. ISO has a large number of member bodies, one or each participating country - BSI in the UK, ANSI in USA, AFNOR in France. Other bodies such as CCITT and ECMA are also represented. The European Conference of Post and Telecommunications Administrations undertake standardization in the field of telephony extending into other facilities provided by PTTs, e.g. digital data networks. National organizations such as the IEEE promulgate standards, e.g. RS 232, equivalent to CCITT V.24 and a local area network standard IEEE 802. See AFNOR, ANSI, ARPA, BISYNC, BSI, CCITT, EGMA, IEEE, IEEE 802, ISO, ITU, local area network, PTT, RS 232, V, X.

proton An electrically positive charged particle in the nucleus of an atom. Compare electron.

PSE See packet switching exchange.

psec Synonymous with picosecond.

pseudocode In computer programming, an arbitrary set of symbols to represent components of a program, i.e. registers, operands, etc.

pseudorandom number In computing, a number, generated by a specific algorithm, to approximate to a random number. Such algorithms are designed to produce numbers with specified statistical properties. See random number.

PSN See public switched network.

PSS In data communications, Packet Switch Stream, a national, public, switched data service provided by British Telecom. It provides full duplex working up to 48 kilobits

per second. See Megastream, Satstream, Kilostream.

PsycInfo A database supplied by American Psychological Association and dealing with psychology. See on line information retrieval.

PTS Files A collection of databases, supplied by Predicasts Inc. and dealing with business and industry. See on line information retrieval.

PTT See Post Telephone and Telegraph.

p-type material In electronics, a semiconductor material doped with an impurity that has electron accepting nuclei. These impurities effectively produce holes that move through the medium providing positive charge carriers. Compare n-type material. See semiconductor devices, hole.

public address system An audio system with a microphone and loudspeaker to enable a speaker to pass information to a large or remote audience.

publication language In computing, a language that does not contain special characters unavailable in common type fonts, i.e. one suitable for publication in books or journals. See font.

public data network In data communications, a network to supply a data transmission service to the public, provided by a public authority or recognized private operating agency.

public dial port In a packet network, a dial-in port providing access to the network from a terminal connected to the public telephone network. Compare private dial port.

public domain In copyright, material which has not been copyrighted or for which the copyright has expired. See copyright.

public key cryptosystem In data security, a method enabling a variety of senders to encode a message for a recipient whilst only the recipient can decode it. The senders use one key, made public, whilst only the recipient is in possession of a second key required to decipher the received messages. See cryptographic key.

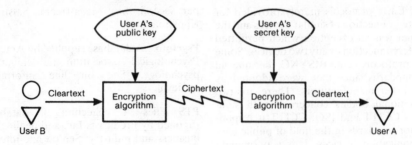

public key cryptosystem

public switched network In communications, a switching system that provides switching transmission facilities to customers.

pulldown In micrographics, the length of film advanced after each exposure.

pull up a line In electronics, to place a voltage corresponding to a specified logic state on an input connection.

pulp In printing, fibrous material of vegetable origin that provides the raw material for paper making.

pulse In electronics, a change in a voltage or current level for a short duration, typically an increase from zero to 5 volts for a few milli- or microseconds.

pulse amplitude modulation In communications, a method of pulse modulation in which the amplitude of a train of pulses is adjusted in accordance with the input signal. See pulse modulation.

pulse code modulation In communications, a technique for transmitting analog information in digital form. The analog signal is sampled, and the sampled value represented by a fixed length binary number. This number is then transmitted as a corresponding set of pulses. In telephony, the sampling rate is 8000 per second. See pulse, analog signal, sampling, pulse modulation.

pulse duration modulation In communications, a pulse modulation technique in which the width of the pulse, in a pulse train, is adjusted in accordance with the input

signal. See pulse modulation. Synonymous with pulse width modulation.

pulse generator In electronics, a device to generate a specified type of pulse or pulse train. See pulse, pulse train.

pulse modulation In communications, a signal transmission system in which the information content is impressed upon a pulse train by adjusting the pulse amplitude (PAM), pulse duration (PDM), pulse position (PPM) or by binary codes based upon the presence and absence of pulses (PCM). See pulse amplitude modulation, pulse duration modulation, pulse position modulation, pulse code modulation.

pulse period In electronics and communications, the time interval between the leading edges of two successive periodic pulses. See pulse, period.

pulse position modulation In communications, a pulse modulation method in which the timing of the individual pulses, in a pulse train, depends upon the modulating signal. See pulse modulation.

pulse regenerator In electronics, a device that accepts a distorted pulse and produces a well shaped one. See pulse.

pulse repetition rate In electronics and communications, the number of pulses per unit time. See pulse.

pulse train In electronics and communications, a series of pulses having similar characteristics. A method of conveying binary information in which the presence, or

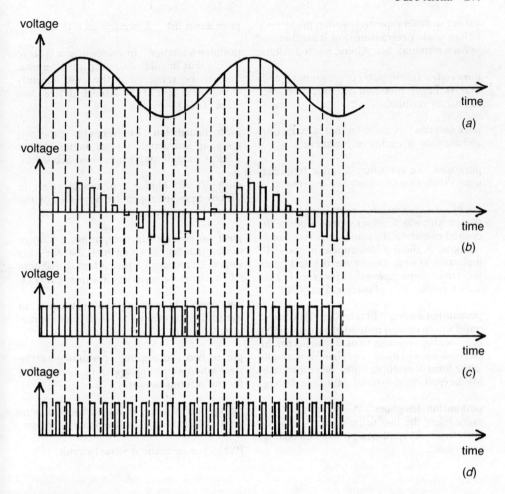

pulse modulation
Three types of pulse modulation: (a) the sampled message signal; (b) pulse amplitude modulation; (c) pulse duration (width) modulation; (d) pulse position modulation.

absence, of a pulse represents a binary one or zero respectively. See pulse, binary code.

pulse width modulation Synonymous with pulse duration modulation.

punched card In computing, a medium for recording data in binary coded format. Characters are recorded by punching a pattern of holes vertically across a stiff paper card and normally 80 characters may be stored. Punched cards have now been largely superseded by floppy disks. Compare paper tape.

punched card code In computing, the relationship between the set of holes punched

vertically across the card and the data it is intended to convey. See hollerith code.

punched tape code See paper tape code.

punching station In punch card equipment, the area on the punch machine where the card is aligned for the punching process. See punched card.

Pure Aloha In packet switching, a technique employed in the Aloha system when packet collision occurs. Retransmission is initiated when the terminal does not receive an acknowledgement within a time out interval but to avoid repeated overlap the interval before packet retransmission is randomized in each terminal. See Aloha, Slotted Aloha.

pure code In computer programming, code that is never modified in execution. See re-entrant routine.

pure notation A notation that is exclusively alphabetical or exclusively numeric.

pure tone In acoustics, a single frequency sound without overtones. See overtones.

purity In television, pertaining to the degree with which colour signals produce the desired colour on the screen of a receiver or monitor. A slight misalignment of the CRT deflection system can cause the red beam (say) to strike phosphor dots for green or blue screen colour. See phosphor dots, CRT.

pushbutton dialing In telephony, the use of pushbuttons or keys instead of a rotary dial to generate the sequence of dialing digits for the establishment of a call. The signal is normally in the form of multiple tones. See touchtone, MF keypad. Synonymous with tone dialing.

pushbutton telephone A system in which users select the line to be used by pressing buttons on a keypad. See pushbutton dialing, touchtone.

push down list Synonymous with stack.

pushdown storage In computing, a storage device that handles data such that the next item to be retrieved is the most recently stored item still in the storage device. See stack, LIFO.

push instruction In computer programming, an instruction to store an item on the stack. Compare pop instruction. See stack.

push off In filming, an optical effect in which one image appears to be pushed off the screen by another.

push up storage In computing, a storage device that handles data such that the next item to be retrieved is the earliest stored item still in the storage device. See queue, FIFO.

put down In printing, an instruction to the printer to change to lower case characters. Compare put up. See lower case.

put to bed In printing, pertaining to the state when a printing apparatus is prepared for the printing action.

put up In printing, an instruction to a printer to change to capitals. Compare put down.

PVC See permanent virtual circuit.

Q

quad See em quad, en quad.

quadding In printing, the action of putting abnormal spacing between words in order to fill out a line. See quad.

quadrophonic A frequency modulation broadcast or audio recording system using four speakers, two in front of and two behind the listener. Compare stereophonic.

quadruplex In video recording, a system using four recording or replay heads on a wheel. See transverse scan.

quadruture error In video recording, a playback error condition that arises if the recording, or reading, heads do not arrive at the edge of the tape at the same relative time. See quadruplex. Synonymous with switching error.

quaint characters See ligatures.

quantifier In relational databases, a term used in a relational calculus expression. There are two quantifiers used, the existential quantifier read as 'there is', and the universal quantifier that is read as 'for all'. See relational calculus.

quantize In communications, to assign one of a fixed set of values to an analog signal as part of an analog to digital conversion process, e.g. in pulse code modulation, an analog signal is sampled, quantized and a corresponding set of binary pulses is produced. See pulse code modulation.

quantizing noise In communications, noise arising from the process of analog to digital and subsequent digital to analog conversion. The quantization process produces discrepancies in the input and output analog signals. See quantize, COMPANDOR.

Qube In cable television, on experimental systems in Columbus, Ohio, where a two way facility has been used to enable viewers to respond to TV programs and vote on referenda.

queue (1) In data structures, a list in which items are added at one end and removed from the other. (2) Processes or items awaiting service on a FIFO principle. Compare stack. See list, FIFO.

queuing theory A branch of probability theory used in the study of queues. Given the statistical properties of the servicing and arrival process, it attempts to predict the statistical properties of the queues, i.e. average length, waiting time, etc.

queuing time In communications, the time spent in waiting to send, or receive, a message due to contention on the line. See circuits, in which the output can vary with minor changes in the relative time of arrival of input pulses. Compare hazard.

qwerty keyboard a converrntional typewriter keyboard with the letters q, w, e, r, t and y on the upper left hand side. Compare azerty keyboard. See word processing.

R

race In electronics, an undesirable state, produced by poor design of digital circuits, in which the output can vary with minor changes in the relative time of arrival of input impulses. Compare hazard.

rack (1) In electronics, a metal frame or chassis for the mounting of items of equipment. (2) In photography, to focus a lens.

radial transfer In computing, the transmission of data between a peripheral unit and another device that is closer to the centre than the peripheral unit.

radiant energy The energy of a sinusoidal wave is proportional to the square of the amplitude of oscillation. See photon.

radiating element In radiocommunications, a basic unit of an antenna designed to produce electromagnetic radiation. See antenna.

radio In communications, a service for the transmission of speech and music by electromagnetic radiation, See radiocommunication, radio waves, electromagnetic radiation, GHz, kHz.

radiocommunication Telecommunication by means of electromagnetic waves at radio frequencies. See radio waves.

radio frequency In communications, any frequency that can be used for communication by means of electromagnetic radiation. The range is considered to extend from a few hertz to 300 gigahertz but radio frequency communication now extends into the infrared and visible light frequency ranges. See fiber optics, giga, hertz, infrared.

radio microphone A microphone combined with a low range radio transmitter, thus requiring no connecting wires to an amplifier, used for studio or location work. See amplifier, transmitter.

radio paging In communications, a method of contacting a user by means of a small portable radio receiver. The caller dials a number on an ordinary telephone and the called party receives a bleep from the pager. Current systems can emit four tones to convey varying information. Other devices can display a numerical, or alphanumerical, message.

radiotelegraphy In communications, the transmission of telegraph codes by electromagnetic radiation. See telegraphy.

radio waves Electromagnetic waves with frequencies in the range 10kHz - 3000GHz. See GHz, electromagnetic radiation, kHz.

radix In a radix numeration system the total value of a numeral represented by a string of characters is the sum of each character multiplied by its weight. The ratio of the weight of one digit to the preceding one is the radix for the number system used, and is always a positive integer. Thus in a hexadecimal system the radix is 16 and the number 123 has the decimal value of 291 = (1x16x16+2x16+3). See base, hexadecimal.

radix point In a radix numeration system, the character, or implied character, that separates the integral part of the numeral from the fractional part, e.g. decimal point. See radix.

ragged centre In printing, ragged setting in which any necessary additional spaces are added equally to the left and right of the text. If the total number of necessary additional spaces is not an equal number then the remaining space is added to the left of the text. See ragged setting.

ragged left In printing, ragged setting with the text set flush with the right hand margin and any necessary additional spaces added to the left of the text. See ragged setting.

ragged right In printing, ragged setting with the text set flush to the left hand margin and any necessary additional spaces added to the right of the text. See ragged setting.

ragged setting In printing, the method used

to adjust the length of a line to its desired measure when one interword space value is used. Additional spaces are added to the right or left of text as necessary giving a ragged appearance on at least one side. See measure, ragged left, ragged right, ragged centre.

raise a line Synonymous with pull up a line.

RAM See random access memory.

RAM disk Synonymous with virtual disk.

RAM refresh operation In computing, an operation necessary because dynamic RAM devices require a periodic rewrite operation to ensure that their contents are retained. See dynamic RAM.

random access In computing, access to data such that the next location from which a word or byte is to be retrieved is independent of the location of previously accessed word or byte. Compare direct access, serial access. See word.

random access memory In computing, (1) a memory chip used with microprocessors, information can be both read from, and written into, the memory but the contents are lost when the power supply is removed, (2) any form of storage in which the access time for any item of data is independent of the location of the data most recently obtained, e.g. immediate access store has a random access capability but magnetic disk does not. See immediate access store, magnetic disk.

random access projector In audiovisual devices, a projector that permits the selection of any sequence of slides independent of their order in the slide tray.

random access storage See random access memory.

random interlace In television, a camera system in which the positioning of horizontal lines of each succeeding vertical field is not fixed and the line spacing may vary in a random manner. Compare positive interlace. See field, interlace.

random number In computing, a number

used to represent a random, or chance, event in games, simulations, etc. See pseudorandom number, simulator, video game.

random process A process in which the output cannot be fully predetermined from a knowledge of the system variables. One in which the outcome depends upon one or more random events.

range The difference between the highest and lowest value that a function or quantity may assume.

ranging figures Synonymous with lining figures.

rank (1) To arrange in ascending or descending order according to some criterion. (2) A measure of the relative position in an array, group, series or classification.

RA paper sizes Synonymous with A, B and C series of paper sizes.

rapid access processing In photography, a method of processing exposed photographic film or paper using high temperature chemistry and shallow bath processing to produce dry products in under two minutes.

raster In computer graphics, and television, a predetermined pattern of lines, that provide uniform coverage of display space.

raster scan In television and computer graphics, a technique for recording or displaying an image by a line by line sweep across the entire display area.

rate center In telephony, a given geogra-

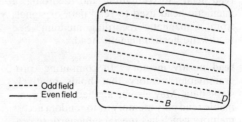

raster scan
A scan with two interlaced fields. A to B and C to D.

phic location used by telephone companies as the reference point to determine the mileage measurements in the determination of inter-exchange rates.

ratemaking   In communications, the process of determining the appropriate level of charges to be set by a common carrier for its services. See common carrier.

ratio   The result of dividing the first specified quantity by the second, e.g. the ratio of 6 to 2 is 3.

rational number   Any number that can be expressed by the ratio of two integers where the divider is nonzero.

raw data   In computing, unprocessed and nonreduced data.

raw tape   (1) In recording, blank magnetic tape not previously used for recording. (2) In printing, unjustified tape. See unjustified tape.

R & D   Research and Development.

read   In computing, to acquire or interpret data from an input device, store or some other medium.

reader   (1) In computing, a device that converts data from one form of storage into another. (2) In printing, one who reads text for a specific purpose. See copyreader.

reader/printer   In micrographics, a reader that produces hard copy enlargements of specified microimages See microform reader/-printer.

read head   In computing and recording, a magnetic head used to read data or signals from a magnetic recording medium. See read/write head, magnetic head.

read mostly memory   In computing, programmable memory that holds relatively static data. May also be applied to programmable read only memory or to random access memory which has special safeguards to prevent overwriting. See programmable read only memory, random access memory.

read only memory   In computing, a storage device whose contents can only be changed by a particular user, by particular operating conditions or by a particular external process. Read only storage can include storage media where the writing action is inhibited by the operating system or by some mechanical device, e.g. a tag on a diskette. The term ROM implies a storage device not designed to be modified by conventional write procedures and which is used to store permanent information in computers and microcomputers, e.g. the operating system and BASIC interpreters are supplied in ROM on microcomputers. See PROM, EPROM, diskette, interpreter, operating system.

read only storage   See read only memory.

read out   In computing, the retrieval of stored data. See read.

read/write head   In computing and recording, a magnetic head capable of both reading and writing actions. See magnetic head.

ready state   In communications, a condition at the DTE/DCE interface that indicates the DTE is prepared to accept an incoming call and the DCE is ready to accept a call request. See DCE, DTE, call request.

realia   Real objects as compared with models or representations of them.

real number   A number that may be represented by a finite or infinite number of digits in fixed radix numeration system. See radix.

realtime   In computing, pertaining to operations that are performed in conjunction with some external process or user and which are required to meet the time constraints imposed by that process or user, e.g. control of an aeroplane guidance system, an on line information service.

realtime clock   In computing, a hardware unit that produces a timing pulse train. The pulses are used to operate interrupts and thus synchronize computer operations with external events. See interrupt, pulse train.

realtime input   In computing, input data received into the system within a time scale, or at instants of time, determined by some other system. See realtime output.

realtime operation See realtime.

realtime output In computing, output data that must be delivered within a time scale, or at instants of time, determined by some other system. See realtime input.

realtime simulation One in which the times taken to perform specified operations on the simulator are equal to the corresponding timings of the real system. Realtime simulation enables components of the real system, including human operators, to operate in conjunction with a computer simulation of the remainder of the system. See simulator.

rear projection In filming, a method using a previously filmed background for a shot. The still, or moving, background is rear projected onto a translucent screen and the performers are filmed in front of this artificial background. Compare front projection.

rear screen A screen located between the projector and audience. It must be manufactured from translucent glass or plastic with a special coating. The slide or film must be reversed, or a mirror or prism used, to provide the correct image for the viewer.

reasonableness check In computing and communications, a test for the existence of a gross error, e.g. by checking that a data value lies within a prespecified range.

recall ratio In library science, the number of documents, retrieved from an index in response to a question on a given theme, divided by the number of documents on the theme known to be indexed. Compare relevance ratio.

receive only typing reperforator In communications, a receiving terminal in a teletypewriter system that prints incoming messages and also punches them on paper tape. Compare RONTR. See teletypewriter.

receive only In communications, terminals or other equipment capable of receiving data or messages but lacking a keyboard or other input device.

receiver In communications and broadcasting, a device used for detecting and decoding information transmitted down a line, or optical fiber, or as a radiated electromagnetic wave.

receiving perforator In communications, a punch converting telegraph type signals into hole patterns on paper tape. See telegraphy. Synonymous with reperforator.

reciprocity law In photography, the density of the developed negative image is proportional to the exposure time. See density.

recognition memory In optical character recognition, a read only memory in the optical character reader holding the bit patterns of characters in the font. This data is pattern matched with the corresponding information from the input character. See bit, read only memory.

reconfiguration To add or to remove components of a system or to change their interconnections.

record (1) In data processing, a collection of related data treated as a unit, e.g. details of name, address, age, occupation and department of an employee in a personnel file. (2) To store signals on a recording medium for later use. Compare field. See logical record, physical record.

record button In recording, a plastic button on video-cassettes that can be removed to prevent re-recording.

record current optimizer In recording, a device that facilitates the setting of the optimum current to the magnetic heads. The current to the recording head is adjusted in small steps and the audio playback voltage is monitored until it just reaches saturation. See magnetic head, saturation.

recorder A device used to make a permanent or temporary record of signals, emanating from an audio or audiovisual source. It will normally have playback as well as record facilities. See video recorder, video tape recorder, audio tape recorder, audio cassette recorder.

record gap　See interblock gap.

recording density　Synonymous with packing density.

recording trunk　In telephony, a line between a local exchange and a long distance office used for operator communications only.

record layout　In data processing, the manner in which the data is organized in the record, i.e. description and size of fields. See field.

record length　In data processing, the number of words or characters in a record. See word, record.

record separator character　In data processing, the indicator specifying the logical boundary between records. See record.

recoverable error　In computing, a condition that enables the program to continue execution after any necessary correcting action has been taken. Compare unrecoverable error.

recovery procedure　In data communications, a process whereby a specified station attempts to resolve erroneous or conflicting conditions arising from some malfunction or external situation in the transfer of data.

rectangular waveguide　In communications, waveguides of rectangular cross section used for the transmission of signals over relatively short distances, e.g. from a transmitter to an antenna. Compare circular waveguide. See waveguide.

rectification　In electronics and communications, the removal of the positive, or negative sections of a waveform. See rectifier.

rectifier　In electronics, a device to convert an alternating current into a direct current. See AC, DC, rectification.

recto　In printing, any right handed, odd numbered page of a book. Compare verso.

recursive routine　In computing, a routine that may be used as a routine of itself, calling itself directly or being called by another routine, one that it itself has called. For example in the computation of $n \times (n-1) \times (n-2)....x 1$, the routine is passed the parameter n, if n = 1 or 0 it returns the value of 1 otherwise it calls itself with the value (n - 1), multiplies the result of the call by n and returns the product. The routine continues to call itself until the value passed is 1 when the value of the routine, i.e. 1 is then returned and the successive calls then receive the routine values.

recursive subroutine　In computing, one that calls itself. The state of the subroutine must be stored in each successive call and the data representing the state is often stored on a stack. See stack, recursive routine.

red tape operation　In computing, an operation on data that is necessary for internal purposes but does not contribute to the final answer.

reduction　In micrographics, a measure of the linear relationship between the original and final image. A reduction of 16:1 is indicated as 16X. See low reduction, medium reduction, high reduction, very high reduction, ultra high reduction.

redundancy　(1) In communications, the fraction of the gross information content of a message that can be eliminated without losing any essential information. In computing and data communications, redundant characters, e.g. parity bits, are added to data to provide a method of detecting errors in transmission or processing. (2) The use of additional equipment or components to provide a backup facility. See parity checking, redundancy checking.

redundancy checking　In computing and data communications, the performance of a calculation on received data and comparison of results with redundant codes to check for certain processing or transmission errors. See redundant code.

redundant code　In computing and communications, additional bits added to characters for error checking purposes, e.g. parity bits and hamming codes. See redundancy checking, hamming code, parity checking.

reel fed   Synonymous with web fed.

reel to reel   Pertaining to the copying of signals, or data, from one reel of tape to another.

reel to reel recorder   A tape recorder using magnetic tape threaded on two reels. Compare cassette recorder.

re-entrant routine   In computing, a routine that may be repeatedly entered and may be entered before prior executions of the same routine have been completed. The calling programs must not, however, change any of the routine's instructions or external parameters. Such routines may be used simultaneously by a number of programs. See pure code.

reference mark   In printing, symbols that direct the reader to a footnote or to a given reference. Commmon reference marks are symbols termed asterisk, dagger, double dagger, section, parallel, and paragraph.

reference retrieval systems   In information retrieval, systems typified by the library card catalog, or other indexes, which provide a reference to a document in response to a general search request.

reference volume   In recording, the magnitude of an electrical signal, usually corresponding to speech or music waveforms, that gives a zero reading on a standard volume indicator. It corresponds to 1 milliwatt of power delivered to an electrical load of 600 ohms at 1000 hertz. See hertz, VUmeter.

reflectance   (1) In optics, the ratio between the quantity of light that is reflected from a given surface and the quantity of light incident on that surface. (2) In optical character recognition, a value assigned to a character or colour of ink relative to its background. Compare transmittance.

reflectance ink   In optical character recognition, an ink with a reflectance approximating to the acceptable paper reflectance level for the reader used. See reflectance.

reflected light   In optics, light incident upon a surface will be partly absorbed, partly transmitted and partly reflected, according to the optical properties of the material and the surface. If the surface is smooth then the rays of a narrow beam of incident light will strike the surface at the same angle, giving a reflected beam with an angle of reflection equal to the angle of incidence. An irregular, rough or matt reflecting surface will however produce diffuse light with the reflected rays having an almost infinite variety of directions.

reflected light meter   In photography, a meter indicating the quantity of light reflected from the subject or action field. See action field.

reflective disk   In video disk, an optical disk in which the laser beam is reflected off the shiny disk surface. Compare transmissive disk. See optical disk.

reflex   In photography, an optical mirror system that permits the viewing of the action field through the camera lens. See action field.

reflex camera   See reflex.

refraction   When light is transmitted through a number of different materials the direction of the rays change at each interface according to the optical properties of the two materials at the interface. See refractive index.

refractive index   In optics, a measure of the angle through which light is bent when it passes through the interface of two transparent media. The ratio of the sine of the angle of incidence to the sine of the angle of refraction is equal to the ratio of the refractive index of the second medium to that of the first. See refraction, sine.

refresh   (1) In computing, a signal sent to dynamic RAM to enable it to maintain its storage contents. (2) In computer displays, the technique of continuously energizing the phosphor coating of a CRT screen to keep the display visible. See CRT, dynamic RAM.

refreshed CRT   In computer displays, a

CRT screen that must be continually refreshed to keep the display visible. Compare storage tube. See refresh, CRT.

refresh RAM   See RAM refresh operation.

refresh rate   In computer displays, the number of times per second that a display is drawn on the screen of a refreshed CRT. See refreshed CRT.

regeneration   (1) In computer graphics, the process of repeatedly producing a display image on a screen of a CRT so that it remains visible. (2) In communications, the process of producing a duplicate of a message or data from an unambiguously recognizable but distorted signal, e.g. a set of on-off pulses attenuated in transmission. See pulse regenerator.

regenerative repeater   In telegraphy, a device used to receive signals, reform them to their original strength and forward them to the next station or repeater. See repeater.

register   (1) In computing and electronics, a memory device, usually high speed, and of limited specified length, e.g. one byte, one word, used for a special purposes, e.g. arithmetic operations. (2) In photography, the accurate superimposition of two images. (3) To react visibly to a stimulus. (4) In printing, a term to indicate the correct relationship of two or more print impressions.

registered design   Features of shape, configuration, pattern or ornament applied to an article by any industrial process or means, that have been registered with the appropriate authority.

register file   In computing, a bank of registers that can be used for the temporary storage of data or instructions. See register.

register insertion   In data communications, pertaining to a technique in which a message to be transmitted, in a local area network, is first loaded into a shift register. The network loop is broken and the shift register inserted either when it is idle or at a point between two adjacent messages. The message to be sent is then shifted out to the network, any message arriving during this period is shifted into the register behind the transmitted message.

Compare control token, daisy chain, message slot. See local area network.

register map   In computer programming, a worksheet used by machine code programmers to record and update computer register contents at appropriate points in the program. See machine code, register.

register marks   In printing, marks outside the job area of a trimmed printed sheet used to ensure an accurate register. See register.

regular reflection   Reflection from a smooth plane surface. See reflected light.

regular 8   In cinematography, 8 millimetre film with forty frames per foot. The perforations are the same size as 16 mm film and there is one perforation per frame line.

regulated power supply   In electronics, a source of voltage or current that holds its output level within specified limits irrespective of given variations in the input voltages or the current drawn from the unit. See power supply.

regulatory agency   In data communications, an agency controlling the specialized and common carrier tariffs. See common carrier, specialized common carrier, tariff.

relation   In databases, a flat file. In a relational database the data is stored as entities and attributes of those entities in two dimensional arrays, e.g. a relation might comprise employee name, employee number, department and salary. See relational database, flat file.

relational algebra   In relational databases, a language that provides a set of operators for manipulating relations, e.g. if there were two relations R1(employee number, employee department) and R2(employee number, project) and a user required to know which departments were involved with a given project then a set of operations would be specified and the resulting relation would comprise a table of departments associated with the project. See join, projection, relation, relational calculus.

relational calculus   In relational databases,

a language in which a user specifies the set of results required from the manipulation of the data. Relational calculus provides a concise unambiguous mathematical notation for statements such as:- take the two relations (employee number, project) and (employee number, department) and produce the relation (department) for project = DYNAMO. The result would be a list of departments whose employees were working on the DYNAMO project. Compare relational algebra. See relation.

relational database A database comprising a collection of relations. The relations may be manipulated and reconfigured by the database management system providing a very high degree of flexibility in the use of the data. See relation.

relational operator A symbol used to compare two values, e.g. > (greater than).

relative address In computer programming, an address specified in terms of its relationship to a given base address. See address.

relative data In computer graphics, values specifying displacements from the actual coordinates in a display space.

relative error Ratio of the absolute error of a quantity to its true, theoretically correct or specified value.

relative motion The motion of one object as observed from another. The motion of object A as seen from object B is the reciprocal of B's motion as observed by A. This effect can be exploited in filming by substituting a camera movement for that of the subject.

relay (1) In communications, a point to point reception and retransmission system. (2) In electronics, a single or multiple switch operated by an electromagnetic effect.

relay center Synonymous with message switching center.

release graphics In videotex, the complementary state to 'hold graphics', in which control characters are displayed as spaces. See hold graphics.

relevance ratio In library science, the number of retrieved documents actually required divided by the total number of documents retrieved in response to a question on a given theme. Compare recall ratio. Synonymous with precision ratio.

reliability The ability of a system to perform its function under specified conditions for a stated period of time.

relief printing A generic term for printing processes in which the inked image is on a raised surface. Compare planographic, intaglio. See letterpress.

relocatable program In computer programming, a program in a format that facilitates the modification of its addresses so that it can be easily relocated. An essential feature of programs executed in a multiprogramming system since, upon execution of one program, other programs may need to be shifted in the internal storage to avoid fragmentation of storage space. See relocate.

relocate In computing, to move a program from one area of internal storage to another, and to adjust its address values, so that it can be executed in its new location.

REM See recognition memory.

remainder The dividend minus the product of the quotient and the divider.

remainders In printing, copies of a book that is no longer selling at its original price.

remanence In ferromagnetic materials, the magnetic flux density that remains when the magnetic field is gradually increased to flux saturation and is then reduced to zero. See flux, ferromagnetic, coercivity, saturation.

remote batch processing See remote job entry.

remote control A system in which the desired control signals are transmitted over some distance, e.g. by connecting wires, radio, ultrasonic waves, etc.

remote job entry In computing, the submission of a job to a peripheral that is connected to the processor via a data link. See data link.

remote station In communications, (1) a station that can call, or be called by, a central station in a point to point switched network, (2) in a multipoint network, a tributary station. See tributary station, point to point connection.

remote terminal In computing and communications, (1) a terminal connected via a data link to a system, (2) a VDU with its own refresh memory, editing facilities and modem interface. See VDU, refresh, MODEM, edit.

repaginate In word processing, an editing facility that permits the operator to change the number of lines in each page after final editing. See edit.

repeat action key Synonymous with typamatic key.

repeater In communications, a bidirectional device used to amplify or regenerate signals in channels. Repeaters are spaced along long communication channels subject to excessive attenuation or interference. See attenuation.

repeating group In data processing, a group in a record that can occur any number of times, e.g. the names of dependants in an employee's file. It is not possible to predetermine the number of fields to be allocated to such a group and records with repeating groups cannot fit into flat files. See record, field, flat file.

reperforator In communications, a device that automatically punches paper tape from received signals.

reperforator transmitter In communications, a combination of a receiving reperforator and tape transmitter that can be used to relay messages from one teletypewriter channel to another. See reperforator, tape transmitter, teletypewriter.

repetitive letter Synonymous with form letter.

repertoire In computing, (1) a complete set

of machine code instructions for a computer, or family of computers, (2) a set of types of instruction for a high level language. See high level language, machine code.

replay In data security, a form of active wire tapping in which a message is first recorded and subsequently re-transmitted down a link. Encryption alone may not be sufficient to protect against this type of attack, since an opponent could simply replay previous ciphertext. See wire tapping.

report program generator In computer programming, a program that can generate other object programs which in turn produce user specified reports from a set of data. See object program.

reprint In printing, the production of subsequent copies of a publication.

reproduce To copy information so that both the original and duplicate are held on similar storage media.

reprogramming In computer programming, changing a program written for one computer so that it will run on another. See program.

reprographic printing A generic term encompassing spirit duplicating, ink duplicating, xerography and small offset printing. See spirit duplicator, xerography, offset printing.

repro proof In printing, a proof produced with great care, on best quality paper for use in photomechanical reproduction. See photomechanical.

reprotyping In printing, typing intended for photomechanical reproduction. See photomechanical.

required hyphen In word processing, a hyphen that is not deleted during repagination. See repaginate.

required page break In word processing, a special break instruction that is not deleted during repagination. See repaginate.

required space Synonymous with protected space.

rerun point In computer programming, an intermediate stage of the program from which the execution may be recommenced in the event of an execution error. A program may have more than one rerun point.

rescue dump In computing, a complete dump of computer storage and states onto a peripheral device so that, in the event of a major system failure, e.g. loss of power supply, the program can be recommenced at the state of the last rescue dump. See dump.

reset In computing, (1) to manually terminate a program on a microcomputer, (2) to restore a register, storage location or storage device to its initial state. (3) In electronics, to switch a flip flop output to zero. See flip flop, register.

reset key In computing, a control key to clear a program from the system; used as a last resort to regain control, e.g. when a program enters an endless loop. See endless loop, reset.

resident software In computing, any program held permanently in memory to provide a service to other programs, e.g. a resident compiler. See software, compiler.

residual error rate In communications, the ratio of the total number of bits, bytes or blocks incorrectly received but uncorrected or undetected by the error control device, to the total number of corresponding units transmitted.

residual magnetism In electronics, the magnetic effect that remains in a material when the external magnetic field is removed. See remanence.

resin covered paper In photography, a photographic high contrast paper used on phototypesetters. See contrast, phototypesetting.

resistance In electronics, an electrical property of a component relating the voltage drop across its terminals to the current

flowing through it. See voltage, Ohm's Law, current.

resistor In electronics, a device connected into a circuit to provide a specified electrical resistance. See resistance.

resolution The ability to distinguish fine detail. See resolving power.

resolver In recording, a unit controlling the speed of an audio playback device for tape or magnetic film. The speed is determined by sync pulses recorded with the original audio track. See synchronization, magnetic film.

resolving power In optics, the maximum number of equal width black and white lines per millimeter discernible in the image of an optical system, e.g. a lens. See resolution.

resonance A situation in which a system has a response to a particular excitation frequency that is much greater than its response to neighbouring frequencies.

resource sharing In computing and communications, the joint use of resources available on a system, or network, by users or peripherals, e.g. microcomputer users in a local area network can share a hard disk drive or printer. See hard disk, local area network.

responder (1) In communications, a device that automatically transmits a predetermined signal when activated by a received signal. (2) In audiovisual aids, a device that allows a student to respond to the teaching material, e.g. answer a multiple choice question. Compare transponder.

response frame In videotex, a viewdata frame that enables a user to send information to an IP, e.g. for booking a hotel room. See IP, frame.

response position In optical mark reading, the area designated for marking information on the form.

response time (1) The time taken by a system to attain a specified state or produce a specified output, after receiving an input. (2) In computing, the time between the gener-

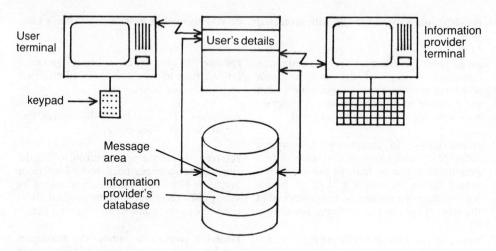

User terminal

keypad →

User's details

Information provider terminal

Message area

Information provider's database

response frame

ation of the last character at the terminal and receipt of the first character of the reply.

restore   In computing, to write data back into memory immediately after a destructive readout. See destructive readout.

reticle lines   In filming, fine guide lines in a camera viewfinder designating various points and areas, e.g. center of frame, television safe action area. See television safe action area.

retouching   In printing and photography, the skilled alteration of halftone images or photographs for improvement or correction.

retree   In printing, pertaining to a substandard batch of paper.

retrieval   In computing, the process of searching for, locating and reading out data.

retrieval center   In large viewdata networks, a computer center that hosts the viewdata base for a given set of users, or area, and receives updates from the update center. See update center.

retrofit   An add on accessory.

retrospective search   In library science, a search request in the form of a call for all

items published on a specific topic since a specified date.

return   In computing, (1) a return jump, (2) a key used to terminate the inputting of information from a keyboard. (3) In electronic typesetting, a code to indicate the end of a line. See carriage return, return jump.

return jump   In computer programming, an instruction terminating a subroutine and causing a branch to the instruction immediately following the most recent subroutine call. See subroutine call, branch.

return to zero signal   In computing, a method of recording in which the reference condition is the absence of magnetization. Compare nonreturn to zero.

Reuters   An international news gathering and dissemination organization. It now provides an extremely comprehensive computer based financial information service.

reveal   In videotex, (1) the facility to produce information on the screen, previously concealed by invocation of conceal mode, with the depression of the reveal key on the user's keypad. It is used for games or quizzes, (2) the mode complementary to the conceal mode. Compare conceal.

reverberation time A measure of the acoustic properties of a room or space, the time taken for sound to become attenuated to one millionth of its initial intensity.

reversal film In photography, a film normally processed so as to produce a positive image after exposure.

reversal intermediate In filming, a second generation duplicate, used for printing to protect the original, reversed so as to make it the same type, positive or negative as the original.

reverse B to W In printing, an instruction to reverse the image from black to white.

reverse channel In communications, a channel provided from receiver to transmitter for low speed control signals.

reverse index In word processing, a facility to move a printer up half a line for the insertion of superscripts.

reverse interrupt In data communications, a control character sequence sent by the receiving station, in a binary synchronous communications system, to request a premature termination of the transmission in progress. See binary synchronous communications.

reverse L to R In printing, an instruction to reverse the image laterally.

reverse P Synonymous with paragraph mark.

reverse Polish notation Synonymous with postfix notation.

reverse reading In printing, reading from right to left as on a letterpress printing surface. See letterpress.

reverse video In computer displays, a VDU facility that enables all, or part, of the data to be displayed as a black image on a white background. Often used to highlight a portion of text. See VDU. Synonymous with inverse video.

revise In printing, pertaining to an additional proof showing that corrections from an earlier proof have been implemented.

RF See radio frequency.

RGB In television, (1) the amplifiers which drive the red, green and blue electron guns in a colour CRT, (2) the phosphor dots on a CRT screen which produce the red, green and blue primary colours. See amplifier, gun, phosphor dots, primary colours, CRT.

rheostat A resistor with a movable wiper arm that can be used to supply a variable, usually DC, voltage. See DC, resistor.

RI See ring indicator.

ribbon cable In electronics, a flat plastic sheathed cable in which the conductors lie parallel to each other.

right angle fold In printing, folding a sheet of paper in half twice, with the second fold at right angles to the first. A standard fold used for book sections.

right justified In computing, a display mode in which leading zeros are appended to the left of the data field until the specified length has been attained. See left justified.

right reading A print, or film, image in the correct lateral orientation with text reading from left to right. Compare wrong reading.

ring (1) In computing, a data structure in which the last pointer of a chain list references the first element in the same list. (2) In communications, a network topology in the form of a ring so that each node is connected only with two neighbours on each side. Compare bus, star. See chain list, local area network.

ring counter In electronics, an electronic counter in which the overflow from the last unit is fed back to the input. See counter.

Ringdoc Pharmaceutical Literature Documentation, a database supplied by Derwent Publications Ltd and dealing with pharmaceuticals and pharmaceutical industry. See on line information retrieval.

ring down   In communications, a method of alerting subscribers or operators by the use of an AC ringing current on a communication line. See AC.

ring indicator   In data communications, a signal from an automatic answering unit to a DTE that it has detected an incoming call and gone off hook. See automatic answering, DTE, off hook.

RIP   In printing, Rest in Proportion, an instruction that all elements are to be reduced or enlarged in the same proportion.

rise time   In electronics, the time taken for a voltage pulse to rise from 10% to 90% of its final value. See pulse.

river   In printing, an undesirable white streak, produced by vertically interconnecting word spaces, that straggles down the text.

RJE   See remote job entry.

RMM   See read mostly memory.

RMS   See root mean square.

RO   See receive only.

roaming   In communications, a capability for travellers to take their telephones on the road. See cellular radio.

robot   A device that can accept input signals and/or sense environmental conditions, process the data so obtained and activate a mechanical device to perform a desired action relating to the perceived environmental conditions or input signal.

robotics   An area of artificial intelligence concerned with robots. See robot, artificial intelligence.

role indicator   In library science, a symbol which is assigned to an index term which designates the role of the term in its context, e.g. part of speech.

roll   In cinematography, (1) a roll of film, (2) rotation of camera around its axis, (3) a command to commence filming and record-ing. (4) In satellites, a rotation about the central axis. See pitch, yaw.

roll back recorder   A magnetic tape recorder with a facility to erase on tape motion reversal, to facilitate a rerun of a mix. See mixing.

rolling ball   In computer displays, a ball, mounted so that an operator has access to a hemispherical part of it, and used to direct the movement of a point on a VDU display. Similar in function to a mouse. See mouse, VDU.

rolling headers   In teletext, the display of all page headers, of a selected magazine, as they are received, providing the viewer with an indication of the transmitted page sequence. See magazine, page header.

rollover   A feature of a keyboard that can continue to send the correct codes when more than one key is depressed at any one time.

roll scroll   See vertical scrolling.

ROM   See read only memory.

ROM cartridge   In computing, a read only memory unit, often containing an educational or game program, mounted in a convenient cartridge and plugged into a microcomputer or video game unit. See ROM, video game.

RONTR   In communications, Receive Only Non Typing Reperforator, a device that receives signals and correspondingly punches a paper tape without a written output. Compare ROTR. See reperforator.

root   (1) In mathematics, a fractional power of a number or quantity. (2) In data structures, the node that represents the starting point for all paths in a tree structure. Compare leaf. See power, tree structure.

root mean square   In electronics, a measure of the amplitude of a waveform. It is equal to the square root of the mean value of the square of the waveform. For sinusoidal voltages it is equal to the amplitude multiplied by 0·7071. See sinusoidal.

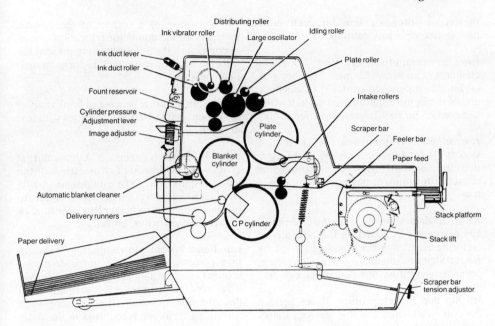

Distributing roller
Ink vibrator roller
Large oscillator
Idling roller
Ink duct lever
Ink duct roller
Plate roller
Fount reservoir
Intake rollers
Cylinder pressure Adjustment lever
Image adjustor
Plate cylinder
Scraper bar
Feeler bar
Blanket cylinder
Paper feed
Automatic blanket cleaner
Delivery runners
C P cylinder
Stack platform
Paper delivery
Stack lift
Scraper bar tension adjustor

rotary press
The method of operation is based on the principle of lithographic offset printing.

rotary camera In micrographics, a type of microfilm camera which photographs documents while they are being moved by a transport mechanism. The document transport mechanism is connected to a film transport mechanism and the film moves during exposure so that there is no relative movement between the film and document image. Compare planetary camera, step and repeat camera. See microfilm.

rotary hunting Synonymous with equivalent service.

rotary press A sheet, or web, fed printing machine in which the printing surface is cylindrical. See sheet fed, web fed.

rotate operation In computing, to shift the contents of a register to the left, or to the right, and directing any overflow bits to the input at the other end. See register.

rotogravure In printing, the photogravure technique using a web fed rotary press. See photogravure, web fed, rotary press.

ROTR See receive only typing reperforator.

round off errors In computing, the errors resulting from the rounding off process. This process is employed when a number is to be stored within a limited number of digits, the least significant remaining digit is incremented if the next digit in succession was greater than, or equal to, half the radix employed, e.g. 0·265 would become 0·27. See radix.

routine In computer programming, a set of instructions to perform a self contained task.

routing In communications, the assignment of a path for a message or telephone call to attain its ultimate destination. See adaptive routing, data communications, directory routing, hot potato routing.

routing page In videotex, an index page giving routes to other pages. See page.

routing table In communications, a table, at a node of a message switching network, indicating the preferred, and sometimes second

preference, outgoing line for each destination. See directory routing.

row In computing (1) the horizontal
elements of an array, (2) one of the horizontal lines on a punched card. (3) In videotex,
one of the 24 information lines each of which
can contain up to 40 characters. See array.

row adaptive transmission In teletext, a
system in which rows containing no information are omitted from the transmission
sequence to improve page access time. See
row.

RSA In data security, a method of public
key cryptography based on the difficulty of
factoring large numbers, and proposed by
Rivest-Shamir-Adleman. See factoring,
public key cryptosystem, knapsack cipher.

RS flip flop In electronics, Reset Set flip
flop, an unclocked bistable device. Pulses
sent alternately to the R and S inputs cause
successive changes of output. Simultaneous
R, S pulses will give an unpredictable result.
See race, flip flop, clock pulse.

RST flip flop In electronics, a clocked RS
flip flop. See RS flip flop.

RS 170 In television, an EIA standard for
monochrome television studio facilities. See
EIA.

RS 232 In data communications, an EIA
approved standard for voltage interface.
Commonly used in microcomputers for serial
transfer of data to peripheral devices. See
EIA, peripheral, V.24.

RS 449 In data communications, a new
standard designed to replace RS 232. See RS
232.

RTECS Registry of Toxic Effects of
Chemical Substances, a database supplied by
US Public Health Service, National Institute
for Occupational Safety and Health
(NIOSH) and dealing with toxicology. See on
line information retrieval.

rubber banding In computing, pertaining
to the flexible movement of interconnecting
lines in computer graphics. In some systems a

cut and paste of a section of the graphic
provides for the automatic relocation of connecting lines, if this facility is not present the
the lines must be erased and redrawn in their
new location.

rubric In printing, heading of book chapter
or section, printed in red to contrast with text
in black.

rule In expert systems, a statement that
enables the likelihood of an assertion, or the
value of an object, to be established. A rule
combines lower level assertions or objects to
produce a value for a higher level assertion or
object. See assertion, object.

rule based system In computing, a system
that consists of a set of antecedent-con-
sequent rules, a database and an executive.
The rules are conditional statements that
describe how to modify the database when
certain patterns are recognised in the data.
The executive looks after pattern matching,
monitoring database changes, deciding which
rule should be executed next and performance of the execution. See database, expert
systems.

ruler In word processing, a line across the
top or bottom of the VDU showing the tab
and margin settings currently in force. See
VDU, tab.

run (1) In computing, execution of a program. (2) In printing, another term for print
run. See print run.

run around In typesetting, the process of
fitting text around an illustration or other
display matter.

run in In printing, the proof correction 'do
not start a new line or paragraph'.

running head In printing, type lines above
the main text giving book and/or chapter
titles.

run on In printing, a term used in price
quotations referring to the cost of increasing
the print quantity.

run through work In printing, use of a
special ruling machine to print continuous

parallel lines from one edge to the other of a sheet.

run time In computing, the time required to complete the execution of a single, continuous object program. See object program.

Rural Electrification Administration A US

department that finances the construction of rural electric and telephone facilities.

rushes Synonymous with dailies.

R/W In computing, Read/Write. See read/write head.

RX See receiver.

S

saccadic movements Brief, rapid eye movements from one fixed point to another, e.g. during reading.

safe area In television, that part of the TV image that can be guaranteed to be seen on a domestic TV receiver. See television safe action area.

salami technique In data security, pertaining to fraud spread over a large number of individual transactions, e.g. a program which does not round off figures but diverts the leftovers to a personal account.

sample and hold circuit In computing, a circuit that samples an analog signal and then holds its output at that value until it takes the next sample. This represents the first stage in an analog to digital conversion process. See analog to digital converter, sampling.

sampling The process of obtaining a group of representative measurements, pertaining to some function, in order to develop information on that function. The measurements may relate to consecutive values of a continuous variable, or to a set of values from some static group of elements. In sampling a continuous signal the sampling rate must be sufficiently high to ensure that the signal can be accurately reconstructed. The theoretical minimum required sampling rate is equal to twice the highest frequency contained in the signal, in the case of PCM for voice signals the sampling rate is usually of the order of 8000 samples per second. See PCM.

sampling interval The time interval between consecutive samples. See sampling.

sans serif In typesetting, a typeface without serifs and constructed from strokes of nearly uniform thickness. Compare serif.

SATCOM In communications, two RCA geostationary communication satellites. See geostationary satellite.

satellite (1) In communications, an earth orbiting radio relay station. A complete satellite communication system comprises the satellite and earth stations which communicate with one another via the satellite. Conventional earth transmitter/receivers, that are not in direct line of sight with each other due to the curvature of the earth, have to rely upon reflection of radio waves from certain layers outside the atmosphere. Satellites are used to receive and retransmit communication signals for telephone, television and data channels. (2) A system operating as a subsidiary of a central system. See earth station, geostationary satellite, satellite computer.

satellite computer A computer performing subsidary operations under the control of another computer. Such a system can relieve a main computer from routine low level tasks, e.g. remote terminal handling, input output functions.

Satstream In data communications, a fully digital service offered by British Telecom which offers satellite communication links, initially over Western Europe. Customers will require a small satellite dish antenna. See X-Stream.

saturation (1) In television, pertaining to the purity of colour signals, a saturated colour implies that it is vivid, e.g. blood red. (2) In recording, pertaining to the state of magnetic materials subjected to a magnetic field. With a sufficiently large field the material saturates and further increases in magnetic field produce no further changes in magnetic flux. See flux, composite colour video signal.

saturation testing In communications, a technique of checking the performance of a communications network by means of a large bulk of messages. It is undertaken to check for system faults that only arise in exceptional circumstances, e.g. the simultaneous arrival of two messages.

save In microcomputers, to store a computer program on an auxiliary storage device, e.g. tape cassette or disk. Compare load.

save area In computing, an area of main storage allocated for the temporary storage of the contents of registers. See register.

sawtooth In electronics, a waveform commonly used in test equipment, so named because it has the shape of a series of saw-teeth, i.e. linearly increasing to a maximum and then decreasing linearly to its minimum value. See waveform.

SBC See single board computer.

S-box In cryptography, a substitution process carried out in the DES algorithm. See DES.

SBS Satellite Business Systems, a communications satellite to provide a private network for corporations and government. See satellite.

scalar A quantity that takes a single numerical value, e.g. height. Compare vector.

scaled factor The factor by which a quantity is multiplied to convert it to its scaled value. See scaling.

scaling (1) A method of readjusting variable values to fit within a specified range. (2) In printing, the process of calculating the degree of enlargement, or reduction, of an original image, for reproduction.

scallop In television, a distortion in the form of a wavy picture.

scan (1) The action of a scanner. (2) In data structures, a procedure to investigate every node in the structure. See scanner, node.

scan area In optical character reading, the area scanned by the reader. See scanner.

scanner (1) A device that examines an object, image or three dimensional space, in a regular manner, and produces analog, or digital, signals corresponding to a physical state at each part of the search area. (2) An instrument that automatically samples or interrogates the states of a system and initiates action in accordance with the information so obtained. (3) In printing, a photoelectric device that detects the relative densities of primary colours in full colour copy to make colour separations. See primary colours, photocell.

scanning device In micrographics, a device on a microfilm reader which permits shifting the film, or the entire optical system, so that different portions of the microfilm, frame or reel may be viewed. See microfilm.

scanning line In television, a single horizontal line traced across the face of a television screen by an electron beam.

scanning spot In television, (1) a small area of the target in the camera tube that is covered by the scanning electron beam, (2) the area of the phosphor screen covered by the electron beam in a display tube. (3) In facsimile, the elemental area of the recording medium examined at a given moment by the reading head during transmission, (4) the elemental area of recording medium acted upon at a given instant by the recording head. See pickup tube.

scanning spot beam In communications, an experimental satellite communications system that broadcasts 600 Megabits per second over multilple areas of 10,000 square miles. See satellite, spot beam.

s caps Synonymous with small caps.

scatter graph A representation of the relationship between two quantities as points on a two dimensional graph when the scatter of the points does not permit a sensible line, or curve, to interconnect the points.

scatter proofs In printing, proofs of illustrations, in photomechanical processing, arranged in a random manner unrelated to layout. See photomechanical, proof.

scavenging Synonymous with browsing.

scheduled circuits In data communications, leased circuits provided by British Telecom specially conditioned for data use. See conditioning.

schema In databases, (1) a map of the overall logical structure of a database, (2) in CODASYL it consists of the data description language entries and is a complete description of all the area, set occurrences, record occurrences and associated data items, and data aggregates as they exist in the database. See area, record, set, data description language, CODASYL.

schematic A diagram of a system's components and their interconnections or interrelationships.

Schottky diode In microelectronics, a diode with a low forward voltage drop but with a higher leakage current than conventional semiconductor diodes. See diode.

Scisearch A database supplied by the Institute for Scientific Information and dealing with science and technology. See on line information retrieval.

scissor In computer graphics, to remove the parts of display elements that lie outside a selected area. Synonymous with clipping.

scope In electronics, an abbreviation for oscilloscope. See oscilloscope.

scrambler In communications, a coding device applied to communications links for security purposes or to avoid harmful repetitive patterns of digital data. Such repetitive patterns may arise in phase modulated systems and produce a zero phase shift over a comparatively long period, with a resultant loss in synchronization between the transmitter and receiver decoders. See phase modulation.

scratch (1) In computing, to free an area of storage so that it can be used for another application. (2) In cinematography, an unintentional abrasive mark on a film.

scratch file In computing, a file used as a work area.

scratch pad memory In computing, a small high speed memory used as a temporary storage for working data.

screen buffer In computing, a buffer used to store the data that is displayed on the screen of a VDU. The display unit accesses this buffer in each display scan. See refreshed CRT, VDU.

screen editor In computing, a text editor which displays a screenful of text; a cursor can be moved to any character position and the corresponding section of text modified. Compare line editor. See text editor.

screen format In computing, the layout or structure of the visual display.

screenful In videotex, the information contents of a full page. See page.

script (1) In typesetting, a typeface based upon handwritten letterforms. (2) In filming, a set of written specifications for the production of a film.

scrolling In computing, the continuous horizontal or vertical movement of a screen display such that new data appears at one edge whilst old data disappears from another. See vertical scrolling, page scrolling.

scroll mode In data communications, pertaining to a terminal with no intelligence. When a key is struck a character is sent over a line and when it is received it is displayed. Compare form mode, page mode.

scumming In printing, a fault in lithography in which the water accepting layer is worn away from nonimage bearing areas. See lithography.

SDI See selective dissemination of information.

SDLC See synchronous data link control.

SDM See selective dissemination of microfiche.

search and replace In word processing, a facility in which every occurrence of a specified string of characters, in stored text, can be automatically replaced by a second specified string, e.g. in correcting a common spelling error.

search key In data processing, the data to be compared with a specific part of each item in a search. See key.

search memory Synonymous with associative storage.

SECAM See video standards.

secondary channel In data communications, a data channel derived from the same physical path as the main data channel but completely independent from it. It carries auxiliary information, at a low data rate, dealing with device control, diagnostics etc. See channel.

secondary colour A colour produced by the combination of two primary colours. See primary colours.

secondary destination In communications, any of the destinations specified in a message except the first.

secondary key In data processing, a key that does not uniquely define a record. A key that contains the value of an attribute other than the unique identifier. Compare primary key. See attribute.

secondary station In communications, a station selected to receive information from a primary station. The designation of secondary status is only temporary, it is produced by the primary station for the duration of the message transmission. See primary station.

secondary storage Synonymous with auxiliary storage.

second generation computer The generation of computers in which solid state components replaced vacuum tubes. Originated in the late 1950's. Compare first generation computer, third generation computer, fourth generation computer, fifth generation computer. See solid state device, vacuum tube.

second normal form In relational databases, a relation is in second normal form if it is in first normal form and every nonprime attribute of the relation is fully functional dependent on each candidate key of the relation. See first normal form, fully functional dependent, nonprime attribute, candidate key, third normal form, normal forms.

second sourcing In microelectronics, (1) the licensing of rights for manufacturing electronic components, typically a microprocessor, (2) the securing of component supplies from two or more separate sources.

sectioning In micrographics, microfilming of an oversize document in two or more parts. See microfilm.

section 214 In communications, an FCC regulation governing the acquisition, leasing, or construction of new telecommunication facilities. See FCC.

sector In computing, a portion of a rotational magnetic storage device that can be accessed by the magnetic heads in the course of a particular rotation. Magnetic disks are divided into circular tracks and each track is then subdivided into sectors holding a block of data. A sector is the smallest element of disk store that can be addressed by the computer. See hard sector, magnetic disk, soft sectored disk, track.

sector chart Synonymous with pie graph.

security In computing, prevention of access to, or use of, data or programs without authorization. See cryptography, data security.

see through In printing, the degree to which an image on an underlying sheet can be seen through a sheet of paper. Compare show through.

segment (1) In computing, a self contained portion of a computer program that can be executed without the entire program necessarily resident in the internal store at any one time. (2) In communications, a section of a message that can be held in a buffer. See buffer.

seize In communications, to gain control of a channel in order to transmit a message.

selecting (1) In manual data processing, the process of extracting a specific card for a certain purpose without changing its relative position. (2) In communications, inviting another station or node to receive messages.

selection sort In computing, a sort routine that continually extracts the extreme value (smallest or largest) from a list and adds it to a second sorted list until the first list is empty. See sort.

selective abstract In library science, an abstract prepared by a librarian and containing a condensation of those parts of the article known to be relevant to the needs of the user. Compare auto abstract, evaluative abstract, general abstract, indicative abstract, informative abstract, slanted abstract. See abstract.

selective calling In communications, (1) a system where remote stations may be called in for transmissions of messages when required, excluding all other stations on the circuit, (2) the facility of a transmitter to select the stations, on the same line, that are to receive the message.

selective dissemination of information In library science, a service for providing users with abstracts which lie within the user's area of interest. A profile defining each area of interest is compiled for the user and stored on a magnetic media for computer processing. Keywords representing documents are automatically matched with the user's profile and abstracts are sent to the user for each match. Compare SDM. See abstract, keyword.

selective dissemination of microfiche In library science, a system which regularly provides large scale microfiche users with microfiche copies of documents corresponding to their areas of interest. Compare SDI. See microfiche.

selective dump In computing, a dump of one or more selected areas of storage. See dump.

selective ringing In telephony, a facility in which only the desired subscriber's telephone on a multiparty line is rung.

selectivity In broadcasting, the discrimination of a radio receiver between two adjacent broadcast carrier signals. See carrier.

selector (1) In electronics, a device that looks for the presence of a control pulse, in a pulse train, and consequently directs the pulse train to the appropriate one of the two lines. (2) In communications, a device used to select a communication line according to a set of dialed up digits. The selector is a complex switch that moves up a band of contacts according to a dialed digit, and then searches along the level attained for another selector to accept the next dialed digits. See pulse train.

selector channel In data communications, a channel designed to operate with only one input output device at any one time. After selection of the input output device the whole message is transmitted byte by byte. See byte.

selenium A chemical element used in photoelectric devices. See photoelectric.

self adapting system A system that is able to adjust its performance characteristics according to its environment and to perceived relationships between input and output signals.

self banking The use of automatic tellers, cash dispensers and communication terminals by individual clients to perform banking transactions. The equipment may be located in a bank, place of work, home etc. Compare home banking.

self checking codes Synonymous with error detection code.

self correcting code Synonymous with error correction code.

self relocating program In computing, a program that can be loaded into any area of main storage, at initialization the program adjusts its address constants so that it can be executed at that location. See relocate.

semantics The study or science of the relationship between symbols and their meaning.

semaphore (1) In communications, a method of signalling characters by the position of two mechanical or human arms. (2) In computing and communications, a method to ensure the synchronization of cooperating processes. It is used to prevent the undesirable interference arising when two processes simultaneously seek to utilize a resource. See deadlock.

semiconductor In electronics, a material with a conductivity midway between that of an insulator and a good conductor. The conductivity is sensitive to temperature, radiation and the presence of impurities. Such materials are used in the manufacture of transistors, diodes, photoelectric devices and solar cells. See transistor, diode, solar cell, photocell, semiconductor devices.

semiconductor devices In electronics, devices manufactured using semiconductor materials. For some purposes impurities are deliberately added to the semiconductor to induce certain conductivity characteristics. The impurities produce additional positive or negative electrical carriers in the material and the result is a p- or n- type semiconductor respectively. Semiconductor devices form the basis of modern electronics because they are rugged, reliable, cheap, small and have a very low power consumption. They replaced the earlier vacuum tube devices. See chip, semiconductor, transistor, vacuum tube.

semiconductor laser In optoelectronics, a small, efficient and rugged laser well suited for use in fiber optics. The device effectively comprises a p-n diode of gallium arsenide. The sides of the crystal are highly polished and electrons are injected into the p-region. Photons produced by electron-hole combinations at the junction region are reflected back into the crystal and produce further combinations. Brightness is adjusted by the current flow. See diode, LASER, n-type material, photon, p-type material, semiconductor. Synonymous with ILD.

semiology See semiotics.

semiotics The study of the nature and use of signs which may be spoken, gesticulated, written, printed or constructed. Synonymous with semiology.

sense (1) To examine in relationship to some specified criterion. (2) In electronics, to determine the state of a particular element of hardware, e.g. a switch, a hole on punched card.

sense switch In computing, a console switch that can be interrogated by a computer program.

sensitometer In photography, a device designed to expose film with an accurately given series of exposures having a systematic progressive relationship.

sensitometric strip In photography, a strip of film exposed in a sensitometer to determine photographic response and/or processing conditions. See sensitometer.

sensor In electronics, a transducer or similar device that produces an output, for monitoring by a system, according to the state of some physical phenomenon. See transducer.

sentinel In computer programming, a marker indicating the beginning or end of a section of information accessed by a program.

separate channel signalling In communications, signalling that utilizes the whole or part of a channel frequency band or time slots in a multichannel system in order to provide for supervisory and control signals for all the traffic channels in the multichannel system. The same time slots or frequency bands that are used for signalling are not used for the message traffic. Compare common channel signalling. See frequency division multiplexing, signalling, time division multiplexing.

separated graphics In videotex, a display option in which the display of an individual mosaic does not fill the whole of its character space. Compare contiguous graphics. See mosaic.

separator Synonymous with delimiter.

sequence An arrangement of items arranged according to a specified set of rules, e.g. items arranged alphabetically, numerically or chronologically.

sequential access In computing, an access mode in which records are obtained from, or placed into, a file in such a way that each successive access to the file refers to the next subsequent record in the file. Compare direct access. Synonymous with serial access.

sequential access storage In computing, a storage device in which the access time depends upon the location of the data and on a reference to data previously accessed. Compare direct access storage, random access memory.

sequential batch processing In computing, a mode of operation in which a run must be completed before another run can be started.

sequential computer One in which events occur one after the other with little or no provision for simultaneity or overlap. Compare parallel computer.

sequential data set In computing, a data set that is organized on the basis of the successive physical location of records on a storage medium, e.g. magnetic tape. See data set, record.

sequential logic In electronics, a logic circuit in which the output depends upon the previous states of the inputs. Compare combinational logic.

sequential operation A mode of operation in which two or more operations are performed one after the other in a specified order.

sequential processing In computing, the processing of records in the order that they are accessed. See record.

serial access Synonymous with sequential access.

serial adder In computing, a digital adder in which addition is performed by adding, digit place after digit place, the corresponding digits of the operands.

serial computer (1) A computer with a single logic and arithmetic unit. (2) A computer which has a specified characteristic that is serial in its operation. Compare parallel computer. Synonymous with sequential computer.

serial input output interface In computing, a device that accepts serial information from a peripheral device, cassette or keyboard, and presents it to the computer, and vice versa.

serial interface In electronics, a device that supports the processing of data a bit at a time. Compare parallel interface.

serializer In computing, a device that converts a space distribution of simultaneous states representing data into a corresponding time sequence of states.

serial operation Pertaining to the sequential or consecutive execution of two or more operations in a single device, e.g. an arithmetic or logic unit.

serial printer In computing and word processing, an output device that prints one character at a time. Compare line printer.

serial transmission In computing and communications, a method of information transfer in which each bit of a character is sent in sequence. Compare parallel transmission.

series circuit In electronics, a circuit in which the components are connected end to end so that the same current flows through each one. Compare parallel circuit.

series connection The connection of units such that the output of one unit is fed to the input of only one other unit. Compare parallel circuit.

series to parallel converter In electronics, a device that accepts the serial input of a word, or byte, on one line and produces a parallel version of that input on n lines (n being the number of bits in the word or byte). Compare parallel to series converter.

serif In printing, the short strokes projec-

	Parallel	Serial
Number of wires	Multiple	One
Amount of data sent (during one bit time)	Multiple bits	One bit only
Cabling costs	High; multicore cable required	Low single wire only
Applications	Inter computer communications; internal computer communications	Connecting low speed terminals and peripherals to a computer

serial transmission
A comparison of serial and parallel transmission.

ting from the principal lines of printed characters. Compare sans serif.

server In computing, a unit at a node of a computer network that provides a specific service for network users, e.g. a printer server provides printing facilities, a file server stores user files. See local area network.

service bureau An organization that provides computing or data processing services for other individuals or organizations.

service center In videotex, the computer center hosting the system for a particular group of users. See update center.

servo Synonymous with servomechanism.

servomechanism A control system that measures the difference between the actual and desired value of a variable, and takes action to reduce that difference. See feedback.

session key In cryptography, a secret key shared by users on a communications network. The key will change from one session to the next. See key management.

session layer In data communications, a layer in the ISO Open Systems Interconnection model. This layer provides for connec-

tions between processes in different hosts. Compare application layer, data link layer, network layer, physical layer, presentation layer, transport layer. See host, Open Systems Interconnection.

set (1) In filming, the physical surroundings and background for a studio scene. (2) A collection of elements with a common property. (3) In printing, a measure of typeface width. (4) A radio or television receiver. (5) In databases, a CODASYL term for a named collection of record types. See set size, CODASYL, record.

set off In printing, a situation in which wet ink on one sheet of paper, that has just been printed, marks the underside of the following sheet on the stack.

set size In printing, the horizontal dimension of a typeface expressed in sets. One set = 1 point, the standard dimension of a point is 0·01383 inches. The set size indicates the horizontal width allocated to a character not the size of the printed image. See point, type size.

set theory The mathematical study of the properties of sets. See set.

set-top convertor In cable television, a device which interfaces the consumer's TV receiver to the network. It will usually contain a frequency changer to enable the receiver to accept any of the wide range of cable signals. It may also contain a decoder to enable authorized subscribers to receive scrambled channels available on premium services. See premium television.

set up time   The time interval between the instruction to start an operation and the time that the operation can commence.

set width   In typesetting, (1) in metal type the width of the body upon which the type character is cast. (2) In phototypesetting, the width of the individual character including the normal amount of space on either side to prevent the characters from touching. See phototypesetting.

sexto   In printing, folded or cut sheet that is one sixth the area of basic sheet size.

sf signalling   See single frequency signalling.

shade   In printing, (1) the result of adding and mixing small amounts of black with basic hue. (2) The degree of black mixed into pure hue.

shaded letter   In printing, an outline letter shaded along one side to give a three dimensional effect of letter and associated shadow. See outline letter.

shadowmask   In television, a perforated mask located immediately behind a television tube screen and used to separate the electron beams producing red, green and blue. See television tubes.

shadow memory   In computing, a memory that has the same range of addresses as another memory and which can be accessed by special address coding. In microcomputers the range of memory that can be addressed is limited by the architecture of the microprocessor and the operating system is sometimes supplied in shadow ROM which can then share address space with the user programs in RAM. See address, microprocessor, operating system, program, RAM, ROM.

shadow ROM   See shadow memory.

shannon   See information content.

Shannon's Law   In communications, a law that provides a measure for the capacity of a communication line in terms of its bandwidth and signal to noise ratio. According to this law the maximum transmission in bits per second is given by W lg (1 + SN) where, W = bandwidth, lg = logarithm to base 2, SN = signal to noise ratio. See bandwidth, signal to noise ratio.

shared file   In computing, a file that may be accessed by two systems. It can provide a means of communication between two computer systems.

shared line   Synonymous with party line.

shared logic   In word processing, the sharing of a central processing unit and a rigid disk store by a number of work stations. See work station.

sheet fed   In printing, pertaining to presses in which paper is fed a sheet at a time. Compare web fed.

shelf life   The period of time before deterioration, or external market forces, renders a material or product unusable.

SHF   See super high frequency.

shielded cable   In electrical transmission, an inner conductor surrounded by an outer grounded metallic braid to protect signals from interference. See coaxial cable, interference.

shift   In computing, a movement of bits in storage to the left or right.

shift codes   In character coding systems, a method of increasing the number of characters which can be associated with a given number of bits. If a 6 bit code is used then 64 characters may be allocated, however, if two of these characters are designated as 'shift' and 'unshift' then they may produce the effect of a shift to and from an alternative character set giving a total of 124 available characters. See escape codes.

shift register   In electronics, a register

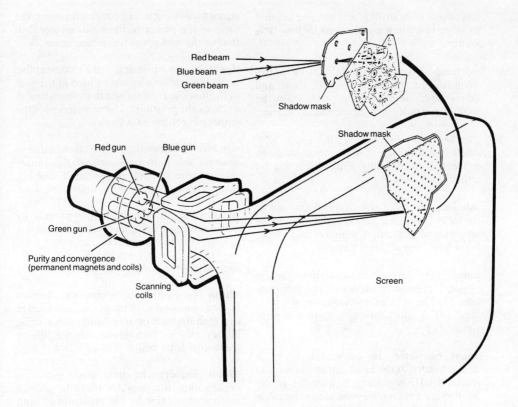

shadow mask
The screen is covered with primary colour phosphor dots in the form of a triad for each colour cell. The metal mask ensures that only the beam with the correct colour signal modulation strikes each dot.

designed for the shifting of data to the left or right. See register.

Ship Movement Service In communications, a safety service for ships and coastal stations restricted to messages relating to the movement of ships.

SHL See studio to head end link.

short circuit In electronics, a very low resistance connection between two electrical points. Usually resulting from an accidental connection.

short wave Radio waves with wavelengths up to 60 meters. See radio waves.

shotgun microphone A highly directional microphone. See unidirectional microphone.

shoulder In printing, the flat non printing area surrounding face of type. See type.

shoulder tap In computing, a technique enabling one processor to communicate with another.

show through In printing, the degree to which an image on a reverse side can be seen through a sheet of paper. Compare see through.

SI Système Internationale. A metric system of measurement units based upon the meter (length), gram (weight), second (time) and amperes (electrical current).

sibilance   In recording, an excessive amount of voice hiss when a consonant such as 's' is spoken.

sideband   In communications, a band of frequencies of a transmitted signal, above and below the carrier frequency, produced by the modulation process. See modulation, carrier.

side bearings   In printing, the space allocated to either side of a character image to prevent it overlapping with characters on either side.

side lobe   In radio communications, one of the lobes between the main and back lobes of an antenna pattern. Compare back lobe, main lobe. See antenna pattern.

signal   (1) An intentional time-varying physical phenomenon conveying information. (2) The physical embodiment of a message. (3) A short message, as in a control signal.

signal converter   In cable television, a device located at the head end to convert the received UHF signals to frequencies in the VHF range for transmission along the cable system. See head end, UHF, VHF.

signal element   In communications, the basic unit by which data is communicated along a channel. Each unit is a state or condition of the channel representing one or more bits of digital information. A unit may be a DC pulse, or an AC signal of certain amplitude, phase or frequency which is recognized and translated by the receiving equipment.

signal generator   In electronics, a device for producing waveforms of various shapes, frequencies and amplitudes, often used for test equipment. See waveform.

signalling   In telephony, (1) the process by which a caller or equipment at the transmitting end informs the called party or equipment that a message is to be communicated, (2) the supervisory information to the caller

that the called party is ready to talk, has hung up or the line is busy.

signal to noise ratio   In communications, the ratio of the power of the required signal to that of the unwanted noise. See noise.

signature   In printing, the consecutive number or letter which is printed at the foot of the first page of a section to enable a binder to check the position and completeness of the gathered sections of a book.

sign bit   In computing, the bit designated to indicate the numerical sign of the binary number with which it is associated. See bit, two's complement, one's complement.

signification   In semiotics, the process by which messages are conveyed to a spectator or receiver. See semiotics.

sign on   Synonymous with log in.

silicon   In electronics, a chemical element having semiconductor properties and used in the manufacture of transistors, solar cells, diodes, etc. See chip, semiconductor, silicon transistor, solar cell.

silicon foundry   In microelectronics, an organisation that enables users to acquire custom built chips by the provision of both design and manufacturing facilities. The user may employ the organisation's computer assisted design facilities to develop the chip design and then the organisation manufactures batches of the chip. See chip, microcomputer.

silicon gate   In microelectronics, a form of MOS technology in which a heavily doped amorphous silicon replaces the usual aluminium gate metallization. See chip, gate, MOS.

Silicon on Sapphire   In microelectronics, a fabrication technique in which MOS devices are built upon a synthetic sapphire substrate providing for higher speed switching than conventional devices. See chip, MOS.

silicon transistor   In electronics, a transistor manufactured from silicon crystal, sometimes preferred to the alternative, germanium transistor, because it has a higher temperature stability. See semiconductor, transistor.

Silicon Valley Santa Clara, California, an area famed for its microelectronic manufacturing plants. See microelectronics.

silk In photography, a sheet of white fabric stretched on a frame to reduce the harshness of lighting on the subject.

SIMD See single instruction stream multiple data stream.

simplex (1) In communications, pertaining to communication in one direction only. (2) In micrographics, an image positioning technique in rotary camera microfilming in which images are photographed across the full width of the film. Compare duplex, half duplex. See microfilm.

simulate To represent the behaviour of one system with another. The two systems need not have the same physical form but they must share the same mathematical model to an acceptable degree of refinement. In many cases the second system is the execution of a computer program. See mathematical model, simulator.

simulator A device designed to simulate a physical system in order to study its performance or for training purposes. In many instances the simulator will be a computer program, or a special purpose computer system which can be used for training or experimentation that would be too expensive, or dangerous, on the original system, e.g. a flight simulator used for airline pilot training. See simulate, analog computer.

simultaneous processing In computing, the performance of two or more computing tasks at the same instant of time. Synonymous with parallel processing.

simultaneous transmission In communications, transmission of control characters, or data, in one direction whilst messages are being received in the other. See duplex.

sin An abbreviation for sine. See sine.

sine The sine of an angle of a right angled triangle is equal to the ratio of the side opposite the angle to the hypotenuse.

sine wave A wave that can be expressed as the sine of a linear function of time or distance. Any periodic function can be decomposed into a series of sine waves and this technique can be used to study the passage of a complex waveform through a circuit or transmission system. See sine, circuit, fourier series, periodic.

single address instruction In computing, a machine language instruction that contains only an operator and one address. See address.

single address message In communications, a message to be delivered to only one destination.

single board computer In computing, a microcomputer or minicomputer using a single printed circuit board for all logic, timing, internal memory and external interfaces. See printed circuit board.

single frequency signalling In communications, the use of tones to give information for control and supervisory purposes on a channel, e.g. to indicate answer or disconnect states on a direct distance dialing system. See direct distance dialing.

single instruction stream multiple data stream In computing, pertaining to a form of parallel computer with a single control unit and multiple arithmetic logic units, each arithmetic logic unit having its own memory. The single control unit allocates execution commands to the arithmetic logic units. Compare MIMD, MISD, SISD. See arithmetic logic unit, control unit, instruction, memory, parallel computer.

single instruction stream single data stream In computing, pertaining to a conventional computer system with a single control unit and a single arithmetic logic unit, which operates upon a single stream of data from memory according to a single stream of instructions. Compare MIMD, MISD, SIMD. See arithmetic logic unit, control unit, instruction, memory.

single operand instruction Synonymous with single address instruction.

single operation In communications, a system which only permits transmissions in one direction at any one time. Thus the system is qualified by suffixes S/O - send only, R/O - receive only, S/R - send or receive. See simplex.

single pole In electronics, a switch or relay which enables connections to only one circuit.

single scan non segmented In video recording, a video tape format that records one television field during each head pass thus permitting freeze framing. See freeze frame, field.

single sideband transmission In communications, a method of signal transmission in which one sideband of the modulation signal is suppressed. The upper and lower sidebands are mirror images about the carrier frequency and thus the suppression of one sideband reduces the power that has to be transmitted without removing any of the information content. Compare suppressed carrier transmission. See modulation, sideband.

sink In communications, a point of data usage in a network. Compare source. Synonymous with data sink.

sink tree In communications, the set of all paths to a destination in a communication network, when fixed routing tables are used. See routing table.

sinusoidal Pertaining to sine waves. See sine wave.

siphoning In cable television, pertaining to the transmission of a program originally available by direct broadcast.

SISD See single instruction stream single data stream.

SITA high level network In communications, Société Internationale de Télécommunications Aeronautique, a network serving airlines with a combination of packet

and message switching facilities. See packet switching, message switching.

SITE In communications, Satellite Instructional Television Experiment, a trial of educational television via satellite, first used by India in 1974. See satellite, educational television.

site polling In communications, a technique in which all the terminals at a given location are polled as a group, with the local controller acting as the supervisor for this purpose. See polling.

sixteen mo In printing, folded or cut sheet that is one sixteenth of basic size.

sixteen sheet In printing, poster size of 305 x 203 cm (120 x 80 inches).

skew (1) In facsimile transmission, a deviation from the rectangular frame due to a lack of synchronism between transmitting and receiving scanner. (2) In optical character recognition, a condition in which a scanned line is not perpendicular to the reference edge or not parallel to preceding and succeeding lines. (3) In printing, the ability to indent text by a varying amount over a specified number of lines. (4) In television, a zig zag distortion. See scan.

skip In computer programming, to ignore one or more instructions in a sequence of instructions.

skip capability In word processing, (1) during editing, the ability to jump over segments of a document leaving the corresponding stored sections unchanged, (2) the ability to insert instructions between skip codes; such instructions are displayed on the screen and on draft copies but not on the final printout.

skip effect In broadcasting, the long distance reflection of radio waves from the ionosphere. See ionosphere.

sky wave In broadcasting, a secondary portion of a broadcast signal radiating skywards, part of which is reflected by the ionosphere. See skip effect, ionosphere.

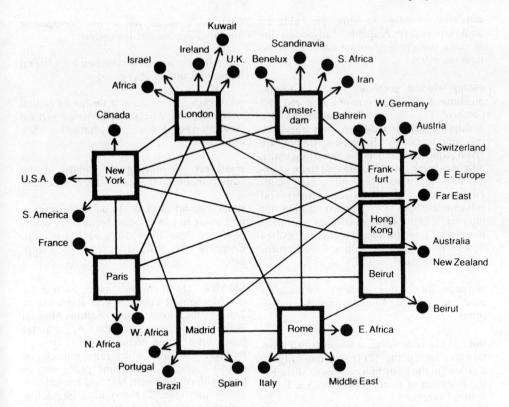

SITA high level network
This network was the first commercial application of packet switching.

slab serif In printing, typeface with square end serifs which may, or may not, be bracketed. See serif, bracketed.

slanted abstract In library science, an abstract which gives emphasis to a particuar aspect of the components of a document so as to cater for the interests of a particular group of readers. Compare auto abstract, evaluative abstract, general abstract, indicative abstract, informative abstract, selective abstract. See abstract.

slash Synonymous with solidus.

slave (1) In computing, a remote system or terminal whose functions are controlled by a central master system. (2) In recording, a recorder dubbing playback from a master.

slew See high speed skip.

slice architecture In computing, a form of chip architecture that enables the cascading of units to increase the word size. See word size, chip architecture.

slide / audiotape In audiovisual devices, a set of slides accompanied with an audiotape recording. Sometimes a signal is available to project the next slide.

slide projector In audiovisual aids, a device containing a light source, and a lens system, to project the image of a slide onto a screen. Some devices have a built in rear viewing screen. The slides may be housed in trays, cartridges and drums. The slide access may be sequential or random.

slide/sync recorder In audiovisual aids, an audio tape recorder capable of advancing one or more slide projectors on cue. See audio tape recorder.

sliding window protocol In data communications, a modified form of a stop and wait protocol. The sending host is allowed to have multiple unacknowledged frames outstanding simultaneously. Successive frames are given sequence numbers in a given range with numbers being reused to prevent them growing without bound. The sending host maintains a record of unacknowledged frames and retransmits them after a specified time out interval, a limit on the maximum permitted number of unacknowledged frames ensures flow control. Compare stop and wait protocol. See frame.

slip page In printing, a galley proof made up on slip but separated out as a page. See galley proof.

slot (1) In computing, a single board position on a back plane. (2) In cinematography, a groove in the body of a camera to allow for the insertion of filters or mattes. See filter, matte, backplane.

Slotted Aloha In communications, a packet broadcast system in which packets are timed to arrive at the receiving station in regular time slots, synchronized for all stations. See Aloha.

slow motion In video disk, the controlled movement of the laser beam from frame to frame at a variable rate less than that of normal play.

slow scan television device A device that compresses the bandwidth of a video signal so that it may be transmitted over a telephone line. The slow speed of transmission mitigates against the communication of moving images. See bandwidth, video signal, video compressor.

SLSI See super large scale integration.

slug (1) In cinematography, a strip of film, either blank or image bearing, used as a leader. (2) In printing, a line of type cast as a

continuous piece on a line composing machine. See leader, linecaster.

slur In printing, a fault caused by a lateral movement during impression.

small caps In printing, a design of capital characters with a height equal to the vertical dimension of lower case characters. See lower case.

small face In printing, the smaller of two sizes available on the same body of typeface.

small scale integration In microelectronics, pertaining to a fabrication technology which produces less than 10 gates per chip. Compare LSI, MSI, SLSI, VLSI. See chip, gate.

SMART (1) In library science, System for the Mechanical Analysis and Retrieval of Text or, more irreverently, Saltons Magical Automatic Retrieval of Text. A computer based information retrieval system devised by Professor Salton which relies entirely, or almost entirely, on machine processing of text, both of document text and natural language questions. The system is interactive with the user provided with a ranked output from the database which may be evaluated by the user and the results of the evaluation fed back for a modified search. In addition to its use as a retrieval system it is able to compare the effectiveness of one retrieval method against another. (2) A term used synonymously with intelligent, e.g. a smart terminal. See intelligent terminal.

smart card A plastic card, the size of a credit card, which acts as an electronic cheque book. It contains a processor and memory for processing debit transactions when used with a point of sale terminal. It is also used to verify the card holder's PIN code and will encrypt/decrypt data exchanged over the telephone network.

smart card

smart terminal   In computing, a terminal that has the capability to process information received or to be transmitted. See terminal. Synonymous with intelligent terminal.

SMPTE   Society of Motion Picture and Television Engineers.

SNA   See systems network architecture.

snapshots   In computing, the complete state of a computer, memory contents, registers, flags, etc. at a selected instant of time. See register, flag.

SNOBOL   In computer programming, StriNg Oriented symBOlic Language. A programming language designed for advanced string manipulation, used in artificial intelligence, compiler construction applications etc. See string, artificial intelligence, compiler.

snow   In television, a momentary picture distortion caused by a weak video signal. See video signal.

s/n ratio   See signal to noise ratio.

soak   In computer programming, a method of detecting program errors and problems by running it under operating conditions while closely supervised by the programmers.

Social Scisearch   A database supplied by the Institute for Scientific Information and dealing with social sciences and humanities. See on line information retrieval.

Sociological Abstracts   A database supplied by Sociological Abstracts Inc. and dealing with sociology. See on line information retrieval.

soft   In recording, pertaining to magnetic materials that become strong magnets when placed in a magnetic field but lose their magnetism when the field is removed. The reading and writing heads of magnetic recorders must be manufactured from soft magnetic material. Compare hard.

soft copy   Information displayed on screen or in audio format. Compare hard copy.

soft sectored disk   In computing, a floppy disk in which one hole in the disk is used to synchronize the beginning of data tracks. Each other sector is identified by recorded sector identification. Compare hard sector.

software   (1) In computing, the programs, procedures, routines and possibly documents associated with the operation of a data processing system. (2) All the non hardware components of certain information systems, e.g. the tapes and documents associated with complex self teaching systems. Compare hardware.

software development process   In computing, the steps of a software development cycle are (a) Problem Statement (b) Design of abstract algorithms and data structures (c) Statement of flow control and data layouts (d) Coding of program in chosen language (e) Preparation of source code in machine readable form (f) Translation to object code (g) Loading of machine code program (h) Run time check and debugging (i) Documentation. See algorithm, data structure, source code, object code, debug.

software documentation   In computing, a complete description of a software system including program listings, data and file layouts, operating procedures, error messages, etc. See software, file, program listing.

software emulation   In computing, a software system, often in microprograms, that enables one computer to execute a program in the machine code of another computer. Often used to minimize reprogramming when one computer system replaces another. See microprogram, emulator.

software engineering   In computer programming, a broadly defined discipline that integrates the various aspects of programming, from writing code to ensuring that budgets are met, in order to produce effective and cost effective software. See software.

software house   In computing, an organization offering software support services to users. See software.

software interrupt   In computing, an interrupt caused by a high priority program requiring the services of the CPU. Compare hardware interrupt. See interrupt, CPU.

software license In computing, an agreement between a user and a vendor of software describing the user's rights to the software. See software.

software maintenance In computer programming, the improvements and changes required to keep programs up to date and ensure effective operation. See software.

software package In computing, a set of programs for a specific purpose.

software support system In computing, a system to test the software developed for special purpose microprocessor systems. The support system executes the object code in the same manner as the microprocessor enabling a programmer to check and debug it. See microprocessor, object code, debug.

solar cell In electronics, a semiconductor device for collecting the sun's radiation and converting the received energy to electrical power. Used for remote communication systems lacking access to conventional power supplies, e.g. satellites. See semiconductor devices, satellite.

solenoid An electromagnetically operated switch.

solid In typesetting, type set with no line spacing between the lines.

solid state device In electronics, a device whose operation depends upon the behavior of electrical or magnetic signals in solids, e.g. transistors, integrated circuits. Earlier electronic and electromechanical devices-vacuum tubes, relays, etc, are not included in this category. See chip, relay, semiconductor, transistor, vacuum tube.

solidus In printing, a diagonal typographic sign.

SOM In data communications, a character in a poll response that precedes the address, or addresses, of any data stations other than the master station that are to receive the message. See polling.

sonic Pertaining to the audible frequency range (20 - 20,000) Hz. See Hz.

sort (1) In computing, to arrange items of data according to the values of certain parts of the data. (2) In printing, a special piece of type. See sort key, special sort.

sort key In data processing, a field of a data record that is used to determine the order of that record in a set of sorted data, e.g. an employee's name when sorting personnel records in alphabetical order of employees' names. See field, record, sort.

SOS See Silicon on Sapphire.

sound (1) A train of compression waves transversing air, or other gaseous, liquid or solid material at a frequency, or combination of frequencies in the range 20 - 20, 000 Hz. (2) In filming, a term for all or any of the aural elements in film production. See Hz.

sound advance In cinematography, the physical distance, in frames or inches, between a point on the sound track and the corresponding visual frame. Necessary because the sound reading head cannot occupy the same space as the camera aperture.

sound effects In filming and broadcasting, sounds produced from electronics, recording or other devices to give the impression of realistic effects.

sound effects library A collection of catalogued sound effects stored on a recording medium. See sound effects.

sound filmstrip projector In audiovisual aids, a filmstrip projector with an associated, or built in, sound reproducing unit. See film strip.

sound head In recording, the device that detects the audio signal from a recording medium. See magnetic head.

sound sheets In recording, a flat magnetic vinyl dictation recording medium.

sound slide projector In audiovisual devices, a slide projector with an associated, or built in, sound reproducing unit. The sound unit may control the slide advance automatically. See slide/sync recorder.

sound synthesizer In electronics, a transducer that produces music or speech from its constituent amplitude/frequency characteristics. See fourier series, speech synthesizer.

sound track In recording, the audio track of a film or magnetic tape.

source (1) In communications, a point of message entry into the system. (2) In electronics, a terminal on an FET. Compare sink. See FET, drain, gate.

source code In computer programming, the original code of a user's program prior to being processed, e.g. compiled, assembled, interpreted. Compare object code. See compiler, assembler, interpreter.

source document (1) In data processing, an invoice, form, voucher or other form of written evidence of a transaction from which the basic data is extracted for processing. (2) In word processing, material from which a secretary prepares final copy.

source language (1) In computer programming, a language in which the user's program is written. (2) In machine translation, the language from which translation is to be made. Compare object language, target language. See assembly language, high level language.

source program In computer programming, a program written in a source language, e.g. FORTRAN, BASIC. See source language, FORTRAN, BASIC.

space (1) A blank column or character. (2) In communications, an impulse, or absence of an impulse, to signify a binary zero condition. (3) In videotex, a character position filled entirely by background colour. Compare mark.

space craft A man made vehicle designed to go beyond the major portion of the earth's atmosphere.

space division multiplexing In commu-

nications, the grouping of more than one physical transmission path. In landline communications, many wire pairs may be combined in one cable; in satellite communications, an antenna can focus a number of spot beams to different geographical locations. Compare time division multiplexing. See spot beam, multiplexing.

space division switching In communications, a method for switching circuits in which each connection through the switch takes a different physical path. Compare time division switching.

space shuttle A manned space vehicle, capable of launching satellites, that can return to earth and be used for another launch.

space station In communications, a station located on an object that is, or is to be, located beyond a major portion of the earth's atmosphere. See station.

space telecommand In communications, the use of radiocommunication for the transmission of control signals to initiate, modify or terminate functions performed by equipment on a space station or another space object. See space station.

space telemetry In communications, the transmission of measurements taken by a space craft, including those relating to the functioning of the craft. See telemetry, space craft.

Spanish n In printing, the letter n with a tilde, giving a sound as if it were followed by the letter y. See tilde, accent.

sparse array In data structures, an array in which most of the entries have a zero value. Uneconomic in storage unless special data structures are used. See array.

speaker Synonymous with loudspeaker.

special effects In filming, (1) any effects unobtainable by straight forward cinematography shooting methods, e.g. explosions, (2) electronic generation of certain graphics effects, e.g. wipes, dissolves. See wipe.

special effects generator In filming, a video

device that produces optical effects, e.g. chroma keying and wiping by electronic means. See wipe, chromakey, special effects.

specialized common carrier In communications, an organization, not a telephone company, authorized by a 1971 FCC decision to provide a domestic point to point communication service on a common carrier basis. See common carrier, FCC, point to point connection.

special purpose Pertaining to systems and devices designed for use in a limited set of applications. Compare general purpose computer.

special sort In printing, a type character not usually included in the font. See font.

specifications The detailed information necessary to describe a task.

specific coding Synonymous with absolute code.

specificity In library science, (1) the extent to which the system permits precision in specifying the subject of a document to be processed, e.g. the specification of a digital computer has a higher specificity than that of a computer, (2) a measure expressing the ratio of non relevant documents not retrieved to the total number of non relevant documents on file. Compare exhaustivity.

specs See specifications.

spectrum A range of frequencies. Electromagnetic radiation manifests itself according to its frequency, ranging through low frequency radio waves, microwaves, infrared heat, visible light, ultraviolet radiation, X rays to gamma and cosmic rays.

spectrum roll off In communications, the attenuation characteristics at the edge of the frequency band of a transmission line or filter. See filter, frequency response.

speech plus In communications, a technique of multiplexing low speed data traffic onto voice grade telephone lines carrying speech. Acceptable speech quality can usually be obtained using less than the whole bandwidth of a voice grade channel and this technique enables up to five teleprinter terminals to be frequency division multiplexed on the same line without noticeably impairing the voice transmission. See frequency division multiplexing, teleprinter, voice grade channel.

speech recognizer In computing, a system that receives spoken word inputs and identifies the message. The system output can then be used to initiate appropriate actions or responses. There are currently four main approaches to the problem of speech recognition, i.e. acoustic signal analysis, speech production, sensory reception and speech perception. The acoustic signal approach treats speech as a signal waveform and uses mathematical techniques to characterize the waveform and hence identify it. The speech production approach looks to capture the essential ways that speech is produced, rate of vibration of vocal chords etc. The sensory perception approach suggests duplicating the human auditory process by identifying the parameters and classifying patterns as is performed in the ear. The speech perception approach suggests the extraction of features that are experimentally established as important to human perception of speech, e.g. voice onset times.

speech synthesis In computing, the production of a sound corresponding to spoken words according to stored text or commands. The current methods fall into two categories, stored digitized sound waveforms and formant synthesis. A sound waveform can be represented by binary digits corresponding to the sampled values of the sound wave intensity, as in pulse code modulation. Digitized speech waveforms are expensive in stored capacity, requiring some 20,000 bits per second of speech, but they provide pleasing outputs as compared with the dalek like utterances of early artificial synthesis devices. The SIRIUS microcomputer uses this technique for operator prompts.

The synchronous serial data adaptor (SSDA) accepts sound bytes from the CPU and produces a serial bit stream for the codec. The serial data is converted, by the codec, to an analog signal which is then filtered to remove high frequency elements produced by the conversion. The sound level is controlled

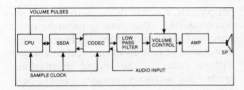

speech synthesis
Fig 1 ACT Sirius speech system.

by the volume control unit and the analog signal is finally sent through an audio amplifier to the loudspeaker. Digitized waveforms can provide single words or tailored phrases but attempts to produce ad hoc sentences by the combination of individual words do not provide the necessary inflection and modulation of human speech.

Formant synthesis is concerned with a form of sound production related to the physiological actions of the vocal tract. The General Instrument speech chip is based on the theory that human speech can be characterized as voiced or unvoiced. When the vocal chords vibrate and the passage of air is not constricted a vowel like sound is produced, i.e. voiced. Voiced sounds like 'l', 'm' or 'ee' have a pitch determined by the rate of vocal chord vibration. Unvoiced sounds such as 's', 'f' and 'sh' have no definite pitch and are produced through constrictions formed by the teeth, tongue or lips.

An impulse generator, producing a signal related to a particular pitch, or a random noise generator, is selected according to whether the sound is voiced or unvoiced. The amplitude of this source signal is adjusted to the appropriate level for the component of sound waveform and the signal is fed to a

digital filter. The output of the digital filter, which is programmed by 12 coefficients to model the human vocal tract, is fed to a pulse width modulator which produces the audio signal. The filter coefficients are generated by a speech synthesis program using linear predictive coding which relates current outputs to a series of previous outputs, thus modelling the characteristic properties of the human speech mechanism. Since these coefficients are inherently related to physiological movements they change fairly slowly and the information rate is only some 10% of that associated with digitized recorded waveforms.

Speech can be considered as a combination of basic speech sounds of a language. A phoneme is the name given to a group of similar sounds in a language and a phoneme may be acoustically different depending upon word position. Each of these positional variants is an allophone of the same phoneme. Speech contains some 10 to 12 allophones per second and 64 allophones can produce a reasonable approximation to English language. This technique therefore only requires an information rate of less than 100 bits per second. The allophone synthesis system provides an unlimited vocabulary since the stored units are sounds - not words. The user, however, has to select the appropriate sounds to represent a given word. See allophone, analog, bit, CODEC, formant, linear predictive coding, noise.

speech synthesizer In computing, a system that receives signals corresponding to text and produces synthetic speech. See phoneme, sound synthesizer.

speed (1) In photography, the light sensitivity of film emulsion. (2) In recording, the rate of movement of the recording material past the reading or writing head. The frequency response of recording devices is a function of the relative speed of the recording medium past the head. In audio recording high fidelity can be attained by increasing the tape speed. In video recording the required frequency response is such that it is not possible to achieve it with a simple linear movement of the tape past the head. Special arrangements, with the heads spinning at an angle to the direction of tape movement, are therefore employed. See frequency response,

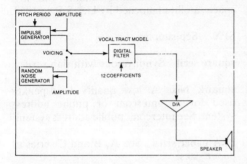

speech synthesis
Fig 2 General Instruments speech synthesis model.

helical scan, quadruplex, transverse scan. video tape recording.

spelling error detection　In word processing, a system holding a dictionary in storage to perform spelling error checking on a document.

spherical aberration　In optics, a fault in a lens causing straight lines to be rounded in the reproduced image.

spike　In electronics, a sharp peaked short duration voltage.

spirit duplicator　In printing, a planographic method using an anilene dye transfer onto plain sheet moistened with spirit, suitable for runs of up to about 100 sheets. See planographic.

splice　In photography and recording, to join two pieces of film or magnetic tape with a special splicing tape.

splicing block　A device to hold the ends of film or tape whilst a piece of splicing tape is applied.

spline　In mathematics, a polynomial function used to approximate to a given curve with a high degree of smoothness.

split keyboarding　In word processing, a system in which keyboarding and editing are performed on one system, and playback on another. See edit.

S plus DX　See speech plus.

spoofing　In data communications, a technique to enable a multiplicity of computers to deal with a variety of terminals. Software emulators running on microprocessors in the channel interfaces make the network appear to the terminal as its own type of computer, and the terminals appear to the computer as its own type of terminal. See channel, emulator, microprocessor, software.

spooling　(1) In computing, Simultaneous Peripheral Operation On Line. The use of auxiliary storage as a buffer when transferring data from the processor to its peripherals. This allows programs using slow peripherals, e.g. line printers, to run to completion quickly, thus making room for other programs in the main store. (2) In recording, movement of tape from one reel to another without being in the record or playback mode. See auxiliary storage, buffer, peripheral.

spot　In cathode ray tubes, the small area on the screen surface which is bombarded by the electron beam.

spot beam　In satellite communications, a narrow antenna beam. Compare earth coverage.

spreadsheet　In computer programming, a software package widely used by managers and accountants. The user is effectively provided with a large grid and he may assign labels, numerical values or formulae, relating numerical values of other squares, to the squares. Thus in financial planning the user may specify that certain squares display the sum of values in corresponding rows or columns. Any alteration in the value of data in a square will result in the automatic update of all related data on the spreadsheet.

sprocket feed　A method of feeding paper, or film, through a device. Toothed gearlike wheels rotate and the pins (or sprockets) on these wheels engage in holes along the edge of the film, or paper, ensuring a positive drive and accurate positioning.

spur　In communications, a junction on a cable distribution system which connects system outlets to the network.

Sputnik I　In communications, the first space satellite launched by U.S.S.R in 1957.

SPX　See simplex.

square serif　Synonymous with slab serif.

squawk box　A low quality loudspeaker used for an intercom or public address system. See intercom, public address system.

SRA paper sizes　See A, B and C series of paper sizes.

SSI　See small scale integration.

stabilization process In photography, a photographic rapid access process utilizing special paper in which a developing agent is incorporated in the emulsion layer, thus allowing fast development. In this process a stabilization bath is substituted for the conventional fixing bath. In phototypesetting it is commonly used for paste up but is not suitable for long term storage. See fixation, phototypesetting, rapid access processing.

stable state The state assumed by a system when the transient effects of all signals and disturbances have died away. See transient.

stack In data structures, a structure in which items are added at the end of a sequential list and can only be retrieved from the same end. Thus a LIFO strategy is employed. Compare queue. See LIFO. Synonymous with pushdown storage.

stack pointer In computer programming, a storage location holding the address of the most recently stored item in a stack. See stack.

stand alone system A self contained system independent of another device, system or program.

stand alone terminal In communications, a terminal that can be directly connected via a modem and is not, therefore, a member of a cluster. See MODEM.

stand alone word processing system A system comprising a single word processing station that does not share the power of a central computer.

standard deviation In statistical measurements, a measure of the spread of values about the arithmetic mean value. See arithmetic mean.

standard document In word processing, the primary document used in automatic letter writing, and merged with variable information to produce the final letter. See variable text, automatic letter writing, boilerplate.

standard interface In computing, a standard physical unit for interconnection of any

peripheral device to the central processing unit. See central processing unit.

standard paragraphs Synonymous with boilerplate.

standards converter In television, a device to convert television signal characteristics, number of lines, number of fields and colour coding from one national standard to another. See video standards.

standby A condition in which a complete resumption of stable operation is possible within a short time. See cold standby, warm standby, hot standby.

standby equipment A duplicate system to be used if the primary unit becomes unusable as a result of malfunction. See standby.

star In communications, a network topology in which each node is connected only to one central controller. Compare ring. See local area network.

start bit In communications and computing, a bit used in asynchronous transmission preceding a serial character and signalling the start of that character. Compare stop bit. See asynchronous transmission.

start element See start bit.

start of header In communications, a control character used at the beginning of a sequence of characters that constitute the address or routing information for the message. See header.

start of text In data communications, a transmission control character that terminates a message heading and indicates that successive characters relate to the text of the message. Compare end of text.

start stop envelope In asynchronous communications, a string of data elements comprising start elements, binary data and stop elements. The envelope can arrive at any time, the receiver remains in an idling mode until the start element arrives and reverts to the idling mode after the stop element is received. See asynchronous transmission, start bit, stop bit.

stat   Synonymous with photostat.

statement   In computer programming, a meaningful expression used to specify an operation and is usually complete in the context of the language used.

state of art   That which can be achieved with currently proven technology and practice, i.e. without further research or development.

static   (1) In audio recording, a popping or crackling noise. (2) In radio transmission, interference produced by abnormal atmospheric effects. (3) A non dynamic system or condition.

static dump   In computing, a dump performed at a particular point in time relative to a machine run, e.g. at the end of the run. See dump.

static memory   In computing, a type of semiconductor memory that does not require periodic refresh cycles. Compare dynamic RAM.

station   In communications, (1) an input or output location of a communication system, it will contain the sources and sinks for the messages and those elements that control the message flow on the link, (2) one or more transmitters and receivers, or a combination thereof, together with the necessary accessory equipment to perform a radiocommunication service, (3) a broadcasting facility assigned a specific frequency. See radiocommunication.

statistical time division multiplexing   In data communications, a version of time division multiplexing in which time slots are only allocated to active terminals. This technique increases the number of terminals that may be connected to a given capacity channel. A buffer memory assembles data and is usually sufficient to store channel characters if traffic temporarily exceeds the multiplexer data link rate. See multiplexer, time division multiplexing.

statmux   See statistical time division multiplexing.

status poll   In communications, a request, initiated by a computer, for information on the current status of a terminal. See polling.

STD   See subscriber trunk dialing.

STDM   See statistical time division multiplexing.

steel engraving   In printing, an intaglio technique in which an image for reproduction is engraved into a steel plate using a chisel shaped tool. Compare etching. See intaglio.

stencil duplicating   In printing, a method of duplication in which ink passes through perforations in a stencil master to form an image. See stencil master.

stencil master   In printing, a sheet with an image of the material to be copied in the form of perforations. See stencil duplicating.

step   In video disk, to advance by one frame either forward or reverse. See frame.

step and repeat camera   In micrographics, a type of microfilm camera which can expose a series of separate images on an area of film according to a predetermined format, usually in orderly columns and rows. See microfilm.

step by step switch   In communications, a switch that is moved to successive positions by line pulses. See selector.

steradion   In optics, a unit solid angle which, having its vertex at the center of a sphere, cuts off an area of the surface of the sphere equal to that of a square with sides of length equal to the radius of the sphere.

stereo   (1) In filming, a positive transparency used for projection of a rear screen background. (2) In printing, a duplicate letterpress plate cast from a mould. (3) Abbreviation for stereophonic. See stereophonic.

stereophonic   An effect of three dimensional sound produced by recording via two separated microphones. The signals from the microphones are recorded or broadcast as separate signals and these signals are played back through two separately spaced loudspeakers. Compare quadrophonic.

stet In typesetting, a proofreader's mark indicating that the copy marked for correction should remain as it was prior to the correction. See proofreading.

still frame audio Synonymous with compressed audio.

still frame In video recording, the continuous reproduction of a stationary helical scan frame or the corresponding effect from a video disk. Synonymous with freeze frame.

stochastic model A mathematical model of a system which incorporates the effects of random events.

stock keeping unit In data processing, an identifier for each item of merchandise.

stop and wait protocol In data communications, a flow control algorithm in which the sending host awaits acknowledgement, from the receiving host, that error free frames have been received before transmitting further frames. Compare sliding window protocol. See frame, host.

stop bit In communications and computing, a bit, used in asynchronous transmission, indicating the end of the character. Compare start bit. See asynchronous transmission.

stop code In word processing, a control code in the body of text that stops playback, or printout, usually to enable the insertion of variable information. See variable text.

stop cylinder press In printing, a cylinder press in which the cylinder remains stationary as the printing bed is returned after being moved out of contact for inking. See cylinder machine, two revolution press.

stop element See stop bit.

stop instruction In computer programming, an instruction indicating the termination of a program execution.

stop list In library science, a list of words or terms, or roots of words, which are considered not to be significant for the purpose of information retrieval and which are excluded from indexing. In automatic indexing systems the computer will be instructed to ignore common terms such as 'and', 'but' etc. included in the stop list. See automatic indexing.

stop motion cinematography A technique to give the trick effect of an instantaneous change, e.g. performers stop their action and an object is placed or removed from the scene. The camera may be stopped during this interval, or the appropriate section of the film removed. On playback the object appears to disappear or materialise.

storage capacity In computing, the quantity of data, measured in bits, bytes or words, that can be held in the memory device. See bit, byte, word.

storage device In computing, a unit into which data can be entered, retained and later retrieved.

storage dump Synonymous with memory dump.

storage tube In computer graphics, a type of CRT that retains its displayed image for an extended period without refreshing from a dynamic store. Compare refreshed CRT. See CRT.

store and forward In communications, a system that stores message packets at intermediate points prior to further transmission. See packet, message switching.

stored program signalling In communications, a technique which enables the sequence of controlling, setting up and clearing down calls by an exchange to be stored as a program within a computer memory. See System X.

story board In filming, a documentary outline of proposed film sequence with sketches, photographs, details of dialog, music, sound effects, etc.

stratified language A computer language that cannot be employed as its own metalanguage. See metalanguage.

streaking Horizontal distortion of a television picture.

strike on   In typesetting, a process of setting type by direct impression, e.g. output of a typewriter composing device. Compare hot type, etch type, cold type.

string   In data structures, a linear sequence of elements, e.g. alphanumeric characters.

string variables   In computer programming, variables that can assume values of strings, usually alphanumeric. See string.

stripping   In communications, the process of extracting the essential information elements of a message by removing the header and tail parts of the message envelope. See header, tail.

strobe   In electronics, a selection signal.

strobing   In television, an effect due to a transverse or rotary movement of an object at a speed counteracting the effect of persistence of vision. See persistence of vision.

stroboscopic effect   A false impression of the speed of revolution of rotating spokes when viewed in a regularly flashing light. It can be used to measure a speed of rotation. See wagon wheel effect.

stroke   (1) In character recognition, an arc or straight line used as a segment of a character. (2) In computer graphics, an arc or straight line used as a segment of a display element. (3) An abbreviation for keystroke. See keystroke.

stroke generator   In computer graphics, a character generator that produces characters composed of strokes. See stroke.

strowger exchange   In telephony, an electromechanical exchange containing switches that move vertically to line up with a bank of contacts and then rotate to engage with one of those contacts. See exchange.

structured programming   In computer programming, a method of designing a program, and associated data structures, that improves clarity, reduces complexity and renders it more amenable to modification and debugging. See data structure, debug.

studio to head end link   In cable television, a fixed microwave link station that transmits signals from the studio to the head end. See head end, microwave transmission.

stunt box   In communications, a device that controls the non printing features of a teletypewriter terminal and recognizes line control characters. See teletypewriter.

STX   See start of text.

stylus   (1) In recording, a transducer in the form of a pointed needle which makes physical contact with a hi fi record. (2) In computer graphics, a hand held pointer for establishing a coordinate position on a display surface, may be used to draw figures or move elements of the display. (3) In video disk, a unit that detects changes in capacitance on a capacitance disk. See capacitance disk, digitizing pad, light pen, transducer.

subaudio frequency   Synonymous with infrasonic frequency.

subliminal   Pertaining to images and sounds below the perception threshold that can influence a subject's behaviour.

subprogram   In computing, (1) a program that is invoked by another program, (2) a part of a larger program that can be compiled independently. See compiler.

subroutine   In computer programming, a sequence of instructions to perform an action that is frequently required in a program or set of programs, e.g. to sort a set of strings into alphabetical order. See open subroutine, closed subroutine.

subroutine call   In computer programming, an instruction which passes control to a subroutine. See subroutine.

subschema   In databases, the application programmer's view of the data. See schema.

subscriber trunk dialing   In telephony, a method by which a user can gain access to exchanges, outside the local area, without operator intervention. Synonymous with direct distance dialing.

subscript (1) In computing, a symbol associated with a name of a set to identify a particular element or subset. (2) In printing, a letter or number that appears below the baseline in a line of printed text. See baseline. Compare superscript.

subset A set of elements, each one of which is a member of another given set. See set.

substitute character In computing, a control character put in place of a character that is recognized to be in error or cannot be represented on a given device, e.g. in videotex received characters with parity errors are displayed as white squares. See parity, videotex.

substrate In microelectronics, the physical material on which a circuit is fabricated. See chip.

subtractive colour mixing (1) In printing, a means of reproducing colours by mixing or superimposing inks, paints or dyes. (2) In photography, a method of analyzing and resynthesizing colours. A scene is filmed with three light filters, representing the primary colours, and black and white negatives of a subject are produced. A dye positive image is produced for each negative with the dye colour complementary to that of the corresponding filter. These dye images are then superimposed to yield a combined transparent positive image. See additive colour mixing.

subtractive primary colours See subtractive colour mixing.

subtrahend The number or quantity sub-

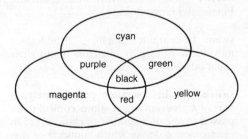

subtractive colour mixing

tracted from the minuend in the subtraction process. See minuend.

subvoice grade channel In communications, a channel with a bandwidth of 240-300 Hz suitable for telegraphy or low speed (up to some 150 bits per second) data transmission, but not for voice messages. Such channels may be leased from a common carrier or derived as subsets of a voice grade channel. Compare voice grade channel. See bit, common carrier, Hz.

suffix notation Synonymous with postfix notation.

summation check In computing, a check based upon the comparison of the sum of digits of a numeral with a previously computed value to indicate any accidental change in the value of a digit during transmission or transcriptions. See redundancy checking.

sun outage In satellite communications, a period in which the system does not function fully due to the relative position of the satellite and the sun. The outage may be caused by the earth's, or moon's, shadow crossing the solar cells or by the satellite passing in front of the sun. See helios noise.

sunshine notice In communications, a notice issued by the FCC stating that members of the public may attend its regulatory proceedings. See FCC.

supercalendered paper In printing, a glossy, but not coated, paper which is produced by being passed through supercalender rolls under high pressure.

supercomputer In computing, an extremely powerful mainframe computer used for complex mathematical calculations demanding high speed and storage, e.g. weather forecasting. Compare fifth generation computer. See mainframe.

supergroup In communications, a collection of five channel groups occupying adjacent bands in the spectrum for the purpose of simultaneous modulation and demodulation. A supergroup comprises 60 voice channels. See channel group, modulation, demodulation, master group.

superheterodyne In radio communications, a method of reception in which the received signal is frequency changed to an intermediate frequency, by a heterodyne process involving a local oscillator. This technique simplifies the design of subsequent amplification stages. See heterodyne, intermediate frequency, amplifier.

super high frequency In communications, frequency range of 3 - 30 GHz. See GHz.

superimposed circuit Synonymous with superposed circuit.

super large scale integration In microelectronics, pertaining to a fabrication technology which produces more than some 100,000 gates per chip. Compare LSI, MSI, SSI, VLSI. See chip, gate.

super master group In communications, CCITT terminology for an assembly of 900 voice channels. See channel group, supergroup, master group.

superposed circuit In communications, an additional channel obtained from one or more circuits, usually provided for other channels, in such a way that all the channels can be used simultaneously and without mutual interference.

superscript In printing, a small character set above the normal level of characters in a typeface. Compare subscript.

super videotex A private videotex system with three sets of attributes: integration with other company information and communication services, integration with word processing and electronic office facilities, integration with computing facilities, e.g. transaction processing and real time updating. See electronic office, transaction processing, videotex, word processing.

supervisor In computing, the section of a control program that coordinates the use of resources and maintains the flow of the processor unit operations.

supervisory program See supervisor.

supervisory sequence In data commu-

nications, a sequence of control characters that performs a defined control function.

supervisory signal In communications, (1) a signal indicating whether a circuit is in use, (2) a signal used to indicate the various operating states of circuit combinations.

superzapping In data security, pertaining to operations which misuse the computer universal access program in order to bypass normal security arrangements and then make illegal modifications to programs or data.

suppressed carrier transmission In communications, the transmission of a modulated wave in which the carrier signal is to some degree suppressed. The carrier conveys no information and its suppression reduces the total power of the transmitted signal. Compare single sideband transmission. See modulation, carrier.

surround sound Synonymous with ambisonics.

SVC See switched virtual call.

swap In time sharing computer systems, to write the image of one job from main into auxiliary storage and to bring another job into the main store from auxiliary storage. See time sharing.

sweep In television, the repetitive movement of the cathode beam over the phosphor screen. There are two sweeps, one which traces horizontal lines, and another moving vertically at a slower rate tracing the assembly of lines into a field. See raster scan, field, line blanking interval, field blanking.

SWIFT Society for Worldwide Interbank Financial Transactions.

swim In computer graphics, an undesired movement of display elements about their usual positions.

switch (1) In computer programming, a part of a program which allows control to be passed to one of a number of choices. (2) In electronics, a device which connects or disconnects an electric circuit.

switchboard In communications, a manually operated system for interconnecting subscribers.

switched network backup In communications, an optional facility enabling a user to specify an alternative path if the primary path is, for some reason, not available.

switched network In communications, any network that uses switching to establish connections.

switched star In cable television, a modern method of cable distribution in which the main cable serves a series of junctions and lines connect the individual subscribers to these junctions. The system has the advantage that the subscriber lines do not have to be of high bandwidth because each subscriber siphons off the signals he requires. Moreover the system facilitates the development of information services which require the user to send signals back up the line. Compare tree and branch.

switched virtual call In packet switching, a connection between two terminals which is created only when it is required, following a call set up procedure. See virtual call service.

switcher Synonymous with vision mixer.

switching In communications, the provision of point to point connections between dynamically changing sources and sinks. See source, sink, circuit switching, message switching, packet switching.

switching center In communications, a location that terminates multiple circuits and has the capability of transferring traffic between circuits or interconnecting circuits.

switching error Synonymous with quadrature error.

switching office Synonymous with switching center.

switch lock See vertical lock.

switch over In computing and communications, a switching action, performed manually or automatically, to remove a faulty unit and connect in an alternative serviceable one.

Switchstream See PSS, X-Stream.

switch train In telephony, a sequence of switches providing the connection between a caller, and a called, telephone.

syllogism In mathematics, a logical statement that involves three propositions: the major premise, minor premise and conclusion. The conclusion is necessarily being true if the premises are true e.g. John likes fishing or singing, John does not like fishing, John likes singing.

symbolic address In computer programming, a name or label representing a storage location. See label.

symbolic language In computer programming, a language for the expression of operation codes and addresses that is more meaningful to a user than machine code representation. See machine code, assembly language.

symbol table In computing, a table produced by a compiler, or assembler, to associate a symbolic name to an actual address or value. See compiler, assembler.

SYMPHONIE An international communications satellite. See satellite.

sync See synchronous.

sync bit In data communications, a bit used for synchronization. See bit, synchronization.

synchronization The process of maintaining common timing and coordination between two or more operations, events or processes.

synchronization pulses In electronics, pulses sent to receiving equipment, by transmitting units, to keep the two units in step.

synchronizer In audiovisual aids, a single function control device. It may receive a signal from another device, e.g. a tape recorder, and perform a single control action, e.g. select a new slide. If used in conjunction with a programmer more complex control functions may be performed with the synchronizer informing the programmer when the next control action is to be undertaken. See programmer.

synchronous Pertaining to two or more processes that require common physical occurrences, e.g. timing pulses for their operation. Compare asynchronous.

synchronous computer A computer in which each event is constrained to wait upon the arrival of a timing signal.

synchronous data link control In data communications, a discipline for the transmission of binary synchronous data communication. Messages are structured into frames with each frame commencing and terminating with a flag. The flag is the character 0111 1110, and bit stuffing is employed to prevent an encoded signal from duplicating a flag. See bit stuffing, binary synchronous communications, flag, frame.

synchronous data network In data communications, a network in which the timing of all network components is controlled by a single timing source.

synchronous detection In communications, a method of recovering the signal from an amplitude modulated waveform. The received waveform is multiplied by a signal of the same frequency and phase as the original carrier. Compare envelope detection. See amplitude modulation, carrier.

synchronous idle character In synchronous data transmission, a transmission control character used by DTE's for synchronism or synchronous correction, particularly when no other character is being transmitted. See synchronous data network, DTE.

synchronous network In communications, a network in which all the communication links are synchronized with a common clock.

synchronous transmission In data communications, a transmission method in which each bit is transmitted according to a given time sequence. It can provide a higher bit rate than asynchronous transmission but requires

that the receiver and transmitter maintain exact synchronization over an extended period. Compare asynchronous transmission. See bit rate.

sync pulses Synonymous with synchronization pulses.

sync tip frequency In video recording, the frequency of the recorded frequency modulated signal corresponding to the TV sync pulse. During sync pulses the voltage level of the video signal is at a minimum and thus the sync tip frequency is the lowest frequency of the recorded frequency modulated signal. See sync pulses, white level, frequency modulation, black level.

syndetic In library science, (1) having entries connected by cross references, (2) coordination of two or more related documents.

synonym (1) A word denoting the same thing as another but suitable to a different context. (2) In computing, one of the records whose key corresponds to the result of a given hashing routine. See hashing.

synoptic In library science, a concise publication in a journal which presents the key ideas and results of a full length article.

syntactic error In computer programming, a programming error in which the statement does not conform to the syntax of the language. Such errors are detected and reported in the translation process. See translator, syntax.

syntax (1) The interrelationship of characters or groups of characters independent of their meaning, interpretation or use. (2) In computer programming, the grammatical rules governing the use of a language.

synthesis Building up of separate elements.

SYSGEN See system generation.

system generation In computing, the process of selecting and modifying an operating system to optimize its performance for a particular hardware configuration and data processing environment. See hardware, operating system.

system library   In computing, the collection of files and data sets in which the various sections of the operating system are held. See operating system, data set.

systems analysis   In data processing, the analysis of an activity or system, often in a commercial context, to determine if and how the system may be improved using computer systems. See feasibility study.

systems network architecture   In data communications, an IBM term for the total description of the logical structure, formats, protocols and operational sequences for transmitting information units through the communication system. The communication system functions are separated into the distinct areas: application layer, function management layer and transmission subsystem layer. This form of architecture enables the end users to be unaffected by the specific communication system services and facilities used for the exchange of information.

System X   In data communications, a new family of digital switching systems which will provide the control and signalling for the Integrated Services Digital Network (ISDN) in the UK. The ISDN is the common data highway which will carry all customer services such as telex, viewdata and telephony, and any new service which will be introduced.

See (a) the Integrated Services Digital Network, (b) Digital Switching and (c) The System X Family.

(a) The Integrated Service Digital Network System X is the central feature of an overall strategy to convert the whole of the existing UK analog trunk network to digital by the early 1990s. There will then be one network with a common family of switching exhanges for the integrated service, as opposed to traditional ad-hoc approach of one network and asociated exchanges for each service, see Fig. 1.

System X is based on the recognition that the telecommunications network can no longer remain primarily a carrier of voice mesages. The anticipated growth of digital services is shown in Fig. 2 and reflects the growth of business data communications.

Sending computer data and text along channels designed for speech requires costly conversion equipment.

Moreover, with the current two-wire switching network numerous signalling systems are used which have limited capacity to convey information about the call and caller. Connection times are slow for calls routed through several exchanges, and calls are

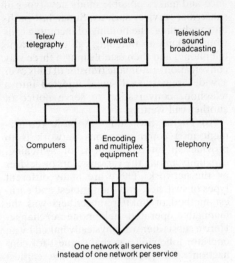

One network all services
instead of one network per service

System X
Fig 1 Integrated services digital network.

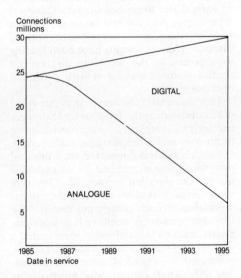

System X
Fig 2 The change from analog to digital switching.

subject to variable transmission losses, noise and distortion.

System X uses digital signals which are handled far more easily than analog voice signals. Messages, whether voice, vision or data can be reduced to a common digital format. Digital transmissions, combined with exchanges run by computers and using digital switching, gives a better economic performance and makes possible many new types of subscriber services such as: Super-fast push-button dialling, the holding of incoming calls while making an outgoing call on the same telephone, and then establishing a three way conversation; automatic transfer of calls over a wide area; special signal injected into a telephone conversation to serve notice of another call waiting.

(b) Digital Switching   A basic requirement in a communications network is to provide an interconnection, or switching, capability among the various users or devices on the network. There are many different types of switches, and the simplest and earliest method of linking subscribers was the manually operated telephone exchange. Here a subscriber was physically linked by an operator following a verbal request for connection. The performance of the earliest exchanges was heavily dependent on the ability of the central control operator, but it was for reasons of security and cost that led to an early desire to replace operators. Nevertheless, ever since the first automatic systems were introduced into a telephone network all subsequent developments have been leading to a return to the flexibility and central control features associated with a manual operator system.

The automatic systems that replaced operators, such as the crossbar and Strowger exchanges, employed electromechanical technology and space division multiplexing. Here each call was connected via a physical path which was maintained for its exclusive use for the duration of the call. The term space division is derived from the spatial separation of each connecting circuit. The Crossbar exchange employed a switching matrix, each element of which represented a crosspoint at which a 'horizontal' inlet can be connected to a 'vertical' outlet if required. The crosspoint contact was mechanically made by the crossbar switch, see Fig. 3.

The development of digital techniques,

and the resulting low cost of crosspoint devices, offered the ability to move from space switching to time switching techniques, such as those used in time division multiplexing (TDM). System X uses a combination of space and time switching for routing digital information, Fig. 4.

In Fig. 4 A transmits information to B, and vice-versa. The signals are PCM and in practice A would be one of 30 incoming time slots, with each time slot it would have 8 bits of information, i.e. 8 wires with either an 0 or 1 being carried on each. Each 8 bit of data is placed in a buffer store in strict rotation under a synchronizing clock. The contents of each buffer of the incoming time switch are then removed during a later time slot and passed down a bus or highway to the space switch. During the same time interval, one electronic crosspoint is operated in the space switch and the information is transferred to the required outgoing time switch. The space switch crosspoint is only operated for a few microseconds, and once it has completed its task, it is used for interconnecting other inputs and outputs, thereby time-sharing the space switch.

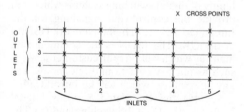

System X
Fig 3 Crossbar switching matrix with crosspoints.

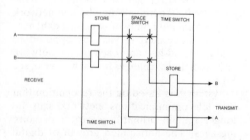

System X
Fig 4 Time-space time switching.

(c) The System X Family. Apart from using digital switching, System X uses stored program signalling (SPC) and Common Channel Signalling. The basis of SPC relies on the fact that in any exchange there is a logical sequence to controlling, setting up and clearing down calls. It is therefore possible to hold the sequence of operations and instructions as a program within computer memory. Common channel signalling is a method of signalling in which a single link causes signalling information for many traffic circuits (typically 960 circuits). This is inherently a more efficient process than separate channel signalling, where there is a separate signalling interface for each transmission channel.

A System X exchange may either be a trunk exchange, where it is known as a digital main switching unit (DMSU), or a local exchange, where it is either a digital local exchange (DLE) or a digital principle local exchange (DPLE). There are two very important features of the System X network:

(i) all exchanges must be synchronized to a common clock for the safe transfer of data

(ii) the service must continue to operate in the event of a failure of part of the network.

Fig. 5 shows the multiple pathways in the system and the requirement for overall network synchronization. The network is arranged as a three level hierarchy, with the national reference clock at level 1.

See common channel signalling, ISDN, PCM, space division switching, strowger

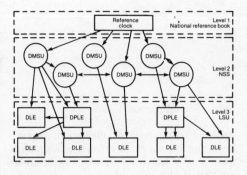

System X
Fig 5 Network synchronization.

exchange, stored program signalling, TDM, telex, viewdata.

SYSTRAN In machine translation, TRANsatlantic SYStem, a widely used fully automatic machine translation system providing translation between pairs of languages - English, French, Russian and Spanish. Current experience indicates that it requires both pre- and postediting for acceptable results. See postediting, pre-editing.

S100 bus In microcomputers, a bus originally designed for the ALTAIR system and now standardized as the IEEE 696 bus. It may be used with both 8 and 16 bit microprocessors. See bus, microprocessor.

T

tab   See tabulation.

table   In computing, a collection of data in a form suitable for ready reference, frequently stored in consecutive storage locations or written in the form of an array. See table lookup, symbol table, array.

table lookup   In computing, a method of determining an unknown quantity by checking for a related known quantity in a table. See table.

tablet   See digitizing pad.

tab memory   In word processing, a facility to store and recall details of tab stops. See tabulation.

tabulating   In data processing, an operation on punched cards, e.g. sorting, collating. See sort, collate.

tabulation   (1) In printing, the action of automatically moving a printing head to a specified position on a line. (2) To produce a table.

tabulation markers   In computing, symbols used to designate protected fields of a visual display or to perform tabulation setting functions. See tabulation, protected field.

tachistoscope   In visual aids, a device for displaying images, or text, for brief intervals of time, usually a fraction of a second.

tachometer lock   In recording, a condition in which the tach pulses from a controlled motor arrive in a required relationship with a set of reference pulses; this condition ensures that the reading head follows the same track, at the same rate, as the original recording head. See tach pulse.

tach pulse   In recording, a pulse derived from the rotation of a motor shaft. The pulse is produced optically, magnetically or mech-

anically whenever a given point on the shaft rotates past a fixed point. See tachometer lock.

TACS   In communications, Total Access Communications System, the standard adopted by the UK Government for the cellular radio system. See cellular radio.

tactile   Pertaining to a sense of touch.

tactile feedback   Use of sense of touch to receive information. See braille marks.

tag   In computer programming, (1) a portion of an instruction, (2) one or more characters attached to a group of data providing information about the group.

tail   (1) In cinematography, the end of a film. (2) In printing, the bottom of a book. (3) In computing, a specified data item indicating the end of a list. (4) In communications, a series of codes to denote the end of a message. See list.

take   (1) In typesetting, a unit of text. It may be one portion of copy taken from a longer piece of matter to be set that is shared among several typesetters. In phototypesetting it refers to the composed matter appearing on one piece of punched paper tape. (2) In filming, a shot or the number of times that a shot has been taken. See copy, matter, paper tape, phototypesetting,

take back   In printing, a proof instruction to a printer to take back a line, or number of lines, of type to a previous page or column. See proof, take over.

take in   In printing, an instruction to a printer, on a proof or manuscript, to take in added copy. See copy, proof.

take over   In printing, a proof instruction to a printer to take a line, or number of lines, of type over to the next page or column. Compare take back. See proof.

talkback In television, a speaker system providing communication between a control room and a television studio.

tandem exchange In communications, a telephone switching office handling traffic among local exchanges. Compare toll office. See local exchange.

tandem switching In telephony, the use of an intermediate switch or switches to interconnect circuits from the switch of one serving central office to the switch of a second serving central office in the same exchange area. See tandem exchange, central office.

tank recorder In recording, a continuous loop recording system.

tape See magnetic tape, paper tape.

tape counter In recording, a device that indicates the length of tape that has passed over the magnetic heads.

tape deck In recording, a tape transport mechanism, read/write heads and preamplifier electronics. Designed to act as a tape recorder with an external sound system. See tape transport.

tape drive In recording, a mechanism to move magnetic tape over reading or writing heads at constant speed and tension and also used for automatic rewinding. See tape. Synonymous with tape transport.

tape guides In recording, rollers or posts to position the tape correctly along its path to the tape drive. See tape drive.

tape library In computing, a secure room with controlled environmental conditions, used to store computer magnetic tapes.

tape punch In computing and communications, a device that punches holes in paper tape according to signals from a computer or a transmitting device. See paper tape.

tape recorder In recording, an electronic mechanical device to record information on magnetic tape for instant playback.

tape slide In audiovisual aids, a 35mm projector which can be synchronized to a magnetic tape commentary.

tape streamer In computing, a tape drive system used as a backup storage device for a fixed head disk unit. See magnetic tape, Winchester.

tape timer In recording, a device that measures the length of tape transported between two reels, usually calibrated in playing time.

tape to card converter In computing, a device, usually off line, that converts information from magnetic tape to punched cards. See off line.

tape transmitter In telegraphy, a device which transmits signals coded on perforated paper tape. See paper tape.

tape transport Synonymous with tape drive.

target In television, the light receptive area of the camera tube.

target language In computer programming and machine translation, the language to which translation is to be made. Compare source language. Synonymous with object language.

target program Synonymous with object program.

tariff In communications, the published set of rates, rules and regulations relevant to the equipment and services provided by a telecommunications common carrier. See common carrier.

TASI In telephony, Time Assigned Speech Interpolation, a technique that reassigns a voice channel for the period that a user pauses in speech. See DSI.

task In computing, a unit of work for the computer.

task list In office systems, a detailed record of work performed by a worker and the average time required to perform the tasks each week.

T carrier In communications, a hierarchy of Bell Telephone digital communication systems designated T1, T2 and T4.

TDM See time division multiplexing.

TDS See transaction driven system.

TEAM In machine translation, Terminology, Evaluation and Acquisition Method. A machine aided translation system developed in Germany, based on an automatic dictionary and term bank, and offering on line interrogation. Its databases give target language equivalents for input terms in eight European languages and it can produce a range of off line translation aids and services. See automatic dictionary, term bank.

tearing In television, a distortion of image produced by a lack of sweep synchronization. See sweep.

telebanking In data communications, a facility to perform client banking transactions over a communication network, e.g. videotex, interactive cable television. See home banking, interactive cable television, self banking, videotex.

telecine In television, a technique for replaying a cine film over television.

Telecom Gold In communications, the British Telecom version of the US Dialcom system which provides a nationwide electronic mail service. Communication is via PSS or the telephone network. Information may also be undertaken with the US Dialcom service. See Dialcom, electronic mail.

telecommunications Essentially communications over a distance. In modern technology the transmission may take one of three forms, i.e. electrical signals along a conductor, electromagnetic radiation or light signals passing along an optical fiber. The signal may, in some cases, have the same shape as the originating signal but in many cases the information to be transmitted modulates a carrier wave. See modulation, electromagnetic radiation, fiber optics.

teleconferencing A system which provides facilities for group communications amongst remote users. See computer conferencing, dial up teleconferencing, picturephone meeting service, video teleconferencing.

telecontrol In communications, the remote control of devices using a telecommunication link.

Teleglobe Canada In communications, the Crown corporation that handles Canada's overseas telecommunications.

telegraphy In communications, (1) a system in which a direct current is interrupted, or its polarity is reversed, in order to transmit a signal code, (2) the branch of telecommunications concerned with the reproduction at a distance of documentary matter originating in written, printed or pictorial form.

teleinformatic services In communications, a CCITT term encompassing all record type non voice, or non speech telecommunication services, e.g. telex, videotex, facsimile. See telex, videotex, facsimile, common carrier.

telematics See télématique.

télématique In communications, a French term coined to describe the combination of computers and telecommunication networks.

telemetering In communications, the remote metering of domestic utility consumption. See telemetry.

telemetry In communications, the transmission of signals derived from measuring devices over long distances.

telemonitoring In communications, the remote monitoring of, usually domestic, measuring devices using a telecommunication link, e.g. reading electricity meters. See telemetering.

Telenet In communications, Telenet Communication Corporation, a packet switching transmission service. See packet switching.

teleordering In publishing, an automated method for book seller purchasing. Book sellers enter orders for books, using ISBN identification, into an intelligent terminal during the day. At the end of the working day a central minicomputer automatically dials up these terminals, over the telephone network, collects the details of orders, and stores the orders in backing storage. This information is then transferred to a mainframe computer where they are processed into a format suitable for the publishers. The minicomputer returns a confirmation or otherwise, for each order to the book seller terminal where it is stored and printed out the following day. Compare teleshopping.

telephone exchange Synonymous with central office.

telephone frequency Synonymous with voice frequency.

telephone repeater A combination of amplifiers, and associated equipment, to compensate for the attenuation of voice signals along a telephone line. See repeater.

telephone set A set of equipment comprising telephone transmitter, telephone receiver, switch hook, dialing unit and associated components.

telephony In communications, a system for the transmission of speech, or other signals coded onto audio frequency signals.

teleprinter Synonymous with teletypewriter.

teleprinter exchange service In communications, a service provided by a common carrier for the interconnection, via dial up facilities, of subscribers' teleprinters. See teleprinter.

teleprinter interface See terminal interface.

teleprocessing In computing and communications, data processing combined with telecommunications, e.g. the use of a telephone network to connect a remote terminal to a computer or to interconnect two computers.

Telesat In communications, a Canadian domestic communications satellite system. See satellite.

teleshopping In communications, the use of a domestic terminal, e.g viewdata, to order goods from a supplier. See viewdata.

telesoftware In computing, the transmission of software to an intelligent videotex terminal, or to a microcomputer programmed to emulate a videotex terminal. See software, videotex.

Télésystèmes-Questel In databases, an information retrieval service operated by Télésystèmes-Questel (France). See on line information retrieval.

Télétel In communications, the French public videotex service.

Teletex In communications, an international business correspondence service defined by CCITT and offered by common carriers. The terminals used are primarily sophisticated electronic typewriters and word processors. See CCITT, common carrier.

teletext In communications, a method of transmitting information, stored on a computer, to domestic television sets suitably adapted. In broadcast services the data signals are transmitted in conjunction with normal TV programs. See videotex.

teletext decoder In communications, a device to enable a domestic TV set to display teletext information. See teletext.

teletype In communications, a term commonly used for a range of teleprinter equipment, e.g. tape punches, reperforators, page printers etc. See tape punch, reperforator, page printer.

teletype compatible terminal In computing, a VDU, or hardcopy terminal, that is compatible with a teletype at the functional or software level. See teletype, VDU.

teletypesetting In printing, a method of using punched paper tape to operate a linecaster. See linecaster.

teletypewriter In communications, (1) a typewriter device capable of transmitting and receiving alphanumeric information over communication channels, (2) a printer used to display information received from a telegraph system. See alphanumeric, telegraphy. Synonymous with teleprinter.

teletypewriter exchange service In communications, an automatic teletypewriter exchange switching service in which customers dial calls from station to station on the network. Provided by Western Union in USA and the Computer Communications Group of the TransCanada Telephone System in Canada.

television In communications, the electronic transmission of pictures and accompanying sound.

television camera An optical and electronic apparatus for translating an optical image into electrical signals suitable for transmission. See pickup tube, television receiver, composite colour video signal.

television cut off In cinematography, the limitation in the area of a film frame when televised. See television safe action area.

television game Synonymous with video game.

television mask In filming, a mask used on a viewfinder, or on material to be filmed, indicating the television safe action area. See television safe action area.

television monitor A device that displays TV pictures received from a recorder, camera or closed circuit system. It has neither a sound system nor the facilities to receive broadcast signals.

television projector A device that projects a TV image onto a screen for viewing by a large audience.

television receiver A device for receiving and reproducing both pictures and sound from broadcast television, or modulated cable system, signals.

television receiver/monitor A device that can be used to display both broadcast and closed circuit TV signals. See television monitor, television receiver.

television safe action area The area of a frame of film which will not be cropped during transmission by television.

television scan A regular series of horizontal scanning lines on a TV screen. The total scan is normally performed in two stages, with the second set of scan lines interlacing the first. See scanning line, video standards, sweep, interlace.

television tubes A television tube accepts an electrical signal and produces a corresponding visual image. The tube is effectively a cathode ray tube with scanning circuits that cause the spot to trace out a series of horizontal lines across the tube. The signal corresponding to the brightness of the image is fed to the electron gun thus varying the intensity of the beam striking the phosphor screen. In colour tubes there are three guns corresponding to the red, green and blue signals. Each gun strikes a corresponding phosphor dot on the screen to produce the appropriate colour. See cathode ray tube, phosphor dots, television scan, gun, shadowmask.

telex In communications, an automatic dial up teletypewriter switching service provided by common carriers. See teletypewriter, common carrier.

Telidon Canadian videotex service using alphageometric coding. See alphageometric, videotex.

Telpak In communications, a pricing arrangement giving a bulk rate for multichannel paths on a two point or multipoint basis.

Telset In communications, the Finnish videotex system. See videotex.

Telstar In communications, a television communications satellite. See satellite.

Teltex In communications, a Western Union service that enables telex subscribers to send telegrams. See telex.

ten pitch See pica.

ten's complement The decimal number resulting from the subtraction of a number from the next highest integral power of 10, e.g. the ten's complement of 69 is 100-69=31. See one's complement, nine's complement, two's complement.

tera A million million, i.e. 10 to the power 12.

terahertz In communications, a frequency of one million megahertz.

term (1) A word or expression that has a precise meaning, in some uses, or is peculiar to a science, art, profession or subject. (2) In library science, a subject heading or descriptor in an index. See descriptor, heading, index.

term bank In databases, a database of terms for specialized vocabularies, stored on a computer, which can provide an on line service and from which mono-, bi- and multilingual dictionaries can be produced as well as a range of glossaries and word lists. A facility that can be employed in machine aided translation but monolingual term banks also have applications areas, e.g. by Standards Organizations.

terminal (1) In communications and computing, an input output device for transmitting and receiving data on a communication line. (2) In electronics, a point for the connection to an electrical unit. (3) In communications, a point in the system where information can be transmitted or received.

terminal handler In communications, a part of a data network that services simple, character stream terminals.

terminal identity In viewdata, codes transmitted by a viewdata terminal to the host computer to establish the identity, and hence authorization, of the user. See viewdata.

terminal interface In computing and communications, the codes and hardware used to control an input output device, or terminal.

terminological data bank See term bank.

ternary A system with three possible states. Compare binary.

tertiary colour In printing, a colour produced by the combination of two secondary colours. See secondary colour.

test data In computing, data developed specifically to test a program or computer system.

test pattern In television, a pattern designed for checking linearity, contrast, resolution and colour of a TV receiver.

text (1) In word processing, a set of alphanumeric characters which convey information. (2) In communications, the information content of a message.

text compression In data communications, pertaining to the elimination of redundant data, e.g. leading zeros, trailing blanks, from a message. See huffman code.

text editing In computing and word processing, the insertion, deletion, movement, correction and copying of stored text. See text editor.

text editor In computing, a program that enables a user to modify and copy programs and text files in a versatile manner. Characters and strings can be inserted, modified, deleted and moved throughout the text. In many cases it is possible to locate automatically a specific string, and to replace every instance of one string by another. See line editor, screen editor.

text move In word processing, the ability to select a portion of text from a stored document and move it to a new position in that, or another, stored document. See text editor.

text processing See word processing.

text retrieval In information retrieval, a computer based system in which the user is provided with a printout, or display, of whole, or part of the relevant document instead of merely references to them. Legal literature was the first field to be covered in this way.

text size   See composition size.

text to speech synthesis   In computing, a system which receives stored text and produces the corresponding spoken output. Design of a comprehensive system involves algorithms to cope with the vagaries of English spelling and pronunciation plus the design of sound synthesizers which can successfully mimic the human voice. A further complication arises from the relationship between the manner of speech and its context, e.g. 'there is a fire in the lounge' can be a welcoming statement to a guest or an urgent warning to a householder. See speech synthesis.

The Computer Database   A database supplied by Management Contents and dealing with computers & computer industry. See on line information retrieval.

thermal imaging   In television, a camera system that responds to the subject's radiated heat rather than light.

thermal noise   In electronics, random signals produced in electronic components with a power proportional to the component's temperature. See noise.

thermal printing   In printing, a process in which heat is transferred from a print head to a substrate to form an image.

thermistor   In electronics, a device that exhibits a definite, reliable and repeatable change of electrical resistance with temperature. The resistance may increase, or decrease, with temperature depending upon the type of thermistor. See resistance.

thick film   In electronics, a method of integrated circuit fabrication in which the components are mounted and interconnected on a ceramic substrate. See chip, integrated circuit.

thimble   A printing element similar to a daisy wheel but bent into a cup shape. See daisy wheel.

thin film   In electronics, a method of integrated circuit fabrication in which thin layers of material are deposited on an insulating base in a vacuum. See integrated circuit, chip, thick film.

thin film memory   In computing, a high speed random access memory device. Magnetic dots are deposited in a thin film of insulating material. A grid of read write heads magnetize, and read, the magnetic state of the dots. See random access memory.

thin window display   In word processing, a single line display of 15 to 32 characters to prompt an operator or display a section of text. Synonymous with marching display.

third generation computer   The generation of computers in which integrated circuits replaced individually wired transistors, originated in about 1964. Compare first generation computer, second generation computer. fourth generation computer, fifth generation computer.

third normal form   In relational databases, a relation is in third normal form if it is in second normal form and every nonprime attribute of it is nontransitively dependent on each candidate key of the relation. See second normal form, nonprime attribute, transitive dependence, candidate key, normal forms.

third party database   In videotex, a database maintained by an IP on a separate computer, from the videotex service, but accessible by a gateway link between the two computers. See gateway, database, IP.

thrashing   In computing, a condition in a virtual storage system where an excessive proportion of CPU time is spent in moving data between the main and auxiliary storage. See CPU, paging, virtual storage.

threaded tree   In data structures, a tree in which additional pointers assist in the scan of the tree. See tree, pointer, scan.

three colour process   In printing and photography, a process that uses all three primary colours. Compare four colour process. See primary colours.

three two pulldown   In video disk, a means of transferring film shot at 24 frames per second into video at 30 frames per second (NTSC). The first film frame is exposed on three video fields and the next film frame is exposed on two fields. See field, frame, NTSC.

throughput   A measure of the amount of useful work performed by a system in a given period of time.

thyristor   In electronics, a semiconductor device that passes only a part of an AC current cycle in relationship to a control voltage. See AC.

tie breaker   In computing, a device that resolves a conflict when two CPUs simultaneously try to access the same peripheral. See CPU, peripheral.

tie line   Synonymous with tie trunk.

tie trunk   In communications, a point to point communication channel linking PBX systems or switchboards. See PBX, point to point connection.

tilde   In printing, an accent in the form of a small wavy line, usually over the letter n. See Spanish n, accent.

time address code   In video recording, a digital timing signal recorded on a longitudinal track that provides a display of real time in hours, minutes, seconds and frames. It is used for editing purposes. See edit.

time base   In electronics, a signal generated to provide an indication of relative timing. In an oscilloscope the time base signal is a waveform that increases linearly to a maximum and then returns rapidly to its reference level before commencing the next sweep. This signal draws the spot horizontally across the face of the tube for the display of waveforms. In television tubes, the spot is similarly traced across the face of the tube but in successive horizontal scans the spot is moved vertically down the screen. See sweep.

time base corrector   In recording, a device to correct the distortion due to a lack of synchronism between the timebase of the recorded signal and that of the playback device. The timing differences are adjusted

with the aid of a short term signal store, e.g. an adjustable delay line. See delay line.

time coded page   In teletext, a page in which additional information is added to its normal magazine and page number, thus permitting a number of pages bearing the same magazine and page numbers to be transmitted in sequence. The additional identification is in the form of a four digit number that may correspond to the time of page transmission. See magazine.

time derived channel   In communications, a channel derived by time division multiplexing. See time division multiplexing.

time display   In teletext, the last eight digits of a teletext page header are reserved for clock time and a receiver may display this information giving a rolling display of current time. See page header.

time division multiple access   In communications, a technique in a time division multiplexing system in which a stream of time slots are allocated to users according to their demand. Compare frequency division multiple access. See time division multiplexing.

time division multiplexing   In communications, a method of allocating a high capacity channel to a number of sender recipient pairs. The information from each sender is allocated time intervals in the main channel and the sections of messages are interleaved, with those from other users, at the channel input. The message segments are separated and the complete messages are reconstructed at the receiving end. The decreasing cost of digital circuitry has rendered time division multiplexing cheaper than frequency division multiplexing which requires expensive analog filter circuits. However it can only be used for digital signals. Analog signals such as voice must be converted into digital form by PCM before they can employ this technique. Compare frequency division multiplexing. See analog signal, digital signal, packet switching. PCM.

time division switching   In communications, a switching method for time division multiplexed channels. Data enters a switching stage in one time slot and emerges in another.

message
signals

low-pass
filters

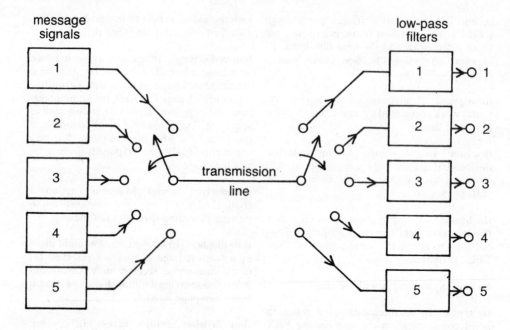

time division multiplexing
An example of TDM in which five message signals are transmitted over the same line.

For switching of pulse code modulation channels, each time slot contains one coded sample, e.g. 8 bits. Compare space division switching. See time division multiplexing, pulse code modulation.

time domain In electronics, pertaining to the analysis of the effect of a linear circuit on a waveform in terms of time rather than frequency. Compare frequency domain. See waveform.

time lapse cinematography A method of filming processes with invisibly slow movements, e.g. growth of a plant. A greater than normal time interval elapses between the exposure of successive frames. Projection at normal speed then provides an apparent speed up of events.

time lapse recorder In recording, a video recorder that is operated intermittently to sample video information. It is used for security and surveillance.

time out In computing, (1) a time interval allotted for certain operations to occur, (2) a terminal feature that logs off a user if an entry is not made before the end of a specified time interval. See log off.

time sharing In computing, a technique that enables a computer to handle simultaneous users and peripherals. Each computer operation is performed in sequence but the high speed of operation, together with the time slice technique, gives the appearance of a simultaneous multiuser service. See time slice.

time shift viewing In video recording, the use of a video cassette recorder to replay a television program at a time more convenient than the original television broadcast.

time slice In computing, a non preemptible interval of processor time allocated to a specific task in a time shared system. All the tasks receive time slices in rotation until they are completed, thus no one task can monopolize the processor. See time sharing.

time study In office systems, a method for the determination of the optimum method of performing various tasks by a detailed study and analysis of the work content of individual component operations.

timing loop In computing, a short computer subroutine that produces a precise time delay, usually of the order of milliseconds. See subroutine.

tinny In recording, an audio output lacking low frequency components.

TIP In computer networks, Terminal Interface Processor, a term originating in the ARPA network to describe a small computer connecting terminals to a packet switching network. See IMP, ARPA, packet switching.

TIR See total internal reflection.

Titus In machine aided translation, a system developed for the Institut Textile de France, which translates abstracts, in the field of textile technology, simultaneously into several languages. Texts are initially edited to make them fit the syntax and vocabulary that the machine can handle.

T junction In electronics, a junction formed to make connection with a cable carrying power or signals.

T network In electronics, a network comprising three elements interconnected in the shape of a letter T.

toggle In electronics, any device having two stable states. See bistable.

toggle switch In electronics, a two position manual switch. See toggle.

token See control token.

toll call In telephony, a call to a connection beyond an exchange boundary. See exchange.

toll center In communications, a switching center where intercity circuits terminate. Usually one local office in a city is designated the toll center and is also used for mileage rate measurement. See switching center.

toll charge In telephony, a charge for a call

outside the local service area of the calling station.

toll office Synonymous with toll center.

toll switching office Synonymous with toll center.

toll switching trunk In communications, a line connecting a local exchange to a trunk exchange, enabling a trunk operator to establish a trunk call for a subscriber. See trunk.

tone A continuous signal, or sound, of one particular frequency.

tone dialing Synonymous with pushbutton dialing.

toner In xerography, the material employed to develop a latent image. See latent image.

tone signalling In telephony, the use of tones to transmit supervisory, address and alerting signals over a circuit. See tone, signalling.

top down method A method of designing a system, or computer program, commencing with a simple overall structure, then successively refining the description of each sub-component, in a similar manner, until a detailed structure is obtained. Compare bottom up method. See programming.

TOPIC In videotex, Teletext Output of Price Information by Computer. The UK Stock Exchange information service. Inputs are received from EPIC, Stock Exchange IP's, Member Firm IP's, External IP's and outputs are available to a nationwide network of viewdata terminals. See EPIC, IP, viewdata.

top of form In word processing, a facility on a character printer that automatically advances the paper by one page.

topology In communications, the form of interconnection of nodes in a network. See bus, node, ring, star.

TOPS See traffic operator position system.

torn tape　(1) In communications, a manual switching system where incoming messages to the switching center perforate paper tape. The tape is removed from the reperforater by manual operators and placed on the appropriate tape reader for signal transmission to the destination. (2) In typesetting, a system where the paper tape output of the computer is torn off and manually transported to the typesetting machine for input. See paper tape, reperforator.

total internal reflection　In optics, a phenomenon that can occur when light travelling in a medium with relatively high refractive index meets an interface with a medium with a lower refractive index. If the angle of incidence is greater than a given critical angle then the light is not refracted but is reflected back into the denser medium. This phenomenon traps light signals in fiber optic devices and results in their transmission along the fiber. See refractive index, fiber optics.

touchpanel switch　A switch that operates by capacitance, resistance or physical contact effects and requires no mechanical movement.

touchscreen　In computing, an input device with which the user indicates a particular choice, or a coordinate position, by touching the appropriate point on a VDU screen. In a common form infrared lamps are affixed to a horizontal and a vertical side of the screen, producing a grid of rays, infrared detectors are aligned on the opposite sides. An interruption of the beams, by the user's finger, produces two signals corresponding to the horizontal and vertical coordinates, for input into the computer. See infrared, VDU.

touchtone　In telephony, an AT&T term for pushbutton dialing. See pushbutton dialing.

Toxline　A database supplied by National Library of Medicine, Toxicology Information Program and dealing with biomedicine, toxicology. See on line information retrieval.

TP　See transaction processing.

TPI　See tracks per inch.

TPS　Transaction Processing System. See transaction processing.

trace packet　In a packet switching network, a packet that causes a report, on each stage of its progress through the network, to be transmitted to the network control station. See network control station.

track　In recording and computing, a path along which data is recorded, on a continuous or rotational medium, e.g. magnetic tape, magnetic disk. In video recording the track is diagonal on the tape. In magnetic disks the data is recorded on a series of circular tracks. Compare sector. See helical scan, transverse scan.

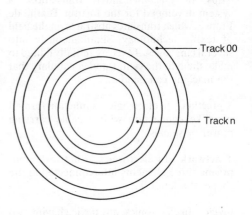

track
The organization of tracks on a floppy disk.

tracking　In video recording, the adjustment of the relative position of the rotating playback head with the recorded track.

tracks per inch　In computing, a measure of the density of tracks on a magnetic disk. Floppy disks typically have upwards from 48 TPI whilst hard disk systems have up to 400 TPI. See floppy disk, hard disk, magnetic disk, track.

tractor feed　See sprocket feed.

traffic　In communications, the signals or

messages handled by a communications system.

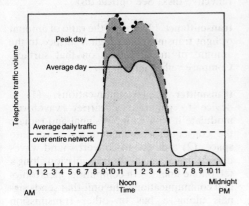

traffic
A typical telephone traffic pattern at a local office.

traffic analysis In communications, a detailed study of a communication system's traffic. It includes a statistical analysis of message headings, receipts and acknowledgements, routings etc., plus a study of the time variations in the volume of traffic and the type of traffic.

traffic matrix In communications, a matrix that records the volume of traffic in a network. The quantity at element (p,q) is a measure of the traffic volume from node p to node q. See node, traffic.

traffic operator position system See traffic service position system.

traffic service position system In telephony, a stored program computer equipped with telephone operator consoles and designed to facilitate the handling of calls requiring operator intervention.

trailer microfiche In micrographics, a microfiche holding the remaining images of multipage document when the total number of pages exceeds the image area capacity of a single microfiche. See microfiche.

trail printer In word processing, a printer which is shared between work stations.

transaction driven system In computing, a mode of operation in which the arrival of a

transaction causes an interrupt of batch processing activities as resources are diverted to deal with the transaction. See batch processing, transaction processing.

transaction processing In computing, a mode of computer usage in which the user enters data and commands from a remote terminal, often over a communication link. The results of the actions are displayed on the terminal. A similar mode of action to multi-access computing; it is often employed when the user is operating with a specific application package. Compare batch processing, multi-access computing. See on line.

transceiver In communications, (1) a radio transmitter and receiver unit in one housing and employing some common circuits, normally used for portable or mobile operations, (2) a terminal device that can both transmit and receive signals.

transcoder In television, a device to convert colour standards, typically from PAL to SECAM and vice versa. See video standards.

transcribe In office systems, to produce a written copy of recorded, or dictated, material in longhand or on a typewriter.

transcriber In computing, the device used to convert the information from a given language of an information recording system to the language of the computer and vice versa.

transcription In office systems, to copy information from one medium to another, or to produce typed copy from a recorded dictation.

transducer In electronics, a device that receives a signal in one physical form and produces an output in another, usually electrical, e.g. a thermocouple produces a voltage proportional to the temperature of the thermocouple junction.

transfer In computing, (1) to copy a block of information and write it into another part of memory, (2) to change control.

transformational coding In computing and communications, the application of a strict set of rules in the transformation of data into a coded form.

transformer   In electronics, a device to change the voltage or current of an AC signal or power supply. See AC.

transient   A condition which exists for a limited period following a change in equilibrium states.

transistor   In electronics, a device manufactured from semiconductor material that can be used to control a current flow in a circuit. There are two basic forms, bipolar and unipolar. The bipolar comprises a sandwich of n-p-n or p-n-p semiconductor materials with three terminals emitter, base and collector, the current flow comprises both positive and negative carriers. In unipolar transistors the terminals are source, gate and drain and the current flow is by majority carrier only. See FET, semiconductor devices.

transitive dependence   In relational databases, an indirect dependence between attributes. Suppose A, B and C are three attributes or distinct collections of attributes of a relation R. If C is functionally dependent on B and B is functionally dependent on A then C is functionally dependent on A, if A is not functionally dependent upon B or B is not functionally dependent on C then C is transitively dependent upon A. See functional dependence.

translator   (1) In computing, a program that translates a program from one computer language to another. (2) In communications, a device that converts information from one system of representation into another, e.g. converting dialed digits into call routing information. See compiler, assembler, interpreter, dial up.

transmission   In communications, the action of sending information from one location to another leaving the source information unchanged.

transmission window   In fiber optics, the wavelength at which an optical cable is most transparent.

transmissive disk   In video disk, an optical disk in which the laser beam is transmitted through the transparent disk. Compare reflective disk. See optical disk.

transmittance   In optics, the ratio of amount of light transmitted through a surface to the amount of incident light on that surface. Compare reflectance.

transmitter   In communications, (1) a device to generate a carrier waveform, modulate it with an input signal and radiate the consequent modulated waveform into space, (2) a device to convert sound waves into electrical signals for transmission along a telephone line. (3) In computing, electronics and communications, the unit that sends signals along a bus or other transmission medium. See bus.

transmitter distributor   In communications, a device that reads and transmits punched paper tape. See paper tape.

transparency   In photography, a positive image, mounted on acetate or glass, used for projection.

transparent   (1) In computing, pertaining to a process, or procedure, invoked by a user without the latter being aware of its existence. (2) In communications, pertaining to a network or facility that allows a signal to pass through it without a change. Compare virtual.

transparent data communication code   A data comminication mode using a code independent protocol. Correct functioning is independent of the code or chracter set. See transparent.

transphasor   In optoelectronics, an optical transistor. It employs a crystal with a refractive index that varies with the intensity of incident light. Interference effects produce a sudden switch in the intensity of the transmitted beam according to comparatively small changes in the intensity of the input beam. It is capable of very high switching speeds. See transistor, refractive index, interference.

transponder   In communications, a device that receives and retransmits signals. In satellite commmunications the received signals are amplified and retransmitted at a different frequency. Compare responder.

transport layer   In data communications, a layer in the ISO Open Systems Interconnection model. This layer provides a transport service ensuring that the bit stream sent by the source arrives intact at the destination. Compare application layer, data link layer, network layer, physical layer, presentation layer, session layer. See bit stream, Open Systems Interconnection.

transposition error   The error arising from the keyboarding of two characters in reverse order.

transputer   In microelectronics, a CMOS chip occupying 45 square millimeters of silicon and comprising a powerful 32 bit microprocessor capable of executing 10 Mips. 4 Kbytes of static RAM are also included on the chip. See bit, byte, chip, CMOS, microprocessor, MIPS, RAM.

transreceiver   Synonymous with transceiver.

transverse scan   In video recording, a method of scanning a videotape in which the one or more heads rotate in a plane at 90 degrees to the direction of motion of the tape and the tape itself is bent into an arc across its width. Compare helical scan. See quadruplex.

travelling wave tube   In electronics, a radio frequency amplifier used in satellite communications. The radio frequency signal travels along a wire helix and an electron beam is aimed along the axis of the helix. When the radio frequency signal travels along the axis at the same velocity as the electrons then the signal and beam interact producing an amplification of the signal. See amplifier.

treble roll off   In recording, pertaining to a gradual attenuation of high frequencies.

tree   See tree structure.

tree and branch   In cable television, a conventional method of cable distribution in which an area is served by a main cable and branches from this cable serve a group of subscribers. The disadvantage of this method is that each subscriber cable must therefore have sufficient bandwidth to carry all available channels. This system is also less suitable for interactive information services. Compare switched star.

tree database   Synonymous with hierarchical database.

tree structure   In data structures, a series of connected nodes without cycles. One node is termed the root and is the starting point of all paths, another one or more nodes termed leaves terminate the paths. A path from any node towards a leaf will never pass through any individual node more than once. It can be used to represent hierarchical structures, e.g. a family tree. See root, leaf, node.

triad   In television, the triangular grouping of red, green and blue phosphor dots on the screen of a shadowmask tube. See shadowmask, RGB.

tribit   In data communications, three consecutive bits. In phase modulated systems a tribit is represented by a phase change of 0, 45, 90, 135...... 315 degrees. See phase modulation.

tributary station   In data communications, any station, other than the control station on a multipoint circuit. It can communicate with the control station only when polled or selected by it.

trichromatic system   Synonymous with three colour process.

trim marks   In printing, marks on a printed sheet that show how it is to be trimmed.

Trinitron   A television colour tube with striped phosphors and an aperture grid. See television tubes.

Trojan Horse   In data security, a program inserted by an attacker in a computer system. It performs functions not described in the program specifications, taking advantage of rights belonging to the calling environment to copy, misuse or destroy data not relevant to its stated purpose. For example, a Trojan

Horse in a text editor might copy confidential information in a file being edited to a file accessible to another. See leakage.

troposphere In radio communications, a layer that extends up to 6 miles above the earth's surface and scatters radio waves. It is more stable than the ionosphere. See ionosphere, tropospheric scatter circuit.

tropospheric scatter circuit In radiocommunications, a channel that uses the troposphere to scatter the radio waves thus providing communication between stations that are not in line of sight. The channels use signals in the UHF range and are employed for communication links of up to 600 miles. They are more reliable than HF channels using ionospheric scattering. See troposphere, ionosphere, UHF, HF.

trouble shoot (1) To seek, locate and repair equipment malfunctions. (2) In computing, to debug. See debug.

trs In printing, an instruction on a manuscript or proof to transpose a character or text.

true descenders In computing, pertaining to displayed, or printed, lower case characters in which the descender appears below the baseline of other characters. See descender.

truncate In computing, (1) to drop the lower order digits of a number, usually to fit it into a limited storage space. (2) In some high level languages it is an instruction to convert a floating point number to an integer. See floating point.

trunk In communications, a circuit, or channel, interconnecting two exchanges or switching units, capable of being switched at both ends and provided with the necessary signalling and terminating equipment. See exchange.

trunk exchange In telephony, an exchange for trunk lines only.

truth table In logic operations, a means of describing the functions of a logical operation, or a circuit containing logic units. The table lists all the possible input states,

together with the corresponding outputs. See AND, Karnaugh map.

TSPS See traffic service position system.

TSW See telesoftware.

TTL In electronics, Transistor Transistor Logic, pertaining to logic devices using direct bipolar transistor to transistor coupling, i.e. directly from collector to base. It is characterized by high sped and low power dissipation. See logic circuit, transistor.

TTL compatible In microelectronics, pertaining to a MOS device that can interface directly with bipolar TTL devices. See MOS, TTL.

TTL Logic In electronics, pertaining to units using bipolar Transistor-Transistor coupled Logic circuits.

TTS See teletypesetting.

tube shield A screen or tube around a CRT display to reduce the effect of reflections. See CRT.

tunable laser A laser that can be made to vary the frequency of its emitted light. See LASER.

tuning (1) To optimize the performance of a system by fine adjustment. (2) In recording, to align a magnetic head to the recorded track.

tuple A related set of values.

Turing machine In computing, a mathematical model of a device that reads data from a tape, moves the tape zero or one position forward or backward, writes to tape and changes one of its internal states. It was invented by Alan Turing, preceding the first electronic computer, and it provides a useful model for theoretical studies in computation. See mathematical model.

turnaround time (1) In office systems, the elapsed time between the despatch and subsequent receipt of material. (2) In communications, the time taken in reversing data flow in a half duplex channel. See half duplex.

turnkey system In computing, a complete system designed for a specific user. The user needs only to switch on the system, the prime contractor accepting full responsibility for system design, installation, supply of hardware, software and documentation.

turtlegraphics In computer graphics, a method of creating images by sending instructions to a 'turtle', represented by the screen cursor, to change direction, move specified distances or move to specified points. Used for educational computer graphics languages. See Logo.

tweeter A small loudspeaker used to reproduce high frequencies. Compare woofer.

twelve mo In printing, cut or folded sheet that is one twelfth of basic size.

twelve pitch See elite.

twisted pair In telephony, a pair of wires forming a local loop. See local loop.

two key lockout A system used to inhibit further keyboard action when two keys are simultaneously depressed. Compare two key rollover.

two key rollover A system that enables two keystrokes to be correctly interpreted when two keys are simultaneously depressed. Compare two key lockout.

two revolution press In printing, a continuously revolving press that makes two revolutions to each impression. Compare stop cylinder press.

two's complement In computing, a method of representing a negative binary number. In this convention a binary number is negated by interchanging the ones and zeros and then adding one to the result. The most significant bit is a sign bit, i.e. a one represents a negative number. Compare one's complement.

two wire circuit In communications, a circuit comprising two conductors insulated from each other, thus providing a go and return channel for signals of same frequency. Compare four wire circuit.

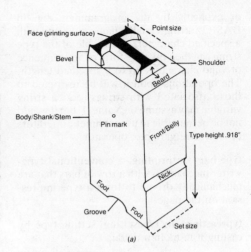

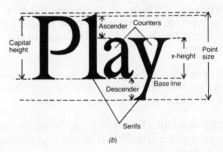

type
(a) parts of a foundry type; (b) elements of typeface.

TWT See travelling wave tube.

TWX See teletypewriter exchange service.

TX See transmitter.

typamatic key A keyboard key that automatically repeats the appropriate character or control action when it remains depressed for more than a given short interval of time.

type In printing, (1) a piece of metal of standard height with a raised image of a character, or characters, on its upper face, (2) images produced by composition systems which do not use metal type, (3) images produced by metal type. (4) In computer programming, pertaining to the range of values and valid operations associated with a variable. Types are declared either implicitly or explicitly by the programmer, e.g. in BASIC a string variable name must end with a specified character. A variable of the type string can then take the form of any sequence of valid characters up to a specified length. The operations upon it will be restricted to those associated with strings, e.g. a string variable may assume the value '1' but it would not be permissible to use arithmetic operators upon it. See variable, operator.

type bar In printing, a conventional typewriter mechanism with a row of bars that are mechanically driven to form a type impression on the page.

typecasting In typesetting, setting type by casting it in molten metal.

typeface (1) In word processing and printing, the face design of a particular type. (2) In printing, the design of a particular set of type. See type.

type height In printing, the standard height of type from the bed of a printing press. It is 0·918 inches in US and UK. See type.

type markup In typesetting, to mark the type specifications on layout and copy for the typesetter.

type matter In printing, type set up in a form ready for printing. See form.

typesetting The putting of text into typeset form on to a medium, usually photographic film or paper, suitable for making printing plates. Typesetting is as old as Gutenberg but now its technology is heavily electronic in nature; instead of the manual assembly of lead type, a computer program in a phototypesetter can govern the output of digitized type forms using CRT or laser beams to image the text on various photographic media. Later developments have been the merging of the text (type) with graphics, e.g. photographs, drawings etc., whilst using the same imaging techniques of CRT or laser. This affords the possibility of electronic composition, i.e. the production of a complete page of text and graphics. This in turn allows the user to produce printing plates directly, without having first to assemble manually the output of the typesetter into columns, pages etc. and combine with graphics.

See (a) Phototypesetting, (b) computer assisted typesetting, (c) digitized type, (d) links with word processing, (e) further developments.

(a) Phototypesetting. Because the output of all modern typesetters is in photographic form, the output device of all electronic typesetting systems is called a phototypesetter. Phototypesetting has passed very quickly though four generations of equipment. The first generation was based on the metal-casting, mechanical equipment that held sway in the printing industry for nearly a hundred years. Instead of injecting molten metal into moulds they substituted light exposing onto film. These modified mechanical typesetters soon gave way in the early 1950's to the second generation based on a totally redesigned approach to the problem of typesetting, using modern electronic components. In one of the most famous of these early second generation models, the Lumitype, several keyboards could power one photounit, each keyboard producing paper tape (fig. 1). This was an important advance since the phototypesetter could set type much faster than anyone could type. The photounit itself projected the use of a strobing light source under the control of the paper tape, i.e. the light would flash when the desired character was between it and the film. The type image was put into the size needed by some form of lens system before exposing onto the film. The spinning disk is the hall mark of the second generation of phototypesetter and they are still a popular kind of typesetter.

The next development resulting in the third generation was the adoption of the cathode ray tube (CRT) as the imaging light source, rather than a flashing, strobing light (fig. 2). The CRT can generate a flying spot of light that can 'paint' the image of the type on the photomaterial. The first version of the CRT typesetter stored its type images in similar fashion to the second generation, in photographic form, but in the later third generation typesetters the type is stored in digital form, See (c).

In the latest generation of typesetter, the fourth, the imaging light source is a laser. These are used for scanning across the page, like a facsimile device, rather than setting the type a character at a time. The advantage of the laser is its great intensity, compared to that of the CRT. This allows the photosen-

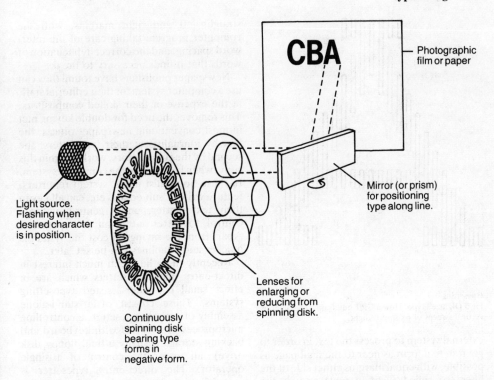

Light source. Flashing when desired character is in position.

Continuously spinning disk bearing type forms in negative form.

Lenses for enlarging or reducing from spinning disk.

Mirror (or prism) for positioning type along line.

Photographic film or paper

typesetting
Fig 1 Schematic diagram of the second optical-mechanical generation photosetter.

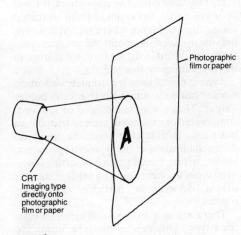

CRT Imaging type directly onto photographic film or paper

Photographic film or paper

typesetting
Fig 2 CRT typesetter.

sitive layer of a lithographic plate to be exposed. This potential has yet to be fully realised but one recent development is to use an electrostatic, xerographic technique with the laser. This results in the elimination of the photographic processing necessary in the other kinds of phototypesetter. In this way the phototypesetter seems to be coming closer to the fast laser output printers such as the Xerox 9700 Electronic Printing System or the 'intelligent copier' which also use digitized type forms.

Both the fourth and third generation of typesetter set type extremely quickly; the fastest CRT typesetters, often used by newspapers, can set out over 3000 newspaper lines per minute. Their great capacity for text is supplied nearly always now by some form of computer system.

(b) Computer associated typesetting. In order to take advantage of the great speed and flexibility of the modern phototypesetter, some form of computer system is used. Although all phototypesetters have a computer housed within them to control their functions, there is still a need for some

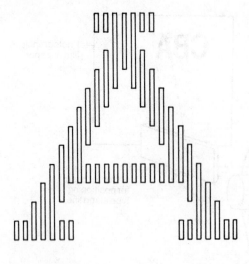

external system to process the text in order to get it in to a form as near to the final page as possible, with equal margins either side of the lines (so called justified text) and in the correct type size and style etc. Such systems are very similar to shared-logic word processing systems in that they comprise a central processing unit, often a minicomputer, with several visual display terminals online to it, with rigid disk storage for the text. Output from the system is either through a lineprinter, for proofing purposes, or through the online phototypesetter.

An operator keys in the text at a visual display terminal, interpolating through the text the various commands necessary to structure the text typographically. Such systems are especially popular in book, magazine and newspaper printers where they can cause the phototypesetting unit to output full pages, made up into columns, with automatic handling of such things as page numbering. Other facilities include the repetitive headings at the head and foot of the page, footnotes and their numbering and the elimination of typographical blemishes such as single line or word paragraph ends at the top or bottom of a page, or ugly spacing of lines or characters. One of the most important functions of these computer systems is simple hyphenation and justification, wherein the text is set with straight left and right margins, with the computer program taking care of the interword spacing, and the correct hyphenation of words that it finds necessary to break.

Newspaper publishers have found they can use a computer system for their editorial staff, at the expense of their skilled compositors. This removes the need for double keying met in most conventional newspaper offices, the first by journalists at their typewriters, the second by the compositors, working from this copy, when keying in to the computer system. In these 'journalist input' system reporters, feature writers, sub-editors etc. can all key in their text matter, under central editorial control, for latter output on the typesetter. Apart from the savings in cost the system is quicker and deadlines can be set later.

Recently there has been much interest in direct-entry phototypesetters which are in effect small computer-assisted typesetting systems. These consist of a stand-alone assembly of a phototypesetter, a controlling microprocessor, a VDU with keyboard and backing storage (usually a dual floppy disk drive), all under the control of a single operator. The direct-entry typesetter is especially popular with the inplant printer and increasing numbers of these are linked up with word processing systems, giving a cheap typesetting facility to large companies, academic institutions and local governments.

(c) Digitized type. The rise of the CRT and laser typesetter has resulted in an increased use of digitized type, where the type forms, previously kept in metal or photographic form, are coded in digital form for storage in the typesetting system (fig. 3).

Type in digital form is extremely important since it can be handled electronically before output. Thus it can be enlarged or reduced, compressed or expanded, slanted to make an italic etc. It also contributes to the total de-mechanization of the typesetting process, leading to fast, trouble-free typesetting. Digitized types are being used by other computer output devices, in particular intelligent copiers.

There are now extensive libraries of digitized type. Originals of the type forms are scanned into special computer systems and converted into, at the most, 3000 by 3000 dot matrixes. These are then examined by the operator who has to fine-tune the initial scanning, based on what is a frankly aesthetic appreciation of the type form. He does this by using an interactive graphics terminal, indicating which individual dots in the array he wants deleted and which he wants inserted. When satisfied he clears the character for computer coding for storage in the typesetting system. This procedure is slow and skilled, and the possession of a full library of digitized type forms is becoming quite a considerable asset. (d) Links with word processing. An important development is the linking of word processing systems with phototypesetters. With such a link over communication lines a word processer user can typeset reports, parts lists, accounts etc. and gain the advantages of a reduction in text area (type taking up less space than typewritten text) whilst retaining legibility, as well as speeding up the typesetting operation by the elimination of the requirement to rekey. Several users are employing microcomputers to 'milk' word processing files of text onto floppy disks for later input into phototypesetters.

(e) Further developments. The most important developments in electronic typesetting are in the area of the computer systems preceding the actual typesetting operation. Thus with the digitizing of type, these type forms can be used with storage tube VDUs to indicate on a screen the precise appearance of the page as it will be set by the phototypesetter before output. Such a facility is termed electronic composition and it allows a great deal of interactivity with the operator, and with other hardware advances (particularly laser typesetters) the ability to place in position previously digitized graphics, for output by the same 'typesetter'. There is thus a convergence of the two kinds of informa-

tion, i.e. type and pictures. See digital typography, phototypesetting, word processing.

type size   In typesetting, the space allocated to a character given in terms of height, width and space. The height is measured in points, the width in sets and the space in ems. The base unit of measurement is 1 point = 0·01383 inches. The em is expressed in terms of height and width except for a square typeface, e.g. an 8pt em represents an 8 pt x 8 set typeface. The space refers to that allocated for the typeface, not the area of the printed image. See em, set, point.

typewriter faces   In printing and office systems, the spacing of print characters on typewriters is provided in two standard sizes, i.e. elite (12 characters to the inch) and pica (10 characters to the inch). See elite, pica.

typing station   In office systems, (1) locations where typing is performed in an organization, (2) the number of units in a word processing system.

typist   In office systems, one whose prime responsibility is to operate a typewriter.

typo   In printing, a typographical error, either typewriting or typesetting. See typesetting.

typographer   In printing, (1) a person who is responsible for the design of a piece of printing, (2) a person who sets type.

typography   In printing, the art and technique of working with type. See type.

UART In computing, Universal Asynchronous Receiver Transmitter, a chip which converts parallel bit streams to serial bit streams and vice versa for asynchronous devices, e.g. a line printer. Compare USART. See parallel transmission, serial transmission.

UHF See ultra high frequency.

UHR See ultra high reduction.

Ukmarc A database supplied by The British Library and dealing with books & periodicals, catalogs. See on line information retrieval.

ULA See uncommitted logic array.

ultrafiche In micrographics, microfiche images reduced by more than 90X. See microfiche.

ultra high frequency In communications, frequency range of 300 - 3000 MHz. See MHz.

ultra high reduction In micrographics, a reduction greater than 90X. Compare low reduction, medium reduction, high reduction, very high reduction. See reduction.

UART
The conversion of serial to parallel, and parallel to serial bit streams.

ultrasonic Air pressure waves at frequencies above audio band.

ultraviolet Electromagnetic radiation in a frequency band just above the visible spectrum with wavelengths from some 200 to 4000 angstrom units. See angstrom.

ultraviolet erasable PROM In computing, a PROM that may be erased by exposure to ultraviolet light which causes stored electrical charges to leak away. See programmable read only memory.

U-matic In recording, a video cassette format for three quarter inch tapes developed by Sony. Compare Beta, VHS.

umbrella IP In videotex, an IP who rents a large number of pages on a public videotex service and then in turn leases them to a number of other organizations, known as sub IP's. See IP.

umlaut In printing, an accented sign used in German language text, indicated by two dots over an a, o or u. See accent.

unary operation In computing, an operation on only one operand, e.g. negation which reverses the sign of a term. See operand.

unattended operation In communications, the automatic transmission and reception of messages without an operator in attendance. Compare attended operation.

unbundling In computing, the operation of selling software, services and training by a computer manufacturer independent of the sale of computer hardware. See hardware, software.

unclocked In electronics, a flip flop that changes state at the time of a change of input. Clocked logic units can only change state at the instant that a clock pulse is applied. See flip flop, clock pulse.

uncommitted logic array   In computing, a matrix of AND and OR gates programmed as a final stage of manufacture to meet specific requirements. Compare programmable logic array. See AND gate, OR gate.

unconditional jump   In computer programming, an instruction to jump to another specified instruction. Compare conditional jump. See branch.

underdevelopment   In photography, the result of using a development time less than that required to bring up the image fully. See developing.

underexposure   In photography, any action that results in an insufficient amount of light reaching the film in the camera or printer.

underflow   In computing, a condition that arises if the result of an arithmetic operation lies between zero and the smallest number that can be represented by the limited number of bits assigned to the fractional binary number. Compare overflow. See bit.

underline   In word processing, a facility to automatically underline text.

underscore   See underline.

unidirectional microphone   In recording, a microphone that has its greatest sensitivity in a given direction. Compare omnidirectional microphone.

Uniform System of Accounts   In communications, a U.S classification of accounts for common carriers. See common carrier.

unipolar   In electronics, a transistor formed from a single type of semiconductor material either n- or p- type. See transistor, FET, p-type material.

unipolar transmission   In telegraphy, a method in which a mark is represented by current on the line and a space by the absence of current. See mark, space, current.

unit buffer terminal   In communications, a

terminal that does not have a communication buffer. See communication buffer.

unit load   In electronics, the electrical load placed on a driver output by a receiver unit. See load.

unit record   In computing, (1) a punched card containing one record, (2) a separate record of information similar to other records. See record.

unit record equipment   In computing, equipment for operation on punched cards, e.g. collators, tabulating machines, etc. See collate.

unit system   In typesetting, a unit obtained by dividing the square of the type size, i.e. em, into vertical segments. Thus a 36 point em is a square of dimension 36 points, an 18 units to the em system divides the square into 18 vertical segments, i.e. each unit would be 2 points width in this example. Units are thus always relative to the typesize. See em quad, point.

Universal Copyright Convention 1952   In printing, an agreement between signatory countries on copyright. See copyright.

Universal Product Code   In computing, an agreed bar coding for product labels giving country of origin, manufacturer, etc. Used for supermarket checkouts, stock control, etc. Compare EAN. See bar code.

universal set   The total set of elements that have a specified property, e.g. 0, 1, 2...9, is the universal set of non-negative, single digit integers. See set.

Unix   In computing, an operating system developed by Bell Laboratories and available for minicomputers and microcomputers. It is favoured by computer scientists. Compare CP/M, MS-DOS. See operating system.

unjustified   In printing, lines of type that line up vertically on one side but are ragged on the other. See ragged setting.

unjustified tape   Synonymous with idiot tape.

unpack In computing, to recover original data from its packed format. See packing.

unprotected field In computing, a part of the display on a VDU that a user can modify. Compare protected field. See VDU.

unrecoverable error In computing, an error that results in a premature termination of a program. Compare recoverable error.

up and down propagation time In satellite communications, the time taken for a signal to travel the distance from earth station to satellite to earth station. For geostationary satellites the up and down propagation time is approximately 540 milliseconds. See geostationary satellite.

UPC See Universal Product Code.

update (1) In computing, to modify stored information with data from recent transactions according to a specified procedure. (2) In word processing, to replace text stored on a file with a revised version.

update center In large viewdata systems, a computer center that accepts database updates and transmits them to retrieval centers. See retrieval center.

up/down counter In electronics, a binary counter that accepts two inputs, one to increase the count and the other to decrease it. See binary counter.

upper case In printing, capital or large size characters. Compare lower case.

uptime In computing, the time that a computer is available for normal operation.

upward compatibility In computing, the capability of one computer to execute programs written for another but not vice versa.

usage sensitive pricing In communications, charges for service based upon usage.

USART In computing, Universal Synchronous Asynchronous Receiver Transmitter, a chip which can be programmed under CPU control for synchronous or asynchronous serial transfer of data between the CPU and an I/O device. See CPU.

USASCII In computing and communications, USA Standard Code for Information Interchange. Synonymous with ASCII.

USASI United States of America Standards Institute.

user action frame See response frame.

user friendly Pertaining to any system designed to be used without extensive operator training and which seeks to assist the user to gain maximum benefit from the system. See menu selection.

user id In computing, a user identification code enabling a computer to recognize, and allocate charges to, a user.

user operated language See problem oriented language, procedure oriented language.

user profile In communications, a definition of the user type of interaction with a network, supplied by the user as a set of parameters, or options, at registration.

user programs In computing, a group of programs written by the user as compared with manufacturer supplied software. See software.

users group In computing, a group of users who share programs, exchange information, etc, on a class of computer systems. Compare closed user group.

user terminal In computing, a terminal employed by a user to communicate with a computer system.

USRT In computing, Universal Synchronous Receiver Transmitter. An integrated circuit device to perform timing of synchronous bit serial data and series-parallel conversion. Compare UART, USART.

utility programs In computer programming, a program supplied for common routine tasks, e.g. copying files.

V

V See V series recommendations of CCITT.

vacuum forming A means of producing a shape on a thin sheet of plastic by placing it on a relief plate and inducing a vacuum between the sheet and the plate.

vacuum guide In recording, a part of the magnetic head assembly that is used to hold the tape in the correct position by a vacuum action. Used in transverse scans when the tape must be curved across its width. See transverse scan.

vacuum tube In electronics, a device with electrodes within an evacuated glass envelope for the control of current flows. An electrically heated cathode produces electrons which are attracted to the anode. Other electrodes are used to control the current flow. It was the basis of early computers, communication and control devices but has now been superseded by solid state devices. See electrode, cathode, anode, solid state device.

validation In computing, a check on input data for correctness against set criteria, e.g. format, ranges, etc. May be performed manually or automatically.

validity checking In computing, (1) a procedure to check that a code group is actually a character of the particular code in use, (2) a data screening procedure wherein data input records are checked for range, valid representation etc. See reasonableness check.

value In printing, the value of a colour is the degree of lightness or darkness relative to a neutral gray scale.

value added service In communications, a communication service using communications common carrier networks for transmission and providing added data services with separate additional equipment. Added services may include store and forward message switching, terminal and host interfacing. See store and forward.

value of service pricing In communications, a pricing system in which the charges are related to the value of the service to the user rather than the costs of the supplier.

variable In computer programming, a quantity that is named in the program and can assume any value, within a valid range for its type, and may be operated upon by any valid operator for that type. See type, operator.

variable area sound track In cinematography, a optical sound track which is divided longitudinally into two components, one essentially opaque and the other essentially transparent. Compare variable hue sound recording, variable density sound track. See optical soundtrack.

variable data Synonymous with unprotected field.

variable density sound track In cinematography, an optical sound track recorded in the form of variable density striations at right angles to the film edge. Compare variable hue sound recording, variable area sound track.

variable hue sound recording In cinematography, a method of sound recording onto a photographic sound track using variations in colour instead of variations in monochrome density or area. Compare variable area sound track, variable density sound track.

variable length record In computing, a record that can have a length independent of the length of other records with which it is associated. Compare fixed length record. See record, file.

variable space In electronic typesetting, the length of a line may need to be altered so that the text is justified and this effect is achieved by varying the space between words. At the time of initial insertion of text this space length is not known so a variable space code is inserted, the actual space length is computed at the appropriate time. See justify, word space.

variable text In word processing, text of a changing nature that is added to recorded text so as to produce the final document. Compare boilerplate.

VCR Video cassette recorder.

VCS See video computer system.

VDE See voice data entry.

VDU See visual display unit.

vector (1) A variable that has magnitude and direction. (2) In computing, a quantity represented by an ordered set of numbers, e.g. a one dimensional array. (3) In computer graphics, a line coupled with its direction. Compare scalar. See array.

vector diagram A diagram in which vectors are represented by straight lines with arrows. The length of the line represents the magnitude of the vector and the direction of the line, as given by its angle and the arrow, represents the direction of the vector. See vector.

vectoring In computing, the process of instructing the program to seek additional instructions from a given storage location. See instruction.

vectoring an interrupt In computing, the process of selecting instructions from a storage location which is a function of the particular interrupt line activated. See interrupt, vectoring.

Veitch diagrams In computing, a diagram in which a boolean function is represented by a set of squares with each square representing one of the possible states of the function. Compare Venn diagram. See boolean algebra, Karnaugh map.

Venn diagram In computing, a diagram in which states are represented by regions drawn on a surface, e.g. if state A represents all men with red hair and state B represents all bachelors, the overlapping area then represents all red haired bachelors.

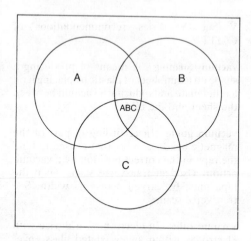

Venn diagram

verification In computing, the practice of keyboarding data twice and automatically performing a character by character comparison. See verify.

verify In computing, to determine whether an operation on data has been performed accurately.

verso In printing, any left handed, even numbered page of a book. Compare recto.

vertical blanking interval In video disk, blanked lines in each field wherein frame numbers, picture stops, chapter stops, white flags etc. are encoded. See chapter stop, field, picture stop, white flag.

vertical format control unit In computing and printing, a method of programming line printers to insert blank lines, often performed using a loop of punched paper tape. See line printer.

vertical justification In printing, the adjustment of interline spacing and the manipulation of text to fit into a specified space on a page or column. See justify.

vertical lock   In recording, a video recording playback condition in which the playback head rotation is in synchronism with the pulses on the control track. See control track, helical scan.

vertical redundancy check   See longitudinal redundancy check.

vertical scrolling   In computing, an action that permits the user to move the screen displayed text up or down, a line at a time, to reveal other parts of the stored text. Text to be viewed from a VDU is often stored in a buffer with a greater storage capacity than that of the screen display. See VDU, screen buffer.

vertical tab   Synonymous with high speed skip.

vertical wraparound   In word processing, the continuation of the cursor movement from the bottom character position in a vertical column to the top character position in the next column. Compare horizontal wraparound.

very high frequency   In radiocommunications, the range of frequencies from 30 - 300 MHz. See MHz.

very high reduction   In micrographics, a reduction in the range 61X to 90X. Compare low reduction, medium reduction, high reduction, ultra high reduction. See reduction.

very large scale integration   In microelectronics, pertaining to the fabrication technology which produces more than some 1000 gates per chip. Compare LSI, MSI, SSI, SLSI. See chip, gate.

very low frequency   In radiocommunications, the range of frequencies from 3 - 30 kHz. See kHz.

vesicular film   In photography, film which has the light sensitive element suspended in a plastic layer and which upon exposure creates strains within the layer in the form of a latent image. The strains are released and the latent image made visual by heating the plastic layer. The image becomes permanent when the layer cools.

vestigial sideband   In communications, a transmission technique of a modulated wave, in which one sideband, the carrier and a small part of the opposite sideband are transmitted on a channel. Compare single sideband transmission, suppressed carrier transmission. See modulation, carrier, sideband.

VET   See visual editing terminal.

vf band   In communications, voice frequency band. See voice frequency.

VHD   In video disk, Very High Density, a capacitance disk in which the stylus is maintained in position by tracking signals encoded on both sides of the information track. See capacitance disk.

VHF   See very high frequency.

VHR   See very high reduction.

VHS   In recording, a video cassette format for half inch tapes developed by JVC. Compare Beta, U-matic.

vide   In printing, used in footnotes to direct reader to a given reference.

video   Pertaining to visual images produced or transmitted by a television system.

video cassette   In recording, a cartridge holding a loop of video tape. See video tape.

video compressor   A device that converts standard television signals to narrow bandwidth for transmission over voice grade channels. It may be used in conjunction with a video expander at the receiving end. See video expander.

video computer system   In computing, a microprocessor system with a primary function of providing a video display, e.g. for video games. See video game.

video confidence head   In recording, a device for checking that the video recorder is actually recording. See video recorder.

video disk   In video recording, a disk which contains recorded television pictures and sound. Video disks share the advantage of

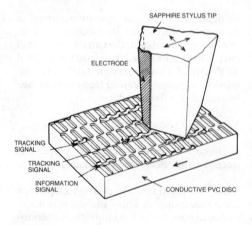

SAPPHIRE STYLUS TIP

ELECTRODE

TRACKING SIGNAL

TRACKING SIGNAL

INFORMATION SIGNAL

CONDUCTIVE PVC DISC

video disk
Fig 1 JVC capacitance video disk with sapphire stylus.

audio hi fi disks in that they can be mass produced using low cost raw materials whereas prerecorded video cassettes require lengthy recording sessions on expensive magnetic tape. However, such disks do not provide the user with the record facilities of video tape and therefore cannot be used for time shift TV viewing. Certain classes of video disk have freeze frame, fast/slow motion and random access search and the disk player can be controlled from a local microprocessor or linked to a microcomputer. These interactive video disk systems provide excellent facilities for education, training, sales promotion etc. Video disks can also be used as mass storage devices with very high information packing density and fast random access.

The video signals are frequency modulated and the resulting sine wave is clipped, this signal is regarded as a series of pulses of constant amplitude and varying duration. When a video disk is encoded with these signals the reading system needs only detect the presence or absence of a pulse. The two major forms of consumer disk are capacitive and optical. In the capacitive disk the reading head, or stylus, acts as one plate of a capacitor and the disk as the other. The disk is produced from conducting material and either the disk, or the stylus, is covered with insulating material to prevent a short circuit between the capacitor plates. The recorded information is in the form of minute pits, as small as

half a micron, which produces the variation in capacitance. Two forms of capacitance disks have been produced. The RCA Selectavision uses a grooved disk; the sole function of the grooves is to guide the stylus over the pitted surface. Stereo sound facilities are available. The disk rotates at 450 RPM (NTSC standard) to give four television frames per revolution. A form of freeze frame, actually showing four frames in cyclic sequence, is therefore feasible with this system. An alternative version of capacitive disk is the VHD system produced by JVC. This is a grooveless disk and the stylus has a much larger surface area which is said to significantly reduce wear. The stylus follows the information track by tracking signals which are encoded in parallel with the video information on the disk.

The speed of rotation 900 RPM (NTSC standard) produces two television frames per rotation, thus providing for better freeze frame viewing. Variable slow or fast speed viewing and true random access to frames is available from this system. Both the RCA and the VHD systems use a protective caddy to reduce damage from dirt, scratches and fingerprints.

The optical disk does not employ a stylus and the information is read by a laser beam which is either reflected or transmitted by the minute encoded pits. Both Philips and Pioneer have manufactured laser disk players using reflective disks whilst a transmissive system has been produced by Thomson CSF. Both sides of optical and capacitive disks can carry video information. In the case of the transmissive disk, however, the disk need not be removed, and turned over, to read the second side, it is merely necessary to change the focal point from one side to the other. The current reflective disk systems are hard compared with the flexible Thomson CSF disk. The optical disks suffer no stylus wear and it is possible to continuously display an individual TV frame with high quality and no disk damage. The playback quality is relatively insensitive to fingermarks etc. on the disk surface and, unlike the capacitive disk, they do not require protective plastic caddys. Since there is no mechanical contact with a reading head the optical disk can rotate at higher speed, 1800 RPM (NTSC standard), giving one TV frame per rotation and therefore very good freeze frame picture quality.

Optical disk players have two modes of

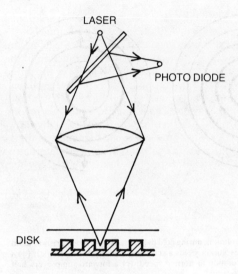

LASER

PHOTO DIODE

DISK

video disk

Fig 2 Philips VLP optical pickup, laser and photo diode.

operation, CAV (constant angular velocity) and CLV (constant linear velocity). In CAV mode the disk is rotated at a constant speed and one frame is recorded on each circular track.

In the freeze frame action the beam jumps back to the start of the frame. Fast and slow motion, forward and reverse play effects are produced by programming the laser beam to jump to appropriate tracks at the start of each frame. In this CAV mode 54,000 individual frames can be accessed but the total playing time per side is only 30 minutes. A CLV disk has a longer playing time, one hour per side, but it is only suitable for continuous play; fast/slow motion, freeze frame and random access to individual frames is not available with these disks. The additional playing time is achieved by recording more frames per circular track and the speed of rotation varies from 1800 RPM when the beam reads tracks on the inner circumference to 600 RPM at the outer circumference. The use of video disks for education, sales promotion etc. is described under interactive video disk systems.

The high quality freeze frame display of optical disks renders them attractive as storage devices for documents. A single frame on a disk occupies a total surface area of 1 square millimeter, compared with 5 square millimeters on a 3000 frame ultrafiche, and can be accessed in approximately 5 seconds. This use of consumer optical disks for document storage is, however, relatively inefficient, in terms of storage capacity, and the data is not suitable for computer or word processor input. With domestic TV sets the limited resolution of 525 (NTSC) or 625 (PAL) systems only provides comfortable viewing of some 960 characters (videotex standard) compared with 4000 characters on a typed page. This not only limits the total capacity of the disk but also presents some inconvenience to the user. The latter problem may, however, be overcome by using special high resolution monitors with 2000 scan lines.

The comparatively low power of the lasers in consumer playback devices does not permit them to be employed as recording devices. Players with record facilities have been demonstrated, they employ non-erasable disks so that each new document can only be recorded on a virgin track and the current devices are very expensive. See capacitance, frame, freeze frame, frequency modulation, interactive video disk systems, micron, NTSC, optical digital disks, PAL, sine wave, time shift viewing.

video display In computing and communications, a device to display visual information, text or graphics, usually a CRT but may also include LED's or plasma panels. See CRT, LED, plasma panel.

video drive In communications, the amplifier and electronic circuits to provide the CRT signals for a videotex display. See videotex, CRT.

video editor In printing, a photocomposition editing device incorporating a CRT. See CRT, photocomposition.

video expander In recording, a memory device capable of storing one frame of video information. Data may be fed in at a slow rate and used to build up a continuously refreshed image on a television monitor. See video compressor.

video game In computing, a special purpose microcomputer producing a graphic display

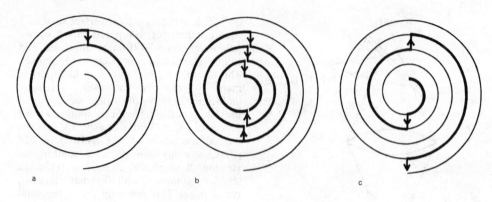

video disk
Fig 3 The different modes of Philips VLP player. Twice per revolution, during field flyback, an opportunity exists to jump from one track to another. (a) a reverse jump after every revolution yields a stationary picture (freeze frame); (b) a reverse jump after every half revolution produces reverse motion at normal speed; (c) a forward jump every half revolution results in three times normal speed forward.

and, usually, receiving inputs from a hand controller, thus enabling the player, or players, to participate in games requiring skills and coordination. In some cases the games may be changed by inserting new ROM cartridges. See ROM cartridge.

video generator   In computing, a device that generates the signals for a TV display according to received commands and signals. See screen buffer.

videogram   In recording, a generic term for video recording systems encompassing video disk and video cassette recorders. See video disk, video cassette.

videographics   In television, the technique of electronic manipulation of pictures.

video layout system   In typesetting, a CRT system used for layout planning prior to photocomposition. See CRT, photocomposition.

video monitor   In recording, a device for viewing a video recording at the time of recording, or afterwards.

video phone   In communications, a uni- or bidirectional broadcast image service using microwave, cable or satellite communication media.

video player   In recording, a device that can playback a video recording but cannot itself make video recordings. See video disk.

video recorder   In recording, a system that can record TV film and sound.

video signal   In television, the signal voltages variations due to picture information and synchronizing pulses. See composite colour video signal.

video standards   In television, there are three international standards. (a) NTSC (National Television Standard Committee). Commonly used in US and Japan. 525 horizontal lines and 60 frames per second. (b) PAL (Phase Alternating Line). Used in Western Europe, Australia, parts of Africa and Middle East. 625 horizontal scan lines, 50 frames per second. (c) SECAM (Sequential Couleur à Mémoire). Used in France, Saudi Arabia and USSR. Similar to PAL but differs in method of producing colour signals.

video tape   In recording, a flexible tape coated with magnetic material upon which video signals can be recorded. See video tape recorder.

video tape recorder   In recording, a video recorder using video tape. Compare video disk. See video tape.

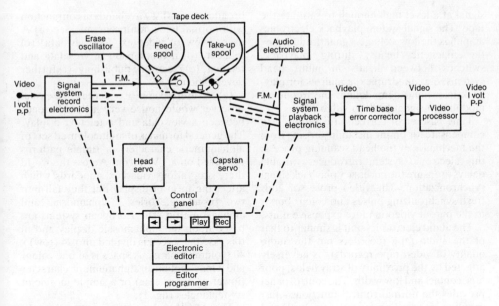

video tape recording

video tape recording A tape recorder for television pictures and sound must deal with signals in the frequency range 0 to 5 Mhz as compared with a 15 kHz bandwidth for audiotape systems. Such high frequencies imply head to tape speeds in excess of 12·7 meters per second; the longitudinal recording track schemes of audio tape recorders cannot therefore be employed because they would involve excessive tape velocities and a one hour recording would require nearly 46 kilometers of magnetic tape. The necessary head to tape speed for video recording is produced by rotating the magnetic heads at a high speed across the width of the tape, as it moves longitudinally at a relatively low speed (12·7 to 3·81 centimeters per second). The signals are thus recorded as a series of diagonal lines across the width of the tape giving a high effective length of recorded track for a reasonable length of tape. A second potential problem of video recording is the number of octaves in the signal range of just above d.c. to 5 MHz; this octave range is reduced by using signal modulation techniques. Given a carrier of 8 MHz the modulated signal ranges from 3 to 13 MHz giving a span of just over 2 octaves. Frequency modulation is nearly always used because of its tolerance to amplitude variations, which occur in tape recording.

The major components of a video tape recorder are tape deck, head servo, capstan servo, signal system record electronics, signal system playback electronics, time base error correction, video processor, audio electronics and control panel.

The tape deck contains a feed spool and a take-up spool to contain the tape. A capstan, usually with a pinch roller to provide traction, controls the longitudinal speed of tape. A rotating head wheel, or drum scanner, with a separate motor drive provide the head speed. This assembly has a form of signal coupling so that the radio frequency signal can be fed to the rotating heads. The audio heads are stationary and the audio tracks are recorded longitudinally with the audio erase head preceding the audio playback/record head. A stationary video erase head is located upstream of the video heads.

The rotational speed and phase of the video heads are controlled electronically by a servo-mechanism on the head motor. The tape speed and phase is controlled by the capstan servo in more expensive devices. This servo-mechanism ensures accurate alignment of the video heads to recorded track during playback.

The signal system record electronics receive the input signal, during recording, and produce the modulated radio frequency signal at a level high enough to saturate the tape. The signal system playback electronics amplifies the low voltage signal produced by the magnetic heads, during playback, switches between heads in multi head systems, e.g. quadruplex, equalizes for playback losses and demodulates the frequency modulation signal back to video.

Time base error correction is required to compensate for timing instability arising from the mechanics of the head scanning process; this electronic system introduces variable delays to ensure the necessary playback signal synchronization. The video processor adds fresh synchronizing pulses and colour bursts to the output video in more expensive units.

The audio electronics unit is similar to that of the audio tape recorders but the audio quality of video tape recorders is adversely affected by the proximity of stray fields, poor tape contact and low width. The control panel provides the normal control functions - fast spooling, forward or reverse, playback and record. See alpha wrap, capstan, colour burst, frequency modulation, helical scan, kHz, magnetic head, MHz, omega wrap, pinch roller, quadruplex, servomechanism, transverse scan.

video teleconferencing In communications, a system providing full audio and visual conferencing facilities. See teleconferencing.

videotex (1) A term proposed for use at the international level instead of viewdata. (2) The term is also used generically to cover teletext, a broadcast videotex service as well as viewdata, a wired videotex service. It is this latter meaning that is considered here. Videotex technology is designed to forge a link between members of the general public and a centralised computer. In its most advanced form it can bring massive reference library, computer power and extensive communication facilities into the home. It has the capability to act as the single most important step in the evolution of the information society. As mentioned in the above entry, the term videotex covers two separate technological developments: viewdata and teletext. In the former case a communication link, providing simple two way communication, is established between the user and host computer through a telephone network. With teletext the information flow is simplex,

broadcast over TV wavebands in conjunction with normal television programs. See (a) A user's view of videotex, (b) viewdata, (c) teletext, (d) a comparison of viewdata and teletext, (e) electronic publishing, (f) further developments.

(a) A user's view of videotex. A casual observer would notice very little difference between a viewdata and a teletext display. The general format is of multicoloured sets of alphanumeric characters or simple patterns displayed on a TV screen. Across the world there are various videotex standards which affect the form of display but they fall into two broad categories - alphamosaic and alphageometric. The European systems are based upon the alphamosaic display and in this case the screen is divided into 24 (row) x 40 (column) spaces. A space is of one colour and it may contain an alphanumeric character (lower or upper case) or a simple mosaic of six rectangles (fig. 1).

The ASCII codes transmitted to the user either provide details of the pattern or character, to be displayed in the character space or set certain attributes for the remainder of the line, e.g. switch to graphics, change colour, etc. The alphamosaic system has the advantage of a simple user decoder system, but in normal operation (i.e. with conventional viewdata terminals) it cannot produce elegant pictures. Even a simple diagonal line has a staircase appearance. On the other hand, the Canadian Telidon system is based upon an alphageometric standard and the transmitted codes can produce simple line drawings, thus Telidon terminals can be more readily used for (say) educational purposes. The access methods of videotex have been designed on a user friendly basis to ensure that no training is required to retrieve information from the database. There are no

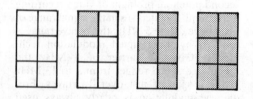

videotex
Fig 1 Coarse 2 × 3 graphic dot matrix.

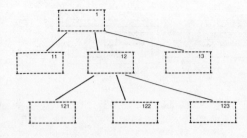

videotex
Fig 2 Videotex tree structure.

complicated log on procedures and the user is guided to the required information by a series of menu choices provided by the display. A simple hand held numeric keypad is used to select the next page to be displayed. For example, suppose a home viewer wishes to check the program at a certain theatre. The first displayed page would provide a very broad choice of subject matter and the associated keypad inputs: (1) government; (2) business; (3) leisure; (4) education; (5) travel. Upon depressing the key for leisure, (3) the next display will appear and provide details of the leisure section of the database; (1) theatre; (2) movies; (3) sport; (4) TV and radio; (5) holidays; (6) hobbies. Depression of key (1) will supply an index of theatres and eventually the desired information page will be displayed.

Videotex organizes its database using a tree structure, although cross references from one section of the database to another are possible (fig. 2).

A user can also access a page directly by keying in the appropriate page number. Each page can be the start of a small 'pamphlet' to 25 additional frames associated with it. The first page is, say, 121a and successive frames are 121b, 121c, etc. Successive depressions of a control key on the keypad will produce frames b, c, d, etc. The simple tree structure and menu selection allows videotex to be employed by a casual user, but this system does not supply the more sophisticated keyword searches that are possible with other database systems.

(b) Viewdata. A schematic diagram of a typical viewdata system is given in fig. 3.

In Prestel, the UK national viewdata service, a user dials up the viewdata computer,

or uses an autodialler, and the computer responds with an opening page giving instructions on how to proceed. Each user keypad depression is converted into audible tones and transmitted to the computer at 75 baud. The computer sets aside a small section of memory for every on line user, receives the user requests, selects the appropriate page from the disk store and transmits the information as ASCII codes at user terminal. Details of the user connect time, page accesses, etc. are recorded by the computer for customer billing. The codes transmitted to the user are stored in the decoder RAM memory, i.e. the screen buffer. The decoder display unit scans this memory, interprets the codes and produces the display on the TV screen.

In viewdata, the user forwards requests to the host computer and it is possible for other information to be similarly transmitted. Thus a response frame can be used as a blank form in which the user inputs appropriate details. For example, a hotel booking service can be provided using viewdata. Information pages provide details of the hotels, prices, location, facilities etc - and a response frame enables the user to input requirements, e.g. type of room, number of nights, dates, etc. The user response information is held in computer store until it is accessed by the hotel reservation unit.

(c) teletext. To a casual observer the only substantial difference between teletext and viewdata is the delay between a keypad depression and the appearance of the page. Teletext, however, is based on a one-way communication over TV broadcast (or cable TV) channels (fig. 4).

In radio broadcasts the signal is continuous, but with TV the picture information is transmitted in synchronism with the raster scan of the TV camera. The picture on the TV screen is produced by varying signals to the cathode ray tube gun as the electron beam scans across the face of the tube. The beam commences in the upper left hand corner of the screen and moves across in a horizontal line; it then jumps back to the left hand side and paints the next line slightly below the previous one, until the whole screen has been covered, at which point the beam flies back from the bottom right hand to the top left hand corner. Thus there are short intervals of time, measured in microseconds, when the spot is relocating itself on the screen, and no

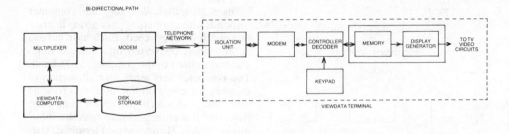

videotex
Fig 3 Elements of a viewdata system.

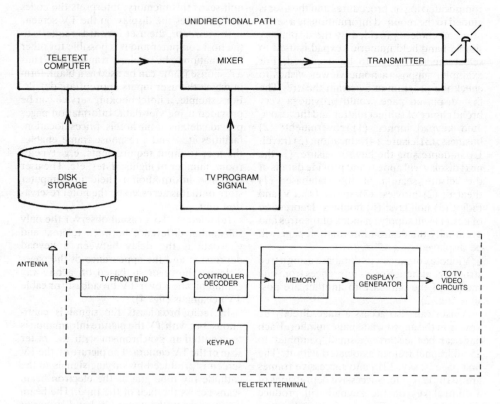

Videotex
Fig 4 Elements of a teletext system.

picture information is transmitted in these flyback periods. A TV broadcast signal therefore has periodic gaps in its picture transmission and it is possible to add a binary pulse train to the normal broadcast signal in these gaps. Teletext, therefore, uses spare capacity on an existing broadcast network and is an efficient and relatively cheap communication technique.

Unlike viewdata, the teletext computer does not respond to user requests, but simply produces each page of the database in rotation. The user requests the desired page, by menu selection, and inserts the page number on the keypad. The teletext decoder compares the page number of the broadcasted incoming page with that requested by the user and 'grabs' the appropriate frame, storing it in a RAM screen buffer, as in viewdata.

(d) a comparison of viewdata and teletext. The essential difference between viewdata and teletext lies in the interactive nature of the former. With viewdata the user selects a page from a very large database and the information is transmitted back over the telephone network. The size of a viewdata base is limited only by the on line disk storage capacity of the host computer and even small systems can contain several hundred thousand pages. A teletext system, however, transmits the whole of its database in a cyclic sequence and the user awaits the selected page to arrive. The actual data transmission rate of teletext is much higher than that of viewdata but, since a user has to wait for the selected page to appear, the system response is much slower. The size of the teletext database is related to the maximum delay that a user can reasonably be expected to tolerate in waiting for a page, and teletext databases therefore only comprise a few hundred pages.

The interactive nature of viewdata also allows it to offer facilities that cannot be supplied with teletext. The response frame technique can be expanded into teleshopping, and a user provided with an alphanumeric keypad may order goods and services from an IP offering such facilities. The response frame, once transmitted, is held for the IP in an electronic mailbox on the viewdata computer. It also permits the viewdata operator to monitor usage of the system and to levy a charge for computer connect time and page access. Teletext, on the other hand, can continuously update a page once selected by a user, thus providing a 'stop press' feature or subtitles associated with particular TV programs. An even more significant advantage of teletext, from a user's viewpoint, is the ease of installation and zero cost operation. Unlike viewdata, the teletext user needs no modem, no registration with the viewdata operator and the decoder can be supplied as an integral part of a domestic TV set. Teletext and viewdata, in spite of their similarities, are not competing systems; each has its own sphere of activities and the two systems can have a symbiotic

relationship: with teletext, stimulating a public awareness of, and interest in, the wider facilities of viewdata.

(e) electronic publishing. Videotex has provided the technology for domestic information retrieval and it has, therefore, generated a requirement for the information that is to be stored in the host computer. A new form of publisher, the Information Provider (IP), has arisen in recent years and such companies provide pages on public viewdata systems. The user is thus offered a variety of small databases supplied by individual IP's and each may be considered as a specialist publication. One IP might concentrate on providing up to date financial information, another supplies a database in the format of a regional newspaper with details of local events, response frames for local hotels and so on. The IPs pay the system operator responsible for operating the viewdata system, and gain their revenue from page access charges. Videotex therefore represents the first step in the generalized electronic provision of information, i.e. electronic publishing.

(f) further developments. Videotex in its basic form may be regarded as a simple information retrieval system for people with no computing expertise. The technology may, however, also be considered as a sophisticated communication network with considerable potential for further applications.

Even with the existing Prestel system within the UK, response frames may be used for a variety of consumer services, e.g. teleshopping and electronic mailboxes. The host computer on a viewdata system may, however, be linked to other remote computers and this 'gateway' concept can therefore convert the domestic viewdata terminal to an input device for a powerful computer network. This development not only enhances the size of the database available to the user, it ensures that response frames communicate directly with suppliers' databases and it offers powerful on line computing services for the home user and small business.

A complementary development is the convergence of the microcomputer and the viewdata terminal. A microcomputer can be enhanced to convert it to act as a viewdata terminal, in many cases by using an appropriate software package, and data supplied by viewdata pages may be fed directly into a microcomputer program. For example, stock exchange prices may be pulled down by viewdata and used to calculate the current value of the user's portfolio. A microcomputer acting as a viewdata terminal can also retrieve a computer program stored as a series of viewdata pages. This method of distributing computer programs over the telephone network is known as telesoftware. It offers a quick and easy method for selling microcomputer programs. The combination of a microcomputer/viewdata terminal and the gateway facility opens up the possibility of a home computer used either as an information retrieval system or else as an intelligent terminal with powerful computing facilities. See alphageometric, alphamosaic, alphanumeric, cathode ray tube, electronic mailbox, fly back, frame, gateway, half duplex, IP, MODEM, Prestel, raster scan, response frame, simplex, teleshopping, telesoftware, teletext, Telidon, tree structure, viewdata.

videotext   (1) The display of textual material on a CRT screen or television set. (2) German term for teletext. See CRT, teletext.

Viditel   In communications, Dutch experimental viewdata system. See viewdata.

viewdata   In communications, an interactive information service using a telephone link between the user and a host computer. The user employs a special terminal or an adaptor linked to a domestic TV set. See videotex.

Viewdata 80   In videotex, a UK specification for terminals with a dedicated module for assembly into the television electronics. The module provides line handling, data communications transport mechanisms with 1200 baud downstream and 75 baud upstream data rates. An integral chip modem is incorporated with automatic telephone number dialing and a locally programmable telephone directory holds six telephone numbers, including two automatic alternates for engaged numbers. This specification also provides a standard for peripheral device connection to the terminal, e.g. alphanumeric keyboard, audio cassette for page store, etc. See baud, chip modem, page store.

virtual   In computing and communications, a description of a facility that is offered to a user, or system, as if it were a physical reality. Compare transparent. See virtual storage.

virtual address   In computing, the apparent address of a location in virtual storage. See virtual storage.

virtual call service   In packet switching, a service in which a logical link is set up prior to transfer. Packets are transferred over the logical link, some of them contain no data but are used for supervisory purposes. During the data transfer phase packet sequence and flow control operations are performed. See virtual circuit.

virtual circuit   In packet switching, a circuit which comprises a path established from source to destination in the network. For the duration of the call all packets, which are not individually addressed, are transmitted through this virtual circuit and arrive in the same order as delivered. Compare datagram.

virtual disk   In microcomputers, a large RAM store which holds some portion of the contents, of a floppy or hard disk, during processing so that operations involving many read or write actions can be speeded up. See floppy disk, hard disk, RAM. Synonymous with RAM disk.

virtual machine   In computing, a simulation of a computer and its associated devices by another computer system. See simulate.

virtual storage   In computing, a large notional main store is made available to the user by mapping the user virtual addresses onto real addresses of auxiliary storage. See auxiliary storage, main storage.

virtual terminal   In computing and communications, an ideal terminal that is defined as a standard for the purpose of uniform handling of a variety of actual terminals. A terminal processor thereafter converts the signals of the real terminal to conform to the standards of the virtual terminal. See terminal.

visible light emitting diode   In microelectronics, a light emitting diode with an output in

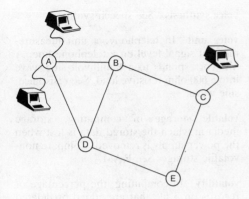

virtual terminal
The vertical terminal concept enables a variety of user terminal types to access a computer network.

the visible range. Some LED's produce infrared radiation. See light emitting diode.

VISICALC   In computer programming, a popular spreadsheet package. See spreadsheet.

vision mixer   In television, a device that selects one of a number of image sources, e.g. cameras, video tape recorders, to provide the broadcast picture, also used for fades, mixes, etc. See mixer.

visual acuity   The ability of the eye to resolve or discriminate fine detail.

visual display terminal   In computing, a device which permits the user to input information to a computer via keyboard, light pen or touchscreen facilities and to view the computer output, text or graphics, on a CRT screen. See light pen, touchscreen, CRT.

visual display unit   See visual display terminal.

visual editing terminal   In typesetting, a visual display terminal used specifically for editing.

visual literacy   Skills developed in interpreting, judging, responding to, and using visual representations of reality.

visual programming   In computer programming, a method of instructing the computer by showing it what to do rather than keying what to do. For example, instead of writing a lengthy and exacting description of the manner that information is to be formatted, for entry into or retrieval from a system, the user draws a corresponding visual representation by (say) manipulating a cursor on a VDU screen. See VDU.

viz   In printing, term used in footnotes meaning 'namely'.

VLED   See visible light emitting diode.

VLF   See very low frequency.

VLSI   See very large scale integration.

voder   In computing, a speech synthesizer. See speech synthesizer.

VOGAD   In communications, Voice Operated Gain Adjusting Device, a unit used in radiocommunications that removes fluctuations in input speech signals and outputs them at a constant level. Compare COMPANDOR.

voice answer back   In computing, an audio response unit that can link a computer system to a telephone network to provide voice responses to enquiries. See voice output.

voice band   In communications, the band of frequencies permitting intelligible transmission of human voice, usually 300 - 3000 Hz. See Hz.

voice bank   In communications, a recording system which can store spoken material for ready access.

voice data entry   In computing, a system which accepts the spoken word as input data or commands. The user speaks into a microphone and a digitized version of the audio signal is compared with that of digitized words held in computer memory. When a reasonable match is found the encoded characters (say ASCII) are often displayed on a VDU for user confirmation prior to input to the computer. Usually a 'training session' is held to provide the computer with examples of the spoken word. Applications include comments from quality control inspectors on production lines, receipt of telephone orders from salesmen, stock checking etc. See speech recognizer, VDU.

voice frequency　See voice band.

voice grade channel　In communications, a channel suitable for the transmission of speech, facsimile, analog or digital data with a frequency range in the audio band, generally about 300 - 3000 Hz. See Hz.

voice guard　In recording, a dictating machine device that emits a loud steady tone if the recording medium is not moving.

voice input　In computing, a device that enables a computer to accept voice commands. See speech recognizer, voice data entry.

voice mail　In communications, a system in which spoken information is digitized and stored either in a network memory or in the appropriate apparatus at the destination for the message. The spoken message is later retrieved by the called party. See voice store and forward.

voice operated device　In telephony, a device used on a circuit to permit the presence of telephone currents to effect desired control. Echo suppressors often use such devices. See echo suppressor.

voice output　In computing, a device that enables a computer to produce output as a spoken word. See speech synthesizer.

voice over　In cinematography or TV, an off screen voice.

voice print　A recorded signal which identifies the voice characteristics of an individual and is used for identification purposes. Compare ear print.

voice recognition　See speech recognizer.

voice store and forward　In communications, a system that transmits and stores voice messages for playback or demand. See store and forward, voice mail.

voice synthesis　See speech synthesis.

voice unit　In telephony, a unit measurement of signal level on a telephone line. A VU corresponds to a 1 millivolt sine wave into a 600 ohm resistive load. See resistance, sine wave.

volatile storage　In computing, storage media in which the stored data is lost when the power supply is removed. Compare non-volatile storage. See RAM.

volatility　In computing, the percentage of records on a file that are added or deleted during a run. See record, file, activity.

volt　In electronics, a unit of electrical voltage. Compare ampere. See voltage.

voltage　In electronics, the electrical pressure across a circuit causing a current flow, or capable of causing a current flow. See volt, Ohm's Law.

volume　(1) The amplitude of sound waves. (2) In printing, a set of printed sheets bound together and forming part or whole of a work. (3) The space occupied. (4) In computing, a storage medium holding data that can be mounted or demounted as a unit, e.g. a disk pack. See disk pack.

Von Neumann　In computing, pertaining to the architecture of a conventional computer. It is characterized by (a) a single computing element incorporating processor, communications and memory (b) linear organization of fixed size memory cells (c) one level address space of cells (d) low level machine language (e) sequential, centralized control of computation, (f) primitive input output capability. Compare data driven, demand driven. See architecture, cell, memory, machine code.

voxel　In computing, a three dimensional pixel. See pixel.

VRC　See vertical redundancy check.

V series recommendations of CCITT　In data communications, a series of recommendations relating to data communications over analog channels.

VSMF In micrographics, Visual Search Microfilm File, a 16mm microfilm catalog of products approved and listed by the US Department of Defense and their suppliers. See microfilm.

VTR See video tape recorder.

VU See voice unit.

VUmeter In recording, a meter on sound recorders and playback devices which indicates variations in sound amplitude.

V.1 In data communications, equivalence between binary notation symbols and the significant conditions of two condition code.

V.2 In data communications, power levels for data transmission over telephone lines.

V.3 In data communications, international Alphabet No 5 for transmission of data and messages.

V.4 In data communications, general structure of signals of International Alphabet No 5 for data and message transmission over public telephone networks.

V.5 In data communications, standardization of data signalling rates for synchronous data transmission in the general switched telephone network.

V.6 In data communications, standardization of data signalling rates for synchronous data transmission on leased telephone-type circuits.

V.10 In data communications, electrical characteristics for unbalanced double-current interchange circuits for general use with integrated circuit equipment in the field of data communications.

V.11 In data communications, electrical characteristics for balanced double-current interchange circuits for general use with integrated circuit equipment in the field of data communications.

V.13 In data communications, answer-back unit simulators.

V.15 In data communications, use of acoustic coupling for data transmission.

V.16 In data communications, medical analog data transmission modems.

V.19 In data communications, modems for parallel data transmission using telephone signalling frequencies.

V.20 In data communications, parallel data transmission modems standardized for universal use in the general switched telephone network.

V.21 In data communications, 300-baud modem standardized for use in the general switched telephone network.

V.22 In data communications, 1200 bit/s duplex modem standardized for use on the general switched telephone network.

V.23 In data communications, 600/1200 baud modem standardized for use in the general switched telephone network.

V.24 In data communications, a CCITT recommendation for an interface for the connection of a data terminal to a modem for serial data transmission. Equivalent to the EIA specification RS232. See EIA, MODEM, serial transmission, RS232.

V.25 In data communications, automatic calling and/or answering on the general switched telephone network, including disabling of echo suppressors on manually established calls.

V.26 In data communications, 2400 bit/s modem standardized for use on four-wire leased circuits.

V.26bis In data communications, 2400/1200 bit/s modem standardized for use in the general switched telephone network.

V.27 In data communications, 4800 bit/s modem standardized for use on leased circuits.

V.27bis In data communications, 4800 bit/s modem with automatic equalizer standardized for use on leased circuits.

V.27ter   In data communications, 4800/2400 bit/s modem standardized for use in the general switched telephone network.

V.28   In data communications, electrical characteristics for unbalanced double-current interchange circuits.

V.29   In data communications, 9600 bit/s modem for use on leased circuits.

V.30   In data communications, parallel data transmission systems for universal use on the general switched telephone network.

V.31   In data communications, electrical characteristics for single-current interchange circuits controlled by contact closure.

V.35   In data communications, data transmission at 48 kilobit/s using 60 to 108 kHz group band circuits.

V.36   In data communications, modems for synchronous data transmission using 60 to 108 kHz group band circuits.

V.37   In data communications, synchronous data transmission at a data signalling rate higher than 72 Kbit/s using 60 to 108 kHz group band circuits.

V.40   In data communications, error indication with electromechanical equipment.

V.41   In data communications, code independent error control system.

V.50   In data communications, standard limits for transmission quality of data transmission.

V.51   In data communications, organization of the maintenance of international telephone-type circuits used for data transmission.

V.52   In data communications, characteristics of distortion and error rate measuring apparatus for data transmission.

V.53   In data communications, limits for the maintenance of telephone-type circuits used for data transmission.

V.54   In data communications, loop test device for modems.

V.55   In data communications, specification for an impulsive noise measuring instrument for telephone-type circuits.

V.56   In data communications, comparative tests for modems for use over telephone-type circuits.

W

WACK In data communications, Wait before transmitting positive ACKnowledgement. A signal sent by a receiving station to indicate that it is temporarily not ready to receive.

WADS See Wide Area Data Service.

wafer In microelectronics, a very thin slice of cylindrically shaped monocrystalline solid rod of silicon, either before or after integrated circuits have been fabricated on it. After fabrication the wafer is cut into square dice, each of which is an integrated circuit. See chip, integrated circuit, silicon.

wafer silicon integration In microelectronics, a chip as large as a wafer developed for high speed computers. In conventional chip technology chips are manufactured on wafers and then cut into individual chips. In subsequent computer manufacture the individual chips are brought together on a circuit and interconnected electrically. This method of computer manufacture results in comparatively long chip interconnections and the speed of the computer is limited by the time taken for pulses to traverse these interconnections. If the complete set of chips and interconnections are manufactured as a single unit on a wafer then the length of interconnections is considerably reduced. The major disadvantage of this technique lies in the problems of guaranteeing fault free chips and interconnections in the wafer manufacturing phase. With conventional chip technology a faulty chip on a wafer can be discarded, with wafer scale integration techniques, however, it is necessary to employ a high degree of redundancy to ensure that a few isolated faults do not cause the whole wafer to be rejected. See chip, redundancy.

wagon wheel effect In filming, a spoked wheel may appear to move in reverse because a spoke moves almost to the position of its nearest neighbour in the interval between shutter openings. See stroboscopic effect.

wait condition In computing, a state in which the processor has suspended program execution whilst waiting for an external signal, e.g. data from a peripheral or an external memory.

wait loop In computing, a subroutine in a computer program that continually loops until a condition external to the program occurs. See loop, subroutine.

walkie talkie In communications, a small portable radio transmitter with limited range.

walk through In computer programming, a process of tracing the logic of a computer program by a structured discussion amongst a small team.

WAMI World Association of Medical Informatics.

WAN See wide area network.

wand In computing, a hand held bar code reader. A typical wand comprises an aluminium tube and illumination from an LED, near the reading end of the tube, is focused by a sapphire sphere onto the reflecting bar code label. Reflected light from the label is focused by the sphere onto a phototransistor higher up the tube interior. See bar code, LED, phototransistor.

warmbody device In computing, a device which can measure a characteristic unique to an individual and check it against recorded corresponding identification information stored in a computer or on a credit card. Compare PIN. See ear print.

warm standby In computing and communications, a backup system which can be switched into operation within a few seconds of an active system malfunction. Compare cold standby, hot standby.

watermark In printing, a faint mark imparted to certain uncoated papers during manufacture to identify the paper mill.

WATS See Wide Area Telephone Service.

watt In electronics, a unit of electrical power produced when one amp flows between a potential difference of one volt. See volt, ampere.

wattage rating In electronics, the maximum power that an electrical component can dissipate under standard operating conditions.

wave A physical activity that increases and decreases, or advances and retreats, periodically as it travels through the medium.

waveband A range of wavelengths.

waveform The graphic representation of the amplitude variations, with time, of a wave. See wave.

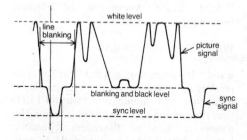

waveform
A typical line in a PAL video transmission showing synchronizing signals.

waveguide In communications, metal tubes used for the transmission of microwave signals. An optical fiber may be considered to be a waveguide for light waves. See circular waveguide, fiber optics, rectangular waveguide.

wavelength The distance between corresponding points on a wave. The wavelength multiplied by the frequency is equal to the speed of the wave, in the case of light and

radio waves the speed is 3 x 10 to the power 8 meters per second. See frequency.

wavelength division multiplexing In communications, a technique that is identical to frequency division multiplexing. The term is applied to the use of different wavelengths for the light signals along an optical fiber. See fiber optics, frequency division multiplexing.

WDM See wavelength division multiplexing.

web In printing, ribbon or reel of paper as formed on paper making machine.

web fed In printing, a machine in which paper is fed from web or reel rather than from flat sheets.

wedge serif In printing, a typeface with triangular serifs. See serif.

weed In computing, to remove undesired items from a file.

weight In printing, (1) a description of the blackness of a typeface, i.e. light, medium, bold, extra bold and ultra bold, (2) the weight of 500 sheets of paper of standard size.

WESTAR A common carrier domestic communications satellite operated by Western Union. See common carrier, satellite.

Westlaw A database supplied by West Publishing Company and others and dealing with business and industry, communications, energy industry, government - US, federal, insurance and insurance industry, labor and employment, law, law -US federal, law - US state, patents, securities - US. See on line information retrieval.

wet on wet In printing, a technique in which one colour is printed on another whilst it is still wet.

wf See wrong font.

wheel graph See pie graph.

wheel printer In computing, a printer with a printing mechanism containing the printing characters on metal wheels.

white flag In video disk, a code that identifies a new film frame. See frame.

white level In television, the maximum value of video signal voltage, i.e. corresponding to the brightest spot on the TV display. Compare black level. See video signal.

white level frequency In video recording, the frequency of the recorded frequency modulated signal corresponding to the white level. This is the maximum frequency of the signal. See white level, frequency modulation, sync tip frequency.

white line In printing, a space between lines of type equal to that left if one line of type is omitted.

white noise In communications, an unwanted random signal with equal power over all frequencies. See noise.

white space reduction See kerning.

Wide Area Data Service In data communicatons, an AT&T service which makes unlimited dial up use of telegraph grade circuits, within a particular geographic area, available to subscribers for a fixed monthly fee. Compare WATS.

wide area network In data communications, a comprehensive multi-mode network connecting large numbers of terminals and computers spread over a wide area. Compare local area network.

Wide Area Telephone Service A flat rate, or measured bulk rate, long distance telephone service provided on an outgoing or incoming call basis.

wideband See broadband.

wideband channel In data communications, channels that operate to 50K bits per second, speed can be increased up to 168K bits per second with special modems. See bit, MODEM.

widow In printing, a short line at the top of a page or column.

widow line In printing, one line of a para-

graph isolated at the top or bottom of a page. See widow.

width In computing, pertaining to the organization of data within a memory device. Solid state memory chips are organized so that one word may be stored in the corresponding position on a number of chips, e.g. a chip may be organized as 1024 units each of 4 bits, 1024-8 bit words of computer data would be stored with each word having the least significant 4 bits in one chip and the most significant 4 bits in the other. See bit, word, RAM, bit slice.

width card In typesetting, an electrical component for insertion into a phototypesetter, or keyboard, to establish the set widths of the type font in use. See font, phototypesetting, set width.

width value In printing, a list or group of widths allocated to a character set. See character set.

Winchester In computing, pertaining to sealed hard disk systems with close tolerance and high performance characteristics patterned upon an IBM disk system. See hard disk.

windows In computer programming, pertaining to a software technique that facilitates the movement of data between packages. The concept is intended to provide extremely user friendly systems for executives who can view the contents of different packages in 'windows' on the VDU screen and cut and paste information from one into another. See cut and paste, Lisa.

wipe In filming, a visual effect in which one image appears to be pushed off the screen by another.

wiper In electronics, the moveable arm of a potentiometer. See potentiometer.

wiper switch In automatic switching, a moving contact on a selector. See selector.

wireless In communications, early name for radio indicating telecommunication not requiring wires between sender and receiver.

wireless microphone See radio microphone.

wire photo In communications, a technique for transmitting a picture by telegraphy. See facsimile.

wire stripping In communications, the removal of miscellaneous codes, from copy sent on an agency wire service network, at a publishing office.

wire tapping In data security, the unauthorized interception of messages. The purpose of passive wire tapping is to disclose message contents without detection whilst active wire tapping involves the deliberate modification of messages, sometimes for the purpose of injecting false messages, injecting replays of previous messages (e.g. to repeat a credit transaction) or deleting messages. Encryption protects against message modification and injection of false messages by making it infeasible for an opponent to create ciphertext that deciphers into meaningful plaintext. Compare between-lines entry, piggyback entry, display, traffic analysis. See browsing.

wire wrap In electronics, a method of making permanent electrical contacts without soldering. Wire is tightly wrapped around a metal post with at least two sharp edges.

woofer A component of a loudspeaker assembly producing low frequency sound waves. Compare tweeter.

word In computing, a group of bits, bytes or characters, considered as an entity, and capable of storage in one memory location.

word break In word processing, the use of a hyphen to split a word at the end of a line so as to avoid obvious gaps. See exception dictionary.

word-frame counter In data communications, a unit to count the number of words received in a frame as they are received. It may also count the number of frames. See frame, word.

word length In computing, the number of bits, bytes or characters in a word. See word.

word processing The preparation of printed matter using automatic typewriting techniques. The term was created first by IBM Germany in the late 1960's to embrace and provide synergy to their burgeoning range of office equipment. They defined the term as 'the range of operations in dictation, transcription, correction, reproduction and distribution required to communicate information in the modern office'. After the early years, however, the term has become associated mainly with the automatic typewriting element of this whole process. Today there are a number of different types of product available to help automate the typing process e.g. electronic typewriters, specialist word processors and the personal computer with the word processing package.

See (a) history, (b) market potential, (c) WP products (d) document distribution, (e) applications.

(a) History. Automatic typewriting has a history that can be traced to the early years of the century, but the modern industry can be traced back directly to a tender from the US Government who required a machine during the second world war which would send personalized letters of condolence from the President to the relatives of the US Militia who lost their lives during this conflict. The tender was won by IBM, who attached a paper tape reader to their electric typewriter, but after the war they sold the developments to others because they could see no commercial benefit. Through the 1950's the machines developed from using a single paper tape reader connected to a typewriter to the machine with a paper reader punch. Thus text could be corrected and recycled, and additional logic was added to provide automatic centering of a heading, reverse indexing to provide sub- and superscripts, justify text on both the left and right hand margins etc. Since those days 20 years ago the machines have developed quite dramatically.

In the middle of the 1960's IBM re-entered the market with specially adapted Selectric typewriters attached to a magnetic tape cassette. Five years on, at the end of the 1960's, they introduced new machines using a magnetic card, where one card recorded the text on one page of the printed document. Almost in parallel, the Scribona company in Switzerland introduced machines also using the specially adapted Selectric typewriter, but

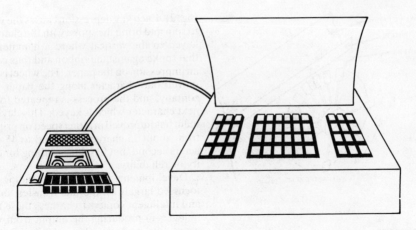

Word processing
Fig 1 An early word processor–a crude link between a cassette recorder and an electro-mechanical typewriter.

attached to a Phillips 'C' series magnetic cassette as the recording medium (fig. 1).

By the middle 1970's the word processor as it is recognized today began to appear when the first machines were introduced using diskettes, screen and daisy wheel printers (figs. 2.3). Also about this time the first shared logic systems began to appear. Since then the external shape of the machines has changed little but with the electronics becoming ever more integrated the functionality of the machines has been under continuous development.

(b) Market potential. Today about 60,000 specialist word processors are in operation within the UK. In addition about 300,000 electronic typewriters and 20,000 personal computers are employed in UK offices dedicated to automating the typing task.

Well in excess of 100 suppliers are attempting to establish their credentials in this market. The prize they are seeking is the approximately 10 million typists in Europe. All their machines will be replaced before the end of the decade by an electronic device which may be an electronic typewriter, a word processor or some form of multifunction workstation. In addition, there are another 40 million clerks and executives working throughout western Europe who at present are largely untouched by technological developments. A market of this size has naturally attracted the traditional suppliers of typewriters, all the small business computer

suppliers have developed their equipment to handle text, and more recently the suppliers of telephone switching equipment have joined the competition.

(c) WP products. The first essential of all word processing is to record keystrokes. Once they are recorded they can be recomposed into different formats, revised without a major retype or played out any number of times to produce individual top copies to a number of recipients. On this basis many electronic typewriters will qualify because, in addition to replacing literally thousands of moving parts with electronic components, many have additional logic to record keystrokes and provide the basic word processing functions listed above.

At present most of the machines are sold with very few additional facilities beyond those of the electromechanical devices they have replaced but experience amongst users suggest that when they grasp the additional functionality available they quickly demand more sophisticated machines. A number of upgrade paths are now available. Some suppliers provide a 'buy back' policy, others provide a screen and a diskette unit with sufficient logic to provide a basic word processing capability.

A specialist word processor or personal computer starts at this point. Both comprise a keyboard, printer, storage and display. The keyboard uses the QWERTY layout developed by Mr Christopher Sholes 100 years ago

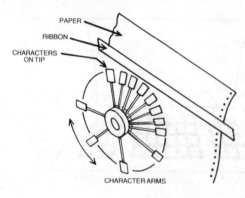

word processing
Fig 2 Daisy wheel. The diameter of the wheel is about three inches; it has ninety spokes with a different character moulded on to the end of each.

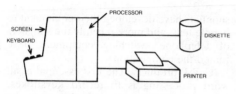

word processing
Fig 3 Stand alone word processor.

to slow down the operator to a speed at which the mechanical linkages in his, the first commercial typewriter, could operate without breaking down too frequently. There are variations on this keyboard in most countries, and many do not have a standard keyboard due to lack of international agreement on standardization. A major area for reconciliation remains over the various punctuation marks and other single key impressions such as fractions, foreign language accents and automatic sub- and superscripts which may be deemed useful on an English keyboard. In addition some function and command keys are also necessary for the word processing environment.

The printer in almost universal use today is the daisy wheel. It is so called because the characters are moulded onto the end of individual spokes, and typically the spokes are connected to a wheel, normally between 90 and 100 spokes per wheel. The wheel is mounted vertically, with a ribbon behind, and the sheet of paper is pressure mounted against a platen as with a normal typewriter

(fig. 2). Each key depression causes the wheel to spin and bring the spoke with the character keyed to the vertical where a hammer hits that spoke against the ribbon and thus causes an impression on the paper. The wheel is then moved one character along the paper horizontally, and the process is repeated for the next character which is keyed. This development has improved printing speed on printout from about 15 characters/second to 45 characters/second, but has done nothing for quality or reliability.

Developments in imaging technology are focussed largely on thermal transfer, ink jet and intelligent copiers to harness these technologies in producing the output from word processing systems. The reasons for this development in different technologies are to reduce noise, increase speed, eliminate the high costs of ribbons and the inability to change typefaces without stopping the machine and physically changing the wheel. Also it is impossible to change type sizes on a daisy printer. Additionally, they offer the potential for colour printing in a compact unit, but at present there are technical limitations (primarily reliability) in their performance.

Today the majority of standalone word processors use floppy diskettes for storage. These devices are flexible magnetic disks, either 8 or 5 inch in diameter, encased in a sleeve with a window for recording and retrieving text. Typically each diskette will store from approximately 150,000 characters to upward of 1 million. Whilst this may sound very large, it is not unusual to find a mature installation with several hundred or even thousand diskettes, at which point the difficulties of recording and handling a library of this size become quite dramatic and the problems of finding and re-using a particular document become acute.

For this reason shared logic or shared resource systems have become popular (fig. 4). In shared logic systems, all the workstations are connected to a single central storage system, and usually share printing and communication resources as well. The problem of supervising a single, large on line store is obviously much less acute, and the other shared resources typically make a more productive and more efficient use of the word processing facilities.

Displays, like so much else in word process-

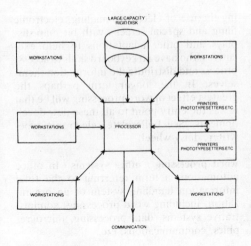

word processing
Fig 4 Shared logic system. Each workstation shares the advantages of a large capacity disk, one or more printers and central system processing power.

ing, have been developed from the data processing industry, and the most common is a 12 or 13 inch diagonal display providing approximately 25 lines of 80 characters of text, known as a partial page. Several companies believed this to be insufficient and have produced a full page display, however none have yet made any massive penetration in the market place and most suppliers have now abandoned it. Thin window displays of less than one line use gas plasma technology although some use LED (Light Emitting Diode). As each character is keyed, it is also displayed in the right hand end of the screen (which is typically situated on the workstation above the keyboard and in front of the printer mechanism), and the other text in the display moves one character to the left, so that the foremost character disappears off the screen. The screen length is between 16 and 45 characters, and the logic of most machines will allow text to be scrolled back for review and possible revision. The value of such screens is to correct conscious errors before they reach the printer, and for simple revisions. Today they are used almost exclusively on electronic typewriters. Experience throughout the market suggests that the screen becomes invaluable during revision typing, and also for difficult composition such as tables.

(d) Document distribution. The aspect of word processing which is becoming increasingly important is distribution. The life cycle of a document has been analyzed as follows: creation, proof reading and revision - 5%, in-out trays of author and receiver - 18%, transmission between author and reader - 77%.

Word processing until recently has largely concentrated on the creation phase in an attempt to speed up this process and make it more efficient. Now electronic mail systems are appearing which are attempting to reduce the times and increase the efficiency of the latter functions. Labour intensive activities such as foot mail are becoming increasingly expensive, and decreasingly efficient. Once the information has been recorded on a system the pressure to transmit it electronically increases. The major reason why such systems are still not used universally is primarily that only recently have user friendly electronic mail systems begun to appear, and also the lack of compatability between different suppliers. The problem is largely one of character and protocol compatibility. The former was standardized for the data processing industry in the 1960's and was defined in terms of transmitting fixed field data from one machine to another. Thus the standard codes (ASCII and EBCDIC) have little in the way of punctuation and nothing for setting margins and tabs, standardizing on the codes and centering or underscoring etc. Some standardization of protocols has been achieved, largely through emulating IBM's protocols.

(e) Applications. When looking at the reasons for rapid growth in the use of word processing it is useful to analyse documents into types: short letters and memos, repetitive standard letters, boilerplating, long revision documents, schedules, application documents.

The standard typewriter with a correcting ribbon remains, arguably, the most productive way of producing unique short letters or memos. As mentioned earlier, the first automatic typewriters were designed to produce personalized standard letters, and this is still a main application area. It is not as cheap a process as preprinting the letters, and typing or writing the individual name and address unless there is a highly sophisticated form of name and address selection (i.e. selecting all the drug stores staying open late on Wednesdays in a certain geographical area, or finding an employee with skills in certain subjects and an ability to speak Arabic, and holding an Israeli entry visa) etc. but it can often be more effective. There are numerous examples in sales letters, debt collection letters, etc.

Boilerplating, is a US term used to define documents which have been compiled from a large library of standard paragraphs, sentences and phrases. Perhaps the most common examples are legal documents such as property conveyances or wills compiled from standard paragraphs and appropriately personalized. In continental Europe this technique is popular for producing sales documents where it is estimated that approximately 70% of the text leaving any office is a repeat of something that was published at least once previously.

Long revision documents are a good example of candidates for a recording system. If every keystroke of the first draft is recorded, then obviously when it is revised a total retype and re-proofread becomes unnecessary. Typically a 40 page document will be revised on an average 3 times by the author, and often further revised by departmental colleagues, before being submitted to the receiver who in discussion may suggest further revisions. If the first draft is recorded then subsequent revision can be produced without a complete retype, and that is a major benefit of word processing.

Many word processing systems have an ability for customization which means that the functions needed to create a document which is produced repetitively, e.g. the Articles of Association for company formation, can be pre-recorded, and the system programmed to create the documentation automatically when the name of the company, and the names and addresses of the shareholders are keyed in.

All the above mentioned developments are designed to produce better documents of the types analysed latterly. Typing productivity increases of between 200% and 700% are already well documented, and no doubt this is the reason why annual installation growth rates of between 30% (screen based word processors) and more than 100% (electronic typewriters) are being recorded.

The more creative suppliers are already looking beyond the use of word processors to improve typing productivity and are evaluating the use of electronic mailing, electronic filing and special screens with bit map displays and other adaptations to help executives who have no keyboard skills to access, process and distribute the information themselves. In the longer term perhaps the greatest effect of word processing will be that it was the entry point to all these new developments. See boilerplate, electronic typewriter, daisy wheel.

word processing / office systems In office automation, a term referring to the total information handling system of an organization, including word processing, administrative systems, data processing, micrographics, communications, etc.

word serial In computing, a parallel data transmission mode in which the words are sent along the bus system one after another. See word, bus, parallel transmission.

word size See width.

word space In electronic typesetting, a code, spaced between words, that will activate the typesetting and produce a nonprinting character or space. See variable space.

words per minute In communications, the rated speed of teletypewriter equipment.

word time In electronic typesetting, the time between the appearance of corresponding parts of successive words from a serial access storage device. See serial access.

work area Synonymous with memory workspace.

working data file In word processing, a file that is either erased at the end of an editing session or converted to a permanent file. See permanent file.

working memory In word processing, the section of memory holding text during the keyboarding, editing or playback processes. See edit, memory.

work station See stand alone word processing system.

World Aluminum Abstracts A database

supplied by the American Society for Metals (World Aluminum Abstracts) and dealing with metallurgy. See on line information retrieval.

World Textiles A database supplied by Shirley Institute and dealing with textiles. See on line information retrieval.

wow In sound recording, a low frequency noise usually produced by regular variations in the speed of a system's mechanical component.

WP See word processing.

WPI World Patents Index, a database supplied by Derwent Publications Ltd. and dealing with patents. See on line information retrieval.

wraparound (1) In computing, the continuation of an operation from the maximum address of working location to the starting address. (2) In word processing, a facility that enables a word to be moved to a succeeding or preceding line, or page, to accommodate insertions and deletions. See vertical wraparound, horizontal wraparound.

wraparound press In printing, a letterpress machine using a curved printing plate wrapped around a cylinder. See letterpress.

write In computing, to record data in a storage device or data medium. Compare read. See storage device.

write after read In computing, a technique that restores the data after the read action in those storage devices in which the action of reading erases the data from the device. See destructive readout.

write enable In computing and recording, a mechanism that enables data or signals to be recorded on a tape. In the absence of this mechanism the tape or disk is protected against any unwanted or accidental over-writing.

writing head In recording, the magnetic head that writes signals onto the storage medium. Compare read head.

writing line In printing, the maximum line length that can be written by a machine, usually expressed in characters or inches.

wrong font In typesetting, a typographic error in which letters of different fonts become mixed. See font.

wrong reading In cinematography and printing, text or graphics that are reversed from left to right. Compare right reading. Synomymous with reverse reading.

X

X In micrographics, pertaining to the degree of reduction. See reduction.

x-axis The horizontal axis of a coordinate graph. Compare y-axis.

xenon flash In typesetting, a high intensity short exposure light source often used in phototypesetting machines.

xerography In printing, a process that first places an electrostatic charge on a plate. Then an image is projected onto the plate causing the charge to dissipate in the illuminated areas, thus allowing an applied coating of resinous powder to adhere only to the uncharged (dark) areas. The powder is then transferred to paper and is fixed by heat. See laser xerography.

x height In printing, the height of the body of the lower case letters, exclusive of ascenders and descenders. Synonymous with z height.

X-Series of recommendations of CCITT In data communications, a series of recommendations for data transmission over public data networks.

X-Stream In data communications, a generic name of four fully digital services, provided by British Telecom - Megastream, Switchstream, Satstream, Kilostream. See Kilostream, Megastream, Satstream, Switchstream.

X-Y plotter In computing, a plotting device that receives x and y, coordinates from a computer and plots a coordinate graph. See coordinate graph.

X.1 In data communications, international user classes of service in public data networks.

X.2 In data communications, international user facilities in public data networks.

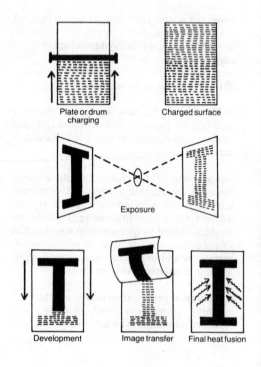

Plate or drum charging — Charged surface — Exposure — Development — Image transfer — Final heat fusion

xerography
The stages in xerographic duplication.

X.3 In data communications, packet assembly/disassembly facility (PAD) in a public data network.

X.4 In data communications, general structure of signals of International Alphabet No 5 code for data transmission over public data networks.

X.20 In data communications, interface between Data Terminal Equipment (DTE) and Data Circuit Terminating Equipment (DCE) for start/stop transmission services on public data networks.

X20 bis In data communications, V.21-

compatible interface between data terminal equipment (DTE) and data circuit-terminating equipment (DCE) for start-stop transmission services on public data networks.

X.21 In data communications, general purpose interface between data terminal equipment (DTE) and data circuit terminating equipment (DCE) for synchronous operation on public data networks.

X.21 bis In data communications, use on public data networks of data terminal equipments which are designed for interfacing to synchronous V-series modems.

X.22 In data communications, Multiplex DTE/DCE interface for user classes 3-6.

X.24 In data communications, list of definitions of interchange circuits between data terminal equipment and data circuit-terminating equipment on public data networks.

X.25 In data communications, interface between data terminal equipment (DTE) and data circuit terminating equipment (DCE) for terminals operating in the packet mode on public data networks.

X.26 In data communications, electrical characteristics for unbalanced double-current interchange circuits for general use with integrated circuit equipment in the field of data communications.

X.27 In data communications, electrical characteristics for balanced double-current interchange circuits for general use with integrated circuit equipment in the field of data communications.

X.28 In data communications, DTE/DCE interface for a start-stop mode data terminal equipment accessing the packet assembly/-disassembly facility (PAD) on a public data network situated in the same country.

X.29 In data communications, procedures for the exchange of control information and user data between a packet mode DTE and a packet assembly/disassembly facility (PAD).

X.30 In data communications, standardization of basic mode-page-printing machine in accordance with International Alphabet No 5.

X.31 In data communications, characteristics, from the transmission point of view, at the interchange point between data terminal equipment and data circuit terminating equipment when a 200-baud start-stop data terminal in accordance with International Alphabet No 5 is used.

X.32 In data communications, answer-back units for 200 bauds start-stop machines in accordance with International Alphabet No 5.

X.33 In data communications, standardization of an international text for the measurement of the margin of start-stop machines in accordance with International Alphabet No 5.

X.40 In data communications, standardization of frequency-shift modulated transmission systems for the provision of telegraph and data channels by frequency division of a primary group.

X.50 In data communications, fundamental parameters of a multiplexing scheme for the international interface between synchronous data networks.

X.50 bis In data communications, fundamental parameters of a 48 Kbit/s user data signalling rate transmission scheme for the international interface between synchronous data networks.

X.51 In data communications, fundamental parameters of a multiplexing scheme for the international interface between synchronous data networks using 10-bit envelope structures.

X.51 bis In data communications, fundamental parameters of a 48 Kbit/s user data signalling rate transmission scheme for the international interface between synchronous data networks using 10-bit envelope structure.

X.52 In data communications, method of encoding anisochronous signals into a synchronous user bearer.

X.53 In data communications, numbering of channels on international multiplex links at 64 Kbit/s.

X.54 In data communications, allocation of channels on international multiplex links at 64 Kbit/s.

X.60 In data communications, common channel signalling for synchronous data applications data user part.

X.61 In data communications, signalling system No 7 - data user part.

X.70 In data communications, terminal and transit control signalling system for start-stop services on international circuits between anisochronous data networks.

X.71 In data communications, decentralized terminal and transit control signalling system on international circuits between synchronous data networks.

X.75 In data communications, terminal and transit call control procedures and data transfer system on international circuits between packet-switched data networks.

X.80 In data communications, interworking of interchange signalling system switched data services.

X.87 In data communications, principles and procedures for realization of international user facilities and network utilities in public data networks.

X.92 In data communications, hypothetical reference connections for public synchronous data networks.

X.93 In data communications, hypothetical reference connection for packet switched data transmission services.

X.95 In data communications, network parameters in public data networks.

X.96 In data communications, call progress signals in public data networks.

X.110 In data communications, routing principles for international public data services through switched public data networks of the same type.

X.121 In data communications, international numbering plan for public data networks.

X.130 In data communications, provisional objectives for call set-up and clear-down times in public synchronous data networks (circuit switching).

X.132 In data communications, provisional objectives for grade of service in international data communications over circuit switched public data networks.

X.150 In data communications, DTE and DCE test loops for public data networks in the case of X.21 and X.21 bis interface.

X.180 In data communications, administration arrangements for international closed user groups (CUG).

X.200 In data communications, OSI Reference Model for CCITT applications.

X.210 In data communications, OSI Layer Service definition on convention.

Y

yaw In satellite systems, a rotation of the satellite about an axis that joins the satellite to the center of the earth. See pitch, roll.

y-axis The vertical axis of a coordinate graph. Compare x-axis.

Younger Committee In computing, a committee which considered the problems of data protection and privacy and reported in 1972. See data protection, privacy.

Z

Z In electronics, the symbol for impedance. See impedance.

zero In logic circuits zero corresponds to the false state. See logic circuit.

zero a device In computing, to erase all the data stored in memory. See memory.

zero fill In computing, to fill an area of memory with zeros. See memory.

zero insertion force In electronics, pertaining to a socket for DIL integrated circuit devices in which a cam action permits a device to be inserted or removed without the application of pressure to the inline pins. See dual in line.

zero lead In electronic composition, a command which inhibits the line feed and sets the second line on top of the first.

zero suppression In computing, the elimination of zeros to the left of the most significant digits of a number, especially before printing.

z height Synonymous with x height.

ZIF See zero insertion force.

zigzag folding See accordion fold.

zoom In photography, to reduce or enlarge the size of the action field by operation of a varifocal lens. See action field.